National Infrastructure Planning Handbook

Fourth edition

National Infrastructure Planning Handbook

Fourth edition

General Editor

Michael Humphries QC
Barrister, Francis Taylor Building

Assistant Editors

James Pereira QC
Barrister, Francis Taylor Building

Hereward Phillpot QC
Barrister, Francis Taylor Building

Contributors

Douglas Edwards QC
Barrister, Francis Taylor Building

Gregory Jones QC
Barrister, Francis Taylor Building

Alexander Booth QC
Barrister, Francis Taylor Building

Richard Honey QC
Barrister, Francis Taylor Building

Mark Westmoreland Smith
Barrister, Francis Taylor Building

Pavlos Eleftheriades
Barrister, Francis Taylor Building and Professor of Public Law, University of Oxford

Cain Ormondroyd
Barrister, Francis Taylor Building

Hugh Flanagan
Barrister, Francis Taylor Building

Rebecca Clutten
Barrister, Francis Taylor Building

Ned Westaway
Barrister, Francis Taylor Building

Isabella Tafur
Barrister, Francis Taylor Building

Caroline Daly
Barrister, Francis Taylor Building

Daisy Noble
Barrister, Francis Taylor Building

Guest Contributors

Ashley Parry Jones
Director, WSP

Vicky Bramhill
Technical Director, WSP

Sean Bashforth
Board Director, Quod

Bloomsbury Professional

LONDON • DUBLIN • EDINBURGH • NEW YORK • NEW DELHI • SYDNEY

Bloomsbury Professional
Bloomsbury Publishing plc
50 Bedford Square, London WC1B 3DP, UK
1385 Broadway, New York, NY 10018, USA
29 Earlsfort Terrace, Dublin 2, Ireland

British Library Cataloguing-in-Publication Data

A catalogue record for this book is available from the British Library.

ISBN: PB: 978 1 52652 489 8
ePDF: 978 1 52652 491 1
ePub: 978 1 52652 490 4

Typeset by Compuscript Ltd, Shannon

Preface

An awful lot has happened since the third edition (2018) of the Handbook and, if anything, the pace of change is accelerating. This Preface is not the place to attempt a general review of national infrastructure planning law and the challenges it faces, but I will venture to identify a few themes that seem to me to be significant.

First, though, a few statistics to illustrate where we are. At the time of writing, there have been some 138 applications for development consent under the Planning Act 2008 regime and, of these, about 100 have been decided and some 8 were withdrawn. Of the decided cases, about 94% were approved. That leaves about 30 undecided applications still in the system. Many of these are at pre-examination, examination or with the Examining Authority for reporting, but many (and some quite old ones) are still with the Secretary of State for decision. It is a feature of the more recent operation of the regime that a disappointingly large number of cases have not been decided by the Secretary of State within the statutory three-month period. There will often be good reason for such delay, although not always; but the delay does rather undermine one of the principal objectives of the system, which was to be *"timely, efficient and predictable"* (Planning for a Sustainable Future, 2007). This will need to be addressed.

What of the new and emerging challenges that the Planning Act 2008 regime is facing?

An obvious challenge over the last couple of years has been the Covid-19 pandemic. Like the rest of the economy, the planning system has had to learn to live with disruption and remote working. This has not been easy, but the Planning Inspectorate, practitioners and, indeed, the public have risen magnificently to the challenge, and applications have continued to be made, examined and determined in large numbers. Virtual hearings have become an accepted (if not, perhaps, welcome) feature of the system, as has the widespread use of pdf documents rather than hardcopy. The tide of the pandemic appears now (hopefully) to be receding, but I suspect that there will be many lessons learnt during lockdown that will be carried forward into the future; and that is a good thing.

A second challenge for the regime arises from the legislative changes resulting from the UK's withdrawal from the European Union. The transition period ended on 31 December 2020 and ushered in the new concept of 'retained EU law'. Whilst withdrawal did not greatly change the Planning Act 2008 itself – although an amended Schedule 6 does introduce the concept of 'relevant retained EU law' – it does have a rather more profound effect on environmental law. I have had to update the text in various of the EIA / SEA / HRA articles in the Handbook and, indeed, introduce a new article to explain the concept of 'retained EU law'. Withdrawal from the European Union has also led to a more profound reappraisal of domestic environmental law and to the passing of the Environment Act 2021; and that leads to a third challenge for national infrastructure planning … Biodiversity Net Gain ('BNG').

In a late amendment to the Environment Bill, the Government extended its proposed BNG regime to Nationally Significant Infrastructure Projects. The Environment Act 2021 introduces some pretty profound changes to the Planning Act 2008, including a new Schedule 2A on BNG. Whilst the new NSIP BNG regime is not yet in force, and so not reflected in the Handbook, changes will include a new section 104(3A) providing that *"… if a relevant national policy statement contains a biodiversity gain statement under Schedule 2A in relation to development of the description to which the application relates, the Secretary of State may not grant the application unless satisfied that the biodiversity gain objective contained in the statement is met in relation to the development to which the application relates"*. At the time of writing, Defra is consulting on Biodiversity Net Gain Regulations and Implementation and has indicated that the Government will apply the BNG regime to NSIPs *"no later than 2025"*.

Which brings me to my fourth great challenge, and perhaps the most profound of all: climate change and the achievement of 'net zero'. The Climate Change Act 2008 came into force on the same day as the Planning Act 2008, and the latter imposes clear duties in relation to climate change at sections 5(8) and 10(3). The original 'target' in section 1(1) of the Climate Change Act was for the Secretary of State to ensure that the 'UK carbon account' for the year 2050 would be at least 80% lower than the 1990 baseline. In June 2019 the Government amended the target to be at least 100% lower; or 'net zero' as it is usually called. The 2050 target is to be achieved by compliance with 5-yearly carbon budgets set following the recommendation of the UK's Committee on Climate Change. The new 'net zero' target has been raised as an issue in the planning system and, in particular, the infrastructure planning system in two principal ways. First, in how major projects should seek to demonstrate compliance with the legal and policy requirements on Government to meet the 'net zero' target and carbon budgets. And, secondly, in the formulation of policy itself, both in the context of the Climate Change Act duties and, as argued by some, in the context of the long-term global temperature objective of the Paris Agreement. This has led to a number of legal challenges to both the grant of development consent for projects and, indeed, the adoption of National Policy Statements ('NPS'). The first ever Planning Act 2008 case to get to the Supreme Court (*R (oao Friends of the Earth) v Heathrow Airport Limited* [2020] UKSC 52) was a challenge to the Airports NPS on climate change / 'net zero' grounds. Such challenges within the Planning Act 2008 regime are likely to continue until the legal framework for considering these issues is more clearly settled by the Courts.

Finally, I will point to the 'Levelling Up' agenda; an issue so central to Government thinking that the Ministry for Housing, Communities and Local Government has now become the Department for Levelling Up, Housing and Communities. Levelling Up is, perhaps, not itself a challenge for the Planning Act regime, but it is certainly a benchmark against which the performance of that regime may come to be measured. To borrow a phrase from above, the *"timely, efficient and predictable"* delivery of development consent for infrastructure will clearly be central to achieving 'Levelling Up' and the operational performance of the regime will, therefore, be key. At the time of writing, the Government has been conducting an Operational Review of the NSIP regime and clearly recognises that it must be fit for the many challenges ahead.

As ever, the National Infrastructure Planning Handbook is intended to help readers navigate the Planning Act 2008 regime. The idea of the Handbook was always to produce a series of self-contained 'articles' on the practical issues that arise. I hope that the Handbook continues to help practitioners and clients alike. I have taken the decision for this edition to omit the Planning Act 2008 case summaries. I have found that the cut-off date for submitting copy to Bloomsbury often falls part way through the appeal process for Court decisions, with the result that the case summaries in the Handbook can end up being out-of-date and, therefore, misleading. The case summaries will, however, continue to appear in the online National Infrastructure Planning Service version of the Handbook, along with all statutory and policy materials.

I am hugely grateful to my fellow editors and authors at Francis Taylor Building ('ftb') who have, once again, contributed articles to the Handbook. I have manged to entice a few additional members of chambers at ftb to write material for this edition and I think this reflects the enormous depth of expertise within chambers. I am also very pleased that, for this edition, we have articles by some eminent external authors. I hope that this adds perspective on the issues from practitioners in other disciplines. All contributors are, of course, listed and their experience given in the profiles set out just after the contents pages.

I would also like to thank the in-house team at Bloomsbury; Jane Bradford, Leanne Barrett and Peter Smith. All have been great supporters of this work and I am very grateful to them for the time and effort they have put into bringing it to fruition. Leanne has been closely involved in the Handbook from its very inception and has been a constant source of encouragement and ideas. Peter has reviewed and corrected the text and cross-references to materials with a degree of diligence and precision that has make the Handbook immeasurably better. Needless to say, any errors and omissions that do remain are entirely my own. Anyway, who would have thought that the crazy idea I had back in 2013/14 to write something on the niche subject of national infrastructure planning would lead to a Handbook now in its fourth edition.

In previous editions, I have thanked my wife, Juliet, and children (and even our dog!) for putting up with me during holidays and weekends when I have worked on the Handbook. These projects really do take a vast amount of time and, again, I thank you for your encouragement and forbearance. For this edition, I will also mention my father who died at the end of 2021. Had it not been for his hard work, support and example, I would not have made it even to the very first rung at the planning Bar. Thanks Dad; I hope I made you proud.

Michael Humphries QC
Francis Taylor Building
March 2022

Contents

Contributors

Francis Taylor Building

Francis Taylor Building (FTB) is a leading set of barristers' chambers specialising in infrastructure planning law. FTB members advise and represent clients on a wide variety of Infrastructure projects promoted under the Planning Act 2008, the Town and County Planning Act 1990, the Transport and Works Act 1992, the Electricity Act 1989, Transport and Works Act Orders or Bills going through Parliament.

FTB members act for promoters, local authorities, statutory consultees and other interested parties on all aspects of planning and compulsory purchase, compensation and land valuation issues where they arise.

Members of chambers work on Infrastructure projects covering Energy, Transport, Business and Commercial, Water, Waste Water sectors, encompassing a wide variety of schemes such as:

Energy – including electricity generation from nuclear, gas, coal and renewables such as onshore and offshore wind farms; energy from waste; solar and tidal; electricity transmission and distribution systems; gas production facilities; underground gas storage facilities; pipelines and Carbon Capture and Storage (CCS) facilities.

Transport – including bridges; tunnels and roads; airports; railways trams and guided bus ways; ports, harbours and marine energy parks.

Water – including reservoirs and desalination plants.

Waste water – including waste water treatment plants and waste water transfer and storage tunnels.

General Editor

Michael Humphries QC

Barrister, Francis Taylor Building

Michael Humphries specialises in all aspects of property development law, but is particularly well known for his major infrastructure planning and compulsory purchase work, where he has acted in relation to some of the largest and most important projects in recent years.

Michael has promoted and advised on some 30 nationally significant infrastructure projects under the Planning Act 2008. A selection of the projects he has been involved in includes the Thames Tideway Tunnel project, the Hinkley Point C Connection project, the Richborough Connection project, the Silvertown Tunnel project, the Wylfa Newydd nuclear power station project, the Manston Airport project and the M25 Junction 10 Improvement project. He also advised Heathrow Airport Limited on the third runway project. As well as his work under the Planning Act 2008, Michael has promoted major infrastructure schemes under the Transport and Works Act 1992, the Town and Country Planning Act 1990, the Electricity Act 1989, the Highways Act 1980, the Gas Act 1965, the Pipelines Act 1962 and, indeed, has petitioned against hybrid Bills in Parliament. Recent non-Planning Act 2008 infrastructure cases include promoting the UK-Denmark interconnector ('Viking Link') and the expansion of Bristol Airport. His recent Court work includes appearing for Heathrow Airport Limited in the High Court, Court of Appeal and Supreme Court in relation to the Airports National Policy Statement challenges. Michael has considerable experience with issues arising from infrastructure and climate change/net zero.

In the *Chambers and Partners* UK Bar guide 2022, Michael was identified as the highest ranked planning silk at the London Bar and he was Environment and Planning Silk of the Year at the 2021 *Chambers and Partners* UK Bar Awards. He was also one of the highest ranked planning silks in the *Legal 500* UK Bar guide 2022. The *Planning Magazine* annual surveys for 2015–2021 ranked Michael as the highest rated barrister for infrastructure planning work in every year.

Recent published comments about Michael have been consistently complimentary and include: *"Michael Humphries QC is widely known as a leading name in infrastructure planning law. He has an excellent reputation for working on projects of all types, especially the often vast NSIPs."* (Chambers, 2022), *"He knows everything you could possibly need to know about planning and environmental law."* (Chambers, 2022), *"He is truly excellent – a very tactical advocate with a huge breadth of knowledge."* (Chambers, 2022) and *"Michael has a knowledge of the infrastructure planning regime that is second to none. He has a good strategic approach to the giving of advice and a nice collaborative nature. He is always accessible and puts clients at ease. Similarly he works well and collaboratively with other counsel brought in to assist in his cases."* (Legal 500, 2022).

Michael helped to found the National Infrastructure Planning Association (NIPA) and is its current Treasurer. He also helped found the Compulsory Purchase Association, was its first Treasurer and has now been made an Honorary Member. He is also a member of the Planning and Environment Bar Association. Michael is also a member of the committee of the Joint Planning Law Conference, Oxford.

Michael was called to the Bar in 1982 and was appointed Queen's Counsel in 2003.

Assistant Editors

James Pereira QC

Barrister, Francis Taylor Building

James specialises in all aspects of planning, environmental, local government and administrative law, compulsory purchase and compensation, and has considerable experience in national infrastructure planning.

James's DCO work includes acting on the Galloper Offshore Windfarm project, the Willington cross-country gas pipeline project, the Whitemoss Landfill project and the International Advanced Manufacturing Plant project. He also has extensive experience in non-DCO infrastructure work and in Court on infrastructure, planning and environmental cases.

James is ranked as a leading planning silk in the *Chambers and Partners* UK Bar guide 2022 and the *Legal 500* UK Bar guide 2022 and comments about him in the directories include: *"James is a real expert in planning and environmental law, excellent with the clients in conference and very good in court."* (Chambers, 2022), *"He has a very calm manner which gives the client confidence and is also completely on top of the brief."* (Chambers, 2022) and *"Calm, articulate, and thorough when it comes to in-depth planning policy. He assists at every stage and presents the case immaculately."* (Legal 500, 2022).

James is a member of the National Infrastructure Planning Association, the Compulsory Purchase Association and the Planning and Environmental Bar Association.

James was called to the Bar in 1996 and was appointed Queen's Counsel in 2014.

Hereward Phillpot QC

Barrister, Francis Taylor Building

Hereward is a hugely experienced and well-regarded silk who acts across the full range of planning work, but is particularly recognised for his infrastructure planning work.

Hereward has an extensive practice in nationally significant infrastructure planning and has promoted a number of major nationally significant infrastructure projects including the Hinkley Point C nuclear power station, the East Anglia One and Navitus Bay offshore wind farms, the Yorkshire and Humber Carbon Capture and Storage project and the Sizewell C nuclear power station project. He also advised the (then) DECC on the Energy National Policy Statements.

Hereward is one of the highest ranked planning silks in both the *Chambers and Partners* UK Bar guide 2022 and the *Legal 500* UK Bar guide 2022. The *Planning Magazine* survey 2021 identified Hereward as the second highest rated barrister for infrastructure work.

Recent published comments about Hereward include: *"Hailed as one of the top barristers acting in infrastructure matters, he frequently appears at inquiries, hearings and higher court cases. Many of the complex development cases he takes on pertain to particularly large or high-profile projects."* (Chambers, 2022); *"Hereward is terrific. He's very responsive and gives valuable views."* (Chambers, 2022); *"Hereward has unparalleled, absolute focus and outstanding intellectual acumen which inspires total trust in his advice. A 'client care champion' who always finds time for urgent advice."* (Legal 500, 2022).

Hereward is a member of the National Infrastructure Planning Association, the Compulsory Purchase Association and the Planning and Environmental Bar Association.

Hereward was called to the Bar in 1997 and was appointed Queen's Counsel in 2015.

Contributors

Douglas Edwards QC

Barrister, Francis Taylor Building

Douglas Edwards practises in the fields of planning, compulsory purchase environment, administrative and local government, highway law and property law. He also has particular expertise in the law relating to common land and greens. He appears regularly for both appellants and local planning and other authorities at inquiries and in the courts.

Douglas has advised on a number of nationally significant infrastructure schemes, including the A30 Improvement project and a major National Grid reinforcement project in Lancashire and Cumbria. Douglas acted for the Mayor of London at the London City Airport planning inquiry and was also advising the Mayor and TfL on the Heathrow third runway project.

In the *Chambers and Partners* UK Bar guide 2022, Douglas is described as *"… a true expert on planning and real estate law, along with town and village greens."* and as *"… calm and thorough."*.

Douglas is a member of the National Infrastructure Planning Association, the Compulsory Purchase Association and the Planning and Environmental Bar Association.

Douglas was called to the Bar in 1992 and was appointed Queen's Counsel in 2010.

Gregory Jones QC

Barrister, Francis Taylor Building

Gregory's practice covers all aspects of administrative law, including judicial review and statutory challenges, town planning, compulsory purchase, environmental law, EU law and public procurement, education, local government and administrative law. Regularly appearing in both public inquiries and the higher courts, Gregory acts on behalf of developers, local planning authorities and third parties.

Gregory has advised on a number of nationally significant infrastructure projects and successfully promoted the Able Marine Energy Park project. He is currently acting for the promoters of the EN1 and EN2 DCO for offshore wind turbines. Gregory has also acted for landowners and others opposing DCOs, including in respect of the East Midlands Gateway project, the Sizewell C project and the London Resorts project.

The *Chambers and Partners* UK Bar guide 2022 says that Gregory *"... is held in high regard for his intellectual ability and knowledge in the area"*, and the *Legal 500* UK Bar guide 2022 says that he is *"Often first choice given his extensive expertise across planning, environment and public law, Greg consistently comes up with novel ideas to tackle complex issues. He fizzes with ideas on how to achieve the best results for clients. Very easy to work with."*.

Gregory is a member of the National Infrastructure Planning Association, the Compulsory Purchase Association and the Planning and Environmental Bar Association.

Gregory was called to the Bar in 1991 and was appointed Queen's Counsel in 2011.

Alexander Booth QC

Barrister, Francis Taylor Building

Alex Booth has a practice which encompasses all aspects of planning, compulsory purchase and environmental law. He regularly appears at Public Inquiries, in the Upper Tribunal (Lands Chamber) and in the High Court, and has also appeared in both the Court of Appeal and the Supreme Court.

Alex has considerable experience of acting and advising in relation to projects under the Planning Act 2008. Projects he has promoted include the Rookery South Resource Recovery Facility, the Northampton Gateway Strategic Rail Freight Interchange, the Riverside Energy Park, and the Southampton-London Esso Pipeline. He also acted for Thames Water in the legal challenges to the Thames Tideway Tunnel development consent.

Alex is highly ranked in the *Chambers and Partners* UK Bar guide 2022 and the *Legal 500* UK Bar guide 2022 and was voted one of the highest rated infrastructure planning silks in the *Planning Magazine* survey 2022.

Published comments on Alex include: *"Alex really cares about his clients, and his passion and drive mean that he consistently achieves great results. He is a highly effective advocate."* and *"He is extremely personable, very bright and commercial."* (Chambers, 2022).

Alex is a member of the National Infrastructure Planning Association, the Compulsory Purchase Association and the Planning and Environmental Bar Association.

Alex was called to the Bar in 2000 and was appointed Queen's Counsel in 2016.

Richard Honey QC

Barrister, Francis Taylor Building

Richard Honey practises as a barrister in public and environmental law, with particular specialisms in judicial review and statutory High Court challenges, infrastructure projects, and compulsory purchase and compensation.

Richard's experience includes schemes under the Planning Act, the Highways Act, the Transport and Works Act and the Electricity Act, and Parliamentary work, including appearances before the Crossrail and HS2 Bill committees for various objectors. Richard has advised National Highways on a number of DCOs and has advised DLUHC and DfT on DCO applications. Recent infrastructure work includes road, rail and flood alleviation schemes, and compensation claims under DCOs.

Having been one of the top-ranked planning juniors, the *Chambers and Partners* UK Bar guide 2022 identifies Richard as a new planning silk and says that he is *"He is a high-flyer and very strong in court."*. The *Legal 500* UK Bar guide 2021 says that Richard is a *"Tenacious litigator and excellent advocate"* and that he is *"Calm and confident, he is a very strong advocate"* and the *Legal 500* UK Bar guide 2022 describes Richard as *"Very hard-working and responsive with great knowledge of compulsory purchase law."*.

Richard is a member of the National Infrastructure Planning Association, the Compulsory Purchase Association, the Planning and Environmental Bar Association and the Parliamentary Bar Mess.

Richard was called to the Bar in 2003 and was appointed Queen's Counsel in 2021.

Mark Westmoreland Smith

Barrister, Francis Taylor Building

Mark is one of the most experienced infrastructure and compulsory purchase juniors at the Bar and has successfully promoted numerous DCOs through examination unled. He is currently promoting the Keadby 3 Carbon Capture Power Station and advised the Government in relation to the Wylfa Newydd Nuclear Power Station, the Aquind Interconnector, Manston Airport and Hornsea Three Offshore Wind Farm. Mark has appeared in a number of Planning Act 2008 challenges in the Courts on a range of issues, and has considerable experience in climate change and net zero litigation.

Mark is a member of the Attorney General's 'A Panel' of junior counsel and was identified as a leading planning junior in the *Chambers and Partners* UK Bar guide 2022, the *Legal 500* UK Bar guide 2022 and in the *Planning Magazine* survey 2021.

Recent published comments say that *"Mark is very adept at cutting through the vast detail and helping shape strategic direction of case. He provides a sensible way forward."* and *"He is thorough and has an excellent ability to put across the facts of a case in a sound and coherent manner."* (Chambers, 2022).

Mark is a member of the National Infrastructure Planning Association, the Compulsory Purchase Association and is a former Assistant Secretary to the Planning and Environmental Bar Association.

Mark was called to the Bar in 2006.

Pavlos Eleftheriades

Barrister, Francis Taylor Building and Professor of Public Law, University of Oxford

Pavlos is a professor of law at Oxford University and a practising barrister at Francis Taylor Building.

He is regularly instructed to advise on issues of EU law, state aid, renewable energy, planning law, education law and human rights. Over the past few years, he has been a regular speaker and commentator on the relations between the European Union and the United Kingdom and has been quoted by the Financial Times and the BBC.

Pavlos was called to the Bar in 2006.

Cain Ormondroyd

Barrister, Francis Taylor Building

Cain undertakes a wide range of planning work, including in relation to infrastructure, and he is particularly known for his environmental law practice.

Cain is an experienced Court advocate and is a member of the Attorney General's 'A Panel' of counsel. He often appears in the High Court on behalf of the (now) Secretary of State for Levelling Up, Housing and Communities and the Secretary of State for the Home Department. He is also frequently instructed by HMRC. Cain has also worked with Friends of the Earth, the Environmental Law Foundation and other public interest groups in relation to environmental law issues.

Chambers and Partners UK Bar guide 2022 says that *"He is a very efficient and thorough advocate. He has a very good grasp of detail."*, *"He is an expert in the field. He is technically excellent and a very good advocate."* and *"His cross-examination style is forensic without being combative."*.

Cain is a member of the National Infrastructure Planning Association, the Compulsory Purchase Association and the Planning and Environmental Bar Association.

Cain was called to the Bar in 2007.

Hugh Flanagan

Barrister, Francis Taylor Building

Hugh specialises in planning and public law, with a focus on infrastructure, housing, compulsory purchase and compensation, and rating. He acts for developers, individuals, central government and local authorities.

Hugh frequently appears in Courts and Tribunals at all levels up to the Supreme Court, as well as at planning inquiries and examinations. He is a member of the Attorney General's 'B Panel' of counsel and an editor of the *Encyclopaedia of Compulsory Purchase and Compensation.*

He has consistently appeared in the *Chambers and Partners* UK Bar guide, the *Legal 500* UK Bar guide and the *Planning Magazine* annual survey as one of the top-rated planning juniors.

The *Chambers and Partners* UK Bar guide 2022 says *"He writes beautifully and is really good with technical analysis. He is a standout junior."*. The *Legal 500* UK Bar guide 2022 says that *"Hugh is calm, clear-minded and incredibly clever. This is reflected in the outstanding quality of his oral and written advocacy, and in the advice that he gives. Clients love him, and very swiftly come to regard him as an invaluable member of the team and their new go-to junior for all planning work. He will go far."*.

Hugh is a member of the National Infrastructure Planning Association, the Compulsory Purchase Association and the Planning and Environmental Bar Association.

Hugh was called to the Bar in 2008.

Rebecca Clutten

Barrister, Francis Taylor Building

Rebecca's practice covers a wide range of planning and related areas of work, but she has a particular focus on infrastructure planning and compulsory purchase and compensation matters. She has acted for and advised utilities, developers, landowners and private individuals, as well as central and local government.

Rebecca has substantial experience in infrastructure planning, having advised and appeared for promoters of DCOs and Transport and Works Act Orders at the application and examination stages, both being led and in her own right. Her experience includes advising and acting for National Grid in respect of the Viking Link Interconnector project, North West Coast Connection project, the Hinkley Point C Connection project, and North London Reinforcement project, the promotion of Network Rail Transport and Works Act Orders, advising and acting as junior counsel for London Underground Limited promoting the Bank Station Capacity Upgrade, and advising and acting for DONG Energy in respect of the Walney Extension Offshore Wind Farm. Her experience includes Parliamentary work, and she recently appeared before the House of Commons Select Committee on High Speed 2.

Rebecca is one of the highest ranked juniors in the *Chambers and Partners* UK Bar guide 2022, the *Legal 500* UK Bar guide 2022 and the *Planning Magazine* annual survey of the planning Bar 2021. Recent published comments say that *"Rebecca is fantastic. She is really user-friendly and a real rising star."* and describe her as *"… extremely bright and fantastic to work with."* (Chambers, 2022), and *"Rebecca's strengths are that she is able to provide clear and concise advice on a number of complex matters. She is always friendly and approachable, with a knack for explaining complex legal matters in an accessible way that distils problems simply and helps us to consider the best solutions. Her work is appreciated and highly commended."* (Legal 500, 2022).

Rebecca is a former Chair of the Compulsory Purchase Association, and a member of the National Infrastructure Planning Association and the Planning and Environmental Bar Association.

Rebecca was called to the Bar in 2008.

Ned Westaway

Barrister, Francis Taylor Building

Ned is a highly regarded junior who accepts instructions in a wide variety of work, in particular across all areas of planning and environmental law.

Ned has considerable experience of major planning and infrastructure cases both under the Planning Act 2008 and preceding legislation. He appeared at examinations into the Able Marine Energy Park on the Humber Estuary, the Thames Tideway Tunnel in London and the Navitus Bay Wind Farm, where he presented the successful objection on behalf of Natural England. He also has an active High Court practice, including major infrastructure challenges, and is on the Attorney General's 'A Panel' of London counsel.

Ned is consistently ranked as a leading barrister in planning and environmental law; the *Chambers and Partners* UK Bar guide 2022 comments that *"He is very good at discerning which way the judge is leaning and what to focus on so as not to waste time."*, whilst the *Legal 500* UK Bar guide says that he is *"Tenacious, highly focused, extremely sharp. He is extremely good with pressing his case and politely and firmly debating with the cream of the Planning judiciary. I would instruct him again in an instant, with absolutely no hesitation. Ned was highly impressive but was also measured in terms of the prospects – really had the confidence of the lay client which is so important. He is at the top of rank in terms of technical knowledge – the whole package."*.

Ned is a member of the Planning and Environmental Bar Association, the current Chair and a trustee of the United Kingdom Environmental Law Association (UKELA) and a visiting researcher at UCL's Centre for Law and the Environment.

Ned was called to the Bar in 2009.

Isabella Tafur

Barrister, Francis Taylor Building

Isabella advises widely on all aspects of planning and infrastructure law and has particular expertise in housing, compulsory purchase and nationally significant infrastructure projects. She has a busy DCO and inquiry practice, and regularly appears in the Courts on planning matters for both Claimants and Defendants.

Isabella has considerable infrastructure experience. She has promoted a number of DCO projects, including Manston Airport, the Lower Thames Crossing, Walney offshore windfarm extension, the Yorkshire and Humber Carbon Capture and Storage project, the A30 trunk road improvement and Able Marine Energy Park; and she has acted for local authorities and interested parties in respect of a number of others, including Sizewell C, East Anglia One (North) and East Anglia Two and Thanet offshore windfarms, and the Lake Lothing Crossing.

Isabella is highly ranked in the *Chambers and Partners* UK Bar guide 2022 and the *Legal 500* UK Bar guide 2022. She was one of the highest rated planning juniors and was in the top ten infrastructure barristers in the *Planning Magazine* survey 2021.

Isabella is a member of the National Infrastructure Planning Association, the Compulsory Purchase Association and the Planning and Environmental Bar Association.

Isabella was called to the Bar in 2009.

Caroline Daly

Barrister, Francis Taylor Building

Caroline has a broad planning practice, but has a particular focus on planning, environment, compulsory purchase and compensation matters. She acts for and advises central and local government, landowners, developers, private individuals, utilities companies and community interest groups.

Caroline acted for the London Borough of Bexley in the Cory Riverside Energy Park project examination and for Highways England in connection with the M25 Junction 10 Improvement project. She is also advising the Department of Levelling Up, Housing and Communities in respect of the suite of new Energy National Policy Statements and the forthcoming review of the National Networks National Policy Statement.

Caroline is currently the third highest rated planning barrister under 35 (*Planning Magazine* survey 2021). She is ranked as 'up and coming' in the *Chambers and Partners* UK Bar guide 2022 and is also ranked in the *Legal 500* UK Bar guide 2022.

Published comments on Caroline include that *"She is hard-working, intelligent and goes that extra mile."*, *"She is willing to pull out the stops to get the desired results."* (Chambers, 2022) and that *"She is able to quickly grasp the detail of the case and provides advice which strengthens the client's case and ultimately leads to success. The quality of her work is always excellent and deadlines are always respected."* (Legal 500, 2022).

Caroline is a member of the National Infrastructure Planning Association, the Compulsory Purchase Association and the Planning and Environmental Bar Association.

Caroline was called to the Bar in 2013.

Daisy Noble

Barrister, Francis Taylor Building

Daisy joined chambers at Francis Taylor Building in October 2018 but is already developing a broad planning law practice, including involvement in a number of major infrastructure, planning and compulsory purchase and compensation cases.

Daisy acted as junior counsel for Bristol Airport Limited at the Bristol Airport expansion planning inquiry (2021) and as junior counsel to the GLA in relation to the inquiry into the proposed tall building known as 'the Tulip' in the City of London (2021). She was also instructed by EDF to advise in respect of the proposed nuclear power station at Sizewell C.

Daisy is currently ranked as one of the top-rated planning juniors (*Planning Magazine* survey 2021).

Daisy is a member of the National Infrastructure Planning Association, the Compulsory Purchase Association and the Planning and Environmental Bar Association.

Daisy was called to the Bar in 2015.

Guest contributors

Ashley Parry Jones

Director, WSP

Ashley is a Director for Planning at WSP, a leading provider of professional land referencing services in the UK. He is a leading expert on the often complex issues arising from the land referencing requirements for major infrastructure development projects.

Over the past 30 years, Ashley has supported many of the UK's high-profile schemes, including Thames Tideway, Heathrow Airport third runway project, HS1 and HS2, Luton Guided Busway, Edinburgh Tram, Crossrail 1 & 2, Silvertown Tunnel, National Highway's M4 J3–12 Smart Motorway scheme, the Manston Airport project, as well as National Grid and Network Rail projects.

Vicky Bramhill

Technical Director, WSP

Vicky is a Technical Director in Land Referencing – DCO Specialist at WSP.

Vicky has worked to deliver land referencing services and produce the relevant documents for Network Rail, Thames Tideway Tunnel, National Highways' M4 Smart Motorway scheme,

Silvertown Tunnel, National Grid's connection projects, National Highways' Stonehenge project and Heathrow Airport third runway project.

She has also supported various non-DCO projects, including Compulsory Purchase Orders, Transport and Works Act Orders and hybrid Bills, such as Thameslink, HS2, HS2 Phase 2, Crossrail and Crossrail 2. In her role at WSP, she has supported projects through consultation, application submission, examination and the land notification / acquisition stages, providing strategic advice for successful delivery of land referencing activities, and guiding, training and directing WSP's specialist team of land referencers.

Sean Bashforth

Board Director, Quod

Sean is a town planner with Quod and an accomplished project manager responsible mainly for large infrastructure and mixed-use proposals. He focuses on providing advice for developers and operators, with particular areas of expertise in strategic planning policy, environmental impact assessment, airport planning and retail planning, including complex mixed-use town centre proposals.

Sean has been involved in a wide range of major development projects, including the expansion of London City and Heathrow Airports. He regularly acts as an expert witness at planning and CPO inquiries and in the Upper Tribunal (Lands Chamber).

Table of Cases

N

P

R

S

T

W

Table of Statutes

Table of Statutory Instruments

Part 1

The Examining Authority and the Secretary of State

Article 1

The Planning Inspectorate

Richard Honey QC, ftb
Michael Humphries QC, ftb

On 1 April 2012 the Planning Inspectorate (also known as PINS) became responsible for operating the planning process for nationally significant infrastructure projects. Before that date, applications for nationally significant infrastructure projects were handled by the Infrastructure Planning Commission (IPC). The IPC was, however, abolished under the Localism Act 2011 and its functions transferred to PINS.

In order to deal with Planning Act 2008 applications, PINS is now organised so that the Director of Operations has two direct reports, being the Head of Operations (Casework) and the Head of Operations (Central Operations). The Head of Operations (Casework) is responsible for four principal teams, being the 'Transport Team', the 'Energy Team', the 'Environment Team' and, currently, 'Project Speed'. Each of these teams itself comprises operational team members and inspector team members (including Examining Inspectors). The Head of Operations (Central Operations) is responsible for the Environmental Service Team giving specialist EIA and land rights advice. An organogram setting out these roles is provided via a link on the PINS National Infrastructure website, and a copy of that organogram (with names removed) is attached to this article.

PINS handles major applications and discharges many of the procedural functions of the Secretary of State under the Planning Act 2008, the Infrastructure Planning (Applications: Prescribed Forms and Procedure) Regulations 2009 and the Infrastructure Planning (Examination Procedure) Rules 2010. This includes the pre-application process, submission of an application, acceptance, pre-examination, examination and reporting.

The Secretary of State has established a formal framework of delegation, delegating nationally significant infrastructure projects actions to the Inspectorate's Chief Executive, who in turn has sub-delegated functions to the Director of Operations.

PINS contact details are:

- The Planning Inspectorate, Temple Quay House, 2 The Square, Temple Quay, Bristol BS1 6PN
  Tel: 0303 444 5000
  Email: NIEnquiries@planninginspectorate.gov.uk.

The Planning Inspectorate's 2019/20 annual report and accounts (p 102) shows that the Inspectorate received over £8.4m in fee income for national infrastructure work, against an operating cost of over £9.1m.

Further information about the Planning Inspectorate can be found at: www.gov.uk/government/organisations/planning-inspectorate.

Also important is the Consents Service Unit (CSU), based within the Planning Inspectorate. The CSU was launched in April 2013 to help provide a 'one-stop-shop' approach to non-planning consents for nationally significant infrastructure projects that are required in addition to any development consent order. The purpose of the CSU is to improve the coordination between the developer, relevant consenting bodies and the Inspectorate, to seek to make the overall consenting process more efficient. The CSU published a 'Prospectus for Developers' that sets out the unit's objectives.

The CSU's contact details are:

- Consents Service Unit, Eagle D, The Planning Inspectorate, Temple Quay House, Temple Quay, Bristol BS1 6PN
  Tel: 0303 444 5000
  Email: NIEnquiries@planninginspectorate.gov.uk.

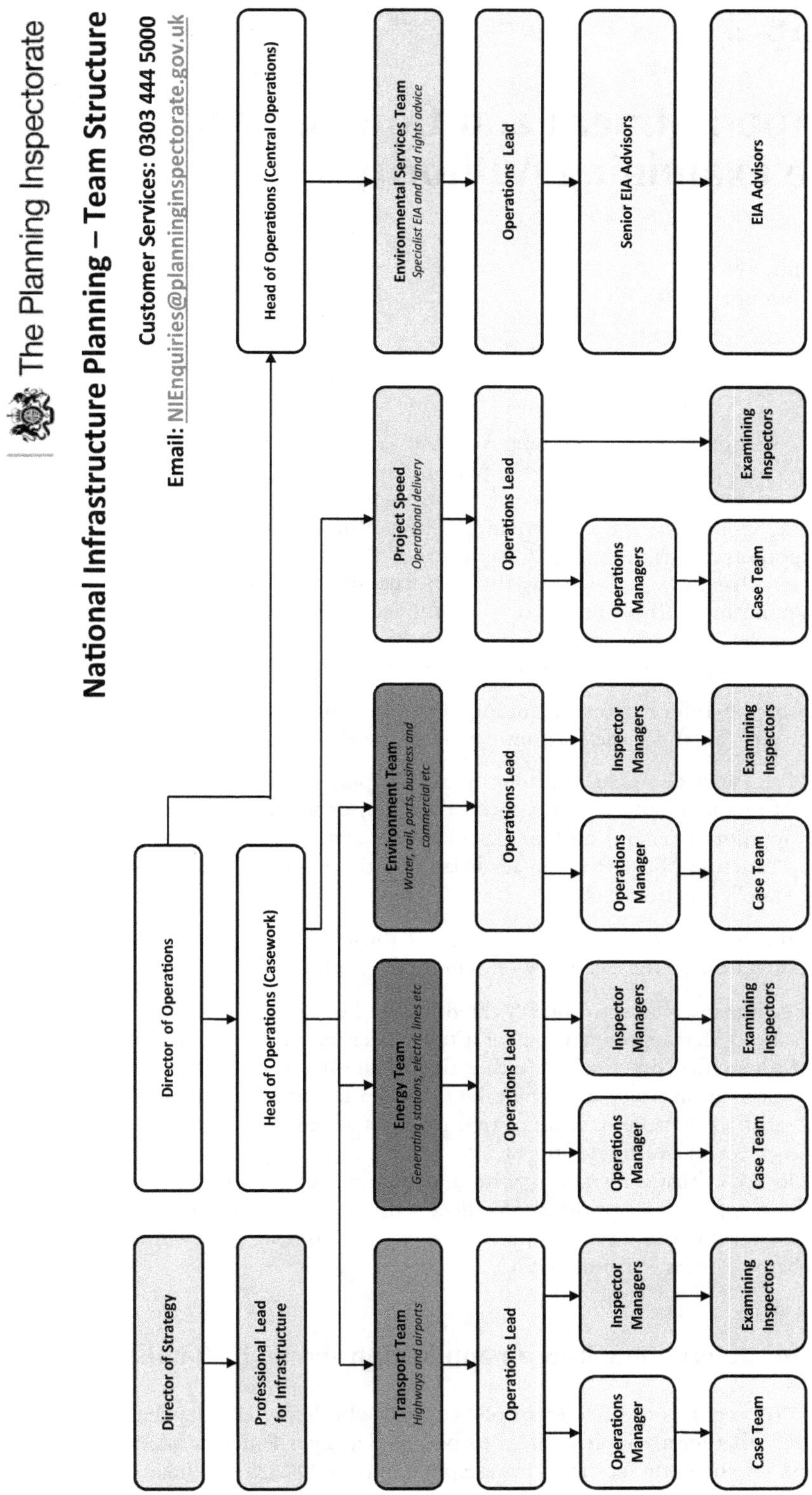
The Planning Inspectorate
National Infrastructure Planning – Team Structure
Customer Services: 0303 444 5000
Email: NIEnquiries@planninginspectorate.gov.uk
Director of Strategy
Professional Lead for Infrastructure
Director of Operations
Head of Operations (Casework)
Head of Operations (Central Operations)
Transport Team
Highways and airports
Energy Team
Generating stations, electric lines etc
Environment Team
Water, rail, ports, business and commercial etc
Project Speed
Operational delivery
Environmental Services Team
Specialist EIA and land rights advice
Operations Lead
Operations Manager
Operations Managers
Inspector Managers
Case Team
Examining Inspectors
Senior EIA Advisors
EIA Advisors

Article 2

The Appointment and Composition of the Examining Authority

Isabella Tafur, ftb
Michael Humphries QC, ftb

Introduction

Pursuant to section 86 of the Planning Act 2008 (PA 2008), the Examining Authority is defined as either a Panel or a single appointed person appointed by the Secretary of State to examine an application for a development consent order. It is for the Secretary of State to determine whether the application should be handled by a Panel (under Chapter 2 of PA 2008) or by a single appointed person (under Chapter 3 of PA 2008). That decision will be made after an application has been accepted by the Secretary of State and a certificate has been received from the applicant confirming that it has complied with the notice and publicity requirements contained in PA 2008, s 56 (and, where applicable, a notice of the persons interested in land to which a compulsory acquisition request relates) (PA 2008, s 61).

Rule 2(1) of the Infrastructure Planning (Examination Procedure) Rules 2010 (as amended) ('the 2010 Rules') defines the Examining Authority as follows:

> '(a) the Panel or single appointed person appointed under section 62 (appointment of members, and lead member, of a Panel) or section 79 (appointment of a single appointed person), and may include one or more members of the Panel allocated a function of the Panel in accordance with section 76 (allocation within Panel or Panel's functions); or
>
> (b) the Secretary of State, in respect of those matters which are the subject of a direction by the Secretary of State under section 95A(2).'

Section 95A was inserted into the PA 2008 by the Localism Act 2011. It enables the Secretary of State to direct that representations of a type specified in his direction may only be made to 'persons of a specified description' (rather than being made in public). It applies where part or all of the examination procedure will take the form of a meeting or hearing and the Secretary of State is satisfied that the making of oral representations at such a meeting or hearing would be likely to result in the disclosure of information as to defence or national security, and that public disclosure of that information would be contrary to the national interest. Examination by persons of a specified description would allow sensitive material to be examined by persons with appropriate security clearance. This procedure was used during the examination of an objection into the Thames Tideway Tunnel DCO.

Criteria for determining how an application should be handled

PA 2008, s 61 requires the Secretary of State to publish the criteria that are to be applied in determining whether an application is to be handled by a Panel or a single appointed person. The criteria are currently set out in paragraphs 12–14 of DCLG's 'Guidance for the examination of applications for development consent' (March 2015). The main criteria which the Secretary of State will consider are: (a) the complexity of the case; and (b) the level of public interest in the outcome (paragraph 12). When looking at the complexity of the case the Secretary of State will consider whether the application raises novel issues for development, raises complex legal or technical considerations, proposes associated development which would require consideration of policy contained in more than a single National Policy Statement ('NPS'), or involves analysis of policy issues because, for example, there is no relevant NPS. In considering the level of public interest the Secretary of State will have particular regard to the likelihood of the examination requiring hearings so that parties can make oral representations about the application.

Transfer of the application from a single appointed person to a Panel

Where the Secretary of State has appointed a single appointed person to examine the application, he may at any time decide that the application should be handled by a Panel instead (PA 2008, s 62). He must publish the criteria to be applied when making such a decision. DCLG's consultation Guidance explains that the Secretary of State will be able to transfer the application to a Panel if he considers the application is more complex than the original assessment indicated and that it requires a wider range of expertise (paragraph 14). The Guidance does not, however, suggest that the Secretary of State can make a decision to transfer the application to a Panel on the basis that it has generated a greater level of public interest than originally anticipated.

Where an application is transferred from a single appointed person to a Panel, the single appointed person may be appointed as a member of that Panel, and may also be appointed as chair of the Panel (PA 2008, s 71). Where such a transfer is effected, it will not always be necessary for the examination procedure to start again. Pursuant to PA 2008, s 71 the Panel may, so far as it thinks appropriate, decide to treat things done by or in relation to the appointed person on the application as done by or in relation to the Panel. In these circumstances it will be the duty of the lead member to ensure that the members of the Panel have the necessary knowledge of the proceedings which took place under the appointed person.

Notifying the parties

The Secretary of State must, before the preliminary meeting, notify all those who have been notified of the accepted application that the Examining Authority has been appointed, and give details of who has been appointed (rule 4 of the 2010 Rules). Where the Secretary of State had originally appointed a single appointed person and subsequently decides that the Examining Authority should be a Panel, he must notify all interested parties of this decision. He must also notify interested parties of any change in the membership of the Panel or appointment of any replacement appointed person, or any direction made under PA 2008, s 95A.

Appointment and replacement of Panels and single appointed persons

The Panel procedure is set out in Chapter 2 of the PA 2008, and the single appointed person procedure in Chapter 3 of the PA 2008. These provision were amended by the Infrastructure Act 2015 with effect from 5 April 2017.

With effect from 5 April 2017, PA 2008, s 65 provides that, where the Examining Authority comprises a panel, it must be made up of a minimum of two and a maximum of five persons, with one of those members (the 'lead member') appointed as chair. If, at any time, a panel has only a single member, another panel member must be appointed (PA 2008, s 68(3)).

Section 75(A1) provides that, if the members of a panel with two members disagree as to a proposed decision by the panel, the view of the lead member is to prevail. Section 75 also provides that the making of a decision by a panel of three or more members is to be by agreement of the majority, subject to the lead member having a second (casting) vote in the event of the same number of members not so agreeing.

A Panel may, instead of undertaking a part of the examination, allocate the undertaking of that part to one or more of its members (PA 2008, s 76). Where it makes such an allocation, anything which is required or authorised to be done by the Panel under Chapter 4 of the PA 2008 in connection with the allocated part of the examination, may be done by or to the member(s) concerned. The findings and conclusions of the member(s) concerned in respect of the matters allocated will be taken to be those of the Panel as a whole, provided the Panel so agreed at the time of making the allocation (or before the allocation was made). Where there is an allocation to two or more members, the making of a decision by the members concerned requires the agreement of all of them. Procedural powers conferred on the Panel for the purposes of its examination of the application can be exercised by the Panel itself and by any one or more of its members (unless the Panel has decided to restrict or prohibit the exercise of procedural powers other than by the Panel itself) (PA 2008, s 77).

Members of the Panel and single appointed persons can resign their positions by giving notice in writing to the Secretary of State, and they can also be removed by the Secretary of State if he is satisfied that they are unable, unwilling or unfit to perform their duties (PA 2008, ss 66 and 80). One of the appointed members of the panel on examining inspectors for the Tidal Lagoon (Swansea Bay) DCO resigned during the examination.

In a Panel, the lead member can be removed from that office without being removed from the Panel altogether. In such circumstances the Secretary of State must appoint another lead member (either from amongst the other members of the Panel or be appointing a new member) (PA 2008, s 69). New members may be appointed by the Secretary of State at any time after the initial appointment of the members (provided the total number does not exceed five), and he must do so if the membership of the Panel falls below three (PA 2008, s 68). He cannot, however, use this power to appoint new members where the Panel ceases to have any members (PA 2008, s 72(5)).

If the Panel ceases to have any members at all, a new Panel must be constituted (PA 2008, s 72). Where a new Panel is constituted, it may decide to treat things done by or in relation to the previous Panel (or treated by the previous Panel as being done by or in relation to that Panel, under PA 2008, s 71(3)) as done by or in relation to the new Panel. The lead member will be responsible for ensuring that the members have the necessary knowledge of the proceedings up until the reconstitution of the Panel.

PA 2008, s 73 makes it clear that the Panel's continuing identity is not affected by any change in its membership; the Panel coming to have only two members or a single member; any change in the lead member; or a vacancy in the office of lead member.

Where a person ceases to be the single appointed person, the Secretary of State must make a new appointment (PA 2008, s 82). Where this happens the new single appointed person may, so far as may be appropriate, decide to treat things done by or in relation to any previous single appointed person as done by or in relation to the new single appointed person (PA 2008, s 82(2)). Where he does so, the single appointed person is under a duty to acquire the necessary knowledge of the previous proceedings on the application.

The functions of the Examining Authority

Regardless of whether it is a Panel or a single appointed person, the functions of the Examining Authority are to: (1) examine the application; and (2) make a report to the Secretary of State on the application setting out: (i) its findings and conclusions in respect of the application; and (ii) its recommendation as to the decision to be made on the application. Its functions must be carried out in accordance with Chapter 4 of the PA 2008 (Examination of applications under Chapter 2 or 3 of PA 2008).

Where the Examining Authority is a Panel, the making of a decision requires the agreement of a majority of its members. The lead member has a casting vote, in the event that the vote is tied.

Appointment of assessors and advisors

Pursuant to PA 2008, s 100, the Secretary of State may, at the request of the Examining Authority, appoint a person to act as an assessor to assist the Examining Authority in its examination of the application. The Secretary of State may only appoint an assessor if it appears to him that the person has the expertise that makes him suitable to provide assistance to the Examining Authority.

The Secretary of State may also appoint, at the request of the Examining Authority, a barrister, solicitor or advocate to provide legal assistance to the Examining Authority in connection with its examination of the application, including carrying out any oral questioning at a hearing on behalf of the Examining Authority.

The role of assessors and legal advisors is to assist the Examining Authority, but those persons do not form part of the Examining Authority.

Where an assessor or a barrister, solicitor or advocate is appointed, the Examining Authority must notify all interested parties of the name of the assessor and/or the details of the legal advisor and, in the case of an assessor, must notify the parties of the particular matters on which the assessor is to assist the Examining Authority (rules 11 and 12 of the 2010 Rules).

DCLG's Guidance explains (paragraphs 66–69) that in most cases the appointment of an assessor is likely to take place at the pre-examination stage, because the initial assessment of the application would usually have identified to the Examining Authority the issues that required further examination with the assistance of an assessor.

DCLG's Guidance also explains (paragraph 70) that the Examining Authority may sometimes need to appoint a professional advocate to ensure evidence is 'tested in the most effective and revealing way'.

Article 3

The Role of the Examining Authority

Isabella Tafur, ftb
Michael Humphries QC, ftb

Introduction

Once the Secretary of State has appointed either a single appointed person or a Panel as the Examining Authority, its role in relation to the application for development consent is governed by PA 2008, ss 74–77 and 83. Article 2 of this work provides further details on the appointment and composition of the Examining Authority.

One of the principal changes introduced by the Localism Act 2011 is that all decisions on development consent applications are now made by the Secretary of State. The role of the Examining Authority is, therefore, limited to examining the application and reporting to the relevant Secretary of State.

Panel

Where the Examining Authority is a Panel, its role is set out in PA 2008, ss 74–77. It must examine the application and prepare a report for the Secretary of State, setting out its findings and conclusions in respect of the application, and its recommendation as to the decision to be made (PA 2008, s 74).

Decisions made by the Panel require the agreement of a majority of its members, and the lead member has a casting vote in the event of a tied vote (PA 2008, s 75). However, the Panel may choose to allocate parts of the examination to one or more members of the Panel (PA 2008, s 76). Where they do so, the findings or conclusions of that member (or those members) will be taken to be the findings and conclusions of the Panel in relation to the allocated matter. If a matter has been allocated to two or more members of the Panel, their decision on that matter requires their unanimous agreement.

Single appointed person

Where the Examining Authority is a single appointed person, its role in relation to the application is governed by PA 2008, s 83. Its functions mirror those set out in PA 2008, s 74 in relation to a Panel: it is to examine the application and prepare a report to the relevant Secretary of State setting out its findings and conclusions in respect of the application and its recommendation as to the decision to be made.

Examination of the application

The functions of the Examining Authority must be carried out in accordance with Chapter 4 of the PA 2008, which governs the manner in which an application should be examined (see PA 2008, ss 74(3) and 83(3)). The Infrastructure Planning (Examination Procedure) Rules 2010 also contain provisions relating to the examination of applications. Articles 83 to 88 of this work consider the 'examination' process in detail.

Article 4

The Legal Status of the Secretary of State in Litigation

Richard Honey QC, ftb
Michael Humphries QC, ftb

Although any Secretary of State or other Minister acts formally on behalf of the Crown, it is important to understand the legal distinction between the Queen and her Ministers. Whilst the Crown retains certain prerogatives and indeed public immunity in litigation (subject to the Crown Proceedings Act 1947), Parliament will normally confer administrative powers and duties on 'the Secretary of State' or 'the Minister' and no such prerogatives or immunity attach to such a Minister acting on the Crown's behalf. This greatly assists the operation of administrative law as it means that all legal remedies are potentially available against a Minister.

It is a well-established principle of constitutional law that powers given to Ministers are normally exercised not by the Ministers themselves but by their officers and, further, that a Minister is not obliged to take an action himself but can act through an officer. In *R v Secretary of State for the Home Department, ex p Oladehinde* [1991] 1 AC 254 at 300–B Lord Griffiths held that 'It is obvious that the Secretary of State cannot personally take every decision … The decision must be taken by a person of suitable seniority in the [Department] for whom the [Secretary of State] accepts responsibility. This devolution of responsibility was recognised as a practical necessity in the administration of government by the Court of Appeal in *Carltona Ltd v Works Commissioners* [1943] 2 All ER 560 and has become known as 'the *Carltona* principle'. Thus it can be said that an act of a duly authorised civil servant is an act of the Minister and, furthermore, that the Minister is legally responsible for the acts of such a civil servant taken in the Minister's name.

It also needs to be recognised that the titles and functions of Ministers and their departments are frequently changed. This is usually effected under the Ministers of the Crown Act 1975. This Act allows the Queen, by Order in Council, to transfer the functions of Ministers and, furthermore, to make changes in departments of the office of Secretary of State. In this regard, such Order in Council may also make a Secretary of State a 'corporation sole' and transfer property etc to a named Secretary of State.

It is in this context that the PA 2008 confers various powers and duties on 'the Secretary of State'. The Act does not, however, identify the particular 'Secretary of State' to which any particular power or duty relates. It is clear, however, from Interpretation Act 1978, Sch 1 that references to 'the Secretary of State' should be taken to mean 'one of Her Majesty's Principal Secretaries of State'. Thus the powers and duties of the Secretary of State are in theory conferred on all the Secretaries of State in existence at the time. This arises because, constitutionally, there is only a single office of Secretary of State although that office may be performed by a number of named Secretaries of State as determined by the Queen in Council.

In practice, however, an application for development consent under the Planning Act 2008 is determined by whichever Secretary of State, or Secretaries of State, have responsibility for the field of activity in relation to which the application relates. Thus, the Secretary of State for Transport in practice determines applications for consent for transport projects. This would include road, rail and port projects. Similarly, the Secretary of State for Business, Energy and Industrial Strategy ('BEIS') makes decisions on energy infrastructure applications.

There may be other roles for a Secretary of State in the DCO process. For example, the power in PA 2008, s 127 (statutory undertakers' land) would be exercised by the Secretary of State who is responsible for the particular affected statutory undertaker's activity (for example, the Secretary of State for Environment, Food and Rural Affairs ('Defra') in relation to a water company).

Legal challenges relating to applications for orders granting development consent are to be brought by judicial review under PA 2008, s 118, and legal challenges relating to National Policy Statements ('NPSs') are to be made by judicial review under PA 2008, s 13. In litigation connected with an application for a development consent order, it will be the Secretary of State responsible for the decision on that application or NPS who would, in practice, be the defendant in any judicial review proceedings. So, for example, the Secretary of State for Transport ('DfT') was the defendant in the judicial review challenges to the designation of the Airports National Policy Statement under PA 2008, s 13, as it was that Secretary of State who had designated the NPS.

In practice, it is usual for the Government Legal Department ('GLD') – formerly known as the Treasury Solicitor's Department ('TSol') – to act on behalf of a Secretary of State in litigation. The GLD website states that it has more than 2,000 employees, of whom around 1,400 are solicitors or barristers. It acts for the majority of central government departments, including the Department on Levelling Up, Housing and Communities (DLUHC), BEIS, Defra and DfT. The GLD operates from its headquarters at: 102 Petty France, Westminster, London SW1H 9GL.

Part 2

National Policy Statements

Article 5

General Procedural Requirements for Designation of an NPS

James Pereira QC, ftb
Michael Humphries QC, ftb

Introduction

A National Policy Statement ('NPS') is a statement issued by the Secretary of State that sets out national policy in relation to one or more type of development falling within PA 2008, s 14. NPSs are formally 'designated' by the relevant Secretary of State (PA 2008, s 5(1) and (2)). In determining an application for development consent, there is a statutory obligation upon the Secretary of State to determine the application in accordance with any relevant NPS, unless certain specified circumstances apply (PA 2008, s 104). NPSs are, therefore, key policy documents within the PA 2008 regime.

Certain important procedural steps must be undertaken before an NPS can be designated. Broadly speaking, these steps relate to publicity and consultation, parliamentary scrutiny and consideration of sustainability (generally, PA 2008, ss 5–10). The High Court has made clear that the procedural requirements that precede the designation of an NPS mean that changes in circumstances relating to the strategic need for a particular type of project should properly be raised by way of a request to the Secretary of State to modify the NPS, rather than as a factor justifying departure from that NPS in any given case: see *R (Thames Blue Green Economy Limited) v Secretary of State* [2015] EWCA Civ 876 (a decision on a judicial review permission application).

The procedural steps are outlined in this section. Reference should be made to the provisions of the Act for the detail.

Publicity and consultation

Prior to the designation of an NPS, or a proposed amendment to an NPS, certain publicity requirements must be met (PA 2008, s 5(4) and (7)). In relation to a 'proposal' to designate an NPS or an amendment to an NPS (PA 2008, s 7(3)), the PA 2008 gives the Secretary of State a discretion to carry out such consultation and arrange for such publicity as the Secretary of State thinks appropriate, subject to certain mandatory requirements being met (PA 2008, s 7(2), (4) and (5)). The Secretary of State must, however, have regard to the responses to such consultation and publicity when deciding whether to proceed with such a 'proposal' (PA 2008, s 7(6)).

Formal consultation is mandatory in relation to such persons and descriptions of persons as may be prescribed (PA 2008, s 7(4)).

In relation to publicity, the Secretary of State must ensure that 'appropriate steps' are taken to publicise the 'proposal' where it identifies one or more locations as suitable or potentially suitable for a specified description of development (PA 2008, s 7(5)). When deciding what publicity is appropriate for these purposes, PA 2008, s 8 requires the Secretary of State to consult the relevant local authorities on the publicity requirements (see PA 2008, s 8(1)–(5) for identification of which local authorities need to be consulted).

The publicity requirements may be satisfied in relation to modified versions of an earlier proposed policy statement, where the Secretary of State thinks that the modifications do not materially affect the policy as set out in the 'earlier proposal' which itself complied with the relevant publicity requirements (see PA 2008, s 6A(1)–(3), to which reference should be made).

Parliamentary scrutiny

A proposed NPS, or amendment to an NPS, must be laid before Parliament (PA 2008, s 9(2)). Before doing so, the Secretary of State must specify the relevant period within which either House of Parliament may make a resolution with regard to the proposal, or a committee of either House may make a recommendation with regard to the proposal (PA 2008, s 6B(4), (6) and (7)). The Secretary of State must lay before Parliament his response to any resolution or recommendation: PA 2008, s 6B(4) and (5).

Following these steps, the proposed policy or amendment to policy can be laid before Parliament, though the formal step of laying the policy before Parliament may need to be repeated in certain circumstances (PA 2008, s 6B(8) and (9)). PA 2008, s 6A(4) contains provision relevant to changes made to the proposed policy after it has been laid before Parliament.

Sustainability

No policy statement can be designated an NPS unless it has first been subject to a sustainability appraisal (PA 2008, s 5(3)). This requirement is intended to satisfy the obligation to carry out Strategic Environmental Assessment pursuant to the SEA Directive 2001/42/EC. A sustainability appraisal that fails to satisfy the requirements of the SEA Directive will be liable to challenge under PA 2008, s 13.

When designating or reviewing an NPS the Secretary of State must also exercise his functions with the objective of contributing to the achievement of sustainable development, in particular with regard to the desirability of mitigating and adopting to climate change and achieving good design (PA 2008, s 10).

These two provisions (PA 2008, ss 5(3) and 10) were the subject matter of the PA 2008, s 13 judicial review challenges to the designation of the Airports NPS that went to the Supreme Court in 2020; see *R (Friends of the Earth and others) v Heathrow Airport Limited* [2020] UKSC 52 (on appeal from [2020] EWCA Civ 214).

Designation as an NPS

Once the consultation and publicity requirements in PA 2008, s 7 have been met, and the parliamentary requirements in PA 2008, s 9 have been discharged, the policy statement can be designated an NPS provided that the statement has been approved by resolution of the House of Commons after being laid before Parliament under PA 2008, s 9(8) and before the end of the 'consideration period', or the 'consideration period' for the statement has expired without the House of Commons resolving during that period that the statement should not be proceeded with (PA 2008, s 5(4)).

The 'consideration period' is defined under PA 2008, s 5(4A) as the period 21 sitting days beginning with the first sitting day after the day on which the statement is laid before Parliament under PA 2008, s 9(8). This period may itself be extended by 21 sitting days or less, and extended more than once, subject to certain procedural requirements (PA 2008, s 6B).

Review and amendment of an NPS

The review of an NPS is discussed in greater depth in article 13 of this work, but in broad terms the position is as follows.

The Secretary of State must review all or part of an NPS where he considers it appropriate to do so (PA 2008, s 6(1) and (2)).

In deciding whether to do so, the Secretary of State must have regard to whether there has been a significant change in circumstances on the basis of which the relevant policy or part of the policy was decided; whether that change was anticipated at the time; and whether, if the change had been anticipated, any of the relevant policy would have been materially different (PA 2008, s 6(3) and (4)).

A review may result in the NPS being amended, withdrawn or left as it is (PA 2008, s 6(5)).

PA 2008, s 6(6) provides that a sustainability appraisal must be carried out before an NPS is amended. The same requirement could be argued to apply to a decision to withdraw an NPS: see, by analogy, *Cala Homes v Secretary of State* [2010] EWHC 2866 (Admin) (decision to revoke Regional Spatial Strategies unlawful unless preceded by SEA).

Amendments to an NPS are subject to similar requirements for consultation, publicity and Parliamentary scrutiny as apply to an NPS itself (PA 2008, s 6(7), referring to PA 2008, ss 7 and 9).

Article 6

NPSs and the Requirement for an Appraisal of Sustainability

Rebecca Clutten, ftb
Michael Humphries QC, ftb

The nature and effect of NPSs

National Policy Statements ('NPSs') are the statutory planning policy statements for nationally significant infrastructure projects in England and Wales. By virtue of PA 2008, s 104, wherever there is an extant NPS (PA 2008, s 104(1)), the Secretary of State must, when determining an application for a DCO, have regard to *inter alia* that relevant NPS (PA 2008, s 104(2)).

Although there are other specified documents and matters to which the Secretary of State must have regard, PA 2008 goes on to provide that, save in specified circumstances (that is, where the circumstances set out in PA 2008, s 104(4)–(8) apply), DCO applications must be decided in accordance with the relevant NPS.

The NPS therefore has a comparable status in the decision making process to the statutory development plan in the determination of applications for planning permission under the Town and Country Planning regime, in that it sets the framework for *inter alia* the nature and scale of development that may be brought forward (cf Planning and Compulsory Purchase Act 2004, s 38(6)).

The need for an assessment of sustainability

As a consequence of their setting of the parameters for development that can be brought forward (and in some cases, such as nuclear, the locations in which development may be brought forward), the NPSs have a significant role to play in determining the nature and scale of environmental, social and economic effects that will in due course occur as a result of such development.

In order to ensure that the policies contained within the NPSs are appropriate in environmental terms, it is therefore vitally important that they be subject to environmental assessment prior to their taking effect upon designation.

The procedure for the preparation and designation of NPSs contained in PA 2008, s 5 makes provision for precisely this. PA 2008, s 5(3) states that, 'Before designating a statement as a national policy statement for the purposes of this Act the Secretary of State must carry out an appraisal of the sustainability of the policy set out in the statement'.

The same requirement applies where the Secretary of State proposes to amend an existing NPS: see PA 2008, s 6(6).

What is required by way of sustainability appraisal?

No guidance is given in the PA 2008, or any related documents, as to precisely what is required as part of an 'appraisal of the sustainability of the policy set out in the statement'.

It is nonetheless clear that, as a minimum, it needs to contain all the information that would be required of a strategic environmental assessment ('SEA') carried out pursuant to the Environmental Assessment of Plans and Programmes Regulations 2004 (as amended) ('the SEA Regulations'), which implemented the requirements of European Directive 2001/42/EC on the assessment of the effects of certain plans and programmes on the environment ('the SEA Directive').

This is because, quite independently of any requirement of the PA 2008 to carry out a sustainability appraisal, a NPS would be a 'plan or programme' for the purposes of the SEA Regulations, which:

> '(a) is prepared for agriculture, forestry, fisheries, energy, industry, transport, waste management, water management, telecommunications, tourism, town and country planning or land use, and
>
> (b) sets the framework for future development consent of projects listed in Annex I or II to Council Directive 85/337/EEC on the assessment of the effects of certain public and private projects on the environment as amended by Council Directive 97/11/EC [the Environmental Impact Assessment Directive])'.

(Annex I or II projects are those projects that are respectively subject to the mandatory carrying out of environmental impact assessment ('EIA'), or exceed specified thresholds and are likely to have significant effects on the environment that necessitate the carrying out of EIA: reg 5. NB reg 6 is irrelevant as no preparatory act relating to a NPS could have occurred before 21 July 2004, NPSs not coming into existence until the commencement of the PA 2008.)

The substantive requirements of the SEA Regulations are set out in Part 3 of the same, with reg 12 requiring the preparation of an environmental report that:

> 'describe[s] and evaluate[s] the likely significant effects on the environment of–
>
> (a) implementing the plan or programme; and
>
> (b) reasonable alternatives taking into account the objectives and the geographical scope of the plan or programme'.

As in the case of environmental impact assessment ('EIA') of development control projects, the report prepared need only to include such of the information referred to in Sch 2 to the SEA Regulations as may reasonably be required, taking account of (a) current knowledge and methods of assessment; (b) the contents and level of detail in the plan or programme; and (c) the stage of the plan or programme in the decision-making process. The authority may in the case of SEA also consider the extent to which certain matters are more appropriately assessed at different levels in that process in order to avoid duplication of the assessment (reg 12(2)).

In *R (Friends of the Earth and others) v Heathrow Airport Limited* [2020] UKSC 52, Lords Hodge and Sales said (para 144) that:

> 'As the Divisional Court and the Court of Appeal held in the present case, the discretion of the relevant decision-maker under article 5(2) and (3) of the SEA Directive as to whether the information included in an environmental report is adequate and appropriate for the purposes of providing a sound and sufficient basis for public consultation leading to a final environmental assessment is likewise subject to the conventional *Wednesbury* standard of review. We agree with the Court of Appeal when it said (para 136):
>
>> "The court's role in ensuring that an authority – here the Secretary of State – has complied with the requirements of article 5 and Annex I when preparing an environmental report, must reflect the breadth of the discretion given to it to decide what information 'may reasonably be required' when taking into account the considerations referred to – first, 'current knowledge and methods of assessment';

second, 'the contents and level of detail in the plan or programme'; third, 'its stage in the decision-making process'; and fourth 'the extent to which certain matters are more appropriately assessed at different levels in that process in order to avoid duplication of the assessment'. These requirements leave the authority with a wide range of autonomous judgment on the adequacy of the information provided. It is not for the court to fix this range of judgment more tightly than is necessary. The authority must be free to form a reasonable view of its own on the nature and amount of information required, with the specified considerations in mind. This, in our view, indicates a conventional 'Wednesbury' standard of review – as adopted, for example, in *Blewett*. A standard more intense than that would risk the court being invited, in effect, to substitute its own view on the nature and amount of information included in environmental reports for that of the decision-maker itself. This would exceed the proper remit of the court."'

This is a hugely important statement of principle on how the courts will approach 'adequacy' in relation to obligations deriving from the SEA Directive and now more specifically, following the UK's withdrawal from the European Union, the SEA Regulations.

By virtue of reg 13, there is also a requirement for consultation upon that environmental report, together with the draft plan or programme to which it relates (reg 13(1)). The consultation must last for a specified period 'of such length as will ensure that the consultation bodies and the public consultees are given an effective opportunity to express their opinion on the relevant documents' (reg 13(4)). Regulation 13(2) contains detailed requirements as to how the consultation exercise is to be carried out.

The 'consultation bodies' are defined in reg 4 of the SEA Regulations, and include agencies such as English Heritage, Natural England and the Environment Agency and, in appropriate cases, the Scottish Ministers/National Assembly for Wales. 'Public consultees' are those whom the authority preparing the plan 'are affected or likely to be affected by, or have an interest in the decisions involved in the assessment and adoption of the plan or programme concerned' (reg 13(2)(b)).

Consultations must also extend, however, to EU Member States if it is considered that the plan or programme is likely to have significant effects on the environment of that Member State (reg 14(1)).

Although not of direct application to appraisals carried out pursuant to PA 2008, the Government's online National Planning Practice Guidance does contain useful guidance on sustainability appraisals and SEA in the context of the local plan preparation process, including a SEA checklist, much of which will apply by analogy. (At the time of writing, the relevant title was 'Strategic environmental assessment and sustainability appraisal', reference ID 11-001-20140306.)

The need for Habitats Regulations Assessment ('HRA')

In addition to the requirement for sustainability appraisal or SEA, the preparation of NPSs will also necessitate the carrying out of an Appropriate Assessment ('AA') for the purposes of the Conservation of Habitats and Species Regulations 2010 ('the Habitats Regulations'), article 61 of which provides that:

'(1) A competent authority, before deciding to undertake, or give any consent, permission or other authorisation for, a plan or project which–

(a) is likely to have a significant effect on a European site or a European offshore marine site (either alone or in combination with other plans or projects), and

> (b) is not directly connected with or necessary to the management of that site,
>
> must make an appropriate assessment of the implications for that site in view of that site's conservation objectives.'

'European site' and 'European marine site' are defined in reg 8, including *inter alia* special areas of conservation and sites of community importance.

As in the case of SEA, consultation on the AA is required. First, with the 'appropriate nature conservation body' to whose responses 'regard must be had', and second, with the public, though only if the competent authority (see reg 7) considers it appropriate (see reg 61(3) and (4)).

By virtue of reg 61(6), the competent authority may agree to the plan or project only after having ascertained that it will not adversely affect the integrity of the European site or the European offshore marine site (as the case may be). This requirement is qualified by the power of the competent authority to show, in cases where an adverse effect on integrity will occur, that there are imperative reasons of overriding public interest ('IROPI') justifying adoption of the plan or project in any event (see regs 61(5) and 62).

It follows from the above that, in the absence of an IROPI justification, a draft NPS could not be designated in circumstances where it had been demonstrated that its provisions would affect the integrity of the European site or the European offshore marine site.

The requirements of any assessment under the Habitats Regulations are discussed in more detail in article 68 of this work.

Taking account of climate change

PA 2008, s 5(7) contains a specific duty on the Secretary of State to give reasons for the policy set out in an NPS, and s 5(8) provides that, 'The reasons must (in particular) include an explanation of how the policy set out in the statement takes account of Government policy relating to the mitigation of, and adaptation to, climate change'. Furthermore, PA 2008, s 10(2) makes clear that, in exercising the powers under s 5 (designating an NPS) and s 6 (reviewing an NPS), the Secretary of State must exercise those functions with the objective of contributing to the achievement of sustainable development and, in so doing, s 10(3) provides that the Secretary of State 'must (in particular) have regard to the desirability of (a) mitigating, and adapting to, climate change …'.

These provisions were central to the challenges by Friends of the Earth ('FOE') and Plan B Earth ('PBE') to the designation of the Airports NPS, finally determined by the Supreme Court in *R (Friends of the Earth and others) v Heathrow Airport Ltd* [2020] UKSC 52.

In relation to the duty under s 5(8) (that is, the duty to have regard to Government policy on climate change), the Court of Appeal had placed reliance on various comments made by Ministers in 2016 on the issue of the Paris Agreement goal of achieving 'net zero' and concluded that this represented the Government's expressly stated policy at the time of designation of the Airports NPS (June 2018), well before the formal adoption of the 'net zero' target in June 2019. The Supreme Court reviewed in detail the meaning of 'Government policy' for the purposes of that section and concluded (paras 101–110) that it means a formal statement of Government policy and not qualified or ambiguous Ministerial Statements recorded in Hansard or a Press Statement. This ground of challenge was, therefore, dismissed.

In relation to the duty under s 10(3), the Supreme Court relied on the three categories of 'consideration' in *R v Somerset CC ex p Fewings* [1995] 1 WLR 1037, namely:

> '… [T]he judge speaks of a "decision-maker who fails to take account of all and only those considerations material to his task". It is important to bear in mind, however,

> … that there are in fact three categories of consideration. First, those clearly (whether expressly or impliedly) identified by the statute as considerations to which regard must be had. Second, those clearly identified by the statute as considerations to which regard must not be had. Third, those to which the decision-maker may have regard if in his judgment and discretion he thinks it right to do so. There is, in short, a margin of appreciation within which the decision-maker may decide just what considerations should play a part in his reasoning process.'

The Supreme Court held that the Paris Agreement on climate change fell into the third category, namely that of considerations to which the decision-maker might have regard if, in its discretion, it thought it right to do so. The Supreme Court also concluded, however, that the Court of Appeal was wrong to have found that the Secretary of State had omitted to consider the Paris Agreement when designating the Airports NPS; on the evidence, he did (paras 114–133). This ground of challenge was also, therefore, dismissed.

Article 7

NPS Consultation and Amendments

James Pereira QC, ftb

Introduction

The designation or amendment of an NPS is subject to requirements concerning consultation and publicity and parliamentary scrutiny. This article explains the statutory framework for consultation under the PA 2008, outlines the general legal principles that apply to lawful consultation, and gives some practical considerations and information.

Although this article focuses on the requirements for public consultation on, and amendments to, NPSs under the PA 2008, other legislation may also be relevant to consultation and publicity. One important such legislative requirement is the need for strategic environmental assessment under the Environmental Assessment of Plans and Programmes Regulations 2004 ('the SEA Regulations'). Other requirements may arise under the Conservation of Habitats and Species Regulations 2017 ('the Habitats Regulations'). In practice, the consultation and publicity on the NPS or a proposed amendment will usually be designed so as to fulfil the requirements of these other legislative regimes as well.

Legal framework

The circumstances that engage the requirements for consultation and publicity are set out in PA 2008, ss 5(4), 6(7) and 6A. The content of the required consultation and publicity is addressed in s 7, as supplemented by s 8.

In respect of a proposed NPS, PA 2008, s 5(4) provides (among other pre-conditions) that a statement may be designated as a national policy statement for the purposes of the PA 2008 'only if the consultation and publicity requirements set out in section 7 ... have been complied with in relation to it'. Therefore, a proposed NPS must always be subject to the statutory requirements set out in section 7.

The position in respect of amendments to an existing NPS is slightly different. Section 6(7) of the PA 2008 provides that the Secretary of State may amend a national policy statement 'only if the consultation and publicity requirements set out in section 7 ... have been complied with in relation to the proposed amendment'. However, by s 6(8), these requirements do not apply '"if the Secretary of State thinks that the proposed amendment (taken with any other proposed amendments) does not materially affect the policy as set out in the national policy statement'. Hence the materiality of the amendment is relevant in deciding whether or not the statutory requirements for consultation and publicity are engaged.

Changes to proposals as a result of consultation: when is a further round of consultation needed?

Section 6A addresses the question of whether further consultation is needed when changes are made to the policy or amendment following consultation and publicity. Not every change will need to undergo a further round of consultation and publicity. A balance must be struck between procedural fairness and the need for consultation and publicity to come to end. The approach to be taken in cases of this kind is found in PA 2008, s 6A(2) and (3).

Section 6A(2) is concerned with situations where an amendment is made to the proposed NPS or an amendment to it, *after statutory consultation* and publicity has taken place. Section 6A(2) provides that the consultation and publicity requirements set out in PA 2008, s 7 are to be treated as having been complied with in relation to a statement of proposed amendment (defined as 'the final proposal') where all of the following three conditions are met:

- The consultation and publicity requirements of section 7 have been complied with in relation to a different statement or proposed amendment (defined as 'the earlier proposal').
- The final proposal is a modified version of the earlier proposal.
- The Secretary of State 'thinks that the modifications do not materially affect the policy as set out in the earlier proposal'.

Section 6A therefore allows the Secretary of State to make non-material modifications to a proposal that has been consulted on, without needing to re-consult on the modification.

Section 6A(3) concerns situations *where there has been further consultation* on an amendment made after an earlier phase of consultation. Section 6A(3) provides that the consultation and publicity requirements set out in PA 2008, s 7 are to be treated as having been complied with in relation to a statement of proposed amendment (defined as 'the final proposal') where all of the following (slightly different) three conditions are met:

- The consultation and publicity requirements of section 7 have been complied with in relation to a different statement or proposed amendment (defined as 'the earlier proposal') *and* in relation to modifications to the earlier proposal (defined as 'the main modifications').
- The final proposal is a modified version of the earlier proposal.
- Either:
  - there are no modifications other than the main modifications; or
  - where the proposal includes modifications other than the main modifications, the Secretary of State 'thinks that those other modifications do not materially affect the policy as set out in the earlier proposal modified by the main modifications'.

The effect of section 6A(3) is that, where 'main modifications' are made to a proposal which materially affect the policy or amendment consulted on earlier, consultation and publicity must take place in respect of those main modifications. Once this has been undertaken, there is no need for further consultation, provided that no further modifications are made or, if they are made, they do not materially affect the earlier proposal as modified and consulted upon.

Note that, while s 6A(2) and (3) gives the Secretary of State a discretion to judge whether changes 'materially affect' the policy set out in the earlier proposal, this discretion will be reviewable on conventional grounds of judicial review.

What are the consultation and publicity requirements?

PA 2008, s 7 sets out the consultation and publicity requirements referred to in sections 5(4) and 6(7).

Section 7(2) provides that, subject to subsections (4) and (5), the Secretary of State must carry out such consultation, and arrange for such publicity, as he or she 'thinks appropriate in relation to the proposal'.

The proposal means either the statement that is proposed to be designated as an NPS, or the proposed amendment to an NPS, as the case may be (s 7(3)). The provision therefore gives the Secretary of State a broad discretion to determine on a case-by-case basis what is required, subject to general principles of public law concerning the requirements for fair consultation and public engagement (discussed below).

As noted, the discretion under s 7(2) is subject to s 7(4) and (5).

Section 7(4) provides that the Secretary of State must consult such persons, and such descriptions of persons, as may be prescribed. Persons were originally prescribed under the Infrastructure Planning (National Policy Statement) Consultation Regulations 2009; however, these regulations were revoked by Town and Country Planning (Revocations) Regulations 2014, Sch 1, para 1 (effective on 14 April 2014). At the time of writing, no further regulations prescribing persons have been made.

Section 7(5) provides that, if the policy set out in the proposal identifies one or more locations as suitable or potentially suitable for a specified description of development, the Secretary of State must ensure that appropriate steps are taken to publicise the proposal. Section 7(5) should be read together with PA 2008, s 5(5)(d), which provides that an NPS may identify one or more locations as suitable or potentially suitable (or unsuitable) for a specified description of development. Not all NPSs have location-specific policies of this kind, so section 7(5) will only be engaged in certain kinds of cases, depending on the content of the policy in question.

PA 2008, s 8 imposes further requirements in cases where section 7(5) is engaged. It provides that, when deciding what steps are appropriate for the purposes of publicising the proposal in a section 7(5) case, the Secretary of State 'must' consult the Greater London Authority, if any of the locations concerned are in Greater London, and each local authority that has within its area any of the locations concerned (s 8(1), (2)). In addition, specific provisions address the need to consult certain local authorities whose areas do not include the locations concerned, but whose boundaries adjoin unitary councils and certain kinds of county council whose areas do include the locations concerned (see s 8(1)(a), (3), (3A) and (5)). In essence, s 8 is a statutory acknowledgement that local authorities have a particular interest in proposals that may impact upon their local area, and particular experience in consulting in their locality. Hence, the requirement for their views to be taken into account when deciding what publicity requirements should apply in a section 7(5) case.

General legal principles relevant to publicity and consultation

It is to be noted that the statute does not prescribe detail about how the consultation and publicity is to be carried out. This does not mean that the Secretary of State is free to consult as he or she chooses. Case law provides general rules that must be complied with for consultation to be lawful.

Known as 'the Gunning principles' from *R v Brent London Borough Council ex p Gunning* (1985) 84 LGR 168, endorsed by the Supreme Court in *R (Stirling) v Haringey London Borough Council* [2014] PTSR 1317 at [25], the four key general principles of note are:

(1) consultation must be at a time when proposals are still at a formative stage;

(2) the proposer must give sufficient reasons for any proposal to permit of intelligent consideration and response;

(3) adequate time must be given for consideration and response; and

(4) the product of consultation must be conscientiously taken into account in finalising any statutory proposals.

In relation to the second principle above, in the present context where the general public cannot be expected to be familiar with all the issues, and the purpose of consultation is to support wide public engagement, providing sufficient reasons for the policy (or proposed amendment) may require a large amount of information to accompany the consultation, including information on realistic alternatives; see, by analogy, *R (Stirling) v Haringey London Borough Council* [2014] PTSR 1317 at [38] and [39]. In practice, consultation on NPSs may include some background material including technical material explaining the reasons for the preferred policy approach. For example, consultation on the Airports NPS included a round of consultation to take into account updated noise and air quality information, and included reference to technical assessments on those impacts. The Government's published 'consultation principles' provide additional practical guidelines which consultation will also usually follow.

Legal challenges arising from consultation

Defective consultation would fall within the ambit of 'anything done, or omitted to be done' under PA 2008, s 13(1), and a challenge on this basis would need to be brought before the end of a period of six weeks beginning with the day after the day on which the statement is designated or, if later, the day on which the statement is published. A claim brought in advance of this date is very likely to be struck out on the basis that the court has no jurisdiction; see, for example, *R (London Borough of Hillingdon Council) v Secretary of State for Transport* [2017] EWHC 121 at [4] and [5].

In the case of defective consultation on an amendment to an existing NPS, although the matter is not free from doubt, it appears that the challenge must be brought before the end of the period of six weeks beginning with the day after the day on which the amendment is made. This appears to be the effect of PA 2008, s13(4) and (5) when read together with s 6(5). On one reading of s 6(5), it is not clear if consultation on a proposed amendment to an NPS is an action carried out in the course of a review (to which s 13(4) applies) or after completing a review (to which s 13(5) applies). However, since the time limits in s 13(4) and (5) relate back to the exercise of power under s 6(5), this uncertainty does not appear to matter.

Practical matters

While the extent and nature of consultation on an NPS or a proposed change to an NPS will vary from case to case, there are some general practical points that can be made.

First, online access to consultations can be gained through the gov.uk website, which has a specific section for consultations. This will describe the nature, dates and duration of the consultation, and provide access to relevant consultation documents. Responses to consultation can also be made online.

Secondly, the key document will be the consultation draft version of the NPS or the proposed amended NPS. This will contain the proposed policy, and the reasons for it, and will usually set out specific consultation questions on which responses are sought. Consultees are, of course, at liberty to make any points they wish irrespective of the questions asked. Details will also be given of other consultation and publicity events, such as local meetings and exhibitions.

Thirdly, there will be other important documents accompanying the draft proposal. One such document will be the 'appraisal of sustainability' for the proposed policy or amendment (s 5(3)). This will contain an assessment of the social, economic and environmental impacts of the proposal, as well as consideration of reasonable alternatives to it, in accordance with the requirements for Strategic Environmental Assessment. Technical appendices to the assessment usually contain more detailed information. Other documents, such as a Habitats Regulations Assessment, will also accompany the draft policy where relevant.

Fourthly, where changes are made to the proposal resulting in a further round of consultation, such further consultation will usually be accompanied by documents explaining the earlier consultation process, how the responses to consultation have been considered, and the reasons for the change being consulted upon. This is to give context to the further consultation round, so as to enable informed responses to be given.

Finally, the designation of an NPS or the adoption of an amendment to an NPS will be accompanied by a post-adoption statement. This is a requirement of the SEA Regulations. The post-adoption statement will explain how environmental considerations and the sustainability appraisal have informed the final policy, how the consultation responses have been taken into account, and the reasons for choosing the version of the policy or amendment that has been adopted, in the light of other reasonable alternatives. The post-adoption statement is therefore a useful source of information on the process and thinking behind the formulation of the final policy.

Article 8

Context for the Identification of Need in NPSs

Rebecca Clutten, ftb
Michael Humphries QC, ftb

Introduction

The Government's stated aim in *Planning for a sustainable future*, the White Paper that preceded the PA 2008, was to create a system for determining applications for nationally significant infrastructure projects that was 'timely, efficient and predictable'.

One of the perceived major obstacles to bringing forward such projects was the absence of clear policy frameworks for all types of nationally significant infrastructure. This resulted in a lack of certainty for promoters and communities, and significant time being spent at public inquiries debating high-level issues including need.

In order to address this problem, the Government proposed the introduction of the national policy statements ('NPSs'), which would 'set out the national need for infrastructure and explain how this fits with other policies such as those relating to economic development, international competitiveness, climate change, energy conservation/efficiency and protection of the historic and natural environment'.

NPSs were subsequently introduced through Part 2 of the PA 2008.

The legislative framework relating to the identification of need

Need in NPSs

The legislative basis for NPSs is found in Part 2 of the PA 2008. By virtue of PA 2008, s 5, the Secretary of State has power to designate a statement that sets national policy in respect of one or more specified descriptions of development.

PA 2008, s 5(5)(a) specifically provides that the Secretary of State may, in particular,

> 'set out, in relation to a specified description of development, the amount, type or size of development of that description which is appropriate nationally or for a specified area'.

PA 2008, s 5(5)(c) empowers the Secretary of State to set out in the NPS 'the relative weight to be given to specified criteria'.

PA 2008, s 5(1) and (5) taken together therefore permit the Secretary of State to identify through NPSs both the need for national infrastructure, and the weight to be attached to that need.

How need is taken into account in determining applications for development consent

The primary provision identifying how national policy on need is to be taken into account when determining applications for development consent is PA 2008, s 104. Section 104 requires that, where there is a designated NPS having effect in relation to development of the description to which the application relates, the Secretary of State must, in deciding the application:

- have regard to that NPS (PA 2008, s 104(2)); and
- determine the application in accordance with it, unless one of the situations identified in PA 2008, s 104(4)–(8) applies (PA 2008, s 104(3)).

The effect of PA 2008, s 104 is therefore to require the Secretary of State to have regard to the national policy position on need, including the weight that it has been determined should to be attached to it, and to determine the application so as to accord with that policy position (including by attaching any prescribed weight to the need for that type of development), save in one of the cases identified in PA 2008, s 104(4)–(8).

Also noteworthy are PA 2008, ss 87 and 106. PA 2008, s 106 entitles the Secretary of State, when determining an application for development consent, to disregard any representations made to him or her relating to the merits of a policy set out in an NPS. PA 2008, s 87 makes similar provision for the Examining Authority.

As a result of these enactments, where the need for infrastructure (and any weight to be attached to the same) has been identified in an NPS, promoters of, and objectors to, schemes will, in effect, be precluded from taking issue with the need as identified.

Designated NPSs

A number of NPSs have now been designated under PA 2008, s 5, as follows:

Energy

- Overarching National Policy Statement for Energy (EN-1) (DECC July 2011)
- National Policy Statement for Fossil Fuel Electricity Generating Infrastructure (EN-2) (DECC July 2011)
- National Policy Statement for Renewable Energy Infrastructure (EN-3) (DECC July 2011)
- National Policy Statement for Gas Supply Infrastructure and Gas and Oil Pipelines (EN-4) (DECC July 2011)
- National Policy Statement for Electricity Networks Infrastructure (EN-5) (DECC July 2011)
- National Policy Statement for Nuclear Power Generation (2 volumes) (EN-6) (DECC July 2011)

Transport

- National Policy Statement for Ports (DfT January 2012)
- National Policy Statement for National Networks (DfT January 2015)
- Airports National Policy Statement (DfT June 2018)

Water, Waste Water, Waste

- National Policy Statement for Waste Water (Defra March 2012)
- National Policy Statement for Hazardous Waste (Defra June 2013)
- Geological Disposal Infrastructure NPS (BEIS October 2019).

Government has also consulted on:

- a draft NPS for Water Resources Infrastructure (Defra) during 2018/19; and
- a suite of new Energy NPSs (BEIS) during 2021.

It is also understood that Government intends to review other NPSs in the context, amongst other things, of its June 2019 commitment in Climate Change Act 2008, s 1(1) to meet 'net zero' by 2050.

Article 9

The Identification of Need in the Energy NPSs

Rebecca Clutten, ftb
Michael Humphries QC, ftb

Introduction

In 2011, DECC (which has since become BEIS) designated the following NPSs under PA 2008, s 5 in relation to energy infrastructure:

- Overarching National Policy Statement for Energy (EN-1) (DECC July 2011);
- National Policy Statement for Fossil Fuel Electricity Generating Infrastructure (EN-2) (DECC July 2011);
- National Policy Statement for Renewable Energy Infrastructure (EN-3) (DECC July 2011);
- National Policy Statement for Gas Supply Infrastructure and Gas and Oil Pipelines (EN-4) (DECC July 2011);
- National Policy Statement for Electricity Networks Infrastructure (EN-5) (DECC July 2011); and
- National Policy Statement for Nuclear Power Generation (2 volumes) (EN-6) (DECC July 2011).

The Overarching Energy NPS (EN-1) together with the relevant technology-specific NPSs (EN2 to EN-6) are intended to set out national policy for energy infrastructure, including that on national need.

Applicants are informed in EN-1 that they should 'ensure that their applications, and any accompanying supporting documents, are consistent with the instructions and guidance in this NPS, the relevant technology NPS and any other NPSs that are relevant to the application in question' (para 1.1.3).

This article is based on the designated Energy NPSs at the time of writing, but it should be noted that BEIS published the 'Energy White Paper: Powering our net zero future' in December 2020, which states as follows:

> 'We will complete a review of the existing energy National Policy Statements (NPS), with the aim of designating updated NPS by the end of 2021.
>
> The suite of energy NPS establish the need for new energy infrastructure and set out a framework for the consideration of applications for development consent. We have decided that it is appropriate to review the NPS, to ensure that they reflect the policies set out in this white paper and that we continue to have a planning policy framework which can deliver the investment required to build the infrastructure needed for the transition to net zero. Work on this review will start immediately, with the aim of designating updated NPS by the end of 2021.

This white paper shows that the need for the energy infrastructure set out in energy NPS remains, except in the case of coal-fired generation. While the review is undertaken, the current suite of NPS remain relevant government policy and have effect for the purposes of the Planning Act 2008. They will, therefore, continue to provide a proper basis on which the Planning Inspectorate can examine, and the Secretary of State can make decisions on, applications for development consent. Nothing in this white paper should be construed as setting a limit on the number of development consent orders which may be granted for any type of generating infrastructure set out in the energy NPS. Other restrictions outside the planning regime (in particular the Emissions Performance Standard) mean that no new coal infrastructure projects can come forward.'

Consultation on the new suite of Energy NPSs was undertaken between 6 September 2021 and 29 November 2021. At the time of writing (early 2022), the new NPSs had not yet been designated.

See the Court of Appeal decision in *R (ClientEarth) v Secretary of State for Business, Energy and Industrial Strategy and Drax Power Limited* [2021] EWCA Civ 43 for an extremely helpful discussion on the proper interpretation of NPSs EN-1 (overarching energy) and EN-2 (fossil fuels). The judgment deals with three important issues, being:

- the proper approach to the interpretation of EN-1 on the assessment of 'need' for generating stations (paras 48–76);
- the proper approach to the interpretation of EN-1 on the approach to greenhouse gas emissions (paras 77–97); and
- the proper application of the s 104(7) / s 104(3) balance (paras 98–110).

Although decided under the NPS for Hazardous Waste, see also the Court of Appeal decision in *R (Scarisbrick) v Secretary of State for Communities and Local Government* [2017] EWCA Civ 787 on the proper approach to 'need' in an NPS. See article 23 of this work for a fuller consideration of that decision.

EN-1: Overarching Energy

EN-1 first sets out the overarching need for energy infrastructure. The Government emphasises that significant new infrastructure will be required not only to meet and secure energy demands in the right location, but also to contribute to the mitigation of climate change (para 2.1.2). The security of supply will be dependent upon factors including having sufficient electricity capacity to meet demand at all times, and having available energy from a diverse mix of technologies (para 2.2.20). Developers are thereby encouraged to bring forward applications for a wide range of energy infrastructure projects.

EN-1 also sets out, in Chapter 3, the Government's position on need in relation to each of the energy infrastructure types for which there is a technology-specific NPS. A summary of the need for each is given below.

Need for electricity generation infrastructure generally

Adopting prudent assumptions as to likely levels of electricity demand, the Government considers that the UK will need at least 113GW of total generating capacity by 2025, some 28GW over and above current capacity. 59GW is anticipated to come from new-build electricity infrastructure. Of that 59GW, 33GW is to come from renewable sources (to meet committed targets), with the remaining 26GW (of which 8GW is already under construction) coming from elsewhere, in a mix to be determined by industry. The Government is supportive of nuclear contributions that that remaining 18GW (para 3.3.22).

Need for renewables electricity generation infrastructure

There is an urgent need for large-scale renewable generation (from sources including onshore and offshore wind, biomass, energy from waste and wave and tidal power), in order to meet the target of sourcing 15% of energy from renewables by 2020, and to facilitate de-carbonisation of the power sector by 2030 (section 3.4).

Need for nuclear electricity generation infrastructure

Nuclear power is one of the key elements of the Government's de-carbonisation strategy, being capable of large-scale deployment and the least expensive source of low-carbon energy (paras 3.5.7–3.5.8). It is also needed to ensure energy security, as uranium prices are less subject to fluctuation than gas and other fossil fuels. The Government therefore seeks the early construction and operation of new stations, in any case before 2025 (para 3.5.9).

Need for fossil fuel electricity generation infrastructure

Fossil fuel generating stations are more flexible than many renewable technologies (which produce energy intermittently) and are considered to remain necessary in order to ensure security of energy supply (paras 3.6.2–3.6.3).

A reduction of emissions from this kind of infrastructure is, however, needed in order to meet carbon reduction targets. The Government considers that carbon capture and storage ('CCS') offers a potential means of achieving such reductions. The Government is therefore seeking to support four commercial-scale demonstration projects for the full CCS chain, and the IPC is directed to take account of the importance placed on these projects in considering applications for CCS projects and infrastructure (paras 3.6.4–3.6.5).

Pending demonstration of the viability of CCS, combustion power stations (300MW or greater) will however need to be carbon-capture ready (i.e. CCS will be adoptable at a later stage) and coal-fired stations will need to demonstrate CCS on up to 300MW of capacity (para 3.6.6).

The need for these CCR fossil fuel stations, and the CCS demonstration projects, is regarded as urgent, as existing capacity will go offline by the end of 2015 (para 3.6.8).

Need for electricity networks infrastructure

The urgent need for additional transmission infrastructure reflects the 'similar' urgent need for new generating capacity to be provided (para 3.7.7). It is recognised that much new generating capacity (particularly wind farms) will be sited in locations where there is little or no existing electricity infrastructure, and it will have to be provided (para 3.7.1).

Need also arises as a result of increasing demands for electricity, which will require a sufficiently robust network to prevent interruptions. A sufficiently robust network will be achieved through making existing infrastructure 'evolve and adapt' and through expansion of the network through new lines (para 3.7.2). The scale of need can be appreciated through consideration of the increases in generation and net electricity flows to 2020 set out in EN-1 (para 3.7.6). Whilst there is an urgent need for transmission and distribution infrastructure generally, it is considered that there is a particular need for new lines of 132kV upwards (para 3.7.10).

The IPC is directed to consider need as demonstrated if it: (a) represents an 'efficient and economical means' of connecting a new generating station; or is (b) reinforcing the network. The cost/benefit of achieving these aims (eg by overhead line or underground cable) and alternatives must however be considered before consent is granted (para 3.7.10).

Need for gas supply infrastructure

Gas infrastructure will continue to be required to meet both domestic (household and industrial) needs, including peaks in demand, and export demand (paras 3.8.2 and 3.8.7). The Government's current assessment is that in order to ensure security of supply, without consumer price risks, additional infrastructure, over and above that which is existing and under-construction, is needed (para 3.8.8).

Particular emphasis is placed on the need for gas (gaseous and liquid) import and storage infrastructure, as the UK's gas production and reserves decline (para 3.8.9). Decisions as to the nature, location, capacity and specification of gas infrastructure are, however, commercial ones for the industry (paras 3.8.13 and 3.8.20).

Need for oil supply infrastructure

The Government considers that the need for oil products will continue to increase in the short-medium term as a result of transport sector dependency, notwithstanding a predicted fall in petrol consumption (para 3.9.2). The need to ensure the security of this supply, and protect against excessive costs, means that new infrastructure for the importation, production, storage and distribution is required (para 3.9.3).

There is a particular focus on the need for pipeline infrastructure, and works associated with the same, the 'significant need' for which the IPC is to take as its starting point in considering applications coming forward (paras 3.9.6–3.9.8).

As a result of the identified need for energy infrastructure, the IPC (now the Examining Authority and/or Secretary of State, but referred to as the IPC for consistency with the original text) is directed to start its consideration of applications with a 'presumption in favour of granting consent to applications for energy NSIPs', the application of such presumption being subject to any more specific and relevant policies set out in the technology-specific NPSs which 'clearly indicate that consent should be refused', and to section 104 of the 2008 Act (para 4.1.2). Need is also a factor which the IPC is directed to take into account in its consideration of where the balance of favour lies on any given application (para 4.1.3).

The weight to be attached to the need for energy infrastructure of all types is also set out in EN-1. Such weight should be 'substantial' but 'proportionate to the anticipated extent of a project's actual contribution to satisfying the need for a particular type of infrastructure' (para 3.2.3).

As in other, non-energy NPSs, the section of EN-1 dealing with Assessment Principles sets out a number of specific policies which require the IPC to weigh in the balance the benefits of the proposed development, which expressly include the stated need for the same (including national need), against various harms which might arise.

These harms include, after mitigation, likely harm to the notified special interest features of a Site of Special Scientific Interest ('SSSI'), in which case the benefits including need should 'clearly outweigh' the harm if consent is to be granted (para 5.3.11). They also include harm to species or sites of principal conservation importance, ancient woodland (by reason of loss or deterioration), and dynamic shorelines (by reason of impacts on sediment flow or other coastal processes) in which case the benefits would need simply to 'outweigh' the harm (paras 5.3.17, 5.3.14 and 5.5.11 respectively).

In the case of designated sites, consent should be granted on sites with national designations (such as Areas of Outstanding Natural Beauty) only in 'exceptional circumstances', where development has been shown to be in the public interest, including by reference to the need for it (para 5.9.9). Regional and local designations should not be used to refuse consent without more (para 5.3.13), and where local landscape impacts arise, the IPC is required to consider whether any adverse impacts are 'so damaging' as to outweigh the benefits, including the need for development of that type (para 5.9.15).

Need is also a factor in decisions as to whether or not to grant consent for development proposals on existing open space, sports and recreational buildings and land. Such proposals should not be consented unless, amongst other things, the decision-maker determines that the benefits of the project (including need) outweigh the potential loss of such facilities (para 5.10.14).

Finally, because of the need for energy infrastructure, the Government's policy is that the IPC is entitled to give little weight to 'speculative assertions of [adverse] socioeconomic impacts [arising from energy development] not supported by evidence' (para 5.12.7).

Whilst no specific reference is made to the weight attaching to the need for the proposed infrastructure, the presumption in favour of consent, and repeated reference to it as benefit of the proposals that must be weighed in the balance, it is clear enough that the weight attached to need by decision-makers is likely to be substantial.

EN-2 to EN-6: the technology-specific energy NPSs

EN 2 to EN-5 inclusive are the technology specific NPSs for energy, providing detailed policy for each of the different kinds of energy infrastructure within the 2008 Act regime.

The majority of the technology-specific energy NPSs do not contain a discrete chapter addressing the need for energy deriving from the technology with which those documents are concerned. EN-2 to EN-6 inclusive (Fossil fuels, Renewables, Gas, Electricity Networks and Nuclear respectively) each cross-refer back to the need identified in Chapter 1.3 of EN-1.

In each case, the need for the energy infrastructure identified in EN-1 is also then reiterated and the IPC is directed, when determining applications for development consent, to 'act on the basis that the need for the infrastructure covered by this NPS [ie the technology-specific NPS in which the statement appears] has been demonstrated' (2.1.2).

A number of the technology-specific NPSs do provide either further commentary on the need that had been identified in EN-1 (for example, emphasising the role a particular technology has to play), or further guidance as to how the need for particular energy infrastructure is to be taken into account by the Secretary of State where particular issues (for example, environmental impacts) arise on any given application. These policies are identified, by NPS, below. NPSs not referred to do not contain any such comment or guidance.

EN-3: Renewable Energy Infrastructure

In addition to the cross-reference to EN-1, EN-3 sets out the principles guiding assessments of applications for each specific type of renewable energy infrastructure covered by the NPS (Biomass and Waste Combustion, Offshore Wind, and Onshore Wind).

There are just two technology-specific references to the need for energy infrastructure. First is the reference, made in Chapter 2.5, to the increasingly important role that energy from waste is anticipated to play in meeting the UK's energy needs.

Second is the reference to balancing the need for offshore wind infrastructure with the impact that the presence of that infrastructure has on recreational craft. It is stated that the IPC should be satisfied that offshore wind schemes have been designed to minimise impacts on such craft. However, in cases where adverse impacts are identified, and no reasonable mitigation is feasible, the IPC is required, 'in view of the level of need for energy infrastructure', to 'weigh the harm caused with the benefits of the scheme', instead of simply refusing the scheme on the basis of that residual harm (para 2.6.166).

EN-4: Gas Supply Infrastructure and Gas and Oil Pipelines

In addition to the cross-reference to EN-1, and in spite of the emphasis on low-carbon energy resources, the continued importance of, and need for, gas and oil energy infrastructure is made clear at the outset of EN-4, which states:

'The efficient import, storage and transmission of natural gas and oil products is crucial to meeting our energy needs during the transition to a low carbon economy. We cannot achieve national objectives relating to security of supply without enabling investment in new infrastructure' (para 1.1.1).

EN-5: Electricity Networks Infrastructure

In addition to the cross-reference to EN-1, EN-5 also emphasises the continued need for electricity networks infrastructure, notwithstanding the emphasis on low carbon resources. It states that:

'The new electricity generating infrastructure that the UK needs to move to a low carbon economy while maintaining security of supply will be heavily dependent on the availability of a fit for purpose and robust electricity network. That network will need to be able to support a more complex system of supply and demand than currently and cope with generation occurring in more diverse locations' (para 1.1.1).

Chapter 2.3 of EN-5 gives specific guidance on circumstances in which the need for electricity infrastructure will have to be weighed in the balance against other factors. It addresses the general assessment principles for electricity networks, and states *inter alia* that, in view of the need for planning to take a holistic approach to the impacts of energy infrastructure development, applications for new generating stations and related infrastructure should, wherever reasonably be possible, be contained in a single application (para 2.3.1).

Where this is not possible or appropriate, and an application for network infrastructure is brought forward in isolation, the IPC will have to have regard to both the need for the network infrastructure identified in EN-1 and the indirect, secondary and cumulative effects that the proposed development is likely to have, and be satisfied that there are no obvious reasons why the necessary approvals for the other element are likely to be refused (para 2.3.3).

Chapter 2.3 goes on to identify two circumstances in which the IPC might consider it appropriate to consider a network infrastructure-only application. One is the situation where 'the project is based on reasonably anticipated future requirements' (also para 2.3.3). It therefore appears that promoters of network infrastructure-only schemes may be required to demonstrate a more specific need for their project, over and above the general need for electricity network infrastructure, which the IPC is directed in Chapter 2.1 to treat as established.

EN-6: Nuclear Power Generation

Whilst EN-6 cross-refers to EN-1, it also contains additional policy relating to need, including the need for early deployment of nuclear technology, if policy ambitions in relation to the de-carbonisation of the energy industry are to be met (paras 2.1.1–2.1.2).

It is worth emphasising the point, however, that NPS EN-6 deals with 'need' in the context of the designated sites capable of deployment before the end of 2025. Of those sites, only the application for the Hinkley Point C DCO was, therefore, examined in the context of there being an NPS that 'has effect' for the purposes of PA 2008, s 104(1)/(3). The application for the Wylfa Newydd DCO recognised that that power station was not capable of being deployed before the end of 2025, and so it was considered under PA 2008, s 105, although it was still argued that NPS EN-6 was important and relevant to the Secretary of State's decision.

Within that context, EN-6 provides that the number of sites identified gives the IPC sufficient flexibility to meet that need, but also to refuse consent on any of those sites, if it considers it appropriate to do so (para 2.4.4). This tends to suggest that the level of national need for nuclear power is not as great as the output from eight stations.

EN-6 also addresses the relationship between the stated urgent need for nuclear power stations to come forward, and the consideration of alternatives. The guiding principle for the IPC in the consideration of alternatives is:

'Whether there is a realistic prospect of the proposed alternative being able to generate a comparable amount of low carbon electricity on a comparable timescale' (para 2.5.2).

This guiding principle applies to both alternative sites and alternative proposals (para 2.5.1).

In relation to flood risk assessments, the IPC is advised that part of the Exception Test applying to developments in flood risk zones does not apply to new nuclear development, in view of *inter alia* the need for that development to come forward (para 3.6.13). It appears that, in view of the continued application of the Exception Test in relation to other development, the need for nuclear development is considered particularly pressing, though it is acknowledged that the policy may also be recognising the greater physical constraints upon the provision of new nuclear facilities (such as the need to be near the sea).

Article 10

The Identification of Need in the Non-energy NPSs

Rebecca Clutten, ftb
Michael Humphries QC, ftb

Introduction

Defra, DfT and BEIS have designated the following NPSs under Planning Act 2008 (PA 2008), s 5 in relation to non-energy infrastructure:

- National Policy Statement for Ports (DfT, January 2012);
- National Policy Statement for Waste Water: A framework document for planning decisions on nationally significant waste water infrastructure (Defra, March 2012);
- National Policy Statement for Hazardous Waste: A framework document for planning decisions on nationally significant hazardous waste infrastructure (Defra, June 2013);
- National Policy Statement for National Networks (DfT, January 2015);
- Airports National Policy Statement (DfT, June 2018); and
- Geological Disposal Infrastructure NPS (BEIS, October 2019).

A further non-energy NPS is also anticipated in relation to:

- Water Resources Infrastructure (Defra).

Ports NPS

The need for new ports infrastructure is set out in Chapter 3 of the Ports NPS, in particular in Chapters 3.4 and 3.5.

The headline in relation to need is that there is a 'compelling need for substantial additional port capacity' in all areas, over the 20–30 year period from 2012 (paragraph 3.4.16). This is based on a number of factors including:

- Demand forecasting, which at 2007 indicated a need for substantial increases in capacity for containers and ro-ro traffic (182% and 101% respectively), and 4% in non-unitised traffic (paragraphs 3.4.2–3.4.3).
- The need to support the offshore wind industry, both in respect of the shipment of parts, and in respect of installation, operation and maintenance facilities (paragraph 3.4.5).
- The need to provide sufficient capacity to facilitate genuine choice and competition for ports users. This may mean capacity in excess of forecast demand. Such capacity also contributes to the resilience of the UK's ports infrastructure (paragraphs 3.4.13–3.4.15).
- To meet growth in the coastal shipping sector, as an alternative to inland freight (paragraph 3.4.14).

There is no specific policy on where such growth should be located. The Government recognises the merit in the provision of a wide range of facilities at a wide range of locations, such as will enable changing market demands and shipping patterns to be met (paragraph 3.4.11).

As for energy infrastructure, the need described is considered to be of a level and urgency that the IPC should 'start with a presumption in favour of granting consent to applications for ports development', subject to PA 2008, s 104 and any other, more specific policies within the NPSs, which 'clearly indicate' that consent should be refused (paragraph 3.5.2).

There are also number of specific policies identified within the Assessment Principles set out in the Ports NPS which require the IPC to weigh in the balance benefits of proposed development, which expressly include the stated need (including national need), against various harms which might arise. The approach is broadly reflective of that taken in relation to energy, and the situations contemplated include where there would, after mitigation, be harm to a SSSI interest or other sites of principal conservation importance, in which case the benefits would need to 'clearly outweigh' the harm (paragraph 5.1.12 and footnote 37, and paragraph 5.5.18), or where open space, sports and recreation facilities would be lost, save where they are surplus to requirements (paragraph 5.13.13).

The impact of national, regional and local land designations, and whether these are capable of outweighing the identified need, is also addressed. Current policy is that regional and local designations should not, of themselves, be a reason for refusing consent (paragraph 5.1.14). In the case of land subject to national designations (National Parks, AONB and the Broads), the IPC is guided that it may grant consent for development in these areas in exceptional circumstances, which expressly include the need for the development (paragraph 5.11.8).

In respect of harm to ancient woodlands (by loss or deterioration) and dynamic shorelines (through impact on sediment flows or coastal processes), permission should only be granted where the benefits, again including national and local need, outweigh those adverse impacts (paragraphs 5.1.15 and 5.1.39 respectively).

Waste Water NPS

The need for new waste water infrastructure is set out in Chapter 2 of the waste water NPS. Policy objectives and demand drivers are set out in sections 2.2 and 2.3. The waste water infrastructure considered to meet that need is set out in section 2.6.

It remains Government policy to reduce the need for waste water capacity, through reductions in water use, increasing use of sustainable drainage systems, separation of surface and waste water sewers, and through decentralisation of waste water treatment infrastructure (i.e. encouraging more local treatment) (section 2.4). However, even with these measures in place, more and better waste water infrastructure will be required to:

- meet the requirements of European and domestic legislation in relation to water body management, waste water and freshwater (paragraphs 2.3.1–2.3.4);
- adapt to the increased pressure on infrastructure resulting from climate change generated events, such as intense rainfall events and reduced river flows (paragraphs 2.3.5–2.3.7);
- meet the additional capacity requirements generated by the expected increase in population growth (paragraph 2.3.8) and also the increase in urbanisation (and corresponding reduction in permeable surfaces) (paragraph 2.3.9); and
- to ensure that existing, dated infrastructure remains fit for purpose or is replaced (paragraph 2.3.10).

Waste water infrastructure projects and improvements required to meet legislative and environmental objectives (which typically overlap) are currently identified by the Environment Agency ('EA') in their National Environment Plan (NEP), which is subject to confirmation by the Secretary of State, and which is scrutinised by OFWAT through water undertakers' business plans (paragraphs 2.5.1–2.5.2).

The NEP currently identifies two projects for which there is a need: improvements at Deephams Sewage Treatment Works ('STW') and the Thames Tideway Tunnel (section 2.6). The need for these, and other projects included in the NEP and said by the EA to be necessary for environmental reasons, is considered to be established (paragraphs 2.5.3–2.5.4).

The urgent need for such infrastructure means that the decision-maker should start with a presumption in favour of granting consent to applications for waste water NSIPs, subject to any more specific and relevant policies in the NPS that 'clearly indicate that consent should be refused', and the requirements of the Planning Act 2008 (paragraph 3.1.2). Further, need is a particular factor which must be taken into account when weighing the benefits and adverse impacts of any proposed NSIP (paragraph 3.1.3).

As for the other NPSs, the Assessment Principles require the decision-maker to weigh in the balance benefits of proposed development, which expressly include the stated need (including national need), against various harms that might arise. These include where there would, after mitigation, be likely to be harm to a SSSI's notified special interest features, to sites or species of principal conservation importance, or ancient woodland, in which case the benefits would need to 'clearly outweigh' the harm (paragraphs 4.5.10, 4.5.13 and 4.5.16).

The impact of national, regional and local land designations, and whether these are capable of outweighing the identified need, is also addressed. Current policy is that regional and local designations should not, of themselves, be a reason for refusing consent (paragraph 4.5.12). In the case of land subject to national designations (National Parks, AONB and the Broads), development should be demonstrated to be in the public interest and consideration of such applications should include an assessment of, amongst other things, 'the need for the development, including in terms of any national considerations [covering both national need and impacts upon the national economy] and the impact of consenting, or not consenting it, upon the local economy' (paragraph 4.7.8).

Need is also a factor in decisions as to whether or not to grant consent for development proposals on existing open space, sports and recreational buildings and land. Such proposals should not be consented unless, amongst other things, the decision-maker determines that the benefits of the project (including need) outweigh the potential loss of such facilities (paragraph 4.8.13).

The need for waste water infrastructure is also a factor which has resulted in a policy that the Secretary of State may reasonably conclude that:

> 'speculative assertions of [adverse] socioeconomic impacts [arising from waste water development] not supported by evidence should be given little weight' (paragraph 4.15.10).

Hazardous Waste NPS

The need for new hazardous waste infrastructure is set out in Chapter 3 of the Hazardous Waste NPS, in particular in sections 3.2 and 3.5.

The headline in relation to need is that there is a need for a 'small number of large facilities' for nationally significant hazardous waste, to deal with a range of hazardous waste arisings (paragraphs 3.3.7 and 3.4.1).

The need for increasing numbers of hazardous waste facilities is a result of:

- the trend toward increased hazardous waste arisings (deriving from both the continuing demand for consumer goods producing such waste, as well as from more waste being classified as hazardous) (section 3.2); and
- the need to meet European and domestic legislative requirements in relation to disposal of waste, in particular the requirements of the Waste Framework Directive (2008/98/EC) for pushing waste up the waste hierarchy (ie improved levels of recycling and re-use) (paragraphs 1.5.3, 3.2.3–3.2.6 and 3.3.5) and for national self-sufficiency in terms of capacity to dispose of hazardous waste (paragraph 3.3.3–3.3.4).

The need for a large number of small facilities arises because of the economies of scale which operate in the waste disposal sector, and in order to avoid cumulative impacts which might be generated by the operation of multiple, smaller sites (paragraph 3.3.6). The author notes that smaller facilities may still come forward through the Town and Country Planning regime.

The Government has not sought to identify particular technologies which should be used, or to identify locations for development, it being considered ill-advised to be too prescriptive when technologies are evolving (paragraph 3.4.1), and because it considers the industry best placed to know where facilities should be located (paragraph 2.4.2). This provides significant flexibility to applicants for hazardous waste developments, as compared to applicants for some other NSIPs.

Broad types of facilities required are however identified, drawing on the 2007 Strategy for Hazardous Waste Management in England (paragraph 3.3.6). The types of facility for which there is an identified need are:

- waste electrical and electronic equipment plants – a small number of larger facilities (paragraph 3.4.3);
- oil regeneration plants – a requirement of at least one new plant already existing at July 2011 (paragraph 3.4.3);
- treatment plants for air pollution control residues;
- facilities to treat oily washes and oily sludges;
- bioremediation/soil washing facilities;
- ship recycling facilities (which covers oil and gas platform recycling) – a mixture of new facilities with capacity to manage both above and below 30,000t of ship(s) pa within the next 10 years (paragraph 3.4.12); and
- hazardous waste landfill sites.

The Examining Authority is directed to examine applications for facilities falling within these categories on the basis that the need for them has been demonstrated (paragraph 3.4.14). Moreover, there is a presumption in favour of granting consent for applications for such facilities where they clearly meet the need for infrastructure identified in the NPS (paragraph 4.1.2). This presumption is subject, as in other NPSs, to the other policies of the Hazardous Waste NSP and also PA 2008, s 104. The need for types of hazardous waste facilities not included on the above list is to be considered on a case-by-case basis, following consultation by the applicant with Defra (paragraph 3.4.1).

The Assessment Principles require the decision-maker to weigh in the balance benefits of proposed development, which expressly include the stated need (including national need), against various harms that might arise. These include where there would, after mitigation, be harm to species or sites of principal conservation importance, or ancient woodland, in which case the benefits would need to 'clearly outweigh' the harm (paragraphs 5.3.14 and 5.3.17).

The impact of national, regional and local land designations, and whether these are capable of outweighing the identified need, is also addressed. Current policy is that regional and local designations should not, of themselves, be a reason for refusing consent (paragraph 5.1.13).

In the case of land subject to national designations (National Parks, AONB and the Broads), development should be demonstrated to be in the public interest and consideration of such applications should include an assessment of, amongst other things, 'the need for the development, including in terms of any national considerations [covering both national need and impacts upon the national economy] and the impact of consenting, or not consenting it, upon the local economy' (paragraph 5.9.7).

The need for hazardous waste infrastructure is also a factor that has led the Government to include guidance that the Secretary of State may reasonably conclude that:

> 'speculative assertions of [adverse] socioeconomic impacts [arising from hazardous waste development] not supported by evidence should be given little weight'.

National Networks NPS

The need for development on national road and rail networks is set out in section 2 of the National Networks NPS (NN NPS).

The NN NPS makes it clear (para 2.1) that the national road and rail networks that connect cities, regions and international gateways play a significant part in supporting economic growth, as well as existing economic activity and productivity and in facilitating passenger, business and leisure journeys across the country. Well-connected and high-performing networks with sufficient capacity are vital to meet the country's long-term needs and support a prosperous economy.

In that context it is then made clear (para 2.2) that there is a critical need to improve the national networks to address road congestion and crowding on the railways to provide safe, expeditious and resilient networks that better support social and economic activity; and to provide a transport network that is capable of stimulating and supporting economic growth. Improvements may also be required to address the impact of the national networks on quality of life and environmental factors.

The NN NPS then sets out specific guidance on:

- paras 2.12–2.27 – the need for development of the national road network, including options for addressing road need (Table 1);
- para 2.28–2.41 – the need for development of the national rail network; and
- para 2.42–2.58 – the need for development of strategic rail freight interchanges.

Airports NPS

The Airports NPS has proved one of the most controversial, and its designation in June 2018 led to the legal challenges that culminated in *R (Friends of the Earth and others) v Heathrow Airport Limited* [2020] UKSC 52. That litigation is dealt with elsewhere in this work, whilst this article will focus on 'need' as established in the Airports NPS.

Perhaps the first point to make is that the Airports NPS does not 'have effect' for the purposes of PA 2008, s 104(2) to all airport development. Paragraph 1.40 is quite clear that:

> 'The Airports NPS has effect in relation to the delivery of additional airport capacity through the provision of a Northwest Runway at Heathrow Airport. It also applies to

proposals for new terminal capacity located between the new Northwest Runway and the existing Northern Runway at Heathrow Airport, as well as the reconfiguration of terminal facilities in the area between the two existing runways at Heathrow Airport. Each of these elements is also capable of constituting a nationally significant infrastructure project.'

However, in paragraph 1.41 the NPS does make clear its status in relation to other airport development, as follows:

> 'The Airports NPS does not have effect in relation to an application for development consent for an airport development not comprised in an application relating to the Heathrow Northwest Runway, and proposals for new terminal capacity located between the Northwest Runway at Heathrow Airport and the existing Northern Runway and reconfiguration of terminal facilities between the two existing runways at Heathrow Airport. Nevertheless, the Secretary of State considers that the contents of the Airports NPS will be both important and relevant considerations in the determination of such an application, particularly where it relates to London or the South East of England. Among the considerations that will be important and relevant are the findings in the Airports NPS as to the need for new airport capacity and that the preferred scheme is the most appropriate means of meeting that need.'

The words 'important and relevant' are a direct reference to the requirements of PA 2008, s 105(2)(b), which would apply to an application for development consent for airport development that is not the Northwest Runway at Heathrow.

The need for additional airport capacity is dealt with at chapter 2 of the Airports NPS, which deals with:

- the importance of aviation to the UK economy;
- the need for new airport capacity;
- the Airports Commission;
- alternatives to additional runway capacity;
- the Airports Commission's shortlisting process; and
- the Government's work.

It is important to note, however, that central to the Government's consideration of need was the policy objective of maintaining the UK's 'hub status'; that is, its status as a major international aviation hub. It was this factor that was at the heart of the decision to select the Northwest Runway option at Heathrow as the scheme that was ultimately supported in the Airports NPS.

The NPS, therefore, reflects the view that:

> 'Having reviewed the work of the Airports Commission and considered the evidence put forward on the issue of airport capacity, the Government believes that there is clear and strong evidence that there is a need to increase capacity in the South East of England by 2030 by constructing one new runway.'

It is chapter 3 of the Airports NPS that sets out the rationale for selecting the Northwest Runway scheme at Heathrow as the 'one new runway', as opposed to the rival shortlisted schemes being a Second Runway at Gatwick or an Extended Northern Runway at Heathrow. This chapter concluded that:

> 'A number of mitigation measures will need to be applied to reduce the impacts of the Heathrow Northwest Runway scheme felt by the local community and the environment.

> Airport expansion is also expected to be accompanied by an extensive and appropriate compensation package for affected parties. With these safeguards in place, the Government considers that the Heathrow Northwest Runway scheme delivers the greatest strategic and economic benefits, and is therefore the most effective and appropriate way of meeting the needs case.'

Following (and indeed before) the Supreme Court's decision in December 2020, a number of parties have asked the Secretary of State to 'review' the Airports NPS under PA 2008, s 6, particularly in the light of the Government's adoption of a 2050 'net zero' carbon target in the June 2019 amendment to Climate Change Act 2008, s 1(1). On 6 September 2021, DfT wrote to individuals or parties who had requested a review of the Airports NPS and made clear that 'the Secretary of State has decided that it is not appropriate to review the ANPS at this time'.

Geological Disposal Infrastructure NPS

Need is dealt with in chapter 3 of the Geological Disposal Infrastructure ('GDI') NPS. The chapter starts (paragraph 3.1) with a broad statement of principle:

> 'There is a technical, ethical and legal need for the safe and secure management of the UK's higher activity radioactive waste in the long term. The development of geological disposal infrastructure is essential because it provides the best available practical means of ensuring the long term safety and security of higher activity radioactive waste.'

The chapter considers:

- the technical need;
- the ethical need;
- the need to meet legal obligations; and
- the need to meet energy and climate change obligations.

The NPS also sets out the need for 'deep boreholes' that will be required for 'investigative purposes at sites that may or may not ultimately be sites of a geological disposal facility' (paragraph 3.3.2).

Chapter 3 concludes with the clear statement (paragraph 3.4.5) that:

> 'The Secretary of State will assess applications for development consent for geological disposal infrastructure covered by this NPS on the basis that need has been demonstrated.'

Article 11

The Status and Role of NPSs within the Planning Act 2008 Regime

Rebecca Clutten, ftb
Michael Humphries QC, ftb

Introduction

National Policy Statements ('NPSs') are the statutory planning policy statements for nationally significant infrastructure projects in England and Wales. They derive from PA 2008, Part 2.

This article explains the status that NPSs have within the PA 2008 regime. Any references to NPSs herein are references to NPSs which have been designated in accordance with PA 2008, s 5. Further information on the requirements for designation can be found in articles 5 and 6 of this work.

PA 2008, s 104: the primacy of the NPS

The primary effect of NPSs is set out in PA 2008, s 104 (decisions in cases where national policy statement applies).

PA 2008, s 104 will apply in respect of any application for development consent for development in relation to which there is an NPS that 'has effect': see PA 2008, s 104(1). Where section 104 applies, the Secretary of State must, when determining an application for a DCO, have regard to *inter alia* that relevant NPS: see PA 2008, s 104(2). Although there are other specified documents and matters to which the Secretary of State must have regard, the PA 2008 goes on to provide that, save in specified circumstances (that is, where the circumstances set out in PA 2008, s 104(4)–(8) apply), the DCO application must be decided 'in accordance with' the relevant NPS (PA 2008, s 104(3)).

The NPS therefore has a comparable status in the decision-making process to the statutory development plan in the determination of applications for planning permission under the Town and Country Planning Act regime. It is important to note, however, that Planning and Compulsory Purchase Act 2004, s 38(6), which requires planning applications to be determined in accordance with the development plan unless other material considerations indicate otherwise, does not apply to applications for development consent under the PA 2008. There is, therefore, no conflict between the requirements of the two regimes.

The PA 2008, s 104(3) concept of 'in accordance with' was considered in the Divisional Court judgment in the Airports NPS challenges: see *R (Spurrier and others) v Secretary of State for Transport* [2019] EWHC 1070 (Admin). At paragraph 329 the Divisional Court held as follows:

> 'Section 104(3) provides that "the Secretary of State must decide [an application for a DCO] *in accordance with* any relevant [NPS] ..." (emphasis added). The italicised phrase appears, analogously, in section 38(6) of the Planning and Compulsory Purchase Act 2004,

> which requires an application for planning permission to be determined "in accordance with the [development] plan …". Just as that means "in accordance with the development plan judged as whole", as [Counsel for the Secretary of State] rightly submits, section 104(3) requires an application for a DCO to be decided in accordance with any relevant NPS judged as a whole, recognising that the statement's policies (or their application) may pull in different directions and that, for example, a breach of a single policy does not carry the consequence that the proposal fails to accord with the NPS (paragraph 4(2) of the Secretary of State's written submissions, citing *R v Rochdale Metropolitan Borough Council ex parte Milne* [2000] EWHC 650 (Admin); [2001] Env LR 22) …'

This is an important statement of principle and means that a decision-maker must look at whether the application is in accordance with any relevant NPS 'judged as a whole' when discharging the duty under PA 2008, s 104(3).

The circumstances in which an application for development consent can be determined otherwise than in accordance with the relevant NPS are as follows (PA 2008, s 104(4)–(8)):

- the SoS is satisfied that to do so would lead to the UK being in breach of any of its international obligations;
- the SoS is satisfied that to do so would lead to him being in breach of any duty imposed on him by or under any enactment;
- the SoS is satisfied that to do so would be unlawful by virtue of any enactment;
- the SoS is satisfied that the benefits of doing so would outweigh the adverse impacts; and
- the SoS is satisfied that to do so would meet any prescribed condition for determining an application otherwise than in accordance with the relevant NPS.

At the time of writing, there are no prescribed conditions as referred to in the last exception.

Again, a comparison can be drawn between these exceptions to the primacy of the NPSs, and in particular the exception at PA 2008, s 104(7) (benefits outweigh adverse impacts), and the ability for applications for planning permission under the Town and Country Planning regime to be determined other than in accordance with the development plan where 'material considerations indicate otherwise'.

In light of the primacy afforded to NPSs, it is vital that applicants explain in detail how their proposals relate to and comply with the NPS 'judged as a whole' and, insofar as they do not, make the case for consent being granted in any event by reference to the exceptions identified. For a decision in which the Examining Authority and Secretary of State did not consider that an NSIP was in accordance with the NPS, see the refusal of the application for the Thanet Extension offshore wind farm DCO (1 June 2020).

Thus promoters will need to consider carefully and establish that:

- the NSIP is 'in accordance with' any material NPS 'judged as a whole'; and
- the exceptions in PA 2008, s 104(4)–(8) to not outweigh the policy support in the NSIP and the benefits of the project.

PA 2008, s 106: restricted challenge to NPS policy

A further effect of the NPSs is set out in PA 2008, s 106, which provides that in determining an application for a DCO the Secretary of State may disregard representations which he considers 'relate to the merits of policy set out in a national policy statement': see PA 2008, s 106. In this regard, clearly, the Examining Authority and Secretary of State must act with *Wednesbury* reasonableness. The practical effect of this is to preclude challenges to the merits of a national policy other than through the NPS consultation process, or at the Secretary of State's discretion.

A similar provision is contained in PA 2008, s 94(8), which allows the Examining Authority to refuse to allow representations at any hearings relating to a DCO application where it considers those representations to relate to the merits of a policy contained in a NPS. Again this power must be exercised reasonably.

Suspension

Effect of suspension of the NPS

It is possible for the Secretary of State to suspend the operation of all or part of an NPS if an unexpected change in circumstances arises that would have led to the policy in the NPS being materially different had that change of circumstances been anticipated at the time: see PA 2008, s 11.

Where such suspension occurs the designation of all or part of the NPS (as the case may be) is treated as withdrawn and, until such time as designation is reinstated, the NPS will not be treated as extant and relevant for the purposes of the duty to determine in accordance with the NPS (PA 2008, s 104) nor, indeed, to the blight provisions referred to further below.

Suspension of the determination of an application

If the SoS considers that a NPS should be suspended and reviewed as a result of an unexpected change in circumstances, and that such review should take place before any given application for a DCO is determined, he has a further power to direct that the examination of the application (if not already completed) be suspended pending that review: see PA 2008, s 108.

NPSs can therefore be a potential source of delay for applicants in the DCO process.

Article 12

Legal Challenges to NPSs

Rebecca Clutten, ftb
Michael Humphries QC, ftb

Introduction

Section 13 of the Planning Act 2008 ('PA 2008') prescribes the means by which legal challenges to National Policy Statements ('NPSs') can be brought, and restricts the time period within which prospective claimants have to lodge their claims.

This article provides information on:

- the circumstances in which PA 2008, s 13 applies;
- the effect of PA 2008, s 13 upon: the mode by which challenges to NPSs and decisions related to them can be brought, the time limit applicable to such challenges, and the date from which time runs in each case;
- the effect of a legal challenge on the status of an NPS; and
- challenges brought to date.

When does PA 2008, s 13 apply?

Broadly speaking, PA 2008, s 13 applies where a person seeks either to challenge an NPS or a decision of the relevant Secretary of State ('SoS') relating to an NPS.

PA 2008, s 13, however, identifies six specific circumstances where a challenge may be brought. Thus a court may entertain proceedings questioning:

- an NPS or anything done, or omitted to be done, by the SoS in the course of preparing an NPS (PA 2008, s 13(1));
- a decision of the SoS not to carry out a review of all or part of an NPS pursuant to PA 2008, s 6 (PA 2008, s 13(2));
- a decision of the SoS to carry out a review of all or part of an NPS pursuant to PA 2008, s 6 (PA 2008, s 13(3));
- anything done, or omitted to be done, by the SoS in the course of carrying out a review of all or part of an NPS pursuant to PA 2008, s 6 (PA 2008, s 13(4));
- anything done by the SoS under PA 2008, s 6(5) after completing a review of all or part of an NPS (that is, amending or doing nothing to an NPS, or withdrawing its designation) (PA 2008, s 13(5)); and
- questioning a decision of the SoS as to whether or not to suspend the operation of all or part of an NPS under PA 2008, s 11 (PA 2008, s 13(6)).

Whilst it is envisaged that that the six circumstances described cover all decisions relating to the designation and subsequent review of NPSs, PA 2008, s 13 is not phrased in such a way as to preclude challenges to other decisions relating to NPSs, should they arise. It contains no drafting comparable to, for example, Town and Country Planning Act 1990, s 284 (as amended), precluding any challenge to the validity of development plans etc, except as provided for in that Part.

It is considered that, in the event that a claimant wished to challenge a decision of the SoS relating to an NPS, but which did not fall within any of the six circumstances referred to in PA 2008, s 13(1)–(6) inclusive, that decision would be treated in the same way as any other decision of a Minister not subject to any statutory provision relating to challenge, that is, ordinary judicial review principles and procedure would apply.

The effect of PA 2008, s 13

Where it applies, PA 2008, s 13 has three main effects:

- it requires a person wishing to bring a challenge to do so by way of judicial review;
- it imposes a time limit of six weeks, within which any application for judicial review must be lodged; and
- it identifies the day from which that time limit runs in each circumstance described.

Challenge by way of judicial review only

The requirement that any challenge to an NPS be brought by way of judicial review has a number of implications for prospective claimants. It requires them to have standing to bring a claim (presently, a 'sufficient interest'), to obtain the permission of the court to bring a claim, and it limits them to challenging the decision on traditional judicial review grounds (ie broadly, irrationality, illegality and procedural impropriety). In other words, there is no direct opportunity to challenge the merit of Government policy in an NPS, as opposed to the legality of such policy.

Furthermore, PA 2008, s 106 provides that, when determining applications for development consent for Nationally Significant Infrastructure Projects, the Secretary of State is entitled to disregard any representations he or she receives relating to the merits of policy set out in an NPS. A similar power to disregard applies to the Examining Authority (PA 2008, s 87).

When read together with PA 2008, s 106, the effect of PA 2008, s 13 is, therefore, to preclude the public at large from challenging the merits of planning policy that has been set at national level, other than through the instigation of the review procedure provided for by PA 2008, s 6.

Date from which time runs

Readers are referred to PA 2008, s 13 (as amended by the Criminal Justice and Courts Act 2015) for details of the date from which the six-week time limit runs in each given circumstance (see PA 2008, s 13(1)–(6) inclusive).

It should be noted that in the section as originally enacted, time ran from the day beginning with the date on which the NPS was designated. The words 'beginning with' in PA 2008, s 13 contrasted with the word 'from' which is used in r 54.5 of the Civil Procedure Rules (CPR) for judicial review challenges generally. In the case of the similarly worded time limit in s 118 this led to two challenges to the Thames Tideway Tunnel DCO being held to be made out of time when the applicants calculated the six weeks from the day after publication of the DCO and their applications for judicial review were dismissed: see *R (Blue Green London Plan and LB Southwark) v Secretary of State for Environment, Food and Rural Affairs* [2015] EWHC 495 (Admin).

Following the decision in these challenges the wording of s 13, in relation to challenges to NPSs, was amended so as to provide that a challenge by way of judicial review must be made within the period of six weeks 'beginning with *the day after*' (emphasis added) the designation of the NPS.

For example: if an NPS was designated and published on 5 January (the circumstance identified in PA 2008, s 13(1)), the first day of the six weeks would be 6 January, and the time for challenge would expire on 17 February.

Accuracy is vital bearing in mind the inability of the court to extend the time limit in cases of error (see below).

The time limit of six weeks is set by statute

The time limit of six weeks for challenges to NPSs is one set by statute (ie by the terms of PA 2008, s 13 and not by the Civil Procedure Rules) and thus it is important to note that the court has no power or discretion to extend it: see *Mucelli v Government of Albania* [2009] 1 WLR 276.

Effect of a challenge

The filing of a claim for judicial review of an NPS has no impact upon its status. The NPS remains extant and valid for the duration of any challenge.

In principle it seems possible that, in appropriate circumstances, the court might exercise its discretion grant to a claimant injunctive relief, preventing decisions being taken in accordance with an NPS the subject matter of a current application for judicial review.

Such a course of action would require the court to balance the harm caused by any policy vacuum that would be created, with any harm caused by determining an application for development consent in accordance with a potentially flawed or unlawful policy. The outcome of any such balancing exercise would represent a judgment on the facts of the given case.

Challenges to date

By early 2022, there were 12 designated NPSs and a further one in draft. These designated NPSs have resulted in just two applications for permission to apply for a judicial review of a designated NPS and one application for judicial review of something done in the course of preparing an NPS.

The application, made by Greenpeace in August 2011, related to the designation of the Nuclear Power NPS ('the Nuclear NPS'). In short, Greenpeace alleged that, in designating the Nuclear NPS at that time, the Government had acted prematurely and had failed to take into account the implications of the nuclear disaster at Fukushima, Japan, which had occurred earlier that year.

Permission was refused in December 2011. Although his reasons for refusing permission have not been published, it was reported in the legal press that Ouseley J considered that the matters upon which Greenpeace argued further evidence was required before a decision could be taken on potentially suitable sites through the NPS – flood risk, off-site electricity supply and on-site emergency controls – were matters upon which evidence would be considered by the (then) Infrastructure Planning Commission and the Office of Nuclear Regulation when determining whether development consent and/or an operating licence should be granted at any site for which an application ultimately came forward.

In January 2017 the High Court gave judgment in *London Borough of Hillingdon v Secretary of State for Transport* [2017] EWHC 121 (Admin). That decision related to a challenge by LB Hillingdon to the Secretary of State for Transport's announcement in October 2016 that the Government had selected the Heathrow north west runway scheme as its preferred option for delivering additional runway capacity in the south-east and that it would bring forward an NPS during 2017 that would include further details and be subject to consultation before final designation. The Court (Cranston J) held that the Government's October 2016 decision on its preferred option was something done in the course of preparing an NPS and, therefore, that PA 2008, s 13(1) precluded any legal challenge until the period of six weeks beginning with the day after designation.

On 18 June 2018 the Secretary of State for Transport designated the Airports NPS that set out the Government's policy on the need for new airport capacity in the South East of England and its preferred location and scheme to meet that need, namely a third runway at Heathrow to the north of the current two runways ('the NWR Scheme'). This led to five challenges on a wide variety of procedural and environmental law grounds, one of which was refused permission on the papers.

[NB There was also an entirely separate claim brought by Heathrow Hub Limited, the developer of an alternative Heathrow expansion scheme (the Extended Northern Runway Scheme). This claim related to competition law issues. The claim was unsuccessful and it is not dealt with further in this work.]

In the first-instance Divisional Court hearing, there were, therefore, four remaining claimants. Mr Spurrier, a litigant in person, raised a number of issues, including pre-determination of consultation and bias in relation to the NPS. In a claim led by the London Borough of Hillingdon ('Hillingdon'), the claimant was a group of five local authorities, Greenpeace and the Mayor of London. This claim related to environmental law issues, including Strategic Environmental Assessment ('SEA') and Habitats Regulations Assessment ('HRA'). Claims were also brought by Friends of the Earth ('FOE') and Plan B Earth ('PBE'). These claims focused primarily on climate change issues related to duties under PA 2008, ss 5(8) and 10(3) and the UK's obligations under the Paris Climate Agreement. All these claims were heard together, with a single judgment being given in respect of all the issues.

The Divisional Court hearing was a rolled-up hearing on permission and the substantive applications. In the case of Mr Spurrier, permission was refused. In the case of Hillingdon, permission was granted on some issues, but the substantive application was then refused on those issues. On the FOE and PBE claims, permission was refused on all grounds. All claims, therefore, failed in the Divisional Court: see *R (Spurrier and others) v Secretary of State for Transport* [2019] EWHC 1070 (Admin).

Hillingdon, FOE and PBE then appealed to the Court of Appeal against (a) the refusal of permission and/or (b) the refusal of the substantive application. Hillingdon was granted permission to appeal, but the Court of Appeal then refused the appeal on all grounds. The Court of Appeal allowed FOE and PBE to appeal against refusal of permission and then granted their substantive applications: see *R (Hillingdon LBC and others) v Secretary of State for Transport* [2020] EWCA Civ 214. This decision resulted in a declaration that the Airports NPS was of no legal effect unless and until the Secretary of State had undertaken a review of it in accordance with the relevant provisions of PA 2008.

Heathrow Airport Limited then appealed to the Supreme Court. The Secretary of State for Transport did not appeal and was not involved in the Supreme Court proceedings. Hillingdon applied to appeal to the Supreme Court against the Court of Appeal's judgment on its substantive grounds, but was refused permission.

The Supreme Court allowed Heathrow Airport Limited's appeal and reversed the Court of Appeal's declaration so that the Airports NPS now continues to 'have effect' for the purposes of PA 2008, s 104: see *R (Friends of the Earth and others) v Heathrow Airport Ltd* [2020] UKSC 52.

The changing fortunes of the different issues raised through the Airports NPS challenges can appear confusing. In broad terms, however, the following is the position. The issues unique to Mr Spurrier were finally determined by the Divisional Court. The issues on which Hillingdon led, broadly the SEA / HRA issues, were finally determined by the Court of Appeal, which confirmed the Divisional Court's decision. The FOE and PBE issues on climate change were finally determined by the Supreme Court, which overturned the Court of Appeal decision on those issues and confirmed the Divisional Court's decision. The relevant parts of the Courts' judgments at the three different levels are introduced, as appropriate, in other articles in this work.

Article 13

Section 6 Reviews of NPSs

Hugh Flanagan, ftb

Introduction

Section 6 of the PA 2008 is the review mechanism for NPSs. The central place of NPSs within the PA 2008 means that the process for their review is potentially of considerable importance. Section 6 is designed to enable an NPS to be kept up to date. As the Court of Appeal has observed, section 6 is 'the process for accommodating changes of circumstances after designation' (*R (Client Earth) v SSBEIS* [2021] EWCA Civ 43 at [105]). At the time of writing, it is not apparent that any section 6 review has been completed, although a decision has been made to review the energy NPSs. The potential for review under section 6 has also been of significance in how the courts have approached the rest of the PA 2008.

This article examines section 6 reviews in three parts. The first considers section 6 in detail; the second considers the place of section 6 in the Act and the infrastructure planning regime as a whole; and the third considers legal challenges regarding section 6.

Part 1: A closer look at section 6

Section 6 provides a detailed framework for the decision as to when to review, matters which should be taken into account in deciding whether to review, outcomes of the review, and the procedure for review.

Section 6(1) contains a discretionary duty. It requires the Secretary of State to review each NPS 'whenever the Secretary of State thinks it appropriate to do so'. Therefore, although the section imposes a duty on the Secretary of State, whether it arises depends on the Secretary of State's discretionary decision as to the appropriateness of review. The discretionary nature of section 6 corresponds to the discretionary nature of the Secretary of State's original power in section 5 to designate an NPS.

Section 6(2) provides flexibility as to whether the review relates to all or part of the NPS. Given the significant scope of many NPSs, that has obvious practical benefits.

Section 6(3), (4) requires the Secretary of State to consider certain matters when deciding when to review all or part of an NPS. Those matters are: (i) whether there has been a significant change of circumstances since the first publication or last review of the NPS; (ii) whether the change was not anticipated at that time; and (iii) if the change had been anticipated, whether any of the policy would have been materially different. Although these are mandatory factors for the Secretary of State to consider in deciding whether to review, they are not expressed as an exhaustive list. Nor does section 6 dictate the outcome to which these matters should lead; the decision as to review remains a discretionary one for the Secretary of State.

The exercise of this discretion could lead to the Secretary of State concluding that there has been a significant change of circumstances that was not anticipated, but that this would not have led to a materially different policy. This was the conclusion reached by the Secretary of State in relation to requests to review the Airports NPS following the Supreme Court's decision in *R (Friends of the Earth and others) v Heathrow Airport Limited* [2020] UKSC 52: see the Secretary of State for Transport's letter dated 6 September 2021, which made it clear that 'the Secretary of State has decided that it is not appropriate to review the ANPS at this time'.

Section 6(5) contains an exhaustive list of options for the Secretary of State on completing a review: (i) to amend the NPS; (ii) to withdraw the NPS's designation as an NPS; or (iii) to leave the NPS as it is.

Section 6(6)–(9) imposes procedural requirements for review. In particular:

- Before amending an NPS, the Secretary of State must carry out a sustainability appraisal of the policy set out in the proposed amendment (s 6(6)).
- An NPS may only be amended if prescribed consultation and publicity requirements have been complied with (s 6(7)). These requirements are contained in section 7, which gives a discretion to the Secretary of State as to what consultation and publicity he considers appropriate, subject to consulting such persons as are prescribed in delegated legislation. The Infrastructure Planning (National Policy Statement Consultation) Regulations 2009 previously prescribed specified persons, but those Regulations have been revoked and not replaced.
- An NPS may only be amended if the parliamentary requirements have been complied with (s 6(7)). These are contained within section 9 and require the Secretary of State to lay the proposed amendment before Parliament. If Parliament resolves that the amendment should not be proceeded with, the Secretary of State may not do so.
- Importantly, the sustainability appraisal, consultation, publicity and parliamentary requirements in section 6(6)–(7) do not apply if the Secretary of State considers that the proposed amendment, taken with any other proposed amendments, does not materially affect the policy as set out in the NPS. Thus, these potentially onerous procedural requirements are avoided if the amendment is a non-material one.

Section 10 requires the Secretary of State, when exercising his functions under section 6, to do so with the objective of contributing to the achievement of sustainable development.

Section 11 provides the Secretary of State with a discretionary power to suspend all or part of an NPS pending review. The power only arises if the Secretary of State considers that certain criteria are satisfied, which are the same as the considerations which section 6(3)–(4) requires the Secretary of State to take into account in deciding when to review, ie that: (i) there has been a significant change of circumstances since the first publication or last review of the NPS; (ii) the change was not anticipated at that time; and (iii) if the change had been anticipated, any of the policy would have been materially different (s 11(2)–(3)). The effect of suspension is that the NPS or the relevant part of it is treated as having been withdrawn pending the outcome of the review.

Part 2: Section 6 in context

The courts have identified the fundamental purpose of the review mechanism in section 6 as being to deal with changes of circumstance. The Divisional Court in *R (Spurrier and others) v SST* [2019] EWHC 1070 (Admin) stated at [107]:

> 'National infrastructure projects often give rise to a host of issues and it is quite possible that relevant considerations will change or evolve after an NPS has been designated, particularly where long lead-in times are involved. For example, the science on climate change or risks to public health from pollution may change, along with solutions for

> addressing such matters. Parliament was clearly aware of this possibility; and provided for it in section 6.'

Review is to be distinguished from amendment of an NPS. Exercise of the power to review may not lead to amendment; having reviewed the NPS, the Secretary of State may withdraw the NPS or leave it as it is, rather than amending it. A decision could be made to withdraw the existing NPS and designate a new NPS under section 5, rather than amending the existing NPS.

By way of example as to the choice of routes available, the Secretary of State stated in the December 2020 Energy White Paper (p 55) that the energy NPSs would be reviewed, but has separately consulted on designating a new NPS for nuclear power (December 2017). The scope of the NPS in question may inform the choice of route: for example, the existing nuclear NPS (EN-6) dealt with sites capable of deployment by the end of 2025, and the new NPS was proposed to deal with sites capable of deployment between 2026 and 2035.

An NPS may be drafted so as to be self-updating to an extent: it may require compliance with standards or targets in force at the point of decision on any DCO application (eg the Airports NPS which (para 5.82) requires consideration to be given to the Government's carbon budgets, which are set on an ongoing basis). An NPS may also itself contain policy as to review, such as the NPS for Waste Water (para 1.1.5) and the NPS for Hazardous Waste (para 1.1.4) which each state an expectation that the Secretary of State will review the NPS 'approximately every five years'.

The scale of what is involved in a section 6 review may vary enormously. At one end of the spectrum, a review could involve a non-material amendment to the NPS which does not trigger the sustainability appraisal, consultation, publicity and parliamentary requirements in section 6(6)–(7). At the other end of the spectrum, the scope of the review could be the whole NPS rather than only part, and the review could require fundamental reconsideration of the basis of the policy. The sustainability appraisal, consultation and publicity requirements in such a case could be very onerous indeed and might not be dissimilar in scope to what was undertaken on original designation of the NPS.

The relationship between any review and emerging development proposals also needs consideration. Section 108 empowers the Secretary of State to suspend an examination of application for a development consent order pending the completion of a section 6 review, if the Secretary of State considers that all or part of the NPS should be reviewed before the application is decided. This is a power only; the Secretary of State could choose to let the examination continue. The decision as to whether to exercise the section 108 power is likely to be highly fact-specific, with relevant considerations including the scope of the review and its likely duration.

Part 3: Section 6 in the courts

Section 13 regulates legal challenges concerning section 6 reviews. A challenge to a decision by the Secretary of State not to review all or part of an NPS under section 6 must be brought by a claim for judicial review and within the period of six weeks beginning with the day after the day of the decision not to carry out the review. Similar provisions apply in respect of challenges to:

- a decision to carry out a review;
- anything done, or omitted to be done, in the course of a review;
- anything done after completing a review (ie amendment or withdrawal of the NPS, or leaving the NPS as it is); or
- a decision as to whether or not to suspend the operation of all or part of the NPS pending the review.

In 2020 a challenge was brought to the Secretary of State's failure to review the Energy NPSs and to consider whether to suspend them, relying on alleged material changes of circumstance regarding climate change (*R (Dale Vince, George Monbiot, The Good Law Project Ltd) v SSBEIS* CO/1832/2020). The claim was withdrawn following the announcement of the decision to review in the December 2020 Energy White Paper.

Any claim regarding section 6 will need to have close regard to the formulation of section 6 in both discretionary and mandatory terms. In light of the considerable amount of discretionary judgement which section 6 vests in the Secretary of State, any challenge may face the familiar high hurdle concerning matters of planning judgement, potentially compounded by the political considerations involved in setting policy on nationally important infrastructure. In *R (ClientEarth) v SSBEIS and Drax Power Ltd* [2020] EWHC 1303 (Admin), Holgate J observed at [43]:

> 'Policy-making in this area involves the striking of a balance in which these and a great many other issues are assessed and weighed. This is carried on at a high strategic level and involves political judgment as to what is in the public interest.'

Section 6 has also informed the response of the courts to legal challenges to development consent orders. It has been held that section 6, rather than an examination of an application for development consent, is the appropriate forum for arguments as to whether a policy needs revising. As the High Court observed in *ClientEarth* (supra) at [249]:

> 'Challenges to the merits of existing policy in a NPS are not a matter for consideration in the examination and determination of individual applications for a DCO. Such policy is normally applicable to many DCO applications and the appropriate forum for arguments of that nature is a review under section 6.'

See also, to similar effect, the Court of Appeal's decision in *R (ClientEarth) v SSBEIS and Drax Power Ltd* [2021] EWCA Civ 43 at [105] and *R (Thames Blue Green Economy Ltd) v SSCLG* [2015] EWCA Civ 876 at [14].

Finally, section 6 has influenced the approach of the courts to relief on a challenge to an NPS. In *R (Hillingdon LBC and others) v SST* [2020] EWCA Civ 214 at [280], on finding the decision to designate the Airports NPS unlawful, the Court of Appeal declined to quash the NPS, but rather declared the designation decision unlawful and of no effect unless and until a section 6 review had taken place. The Court further refused to make a mandatory order requiring the Secretary of State to undertake a review, having regard to the discretion given to the Secretary of State under section 6.

Part 3

Nationally Significant Infrastructure Projects

Article 14

General Characteristics of an NSIP

Alex Booth QC, ftb
Michael Humphries QC, ftb

Nature of development

There is no single, over-arching definition of a 'nationally significant infrastructure project' ('NSIP') contained in the PA 2008. The closest that the legislation comes to providing such definition is at PA 2008, s 14, of which subsection (1) provides a list of 16 types of development which may potentially comprise an NSIP.

The spectrum of development identified in PA 2008, s 14(1) is diverse. It ranges from highways and harbours to reservoirs and railway infrastructure. Further, whilst the list provided at PA 2008, s 14(1) is expressed in exhaustive terms, the 2008 Act confers on the Secretary of State an express power both to add new types of development to that list, and to remove existing ones from it: see PA 2008, s 14(3).

When seeking to understand the scope of development which may currently be classified as an NSIP, one can at least note that the various developments cited all fall within one of five categories, namely: energy, transport, water, waste water and waste. Indeed, even the Secretary of State's power to identify a new form of development as comprising an NSIP is subject to this same restriction, since only development falling within these five categories of infrastructure may be newly classified as an NSIP.

Currently, the 16 types of NSIP project identified in PA 2008 comprise:

- generating stations (PA 2008, s 15);
- electric lines (PA 2008, s 16);
- underground gas storage facilities (PA 2008, s 17);
- LNG facilities (PA 2008, s 18);
- gas reception facilities (PA 2008, s 19);
- gas transporter pipelines (PA 2008, s 20);
- other pipelines (PA 2008, s 21);
- highways (PA 2008, s 22);
- airports (PA 2008, s 23);
- harbour facilities (PA 2008, s 24);
- railways (PA 2008, s 25);
- rail freight interchanges (PA 2008, s 26);
- dams and reservoirs (PA 2008, s 27);

- transfer of water resources (PA 2008, s 28);
- waste water treatment plants (PA 2008, s 29); and
- hazardous waste facilities (PA 2008, s 30).

In addition, the Infrastructure Planning (Waste Water Transfer and Storage) Order 2012, made under PA 2008, s 14(3), extended the 16 types of NSIP project to include a further type, being infrastructure for the transfer and storage of waste water with a capacity of over 350,000 cubic metres.

Note also that the effect of Growth and Infrastructure Act 2013, s 26 was to amend PA 2008, s 35 to allow the Secretary of State to direct that certain business and commercial projects be treated as development for which development consent is required.

Scale of development

Whilst only development relating to the five categories identified may comprise an NSIP, it goes without saying that not all development within those categories will do so. The question of whether a development will comprise an NSIP turns largely on the scale of development in question. That is to say, it is only in circumstances where the development comprises infrastructure of a particular scale that the consenting procedure of the 2008 Act will be engaged.

As to whether development is of sufficient scale to merit classification as an NSIP, it is necessary to consider whichever is applicable of the various statutory thresholds contained in PA 2008, ss 15–30 (and, indeed, the Infrastructure Planning (Waste Water Transfer and Storage) Order 2012, as above). These provisions, which are discussed in articles 15 to 23 of this work, provide, in respect of each of the various (now) 17 types of development, a threshold couched in terms of scale or capacity that is used to determine whether or not the development proposed must be regarded as an NSIP or not.

Although all NSIPs are, by definition, 'nationally significant' it would not be right to conclude that they will all necessarily comprise development on a 'grand' scale; indeed, this has been one of the issues that taxed Government and practitioners alike in the early years of the new regime. An obvious example relates to 'electric lines'. The definition in PA 2008, s 16, as originally drafted, was such that an electric line of 132 kilovolts and above was 'nationally significant' even if it only comprised a single tower and span. The thresholds in s 16 were amended by the Planning Act 2008 (Nationally Significant Infrastructure Projects) (Electric Lines) Order 2013 to exclude, for example, a project where the length of the line (when installed) will be less than two kilometres in length. Other changes to the original thresholds may be anticipated over time as the new regime beds down.

A further threshold issue relates to 'extensions'. Many of the types of NSIP in PA 2008, ss 15–30 are defined by a threshold that relates to both 'construction' or 'extension' of a project. By way of example, the construction or extension of a generating station is an NSIP where its capacity is more than 50 megawatts. This may, however, appear a relatively modest 'extension' to an existing (say) 1,500 megawatt combined cycle gas turbine generating station (circa 3%). Again, this may be an issue that the Government will need to tackle as the regime matures.

Article 15

Generating Stations

Michael Humphries QC, ftb

Introduction

This article examines some of the legal issues arising in relation to the construction or extension of an on-shore generating station within the meaning of section 15 of the Planning Act 2008 ('PA 2008').

The thresholds for a generating station to fall within the PA 2008

The statutory framework within which the construction or extension of a generating station may become a nationally significant infrastructure project ('NSIP') requiring development consent is set out in the PA 2008.

PA 2008, s 31 provides that:

> 'Consent under this Act ("development consent") is required for development to the extent that the development is or forms part of a nationally significant infrastructure project.'

For these purposes, PA 2008, s 32(1) defines the term 'development' as having the same meaning as it has in the Town and Country Planning Act 1990 ('the 1990 Act'), and section 55(1) of that Act states that '"development" means the carrying out of building, engineering, mining or other operations in, on, over or under land, or the making of any material change in the use of any buildings or other land'.

Thus, to come within the PA 2008 regime at all, there must be 'development', as so defined, and for that development to require 'development consent' it must be, or form part of, a nationally significant infrastructure project.

Section 14(1) of the PA 2008 provides that:

> '(1) In this Act "nationally significant infrastructure project" means a project which consists of any of the following–
>
> (a) the *construction* or *extension* of a generating station; ...' (emphasis added)

Section 15 further provides that:

> '(1) The construction or extension is within section 14(1)(a) only if the generating station is or (when constructed or extended) is expected to be within subsection (2) or (3).
>
> (2) A generating station is within this subsection if–
>
> (a) it is in England or Wales,

(aa) it does not generate electricity from wind,

(b) it is not an offshore generating station, and

(c) its capacity is more than 50 megawatts.'

[NB Subsection (3) relates to offshore generating stations and is considered in article 16 of this work.]

It is worth noting, however, that Wales Act 2017, s 39 amends PA 2008, s 15 by the insertion of a new subsection (3A) that raises the threshold for generating stations in Wales to 350 MW, although at the time of writing that amendment had not been brought into force, save in relation to a related amendment to PA 2008, s 115 in respect of associated development.

Construction of a generating station

The term 'construction' appears to relate to the development of a new generating station, or the term 'extension' would become redundant.

Whilst the capacity threshold for a generating station to fall within the PA 2008 regime is that 'its capacity is more than 50 megawatts' (PA 2008, s 15(2)(c)), in practice the concern about the term 'capacity' for many smaller projects has focused rather less on the minimum threshold of 50 MW and rather more on not exceeding 299 MWe. This arises from the requirements of the (former) EU Large Combustion Plant Directive (2001/80/EC) that imposes a threshold of 300 MWe above which development consent may not be granted for certain types of plant without demonstrating that they are carbon capture ready ('CCR'). The Directive threshold is expressed in 'MWe', which means 'megawatt electricity'. The Carbon Capture Readiness (Electricity Stations) Regulations 2013 ('the CCR Regulations'), by contrast, state that the Secretary of State must not make a DCO for the construction of a combustion plant with a 'rated electrical output' of 300 MW or more. This difference in language is not altogether helpful. A related issue centres, therefore, on the meaning of the term 'output'.

The practical solution to this issue was arrived at in the Progress Power DCO where the 'authorised development' (Schedule 1 Work No 1) was defined as a '... generating station ... with a gross electrical output of 299 MWe ...'.

The Secretary of State's decision letter observes as follows (paras 57 and 58):

> 'As the Development will have a maximum output of 299 MW the Secretary of State notes that the Development is just below the threshold of 300 MW where it would be subject to the requirement set out in EN-1 and the Carbon Capture Readiness (Electricity Generating Stations) Regulations 2013 ("the CCR Regulations") for the plant to be carbon capture ready.
>
> The Secretary of State notes that discussion took place around the definition of "output" and whether this should be the gross output of the generating plant or the net output exported from the site after allowing for transformer and other losses. The ExA noted that it was important that the definition of output used is consistent with Directive 2009/31/EC and the CCR Regulations. The ExA argued that the purpose the Directive and CCR Regulations is to control emissions and that the scale of emissions is therefore determined by the gross output. The Secretary of State notes that the EA also considered that gross output should be used and therefore agrees with the ExA's conclusion that a gross output definition would be consistent with the legislation.'

Thus the Progress Power formula is clearly acceptable to the Secretary of State.

Extension of a generating station

In order to analyse the question of whether development amounts to an 'extension' of an existing generating station for the purposes of PA 2008, s 15, it is worth considering the following issues:

(a) the meaning of the expression 'generating station'; and

(b) the meaning of the terms 'extension' and 'extend'.

The meaning of the expression 'generating station'

Section 235 of the PA 2008 provides that:

> '"generating station" has the same meaning as in Part 1 of the Electricity Act 1989 (see section 64(1) of that Act)'

The only definition of the expression 'generating station' in section 64(1) of the 1989 Act provides as follows:

> '"generating station", in relation to a generating station wholly or mainly driven by water, includes all structure and works for holding or channelling water for a purpose directly related to the generation of electricity by that station'

This definition is clearly intended to be non-exhaustive, but there is no further relevant definition of 'generating station' in either the PA 2008 or the 1989 Act.

The expression 'generating station' was considered, however, in the High Court decision of *R (Redcar and Cleveland BC) v Secretary of State for Business, Enterprise and Regulatory Reform and EDF Energy* [2008] EWHC 1847 (Admin). The claimant local authority in that case applied for judicial review of a decision of the defendant Secretary of State granting section 36 consent for an offshore wind farm. In that case the interested party (EDF Energy) had applied for consent for a wind farm with up to 30 wind turbines situated 1.5km offshore. The local authority had raised various objections to the proposed wind farm, including the proximity to the shoreline and visual impact of the wind farm, the effect on birds and marine ecology, and the adverse effect on the regeneration of the local area. Despite these objections, the Secretary of State granted consent under section 36. The local authority contended, amongst other things, that the consent was invalid because the offshore turbines were not a generating station for the purpose of section 36 of the 1989 Act, as they were not capable of providing consumable power by themselves.

Sullivan J held as follows on the issue of whether the turbines themselves were a generating station:

> '... it does not follow that the wind farm comprised in the section 36 application could not properly be described as a "generating station" for the purposes of that section. In ordinary language a "station" is simply a place, building or structure where a particular activity occurs. Thus, we speak of police stations, polling stations, railway stations, et cetera. *A non-technical description of a "generating station" would simply be a building or structure where electricity is generated.* The nature of the building or structure will depend on the means of generation: wind, water, coal, nuclear power, et cetera. *An application for consent under section 36 may include ancillary facilities, such as transformers, substations and associated cabling, and, for example, coal stockpiles and handling equipment if the generating station is coal-fired, et cetera. Whether or not such ancillary facilities are included in any section 36 application will depend upon the facts of the individual case, including, in particular, the physical proximity of*

> *the ancillary facilities to the turbines themselves*. In the case of an oil or coal-fired generating station the turbines and some or all of the ancillary facilities may well be housed in one building or structure or complex of buildings or structures. In the case of an offshore wind farm the turbines may well be separated by many kilometres of territorial waters from the ancillary facilities onshore. In the former case it will be sensible to include all of the elements of the scheme, including any ancillary facilities, in one application under section 36. In the latter case it will not, not least since the environmental implications of the offshore turbines may well be entirely divorced from the environmental impact of the onshore facilities many kilometres distant.' (emphasis added)

This passage appears to draw a distinction between (a) development that comprises a 'generating station' itself, which development would seem to include the generator, turbines and other equipment used to actually generate electricity, and (b) 'ancillary facilities', such as transformers, substations and associated cabling, and, for example, coal stockpiles and handling equipment if the generating station is coal-fired. It appears that a section 36 consent for a generating station may, but does not have to, also include consent for ancillary facilities.

The meaning of the terms 'extension' and 'extend'

The Oxford English Dictionary ('OED') definition of the word 'extend' includes 'to spread out in area' and 'to widen, enlarge (boundaries); to enlarge the area of', and the definition of the word 'extension' includes 'the action or process of spreading out in area'. It may be thought that these dictionary definitions fairly reflect the common usage meanings of these words.

The term 'extension', in relation to a 'generating station', is defined in PA 2008, s 235 as having the meaning given by section 36(9) of the Electricity Act 1989 (the 1989 Act). The PA 2008 gives no further direct assistance as to the meaning of 'extension' in relation to a generating station.

Section 36(9) of the 1989 Act provides that:

> '(9) In this Part "extension" in relation to a generating station, includes the use by the person operating the station of any land or areas of waters (wherever situated) for a purpose directly related to the generation of electricity by that station and 'extend' shall be construed accordingly.'

Within the 1989 Act the statutory definitions of 'extension' and 'extend' in section 36(9) apply *inter alia* in the context of section 36(1), which states that:

> '(1) ... a generating station shall not be constructed at a relevant place ... and a generating station at such a place shall not be extended or operated except in accordance with consent granted by the Secretary of State.'

It can be seen from the above, therefore, that the use of the term 'extension' and 'extend' in relation to a generating station in the PA 2008 adopts the definition of that term in the 1989 Act. PA 2008, s 33(1)(h) appears to be intended to avoid duplication between the two consenting regimes.

There are a number of points to be made in relation to section 36(9) of the 1989 Act, as follows:

(1) It is clear from the word 'includes' that the word 'extension' may comprise circumstances other than those set out in section 36(9). This is not, therefore, an exhaustive definition of the meaning of the term 'extension' but the identification of one aspect of its meaning. The definition would read very differently if, instead of 'includes', it had said 'means'.

(2) The definition emphasises that the 'use' is of 'any land or areas of waters (wherever situated)'. This appears to suggest that geographical location is not an important qualifier to what is or is not an 'extension', as an extension may occur on *any* land or areas of waters (*wherever* situated).

(3) The 'use' of the land in section 36(9) must be for 'a purpose directly related to the generation of electricity by that station'. These words echo those in section 90(5) of the 1990 Act (above). The inclusion of the word 'directly' does seem to qualify the word 'related', such that a use that is merely related (ie not 'directly' related) to the generation of electricity by that station would not be an extension. The words 'generation … by that station' are also an important qualifier. In other words, the use of the land has to be 'directly' related to the 'generation' of electricity by 'that' station (ie the existing station and not some other station).

(4) The limitation in section 36(9) to use 'by the person operating the station' should not be stretched too far. It would be difficult to argue that development was not an extension simply because it was undertaken by a legally separate, but related, company.

The language in section 36(9) that defines 'extension' as including the use of land for 'a purpose directly related to the generation of electricity by that station' appears to be important and sets a context for its meaning generally. It also supports the proposition that not all development at an existing power station amounts to an 'extension' for the purposes of section 36 of the 1989 Act and PA 2008, s 15.

Whilst the meanings of the terms 'extension' and 'extend' in the PA 2008 and 1989 Act have not been considered by the Courts, the meaning of 'extend' was considered in relation to section 11 of the Electricity (Supply) Act 1919 (the 1919 Act), although only in 1923. In *Attorney-General v Ealing Corporation* [1924] 2 Ch 545, Romer J had to consider section 11 of the 1919 Act, which stated that:

> '… it shall not be lawful for any authority, company, or person to establish a new or extend and existing generating station … without the consent of the Electricity Commissioners …'

Ealing Corporation needed to increase the capacity at an existing generating station to meet anticipated electricity demand and so substituted four generating sets within the station, with a combined capacity of 300 kW, with a single (smaller) turbo alternator with a capacity of 2000 kW. The Corporation did so, however, without having obtained the consent of the Electricity Commissioners under section 11 (above). The question was whether the replacement of the generating plant with smaller, but higher-capacity plant, was an extension of the generating station.

Romer J found (p550) as follows:

> 'I turn, therefore, to the question of whether the defendants have extended their plant. That depends on whether s 11 of the Act merely prohibits an extension in size, or whether it also prohibits an extension in capacity. In my opinion, it prohibits both.'

and later (p551) that:

> 'It is not, perhaps, the most appropriate way of describing such an increase to call it an extension of the plant. But a person who extends the capacity of his plant may not inaccurately be said to extend his plant and, in my opinion, the prohibition in s 11 of the Act against extending the plant used for generating electricity covers an extension of the plant's capacity.'

Whilst these observations need to be seen in the context of the 1919 Act, they are nevertheless instructive and appear to indicate that development that results in an increase in capacity would amount to an 'extension'.

This may be helpful in understanding the meaning of the term 'extension' in the context of PA 2008, s 15. This provision defines 'thresholds' for the construction or extension of a generating station by reference to 'capacity', rather than physical extent: see PA 2008, s 15(2). It is clear generally from the provisions of the PA 2008 that its purpose was to introduce a new system of planning control over infrastructure projects of 'national' importance. This may be important in interpreting the word 'extension'. As Lord Mance put it in *Bloomsbury International v Department for Environment, Food and Rural Affairs* [2011] UKSC 25 at para 11:

> 'In matters of statutory construction, the statutory purpose and the general context scheme by which it is to be put into effect are of central importance. They represent the context in which individual words are to be understood.'

Thus 'capacity' may be a further qualifier within the definition of 'extension'. This accords with a purposive reading of the term 'extension' whereby, for example, it would be difficult to see how the physical enlargement of the control room at a generating station of 250 MW, to allow (say) new monitoring and control equipment to be installed, could be an 'extension' amounting to a project of national significance; even though that physical extension might be 'directly related' to the 'generation' of electricity 'by that station'.

Capacity may, therefore, be an additional aspect of the term 'extension' that needs to be taken into account in determining whether there has been an extension of a generating station such as to make it a nationally significant infrastructure project.

The above analysis leads to a number of broad questions that may be asked in considering whether there is 'extension' of a generating station requiring development consent under the PA 2008:

(a) Is what is proposed 'development' for the purposes of the PA 2008?

(b) If what is proposed is 'development', then it is necessary to determine whether that development is an 'extension' of a generating station by asking;

  (i) what is the generating station for the purposes of any 'extension';

  (ii) has the proposed development 'extended' the generating station itself, or has it merely added or extended an 'ancillary facility';

  (iii) is the proposed development 'directly related' to the 'generation' of electricity 'by that power station'; and

  (iv) does the proposed development increase the 'capacity' of the generating station?

(c) If what is proposed is an 'extension' of a generating station, does the generating station (once extended) fall within the thresholds in PA 2008, s 15?

Conclusions

In most cases, it will be clear whether development is the 'construction' or 'extension' of a generating station falling within PA 2008, s 15. The analysis above should, however, be of some assistance in considering cases where that judgement is not immediately obvious.

Article 16

Offshore Generating Stations

Alex Booth QC, ftb
Michael Humphries QC, ftb

Introduction

PA 2008, s 14(1)(a) identifies development comprising 'the construction or extension of a generating station' as a category of NSIP.

This article is concerned with a sub-category of this type of NSIP, namely construction/extension of offshore generating stations. Such projects require discrete consideration because of the discrete provisions and guidance which govern their delivery (as distinct from that of onshore facilities); these in turn reflect the particular nature of the impacts to which offshore facilities may give rise (such as those on shipping and fisheries), and also the degree to which offshore facilities may lie remote from human habitation.

The relevant capacity thresholds which determine whether any such project in England and Wales falls to be considered as an NSIP (and thus consented under PA 2008) are set out in PA 2008, s 15. Different capacity thresholds apply to onshore generating stations. As regards offshore stations, the relevant provision is currently PA 2008, s 15(3). However, since April 2018, different thresholds have applied to generating stations off the coasts of Wales and England (see further below).

The locational requirement for this particular sub-category of NSIP is set out in PA 2008, s 15(4), which provides that a generating station will be regarded as being 'offshore' in circumstances where it is situated in waters in or adjacent to England and Wales up to the territorial limit, or else in a Renewable Energy Zone (other than one for which Scottish Ministers have functions).

To date, development consent has been granted in respect of two categories of offshore generating stations: offshore wind farms, and tidal lagoons. Numerous DCOs have of course been granted in respect of the former, with many of those projects operational. Examples of DCOs more recently granted for this type of NSIP include:

- the Norfolk Boreas Offshore Wind Farm Order 2021 (SI 2021/1414) – 158 wind turbine generators with a maximum generating capacity of up to 1,800 MW;
- the Hornsea Three Offshore Wind Farm Order 2020 (SI 2020/1656) – 300 wind turbine generators with a maximum generating capacity of up to 2,400 MW;
- the East Anglia THREE Offshore Wind Farm Order 2017 (SI 2017/826) – 172 wind turbine generators with a maximum generating capacity of up to 1,200 MW;
- the Hornsea Two Offshore Wind Farm Order 2016 (SI 2016/1104) – 360 wind turbine generators with a maximum generating capacity of up to 1,800 MW; and
- the Triton Knoll Electrical System Order 2016 (SI 2016/880) – 288 wind turbine generators with a maximum generating capacity of up to 1,200 MW.

The only DCO yet granted in respect of a tidal lagoon project is the Swansea Bay Tidal Generating Station Order 2015 (SI 2015/1386). In January 2017 the Hendry Review provided broad support for this emerging technology, with the author stating that:

> '... the evidence is clear that tidal lagoons can play a cost effective role in the UK's energy mix ... tidal lagoons would help deliver security of supply; they would assist in delivering our decarbonisation commitments; and they would bring real and substantial opportunities for the UK supply chain.'

In June 2018, however, the Secretary of State for BEIS announced that the Swansea Bay Tidal Lagoon project and the programme of lagoons 'do not meet the requirements for value for money' and progress temporarily stalled; however, in its Energy White Paper 'Powering our Net Zero Future' (December 2020), the Government stated that 'We will consider the role of wave and tidal energy, following further evaluation of the commercial and technical evidence'. During late 2021, BEIS undertook consultation as part of its review of the suite of energy NPS, but at the time of writing the outcome of that review in not known.

[NB The Swansea Bay Tidal Lagoon DCO was the subject matter of a CPR Part 8 claim seeking a declaration as to the status of the DCO; see *Tidal Lagoon (Swansea Bay) Plc v Secretary of State for Business, Energy and Industrial Strategy* [2021] EWHC 3170 (Admin).]

Statutory requirements for NSIP classification

'Generating station'

The term 'generating station' is defined in PA 2008, s 235(1), with the definition borrowing from that set out in section 64 of Part 1 of the Electricity Act 1989. The latter gives a non-exhaustive definition of generating station, stipulating that:

> 'in relation to a generating station wholly or mainly driven by water, [the generating station] includes all structures and works for holding or channelling water for a purpose directly related to the generation of electricity by that station.' (section 64(1))

This definition is relevant to hydro-electrical facilities such as tidal lagoons, but has no broader application. Of more assistance is the approach adopted in *R (Redcar and Cleveland BC) v Secretary of State for Business, Enterprise and Regulatory Reform* [2008] EWHC 1847 (Admin), where Sullivan J held (at para 18) that, for the purposes of the Electricity Act 1989, the term 'generating station' should be understood as meaning simply 'a building or structure where electricity is generated'.

As with other NSIPs, there is debate as to the extent to which development may comprise part of an NSIP, or instead comprise associated development (regarding which, see further below). The Hornsea One Offshore Wind Farm Order 2014 (SI 2014/3331) is perhaps typical in restricting the development granted as part of the NSIP to items such as turbines, subsea inter-array circuits and offshore accommodation platforms. However, a somewhat more flexible approach has occasionally been adopted in Wales, where the power of the Secretary of State to grant consent for associated development has historically been restricted: see further below, and article 40 of this work. Such approach has entailed consenting, as part of the NSIP, infrastructure which might otherwise be thought associated development. In this regard the Swansea Bay Tidal Generating Station Order 2015 (SI 2015/1386) appears to consent, as part of the NSIP, related infrastructure that is not necessary for generating electricity.

'Construction' or 'extension'

PA 2008, s 14(1)(a) embraces both the 'construction' and 'extension' of a generating station, in circumstances where the generating station satisfies both the locational and capacity requirements when the relevant works of development (whether construction or extension) have been completed.

In this context, PA 2008, s 235(1) provides that the term 'construction' should have the same meaning as in Chapter 2 of Part 2 of the Energy Act 2004 ('EA 2004') in relation to 'renewable energy installations'. Under section 104(3)–(5) of the EA 2004, the term 'renewable energy installation' embraces, amongst other things, 'an offshore installation used for purposes connected with the production of energy from water or winds', which would include a wind farm or tidal lagoon. For such projects, by virtue of section 104(1) of the EA 2004, operations comprising installation, commissioning or assembly will amount to construction, as will the attaching or placing of development on the sea bed.

'Extension' is defined by PA 2008, s 235(1) with reference to section 36(9) of the Electricity Act 1989, and so provides that the term includes 'the use by the person operating the station of any land or area of waters wherever situated for a purpose directly related to the generation of electricity by that station'.

Some limited further guidance as to the concept of 'extension' is provided in the report of the Examining Authority into the Burbo Bank Extension Offshore Wind Farm Order 2014 (SI 2014/2594), at paragraphs 2.4–2.8. That application proposal was described as an 'extension', and indeed satisfied the criteria set by the Crown Estate in respect of the grant of additional leases adjacent to existing operational wind farms. However, the project amounted to a major proposal in its own right, and satisfied the various defining criteria of an offshore generating station NSIP in and of itself. Indeed, the application proposal was larger than the existing wind farm (40 sq km as opposed to 10 sq km), the number of turbines proposed was greater than those of the existing wind farm (69 turbines as compared to 25 turbines), whilst the turbines proposed were taller than those of the existing wind farm. Further, the Examining Authority noted that, in electrical system and grid connection terms, the proposals would not share the same infrastructure as the existing wind farm. As such, whilst the proposal was nominally promoted as an extension, it did not present as such for the purposes of the PA 2008.

It appears that the intention in drafting PA 2008, s 14(1)(a) so as to include the 'extension' of a generating station as an NSIP is to enable proposals that are not nationally significant in their own right to be dealt with under the PA 2008 where they add capacity to generating stations that are nationally significant, or will be so when extended.

Capacity thresholds

The construction or extension of an offshore generating station in waters adjacent to England, up to the seaward limits of the territorial sea or in an English Renewable Energy Zone, requires the grant of a DCO in circumstances where it is expected to have capacity of at least 100 MW; see PA 2008, s 15(3).

The effect of the Wales Act 2017, however, was to increase the capacity threshold for Welsh offshore generating stations under the PA 2008 to 350 MW where those stations are located in territorial waters off the coast of Wales or the Welsh Zone (as defined by Government of Wales Act 2006, s 158). This reflects a new devolution settlement, devolving responsibility to the Welsh Assembly for developments comprising generating station projects up to 350 MW.

The new devolution arrangements implement the recommendations of the Commission on Devolution in Wales. The Commission concluded that devolving the consenting of generating stations of under 350 MW to Wales would deliver greater accountability and enable Wales to better develop its energy resources: see the report entitled 'Empowerment and Responsibility: Legislative Powers to Strengthen Wales' (March 2014), at paragraph 8.2.19.

Marine licence

By its very nature, an NSIP comprising of an offshore generating station will be located in either English and/or Welsh territorial waters, or else lie in a Renewable Energy Zone. Accordingly, it will require at least one marine licence by virtue of the Marine and Coastal Access Act 2009. By way of illustration, although the turbines of the Burbo Bank Extension Offshore Wind Farm lie in English waters, the NSIP connects to the grid in Wales and part of the grid connection is in Welsh territorial waters; thus it requires both an English and a Welsh marine licence.

However, whilst PA 2008, s 149A provides for a DCO to include the grant of a deemed marine licence in relation to development in English territorial waters and the Renewable Energy Zone, no equivalent provision exists in relation to Wales. Thus, where a Welsh marine licence is required, application must be made to Natural Resources Wales ('NRW'). Wales Act 2017, s 47 provides that NRW is the relevant licensing authority not only for Welsh inshore waters (up to 12 nautical miles) but also for the Welsh offshore region.

Associated development

The guidance issued by DCLG in April 2013 ('the Guidance'), regarding 'associated development' in England, lists (at Annex B) examples of associated development specific to offshore generating station projects. The list includes the following:

- onshore substations,
- harmonic filter compounds,
- overhead/underground lines,
- jointing pits,
- sealing end compounds,
- sea-land cable interface buildings and structures,
- converter stations and associated storage,
- facilities for additional sub-sea cables to offshore platforms, and
- additional circuit breakers or circuit breaker bays on an offshore platform.

Whilst this list is helpful in identifying examples of development that would ordinarily fall to be considered as associated development, it should be noted that paragraph 12 of the Guidance expressly provides that the list is illustrative only, and thus should not be taken to be exhaustive. Accordingly, in determining if development is properly to be regarded as associated development in respect of any particular project, whether or not it is identified within Annex B of the Guidance, regard should be had to the various core principles identified in paragraph 5 of the document.

A further point to note, as regards associated development in the particular context of offshore generating stations, is the observation contained in the Guidance to the effect that the Secretary of State may consider it appropriate for a degree of overcapacity to be provided in respect of the associated transmission infrastructure for an offshore generating station, having regard to the potential for future projects to make use of that infrastructure. However, it should also be noted that the observation is made in respect of '*planned* future projects' (emphasis added); thus provision of overcapacity will not be endorsed merely on the prospect that some, as yet unidentified, scheme may potentially come forward and make use of that excess capacity.

As already noted, the position as regards associated development in Wales has historically been markedly different to that in England; powers to consent such development have been very much restricted. However, Wales Act 2017, s 43 confers on the Secretary of State power to consent associated development for offshore generating stations where capacity will be more than 350 MW. It is anticipated that the DCLG guidance, whilst not applicable to Wales, may nevertheless be relied on in such cases until further guidance is published, as indeed it was by the Examining Authority in respect of the Brechfa Forest West Wind Farm Order 2013 (SI 2013/586), in the context of an onshore generating station.

The issue of whether development can be lawfully consented as part of an NSIP has already proven to be a point of dispute in respect of tidal lagoon projects, which by their nature (located relatively proximate to the shoreline) may bring opportunities for development of a waterfront area. In this regard, the promoters of the Swansea Bay Tidal Generating Station Order 2015 (SI 2015/1386) sought permission within the DCO application for a recreational facility and visitor attractions. The Welsh Government objected to these elements of the scheme on the basis that they should be subject to the approval of local planning authorities in Wales. The Examining Authority accepted that a recreational facility and visitor attraction could not be lawfully consented under the PA 2008 (see section 4.1 of the Authority's report). However, it found that any development necessary to ensure appropriate mitigation and the integration of the scheme with its surroundings would form essential parts of the generating station (see paragraph 4.1.37 of the Authority's report).

Article 17

Offshore Projects – Defining 'Offshore'

James Pereira QC, ftb
Michael Humphries QC, ftb

Introduction

PA 2008, s 15 provides that the construction or extension of an offshore generating station is within the description of nationally significant infrastructure projects under PA 2008, s 14(1) if, when constructed or extended as the case may be, it is expected to be either within PA 2008, s 15(3) or (3B).

PA 2008, s 15(3) concerns English offshore generating stations. It provides that a generating station is within the subsection where:

'(a) it is an offshore generating station; and

(b) its capacity is more than 100 megawatts.'

PA 2008, s 15(3B) concerns Welsh offshore generating stations. It provides that a generating station is within the subsection where:

'(a) it is in waters adjacent to Wales up to the seaward limits of the territorial sea, or in the Welsh zone, and

(b) its capacity is more than 350 megawatts.'

The definition of 'offshore'

PA 2008, s 15(4) provides that an 'offshore' generating station is a generating station that is:

'(a) in waters in or adjacent to England up to the seaward limits of the territorial sea; or

(b) in a Renewable Energy Zone, except the Welsh Zone or any part of a Renewable Energy Zone in relation to which the Scottish Ministers have functions.'

PA 2008, s 15(5) provides that 'Welsh Zone' has the meaning given in s 158 of the Government of Wales Act 2006.Each of these matters is discussed below.

Waters in or adjacent to England and Wales up to the seaward limits of the territorial sea

The 'territorial sea' is the adjacent belt of sea that extends beyond a state's land territory and its internal waters, over which a state has sovereignty under the United Nations Convention on the Law of the Sea and rules of customary international law. The UK is a signatory to the UN Convention (Cmnd 4524).

By Territorial Sea Act 1987, s 1, the territorial sea of the UK extends up to 12 nautical miles measured from baselines established by Order in Council, unless otherwise provided.

For ease of reference, the UK Government has produced maps showing the extent of the UK's territorial waters, and these are available online.

Renewable Energy Zones

Renewable Energy Zones are areas of water *outside* the UK's territorial sea where the UK claims exclusive rights to the production of energy from water and wind for the purposes of Energy Act 2004, s 84. The Renewable Energy Zone for the UK was originally designated by the Renewable Energy Zone (Designation of Area) Order 2004 (SI 2004/2668), but that Order was repealed and replaced by the Exclusive Economic Zone Order 2013 (SI 2013/3161) which was part of a suite of Orders creating an exclusive economic zone beyond the UK territorial waters, consistent with powers conferred by the UN Convention on the Law of the Sea.

The term 'Welsh Zone' is defined in s 158 of the Government of Wales Act 2006 and means:

> '... the sea adjacent to Wales which is—
>
> (a) within British fishery limits (that is, the limits set by or under section 1 of the Fishery Limits Act 1976), and
>
> (b) specified in an Order in Council under section 58 or an order under subsection (3).' The area within which the Scottish Ministers have responsibility for energy installations was designated by the Renewable Energy Zone (Designation of Area) (Scottish Ministers) Order 2005 (SI 2005/3153) and reflects the territorial extent of Scotland under the terms of the Scotland Act 1998.

The areas themselves are described in the Schedules to each Order by reference to points on longitude and latitude. However, for ease of reference, maps have been produced showing the extent of each area, and these are available online.

Article 18

Electric Lines

Michael Humphries QC, ftb

Introduction

Unlike many forms of development that have come within the ambit of the Planning Act 2008 ('PA 2008'), overhead lines already had a bespoke consenting regime under the Electricity Act 1989 ('the 1989 Act'). The 1989 Act has survived the new regime and so in some senses the two regimes existing in parallel, divided only by the 'thresholds' in the PA 2008.

PA 2008, s 14(1)(b) provides that:

> '(1) In this Act "nationally significant infrastructure project" means a project which consists of any of the following–
>
> ...
>
> (b) the installation of an electric line above ground; ...'

However, the expression 'the installation of an electric line above ground' needs first to be understood in the context of the 1989 Act. Section 37 of the 1989 Act (as amended by the PA 2008) provides, *inter alia*, that:

> '(1) Subject to subsections (1A) to (2) below, an electric line shall not be *installed or kept installed* above ground except in accordance with a consent granted by the Secretary of State.
>
> (1A) So far as relating to the installation of an electric line, subsection (1) is subject to section 33(1) of the Planning Act 2008 (exclusion of requirement for other consents for development for which development consent required).
>
> (1B) So far as relating to keeping an electric line installed, subsection (1) does not apply if keeping the line installed is authorised by an order granting development consent under the Planning Act 2008.' (emphasis added)

Thus, whereas, for other nationally significant infrastructure projects in PA 2008, ss 15–30A, the development is often described as 'the construction or extension' or 'the construction or alteration' of a project, for PA 2008, s 16 it is 'the installation' of an electric line above ground. This directly reflects the terminology in the 1989 Act.

The effect of section 37(1A) and (1B) of the 1989 Act, however, is to carve out of the 1989 Act regime those projects that fall within the PA 2008 regime; that is, that fall within the PA 2008, s 16 thresholds and are not otherwise excluded from PA 2008, s 16.

Some issues

This article will first examine the scope and application of PA 2008, s 16 under a number of issue headings.

Geographic coverage

The first part of PA 2008, s 16 sets geographic parameters for overhead line projects, as follows:

> '(1) The installation of an electric line above ground is within section 14(1)(b) only if (when installed) the electric line will be–
>
> (a) wholly in England,
>
> (b) wholly in Wales,
>
> (c) partly in England and partly in Wales, or
>
> (d) partly in England and partly in Scotland, subject to subsection (2).
>
> (2) In the case of an electric line falling within subsection (1)(d), the installation of the line above ground is within section 14(1)(b) only to the extent that (when installed) the line will be in England.'

Whereas most forms of nationally significant infrastructure project are unlikely to straddle national boundaries within the UK, that is not the case for long linear projects such as overhead lines, and so the clarification of the geographic parameters for such projects is important.

Electric line above ground

PA 2008, s 16(1) (above) also makes it clear that it relates to 'an electric line above ground'. That does not prevent a development consent order from including a length of underground cable, but it would appear to be the position that that part of an electrical connection project that comprises the 'electric line above ground' must itself satisfy the thresholds (see below) to bring the whole project within section 16.

The Hinkley Point C Connection project, for example, included some 48.5km of 400kV overhead line and some 8.5km of 400kV of underground cables. The decision is not explicit about whether the underground cable forms an 'integral part' of the project or whether it should be regarded as 'associated development' (see para 12 of the DCLG Guidance on Associated Development). The better view would appear to be that it is an integral part of the overhead line project.

The Triton Knoll Electrical System project comprised a 66km offshore cable and a 60km onshore cable to connect the previously consented Triton Knoll offshore wind farm to a National Grid substation in Lincolnshire. Being an underground cable, the project did not fall within PA 2008, s 16, but the Secretary of State in that case issued a section 35 direction that the project be treated as a nationally significant infrastructure project and thus brought within the PA 2008 regime. Development consent was granted in September 2016.

Other criteria for the overhead line to fall within the PA 2008 regime

PA 2008, s 16(3) provides a number of important thresholds and other exclusions for overhead lines, including:

> '(3) The installation of an electric line above ground is not within section 14(1)(b)–
>
> (a) if the nominal voltage of the line is expected to be less than 132 kilovolts,
>
> (aa) if the length of the line (when installed) will be less than two kilometres,

(ab) …

(b) to the extent that (when installed) the line will be within premises in the occupation or control of the person responsible for its installation …'

The England and Wales electricity supply industry comprises the transmission network operator, National Grid, that operates the system at high voltages (400kV and 275kV) and the distribution network operators ('DNO'), such as UK Power Networks and Western Power Distribution, that operate the system at lower voltages, including at 132kV.

Thus the voltage threshold at PA 2008, s 16(3)(a) will catch all National Grid overhead lines and any DNO overhead lines at 132kV and above.

The length threshold at PA 2008, s 16(3)(aa) is intended to exclude short lengths of overhead line that could not properly be regarded as 'nationally' significant. These will still require section 37 consent, however, under the 1989 Act procedures.

That part of any overhead line project within premises in the occupation or control of the person responsible for its installation does not require development consent. This will usually relate to the ends on a connection project within an existing substation, where the operator has existing permitted development rights under Part 15 Class B of Schedule 2 to the Town and Country Planning (General Permitted Development) (England) Order 2015 in England and Part 17 Class G of Schedule 2 to the Town and Country Planning (General Permitted Development) Order 1995 in Wales.

Special provisions for the replacement of existing lines

PA 2008, s 16 now makes special provision for the situation that can arise where an existing electric line needs to be uprated (ie its nominal voltage increased) in circumstances where no significant changes are made to the physical infrastructure. PA 2008, s 16(3)(ab) was added by the Planning Act 2008 (Nationally Significant Infrastructure Projects) (Electric Lines) Order 2013 ('the 2013 Order'). PA 2008, s 16(3)(ab) provides as follows:

'(3) The installation of an electric line above ground is not within section 14(1)(b)–

…

(ab) if–

(i) the line will replace an existing line,

(ii) the nominal voltage of the line is expected to be greater than the nominal voltage of the existing line (but see subsection (3A)),

(iii) the height above the surface of the ground of any support for the line will not exceed the height of the highest existing support or support which is being replaced by more than 10 per cent, and

(iv) where the line is to be installed in a different position from the existing line, the distance between any new support and the existing line will not exceed 60 metres and the existing line will be removed within twelve months from the date on which the installation of the line which replaces it is complete.'

Where PA 2008, s 16(3)(ab) applies, however, the uprating of an existing line may still need section 37 consent under the 1989 Act. Whilst National Grid's North London Reinforcement Project was a project for the uprating of a 14km existing 275kV overhead line to 400kV, the application was made in August 2012 and so pre-dated the making of the 2013 Order that introduced the above exemption and that in PA 2008, s 16(3)(aa) (above).

There is one important caveat to the above exemption as set out in PA 2008, s 16(3A):

> '(3A) Paragraph (ab)(ii) of subsection (3) (condition that nominal voltage of line expected to be greater than nominal voltage of existing line) does not apply if any part of the line (when installed) will be within a European site or an SSSI.'

Thus, where an existing line is to be replaced in a European site (see definition in PA 2008, s 16(4)) or an SSSI, it will not fall within the exemption if its nominal voltage is to be increased and development consent under the PA 2008 will still be required.

Good practice

So far, National Grid and the DNOs have successfully promoted a number of transmission and distribution network projects. In addition, a number of other overhead lines and cables have been brought forward by the developers of onshore and offshore generating stations to connect their projects to local substations on the transmission or distribution network.

Thus a reasonable amount of experience on electrical connections has now been accumulated and best practice developed. This article will now examine some of the more important themes to emerge.

Options appraisal

Long linear projects pose particular problems for options appraisal. For electrical connections, one end of the project will often be fixed (usually at or near a proposed generating station), but the other end will often be much more footloose (there may, for example, be a number of existing substations into which an overhead line could connect). Furthermore, the route between the two ends of any proposed connection may be numerous and present conflicting technical, environmental and cost effects. Appropriately balancing such effects is hugely important and often the subject matter of challenge by those potentially affected.

Transmission and distribution network operators also have to comply with their legal duty 'to develop and maintain an efficient, co-ordinated and economical system of electricity distribution' (section 9(1) of the 1989 Act).

To help it undertake appropriate and effective options appraisal, National Grid Electricity Transmission ('NGET') now undertakes an updated phased options appraisal process, as follows:

- Strategic proposal: During this phase, NGET explores whether new infrastructure needs to be built. This process concludes with a Strategic Options Report, which reports on the outcome of assessment into the feasibility of different technologies and geographical connection points.
- Options identification and selection: A broad study area is established, within which potential route corridor options are identified. NGET then produces a Corridor and Preliminary Routing and Siting Study which indicates a preferred route corridor. NGET then identifies graduated swathes and siting areas within the preferred route corridor. NGET then undertakes non-statutory consultation on the project.
- Defined proposal and statutory consultation: Using feedback from non-statutory consultation and other technical information, NGET will then identify an updated design proposal

for statutory consultation. The 'defined proposal' will also be described in a Preliminary Environmental Information Report ('PEIR').

- Assessment and land rights: Feedback from statutory consultation and information from additional environmental surveys and engineering input is used to refine the design for application. During this phase, NGET also conducts detailed discussions with relevant landowners about the use of their land. During this phase, an Environmental Statement will be produced to support the DCO application for the proposed project.

This type of process gives a structured approach to project optioneering and assists both the promoter and consultees / landowners.

Flexibility

Some flexibility in the precise locations of pylons, and thus their conductors, is essential for any substantial connection project. Precise pylon location cannot be fixed before detailed land survey of the entire line, and micro-siting of pylon locations also allows adverse local ground conditions (eg rock or bog), farming practices (eg turning circles for machinery or the location of land drains) or unexpected archaeological remains or ecological to be taken into account, where appropriate. Such flexibility will usually be required laterally and longitudinally, but also vertically, as pylons come in fixed unit sizes and ground levels may vary depending on precisely where the pylon is located.

Section 37 consents always allowed 'tolerances' around the 'centre line' of an overhead line and this practice has been broadly copied in the use of 'limits of deviation' on works plans and sections accompanying an application for development consent.

Applications for development consent for overhead lines are often accompanied by 'indicative' plans and sections showing pylon positions and heights. Whilst these are helpful in showing anticipated pylons locations, they cannot fix such locations for the reasons indicated above. For the Hinkley Point C Connection DCO the Secretary of State agreed to the following DCO requirement in respect of National Grid's indicative 'design drawings':

> '3. (1) The authorised development must be carried out *in general accordance with* the design drawings.
>
> (2) The authorised development will not be in general accordance with the design drawings to the extent that any departure from the design drawings gives rise to any materially new or different environmental effects from those assessed in the Environmental Statement.' (emphasis added)

This appears to represent a reasonable compromise between the need for some flexibility and the need also for the development and its environmental effects to be properly controlled.

Environmental impact assessment of flexibility

Paragraph 1(a) of Schedule 4 to the Infrastructure Planning (Environmental Impact Assessment) Regulations 2017 ('the 2017 EIA Regulations') requires that an Environmental Statement include:

> 'A description of the development, including in particular–
>
> (a) a description of the location of the development;
>
> (b) a description of the physical characteristics of the whole development ...'

and paragraph 5(a) requires the Environmental Statement to set out:

> 'A description of the likely significant effects of the development on the environment resulting from, inter alia–
>
> (a) the construction and existence of the development, including, where relevant, demolition works; …'

Thus it is clear that an Environmental Statement will have to identify any flexibility in the location and physical characteristics of a development and, indeed, will have to describe the likely significant effects of the development subject to that flexibility. This is exactly the issue that arose in the Rochdale Envelope cases.

In *R v Rochdale MBC ex p Milne (No 2)* [2001] Env LR 22, Sullivan J (as he then was) said as follows in the context of applications for outline planning permission:

> 'Provided the outline application has acknowledged the need for details of a project to evolve over a number of years, within clearly defined parameters, provided the environmental assessment has taken account of the need for evolution, within those parameters, and reflected the likely significant effects of such a flexible project in the environmental statement, and provided the local planning authority in granting outline planning permission imposes conditions to ensure that the process of evolution keeps within the parameters applied for and assessed, it is not accurate to equate the approval of reserved matters with "modifications" to the project. The project, as it evolves with the benefit of approvals of reserved matters, remains the same as the project which was assessed.'

Thus the concept of environmentally assessing parameters, or the 'Rochdale Envelope' as it became known, is one now recognised and accepted by the Courts.

PINS Advice Note 9 (version 3) gives the following guidance:

> '4.10 The ES should support the application for a DCO and must contain clear information presenting the significant effects applicable to the Proposed Development. If flexibility is sought it will be necessary for the ES to include information taking into account the variations applicable to the Proposed Development.
>
> 4.11 The ES should explain the reasons that lead to the uncertainty to characteristics of the Proposed Development in order to justify the flexibility sought. Applicants should take care to ensure that the approach taken in the assessment is not overly complex, as this may impede the understanding of the assessment and the finding of likely significant effects.
>
> 4.12 Establishing a robust worst case scenario(s) for the purposes of assessment is a particular challenge where there is a large degree of uncertainty and extensive flexibility in the DCO is sought. Applicants should carefully consider the approach to assessing uncertainty and understand how this will influence the complexity of their assessment in the ES. The characteristics of the Proposed Development that are yet to be finalised should be clearly identified in the description of the development in the ES. The Applicant should consider whether it is possible to robustly assess a range of impacts resulting from a large number of undecided parameters. The description of the development in the ES must not be so wide that it is insufficiently certain to comply with requirements of the EIA Regulations.'

The Advice Note also sounds the following caution:

> '5.2 Implementation of the Rochdale Envelope assessment approach should only be used where it is necessary and should not be treated as a blanket opportunity to allow

> for insufficient detail in the assessment. Applicants should make every effort to finalise details applicable to the Proposed Development prior to submission of their DCO application. Indeed, as explained earlier in this advice note, it will be in all parties' interests for the Applicant to provide as much information as possible to inform the Pre-application consultation process.'

These issues may be particularly pertinent when assessing the environmental effects of overhead lines.

Land and rights

Overhead lines will often require the acquisition of both land and rights (eg the Hinkley Point C Connection project DCO) and sometimes just rights (eg the Richborough Connection project DCO). Typically, rights will be sufficient for the pylons and conductors and, indeed, underground cables, but a freehold interest in land may be needed for sub-stations or sealing-end compounds. Rights will also be required for the long-term maintenance of an overhead line and/or underground cable. Rights and/or a power to use land temporarily are also likely to be required for the construction of an overhead line and/or underground cable, including for access to construction areas.

Clearly, the land and rights sought through a DCO will have to take into account the limits of deviation for the project, and a promoter will have to set out the compelling case in the public interest (PA 2008, s 122(3)) for the acquisition of land and rights over a wider area than will ultimately be required.

Article 19

Highways

James Pereira QC, ftb
Michael Humphries QC, ftb

Introduction

Section 14(1)(h) of the PA 2008 includes within the list of NSIPs the category 'highway-related development'. However, it is only highway-related development that satisfies the relevant criteria set out in PA 2008, s 22 that will require a DCO. It is important to note that section 22, as originally enacted, was replaced with a new PA 2008, s 22 with effect from 24 July 2013. The new PA 2008, s 22 was introduced by article 3 of the Highway and Railway (Nationally Significant Infrastructure Project) Order 2013 ('the 2013 Order'). The replacement PA 2008, s 22 was introduced because of concerns that the thresholds in the original version were too low, so that the PA 2008 procedures were being imposed upon highway-related development that was not truly of national significance. In addition, it was recognised that the original version of PA 2008, s 22 lacked clarity, which was giving rise to uncertainty as to whether a DCO was required and hence delays in progressing important infrastructure proposals (see, generally, the Government's consultation documents on the draft 2013 Order, 'Nationally significant road and railway schemes: changes to the Planning Act 2008 definitions' (DoT, 18 December 2012 (the consultation) and 3 June 2013 (the response to consultation)).

The current PA 2008, s 22 seeks to overcome these concerns by providing clearer criteria, including size thresholds, which must be satisfied before highway-related development will require a DCO.

Construction, alteration and improvement of highways: definitions

For highway-related development to require a DCO it must comprise one of three categories of development, and meet certain criteria applicable to each of the three categories. The categories are the construction, alteration and improvement of the highway. Relevant definitions are found in PA 2008, s 235(1).

The term 'highway' is defined in PA 2008, s 235(1) as having the same meaning as it has under section 328 of the Highways Act 1980 ('HA 1980'). By HA 1980, s 328(1), 'highway' means the whole or part of any highway other than a ferry or a waterway. By HA 1980, s 328(2), where a highway passes over a bridge or through a tunnel, that bridge or tunnel is to be taken as part of the highway.

It will be noted that the definition of highway is tautologous, since it includes the word 'highway' within the definition. It is relevant to consider the common law definition of highway. At common law, a highway is 'a way over which there exists a public right of passage, that is to say a right for all of Her Majesty's subjects at all seasons of the year freely and at their will to pass and re-pass without let or hindrance' (*ex p Lewis* (1888) 21 QBD 191 at 197). This definition will be of relevance under the PA 2008.

The term 'Highway Authority' is defined under PA 2008, s 235 as having the same meaning as it has under Highways Act 1980, ss 1 to 3, which set out in detail the different highway authorities that may exist in law and the highways to which they relate. Reference should be made to those sections of the Highways Act 1980 in relation to the facts of any particular case. Only general guidance can be given here. Generally, though not always, a Unitary Authority will be the highway authority for roads within its area, a county council of a district will be the highway authority for roads within its county area, Transport for London is the highway authority for certain roads within London, and the Secretary of State will be the highway authority for certain major roads, such as motorways and trunk roads.

The term 'construction' is not given a specific definition (in this context) under PA 2008, s 235(1). It should therefore be given its ordinary meaning. So 'construction' would usually be concerned with the physical making or laying out of a new highway.

The term 'alteration' is defined under PA 2008, s 235 as including stopping up, diverting, improving, raising or lowering the highway. The definition is not, however, exhaustive and other kinds of works to an existing highway, which can properly be termed an alteration to that highway, are likely to fall within this expression.

The term 'improvement' in relation to a highway is defined under section 235 as having the same meaning as it has under the Highways Act 1980. Section 329(1) of the Highways Act 1980 defines 'improvement' as 'The doing of any act under powers conferred by Part V of this Act, and includes the erection, maintenance, alteration and removal of traffic signs, and the freeing of a highway or road-ferry from tolls'.

Part V of the Highways Act 1980 sets out specific acts that are deemed to be highway improvements. There is a general power of improvement given by Highways Act 1980, s 62(2) in respect of highways maintainable by the highway authority carrying out the improvements. This power is then subject to specific kinds of improvement that are excluded from the general power and for which specific powers must be found. The specific powers are set out in the rest of Part V of the Highways Act 1980.

It is important to note that highway improvements which are carried out by a highway authority within the boundaries of a road may be exempt from the definition of development under section 55 of the Town and Country Planning Act 1990. The exemption does not apply where they are likely to have significant adverse environmental effects: see Town and Country Planning Act 1990, s 55(2)(b). This proviso seeks to give effect to obligations arising out of the Environmental Impact Assessment Directive.

Relevant criteria for the construction, alteration or improvement of highways

PA 2008, s 22 contains detailed criteria in relation to each of the three categories of highway-related development. Reference should be made to its provisions in relation to any particular case. The text below considers certain issues that arise on the wording of the section.

The location of the highway and the requirement for the Secretary of State to be the highway authority

None of the three categories of development (construction, alteration or improvement of a highway) will require a DCO unless the highway falls entirely within England and the Secretary of State is or will be (in the case of a newly constructed highway) the highway authority for the highway: see PA 2008, s 22(2)(a) and (b), (3)(a) and (b), and (5)(a) and (b).

A question arises as to whether this criterion is satisfied by highway-related development where the Secretary of State is or will be the highway authority for part only of the highway. The drafting of PA 2008, s 22 does not clearly identify whether such a highway will be caught by PA 2008, s 22 or not. However, since the definition of highway includes the whole or part of any highway (see Highways Act 1980, s 328(1)), this criterion can be read as being met where the Secretary of State is or will be the highway authority for at least part of the highway as constructed, altered or improved.

The application of size thresholds to development consisting of the construction and alteration of highways

The construction or alteration of a highway will not be highway-related development falling within PA 2008, s 14(1)(h) unless the area of development is greater than the relevant limit set out under PA 2008, s 22(4) (PA 2008, s 22(2)(c) and (3)(c)).

The limits under PA 2008, s 22(4) are as follows:

(a) in relation to the construction or alteration of a motorway, 15 hectares;

(b) in relation to the construction or alteration of a highway, other than a motorway, where the speed limit for any class of vehicle is expected to be 50 miles per hour or greater, 12.5 hectares; and

(c) in relation to the construction or alteration of any other highway, 7.5 hectares.

The 'area of development' is then defined under PA 2008, s 22(9) as follows:

(a) in relation to construction of a highway, it means the land on which the highway is to be constructed and any adjoining land expected to be used in connection with its construction;

(b) in relation to alteration of a highway, it means the land on which the part of the highway to be altered is situated and any adjoining land expected to be used in connection with its alteration.

In relation to the definition of 'area of development', a number of points arise.

First, 'in connection with [the] construction' of the highway is not defined in the PA 2008. The words should therefore be given their natural meaning. The land to be included is therefore land that the developer expects to use in connection with the works of construction or alteration (as the case may be), rather than land which may be needed for other development that is part of the scheme, such as associated development. The land to be included would normally comprise construction and works compounds and the like. This approach is supported by the fact that the size thresholds were based upon the size of the works areas required to construct or alter a single junction on the various categories of road that make up the Secretary of State's network (see page 6 of the Government's response to the consultation on the changes proposed in the draft 2013 Order (June 2013)).

Secondly, to be included within the 'area of development' such land must be 'expected to be used' in connection with the construction and also be 'adjoining' the highway. The legislation therefore expects that all land that the developer expects to use in connection with the construction or alteration will be included within the application for the DCO (since otherwise the thresholds could be circumvented). However, the use of the word 'adjoining' suggests that construction compounds which are remote from the land on which the highway is to be constructed are not to be included in the calculation of the threshold.

Thirdly, what approach should be taken in cases where part but not all of the highway being constructed or altered is (or will) be a highway for which the Secretary of State is (or will) be the highway authority. In such a case, should the area of development only include those works areas expected to be used in connection with the Secretary of State's part of the highway, or should it include works areas expected to be used in connection with the construction or alteration of the entire highway? The position is unclear. However, it may be thought that limiting the area of development to that expected to be used in connection with the Secretary of State's highway was more in keeping with the underlying objective of the changes to PA 2008, s 22, and with the basis upon which the sizes of the thresholds were chosen.

The need for significant environmental effects for development consisting of the improvement of a highway

In addition to the criteria already referred to, the improvement of a highway will not be highway-related development falling within PA 2008, s 14(1)(h) unless the improvement is likely to have a significant effect on the environment (PA 2008, s 22(5)). This should be read as having the same meaning as the equivalent term under the Environmental Impact Assessment Regulations and Directive. For guidance on the approach to be taken to the assessment of whether development has significant environmental effects, see *R (Loader) v Secretary of State* [2012] EWCA Civ 869.

Alteration of a highway that is necessary as a result of development with planning permission

In certain circumstances the alteration of a highway is necessary as a result of a development that already has the benefit of a grant of planning permission. Such alterations will not be highway-related development falling within PA 2008, s 14(1)(h) if the developer has asked for the alteration to be made to the highway: see PA 2008, s 22(7). Note however that the alteration must be 'necessary' as a result of the development that has planning permission. This would appear to be an objective test. It would not be satisfied where the alteration were merely desirable.

Effect of requirement for development consent on certain statutory orders under the Highways Act 1980 and the New Roads and Street Works Act 1991

PA 2008, s 33(4) provides a list of statutory orders under the Highways Act 1980 and the New Roads and Street Works Act 1991 that may neither be made nor confirmed in relation to a highway or in connection with its construction, improvement or alteration, where development consent is required for that construction, improvement or alteration. Reference should be made to PA 2008, s 33(4) for the list of orders in question.

Limited exemption from the requirement for development consent where certain statutory orders under the Highways Act 1980 or the New Roads and Street Works Act 1991 have already been made

However, where an order listed under PA 2008, s 33(4) has *already* been made, the construction, improvement or alteration of the highway may be exempt from the requirement for development consent by reason of either PA 2008, s 22(6) or (8). Reference should be made to the detailed wording of those provisions in relation to any particular case.

Associated development

Some highway-related development may include associated development. The Guidance on associated development applications for major infrastructure projects (DCLG, April 2013), lists the following as examples:

- replacement roadside facilities where this becomes necessary due to the elimination of an existing facility by highway improvement;
- infrastructure associated with cycle/pedestrian access;
- off-site landscaping, habitat creation and other environmental works;
- off-site drainage works;
- alteration/diversion/stopping up of local roads, accesses and other rights of way; and
- off-site diversion of statutory undertakers' equipment.

The (now withdrawn) Highways England Interim Advice Note ('IAN') 134/10 included Motorway Service Areas, Rest Areas and Truck Stops as examples of 'associated development'. This suggests that highways 'associated development' may include reasonably significant forms of development, although the IAN itself is no longer authority for these particular examples.

Note that some highways works will comprise associated development for other kinds of NSIPs. The Guidance on associated development applications for major infrastructure projects (DCLG, April 2013) lists access arrangements and demand management measures as examples.

NPS for National Networks

In December 2014 the Department for Transport designated the National Policy Statement for National Networks ('the NN NPS') setting out national policy for certain transport infrastructure, including the national road network. The NN NPS provides the policy framework within which 'highway-related development' falling within PA 2008, ss 14(1)(h) and 22 will be considered under PA 2008, s 104. The NN NPS outlines 'wider Government policy' on national network (including such issues as road tolling and charging), sets out 'assessment principles' on a range of issues and explains the approach to be taken to the consideration of 'generic impacts' (such as biodiversity and the historic environment).

Article 20

Harbour Facilities

Mark Westmoreland Smith, ftb
Michael Humphries QC, ftb

Introduction

This article is concerned with the construction or alteration of harbour facilities. It examines the thresholds for such development to come within the PA 2008 regime and some recent changes as a result of the Wales Act 2017.

Harbour facilities

By virtue of PA 2008, s 14(1)(j), the construction and/or alteration of harbour facilities is capable of being an NSIP. Whether or not the construction and/or alteration of harbour facilities comprises an NSIP for the purposes of the PA 2008 is determined by reference to the criteria laid down in PA 2008, s 24. These criteria can be divided into two categories: geographical limits, and minimum handling thresholds.

Geographical limits

The construction or alteration of harbour facilities is capable of being within PA 2008, s 14(1)(j) only if the harbour facilities are or would be in England or Wales or in waters adjacent to England or Wales up to the seaward limits of the territorial sea.

Handling thresholds

The minimum handling thresholds relate to the expected handling capacity of the proposed or altered facility.

In order to qualify as an NSIP, where the project involves the construction of a harbour facility, the facility proposed must be expected to be capable of handling the embarkation or disembarkation of at least the 'relevant quantity' of material per year.

For the alteration of an existing harbour facility to qualify, the effect of the alteration must be expected to be to increase the quantity of material the embarkation or disembarkation of which the facilities are capable of handling by at least the 'relevant quantity' per year.

'Relevant quantity' has the following meanings:

- In the case of facilities for container ships (defined as ships which carry all or most of their cargo in containers), 500,000 TEU. [A TEU is defined, in turn, as a 20-foot equivalent unit which is, in effect, a 20-foot long container that can be transferred easily between modes of transport – eg ship to rail or road.]

- In the case of facilities for Ro-Ro ships (a ship which is used for carrying wheeled cargo), 250,000 units (unit here meaning any item of wheeled cargo, whether or not self-propelled).
- In the case of facilities for cargo ships (defined as a ship used for carrying cargo) of any other description, 5 million tonnes.

Where the facility in question handles or is proposed to handle more than one type of ship, the threshold is a weighted sum equivalent to the above figures taken together; described in PA 2008, s 24(3)(d) as 'an equivalent quantity of material'. PA 2008, s 24(4) and (5) sets down the precise meaning of an equivalent quantity of material and the means of calculating whether or not a proposal meets that threshold.

PA 2008, s 24(4) provides that facilities are capable of handling an equivalent quantity of material if the sum of the relevant fractions is 1 or more.

The calculation of the relevant fraction is provided by PA 2008, s 24(5), which sets out three fractions to be summed in order to work out whether the total capacity is an equivalent amount. The fractions are:

- Container ships: x / 500,000, where x is the number of TEU that the facilities are capable of handling.
- Ro-Ro ships: y / 250,000, where y is the number of units that the facilities are capable of handling.
- Cargo ships of any other description: z / 5,000,000, where z is the number of tonnes of material that the facilities are capable of handling.

For example, would a proposed development that anticipated handling 100,000 TEUs, 150,000 Ro-Ro units and 2,000,000 tonnes of other cargo exceed the NSIP threshold?

Container:	100,000 / 500,000	=	1/5th
Ro-Ro:	150,000 / 250,000	=	3/5ths
Other cargo:	2,000,000 / 5,000,000	=	2/5ths
Sum of relevant fractions:		=	6/5ths (or 1 and 1/5th)

In this example, the sum of the relevant fractions is greater than 1 and, therefore, the threshold is exceeded and the development would be an NSIP.

Effect of the Wales Act 2017

From 1 April 2018, PA 2008, s 24 was amended by Wales Act 2017, s 33 such that, for harbour facilities in Wales to come within PA 2008, s 14(j), they must not only be wholly in Wales or in waters adjacent to Wales up to the seaward limits of the territorial sea, but must also be, or form part of, a 'reserved trust port'.

A 'reserved trust port' has the meaning given in Wales Act 2017, s 32. A reserved trust port is a harbour that is owned or managed by a harbour authority that is a relevant port authority within the meaning of the Ports Act 1991 and that meets the annual turnover requirement set out in section 11 of that Act (£5m per annum). The annual turnover requirement has to be met in two of the previous three accounting years.

The main reserved trust ports in Wales are Carnarfon, Milford Haven and Newport.

Harbour NSIPs

To date, there have been three ports projects that have passed through the PA 2008 regime. Those are:

- Able Marine Energy Park Development Consent Order 2014 (SI 2014/2935).
- York Potash Harbour Facilities Order 2016 (SI 2016/772).
- Port of Tilbury (Expansion) Order 2019 (SI 2019/359).

Article 21

Railways

Alex Booth QC, ftb
Michael Humphries QC, ftb

Introduction

This article is concerned with PA 2008, ss 14(1)(k) and 25. The former provides that works for the 'construction or alteration of a railway' may comprise an NSIP, and the latter sets out the statutory thresholds that determine whether the construction or alteration of a particular rail project will comprise an NSIP. This category of NSIP is distinct from the construction of a rail freight interchange, provision for which is made by PA 2008, ss 14(1)(l) and 26. In this regard, PA 2008, s 25(3) expressly excludes development falling within PA 2008, s 14(1)(k) to the extent that the railway the subject of the works does or will form part of such a freight interchange.

Early in the life of the PA 2008 regime, there were a number of DCOs granted in respect of 'Rail NSIPs', all of which have entailed the 'construction' of a railway. These include:

- the Ipswich Rail Chord (SI 2012/2284),
- the North Doncaster Rail Chord (SI 2012/2635),
- the Redditch Branch Enhancement Scheme (SI 2013/2809), and
- the Norton Bridge Area Improvements Scheme (SI 2014/909).

In passing, it is perhaps worth noting that this clutch of DCOs were all granted prior to the designation of the relevant NPS; the National Policy Statement for National Networks was published in draft in 2013, before being designated in December 2014.

Since then, there have been notably few Rail NSIPs, although during 2020 North Somerset Council made an application for the Portishead Branch Line – MetroWest Phase 1 DCO, and the Western Rail Link to Heathrow had been notified to PINS.

A point to note is that significant changes were made to PA 2008, s 25 by the Highways and Railway (Nationally Significant Infrastructure Project) Order 2013 (SI 2013/1883), which introduced additional requirements that any railway scheme must now meet in order to classify as an NSIP (see, in particular, PA 2008, s 25(1)(ba) and (2)(ba)). Significantly in this regard, works of construction or alteration must now include the laying of a continuous stretch of track measuring 2 kilometres or more. One project consented by means of a DCO prior to the making of the 2013 Order would now no longer fall within the statutory definition of a 'Rail NSIP'; in the case of the Ipswich Rail Chord, the relevant length of track did not exceed 1.5 kilometres.

'Construction' versus 'alteration'

PA 2008, s 14(1)(k) embraces both the 'construction' and 'alteration' of a railway. The Act provides definitions of both these terms (PA 2008, s 235), but neither definition applies to rail-related infrastructure. Thus the words must be given their natural meaning.

Statutory requirements for NSIP classification

General observations

The statutory requirements in respect of proposals to 'construct' a railway are all but identical to those relating to the 'alteration' of one. In summary, it is necessary:

(a) that the works (whether of construction or alteration) be undertaken wholly in England;

(b) that the railway (ie that part newly altered or constructed) be part of a network operated by an approved operator; and

(c) that the works (whether of construction or alteration) not comprise permitted development.

Further, and following the 2013 Order, it is also necessary that the newly altered or constructed stretch of railway includes a length of track that is both:

(a) of more than 2 kilometres continuous length, and

(b) not located on land which previously comprised the operational land of a railway undertaker.

It is important to note the distinction between how these two sets of requirements take effect. The former are, at least arguably, absolute requirements. That is, it would appear necessary that the entirety of the length of railway undergoing alteration or construction satisfy the requirements as to location (ie that it be located 'wholly in England') and operation (ie that it 'be part of a network operated by an approved operator'), and that none of the works comprising the NSIP amount to permitted development. Such interpretation of the legislation would appear to follow from the decision in *R (Gate on behalf of Transport Solutions for Lancaster and Morecambe) v Secretary of State for Transport* [2013] EWHC 2937 (Admin). Notwithstanding that the development at issue in that case comprised a highway scheme (the M6-Heysham Link), the reasoning of Turner J regarding the wording of PA 2008, s 14 applies equally to railway development as to road. In particular, in *Gate* the Court emphasised that PA 2008, s 14(1) provides that an NSIP is a project which 'consists' of (as opposed to 'includes') the various categories of development there identified. On this basis, and given that PA 2008, s 25(1) and (2) stipulate that development will fall within the terms of PA 2008, s 14(1)(k) 'only' if the criteria as to location / operation / permitted development are met, it would appear that the requirements must be satisfied by the entirety of the NSIP.

This position can be contrasted with the requirements imposed by the 2013 Order, both of which may be satisfied by part of the length of the railway undergoing alteration or construction. In such circumstances there is no necessity for the entirety of the railway to meet those requirements.

Networks and approved operators

As noted above, in order for development to comprise an NSIP, the track the subject of the works must form part of a network operated by an approved operator. The term 'approved operator' is defined by PA 2008, s 25(4)–(6), whilst PA 2008, s 25(7) provides that the term 'network' should have the definition contained in Railways Act 1993, s 83(1). This identifies a network as:

(a) any railway line, or combination of two or more railway lines, and

(b) any installations associated with any of the track comprised in that line or those lines,

which constitute a system of track and installations used for and in connection with the support, guidance and operation of trains.

Very often there will be no difficulty as regards these particular requirements, since the majority of Rail NSIPs will be likely to comprise track constructed either by an operator (such as Network Rail) for the purpose of extending / improving its network, or by the developer of some other significant project (presumably to provide access in connection with that project's construction or operation) with the intention that it be passed to an operator as part of its network.

However, there may be circumstances where significant stretches of track are constructed as 'private' railways in the context of large infrastructure projects. Where track is not intended to be made over to an operator as part of its network, such a railway – however extensive – will fall outside the definition of an NSIP; although it may be 'associated development'.

Operational land

PA 2008, s 25(2A) provides an important qualification to the general extent of PA 2008, s 25 in that the construction or operation of a railway is not within PA 2008, s 14(1)(k) to the extent that it takes place on the operational land of a railway undertaker unless that land was acquired for the purposes of the construction or alteration.

In this context, PA 2008, s 25(7) stipulates that the term 'operational land' will have the meaning provided for by the Town and Country Planning Act 1990. The relevant provision of the TCPA 1990 is s 263, subject to the qualification provided by s 234.

Permitted development

A railway development will not comprise an NSIP in circumstances where part or all of it comprises 'permitted development'. In this context the relevant permission is that granted pursuant to Class A of Part 8 of Schedule 2 to the Town and Country Planning (General Permitted Development) Order 2015 (SI 2015/596), which provision authorises the carrying out of development by railway undertakers on their operational land where such development is required in connection with the movement of traffic by rail.

However, paragraph A.1(a) of Class A excludes from the scope of the permission any development which comprises 'the construction of a railway'. Further, and more broadly, Article 3 of the 2015 Order engages to exclude development requiring environmental impact assessment. Thus the majority of railway works that would fall to be classed as an NSIP are unlikely to be excluded from the PA 2008 regime because they are 'permitted development'.

Development to be consented

NSIP

The definition of the term 'railway' in the PA 2008 borrows from Transport and Works Act 1992, s 67(1); see PA 2008, s 235. That provision defines a 'railway' as a system of transport employing parallel rails which:

(a) provides support and guidance for vehicles carried on flanged wheels, and

(b) forms a track which either is of a gauge of at least 350 millimetres or crosses a carriageway (whether or not on the same level), but

(c) does not include a tramway.

Having regard to this definition, it would appear that the PA 2008 does not intend that the definition of a Rail NSIP should embrace the construction of items such as 'station' development; platforms, ticket offices and similar; again, this may be subject to consideration of whether any such development may be 'associated development'. Rather, it appears to intend that the NSIP itself comprise only the infrastructure along which (rail) traffic will pass. This would of course include rails, sleepers and ballast, but also includes matters such as the embankments and cuttings in/on which such infrastructure sits.

Such relatively narrow approach is consistent with that adopted in respect of the DCOs issued to date. In this regard, by way of example, the Redditch DCO confined the scope of the NSIP (Work No 1) to what might broadly be termed 'the railway line', being the infrastructure along which trains would travel, with all other matters comprising 'associated development'. Such 'associated development' included the 'construction of a new station platform …' (Work No 2), and the 'construction of a new footbridge to connect from the existing platform …' (Work No 3).

In this context, one might have expected signalling equipment/infrastructure to form part of the 'system of transport' comprising the railway, and thus the NSIP. However in the Redditch DCO 'signal equipment buildings' (Work Nos 6 and 7) and other 'signalling works' were consented only as 'associated development'.

Notwithstanding what is said above, it would appear that the system does admit of some flexibility. In this regard the Ipswich Chord DCO included within the terms of the NSIP not only works to embankments but also the construction and reconstruction of bridges; similarly the Doncaster Rail Chord NSIP included the construction of temporary haul roads. Perhaps the broadest approach to what may comprised part of the NSIP is that adopted in the Norton Bridge Area Improvements DCO, which included not only the line itself, but also:

> '… all associated items that comprise a railway including track, cess drainage, combined troughing and walking route, overhead line electrification … signalling, telecommunications and cutting or embankment earthworks, maintenance access track, crest drainage … and boundary fencing.'

Associated development

A narrow interpretation as to the extent of the NSIP is consistent with what is said in the (then) DCLG 'Guidance on associated development applications for major infrastructure projects'. In this regard, the DCLG Guidance identifies in Annex B development that may constitute 'associated development' connected with a 'Rail NSIP'. Examples of such development include:

- the construction of new railway stations, and improvements, alterations and extensions to existing stations (new footbridges, platforms extensions, ticket halls;
- the construction/alteration of maintenance depots and marshalling yards; and
- the provision of pressure relief or ventilation shafts (and access to them).

The DCOs granted to date have delivered a myriad of items as 'associated development'; these have included matters such as:

- the construction of bridges (both vehicular and pedestrian);
- the diversion of other infrastructure (roads and pipelines); and
- the diversion of other linear features (footpaths and rivers).

Contiguity of development

There is no requirement that the scheme of proposed works comprise a contiguous 'whole'. The closest the PA 2008 comes in this regard are the equivalent stipulations in PA 2008, s 25(1)(b) and (2)(b) that the stretch of track the subject of the construction / alteration be part of a network operated by an approved operator (see above).

However, it would appear that, so long as the railway that is subject to the works undertaken (whether of construction or alteration) forms part of such a network, it may form part of the same NSIP. This may be of some significance in circumstances where a party is seeking to carry out various works in various different locations that are not geographically proximate. In such a scenario it would arguably be sufficient if only one of those works satisfied the requirements regarding length of track and operational land – imposed by PA 2008, s 25(1)(ba) and (2)(ba) – in order for all the remainder to comprise part of an NSIP.

Policy

As noted above, the National Networks NPS was designated in December 2014. The document provides detailed guidance not only in respect of Rail NSIPs promoted pursuant to PA 2008, s 14(1)(k), but also highways and rail freight interchange development.

The guidance is extensive, and those promoting or objecting to applications seeking development consent for the construction / alteration of railways will of course need to consider it in detail so as to ascertain whether a proposal is compliant with the NPS for the purposes of the presumption contained in PA 2008, s 104(3). However, by way of generality it should be noted that the National Networks NPS contains a strong presumption in favour of railway-related development, both in terms of freight and in terms of passenger traffic, where that development will improve the performance of the rail network. In this regard the following paragraphs are worthy of particular note:

- 'The Government has … concluded that at a strategic level there is a compelling need for development of the national networks – both as individual network and as an integrated system. The Examining Authority and the Secretary of State should therefore start their assessment of applications for infrastructure covered by this NPS on that basis' (paragraph 2.10)
- 'Rail transport has a crucial role to play in delivering significant reductions in pollution and congestion …' (paragraph 2.35)
- 'The Government has therefore concluded that at a strategic level there is a compelling need for development of the national rail network …' (paragraph 2.36)
- 'Modal shift from road and aviation to rail can help reduce transport's carbon emissions, as well as providing wider transport and economic benefits. For these reasons, the Government seeks to accommodate an increase in rail travel and rail freight where it is practical and affordable by providing for extra capacity' (paragraph 2.40).

Thus, to the extent that proposed development may have some adverse impact – in terms of planning considerations such as heritage and visual impact – any such impacts must be assessed in policy context that is supportive as a matter of principle. Clearly, however, such policy support in no way excuses rail-related development from compliance with the many and onerous requirements relating to 'environmental impact assessment' and, where necessary, 'appropriate assessment'.

Article 22

Rail Freight Interchanges

James Pereira QC, ftb
Michael Humphries QC, ftb

Introduction

Under PA 2008, s 26, the construction and alteration of a rail freight interchange ('RFI') will be an NSIP, provided that the thresholds and criteria in the legislation are met. The policy guidance on RFIs is found within the NPS for National Networks (December 2014).

The requirements of PA 2008, s 26 are considered below.

What is a rail freight interchange?

There is no definition of an RFI in the legislation. The NPS for National Networks (December 2014) explains at paragraph 2.43 that:

> 'Rail freight interchanges (RFI) enable freight to be transferred between transport modes, thus allowing rail to be used to best effect to undertake the long-haul primary trunk journey, with other modes (usually road) providing the secondary (final delivery) leg of the journey.'

In fact, the NPS uses the term 'strategic rail freight interchange' ('SRFI') to describe rail freight interchanges that qualify as NSIPs (see paragraph 1.1 of the NPS). So, although the term 'strategic' is not used in the legislation, it is clear that the NPS in referring to SRFIs is referring to the same development as RFIs that meet the thresholds and criteria to be NSIPs under the PA 2008.

Paragraph 2.44 explains that:

> 'The aim of a strategic rail freight interchange (SRFI) is to optimise the use of rail in the freight journey by maximising rail trunk haul and minimising some elements of the secondary distribution leg by road, through co-location of other distribution and freight activities. SRFIs are a key element in reducing the cost to users of moving freight by rail and are important in facilitating the transfer of freight from road to rail, thereby reducing trip mileage of freight movements on both the national and local road networks.'

Footnote 42 of the NPS states as follows:

> 'A strategic rail freight interchange (SRFI) is a large multi-purpose rail freight interchange and distribution centre linked into both the rail and trunk road system. It has rail-served warehousing and container handling facilities and may also include manufacturing and processing activities.'

In the light of the NPS, it appears that the essence of an SRFI is that it provides facilities for the reciprocal transfer of goods to and from the rail network, to and from other modes of transport. The extent to which other uses, such as manufacturing and processing activities, might be included within an SRFI application is discussed later in this section.

Threshold requirements and other criteria

To qualify as an NSIP, the proposed new RFI must, when constructed, be 'expected to' meet each of the conditions set out in PA 2008, s 26(3)–(7). These are that it must:

- be in England (PA 2008, s 26(3)(a));
- be part of a railway network in England (PA 2008, s 26(5));
- be on land of at least 60 hectares in area (PA 2008, s 26(3)(b));
- be capable of handling consignments of goods from more than one consignor and to more than one consignee (PA 2008, s 26(4)(a));
- be capable of handling at least four good trains per day (PA 2008, s 26(4)(b)); 'goods train' is defined as a train (excluding any locomotive) that consists of rolling stock designed to carry goods (PA 2008, s 26(9)); and
- include warehouses to which goods can be delivered from the railway network in England, either directly or by means of another form of transport (PA 2008, s 26(6)).

RFIs that form part of a military establishment are expressly excluded from the regime (PA 2008, s 26(7)). A military establishment is defined as an establishment intended for use for naval, military or air force purposes or for the purposes of the Department of the Secretary of State responsible for defence (PA 2008, s 26(9)).

The terms 'network', 'rolling stock' and 'train' are given the same meaning as under Railways Act 1993, s 83(1) (PA 2008, s 26(9)).

Alterations to an RFI

Alterations to an RFI will qualify as an NSIP where the same criteria are expected to be met following the alteration, save that the land area criteria applied to an alteration is that it must increase, by at least 60 hectares, the land on which the RFI is situated (PA 2008, s 26(2)).

The inclusion of other uses within an RFI application

It is in the nature of RFIs that other uses, such as processing and manufacturing uses, may find it advantageous to locate within an RFI site. This is because the SRFI will facilitate the receiving of raw materials and dispatching new products by rail or road. While footnote 42 in the NPS (quoted above) suggests that processing and manufacturing uses can be found on an SRFI, such uses are likely to be an end in themselves, and so are unlikely to qualify as associated development under the PA 2008.

In the East Midlands Gateway Rail Freight Interchange and Highway Order 2016, the accommodation of other primary uses was allowed for through the drafting of the Order.

Regulation 5(2) of the Order provided as follows:

> 'It does not constitute a breach of the terms of this Order, if, following the coming into force of this Order, any development, or any part of a development, is carried out or used within the Order limits under planning permission granted under the 1990 Act.'

This provision was recognised by the Examining Authority as providing flexibility to accommodate the commercial requirements of future occupiers who could not be known at the time, and to provide flexibility to accommodate future uses that would fall outside the PA 2008 but which could be granted planning permission (Examining Authority's report, paragraphs 7.1.18 and 7.1.21).

DCOs granted for RFIs and alterations to RFIs

DCOs granted under this section include:

- The East Midlands Gateway Rail Freight Interchange and Highway Order 2016 (granting development consent for a new rail freight interchange and highway infrastructure at Castle Donnington, Leicestershire);
- The Daventry International Rail Freight Interchange Alteration Order 2014 (granting development consent to expand the existing Daventry International Rail Freight Interchange Terminal);
- The Northampton Gateway Rail Freight Interchange Order 2019 (granting development consent for the construction, operation and maintenance of a new Strategic Rail Freight Interchange and associated infrastructure adjacent to Junction 15 of the M1 in Northamptonshire); and
- The West Midlands Rail Freight Interchange Order 2020 (granting development consent for the construction, operation and maintenance of a new Strategic Rail Freight Interchange and associated infrastructure close to Junction 12 of the M6 Motorway in South Staffordshire District).

Article 23

Hazardous Waste Facilities

Mark Westmoreland Smith, ftb
Michael Humphries QC, ftb

Introduction

Section 14 of the PA 2008 identifies those 'types' of project that are 'nationally significant infrastructure projects' ('NSIPs') for the purposes of the PA 2008 regime; subject to the thresholds set by PA 2008, ss 15–30. PA 2008, s 14(1)(q) states that a project consisting of 'the construction or alteration of a hazardous waste facility' is an NSIP; this is subject to the thresholds set out in PA 2008, s 30.

This article considers the scope and effect of these provisions.

Commencement

PA 2008, s 14(1)(p) came into effect on 26 November 2008 for the purposes of making orders (other than development consent orders), regulations or rules relating to its exercise; but, for all other purposes, that section and PA 2008, s 30 came into effect on 1 October 2011.

Thresholds and geographical issues

The effect of PA 2008, ss 14(1)(p) and 30 together is that:

- the 'construction' of a hazardous waste facility is a nationally significant infrastructure project where:
  - the facility (when constructed) will be in England;
  - the main purpose of the facility is expected to be the final disposal or recovery of hazardous waste; and
  - it is expected to have the capacity of, in the case of the disposal of hazardous waste by landfill or in a deep storage facility, more than 100,000 tonnes per year and, in any other case, more than 30,000 tonnes per year; and
- the 'alteration' of a hazardous waste facility is a nationally significant infrastructure project where:
  - the facility is in England;
  - the main purpose of the facility is expected to be the final disposal or recovery of hazardous waste; and
  - the alteration is expected to have the effect, in the case of the disposal of hazardous waste by landfill or in a deep storage facility, to increase by more than 100,000 tonnes per year the capacity of the facility and, in any other case, to increase the capacity of the facility by more than 30,000 tonnes per year (irrespective of whether the capacity of the original facility exceeded the thresholds).

PA 2008, s 14(1)(q) relates, therefore, to hazardous waste facilities in England only. In Scotland, Wales and Northern Ireland, planning consents for all hazardous waste projects are devolved to the Scottish Government, Welsh Government and Northern Ireland Executive respectively.

Development consent for development that is 'associated' with the construction or alteration of a hazardous waste facility within PA 2008, s 14(1)(q) (ie 'associated development' under PA 2008, s 115) is also restricted to England.

It is worth noting that the thresholds for both 'construction' and 'alteration' are set by reference to the 'capacity' or 'increased capacity' of the facility, and not its intended or likely throughput; this is important.

Where a proposed hazardous waste development in England does fall below the thresholds in PA 2008, s 30, the applicant may request the Secretary of State to issue a PA 2008, s 35 Direction to the effect that the project should be treated as an NSIP such that an application for development consent could be considered under the PA 2008 regime.

Definitions within PA 2008, s 30

PA 2008, s 30 contains a number of defined terms, some of which are defined in other legislation.

PA 2008, s 30(5) defines the terms:

- 'disposal',
- 'hazardous waste', and
- 'recovery',

by reference to the Hazardous Waste (England and Wales) Regulations 2005 and, in particular, reg 5 of those Regulations.

Regulation 5(2) defines 'disposal' to mean 'any operation which is not recovery even where the operation has as a secondary consequence the reclamation of substances or energy (Annex I of the Waste Directive sets out a non-exhaustive list of disposal operations)'.

Regulation 5(2) defines 'recovery' to mean 'any operation the principal result of which is waste serving a useful purpose by replacing other materials which would otherwise have been used to fulfil a particular function, or waste being prepared to fulfil that function, in the plant or in the wider economy (Annex II of the Waste Directive sets out a non-exhaustive list of recovery operations)'.

In both cases 'the Waste Directive' means Directive 2008/98/EC of the European Parliament and of the Council on waste.

Regulation 5(2) defines 'hazardous waste' by reference to reg 6, which states that:

> 'Subject to regulation 9, a waste is a hazardous waste if it is–
>
> (a) listed as a hazardous waste in the List of Wastes;
>
> (b) listed in regulations made under section 62A(1) of the 1990 Act; or
>
> (c) a specific batch of waste which is determined pursuant to regulation 8 to be a hazardous waste,
>
> and the term 'hazardous' and cognate expressions shall be construed accordingly.'

Regulation 9 identifies specific waste to be treated as non-hazardous and the term 'List of Wastes' is refined in reg 4.

Essentially, 'hazardous waste' is waste that contains one or more hazardous properties that may cause harm to human health or the environment. It does not include waste classified as radioactive waste under the Environmental Permitting (England and Wales) Regulations 2010 (except in the limited circumstances where such waste does not require a permit because it falls under an exemption provision), such that facilities for the disposal or recovery of radioactive waste do not fall to be considered as an NSIP under PA 2008, ss 14(1)(p) and 30.

Note, however, that the National Policy Statement for Hazardous Waste (June 2013) (see below and paragraph 2.2.1 of the NPS) states that proposals for hazardous waste facilities that handle a relatively small proportion of low-level radioactive waste ('LLW') alongside hazardous waste may fall within the scope of the NPS and PA 2008, ss 14(1)(p) and 30.

The term 'deep storage facility' in PA 2008, s 30 is defined by sub-s (6) to mean a facility for the storage of waste underground in a deep geological cavity.

NPS for Hazardous Waste

The National Policy Statement for Hazardous Waste was published in June 2013 and will be used by the Secretary of State as the 'primary basis' for decision on development consent applications for hazardous waste infrastructure falling within the 2008 Act regime in England (para 1.1.1).

The NPS sets out a summary of the Government's policy on Hazardous Waste, the main objectives of which are (section 2.1 summary):

- To protect human health and the environment – stringent legislative controls are in place to control the management of waste with hazardous properties.
- Implementation of the waste hierarchy – to produce less hazardous waste, using it as a resource where possible and only disposing of it as a last resort.
- Self-sufficiency and proximity – to ensure that sufficient disposal facilities are provided in the country as a whole to match expected arisings of all hazardous wastes, except those produced in very small quantities, and to enable hazardous waste to be disposed of in one of the nearest appropriate installations.
- Climate change – to minimise greenhouse gas emissions and maximise opportunities for climate change adaptation and resilience.

The NPS concludes that a small number of large facilities (ie with a capacity above the NSIP thresholds) are likely to be needed to meet the expected increase in arisings in hazardous waste (para 3.3.7 and see section 3.1 Summary of Need).

Having set out Government policy on hazardous waste (Part 2) and the need for large-scale hazardous waste infrastructure (Part 3), the NPS then sets out in detail:

- the Assessment Principles for hazardous waste infrastructure (Part 4), and
- the Generic Impacts to be considered by the Planning Inspectorate when examining an application for hazardous waste infrastructure (Part 5).

The Court of Appeal decision in *R (Scarisbrick) v Secretary of State for Communities and Local Government* [2017] EWCA Civ 787 contains a helpful discussion on the proper approach to 'need' in an NPS. The judgment makes clear that, in considering whether any relevant project is capable of meeting the identified need in the NPS, the Secretary of State had to start with an assumption that a national need for such projects had been established, but that is not the end of the exercise. The Court held that:

> '30. When determining an application for a development consent order, the Secretary of State must proceed as section 104 of the 2008 Act requires. The considerations bearing on his decision will include the policy need established in the NPS, any specific regional or local need for the development, any planning benefits, and the likely effects of the development on the environment. Where the development is proposed in the Green Belt, as in this case, the making of the decision must be approached as the relevant policy in the NPS requires.
>
> 31. Implicit in all this is that the weight to be given to particular considerations, including the need identified in the policy in section 3.1 of the [Hazardous Waste] NPS, will always be a matter for the exercise of the Secretary of State's planning judgment in the particular circumstances of the case. The need identified and established in the policy must be given appropriate weight in the making of a decision on an application for a development consent order, but it will not necessarily carry decisive or even significant weight when the planning balance is struck. The weight to be given to that need, case by case, is not prescribed, either in the policy in section 3.1 or elsewhere in the NPS. It will not necessarily increase with the scale or capacity of a particular proposal. The policy does not place a "trump card" or a "blank cheque" in the hands of a developer. Nor does it provide the Secretary of State with "carte blanche" to grant consent, without carrying out a proper balancing exercise in which the need identified and established in the policy is given the weight it is due in the decision on the project in hand, no more and no less. The need identified in section 3.1 will always be a material factor in a case where the policy applies. It will only be met, and can only be met, by individual developments of the relevant types. In this sense it is truly a need for an individual project of a relevant type, and will count in favour of any such project when the decision is made. But the policy does not mean that the bigger the project, the greater is the need for it – or, as [counsel for the appellant] put it (in paragraph 35 of his skeleton argument), "the sky seems to be the limit". That is not what the policy says, and not how it should be understood.'

A number of specific points emerge from this, as follows:

- 'policy need' is established by an NPS, but may be supplemented by any 'specific regional or local need' and by any 'planning benefits';
- the 'weight' to be given to any need established in an NPS is a matter for the exercise of the Secretary of State's planning judgement;
- the need established in the NPS should be given 'appropriate weight', but it will not necessarily carry decisive or even significant weight when the planning balance is struck;
- the weight to be attached to the policy need will not necessarily increase with the scale of the project; and
- where the policy need can only be met by projects of a relevant type, that need is truly a need for an individual project of the relevant type and that will count in favour of such a project.

The King's Cliffe application

To date there has been a single application under PA 2008, ss 14(1)(p) and 30 for the alteration of existing and the construction of new facilities for the recovery and disposal of hazardous waste and disposal of low-level radioactive waste at the East Northants Resource Management Facility, Stamford Road, Northamptonshire, known as 'King's Cliffe'.

During the examination itself and at the time the Examining Authority came to report (22 April 2013), only the draft NPS (July 2011) was available. As a result the Examining Authority's Report was based on the approach set down in PA 2008, s 105 ('Decisions in cases where no national policy statement has effect'). The NPS was, however, adopted on 6 June 2013, about five weeks before the Secretary of State's decision letter (11 July 2013). The Secretary of State, therefore, determined the application under PA 2008, s 104 ('decisions in cases where national policy statement has effect'). He did not, however, consider the changes between the draft and the final versions of the NPS significant enough to warrant further consultation.

A further interesting feature of this case was a jurisdictional point. As can be seen from the description of development above, that the application included the disposal of low-level (radioactive) waste ('LLW'). Given that the definition of hazardous waste does not include radioactive waste, the Examining Authority asked the applicant (Augean) to set out how LLW fell within PA 2008, ss 14(1)(p) and 30.

Paragraphs 2.2.4–2.2.7 of the Examining Authority's Report states as follows:

> 'LLW is not included in the definition of hazardous waste specified in section 30(5) of PA 2008 and I therefore asked Augean to provide a legal submission setting out why, and on what basis, it considered it appropriate to include the disposal of low-level waste in the draft DCO when this is not hazardous waste as defined in PA 2008. In its response Augean referred to section 115 of PA 2008.20 This states in subsection (1) that "development consent may be granted for development which is (a) development for which development consent is required: and (b) associated development." Augean considered that disposal of LLW in the hazardous landfill facility can fall within either of these categories. Section 31 states that "consent under this Act (development consent) is required for development to the extent that the development is or forms part of a nationally significant infrastructure project." In Augean's view use of the words "forms part of" demonstrates that the development does not itself have to constitute an NSIP but also that the development can form part of an NSIP. In addition section 30 which defines hazardous waste NSIPs states that "the main purpose of the facility is expected to be the final disposal or recovery of hazardous waste." Augean argued that the facility would continue to be an NSIP notwithstanding that activities subsidiary to the main purpose of disposal of hazardous waste are carried on. Such subsidiary activities could for example include the disposal of other appropriate waste types.
>
> Augean concluded on this point that "It is considered that Sections 30 and 31 of the Act allow for the disposal of LLW in the hazardous landfill facility NSIP provided that it is subsidiary/subordinate to the main purpose of the NSIP which requires development consent. It is therefore development for which development consent is required and it is correct to characterise it as integral."
>
> Augean considered whether the disposal of LLW might also be regarded as associated development and be included in the DCO on that basis. Drawing on revised guidance on associated development put out for consultation by DCLG in April 2012 Augean concluded that the Secretary of State would have sufficient flexibility to make his decision on a case by case basis and that "the disposal of LLW would fit well within the tenor of the proposed amended core principles."
>
> The draft DCO submitted by Augean with the application does not identify LLW as associated development and in this report I have considered it as an integral part of the development for which consent is sought not as associated development. Consideration

> is given later in this report to whether the inclusion of LLW as part of the waste to be disposed of at the site has any implications in terms of this proposed development remaining an NSIP.'

On this issue the Examining Authority concluded at paragraph 5.134 that:

> 'A hazardous waste facility is classified as an NSIP if, inter alia, "the main purpose of the facility is expected to be the final disposal or recovery of hazardous waste" (s30(1)(b) PA 2008). That leaves scope for some other activity to form part of the facility. In my view it is reasonable, as considered earlier at paragraphs 2.24 to 2.27, for disposal of LLW to be included as part of the proposed development for which development consent is being sought as long as that does not prevent the NSIP from being used for its "main purpose".'

The Secretary of State considered this issue and agreed with the Examining Authority's conclusion (para 24). A total limit on the amount of LLW was imposed, however, to ensure that the disposal of hazardous waste remains the main purpose of the NSIP.

Part 4

Requirement for Development Consent

Article 24

When Development Consent is Required

Mark Westmoreland Smith, ftb
Michael Humphries QC, ftb

Introduction

Although brief, Part 4 of the PA 2008 is pivotal to the entire regime, as it sets out when development consent is required. It is this Part of the PA 2008 that also ensures various other consents are not required for NSIPs, which was one of the principal objectives behind the new regime. As a result, there is much cross-referencing to other Acts in order to disapply the need for consents other than development consent for NSIPs. This makes the navigation of this Part somewhat difficult.

The requirement for development consent

PA 2008, s 31 is the key provision and provides as follows:

> 'Consent under this Act ('development consent') is required for development to the extent that the development is or forms part of a nationally significant infrastructure project.'

Two concepts require consideration, being:

- 'development', and
- 'is or forms part of a nationally significant infrastructure project'.

'Development'

PA 2008, s 32 defines the term 'development' for the purposes of the PA 2008. It provides that, subject to PA 2008, s 32(2) and (3), 'development' has the same meaning as in the Town and Country Planning Act 1990 ('TCPA 1990').

'Development' is defined by TCPA 1990, s 55 as being 'the carrying out of building, engineering, mining or other operations in, on, over or under land, or the making of any material change in the use of any buildings or other land', subject to further definitions and exclusions set out in that section.

The construction or alteration of nationally significant infrastructure projects will almost always involve some form of operational development (ie building, engineering, mining or other operations) and so clearly fall within the PA 2008, s 32 definition for the purposes of the PA 2008. Perhaps less clear, however, is that development comprising a 'material change of use' and for that reason the Act provides some clarification in PA 2008, s 32.

The effect of PA 2008, s 55(2) is that:

- the conversion of a generating station with a view to it using crude liquid petroleum, a petroleum product or natural gas as a fuel source (PA 2008, s 32(2)(a));
- starting to use a cavity or strata for the underground storage of gas (PA 2008, s 32(2)(b)); and
- an increase in the permitted use of an airport (PA 2008, s 32(2)(c)),

are all treated as a 'material change of use' and therefore fall within the meaning of 'development' for the purposes of the development consent regime. This clarification is helpful.

The conversion of generating stations

The effect of the provision relating to generating stations makes clear that the conversion of such a station with a view to its using certain fossil fuel types is a material change of use and, therefore, 'development' for the purposes of the PA 2008. Interestingly, the conversion of such a station to the use of non-fossil biofuels is not so brought within the definition of development; although such a conversion could still require consent under Electricity Act 1989, s 36 depending on the particular circumstances.

Until June 2013, the provision relating to the conversion of generating stations to the use of certain fossil fuels had to be understood in the context of Energy Act 1976, s 14 under which the Secretary of State was able to control the fuelling of new or converted power stations. However, Energy Act 1976, s 14 has been repealed by the Growth and Infrastructure Act 2013, s 18 (effective 25 June 2013). Section 14 of the 1976 Act implemented EU Directive 75/404/EEC on the restriction on the use of natural gas in power stations and Directive 75/405/EEC concerning the restriction on the use of petroleum products in power stations. Both Directives have since been repealed (EC/75/404 in 1991 and EC/75/405 in 1997) and the policy objectives behind Energy Act 1976, s 14 (arising in response to market conditions for gas and petroleum products in the 1970s) no longer exist.

Although the conversion of a generating station to the use of certain fossil fuels is a material change of use, and therefore 'development' for the purposes of the PA 2008, such development will only be an NSIP requiring development consent if the 'construction' or 'extension' of that generating station exceeds the thresholds in PA 2008, s 15.

Thus the conversion of a generating station to the use of fossil fuels that was *not* (i) the construction or extension of a generating station in England or Wales with a capacity of more than 50MW, or (ii) the construction or extension of an offshore generating station of more than 100MW, would not be an NSIP for the purposes of the PA 2008 and would not, therefore, require development consent.

The use of natural porous strata for underground gas storage

There are broadly two forms of underground gas storage development being (i) the creation of gas storage caverns in underground salt deposits by solution mining, and (ii) the use of natural porous strata (eg depleted gas production fields). The first of these clearly involves 'operational' development, whilst the second may simply amount to a change of use. What PA 2008, s 32(2)(b) makes clear, however, is that such a change of use is a 'material' change of use for the purposes of the PA 2008 regime.

Again, although such a use of porous natural strata may amount to a 'material change of use' and therefore comprise 'development' for the purposes of the PA 2008, it will only be an NSIP requiring development to the extent that such development 'is starting to use underground gas storage facilities' in England or Wales above the relevant 'working capacity' or 'maximum flow rate' threshold in PA 2008, s 17.

Increase in permitted use of an airport

Clearly operational development comprising the 'construction' or 'alteration' of an airport will be an NSIP, subject to the thresholds in PA 2008, s 23. The effect of PA 2008, s 32(2)(c), however, is to make an increase in the permitted use of an airport a 'material change of use'. Such a change of use could, potentially, involve no operational development, but still be an NSIP by virtue of PA 2008, s 23(1)(c) and (7).

PA 2008, s 23(1)(c) relates to 'an increase in the permitted use of an airport in a case within subsection (7)'; which sets an annual passenger or air transport movement threshold. The words in PA 2008, s 23(1)(c) reflect those in PA 2008, s 32(2)(c). The important words here are 'permitted use'. The term 'permitted' is defined in PA 2008, ss 32(4) and 23(9) as meaning permitted by planning permission or development consent. At present, no airport has been permitted by development consent and so, for all practical purposes, this means permitted by planning permission.

More important, however, is that, currently, very few UK airports have a level of 'use' – in terms of annual passenger numbers or air transport movements – that is controlled by the terms of any planning permission. Heathrow and Stansted airports do have planning conditions limiting the use of the airport, but most do not. Thus the application of the 'material change of use' in PA 2008, s 32(2)(c) may be of relatively limited scope.

The decision of Dove J in *R (Ross) v Secretary of State for Transport* [2020] EWHC 226 (Admin) makes clear that, in determining whether a proposed alteration to an airport would 'increase by at least 10 million per year the number of passengers for whom the airport is capable of providing air passenger transport services' such as to make it an NSIP under PA 2008, s 23(5), the Secretary of State had to assess what increase in capacity could realistically be achieved, not what might technically or arithmetically be possible. This is important clarification and resulted in an intended expansion of Stansted Airport not being an NSIP, but being considered under the TCPA 1990 regime instead.

PA 2008, s 32(3) further clarifies the meaning of 'development' for the purpose of the PA 2008 by making it clear that the following is development (to the extent that they would not be otherwise):

- works for the demolition of a listed building or its alteration or extension in a manner which would affect its character as a building of special architectural or historic interest;
- demolition of a building in a conservation area;
- works resulting in the demolition or destruction of or any damage to a scheduled monument;
- works for the purpose of removing or repairing a scheduled monument or any part of it;
- works for the purpose of making any alterations or additions to a scheduled monument; and
- flooding or tipping operations on land in, on or under which there is a scheduled monument.

In short, this provision ensures that the development consent regime is aligned with the Planning (Listed Buildings and Conservation Areas) Act 1990 and the Ancient Monuments and Archaeological Areas Act 1979. Where development consent is required for development, PA 2008, s 33(1)(f), (g), (i) and (j) then removes the requirements for consent under those other Acts and thereby removes the need for multiple consents for the same development.

'Is or forms part of a nationally significant infrastructure project'

Development consent is only required for development under PA 2008, s 31 to the extent that it is, or forms part of, a nationally significant infrastructure project. The determination of what is, or forms part of, an NSIP needs to be considered by reference to PA 2008, s 14 in combination with the thresholds in PA 2008, ss 15–30.

PA 2008, s 31 required development consent for two broad types of development, being:

- development that is an NSIP; and
- development that forms part of an NSIP.

Different issues arise in relation to each.

Development that is an NSIP

A consideration of PA 2008, ss 14 and 15–30 reveal three aspects that need to be considered, namely:

- an action;
- a type of project; and
- a relevant threshold.

The various types of project identified in PA 2008, ss 14 and 15–30 are usually preceded by what might be described as an 'action'; for example, the 'construction or extension' of a generating station, or the 'construction or alteration' of a waste water treatment plant. Even those types of development that do not have an associated 'action' in the various sub-categories within PA 2008, s 14(1), and there are four of them, still have such 'actions' in their corresponding threshold section (ie PA 2008, ss 15–30). So, for example, PA 2008, s 14(1)(h) is simply' highway-related development', but PA 2008, s 20 makes it clear that the NSIP must be the 'construction', 'improvement' or 'alteration' of a highway.

PINS has made it clear that it will expect an applicant to specify, to use the example above, whether PA 2008, s 20 development is the 'construction', 'improvement' or 'alteration' of a highway; that is, to specify what 'action' is engaged. It is worth noting that an 'action', so called, is not the same as the limb of operational development, in that, extending the example, the 'construction', 'improvement' or 'alteration' of a highway may all be classified as 'engineering operations'.

The various terms to describe what this article has referred to as an 'action' are often derived from the predecessor legislation and are, no doubt, maintained, as development below the relevant threshold would still be determined under that predecessor legislation. Thus PA 2008, ss 14(1)(b) and 16 refer to the 'installation' of an electric line above ground, echoing the language in Electricity Act 1989, s 37.

The next aspect to consider is the 'type of project' identified in PA 2008, ss 14 and 15–30. In some cases the threshold section does further define the type of development, but often it does not. So, for example, PA 2008, s 18(3) defines what is meant by an 'LNG facility', but PA 2008, s 24 does not define the term 'harbour facility'.

Even where a type of project is further defined, however, there still seems to be considerable scope as to what is properly described as being, for example, a 'hazardous waste facility': see the Examining Authority's Report (paras 2.24–2.27 and 5.134) and Secretary of State's decision (para 24) on the East Northants Resource Management Facility (aka 'King's Cliffe') DCO application.

This raises wider the issue as to whether development normally constructed together with a particular form of infrastructure (for example, a generating station) can properly be described as being 'part of' that type of development', as opposed to 'associated development' within PA 2008, s 115. This issue is particularly relevant in Wales where, subject to the exception in PA 2008, s 115(4), a development consent order cannot include 'associated development'. In this regard the Examining Authority's comments in its report into the Brechfa Forest West wind farm DCO application are interesting (see paras 4.139–4.146).

The final aspect to consider is the relevant threshold. For the most part, these are quantitative and set by reference to an aspect of the scale or capacity of the particular development. These thresholds are considered in more detail in other parts of this work.

Development that forms part of an NSIP

Clearly, many of the above considerations relate to development that forms 'part of' an NSIP, but additional points are also potentially relevant.

A development may form 'part of' an NSIP because it is a phase of a larger project. Thus, for example, an early phase of an offshore generating station, that was itself below the threshold in PA 2008, s 15(3), would nevertheless require development consent under PA 2008, s 31 if it was 'part of' a larger offshore generating station that was above that threshold. The words 'part of' in this context are clearly intended to prevent the 'salami slicing' of projects to bring them under a relevant threshold.

Issues do then arise as to whether a development below the relevant threshold would be within the PA 2008 regime if it was an early phase of a much larger project that was not expected to be promoted for some years. In other words, when does a phase of a project become a separate project? At the moment, no clear guidance exists and the issue will have to be approached on its own facts, if and when it arises.

Article 25

Secretary of State's Direction that a Project is of National Significance

Michael Humphries QC, ftb
Mark Westmoreland Smith, ftb

Introduction

Under PA 2008, s 35 a project which falls outside of the relevant thresholds for NSIPs may, nonetheless, be treated as an NSIP on the direction of the Secretary of State. This procedure was little used until it was significantly amended by the Localism Act 2011 and again by the Growth and Infrastructure Act 2013. It now represents a useful mechanism by which certain projects that fall below the thresholds for national significance in PA 2008, ss 15–30A may, nevertheless, be brought within the development consent regime.

Section 35 directions

Section 35 starts by making it clear that the Secretary of State may give a direction for development to be 'treated' as development 'for which development consent is required'. This is a clear reference to PA 2008, s 31 which provides that 'Consent under this Act ("development consent") is required for development to the extent that the development is or forms part of a nationally significant infrastructure project'. This again brings in s 14 (nationally significant infrastructure projects) and the various thresholds in ss 15–30A. Thus, where the Secretary of State has made a s 35 direction in relation to development, it is to be 'treated' as an NSIP.

Section 35(2) provides, however, that the Secretary of State may only give a direction if:

'(a) the development is or forms part of–

(i) a project (or proposed project) in the field of energy, transport, water, waste water or waste, or

(ii) a business or commercial project (or proposed project) of a prescribed description,

(b) the development will (when completed) be wholly in one or more of the areas specified in subsection (3), and

(c) the Secretary of State thinks the project (or proposed project) is of national significance, either by itself or when considered with–

(i) in a case within paragraph (a)(i), one or more other projects (or proposed projects) in the same field;

(ii) in a case within paragraph (a)(ii), one or more other business or commercial projects (or proposed projects) of a description prescribed under paragraph (a)(ii).'

The first thing to note is that the 'fields' of infrastructure project in respect of which a s 35 direction may be made extend to the full range of such fields identified in s 14(6). Thus any 'type' of infrastructure project that could be an NSIP may (if it is below a ss 15–30A threshold) become the subject matter of a s 35 direction.

The second thing to note, however, is that s 35 allows certain 'prescribed' business or commercial projects to be brought within the PA 2008 regime. Certain types of business and commercial project have been prescribed by the Infrastructure Planning (Business and Commercial Projects) Regulations 2013. Article 26 of this work looks more closely at such projects.

The 'areas' specified in subsection (3) are (a) England or waters adjacent to England up to the seaward limits of the territorial sea; and (b) in the case of a project for the carrying out of works in the field of energy, a Renewable Energy Zone, except any part of a Renewable Energy Zone in relation to which the Scottish Ministers have functions.

Where all or part of a development is or will be in Greater London and is a prescribed business or commercial development, the Secretary of State may only give a direction with the consent of the Mayor of London (PA 2008, s 35(4)).

The Growth and Infrastructure Act 2013 substituted a new s 35ZA (Directions under section 35: procedural matters) and s 35A (Timetable for deciding requests for directions under section 35).

Procedure

PA 2008, s 35ZA sets out a number of procedural matters relating to s 35 directions.

Limitations

First, PA 2008, s 35ZA(1) limits the power to give a direction in relation to projects in the field of energy, transport, water, waste water or waste to circumstances where there has been no prior application for planning permission or, indeed, any other consent mentioned in PA 2008, s 33.

Secondly, with regards to commercial and business projects, PA 2008, s 35ZA(2) makes it clear that a s 35 direction in respect of such development may only be made in response to a 'qualifying request' made by:

- a person who proposes to carry out the development to which the request relates;
- a person who has applied, or proposes to apply, for planning permission, or various other consents in PA 2008, s 33(1) or (2); or
- a person who, if a PA 2008, s 35 direction is made, proposed to apply for development consent in respect of the proposed development.

It is clear, therefore, that for business and commercial projects, a 'qualifying request' may be made not only by someone who has already applied for planning permission for development (by contrast to projects in the fields of energy, transport, water, waste water or waste), but also by someone proposing to apply for such permission.

In practice, the need to draft a development consent order, and provide certain other documents that would normally accompany an application for development consent, will mean that there will be considerable time and procedural advantages in making a 'qualifying request' before making a planning application and, if a PA 2008, s 35 direction is made, proceeding under the PA 2008 regime from the outset. Any other approach is likely to waste considerable time and resource.

Determining a 'qualifying request'

In considering whether to make a PA 2008, s 35 direction, the Secretary of State can:

- direct an authority to whom an application for planning permission (or other PA 2008, s 33 consent) for the relevant project has been or is proposed to be made – that is, 'a relevant authority' as defined by PA 2008, s 35ZA(11) – to take no further action in relation to the application, or proposed application, until the Secretary of State has decided whether to give the direction (PA 2008, s 35ZA(7)); and
- require a relevant authority to provide any information required for the purpose of enabling the Secretary of State to decide whether to and in what terms give a direction under PA 2008, s 35 (PA 2008, s35ZA(8)).

Making a PA 2008, s 35 direction

The Secretary of State must give reasons for a decision to grant a direction (PA 2008, s 35ZA(10)). Interestingly, there is no statutory requirement for providing reasons in relation to a refusal of a 'qualifying request'. However, it is suggested that the Secretary of State would be well advised to provide reasoning in relation to all determinations of 'qualifying requests', whatever the outcome. Examples of 'reasons' that the Secretary of State has giving for making directions are set out towards the end of this article.

If a PA 2008, s 35 direction is made, then the Secretary of State may:

- if an application for planning permission (or other PA 2008, s 33 consent) has been made, direct that that application is be treated as an application for development consent; and
- if a person proposes to make an application for planning permission (or other PA 2008, s 33 consent or authorisation), direct that the proposed application be treated as a proposed application for development consent (PA 2008, s 35ZA(3)).

A relevant authority must refer the application, or proposed application, to the Secretary of State instead of dealing with it themselves once a direction has been made (PA 2008, s 35ZA(6)).

Ability to modify the PA 2008 and other Acts

Whilst PA 2008, s 35ZA(5) provides that a PA 2008, s 35 direction may provide that specified provisions of the PA 2008, or any other Act, shall have effect in relation to an application with any specified modifications or be treated as having been complied with, the Secretary of State is likely to use this power sparingly for fear of creating some procedural unfairness and, therefore, potential target for challenge. Developers considering making a 'qualifying request' would be well advised, therefore, to anticipate having to comply with the pre-application and application requirements of the PA 2008 regime.

Timetable for deciding a section 35 request

Where the Secretary of State receives a 'qualifying request' for a s 35 direction, the decision on that request must be made before the end of 'the primary deadline' (PA 2008, 35A(2)), that is, the end of the period beginning with the day on which the Secretary of State receives the qualifying request.

The primary deadline does not apply, however, where the Secretary of State has asked the person who made the request to provide information for the purposes of enabling the Secretary of State to decide (a) whether to give the direction requested, and (b) the terms in which it should be given. Where the person who has made the request provides the information asked for within 14 days on being so asked, the Secretary of State must decide the request within 28 days beginning on the day when the information asked for is received (PA 2008, s 35A(4)).

The effect of a section 35 direction

A further point of some importance is whether an application for development consent for a project below the PA 2008 thresholds, but where a direction has been made under PA 2008, s 35, can be determined under PA 2008, s 104, or whether it should be determined under s 105.

This point was in direct issue in the application for the Silvertown Tunnel DCO that fell below the threshold in PA 2008, s 22 for a highways-related NSIP, but was made the subject of a PA 2008, s 35 direction. The Secretary of State's decision letter (3 August 2017) said (paras 8–10) as follows:

> '8. On 26 June 2012, the Secretary of State for Transport made a direction under section 35 of the 2008 Act that he was satisfied that the Silvertown Tunnel development is "nationally significant". Although currently falling outside the definition of a "nationally significant infrastructure project", as provided for in section 14 of the 2008 Act, he directed that the development, together with any matters associated with it, be treated as development for which development consent is required. …
>
> 9. Given that the application only falls to be considered under the 2008 Act by virtue of this Direction, the Panel gave careful consideration to the issue of whether it should be considered under section 104 or section 105 of the 2008 Act. Consideration is given under section 104 when a National Policy Statement ("NPS") has effect in relation to the development to which the application relates. In this instance the Secretary of State must have regard to the relevant NPS, any appropriate marine policy documents produced in accordance with section 59 of the Marine and Coastal Access Act 2009, any Local Impact Reports ("LIR") submitted and to any other matters that the Secretary of State considers to be both important and relevant … If section 104 does not apply then the Secretary of State must consider an application under section 105, where the Secretary of State must have regard to any LIRs submitted and to any matters prescribed in relation to development of the description to which the application relates and any other matters that the Secretary of State considers to be both important and relevant … The Secretary of State notes arguments from the Applicant in favour of considering the application under a section 104 and comments from interested parties on this issue … The Secretary of State notes the Panel's reasoning and conclusions that the application falls to be considered under section 104 recognising that the same matters will need to be addressed whether the application is considered under section 104 or section 105 … The Secretary of State agrees with this approach.
>
> 10. Therefore, as required by s104(3) of the 2008 Act, the Secretary of State has considered this application in accordance with the designated National Policy Statement for National Networks ("NPSNN"), (subject to certain exceptions which are not relevant in this case). …'

This clearly indicates that being an application for a project brought into the PA 2008 regime by virtue of a PA 2008, s 35 direction does not preclude that application from being determined pursuant to PA 2008, s 104.

This position appeared to be reasonably well settled until the Secretary of State adopted the opposite position in *EFW Group Ltd v Secretary of State for Business, Energy and Industrial Strategy* [2021] EWHC 2697 and the Court held at [60] that:

> 'The question arises as to whether or not the section 35 direction which was made in relation to [the project] has the effect of bringing it within the scope of the decision-making framework pursuant to section 104. In my view it does not. I am unable to accept the submission that the terms of section 35(1) have the effect of turning a project or development which does not fall within the definition of NSIPs provided within sections 14 and 15 of the 2008 Act into a project which has such a designation. The words "be treated as development for which development consent is required" simply have the effect of making the proposed development subject to the decision-making framework contained within the provisions of the 2008 Act. They do not change the understanding of the proposal as not being within the definition of an NSIP, any more than they change the physical nature of what is comprised within the development. More particularly, they cannot have the effect of altering the scope of an NPS which has been drafted specifically to apply only to those projects that are within the definition of an NSIP.'

The Claimant in that case was refused permission to appeal to the Court of Appeal and the correct position is, therefore, as set out in the *EFW Group* decision; in other words, that a section 35 direction does not bring an application within the ambit of section 104.

Examples of directions to date

In addition to the Silvertown Tunnel, the following give examples of the reasons for making section 35 directions:

- Norwich Northern Distributor Road, Norfolk County Council, Transport, 9 August 2013:
  - Reasons: It would provide a direct connection to and from an international airport to the Trans-European Network-Transport and the Strategic Road Network, it would aid national growth by supporting over 135ha of proposed employment growth and improved connections to/ from the Great Yarmouth Enterprise Zone which supports the offshore energy industry.
- Triton Knoll Offshore Windfarm, RWE Npower Renewables Limited, Energy (grid connection infrastructure), 14 November 2014:
  - Reasons: Need to deliver the electricity from the windfarm into the national grid, benefits of being determined by the same decision maker as the wind farm and benefits of having the entire connection being examined under the same consent regime and removing the need for Marine Management Organisation and local planning authority consents.
- The London Resort, London Resort Companies Holdings, Business and commercial, 9 May 2014:
  - Reasons: Significant economic impact, important in driving growth in the economy, an impact wider than a single local authority area and physical size also relevant.
- International Advanced Manufacturing Park, Sunderland City Council and South Tyneside Council, Business and commercial, 15 September 2015:
  - Reasons: Significant economic impact, important in driving growth in the economy, an impact wider than a single local authority area and physical size also relevant.

- Lake Lothing Third Crossing, Lowestoft, Transport, 22 March 2016:
  - Reasons: forms part of a TEN-T network, would act as a tactical diversion when the A12/A47 bascule bridge is closed, supports growth and connectivity.
- Wheelabrator Kemsley North generating station, Wheelabrator Technologies Inc, Energy, 27 June 2018:
  - Reasons: WKN sits on the same site as two other projects of national significance which are or will be the subject of applications for development consent, namely Wheelabrator's K4 replacement Combined Heat and Power ('CHP') plant (accepted for examination by the Planning Inspectorate on 26 April 2018) and the proposed upgrade to Wheelabrator's K3 Energy from Waste ('EfW') plant to be submitted to the Planning Inspectorate early in 2019. K3 will be applied for at the same time as an application for consent will be sought for WKN. Cumulatively, these developments located on the same site will comprise a significant facility of national sustainable energy supply, with up to 174 MW combined capacity when all plants are operational. In addition, the project will benefit from K3 and WKN being assessed comprehensively at the same time, through the same streamlined process and in a consistent manner by the same decision maker, avoiding duplication of work and reducing the burden on the local planning authority. It will also simplify the consideration of any likely significant environmental effects for both projects.
- AQUIND Interconnector, AQUIND Limited, Energy, 30 July 2018:
  - Reasons: The two giga-watt capacity of the proposed development is similar in terms of electrical capacity to a generating station that would qualify to be considered under the PA 2008 process as nationally significant. By progressing the proposed development through the PA 2008 development consent process, it would provide the certainty of a single, unified consenting process and fixed timescales. It will reduce the need to apply for separate consents from the Marine Management Organisation and local planning authorities.
- East West Rail between Bedford and Cambridge, East West Rail Company, Transport, 29 August 2019:
  - Reasons: The new railway works between Bedford and Cambridge is of national significance because the scheme by itself, and as part of the East West rail link, will:
    - provide a vital step in the development of a strategic transport corridor that will unlock major development opportunities and enable transformational growth around existing towns and cities;
    - improve east-west rail connections and have the potential to increase the labour market catchment areas for key towns and cities, opening up new opportunities for collaboration and job growth; and
    - create a direct link between East Anglia and central and southern England, delivering benefits for passengers and businesses both regionally and nationally.
- Nautilus Interconnector, National Grid Ventures, Energy, 29 April 2019:
  - Reasons: The proposed development forms part of the proposed project, known as the Nautilus Interconnector. The proposed project is of national significance, having taken into account in particular that it has a proposed capacity of 1,400 MW. That capacity is equivalent to the capacity of a generating station that would qualify to

be considered under the PA 2008 process as nationally significant. By progressing the proposed development through the PA 2008 development consent process, it would provide the certainty of a single, unified consenting process and fixed timescales.

- Net Zero Teesside Project, Oil and Gas Climate Initiative etc Holdings, Energy, 17 January 2020:
  - Reasons: The specified elements of the proposed project, when taken together with the other elements of the proposed project as defined in the letter of 25 November 2019, are of national significance; and by progressing the proposed project through the PA 2008 development consent process, it would provide the certainty of a single, unified consenting process for the whole project within fixed timescales.

Article 26

Business and Commercial Development

Michael Humphries QC, ftb

Introduction

Whilst the Planning Act 2008 (PA 2008) was originally conceived as a means of improving the process for delivering major infrastructure projects, its success has attracted the attention of those seeking to provide the same benefits for other forms of development and, in particular, major business and commercial development.

The PA 2008 regime has a number of features that may be attractive to major business and commercial developers, including:

- a (largely) single consenting regime;
- a single application across local authority area boundaries;
- determination by the Secretary of State;
- fixed timetables; and
- the ability for private developers to promote the compulsory purchase of land.

Whilst some of these benefits may be available to developers with the support of a host local planning authority, such support is not always forthcoming. In consequence, during 2012 the Government decided to extend the PA 2008 regime to include business and commercial projects.

The timetable for the amendments

On 6 December 2012 the Government announced, by written Ministerial statement, a series of reforms to the PA 2008, including a commitment to extend the development consent regime to business and commercial projects.

On 22 November 2012 a consultation paper was published seeking views on the form of any extension of the PA 2008 to business and commercial development.

On 23 April 2013 the Growth and Infrastructure Act 2013 was enacted giving effect to the Government's proposals as refined following consultation. Section 26 of the 2013 Act made amendments to the PA 2008 by substituting PA 2008, s 35 with a replacement s 35 and inserting a new PA 2008, s 35ZA.

The Infrastructure Planning (Business or Commercial Projects) Regulations 2013 (SI 2013/3221) ('the BCP Regulations') were made on 17 December 2013 and came into force the following day. It was the coming into force of the BCP Regulations that effectively 'switched on' the PA 2008 regime for business and commercial development.

On 29 October 2013, DCLG deposited in the libraries of House of Commons and the House of Lords a 'Policy Statement' entitled 'Extension of the nationally significant infrastructure planning regime to business and commercial projects'. This is, currently, the only DCLG guidance on the operation of the new business and commercial regime.

The new PA 2008, ss 35, 35ZA

PA 2008, s 35 gives the Secretary of State power to give a direction for development to be treated as development for which development consent is required, inter alia, if the development is or forms part of 'a business or commercial project (or proposed project) of a prescribed description', will be in England or English waters, and the Secretary of State thinks that the project is of 'national significance' either by itself or when considered with one or more other business or commercial projects (or proposed projects) (see PA 2008, s 35(2)).

PA 2008, s 35ZA sets out various procedural matters in relation to directions given by PA 2008, s 35. Most importantly, for business and commercial projects, PA 2008, s 35ZA(2) make it clear that a PA 2008, s 35 direction in respect of such development may only be made in response to a 'qualifying request' made by:

- a person who proposes to carry out the development to which the request relates;
- a person who has applied, or proposes to apply, for planning permission (or various other consents in PA 2008, s 33(1) or (2)); or
- a person who, is a PA 2008, s 35 direction is made, proposed to apply for development consent in respect of the proposed development.

This is important as it is clear that a 'qualifying request' may be made not only by someone who has already applied for planning permission for development, but also by someone proposing to apply for such permission. In practice, the need to draft a development consent order, and provide certain other documents that would normally accompany an application for development consent, will mean that there will be considerable time and procedural advantages in making a 'qualifying request' before making a planning application and, if a PA 2008, s 35 direction is made, proceeding under the PA 2008 regime from the outset.

If a PA 2008, s 35 direction is made, then PA 2008, s 35ZA(3) makes it clear that the Secretary of State may:

- if an application for planning permission (or other PA 2008, s 33(1), (2) consent) has been made, direct that that application be treated as an application for development consent;
- if a person proposes to make an application for planning permission (or other PA 2008, s 33(1), (2) consent), direct that the proposed application be treated as a proposed application for development consent.

Geographical scope of the provisions

As stated above, the new business and commercial provisions in section 35 only apply to development in England and English waters; not to development in Wales. This reflects the devolution settlement in Wales.

It is also worth noting that, if all or part of the business or commercial development is in London, the Secretary of State will only make a section 35 direction with the consent of the Mayor of

London (see PA 2008, s 35(4)). It is also clear that that consent should be obtained before making any 'qualifying request' to the Secretary of State (see the DCLG 'Policy Statement').

Types of business and commercial development

As stated above, PA 2008, s 35(2) provides that a 'qualifying request' may only be made in respect of 'a business or commercial project (or proposed project) of a prescribed description' (PA 2008, s 35(2)(a)(ii)). It is the BCP Regulations that 'prescribe' the descriptions of development in respect of which a direction may be made.

Regulation 2 provides that the descriptions of business and commercial project (or proposed project) in reg 2(2) are 'prescribed' for the purposes of PA 2008, s 35(2)(a)(ii).

Regulation 2(2)(a) states that a project must be of a description that 'consists wholly or mainly' of development within reg 2(2)(a)(i) or (ii). Thus it is clear that development forming part of a project falling within the prescribed description can be authorised, if it meets the other requirements in PA 2008, ss 35 and 35ZA.

Regulation 2(2)(a)(i) identifies development comprising the 'construction of buildings or facilities' for the purposes of one or more of the matters in the Schedule to the BCP Regulations. The Schedule identifies the following matters:

- Office use.
- Research and development of products and processes.
- An industrial process or processes [see the definition of 'industrial process' in reg 1(2)].
- Storage or distribution of goods.
- Conferences.
- Exhibitions.
- Sport.
- Leisure.
- Tourism.

Regulation 2(2)(a)(ii) identifies a further form of development, being the winning and working of minerals in, on or under land. The term 'minerals' for these purposes is defined in BCP Regulations, reg 1(2), but there is a specific exception for the winning or working of 'peat, coal, oil or gas' (see BCP Regulations, reg 2(2)(b)(i)). So, for example, 'fracking' would not currently fall within BCP Regulations, reg 2(2)(a)(ii) and would not, therefore, be development of a prescribed description for the purposes of a PA 2008, s 35 direction.

Establishing national significance

The DCLG consultation on business and commercial development included numerical 'thresholds' for the scale of such development if it was to a regarded as nationally significant. Such thresholds reflected the approach adopted for nationally significant infrastructure projects within PA 2008, ss 15–31.

In the event, the BCP Regulations do not have numerical thresholds to indicate national significance, but leave this as a matter of judgement for the Secretary of State on a case-by-case basis.

The DCLG 'Policy Statement', however, does set out the Secretary of State's intended approach to the issue of national significance, as follows:

> 'In considering whether a project is of national significance, the Secretary of State will consider all relevant matters, including:
>
> - whether a project is likely to have a significant economic impact, or is important for driving growth in the economy;
> - whether a project has an impact across an area wider than a single local authority area;
> - whether a project is of a substantial physical size – further details are set out below; or
> - whether a project is important to the delivery of a nationally significant infrastructure project or other significant development.
>
> The Secretary of State will reach a decision on any request on the basis of the information provided by developer. The Secretary of State will also consider any matter which the Secretary of State considers relevant to whether a direction should be made. This will include:
>
> - whether a project is likely to require multiple consents or authorisations, and which, in consequence, would benefit from the single authorisation process offered by the nationally significant infrastructure regime;
> - whether the project is related to a nationally significant infrastructure project being brought forward at the same time and therefore would benefit from the scheme being considered as a single application through the PA 2008 regime.
>
> Each request will be considered on its own merits, but the Secretary of State would expect those developers who are thinking of asking for a direction to bear in mind the following.
>
> Although size in itself will not be the determining factor in whether a project is nationally significant or not, the Secretary of State would not normally expect to receive requests for directions in relation to projects that are not of a substantial size. For example, the Secretary of State would not normally expect to receive requests for construction projects where the gross internal floorspace to be created by the project is less than 40,000m2; for leisure, tourism and sports facilities where the area to be developed is less than 100 hectares; or for sports stadia where the seating capacity is less than 40,000 seats.
>
> For minerals projects, the Secretary of State would not normally expect to receive requests for projects unless they involve the extraction of a strategically important industrial mineral, or extraction of a mineral on a significant scale, for example where the surface or underground area was over 150 hectares.'

As stated above, this is currently the only guidance on the operation of the regime in relation to business and commercial projects.

Exclusions from the new provisions

As identified above, the winning or working of 'peat, coal, oil or gas' is expressly excluded from the descriptions of business or commercial projects prescribed for the purposes of PA 2008, s 35(2)(a)(ii) (see BCP Regulations, reg 2(2)(b)(i)).

A rather more significant exclusion, however, for many business or commercial projects is the exclusion of 'the construction of one or more dwellings' (see BCP Regulations, reg 2(2)(b)(ii)). This follows the provisions of PA 2008, 35(5) which makes it clear that regulations made under PA 2008, s 35(2)(a)(ii) may not prescribe a description of project which includes the construction of one or more dwellings. It also reflects the approach taken in the PA 2008 generally towards 'associated development', which may not include the construction of one or more dwellings (see PA 2008, s 115(2)(b)).

Thus a mixed-use business, commercial and residential development could not be the subject-matter of a PA 2008, s 35 direction and brought under the PA 2008 regime. In such circumstances, any direction could only be made in respect of the business and commercial element.

National Policy Statements

It seems reasonably clear that the Department for Levelling Up, Housing and Communities (DLUHC) does not intend, certainly for the foreseeable future, to publish a National Policy Statement (NPS) for business and commercial development. In reality, such development is likely to be far too varied in character to be easily susceptible to a single NPS establishing need and identifying potential impacts.

A consequence of this, however, is that business and commercial projects promoted through the PA 2008 regime will not benefits from the presumption in PA 2008, s 104(3), but will have to be considered under PA 2008, s 105.

In deciding an application where there is no NPS, PA 2008, s 105(2) requires the Secretary of State to have regard to:

> '(a) any local impact report (within the meaning given by section 60(3)) submitted to the [Secretary of State] before the deadline specified in a notice under section 60(2),
>
> (b) any matters prescribed in relation to development of the description to which the application relates [none have been prescribed], and
>
> (c) any other matters which the Secretary of State thinks are both important and relevant to the Secretary of State's decision.'

Opting-in to the PA 2008 regime

It is important to recognise that the effect of the substituted PA 2008, s 35 and new PA 2008, s 35ZA is not to require the prescribed forms of business and commercial development to be dealt with under the PA 2008 regime, but simply to give the promoters of such development the opportunity to make a 'qualifying request' to be brought within the regime by a PA 2008, s 35 direction.

Before making such a 'qualifying request', promoters will have to consider a number of tactical issues, including:

- the effects on their prospect of success;
- whether they would have needed to apply to more than one local planning authority;
- the likely timescales for achieving development consent;
- the potential effect on relations with the local planning authority and other stakeholders;

- the need for land assembly; and
- the need for other consents.

Making a 'qualifying request' – procedure

A 'qualifying request' must both specify the development to which it relates and explain why the requirements of PA 2008, s 35(2) are met (see PA 2008, s 35ZA(11)).

The decision-maker for business and commercial development applications is the Secretary of State for Communities and Local Government and it is, therefore, to that Secretary of State that any 'qualifying request' should be made.

To enable the Secretary of State to make a decision within the statutory deadline of 28 days (PA 2008, s 35A), developers should provide the following with each request:

- details about the nature of the project including its size;
- the relevant local planning authority or authorities; confirmation that the project falls within the prescribed description; and
- reasons why the Secretary of State should consider the project of national significance.

Applicants should also have regard to the BCP Regulations and ensure that their project meets the requirements set out within them.

Preparing an application for development consent following a PA 2008, s 35 direction

Whilst PA 2008, s 35ZA(5) provides that a PA 2008, s 35 direction may provide that specified provisions of the PA 2008, or any other Act, shall have effect in relation to an application with any specified modifications or, indeed, be treated as having been complied with, the Secretary of State is likely to use this power sparingly for fear of creating some procedural unfairness and, therefore, potential target for challenge.

Developers considering making a 'qualifying request' would be well advised, therefore, to anticipate having to comply with the pre-application and application requirements of the PA 2008 regime. These are covered in articles 29 to 33 of this work.

PA 2008, s 35 directions for business and commercial development

Business and commercial schemes have now started to come forward under the PA 2008 regime and, on 9 May 2014, the Secretary of State for Communities and Local Government made the first PA 2008, s 35 direction for business and commercial development in respect of the London Paramount project in Kent. Since then, on 15 September 2015, a further PA 2008, s 35 direction for business and commercial has been made in respect of the International Advanced Manufacturing Plant project in Sunderland.

Article 27

Related Housing Development

Hereward Phillpot QC, ftb
Michael Humphries QC, ftb

Introduction

As part of a wider attempt to increase the supply of new housing, the Government has introduced amendments to the Planning Act 2008 ('PA 2008') so as to allow development consent to be granted for housing development that is related to a Nationally Significant Infrastructure Project ('NSIP').

The amendments were introduced by Housing and Planning Act 2016 ('HPA 2016'), s 160, which came into force on 6 April 2017 (Housing and Planning Act 2016 (Commencement No 5, Transitional Provisions and Savings) Regulations 2017), and are explained further in guidance published by the (then) DCLG in March 2017 entitled 'Guidance on Nationally Significant Infrastructure Projects and Housing, March 2017' ('the DCLG Guidance on NSIPs and housing').

The law

HPA 2016, s 160 amends PA 2008, s 115 to add 'related housing development' to the categories of development for which development consent can be granted under the PA 2008. It should be noted that related housing development is an entirely new category, and not a sub-category of 'associated development'.

'Related housing development' is defined in section 115(4B) as follows:

> '"Related housing development" means development which–
>
> (a) consists of, or includes the construction of one or more dwellings;
>
> (b) is on the same site as, or is next to or close to, any part of the development within subsection (1)(a) [that is, the NSIP itself], or is otherwise associated with that development (or any part of it);
>
> (c) is to be carried out wholly in England; and
>
> (d) meets the condition in subsection (4C).'

Note, in relation to 'includes' in (a) above, that paragraph 13 of the DCLG Guidance on NSIPs and housing helpfully clarifies that housing development would include the sort of local infrastructure normally associated with housing. This would include, for example, estate roads, drainage etc. There must, however, come a point at which the limits of this concept are reached. An application that included, say, a local convenience shop to serve the housing would raise the issue of whether what was proposed was now a (housing-led) mixed-use development, as opposed to housing *per se*.

Subsection (4C) confines the scope of the new provision to cases where the NSIP is in England and/or in waters adjacent to England up to the seaward limits of the territorial sea.

It should be noted that the term 'dwellings' is not defined in the statute. However, these amendments to the PA 2008 have been introduced after the High Court has considered and defined the meaning of this term within the statute in the case of *R (Innovia Cellophane Ltd) v Infrastructure Planning Commission* [2011] EWHC 2883 (Admin). It seems reasonable to assume that, had Parliament thought it necessary to apply a different meaning to that which the court had given the term in the context of the PA 2008, it would have taken the opportunity to do so.

In the *Innovia* case, Cranston J interpreted 'dwelling' consistently with the interpretation given to the word 'dwelling-house' in the context of the Town and Country Planning Acts ('TCPA'). Hence, dwellings were buildings that ordinarily afford the facilities required for day-to-day private domestic existence – a characteristic lacking in (*inter alia*) hostels and similar places where people may eat, sleep and perhaps spend 24 hours a day.

Cranston J distinguished dwellings from hostels 'and other forms of non-permanent accommodation which is not self-contained'. The concept of the accommodation being private or self-contained (ie the essential facilities are not shared) seems to be central. It was the key feature that was identified in the earlier TCPA authorities relied upon and said to provide the correct interpretation (paragraph 28).

There remains some uncertainty as to the significance of the reference by Cranston J to 'non-permanent' accommodation. On the one hand, it could refer to the limited life of the buildings to be constructed. In paragraph 30 of the judgment, it seems to be used in that context, differentiating between 'permanent accommodation', which has 'long term impacts for housing land supply', and 'campus type accommodation' 'with its limited life'. However, in the context of what is said in paragraph 28 of the judgement on 'the correct interpretation of the term "dwelling" in section 115' (paragraph 29), it could relate to the permanence or otherwise of the individual occupation, as opposed to the permanence of the building. So, for example, a hotel or a residential school (which were examples given in the earlier case of *Gravesham BC v Secretary of State for the Environment* (1982) 47 P&CR 142 at paragraph 27 of the judgment) is likely to be a permanent building, but not somewhere that people would be expected to live on a permanent basis. (See also *Moore v Secretary of State for the Environment* (1982) 47 P&CR 142; *Panayi v Secretary of State for the Environment* (1985) 50 P&CR 109 and *Commercial and Residential Property Development Co Ltd v Secretary of State for the Environment* [1982] JPL 513, which also point towards the key factor being duration of stay rather than the life of the building.) Whatever was meant by 'non-permanent', however, it seems likely that, unless the accommodation is self-contained, it would not be a dwelling.

No limit has been placed on the categories of NSIP that may include an element of housing. The decision as to when the inclusion of an element of housing is appropriate has, to that extent, been left to developers.

The ability to include an element of housing also extends to any projects that have been directed to come within the PA 2008 regime under PA 2008, s 35. It has been made clear by the Government in the Guidance that any housing element within such a project will not form part of the assessment of national significance, and will not be a factor in deciding whether a direction should be issued.

The DCLG Guidance on NSIPs and housing

PA 2008, s 115(7) requires the Secretary of State to take into account 'any matters set out in guidance published by the Secretary of State' when deciding an application for development consent that includes related housing development.

The DCLG Guidance on NSIPs and housing covers the following matters:

- the types and location of infrastructure project where housing may be included in an application for development consent;
- the circumstances where housing might be consented;
- the maximum amount of housing that may be consented;
- the location of housing that may be consented; and
- some of the factors that may be taken into account in deciding applications for development consent that include an element of housing.

It is clear that any developer contemplating including related housing development within an application will need to pay close attention to the DCLG Guidance on NSIPs and housing. However, it should be remembered that the guidance does not and, indeed, could not alter the scope and effect of the statutory provisions, and it will be important to ensure that what is proposed falls within the scope of PA 2008, s 115, properly interpreted.

When reading the DCLG Guidance on NSIPs and housing, it is essential to take note of what is said in footnote 3 to paragraph 13. This makes clear that, for the remainder of the document, unless otherwise specified, the term 'housing' means 'related housing development' as defined by the amended PA 2008, s 115. It becomes particularly important to have this in mind in order to minimise the scope for potential confusion when the terms 'housing', 'accommodation' and 'dwellings' are used later in the document. This was a problem with the draft version of the guidance, and it appears that footnote 3 was inserted to address it.

Guidance on the application of PA 2008, s 115(4B)(b)

Paragraph 11 of the DCLG Guidance on NSIPs and housing sets out the Government's approach to the requirement in PA 2008, s 115(4B)(b) that related housing development must be 'on the same site as, or next to or close to' any part of the NSIP 'or is otherwise associated' with the NSIP.

It states as follows:

> 'The effect of this is to allow housing to be granted development consent in two specific circumstances:
>
> (i) where there is a functional need for the housing in terms of the construction or operation of a project. For example where housing (rather than temporary accommodation) is needed for construction workers, or to support a 24 hour presence on the site for key workers;
>
> (ii) where the housing is not functionally linked to the infrastructure project but is in geographical proximity to the project. For example, housing which is within the boundary of an infrastructure project such as a business and commercial project that includes housing, or housing that is adjacent to or in close proximity of a nationally significant project (eg a rail station on a railway line).'

Housing included on the basis of geographical proximity

In order for housing to be regarded as sufficiently close to come within this category, it should be within one mile of any part of the NSIP (not any associated development) for which development consent is sought. It is not made explicit whether all of the housing must be within this one-mile limit, or only the closest units. The former may be more likely, but there must be some uncertainty as to precisely how this will be applied in practice.

Housing which is included within an application on the basis of geographical proximity is subject to a number of limits, tests and other matters which are different from those set out for housing included on the basis of a functional link.

In both cases, there is a limit of 500 placed on the number of dwellings that can be included, but the terms in which that limit are expressed differ.

Where the case is made on the basis of geographical proximity, the DCLG Guidance on NSIPs and housing states that the reason for the limit is because of the importance of ensuring that the local planning process is not undermined. However, the limit is not expressed in absolute terms. The guidance says that 'it is very unlikely that the Secretary of State will consent more than 500 dwellings', which leaves the door at least slightly ajar for an applicant to seek to justify a higher number in an exceptional case. There would be risks involved in doing so, not least because paragraph 40 of the guidance explains that the Secretary of State is 'very unlikely' to accept an application for more than 500.

Housing proposals in this category would be expected to include a percentage of affordable housing in accordance with any applicable policy in the Local Plan, secured by means of a section 106 agreement with the local planning authority (paragraph 23). There is no equivalent expectation on applications based on functional need.

Any application would need to include an assessment of the impact of the proposed housing in terms of Local Plan provision and local housing supply. It is to be noted that this is not a requirement where an application is made on the basis of functional need. This may be because, if permanent housing is proposed on the basis of an ongoing functional need driven by the requirements of the NSIP whilst operational, this should do no more than enable the project to 'consume its own smoke' in terms of impact on the balance of housing supply and demand locally.

Housing provided on the basis of a functional need

Developers should expect the Examining Authority to carefully scrutinise the justification advanced for any housing said to be required to meet a functional need (paragraphs 28 and 37). The functional need for housing (as opposed to temporary accommodation) may arise during the construction or operational phases.

Whilst housing provided on the basis of a functional need would normally be expected to be close to the NSIP, the DCLG Guidance on NSIPs and housing recognises that wider sustainability considerations (such as ease of access to facilities) may make it more appropriate to locate housing in a local town (paragraph 25).

Housing applications within this category are also subject to a limit of 500, but the limit is expressed in absolute terms as a 'maximum' number that 'could be granted' (paragraph 18).

Paragraph 19 of the DCLG Guidance on NSIPs and housing is particularly important:

> 'There may be some situations where a developer chooses to provide housing for construction workers (as opposed to temporary accommodation) which is of a standard that will allow this housing to be retained as, or converted to, permanent dwellings once construction of an infrastructure project is complete. In such cases, accommodation for more than 500 workers may be consented for the construction phase of the project

as long as this is subsequently converted so that the number of permanent dwellings after any conversion is 500 or less. The requirement for conversion should be included within the Development Consent Order.'

This is one of those passages of the guidance which would be difficult to unpick were it not for footnote 3 and the clarification it provides as to what is meant by the use of the term 'housing'. With that clarification in mind, it seems that what is contemplated is a development where what is initially constructed would qualify as 'dwellings' and thus 'related housing development'. So the reference to 'conversion' is not a reference to conversion from temporary accommodation (ie a form of associated development) to 'related housing development', but rather works of conversion to alter the form of the housing that has been constructed (and possibly thereby reducing the number of dwellings) for the purposes of permanent retention.

The possibility of seeking to retain temporary worker accommodation (ie associated development) after the construction of the NSIP is complete is addressed in paragraph 20. It notes that the scope for seeking consent for such temporary accommodation is unchanged and that there is no limit on the number of units that can be included. The DCLG Guidance on NSIPs and housing continues as follows:

> 'However the accommodation will be expected to be removed or demolished once construction of an infrastructure project is complete unless a separate planning permission (under the Town and Country Planning Act 1990) has been granted for its retention.'

This would appear to signal a more flexible approach than was shown in response to the application for temporary worker accommodation associated with the construction of the Hinkley Point C nuclear power station in Somerset, where arguments in favour of a similar approach were rejected and a requirement was imposed that obliged the developer to demolish the accommodation once the construction of the NSIP was complete.

Care is needed with this approach, because the effect of any requirement imposed that required removal or demolition would remain, even if planning permission was subsequently granted under the separate TCPA regime for a material change of use of the building. Therefore the requirement itself would need to be expressed in conditional terms in order for such an approach to be effective.

General guidance on assessment that applies to both categories of related housing development

Where specific policies in the National Planning Policy Framework ('NPPF') indicate that development should be restricted, the DCLG Guidance on NSIPs and housing states (at paragraph 21) that 'a lower number of dwellings, or no housing at all, is likely to be appropriate'. Such applications will be assessed against the relevant policies in the NPPF and the development plan (paragraph 22).

The Examining Authority will give careful consideration to the amount and location of any proposed housing, assessed against the relevant policies in the NPPF and supporting guidance. The policies of the development plan are likely to be treated as an important and relevant consideration (paragraphs 28 to 30).

Local Authorities' Local Impact Reports should consider any specific impacts likely to arise from the proposed housing (eg on the local housing market and housing supply).

General guidance on the scope and content of applications

The expectation is that applications for related housing development will be in outline, rather than detailed. Sufficient detail must nevertheless be provided so that the Secretary of State can properly assess the impacts of the housing development when taking a decision whether or not to grant development consent (paragraph 35).

The DCLG Guidance on NSIPs and housing includes a reminder that the obligation in the Infrastructure Planning (Applications: Prescribed Forms and Procedure) Regulations 2009, to include with the application 'any other plans, drawings or sections necessary to describe the proposals for which development consent is sought, showing details of design, external appearance, and the preferred layout of buildings or structures, drainage, surface water management, means of vehicular and pedestrian access, any car parking to be provided, and means of landscaping', applies equally to any related housing (paragraph 36).

Decision-making and post-consent changes

The DCLG Guidance on NSIPs and housing explains that the Secretary of State can refuse consent for some or all of the proposed housing, but nevertheless grant consent for the rest of the proposed project, if he considers that the adverse impacts of the housing outweighs the benefits of the development as a whole (paragraph 44). That formulation is important, because it suggests placing in the positive side of the balance not only the benefits of the housing but also the benefits of the development as a whole (ie including the NSIP).

An application to change a made DCO so as to add related housing 'may' be a change for which a fresh application for development consent is required. That is particularly the case if consent is sought for a significant amount of housing where little or no housing was originally consented (paragraph 45). The additional delay and expense involved in making a fresh application may well limit the extent to which developers with the benefit of an existing DCO will be able to take advantage of the subsequent legislative changes to go back and seek to add an element of housing to their project.

Enforcement is available if the housing is built but not the NSIP to which it related. Thus, housing developers could not seek to use a putative NSIP as a vehicle for delivering housing if that NSIP was not itself genuinely viable and deliverable.

Comment

Housing development tends to be highly controversial in England, sometimes more so than proposals for NSIPs. Promoters will therefore need to keep that well in mind when weighing up the pros and cons of seeking to include related housing within their applications.

There has been a great deal of litigation in the Planning Court and the appellate courts as to the meaning and effect of the housing policies in the NPPF, and any promoter engaging in the business of promoting housing for the first time would need to understand that they are entering fast-moving and, at times, distinctly murky waters, strewn with hazards.

Furthermore, there may be a limited number of NSIPs that require the provision of (more expensive) housing rather than (cheaper) temporary accommodation for construction workers. Similarly, few are likely to require any substantial housing for functional reasons during the operational phase.

That said, the potential financial incentives to include an element of housing could be substantial, and it seems reasonable to expect that some will consider the additional risks, work and complexity involved to be worth it.

There could be much more scope for including housing based on geographical proximity, not least because of the absence of any limit on the type of NSIP to which such a proposal can relate.

The level of risk reflects the fact that there are a number of areas in respect of which the DCLG Guidance on NSIPs and housing is silent (for example, the approach that would be taken to applications for powers of compulsory acquisition to enable the delivery of related housing). Where the housing is based on a functional need associated with the NSIP, the case for compulsory acquisition may be little different from the case that would need to be put together in relation to temporary worker accommodation (although there may be different or additional issues relating to the choice between powers of temporary possession and compulsory acquisition, and the extent of the land take needed), drawing upon the need for and benefits of the NSIP with which it is associated. However, where the case is based on geographical proximity rather than any functional relationship, the case for compulsory acquisition may need to be freestanding in terms of need, benefit and alternatives. That is likely to be more challenging.

Interesting questions also arise in relation to the extent to which it would be legitimate for related housing to influence the design and location of the NSIP itself. For example, would it be objectionable for the route of a linear NSIP to be determined, in part, by the desire to bring a suitable housing site within the one-mile distance set by the guidance?

The combination of financial incentive, complexity and uncertainty makes it likely that this article will need to be updated on a regular basis, as the issues are identified and resolved through decision-making and litigation.

Article 28

Pre-application Project Development

Hereward Phillpot QC
Hugh Flanagan

Introduction

This article is arranged in three parts.

The first part seeks to put the pre-application project development process into context, explaining its particular importance under the PA 2008 and the various ways this can manifest itself at the examination stage.

The second part considers the practical issues for scheme promoters of internal governance and documentation of the pre-application project development process, so as to improve the prospects of success in examination.

The third part considers the scope to involve others from outside the promoter's team in developing the scheme through consultation and engagement.

Part 1: The importance of pre-application project development under the PA 2008

The PA 2008 process is deliberately front-loaded, with projects intended to be developed in a staged and carefully considered manner with extensive third party (including public) involvement. It is also a process that does not enable problems in project development to be rectified easily post-acceptance.

The Act provides for a relatively rapid and tightly timetabled process from acceptance to determination. Successful operation of that process depends to a significant extent on the promoter having flushed out the key issues through the pre-application stages, and submitting a scheme that has been shaped by a careful consideration of those issues. That is not to say that all concerns raised along the way will have been resolved, but they will at least have been understood and taken into account.

There are three key practical points arising from those considerations.

The difficulty in making material changes post-acceptance

First, whilst some post-application change is possible, and an element of flexibility will always be required to deal with points raised in relevant representations or in new data or guidance, making material changes can be challenging and needs to be justified.

A key difficulty in seeking to make material changes post-acceptance is that time is not on the promoter's side. PINS may, exceptionally, be willing to delay the start of the examination to cater for late changes, but not for long. Making material changes to big and complex infrastructure projects may take longer than PINS is willing to tolerate.

The Rail Central Strategic Rail Freight Interchange application provides a useful illustration. In that case, problems emerged after acceptance with the assessment and design of the proposed highways works. PINS was persuaded to defer the date of the Preliminary Meeting (and hence the start of the examination) to enable the necessary further assessment and design work, and engagement with Interested Parties, to be undertaken. That agreement, however, was on the basis of adherence by the promoter to a particular timetable. The programme slipped because the further assessment and design work proved less straightforward than hoped, and the timetable could not be met. Eventually, PINS's patience was exhausted and the promoter was left with no option but to withdraw the application.

Scrutiny of pre-application project development at the examination stage

Second, in circumstances where the need for the proposed development is often uncontroversial, but meeting it may well cause significant residual harm, the focus of objections and examination can shift to considering potential alternative and less harmful ways of meeting the need.

Sometimes the relevant NPS policy will seek to place limits on the consideration of alternatives (see eg NPS EN-1, section 4.4), but sometimes the policy may itself necessitate such consideration (an example would be where major development is proposed in an Area of Outstanding Natural Beauty). Furthermore, where compulsory acquisition of land is proposed, demonstrating that there is a compelling case for taking the land in question may require an explanation of why that land was selected rather than other land.

In those circumstances, the examination process can include delving into the promoter's internal decision-making process, looking at the contemporaneous documentation of that process and questioning the choices made. This is not uncommon in examinations, and in extreme cases can prove onerous for the promoter. The Thames Tideway Tunnel examination is an example from the extreme end of the spectrum. In that case, some of the work sites selected were predicted to give rise to significant noise and associated disturbance to local residential amenity over an extended period, and these sites had changed during the pre-application stages as a result of responses to consultation, new sites becoming available, changes of drive strategy etc. The ExA made this decision-making process a main focus of the examination, with the first set of written questions including the following:

> 'Q.14.1 Provide details and evidence for each site with full documentation and details of how the selection process was undertaken (including professional judgment and any methodology or parameters applied) and how the responses were taken into account.
>
> Q.14.3 Within each of the five parameters [engineering, planning, environment, community and property] there were a number of "considerations". How was each consideration taken into account to form the overall assessment for that parameter? Provide evidence that this was applied consistently and impartially across all sites and provide details of all those who undertook the assessment with their relevant qualifications.'

Preparation of application documents

Third, a properly designed and documented project development process should form the backbone of the case for the project, central to the drafting of the key application documents:

- *The Statement of Reasons:* explaining and justifying the proposed land take, consideration of alternatives to compulsory acquisition, and the account taken of impacts on third party land when developing the proposal.

- *The Environmental Statement:* the consideration of alternatives, including how the environmental impacts of alternatives were taken into account.
- *Consultation Report:* compliance with the PA 2008, s 49(2) duty to take account of feedback.
- *Planning Statement:* the quality of the application proposal, and the care taken in its preparation; avoidance, minimisation and mitigation of adverse effects; and alternatives.
- *Project Development Report:* some applications may benefit from the preparation of a freestanding comprehensive document to explain the process, which enables other documents to be more concise, minimising repetition and the risk of inconsistency.

In exceptional cases, the application may be prepared and submitted on the basis that a choice between options is left for the decision-maker (see eg the National Grid Hinkley Point C Grid Connection project). In those cases, the application material will need to demonstrate why it has not been possible to decide on one option, and that the mechanism is not being used as a substitute for a proper options appraisal (see DCLG Pre-application Guidance at [105]). This will require a clear explanation of, and reliance on, the rigour and robustness of the applicant's internal decision-making process.

Alternatives in the Courts

The decision of the High Court in *R (Save Stonehenge World Heritage Site Ltd) v Secretary of State for Transport* [2021] EWHC 2161 (Admin) contains a very helpful discussion (at paras 242–290) on the law relating to 'alternatives' in cases decided under the Town and Country Planning Act 1990 and then applies those principles to the circumstances of the proposed A303 Amesbury to Berwick Down DCO that included a 3.3km long tunnel through the Stonehenge World Heritage Site. In that case the Court of Appeal held (at para 277) that an alternative to the proposed tunnel was not just a relevant consideration that the Secretary of State could choose whether or not to take into account, but was 'an obviously material consideration which the SST was required to assess' and the decision to grant development consent was, accordingly, quashed.

Part 2: Governing and documenting the process

A robust, thorough and properly documented process, undertaken within a framework of appropriate governance, is an essential part of pre-application project development and minimising risk to the project. Documentation and governance are internal matters for the promoter, but they need to be undertaken on the basis that they will be examined externally in public. These issues are explored under the following headings: what is expected of a promoter; following a process; documenting the process; and decision-making and governance.

What is expected of a promoter

The significant powers granted by the PA 2008 to promoters (for example, in respect of compulsory acquisition) give rise to particular expectations on the part of the ExA, which are more demanding than in other areas of the planning system. In order to satisfy those expectations, there is a need for a rigorous internal project development process, where options are thoroughly and objectively explored.

DCO project development should be approached on the basis that it is an objective attempt to find the optimal solution (which may not be the least environmentally harmful solution in all cases) to meeting the infrastructure need and dealing with any constraints. Time, funding and commercial pressures have the potential to divert from that path. While viability and deliverability are, of course, legitimate and important considerations, a promoter needs to be able to show that any role they have played in project development is justified and evidence-based. Transparency in documentation and governance is an essential part of that.

Following a process

Consideration should be given to creating a structured project development process at the outset and being prepared to stick to it. What that process will look like may be highly project-specific, but it should be a clear and reasoned explanation of how you intend to go about designing a project and meeting specified objectives. Relevant matters are likely to include identifying what workstreams will be necessary, how the workstreams relate to each other, what their outputs are intended to be, and the timing and phasing of the process. Regard should be had to the requirements of the PA 2008 when designing this process. It is important, for example, to be able to show that the process allows for sufficient time for consultation to take place on the project being developed, and for consultation responses to be taken into account. A process that did not leave adequate time for these necessary steps would give ammunition to opponents of the project.

A stand-alone project development process document, created at the start of the process, is likely to be useful. Regard can be had to it by project designers, those involved in project governance, and the ExA should they so wish. Consideration should be given to whether it is an iterative document, capable of being adjusted if timings or workstreams change.

Indeed the project development process may need to allow for flexibility. It may be necessary to envisage how steps can be re-taken in light of the output of assessment or consultation responses. Generally, the extent of flexibility is an important matter to consider at the outset. A project development process needs to be firm enough to stand up to scrutiny, but at the same time, if the process is too rigid, that may create problems for the designers. For example, it may be considered reasonable for the process document to say that testing of options may lead either to an option being adopted, or to further testing with new options being required. Likewise, projects can require more rounds of consultation than originally envisaged. Back-checking is also an important part of flexibility. If new evidence comes to light, back-checking to ensure that the project remains appropriate in light of that evidence is legitimate and, indeed, important. Care needs to be taken, however, that back-checking is not used to retro-fit a 'process' onto decisions taken without one.

Documenting the process

Documenting the project development process contemporaneously, and not leaving it until the final decision, is a fundamental discipline. Project development for major infrastructure projects can be a very long process and, unless it is methodically documented as it progresses, it may be impossible to explain in sufficient detail what took place and why. The ExA may ask about the reasons for a specific step taken several years ago. A properly documented process means that the promoter is likely to be able to give a sufficiently detailed and prompt answer so as to satisfy the ExA. Version control is an important issue in this context: documents need to be finalised and dated, not left in multiple drafts of uncertain date.

Decision-making and governance

Both the substance and structure of decision-making need consideration as part of pre-application project development. In relation to the former, setting out in advance evaluation criteria by which decisions will be taken may assist in showing that project development has been a methodical and evidence-based process, and that commercial pressures have not undermined the integrity of the process.

In relation to the latter, any process document is likely to need to set out the structure of decision-making, ie who is to take decisions and as part of what governance arrangements. The identity of decision-makers is likely to need careful consideration, and regard should be had to the fact that those individuals may need to give evidence at the examination justifying the decisions taken. The need for review procedures is equally important. Roles may need to be allocated to check and challenge decisions in order to ensure that they are robust and avoid groupthink.

Part 3: Involving others in the process

This final part considers the two main means of involving others in the process: consultation and engagement.

Consultation

In order for feedback from consultation to play an effective part in the pre-application project development process, it is important for promoters to give careful thought to what they want to know, and when they need to know it.

Most big infrastructure projects are developed under some timetable pressure, with key decisions needing to be made by particular dates so as to keep to a timetable. In order for consultation to be effective in those circumstances, relevant input from consultees needs to be fed into that process at the right time so that it can be taken into account.

That requires careful planning, because fair and effective consultation takes time to prepare and carry out, and it also takes time to process the responses received so that they can systematically be assessed and fed into the decision-making process before it is too late to make a difference.

It also requires thought to be given to the input that is likely to be of most use to the promoter's team at the relevant stage of decision-making. All too many consultations effectively take the form of: 'Here are our current proposals – what do you think?'. That simplistic approach is unlikely to elicit the most helpful responses, compared to something which is more specific and targeted. For example, if project development is at an early stage, it may be helpful to flush out any concerns about the promoter's approach to decision-making before it is too late by asking about the criteria and/or weighting that are intended to be used.

One of the pillars of effective and adequate consultation with other parties is providing sufficient information to enable them to make an informed response.

That is reflected in the provisions which govern the sharing of preliminary environmental information with consultees. Preliminary environmental information is defined in the Infrastructure Planning (Environmental Impact Assessment) Regulations 2017, reg 12(2) as the information reasonably required for the consultation bodies to develop an informed view of the likely significant effects of the proposed development.

As the likely significant effects of options are considered and appraised, informing the choices as to the nature and parameters of the project for which consent will be sought, possible ways of avoiding and mitigating those effects should be examined and recorded. In that way, environmental impact assessment by the promoter should be seen as an integral part of project development, enabling a properly informed decision to be made about the ultimate content of the application.

Interested Parties will often be able to provide helpful insights to feed into that decision, but only if they are given the right information at the right time. Promoters and those advising them will therefore need to put themselves into the shoes of consultees and consider what information they would want to see in order to express an informed opinion.

The more that can be shared, the more likely it will be that the feedback received will be of assistance in developing a robust scheme that is ready to withstand the rigours of the examination process.

Engagement

Formal rounds of consultation will often represent the tip of the iceberg in terms of the involvement of other parties in the pre-application project development process. Much of that involvement may well take the form of active and regular engagement.

For example, it can often be highly productive to establish regular working groups with those who can offer useful insight and input to the process. This need not be confined to obvious candidates such as local planning and highway authorities and bodies such as Natural England and the Environment Agency, but can be extended to statutory undertakers, end users of the proposed infrastructure (where appropriate), and local residents and interest groups.

The potential benefits to a promoter of such regular constructive engagement can be significant.

Some advantages are obvious, such as gaining insights and information at an early stage without having to wait for a round of consultation to be undertaken and processed.

Others are perhaps more subtle, but no less important. If engagement is undertaken correctly, it not only builds trust but also enhances mutual understanding. The promoter reduces the risk of overlooking or misunderstanding potential local impacts, but also has an opportunity to impart an understanding of the practicalities and constraints that must be accommodated if the project is going to work. It is also a useful opportunity for both parties to develop a shared understanding of the relevant policies that will govern the assessment and determination of the application in due course, and to shape their approaches accordingly.

The benefits of such an approach tend to be felt by both sides, and it can help make the subsequent examination process more constructive, effective and better informed. Those who refuse to engage constructively risk losing the sympathy of the ExA.

Part 5

Pre-application Procedures

Article 29

Legal Requirements for the Statement of Community Consultation

Rebecca Clutten, ftb
Michael Humphries QC, ftb

Introduction

The Planning Act 2008 ('PA 2008') places prospective applicants for development consent under an obligation to consult the local community about their proposals. Before any such consultation takes place, however, applicants are required to prepare a statement 'setting out how the applicant proposes to consult, about the proposed application, people living in the vicinity of the land': see PA 2008, s 47(1). This document is known as a Statement of Community Consultation ('SOCC').

Once a SOCC is prepared, the applicant is under a statutory duty to both publicise the document in the manner specified in PA 2008 and carry out its consultation in accordance with the proposals identified in it: see PA 2008, s 47(7).

This article provides information on:

- the preparation of the SOCC;
- consulting in accordance with the SOCC; and
- revisions to the SOCC.

Preparing the SOCC

The content of the SOCC

Save insofar as relates to environmental information (considered further below), there are no specific requirements as to the information the SOCC is to contain. Typically, however, SOCCs which have been submitted with accepted applications include details of:

- the project, including its scale and the positive and negative benefits which might arise;
- how consultation is to be carried out, in terms of the methods of consultation to be employed, any phasing of consultation, and provisional periods allowed for responses;
- the information to be provided to consultees (at each stage for phased consultations);
- who it is proposed to consult; and
- how feedback is to be captured and recorded.

The former (now withdrawn) PINS Advice Note 16, 'The developer's pre-application duties' (April 2012) (pages 4–5), also suggested that: a SOCC should include details of PINS's role as examining authority; attention should be drawn to any relevant National Policy Statements (NPSs) and their status; and details of any other consultations taking place in the area should be noted (to demonstrate that the applicant has had regard to the need to avoid 'consultation fatigue' when programming its own consultation process).

As to the methods of consultation that are to be set out in a SOCC, the DCLG Guidance on the pre-application process (March 2015) states that:

> '"Guidance on Community Engagement for Onshore Wind Developments" provides useful non statutory guidance on approaches to assist developers and local communities in considering how best to engage with one another. This guidance should be read alongside "Guidance on Community Benefits for Onshore Wind" which promotes good practice and sets out principles and expectations for developers, local authorities and communities. Both sets of guidance may be of benefit to pre-application consultation for other types of developments.'

In relation to environmental information, reg 12 of the Infrastructure Planning (Environmental Impact Assessment) Regulations 2017 requires that the SOCC contain:

- a statement as to whether the development for which the applicant proposes to make an application is EIA development; and
- if that development is EIA development, how the applicant intends to publicise and consult on the preliminary environmental information ('PEI').

Although a previous version of PINS Advice Note 15 contained a statement suggesting that the PEI must be available at the time the preparation of the SOCC is consulted on (on which, see further below), that advice has now been withdrawn and the Inspectorate has confirmed, in its Register of Advice, that the level of environmental information to be made available is a matter for the applicant. The level of information provided must, however, be enough to enable meaningful consultation. In practice, this means that a local authority must have sufficient information about the environmental impacts of the project to be able properly to advise who should be consulted: see the PINS Register of Advice, Response to Marcus Bate of Pinsent Masons (dated 12 December 2011), and Response to Ben Wallace of ESBI Investments (dated 26 January 2012).

Consultation on the draft SOCC

The proposed content of the SOCC must itself be consulted upon. Applicants are required to contact all those local authorities in whose area the land subject of the proposed application falls to ascertain their views as to what the statement should contain: see PA 2008, s 47(2) referring to s 43(1).

Some NSIPs may have impacts that extend beyond the boundaries of the authority in which the land upon which the project proposed is situated. In such cases, applicants are well advised to consult with potentially affected parties in those extended areas, and DCLG Guidance suggests that the intention to consult people in a wider area should be made clear in the SOCC: see paragraph 36 of the DCLG Guidance on the pre-application process (March 2015). If such extended consultation is to be undertaken, it is also advisable for the applicant to include any authorities for those areas in its consultation on the content of the SOCC, notwithstanding the absence of a statutory obligation to do so.

In order to canvass the relevant local authorities' views on the SOCC, the applicant must send to them 'the consultation documents'. There are no statutory requirements as to the contents of the consultation documents, and they are simply defined in PA 2008, s 47(4) as 'the documents supplied to the local authority by the applicant for the purpose of consulting the local authority under subsection (2)'. In practice, however, applicants usually send to the relevant local authorities a draft SOCC and sample consultation materials, along with details of the aspects of it upon which the local authorities' views are sought.

DCLG Guidance on the pre-application process (March 2015) identifies (at paragraph 39) various aspects of the content upon which applicants should seek local authority input. These include but need not be limited to:

- the size and coverage of the proposed consultation exercise;
- the appropriateness of the techniques proposed, including electronic techniques;
- the design and format of consultation materials;
- the issues to be covered in the consultation materials;
- suggested times and locations for public consultation events;
- local bodies and representative groups who should be consulted; and
- timescales for consultation.

Once it has received 'the consultation materials', a local authority has 28 days within which to respond. Applicants should remind local authorities of the deadline when providing the consultation materials. An applicant has a statutory obligation to 'have regard' to any consultation responses received by the applicant before the expiry of the 28-day deadline (that is, up to and including the 28th day), but consideration of any received after that time will be at the applicant's discretion.

The DCLG has noted that 28 days is a short timescale and suggests that applicants undertake informal 'pre-consultation consultation' to iron out any issues that might arise in advance: see the DCLG Guidance on the pre-application process (at paragraph 37).

The obligation to 'have regard' to local authority responses does not mean that an applicant is under an obligation to give effect to any suggestions made, or to address all issues raised. Where an applicant is unable or chooses not to do so, however, the reason for adopting that course of action should be clearly explained in the application documentation.

The Planning Inspectorate may also be able to offer guidance in cases where applicants and local authorities are unable to agree on the consultation process: see the DCLG Guidance on the pre-application process (at paragraph 40).

Although local authorities are usually willing to engage with applicants in relation to the SOCC, it is not unheard of for some authorities to fail to respond. In such cases, the applicant must satisfy itself that (and be able to explain in the application document how) its consultation proposals will ensure that all affected and interested parties (including 'hard to reach' and minority groups) have an opportunity to engage with and comment upon the proposals.

Publicising the SOCC

Pursuant to PA 2008, s 47(6), once an applicant has prepared its SOCC, it must:

- make the statement available for inspection by the public 'in a way that is reasonably convenient for people living in the vicinity of the land';
- publish in a newspaper circulating in the vicinity of the land a notice stating where and when the SOCC can be inspected; and
- publish the statement in such a manner as may be prescribed.

In respect of the first requirement, there is no existing law or guidance on how an applicant should determine whether a location for inspection is 'reasonably convenient for people living in the vicinity of the land'. What would be 'reasonably convenient' location or locations is perhaps best explored with the local authorities during the consultation SOCC. It is considered that, if an applicant makes its SOCC available in a manner suggested by the relevant local authority or authorities, the Examining Authority is unlikely to find non-compliance with the requirement.

It is important to note, however, that, following the coming into force of the Infrastructure Planning (Publication and Notification of Applications etc) (Amendment) Regulations 2020, applicants no longer need to place paper copies of the SOCC on deposit at locations in the vicinity of the proposed development. Instead, applicants should make the SOCC available for inspection online. PINS Advice Note 14: 'Compiling the consultation report' (version 3) states (para 3.15) that evidence that this has been done should be provided in the consultation report – for example, a screen shot of the relevant webpage showing the published SOCC (including the full website address and relevant telephone number for enquiries, as required by the 2020 Regulations) and confirmation that the public could access the webpage free of charge.

Consulting in accordance with the SOCC

Once plans are finalised and publicised, consultation must be carried out in accordance with the contents of the SOCC: see PA 2008, s 47(7).

There is also a duty, under PA 2008, for applicants to take into account responses received to consultation carried out in accordance with the SOCC.

Before an application is accepted for examination, the Examining Authority will contact the relevant local authorities (ie those who were or should have been consulted on the SOCC) to ask for their views on the adequacy of the consultation carried out in accordance with the SOCC. Local authorities are therefore able to explain whether or not they agreed with the contents of the SOCC and highlight any feedback given which the applicant did not address and, furthermore, state whether they consider consultation to have been carried out in accordance with the SOCC.

Although the ultimate decision as to whether or not an application is to be accepted rests with the Examining Authority, which will take into account a range of factors, it is important to try to ensure that any disagreements between an applicant and relevant local authorities about the adequacy of consultation are resolved prior to submission of the application. It is also important for applicants to be open in their application materials in disclosing any incidents where pre-application consultation has not met any SOCC requirement. This needs to be seen in the context of the somewhat more relaxed requirement in PA 2008, s 55, following amendment by the Localism Act 2012, for the Secretary of State to conclude that 'the application … is of a standard that the Secretary of State considers satisfactory'.

Revisions to the SOCC

There is no formal mechanism for revising the SOCC once it has been published. Experience has, however, shown that revisions are sometimes necessary (for example, because there is more or less public interest in the proposals than was anticipated). In such cases, because applicants are in effect producing a new SOCC, they would be well advised to undertake the same process as was carried out in relation to the first SOCC.

PINS Advice Note 14: 'Compiling the consultation report' (version 3) does state (para 3.17) that, where more than one SOCC was prepared for a project (for example, where a SOCC was subject to one or more updates), the consultation report should include a narrative about why the SOCC was reviewed and updated.

Best practice indicates that it may be possible to draft a SOCC such that it may not need to be revised to allow for further consultation. The DCLG Guidance on the pre-application process (March 2015) states (para 76) that:

> 'In circumstances where a particular issue has arisen during the pre-application consultation, or where it is localised in nature, it may be appropriate to hold a non-statutory, targeted consultation. A developer's Statement of Community Consultation should be drafted so that it does not preclude this approach.'

Article 30

Section 42 Consultation

Isabella Tafur, ftb
Michael Humphries QC, ftb

Introduction

The extensive pre-application procedure is a distinctive feature of the PA 2008 regime and early consultation is a key feature of that regime. The rationale for the 'front-loaded' approach to consultation is that effective engagement at an early stage in the project's development will lead to applications which are better developed and understood by the public, so that, by the time they come before the Secretary of State, most important issues will have been raised and, where possible, resolved. That, in turn, allows for shorter and more efficient examinations.

The pre-application procedures are set out in Chapter 5, Part 2 of the PA 2008. The duty to consult is contained in PA 2008, ss 42 (in relation to prescribed persons, landowners, etc) and 47 (in relation to the local community). DCLG has produced 'Guidance on the pre-application process' which sets out advice on pre-application process under both PA 2008, ss 42 and 47.

This article in concerned with PA 2008, s 42 consultation.

Who must be consulted

PA 2008, s 42(1) sets out the categories of person who must be consulted prior to the submission of a DCO application. They are as follows.

Prescribed persons

PA 2008, s 42(1)(a) and Infrastructure Planning (Applications: Prescribed Forms and Procedure) Regulations 2009 ('the APFP Regulations'), reg 3 prescribe a number of persons who must be consulted in certain circumstances. Those persons and the circumstances in which they must be consulted are set out in Schedule 1 to the APFP Regulations. They include, for example, the Welsh Ministers, Scottish Executive and relevant Northern Ireland Department in respect of applications likely to affect land in Wales, Scotland and Northern Ireland respectively; parish councils; the Health and Safety Executive; and certain statutory bodies such as Natural England, the Environment Agency and Historic England.

PINS Advice Note 11: 'Working with public bodies' (version 4) provides a short explanation of the framework governing the involvement of relevant consultees in the pre-application process. It is supplemented by a number of Annexes to assist in understanding the roles of particular consultees (including Natural Resources Wales, Natural England, the Environment Agency and Nuclear Regulators).

The Marine Management Organisation

Pre-application consultation must take place with the Marine Management Organisation ('MMO') where the proposed development would be likely to affect:

(a) waters in or adjacent to England, up to 12 nautical miles from the low-water mark around the coast;

(b) an exclusive economic zone (designated in Schedule A to the Exclusive Economic Zone Order 2013, SI 2013/3161, pursuant to Marine and Coastal Access Act 2009, s 41), except any part of such an area in relation to which the Scottish Ministers have functions;

(c) a renewable energy zone (designated in paragraph 3 of the Exclusive Economic Zone Order 2013, pursuant to Energy Act 2004, s 84), except any part of such an area in relation to which the Scottish Ministers have functions;

(d) an area designated under Continental Shelf Act 1964, s 1(7).

Annex B to Advice Note 11 (version 4) contains guidance on pre-application consultation with the MMO. In particular, it provides a list of the information that the MMO wishes to receive at the pre-application stage, including maps/charts of the site, an outline of the project options, and details of any hazardous materials associated with the construction or operation of the project.

Certain local authorities

Host or neighbouring local authorities must be consulted, in accordance with PA 2008, ss 42(1)(b) and 43.

The Greater London Authority

If the land is in Greater London, consultation must take place with the Greater London Authority (PA 2008, s 42(1)(c)).

Persons with an interest in land

Consultation must take place with persons with an interest in land, as identified in PA 2008, s 44. A person will fall within the categories in PA 2008, s 44 if the applicant, after making diligent enquiry, knows that the person is an owner, lessee, tenant or occupier of the land in which the project is located, is interested in the land or has power to sell and convey or to release the land, or who would or might be entitled to make a 'relevant claim' if the DCO was made and implemented.

A 'relevant claim' is defined in PA 2008, s 44(6) as a claim for compensation under the Compulsory Purchase Act 1965 or Land Compensation Act 1973 or for injurious affection under PA 2008, s 152(3). This would include, broadly, persons who may not own an interest in land being acquired, but who may suffer injurious affection and/or be entitled to rights or restrictions over the land to be acquired that will be interfered with or extinguished.

DCLG's Guidance on the pre-application process recognises that land interests change over time and that new or additional interests may emerge after the consultation has taken place, but before submission of the application. In such circumstances, the Guidance suggests that the applicant should provide a proportionate opportunity for the new person with an interest in land to make their views known on the application. Where the new interests are identified shortly before the submission of the application, the applicant should be proactive and helpful in ensuring that the person understands how they can engage with the process if the application is accepted for examination.

Timetable for consultation

PA 2008, s 45 provides that the applicant must allow at least 28 days for consultation responses to be submitted (beginning with the day after the date on which the person receives the consultation documents). Consultees must be notified of that deadline for submitting representations.

Duty to notify the Secretary of State

The applicant must supply a copy of the consultation information provided to the consultees under PA 2008, s 42 to the Secretary of State prior to submitting the information, pursuant to PA 2008, s 46.

Article 31

General Principles relating to Consultation

Richard Honey QC, ftb
Michael Humphries QC, ftb

Introduction

This article focuses on the general common law principles relating to 'consultation' as established through case law. Articles 29, 30, 32 and 33 of this work examine the specific legal duties and guidance relating to consultation under the PA 2008.

The duty to consult

There is no general duty to consult. In particular circumstances, however, a duty to consult might arise. In *R (Harrow Community Support Ltd) v Secretary of State for Defence* [2012] EWHC 1921 (Admin), Haddon-Cave J said that 'when decisions will have a specific impact on a definable group, fairness and natural justice may entail a duty to consult with those affected by the decision depending on the context of the decision' (para 28). He went on to say (para 29):

> 'A duty to consult does not arise in all circumstances. If this were so, the business of government would grind to a halt. There are four main circumstances where consultation will be, or may be, required. First, where there is a statutory duty to consult. Second, where there has been a promise to consult. Third, where there has been an established practice of consultation. Fourth, where, in exceptional cases, a failure to consult would lead to conspicuous unfairness. Absent these factors there will be no obligation to consult.'

Fundamental rules of proper consultation

Where a duty to consult arises, or where a consultation is voluntarily undertaken, the consultation must be undertaken properly. Lord Woolf MR said in *R v North & East Devon Health Authority, ex parte Coughlan* [2001] QB 213 at paragraph 108 that 'whether or not consultation of interested parties and the public is a legal requirement, if it is embarked upon it must be carried out properly'.

Fair consultation involves giving the persons consulted a fair and proper opportunity to understand fully the matters about which they are being consulted and to express their views, with the person undertaking the consultation thereafter considering those views properly and genuinely (*R v Secretary of State for Trade and Industry, ex p Unison* [1996] ICR 1003).

Four fundamental principles of consultation have been set out by the courts in a number of places and were helpfully summarised by Lord Woolf MR in *Coughlan* at para 108 where he stated that:

> 'To be proper, consultation must be undertaken at a time when proposals are still at a formative stage; it must include sufficient reasons for particular proposals to allow those

consulted to give intelligent consideration and an intelligent response; adequate time must be given for this purpose; and the product of consultation must be conscientiously taken into account when the ultimate decision in taken.'

These four fundamental principles will now be examined in a little more detail.

Consultation must be carried out at a time when proposals are still at a formative stage

In relation to the first principle, it has been said that 'the requirement that consultation must be at a time when proposals are at a formative stage can be expressed as a requirement that the decision maker has not pre-determined the issue upon which he goes out to consultation, i.e. that he has an open mind. That said … to have an open mind does not mean an empty mind': see *Royal Brompton and Harefield NHS Foundation Trust v Joint Committee of Primary Care Trusts* [2011] EWHC 2986 (Admin) at para 16.

Consultation requires that there must be a real opportunity for those consulted to make representations to the decision-maker. The decision-maker should keep a 'responsive and open mind' (*R v Warwickshire City Council, ex p Boyden* [1991] COD 31 at p32) and a 'receptive mind' (*R (Partingdale Lane Residents' Association) v Barnet LBC* [2003] EWHC 947 (Admin) at para 45).

It is well-established that there can be consultation on a 'preferred option'. The fact that a provisional view has been taken, or a preferred option identified, does not prevent a consultation exercise being conducted in good faith at a stage when the position is still formative in the sense that no final decision has yet been made. There is no conflict between a person keeping an open mind and consulting on the preferred route; it is permissible to consult on proposals rather than options which are not being proposed: see *R (Bailey) v Brent LBC* [2011] EWHC 2572 (Admin) at para 90.

The consultation must give sufficient reasons for any proposal to allow intelligent consideration and response

In relation to the second rule, Lord Woolf MR said in *Coughlan* at paragraph 112 that the 'obligation is to let those who have a potential interest in the subject matter know in clear terms what the proposal is and exactly why it is under positive consideration, telling them enough (which may be a good deal) to enable them to make an intelligent response'.

A consultation document must present the issues in a way that facilitates an effective response. It must be clear to the general body of respondents. It must present the available information and the options fairly. It has been said that 'the object of requiring fairness is to ensure high standards in decision-making by public bodies, and to enable responses to be made which will best facilitate a sound decision as a result': see *R (Royal Brompton and Harefield NHS Foundation Trust) v Joint Committee of Primary Care Trusts* [2012] EWCA Civ 472 at para 11.

If, during a consultation process, prior to the final decision-making, a new factor or new material emerges which is of potential significance to the decision to be made, fairness may demand that the consultees should be given an opportunity to deal with it: see *R (Edwards) v Environment Agency* [2006] EWCA Civ 877 at para 94.

Similarly, if circumstances change, or what is preferred changes, there may be a duty to re-consult. This will not be the case if the change is trivial, but if there is a fundamental difference between the proposals consulted upon and what is to be adopted, then there would be a requirement for a fresh consultation: see *R (M) v Croydon LBC* [2013] EWCA Civ 116 at paras 22–23.

In *R (Devon CC) v SSCLG* [2010] EWHC 1456 (Admin), it was held that a change in approach during a consultation was unfair and deprived the affected councils of the opportunity to make their case in the consultation process (para 98). In that case, there had been a last-minute change of stance with which the consultees had no chance to anticipate and deal (para 81).

Adequate time must be given for consultation and response

In relation to the third rule, case law sets no prescribed time period for consultation although it is clear that 'adequate' time must be given. Consultation periods can be shorter than usual if there are good reasons for the urgency. Conversely, it has been held that a consultation period of one month including Christmas was too short in the circumstances of a particular case (*R (Green) v Gloucestershire CC* [2011] EWHC 2687 (Admin)).

The courts have rejected the argument that 'a decision-maker can routinely pick and choose whom he will consult', holding that 'a fair consultation requires fairness in deciding whom to consult as well as fairness in deciding the subject matter of the consultation and its timing': see *R (Milton Keynes Council) v SSCLG* [2011] EWCA Civ 1575 at para 32.

The product of consultation must be conscientiously taken into account in finalising the proposals

In relation to the fourth rule, the representations should form 'part of the matrix of the decision-making process': see *R v Warwickshire City Council, ex p Boyden* (1991) COD 31 at p 32. The burden created by this rule should not be under-estimated. An example is the HS2 judicial review, where it was held that the consultation on blight and compensation was so unfair as to be unlawful because a particular important consultation response was not conscientiously considered (*Buckinghamshire County Council & Ors v Secretary of State for Transport* [2013] EWHC 481 (Admin)).

Unlawful consultations

Fairness is an intrinsic part of consultation: see *R (Edwards) v Environment Agency* [2006] EWCA Civ 877 at paras 90–94 and 102–106. The substantive test of lawfulness is whether a consultation process was so unfair as to be unlawful. The Court will judge on an objective basis whether the process has been so unfair as to be unlawful in all the circumstances: see *R (JL Baird) v Environment Agency* [2011] EWHC 939 (Admin) at para 51.

It has been held that, provided the fundamental requirements of consultation are observed, a decision-making authority has a comparatively wide discretion as to how the process is carried out, bounded only by irrationality (*R (Wainwright) v Richmond upon Thames LBC* [2001] EWCA Civ 2062 at para 11). The threshold to be applied was considered by Sullivan J in *R (Greenpeace) v Secretary of State for Trade and Industry* [2007] EWHC 311 (Admin), where he said at paragraph 62:

> 'A consultation exercise which is flawed in one, or even in a number of respects, is not necessarily so procedurally unfair as to be unlawful. With the benefit of hindsight it will almost invariably be possible to suggest ways in which a consultation exercise might have been improved upon. That is most emphatically not the test. It must also be recognised that a decision-maker will usually have a broad discretion as to how a consultation exercise should be carried out.'

If it is alleged that a consultation process is unfair, clear unfairness must be shown (*Royal Brompton* at para 13). 'In reality, a conclusion that a consultation exercise was unlawful on the ground of unfairness will be based upon a finding by the court, not merely that something went wrong, but that something went "clearly and radically" wrong' (*Greenpeace* at para 63).

It is not necessary to show that the consultation was in general unfair, merely that it was unfair in relation to a group of persons affected (*Royal Brompton* at para 14).

The aspects of alleged unfairness should be reviewed both individually and in aggregate, as an individual aspect of unfairness may seem trivial on its own but, when seen with other aspects of unfairness, it may acquire greater significance (*Royal Brompton* at para 12).

Article 32

Section 48 Publicity

Hereward Phillpot QC, ftb
Michael Humphries QC, ftb

Publicity requirements

PA 2008, s 48(1) imposes a duty on the applicant to 'publicise the proposed application in the prescribed manner'. The detailed requirements for publicising the application are to be found in the Infrastructure Planning (Applications: Prescribed Forms and Procedure) Regulations 2009 ('the APFP Regulations').

In addition to the requirements imposed by the APFP Regulations, PA 2008, s 50(3) imposes a duty on the applicant to have regard to any guidance issued by the Secretary of State about how to comply with those requirements.

Infrastructure Planning (Applications: Prescribed Forms and Procedure) Regulations 2009

Regulation 4 of the APFP Regulations prescribes the manner in which an applicant must publicise a proposed application.

The notice must be published for at least two successive weeks in one or more local newspapers, once in a national newspaper and once in the London Gazette (if land in Scotland is affected, it must also be published in the Edinburgh Gazette). It must also be published other specialist publications (Lloyd's List and an appropriate fishing trade journal) where the proposal relates to offshore development.

Although the meaning of 'successive weeks' is not defined, it does not appear to mean every day for two weeks. Rather, the notice must be published once a week for two successive weeks. That is reflected in the DCLG Guidance on the pre-application process (at paragraph 58), which refers to 'the two required local newspaper advertisements'.

Regulation 4 also identifies what the notice must include, namely:

- the name and address of the applicant;
- a statement that the applicant intends to make an application for development consent to the Secretary of State;
- a statement as to whether the application is EIA development;
- a summary of the main proposals, specifying the location or route of the proposed development;
- a statement that the documents, plans and maps showing the nature and location of the proposed development are available for inspection free of charge at the places (including at least one address in the vicinity of the proposed development) and times set out in the notice;

- the latest date on which those documents, plans and maps will be available for inspection (being a date not earlier than the deadline in sub-paragraph (i));
- whether a charge will be made for copies of any of the documents, plans or maps and the amount of any charge;
- details of how to respond to the publicity; and
- a deadline for receipt of those responses by the applicant, being not less than 28 days following the date when the notice is last published.

Applicants would be well advised to pay close attention to the precise terms of each of these requirements, and to ensure that the notices that they publish satisfy them in all particulars. Inevitably, however, there will be occasions when notices are published which fall short of meeting the precise terms of the requirements. In those circumstances the Secretary of State will need to make a judgment as to whether any departure from the requirements is so significant that the applicant has failed to comply with the requirements of Chapter 2 of Part 5 of the PA 2008. If it is, then the application will not be accepted (PA 2008, s 55(3)(e)).

The degree of force with which an objector could argue that a departure should lead to the application being rejected would be likely to depend in large part on whether an individual or individuals could demonstrate a plausible case that they were substantially prejudiced as a result.

The Thames Tideway Tunnel project provides an example of a project where the PA 2008, s 48 notice involved two inadvertent departures from the requirements, but where this was not judged to be so significant as to justify a decision not to accept the application. In that case the Planning Inspectorate noted in its section 55 checklist that the notice did not explicitly state that the documents, plans and maps showing the nature and location of the proposed development were available free of charge, and did not state whether a charge would be made for copies of those documents. Thames Water had itself drawn attention to these departures in the checklist submitted with the application, and set out its reasons for arguing that they were not material. Whilst some objectors sought to persuade the Planning Inspectorate that this was a significant omission, they did not succeed. The Planning Inspectorate concluded that the omissions did not render the notice a nullity, and that it would be unreasonable to conclude as a result of the omission that the applicant had failed to comply with Chapter 2 of Part 5.

Infrastructure Planning (Environmental Impact Assessment) Regulations 2017

Regulation 13 of the Infrastructure Planning (Environmental Impact Assessment) Regulations 2017 requires that, where the proposed application is an application for EIA development, the applicant must, at the same time as publishing the PA 2008, s 48 notice, send a copy of that notice to the consultation bodies and to any person notified to the applicant in accordance with reg 11(1)(c).

Timing of pre-application publicity

DCLG Guidance

Paragraph 58 of the DCLG's guidance on the pre-application process describes the PA 2008, s 48 publicity as 'an integral part of the local community consultation process'. It advises that, where possible, the first of the two required local newspaper advertisements should coincide approximately with the beginning of the consultation with communities. However, the guidance also acknowledges that because of the detailed information required for publicity under reg 4 of the APFP Regulations (see above) 'aligning publicity with consultation may not always be possible, especially where a multi-stage consultation is intended'.

PINS Guidance

The Planning Inspectorate's (now withdrawn) Advice Note 16 (April 2012) was similarly limited in the advice it offered in relation to the PA 2008, s 48 stage, but did suggest it would be 'helpful' if the deadline for responses to PA 2008, s 48 publicity were 'as close as possible to deadlines given to landowners and local authorities etc in the s 42 consultation'.

Relationship to pre-application consultation

The DCLG Guidance and the now withdrawn PINS Advice Note 16 (April 2012) documents thereby raise, but do not fully resolve, the issue of how the PA 2008, s 48 publicity stage relates to the overall process of pre-application consultation. For smaller and less complex proposals, there may be no difficulty in undertaking pre-application consultation and PA 2008, s 48 publicity at the same time. In larger and more complex cases with multi-stage consultation, however, it may simply be impractical to do that whilst complying with the detailed information requirements set down by reg 4 of the 2009 Regulations. In such circumstances there does not appear to be any objection in principle to PA 2008, s 48 publicity being undertaken following PA 2008, ss 42 and 47 consultation and this was certainly the approach adopted in respect of the Thames Tideway Tunnel project.

Feedback on PA 2008, s 48 publicity

The applicant must have regard to any relevant responses received to section 48 publicity when deciding whether the application that it is actually to make should be in the same terms as the proposed application (PA 2008, s 49(2)).

PA 2008, s 37(3) requires the applicant to submit with his application a consultation report. That report must give details of what has been done in compliance with PA 2008, ss 42, 47 and 48, any relevant responses and the account taken of any relevant responses. This is a useful discipline, because it forces the applicant to engage with the responses it receives at each stage, including what is said in response to PA 2008, s 48 publicity. In writing up the responses, it is important to provide sufficient information so that the reader can understand why changes were or were not made (as the case may be) in response to representations. The Planning Inspectorate can be expected to scrutinise the consultation report with some care to ensure that this has been done carefully and conscientiously.

Article 33

Taking Consultation into Account

Hereward Phillpot QC, ftb
Michael Humphries QC, ftb

The requirements of PA 2008, s 49

Where an applicant has complied with the duties to consult upon and to publicise the proposed application pursuant to PA 2008, ss 42, 47 and 48, and proposes to go ahead with making an application, PA 2008, s 49(2) imposes a duty to first take account of responses to consultation and publicity.

The terms of the duty are expressed as follows:

> 'The applicant must, when deciding whether the application that the applicant is actually to make should be in the same terms as the proposed application, have regard to any relevant responses.'

'Relevant responses' are defined in PA 2008, s 49(3) as those responses received to consultation and to publicity before the deadlines imposed in each case.

In complying with its duty under PA 2008, s 49, the applicant must have regard to any guidance issued by the Secretary of State about how to comply with the requirements of PA 2008, Pt 5, Ch 2 (PA 2008, s 50(1) and (3)).

Compliance with this duty must be demonstrated to the satisfaction of the Secretary of State at the stage of acceptance: see PA 2008, s 55(3)(e), which provides that the Secretary of State may accept the application only if he concludes that the applicant has complied with the pre-application procedures in PA 2008, Pt 5, Ch 2. The key documents to which the Secretary of State is likely to refer in forming a view about the applicant's compliance or otherwise with the duty under PA 2008, s 49 are those to which he is obliged to have regard pursuant to PA 2008, s 55(4): namely, the Consultation Report received under PA 2008, s 37(3)(c), and any adequacy of consultation representation received from a local authority consultee. PA 2008, s 55(4)(c) also obliges the Secretary of State to have regard to the extent to which the applicant has had regard to any guidance issued under PA 2008, s 50.

DCLG Guidance

The DCLG Guidance 'Planning Act 2008: Guidance on the pre-application process' (March 2015).

Paragraph 18 of the DCLG Guidance lists a series of potentially significant benefits for all parties that can be brought about by the early involvement of local communities, local authorities and statutory consultees. These include allowing members of the public to influence the way projects are developed and how they are integrated into the community, resolving misunderstandings, allowing applicants to obtain important information about the likely impacts of the scheme, enabling potential mitigation measures to be considered and in some cases built into the project, and so on. In order to realise these benefits, however, it is essential that applicants comply with their duty under PA 2008, s 49 and approach the responses received to consultation and publicity with a genuinely open mind. Applicants must be willing to learn from the feedback from consultation and, where it is justified, to adapt their proposals in response.

The DCLG Guidance also rightly emphasises that it is more difficult to make changes to an application once it has been accepted for examination and explains that this is why it is important that issues are made known and explored during pre-application consultation and prior to finalising the application. See also on this issue the DCLG Guidance 'Planning Act 2008: Guidance for the examination of applications for development consent' (March 2015) at paragraphs 109 to 115.

Applicants are advised in the DCLG Guidance 'Planning Act 2008: Guidance on the pre-application process' (March 2015) to ensure that their Consultation Report sets out specifically what the applicant has done in compliance with the requirements of the PA 2008, secondary legislation, the DCLG Guidance and any relevant policies, guidance or advice published by Government or the Planning Inspectorate. The report should also set out how the application has been influenced by relevant responses to consultation, outlining any changes made as a result, and explain why responses advising on major changes to a project were not followed (paragraph 80).

Applicants need not agree to all suggestions made in response to consultation, but they are required to take them into account. In practice, demonstrating that they have done so requires a clear and coherent explanation as to why a particular suggestion has not been adopted. Formulaic or 'standard' responses to points raised by consultees are not sufficient – the response must engage with the issue raised and enable the reader to understand why it is that a particular suggestion was or was not accepted.

Other relevant aspects of the DCLG Guidance are considered below.

PINS Advice Note

PINS Advice Note 14: 'Compiling the consultation report' (version 3) states (para 2.1) that the purpose of a consultation report is to explain how the applicant has complied with the pre-application consultation requirements set down in the PA 2008, in particular:

- the requirement to consult with prescribed consultees (s 42);
- the requirement to consult with the community (s 47);
- the requirement to publicise the proposed application (s 48); and
- the requirement to have regard to consultation responses (s 49).

It should also, however, explain non-statutory consultation that takes place outside the requirements of the PA 2008 so that the Secretary of State is given an understanding of all of the consultation activity relevant to a particular project. Furthermore, applicants should use the consultation report to demonstrate compliance with PA 2008, s 50 (the duty to have regard to any statutory guidance issued by the Secretary of State) by illustrating how relevant statutory guidance has been followed. Where an applicant has diverged from any guidance, this should be robustly justified in the consultation report.

Given the diversity of the projects that may use the PA 2008 process, PINS Advice Note 14 (version 3) makes it clear (para 3.1) that it is not appropriate for the Planning Inspectorate to issue prescriptive 'one size fits all' advice. Based on experience, however, section 3 then sets out some helpful guidelines about format and structure.

Section 3 provides guidance on:

- introductory text;
- multi-stage consultations;
- the duty to consult (s 42);
- the duty to consult the local community (s 47);
- the duty to publicise (s 48);
- non-statutory consultation and engagement;
- EIA Regulations consultation; and
- report appendices.

It is essential that a consultation report should demonstrate compliance with PA 2008, s 49 by providing evidence that consultation responses have been taken into account during preparation of the application. Where the level of response is significant, PINS Advice Note 14 suggests (para 4.2) that

> 'it may be appropriate to group responses under headline issues. Care must be taken to ensure that in doing this the responses are not presented in a misleading way or out of context from the original views of the consultee. An explanation of the process by which consultation responses were grouped and organised (coded) is helpful, including any safeguards and cross checking that took place to ensure that the responses were grouped appropriately.'

It is clear, therefore, that the consultation itself should be carried out in a way that allows the submission of a robust and detailed report at application stage.

General case law on taking consultation into account

There is a well-developed body of case law that addresses what is necessary to ensure that consultation is adequate, including the requirement for a conscientious and open-minded consideration of relevant matters.

The requirements were neatly summarised in *R v North and East Devon Health Authority, ex parte Coughlan* [2001] 2 QB 213 at para 108:

> 'To be proper, consultation must be undertaken at a time when proposals are still at a formative stage; it must include sufficient reasons for particular proposals to allow those consulted to give intelligent consideration and an intelligent response; adequate time must be given for this purpose; and the product of consultation must be conscientiously taken into account when the ultimate decision is taken'.

The courts have elaborated upon that final requirement, explaining that an applicant must embark upon the consultation process prepared to change course, if persuaded by it to do so (*R v London Borough of Barnet, ex parte B* [1994] ELR 357 at 375C).

The duty to take responses conscientiously into account does not equate to a duty not to make a decision without the prior agreement or consensus of the consultees (*R (Smith) v East Kent Hospital NHS Trust* [2002] EWHC 2640 (Admin)). In other words, there is no obligation to agree with the points made by consultees, but it is necessary to show that they have been properly considered and that the reasons for disagreeing with them are rational and properly articulated.

A practical consideration to keep in mind is that in order to demonstrate that responses have conscientiously been taken into account, sufficient time for that to happen must be allowed between the receipt of the response and the final decision. If a consultation response raises complex technical matters, requiring expert consideration, the applicant will need to have allowed itself time – and obtained any necessary expert input – to be in a position properly to have regard to those matters.

The authorities also serve to underline the importance of adequately capturing the reasons why a particular suggestion made in response to consultation has not been accepted, at the time that the decision is made (in the PA 2008 context, this would be in the consultation report). Late reasons proffered for taking a particular decision, particularly if provided in response to a subsequent legal challenge to the adequacy of consultation, will be approached with an appropriate degree of scepticism by the courts and are unlikely to be accepted (see eg *R (Medway Council and others) v Secretary of State for Transport* [2002] EWHC 2516 (Admin); *R (Nash) v Chelsea College of Art and Design* [2001] EWHC 538 (Admin)).

Changing a proposed project in response to consultation

The DCLG Guidance acknowledges (para 70) the tension between consulting early but also having project proposals that are firm enough to enable consultees to comment. The DCLG Guidance seeks to reconcile this tension by making clear (paras 70–71) that:

> '... applicants are encouraged to consider an iterative, phased consultation consisting of two (or more) stages, especially for large projects with long development periods. For example, applicants might wish to consider undertaking non-statutory early consultation at a stage where options are still being considered. This will be helpful in informing proposals and assisting the applicant in establishing a preferred option on which to undertake statutory consultation.
>
> Where an iterative consultation is intended, it may be advisable for applicants to carry out the final stage of consultation with persons who have an interest in the land20 once they have worked up their project proposals in sufficient detail to identify affected land interests.'

The courts have accepted that it is lawful to define the parameters of public consultation so as to exclude an option or options (*R (Medway Council and others) v Secretary of State for Transport* [2002] EWHC 2516 (Admin)).

A number of applicants have successfully adopted this staged approach, whereby the options are consulted upon and then narrowed down through an initial round (or rounds) of informal non-statutory consultation, and then statutory consultation is undertaken on a more firm proposal. National Grid, for example, has developed such an approach informed by its early experiences of the PA 2008 process, which it now adopts for all of its grid connection projects.

The DCLG Guidance (paras 73–75) offers the following advice in relation to the procedural implications of making changes to a proposed project in response to the formal statutory public consultation:

> 'Applicants are not expected to repeat consultation rounds set out in their Statement of Community Consultation unless the project proposals have changed very substantially. However, where proposals change to such a large degree that what is being taken forward is fundamentally different from what was consulted on, further consultation may well be needed. This may be necessary if, for example, new information arises which renders

> all previous options unworkable or invalid for some reason. When considering the need for additional consultation, applicants should use the degree of change, the effect on the local community and the level of public interest as guiding factors.
>
> Where a proposed application changes to such a large degree that the proposals could be considered a new application, the legitimacy of the consultation already carried out could be questioned. In such cases, applicants should undertake further re-consultation on the new proposals, and should supply consultees with sufficient information to enable them to understand the nature of the change and any likely significant impacts (but not necessarily the full suite of consultation documents), and allow at least 28 days for consultees to respond.
>
> If the application only changes to a small degree, or if the change only affects part of the development, then it is not necessary for an applicant to undertake a full re-consultation. Where a proposed application is amended in light of consultation responses then, unless those amendments materially change the application or materially changes its impacts, the amendments themselves should not trigger a need for further consultation. Instead, the applicant should ensure that all affected statutory consultees and local communities are informed of the changes.'

In these respects the Guidance reflects the approach that has been adopted by the courts in considering the need for re-consultation where proposals change (see eg (*R (Smith) v East Kent Hospital NHS Trust* [2002] EWHC 2640 (Admin)).

Ultimately the applicant and its advisors are left to form a judgment as to whether their proposed changes fall on one side of the line or the other. In view of the emphasis placed upon the importance of the pre-application consultation process, and the 'sudden death' nature of the rigorous PA 2008, s 55 acceptance process, applicants tend in practice to be fairly cautious.

Where the judgment is reached that the changes are so significant as to warrant re-consultation, then, as stated above, the DCLG Guidance suggests that consultees should be supplied with sufficient information to enable them to fully understand the nature of the change and any likely significant impacts – but not necessarily the full suite of consultation documents – and allow at least 28 days for consultees to respond (paragraph 74). This approach of a 'targeted' re-consultation can help to reduce the burden on the applicant, and was successfully adopted by Thames Water Utilities Limited in the pre-application consultation process for the Thames Tideway Tunnel proposals.

Where proposed changes made in response to consultation are judged to be more limited and not to require re-consultation, the DCLG Guidance suggests that instead the applicant should ensure that all affected statutory consultees and local communities are informed of the changes (paragraph 75).

Part 6

Information and Surveys

Article 34

Obtaining Information about Interests in Land

Douglas Edwards QC, ftb
Michael Humphries QC, ftb

Introduction

PA 2008, s 52 comprises a detailed procedure for the obtaining of information concerning the interests held in land affected by a DCO as well as the identity of those who may be entitled to compensation.

In practice, the detailed requirements for pre-application consultation and the requirement in particular to notify the Secretary of State of those affected by proposed compulsory acquisition within a DCO is likely to lead to this provision becoming well used.

However, the power to seek such information is limited and is exercisable only following compliance with particular and strict procedural requirements, no doubt at least in part being a recognition of the fact that compelling an individual to disclose information may be considered an infringement of privacy.

PA 2008, s 52 is the subject of PINS Advice Note 4.

The purpose of PA 2008, s 52 and the time at which it may be used

PA 2008, s 52 is available both where a person 'is applying' and where a person 'proposes to apply' for an order granting development consent (PA 2008, s 52(1)). This reflects the purposes of the exercise of the power (PA 2008, s 52(1)), being to enable to person proposing or promoting a DCO to comply with:

- Chapter 2 of Part 5 of PA 2008 (ie pre-application procedure and in particular the duty under PA 2008, s 44 to consult owners, lessees, tenants and occupiers of land affected by the DCO); or
- Chapter 1 of Part 6 of PA 2008 (eg notification of an accepted application under PA 2008, s 56 and notice to those whose interests are to be acquired under PA 2008, s 59).

In practice, it is at the pre-application stage that the power is likely to be of most use. Since an applicant will generally be expected to have fully identified relevant interests in land to be compulsory acquired, it is only exceptionally that the power is likely to fall to be exercised after the DCO application has been made and accepted, possibly where it is known that an interest in land has changed since the original request for information.

The requirement for the Secretary of State's consent

In broad terms, a PA 2008, s 52 notice may require:

- information about landowners or those with an interest in land (PA 2008, s 52(2)), and/or
- information about those who may be able to make a 'relevant claim' (PA 2008, s 52(2A)).

These types of notice are discussed later in this article. In both cases, however, a notice requesting information may not be served without the consent of the Secretary of State.

PINS Advice Note 4 (version 6) sets out the procedure to be followed and the information required by the Secretary of State where his consent is sought under PA 2008, s 52. The information should be provided, in a folder with tabs for the information, as follows:

- A1 – Contact details
- A2 – Description of the project requiring development consent
- A3 – Explanation of why authorisation is needed, having regard to the criteria for a s 52 authorisation
- A4 – Identifying the proposed recipient(s)
- A5 – Plans identifying the land for which information about interests is sought
- A6 – Information to demonstrate that the Applicant has acted reasonably and has been unreasonably refused the information sought
- A7 – Evidence of notifying the proposed recipient(s) that a request for authorisation has been made to the Planning Inspectorate
- A8 – Duration for which s 52 authorisation is sought
- A9 – Check list.

Each of these headings is then further elaborated on in the Advice Note.

With regard to A3 above, PINS Advice Note 4 (version 6) states that:

> 'An explanation should be provided by the Applicant as to how service of a land interest notice will enable compliance with the pre-application consultation duties, or the requirement to notify persons of an accepted application, and to give notice to persons interests in land to which a compulsory acquisition request relates. It will be for the Applicant to seek their own legal advice as to how to best address these matters.'

This advice reflects a recognition that the service of a notice under PA 2008, s 52 on an individual is potentially intrusive and onerous, particularly given the criminal sanctions that apply to non-compliance with such a notice (about which, see below). The Secretary of State will need to be satisfied that the service of the notice is therefore genuinely required.

A fee is payable when seeking the consent of the Secretary of State under PA 2008, s 52. The fee is currently set at £1,500 – see reg 3(1) of the Infrastructure Planning (Fees) Regulations 2010 (as amended).

PA 2008, s 52 as a 'last resort'

There is no statutory requirement to seek any required information voluntarily before making a request under PA 2008, s 52. Advice Note 4 clearly indicates, however, that applicants should seek to obtain any required information directly before recourse is had to PA 2008, s 52.

Reference is made in Advice Note 4 (version 6) to the DCLG Guidance on the Infrastructure Planning (Fees) Regulations 2010, which comments in relation to PA 2008, s 52 (at para 3 of the annex) that:

> 'Applicants are expected to act reasonably, first seeking to obtain relevant information or permission to access land directly before seeking authorisation under these provisions.

> Specifically, applicants should only submit requests for those aspects of information … where they consider they have been reasonably refused that information.'

The same Guidance at paragraph 6 provides that requests under PA 2008, s 52 should only be made as a 'last resort'. Advice Note 4 (version 6) continues as follows:

> '… an Applicant will be expected to demonstrate reasonable efforts made to obtain information about interests in the land identified in green on Plan A prior to making the s 52 authorisation request(s) to the Planning Inspectorate, and explain why in their opinion, they have been unreasonably refused that information.'

Advice Note 4 provides detailed guidance as to the form of the correspondence and dialogue that is expected to have taken place. Evidence of such correspondence and dialogue (or efforts to stimulate such a dialogue) should be submitted to the Secretary of State with any request under PA 2008, s 52.

As a matter of policy, therefore, the Secretary of State will wish to see other opportunities to obtain the requisite information exhausted before recourse is had to PA 2008, s 52. Thus an applicant should have a detailed strategy in place to obtain the required information before the PA 2008, s 52 procedure is engaged. Moreover, an evidence base should be assembled to demonstrate the implementation of this strategy. It is this evidence base that will need to be provided to the Secretary of State in the event that it ultimately becomes necessary to seek a notice under PA 2008, s 52.

Consultation

There is no statutory duty on an applicant, or on the Secretary of State, to consult with 'affected persons' when making or considering a request under PA 2008, s 52.

However, Advice Note 4 (version 6) makes it clear that an applicant is required to serve a copy of the PA 2008, s 52 notice request, and all accompanying documents, on all proposed recipients of the notice if it were to be served. The letter accompanying service of the request and information should notify the recipient that he/she may make comments on the authorisation request not less than 14 days starting the day after the expected date of receipt of the notification by the proposed recipient(s). The applicant will be given an opportunity to respond to any comments received before the Secretary of State makes a decision on the request.

Types of PA 2008, s 52 notice

As stated above, in substance PA 2008, s 52 provides for two types of notice to be served with the Secretary of State's consent.

First, a notice may be served under PA 2008, s 52(2) requiring 'the recipient' to give the name and address of any person the recipient believes is one or more of the following, namely:

- an owner, lessee, tenant (whatever the tenancy period) or occupier of the land;
- a person interested in the land;
- a person having power:
  - to sell and convey the land, or
  - to release the land.

It is worth noting that 'the recipient' of the notice does not have to be one of the persons identified in PA 2008, s 52(2). The 'person' on whom a notice may be served under PA 2008, s 52(2) (ie 'the recipient') may be any one of those identified in PA 2008, s 52(3), namely:

- an occupier of the land,
- a person who has an interest in the land as freeholder, mortgagee or lessee,
- a person who directly or indirectly receives rent for the land, and
- a person who, in pursuance of an agreement between that person and a person interested in the land, is authorised to manage or arrange for the letting of it.

Thus a managing agent could be 'the recipient' of a notice in respect of the landowner's interest in the land.

It is also worth noting that the notice may require 'the recipient' to give the applicant in writing 'the name and address' of any of the types of person identified in PA 2008, s 52(2). Thus a notice must be carefully drafted so as to specify the full range of interests in respect of which 'the recipient' may be able to supply 'names' and 'addresses'.

The reference above to a 'person interested in the land' would certainly include those with an 'interest in land' as defined in Law of Property Act 1925, s 1 (in order words, easements and 'profit a prendre' etc), and would appear also to include persons with an equitable interest, such as the interest of a tenant for life under a settlement. The name and address of any mortgagee would also fall within PA 2008, s 52(2).

Secondly, a notice may be served under PA 2008, s 52(2A) requiring 'the recipient' to give the name and address of any person who, 'if the order sought by the application or proposed application were to be made and fully implemented, would or might be entitled':

- as a result of implementing the order,
- as a result of the order having been implemented, or
- as a result of the use of the land once the order has been implemented,

to make a 'relevant claim'.

Again, 'the recipient' of any such notice must be a person identified in PA 2008, s 52(3).

A 'relevant claim' is defined in PA 2008, s 52(14) and comprises a claim under Compulsory Purchase Act 1965, s 10, Land Compensation Act 1973, Part 1 or PA 2008, s 152(3). In substance, this provision covers an entitlement to statutory compensation for injurious affection or other harm arising from the carrying out of the proposed development and its operation, where no land is acquired.

A notice served under PA 2008, s 52(2A) must explain the circumstances in which a person would be entitled to compensation as mentioned in that subsection: see PA 2008, s 52(5A).

Clearly, any determination as to persons who 'would or might' be entitled to make a relevant claim will involve careful judgments as to potential environmental impacts that will have to be clearly justified in making any application for a PA 2008, s 52 notice under PA 2008, s 52(2A).

The form of notice and period for response

There is no statutory form of a notice to be served under PA 2008, s 52. PA 2008, s 52(4) does, however, identify certain formal requirements, including drawing the recipient's attention to the fact that a criminal sanction arises in cases of non-compliance. These are mandatory requirements for a notice.

The notice must be in writing and must specify the deadline by which a response must be given. That deadline must be not earlier than the end of 14 days beginning with the day on which the notice is served on the recipient (PA 2008, s 52(5)). Provisions for service of notices under the 2008 Act are set out in PA 2008, ss 229 and 230.

Failure to comply with a notice

A failure to comply with a notice served under PA 2008, s 52, without reasonable excuse, amounts to a criminal offence (PA 2008, s 52(6)), as does the giving of information which is false in a material respect and which, when it was given, the person knew or ought reasonably to have known to be false (PA 2008, s 152(6) and (7)).

Other statutory powers for obtaining information about interests in land

There are several other statutory provisions by which persons may be compelled to disclose the existence of interests in land. Local Government (Miscellaneous Provisions) Act 1976, s 16 is a well-used example and is available to local authorities in respect of 'a function conferred' on that local authority by any enactment. A similar power is available under Town and Country Planning Act 1990, s 330 in the context of functions arising under that Act. Furthermore, for the purposes of compulsory acquisition, Acquisition of Land Act 1981, s 5A entitles an 'acquiring authority' to serve a notice to secure 'information about land in relation to which an acquiring authority is entitled to exercise a power of compulsory purchase'.

These powers are, however, related to 'functions' of public authorities under other legislation and it seems questionable that they could be used, even by such authorities, for the purpose of promoting an application for a development consent order.

Article 35

Rights of Entry

Douglas Edwards QC, ftb,
Michael Humphries QC, ftb
Rebecca Clutten, ftb

Introduction

PA 2008, s 53 introduced, with safeguards, a wide-ranging power for those proposing or promoting a DCO to enter private land for the purpose of the carrying out of surveys etc.

As is to be expected, however, that power:

- is limited to surveys required for specified purposes;
- requires ministerial consent; and
- is subject to the payment of compensation.

PINS have published guidance, in the form of Advice Note 5, in respect of PA 2008, s 53.

The power

PA 2008, s 53(1) provides that any person duly authorised in writing by the Secretary of State may, at any reasonable time, enter land:

- for the purpose of surveying and taking levels of it, or
- in order to facilitate compliance with provisions made under an Act for the purpose of implementing the Environmental Impact Assessment Directive (85/337/EEC), the EU Habitats Directive (92/43/EC) or any EU instrument replacing those Directives (PA 2008, s 53(1A)),

in connection with:

- an application for a DCO which has been accepted by the Secretary of State, whether in relation to that land or other land (PA 2008, s 53(1)(a));
- a proposed application for a DCO (PA 2008, s 53(1)(b)), where it appears to the Secretary of State that the proposed applicant is considering 'a distinct project of real substance' (PA 2008, s 52(2)); or
- an order granting development consent that includes provision authorising the compulsory acquisition of that land or of an interest in or a right over it (PA 2008, s 53(1)(c)).

It is clear, therefore, that the power to enter land pursuant to PA 2008, s 53(1) is exercisable (i) before a DCO application has been made, (ii) when that application has been accepted, and (iii) after the DCO has been granted, albeit only in respect of those aspects of the order which concern compulsory acquisition. It is likely to be in the first of those situations that the power will be of most utility and, in particular, in the context of the design of the scheme or for the purposes of the preparation of the environmental statement or habitats regulations assessment.

The power to enter land for the purpose of surveying that land under PA 2008, s 53(1) includes a power to search and bore for the purposes of ascertaining the nature of the subsoil or the presence of minerals or other matter in it (PA 2008, s 53(3)). This power may be particularly relevant for projects such as underground gas storage facilities within PA 2008, s 17. This power is, however, subject to a requirement to give notice of an intention to search and bore etc (PA 2008, s 53(9)) and the authority of the 'appropriate Minister' (see PA 2008, s 53(10)) if the land in question is held by a statutory undertaker and that undertaker objects on the ground that the works would be 'seriously detrimental' to the carrying on of their undertaking.

Section 53(3A) provides that the power to enter land to facilitate compliance with provisions made under any Act for the purpose of implementing the two identified EU Directives (above) includes a power to take, and process, samples of:

- air,
- water,
- soil or rock,
- flora,
- bodily excretions, or dead bodies, of non-human creatures, or
- any non-living thing present as a result of human activity.

Thus, and by way of example, samples of contamination on the land could be taken to facilitate compliance with the Infrastructure Planning (Environmental Impact Assessment) Regulations 2017 that implemented the EU EIA Directives. Living fauna could not, however, be taken from the land.

It will be apparent from the above that the power is limited to certain specific purposes. As will be made clear below, in considering whether to grant the power to enter private land under PA 2008, s 53, the Secretary of State requires clear and specific detail of the nature of the surveys etc to be carried out.

The requirement for the Secretary of State's consent

A right to enter private land pursuant to PA 2008, s 53 is subject to the consent of the Secretary of State.

The procedure for applying for consent and the information which the Secretary of State requires for the purposes of such an application is set out in PINS Advice Note 5.

There is no prescribed form of application and an application should, therefore, be made by letter. PINS Advice Note 5 (version 6) provides that 'To demonstrate that the proposed project is one "genuinely requiring entry onto the land" the Applicant should provide an explanation as to why entry is required, bearing in mind whether entry is sought under the provisions of s 53(1) and/or s 52(1A) of the PA 2008.'

PINS Advice Note 5 (version 6) indicates that an application under PA 2008, s 53 should include all the information listed below in a folder with the following tabs:

- A1 – Contact details
- A2 – Description of the project requiring or granted development consent

- A3 – Explanation of why authorisation is needed, having regard to the criteria for s 53 authorisation
- A4 – Details of the proposed surveys and works
- A5 – Identifying persons with interest
- A6 – Plans identifying the land for which authorisation to enter is sought
- A7 – Information to demonstrate that the Applicant has acted reasonably and has been unreasonably refused access to the land
- A8 – Evidence of notifying the persons with interest that a request for authorisation has been made to the Planning Inspectorate
- A9 – Duration for which s 53 authorisation is sought
- A10 – Any conditions subject to which the Applicant thinks any s 53 authorisation should be granted
- A11 – Check list.

PINS Advice Note 5 (version 6) gives more detailed guidance in relation to each of these items. A fee is payable by a developer for making an application under PA 2008, s 53 and this should also accompany the application.

What runs though the guidance in PINS Advice Note 5 (version 6) is a requirement for a detailed and full justification as to why entry is genuinely necessary, no doubt in recognition of the conflict with privacy and the right to quiet enjoyment of land which the exercise of the powers of entry may generate.

This is particularly the case in respect of a proposed application for a DCO where the developer may itself be a private person and, as stated above, the Secretary of State must be satisfied that 'the developer is considering a distinct project of real substance which genuinely requires entry onto the land'.

Moreover, PINS Advice Note 5 (version 6) offers clear instruction as to the level of detail required of the proposed surveys etc:

> 'The Applicant should clearly specify what surveys they intend to carry out, outline their methodology and provide an explanation as to why the surveys are connected with the proposed / accepted for examination / consented DCO.
>
> The following information should be provided in relation to each authorisation request:
>
> - the scope of the surveys and whether these have been agreed with the relevant regulatory/environmental bodies;
> - survey area, timescale and period, including an indication of whether or not repeat visits would be required, and
> - any other survey requirements including access into buildings, and night-time surveys.'

As with applications under PA 2008, s 52, there is no express requirement for a developer to exhaust all opportunities by informal means to secure entry onto land for surveys etc, before making an application under PA 2008, s 53. However, PINS Advice Note 5 (version 6) makes clear that it is the Secretary of State's policy that an Applicant will be expected to demonstrate the reasonable efforts made to obtain entry onto the land. As such, a developer would be well advised to maintain a documentary record of all correspondence, requests for entry and dialogue that has been had with each landowner before making an application to the Secretary of State under PA 2008, s 53.

Applicants are advised to ensure that they allow sufficient time for the PA 2008, s 53 authorisation to be obtained ahead of the requirement to enter land. Applications are understood to take in the order of five to 12 months to process.

The exercise of a power of entry under PA 2008, s 53

A person authorised by the Secretary of State to enter land must serve not less than 14 days' notice of intended entry onto land, where that land is occupied (PA 2008, s 53(4)(b)). Where invasive surveys are to be undertaken under PA 2008, s 53(3) to establish the nature of subsoil and the presence of minerals, then as stated above, the intention to do so must be specified in the notice (PA 2008, s 53(9)). The person entering the land must also produce evidence of the authority to enter and the purpose of entry if requested to do so (PA 2008, s 53(4)(a)), and must comply with any conditions subject to which authorisation of the Secretary of State was given (PA 2008, s 53(4)(c)).

A person who wilfully obstructs a person authorised to enter land under PA 2008, s 53(1) is guilty of an offence (PA 2008, s 53(5)).

Compensation

Where the exercise of a right of entry or the carrying out a survey causes 'damage to land or chattels' compensation may be recovered by the person suffering the damage from the person exercising the right of entry (PA 2008, s 53(7)) and any question of disputed compensation must be referred to and determined by the Upper Tribunal (PA 2008, s 53(8)). It is of note that this right to compensation appears to be limited to physical damage to land or to chattels, and not to any consequential economic loss.

The courts have confirmed that the Secretary of State is not obliged to take into account any losses that might be suffered as a result of entry onto land pursuant to an authorisation granted under PA 2008, s 53 (*R (Dowley) v Secretary of State for Communities and Local Government* [2016] EWHC 2618 (Admin)).

Crown land

By PA 2008, s 54, the right of entry provided for by PA 2008, s 53(1)–(3A) applies to Crown land subject to certain exceptions. Two, in particular, are worthy of note.

First, a person must not enter Crown land unless that person has the permission of (i) a person appearing to be entitled to give such permission, or (ii) the appropriate Crown authority (PA 2008, s 54(2)).

Secondly, the requirements within PA 2008, s 53(4), including the requirement to give 14 days' notice of intended entry onto occupied land, as well as the criminal sanction for obstruction, are disapplied in respect of Crown land.

Other powers of entry for the carrying out of surveys etc

There are other legislative provisions that may be available to applicants, and in particular statutory undertakers, that authorise entry into land to carry out surveys. By way of example, Electricity

Act 1989, Sch 4, para 10 provides the following power to enter land for electricity 'licence holders' (that is, generating companies, transmission companies and distribution companies holding a licence under s 6 of the 1989 Act):

> '(1) Subject to the following provisions of this paragraph and without prejudice to any other right of entry, a person authorised in writing by a licence holder may, at any reasonable time, enter upon and survey any land for the purpose of ascertaining whether the land would be suitable for use for any purpose connected with the carrying on of the activities which the licence holder is authorised by his licence to carry on.
>
> (2) A person authorised to enter upon any land under this section shall not demand to do so as of right unless–
>
> (a) 14 days' notice of the intended entry has been given to the occupier; and
>
> (b) if required to do so, he has produced evidence of his authority.
>
> (3) The powers conferred by this paragraph shall not be exercisable in relation to land which is covered by a building or will be so covered on the assumption that any planning permission which is in force is acted on.
>
> (4) The power to survey land conferred by this paragraph includes power to search and bore for the purpose of ascertaining the nature of the subsoil; but works may not be carried out on the land for this purpose unless–
>
> (a) notice of the proposed works is included in the notice given under sub-paragraph (2) above; and
>
> (b) where land is held by statutory undertakers who object to the works on the ground that the carrying out of the works would be seriously detrimental to the carrying on of their undertaking, the Secretary of State gives his consent.
>
> (5) Where any person exercises any powers conferred by this paragraph, the licence holder by whom he was authorised shall make good any damage done to the land.
>
> (6) In this paragraph "building" includes any garden, yard, outhouses and appurtenances belonging to or usually enjoyed with a building.'

The Schedule 4, paragraph 10 power is subject to a compensation provision in the following terms (Sch 4, para 11(2)):

> 'Where in the exercise of any power conferred by or under paragraph ... 10 above any damage is caused to land or to moveables, any person interested in the land or moveables may recover compensation in respect of that damage from the licence holder on whose behalf the power is exercised; and where in consequence of the exercise of such a power a person is disturbed in his enjoyment of any land or moveables he may recover from that licence holder compensation in respect of that disturbance.'

Whilst the Schedule 4 provisions have some similarities with those under PA 2008, s 53, there are clear differences, including:

- the Schedule 4, paragraph 10 power does not require the authorisation of the Secretary of State, but may be exercised on the authority of the 'licence holder';
- the Schedule 4, paragraph 10 power may not be exercised over land covered by a building, as defined; and

- compensation under Schedule 4, paragraph 11 may be recovered in respect of 'damage' to land and moveables and, furthermore, in respect of disturbance to a person's enjoyment of his land.

Electricity 'licence holders' clearly have an alternative procedure to that available under PA 2008, s 53 for obtaining entry onto land for the purpose of surveys etc. Similar provisions granting rights of entry are available to other statutory undertakers.

The courts have also confirmed that those falling within the definition of 'acquiring authority' for the purposes of Housing and Planning Act 2016 ('HPA 2016'), s 172 may elect to use that power of entry in connection with a proposed application for development consent under PA 2008 (*R (Sawkill) v Highways England Company Limited* [2020] 1 WLR 3661). Although the judgment in *Sawkill* contains *obiter* comments suggesting that the use of the HPA 2016, s 172 power is confined to those applicants for DCOs who enjoy powers of compulsory legislation deriving from legislation other than PA 2008 (as did Highways England in that case), it is understood that at least one other promoter without such powers has obtained a warrant under HPA 2016, s 173 (enabling it to enforce entry pursuant to s 172) on the basis that it was an 'acquiring authority' for the purposes of HPA 2016, s 172 notwithstanding those remarks. The point remains to be addressed by the Senior Courts but the editors of this article consider that the ordinary and natural meaning of the definition of 'acquiring authority' will include persons who could be authorised to acquire land pursuant to PA 2008, s 122 absent any other power.

Promoters will therefore need to consider carefully whether alternative rights may be available and, where they are available, the relative advantages and disadvantages of each.

Part 7

Making an Application

Article 36

Application Documentation

Isabella Tafur, ftb
Michael Humphries QC, ftb

Introduction

PA 2008, s 55 is concerned with the acceptance of applications for DCOs. PA 2008, s 55(3)(f) provides that one of the matters about which the Secretary of State must be satisfied before accepting an application for a DCO is that:

> '… the application (including accompaniments) is of a standard that the Secretary of State considers satisfactory.'

PA 2008, s 55(5A) provides as follows:

> 'The Secretary of State when deciding whether the Secretary of State may reach the conclusion in subsection (3)(f) must have regard to the extent to which–
>
> (a) the application complies with the requirements in section 37(3) (form and contents of application) and any standards set under section 37(5), and
>
> (b) any applicable guidance given under section 37(4) has been followed in relation to the application.'

Therefore, quite apart from the other matters set out in PA 2008, s 55, the Secretary of State has a general discretion not to accept an application if the form and content (as opposed to the merits) of the application is not satisfactory in some way. Given the scale and complex nature of NSIPs, together with the focus on written examination under the PA 2008, the power to 'not accept' an application for being of an inadequate standard is necessary and understandable.

An application for development consent should, therefore, satisfy the requirements of PA 2008, s 37 and, in addition, reg 5 of the Infrastructure Planning (Applications: Prescribed Forms and Procedure) Regulations 2009 ('the APFP Regulations'). Important amendments were made to these, and other, regulations by the Infrastructure Planning (Publication and Notification of Applications etc) (Amendment) Regulations 2020 to accommodate publicity for, and inspection of, application documents following the Covid-19 pandemic.

Regulation 6 of the APFP Regulations also deals with the particular requirements for specific types of project, and is explored further in article 37 of this work. In addition, national policy statements (NPSs) for particular types of infrastructure may also require applicants to supply other specified information as part of the application.

DCLG has published guidance in the form of the 'Nationally significant infrastructure projects – Application form guidance' (DCLG Guidance on application forms), and PINS Advice Note 6: Preparation and Submission of application documents (version 10) also gives detailed advice on how application documents should be prepared, organised and submitted to the Planning Inspectorate.

The application must specify the development to which it relates (PA 2008, s 37(3)(a)) and be made in the prescribed form (PA 2008, s 37(3)(b)), which is currently set out at Sch 2 to the 2009 Regulations. Section 2 of the DCLG Guidance on application documents (paragraphs 10–48) set out detailed guidance on completing the numbered boxes in the prescribed application form.

The application form requires the applicant to provide a brief explanation of why the application falls within the development consent regime, and a brief non-technical summary of the development proposal and of the location or route of the development (with reference to appropriate plans).

The form also requires the applicant to indicate (with appropriate references) whether any associated development is included in the application and to give references for certain documents, including the consultation report, copies of newspaper notices, the draft order and explanatory memorandum, and the land and works plan.

Where relevant, references must also be given to a number of other documents, such as the environmental statement and, if the application seeks authorisation for compulsory acquisition the statement of reasons, funding statement and book of reference (which comply with reg 7 of the 2009 Regulations).

The DCLG Guidance on application forms (para 7) encourages applicants to avoid using complex or technical terminology in the application form. PINS Advice Note 6 (version 10) updates PINS previous advice of paper copies of applications and states (para 3.1) that:

> 'The Planning Inspectorate is committed to the UK Government's 'digital by default' approach set out in the Civil Service Reform Plan. The examination of nationally significant infrastructure projects (NSIPs) under the Planning Act 2008 has since its inception been a mostly electronic process. The Planning Inspectorate has (until now) requested one or more full printed copies of the documents comprising the Applicant's application at the point of its submission. However, following a trialled alternative approach, and having had regard to the relevant requirements and feedback from consultees, the Planning Inspectorate no longer requires Applicants to submit their application documents in printed copy at the point of submission. The Planning Inspectorate would prefer electronic applications to be provided on a Universal Serial Bus (USB) storage device. Although the Planning Inspectorate can accept Compact Disc (CD) or Electronic Versatile Disc (DVD) as a form of electronic application it is not our preference to do so.'

PINS Advice Note 6 (version 10) also says (para 1.3), importantly, that:

> 'Applicants are strongly encouraged to hold pre-application discussions with the Planning Inspectorate about how their application information should be prepared and submitted well in advance of formal submission. The Planning Inspectorate's pre-application service for Applicants 'Prospectus for Applicants' is available on the National Infrastructure Planning website Prospectus for Applicants page.'

The consultation report

The application must be accompanied by the consultation report (PA 2008, s 37(3)(c)), which explains what has been done in compliance with PA 2008, ss 42 (duty to consult), 47 (duty to consult local community) and 48 (duty to publicise) in relation to the application, gives details of any relevant responses (defined in PA 2008, s 49(3)) and of the account taken of the relevant responses. Articles 29 to 33 of this work consider the pre-application consultation requirements of the PA 2008.

Prescribed documents and information

Pursuant to PA 2008, s 37(3)(d) the application must also be accompanied by documents and information of a prescribed description. Regulation 5(2) of the APFP Regulations sets out what constitutes the prescribed documentation and information. It requires an application to be accompanied by the following:

(a) An environmental statement and any scoping or screening or scoping opinions and directions (where applicable).

(b) The draft proposed order.

(c) An explanatory memorandum explaining the purpose and effect of the provisions in the draft order.

(d) A book of reference (where applicable) which complies with the requirements in reg 7 of the 2009 Regulations.

(e) A copy of any flood risk assessment.

(f) A statement dealing with whether the proposal engages one or more of the matters set out in Environmental Protection Act 1990, s 79(1) (statutory nuisances) and, if so, how the applicant proposes to mitigate or limit them.

(g) A report identifying any European site to which reg 48 of the Conservation (Natural Habitats &c) Regulations 1994 applies or any Ramsar site, which may be affected by the proposed development, together with sufficient information that will enable the Secretary of State to made an appropriate assessment of the implications for the site, if required by reg 48(1).

(h) A statement of reasons and a statement indicating how an order containing the authorisation of compulsory acquisition is proposed to be funded (where the proposed order would authorise the compulsory acquisition of land or an interest in or right over land). The DCLG Guidance on application forms explains that the statement of reasons must set out why the compulsory acquisition is necessary to enable to proposed development to proceed, and that the funding statement must contain sufficient information to enable the Secretary of State to be satisfied that, if such powers are granted, the proposed development is likely to be undertaken and not prevented due to difficulties in obtaining the requisite funding.

(i) A land plan identifying:

    (i) the land required for, or proposed by the development;

    (ii) any land over which it is proposed to exercise powers of compulsory acquisition or any right to use land (where applicable);

    (iii) any land over which it is proposed to extinguish easements, servitude and other private rights; and

    (iv) where the land includes special category land and replacement land, that land.

(j) A works plan showing, in relation to existing features:

    (i) the proposed location or (for a linear scheme) the proposed route and alignment of the development and works; and

    (ii) the limits within which the development and works may be carried out and any limits of deviation provided for in the draft order.

(k) A plan identifying any new or altered means of access, stopping up of streets or roads or any diversions, extinguishments or creation of rights of way or public rights of navigation (where applicable).

(l) A plan with accompanying information identifying (where applicable):

(i) any statutory or non-statutory sites or features of nature conservation such as sites of geological or landscape importance;

(ii) habitats of protected species, important habitats or other diversity features; and

(iii) water bodies in a river basin management plan,

together with an assessment of any effects on such sites, features, habitats or bodies likely to be caused by the proposed development.

(m) A plan (where applicable) with accompanying information identifying any statutory or non-statutory sites or features in the historic environment, including scheduled monuments, World Heritage sites, listed buildings and other historic structures, archaeological sites and registered battlefields, together with an assessment of any effects on such sites, features or structures likely to be caused by the proposed development.

(n) A plan with accompanying information identifying any Crown land (where applicable).

(o) Any other plans, drawings and sections necessary to describe the proposals for which development consent is sought, showing details of design, external appearance, and the preferred layout of buildings or structures, drainage, surface water management, means of vehicular and pedestrian access, any car parking to be provided, and means of landscaping.

(p) Any of the documents prescribed by reg 6 (Matters prescribed in relation to applications for specific types of projects) which are relevant to the particular project.

(q) Any other documents considered necessary to support the application.

(r) If requested by the Secretary of State, three paper copies of the application form and supporting documents and plans.

Regulation 5(3) provides that any plans, drawings or sections required to be provided must be no larger than A0 in size, must be drawn to an identified scale (not smaller than 1:2,500) and, in the case of plans, must show north. Where a plan comprises three or more separate sheets, a key plan must also be provided, showing the relationship between the different sheets (reg 5(4)).

Order and format of application documents

PINS Advice Note 6 (version 10) deals with the order and format of documents submitted with the application.

The order in which the documents should be organised is set out at Table 1 to PINS Advice Note 6 (version 10). For more detailed guidance, regard should be had to that Table but, in summary, the order of the documents should be as follows:

- Application form.
- Plans/drawings/sections.
- Draft development consent order.
- Compulsory acquisition information.
- Reports/statements.

- Environmental impact assessment and habitat regulations information.
- Photographs.
- Other media.
- Additional information for specific types of infrastructure.
- Other documents.

Appendix 1 to the Advice Note sets out guidance on preparing a technical index to accompany an NSIP application and Appendix 2 comprises an Excel Spreadsheet 'Electronic Application Index'.

PINS Advice Note 6 (version 10) also makes clear that the structure advocated should be applied to both electronic and printed copy versions of the application.

Summaries

Each document submitted to PINS should include a summary of the key issues contained within the document, which should be no longer than 1,500 words, or 10% of the original document size. Summaries should clearly and accurately highlight the main points and direct the reader to the evidence on which they are based.

References

Each document and plan submitted with the application should be referenced with the following:

- The Proposed Development name;
- A document or plan title;
- A unique document or plan reference number;
- The appropriate reg 5(2) paragraph number to which the document relates;
- The date of production of the document or plan; and
- A chronological note of any revisions made to the document or plan, including the revised document or plan.

Pagination, paragraph numbers and font

PINS also sets out the following guidance in paragraph 8.1 of Advice Note 6 (version 10):

> - 'Each application document must be paginated and paragraphs, tables and figures must be numbered. The paragraphs within appendices should also be numbered.
> - Hard copy textual documents should, as far as possible, be printed on both sides of each page.
> - Electronic application documents should have a maximum file size of 50MB each and wherever possible should be in PDF format.
> - Each document should contain a table of contents setting out the chapter or topic headings, unless it comprises a short statement of no more than two A4 sized pages.

- Where the document comprises a plan or plans, these must be clearly labelled in the bottom right hand corner with 'title page' information. A list of revisions should be produced so at any stage it is easy to identify the latest version of the plan or document.
- A glossary should be included for each written document in order to provide clarification of meaning for all readers (including the general public).
- The main body of text in reports should have a minimum font size of 12pt using a clear font such as Arial or Verdana (for further information refer to Royal National Institute for the Blind's clear print design guidelines).
- Any references made to relevant documents (eg a National Policy Statement, development plan or other document which are to be relied on) should be made to the specific passage, policy or relevant part of the document. Imprecise referencing with links to entire documents are usually unhelpful, and the need for clarification may cause delays in the process.
- Video or audio information should not be submitted except by prior agreement with the Inspectorate as it will not be certain that all interested parties involved will have the appropriate equipment to view the information.
- Application documents **must not include hyperlinks** to documents/evidence outside of the application documents eg technical reports or guidance hosted on an applicant's or third party's website. The Examining Authority, Interested Parties and the Secretary of State cannot rely on documents/evidence that the Inspectorate cannot directly control in respect of availability and content (including from a UK GDPR perspective). Applicant's should endeavour to establish processes that completely avoid the use of hyperlinks when preparing application documents for submission. Any hyperlinks of this type will be redacted from application documents by the Inspectorate prior to publication.'

Photographs

Any photographs should be correctly labelled, annotated and dated. The location at which photographs have been taken should be identified on a map/plan. Specifications of the camera and type of lens used must also be provided.

Paragraph 7.2 of PINS Advice Note 6 (version 10) advises that, 'Applications should not include photographs that could be used to identify a person who has not consented to their image being published. Such images will not be considered as part of an application and will be returned to the Applicant'.

The scale of plans and drawings

Any plans, drawings or cross-sections provided in the application should be consistent with the requirements set out in the Infrastructure Planning (Applications: Prescribed Forms and Procedure) Regulations 2009 – that is, no larger than A0 size, showing the direction of North and, for onshore developments, drawn to an identified scale no smaller than 1:2,500. Greater flexibility is, however, provided for the scale of plans for offshore developments to avoid pages of maps showing empty sea.

PINS Advice Note 6 (version 10) also states (para 12.2) that:

> 'Applicants are encouraged to discuss plan scaling with the Planning Inspectorate in advance of the submission of the application. The scale used for each plan, drawing or section should ensure that each clearly and accurately depicts the Proposed Development. Equally, electronic application documents should be provided with suitable resolution in this regard. A scale bar should also be included on each plan in order to prevent any ambiguity when dimensions or distances are measured on any copies of the plans, or electronically. Applicants should notate key dimensions and measurements on each plan, drawing or section (eg showing proposed distances from a proposed building to the boundary of the site or the heights of key buildings within a scheme).'

The Advice Note (para 12.3) does recognise, however, that, 'Linear schemes may require a sequence of drawings to depict the full extent of the Proposed Development. Where sequenced drawings/ sections are provided a key plan and sequence/section notation should also be provided'.

Appendices

PINS Advice Note 6 (version 10) acknowledges (section 13) that appendices are useful for setting out factual, technical and other material upon which the main body of information is based in an ordered and readily identifiable form.

Appendices must be referenced and indexed and divided by section dividers. The relevance of the appendices must be clearly explained in the document to which they relate.

Fees

At the time when the application is made, the applicant must pay the correct fee to PINS. The fee is currently £6,750; see the Infrastructure Planning (Fees) Regulations 2010, reg 5 (as amended).

Checklist

Appendix 3 to PINS Advice Note 6 (version 10) contains a 'Section 55 Acceptance of Applications Checklist' to assist decision-makers in determining whether or not to accept an application for examination.

It may be useful for applicants to refer to the checklist in preparing their applications for submission, to ensure that all requirements have been satisfied. Indeed, many applicants submit a copy of the completed checklist with their application.

This checklist is also a useful tool for applicants, as it forces them to review whether procedural requirements that will be considered in determining whether to accept an application have been correctly completed.

Assistance from the Planning Inspectorate

As noted earlier in this article, PINS Advice Note 6 (version 10) strongly encourages applicants (para 1.3) 'to hold pre-application discussions with the Planning Inspectorate about how their application information should be prepared and submitted well in advance of formal submission. The Planning Inspectorate's pre-application service for Applicants "Prospectus for Applicants" is available on the National Infrastructure Planning website Prospectus for Applicants page'.

Article 37

Prescribed Matters for Certain Types of Project

Rebecca Clutten, ftb
Michael Humphries QC, ftb

All applications for development consent must satisfy the requirements of PA 2008, s 37 and reg 5 of the Infrastructure Planning (Applications: Prescribed Forms and Procedure) Regulations 2009 ('the APFP Regulations').

For some projects, however, reg 6 of the APFP Regulations requires the production of additional, technology-specific documents. This article identifies those requirements and, where appropriate, gives or identifies guidance in respect of their production.

Technologies with additional prescribed matters

As set out above, reg 6 of the APFP Regulations identifies certain types of project in respect of which additional information is prescribed. The technologies subject to additional prescribed matters are as follows:

(a) onshore and offshore generating stations;

(b) highway-related development;

(c) construction or alteration of a railway;

(d) construction or alteration of harbour facilities;

(e) construction of a pipeline;

(f) construction of a hazardous waste facility; and

(g) construction of a dam or reservoir.

The requirements relating to each project type are set out in turn below.

Onshore generating stations

Regulation 6(1)(a)(i) of the APFP Regulations requires that an application for an onshore generating station (other than a gas fuelled generating station) be accompanied by a statement setting out who will be responsible for designing and building the connection to the electricity grid.

In the case of gas fuelled generating stations, the requirement set by reg 6(1)(a)(ii) is for a statement setting out who will be responsible for designing and building the gas pipeline connection to the proposed station.

This information is typically provided in a document entitled 'Grid Connection Statement' or 'Gas Connection Statement', as the case may be. Examples can be found on the Planning Inspectorate's website in the documentation accompanying previously consented generating facilities.

Offshore generating stations

Where an application is for an offshore generating station, reg 6(1)(b) requires that the applicant provide: (i) details of the proposed route and method of installation for any cable; and (ii) a statement as to whether applications will be made for safety zones. (Safety zones are exclusion zones around offshore generating structures, designed to ensure the safety of those coming into proximity to them, both in the construction and operation phases of a project.)

This information is typically provided in two discrete documents, often called the 'Safety Zone Statement' and the 'Grid Connection and Cable Statement', respectively. Examples can be found on the Planning Inspectorate's website in the documentation accompanying previously consented offshore windfarms.

Highway-related development or the construction or alteration of a railway

Regulation 6(2) requires that applications for highway-related development or the construction or alteration of a railway must be accompanied by section drawings 'accompanied by suitable horizontal and vertical scales, [and] which show, by reference to Ordnance Survey or Chart datum' the following:

'(a) the levels of proposed works, including in particular *and where relevant*:

  (i) ground levels;

  (ii) the height of every proposed bridge, viaduct, aqueduct, embankment and elevated guideway;

  (iii) the depth of every proposed cutting and tunnel;

  (iv) the levels of the bed of any tidal waters or inland waterway in which it is proposed that any works should be situated;

  (v) the height of every structure or device (including a cable, but not catenary and related equipment) intended to be erected above, on or below the surface of, or on or beneath the bed of tidal waters or an inland waterway; and

  (vi) drainage outfall details for highways;

(b) a cross section of every intended tunnel and any altered gradient of a carriageway or a way forming part of a guided transport system on either side of every level crossing, bridge, tunnel or underpass which would carry the carriageway or way or through which it would pass.' (emphasis added)

Construction or alteration of harbour facilities

By virtue of reg 6(3), applications for the construction or alteration of harbour facilities must be accompanied by a statement setting out why the making of the development consent order is desirable, in one of two respects:

(a) in the interests of securing the improvement, maintenance or management of the harbour in an efficient and economical manner; or

(b) facilitating the efficient and economic transport of goods or passengers by sea or in the interests of the recreational use of sea-going ships.

Although the two interests are described disjunctively, making clear that it is not necessary for an application to promote both, if a project is in fact desirable in both respects, then there is no reason why an applicant should not set out in the statement how both interests are served by its proposal.

In harbour facility applications the prescribed information can acceptably be included within the Planning Statement: see, for example, the York Potash Harbour Facility application.

Construction of a pipeline

Regulation 6(4) requires that applications for the construction of a pipeline are accompanied by details of the following:

(a) the name of the proposed pipeline;

(b) the owner of the proposed pipeline;

(c) the start and end point of the proposed pipeline;

(d) the length of the proposed pipeline in kilometres;

(e) the external diameter in millimetres of the proposed pipeline;

(f) what will be conveyed by the proposed pipeline; and

(g) whether the grant of any rights in land or consents to road or river crossing works are required and if so whether they can be obtained by agreement.

It is suggested that each of these matters (with the possible exception of (a) and (b)) would necessarily be covered by any description of the project that was fit for purpose. However, in the applications made to date, this information has typically been provided in a separate 'Regulation 6' or 'Additional Information' document.

Construction of a hazardous waste facility

Pursuant to reg 6(5), applications for the construction or alteration of a hazardous waste facility must be accompanied by a statement detailing the proposed purpose of the facility and an estimate of the annual capacity of the plant for the final disposal or recovery of hazardous waste.

As in the case of the matters prescribed in respect of pipeline applications, it is suggested that these matters would necessarily be covered by any description of the project that was fit for purpose.

Construction of a dam or reservoir

By virtue of reg 6(6), applications for the construction of a dam or reservoir must be accompanied by a statement setting out what, if any, recreational amenities will be made available.

Inclusion of the prescribed information within the application form

Where reg 6 applies, the DCLG Guidance on application forms states, at paragraph 40, that a brief description of the information being submitted should be stated within Box 22 of the development consent application form, with any more detailed information being set out in an accompanying document, appropriately referenced.

Paragraph 40 further explains that, where this information is contained within other documents already cited on the application form, then those documents should be identified in Box 22, rather than duplicating the information within additional documents.

The PINS Advice Note 6 (version 10) also includes, at Table 1 (following para 20), details of the suggested order in which documentation is submitted with an application. That Table indicates that documentation required pursuant to reg 6 should follow after the Environmental Statement, any photographs and other media. This recommendation assumes, however, that the prescribed information is not already included within any other category of document, in which case the advice against duplication ought to be followed.

National Policy Statements

In addition to the legislative requirements placed on applicants by PA 2008, s 37 and regs 5 and 6 of the APFP Regulations, it should be recalled that the National Policy Statements (NPSs) also specify further information that the Secretary of State will expect to see included within their applications. Although the requirements contained in NPSs are not 'prescribed' and, as such, are beyond the scope of this article, applicants should be aware that the DCLG Guidance on application forms makes clear, at paragraph 4, that a failure to include this information *may* lead to the Secretary of State refusing to accept an application.

Part 8

Contents of a Development Consent Order

Article 38

Defining the Nationally Significant Infrastructure Project

Alex Booth QC, ftb
Michael Humphries QC, ftb

Introduction

There is no single, over-arching definition of a 'nationally significant infrastructure project' ('NSIP') contained in the PA 2008. The closest that the legislation comes to providing such definition is at PA 2008, s 14, of which subsection (1) provides a list of (now) 18 'types of project' that may potentially comprise an NSIP.

The spectrum of development identified in PA 2008, s 14(1) is diverse. It ranges from highways and harbours to reservoirs and railway infrastructure. However, when seeking to understand the scope of development that may currently be classified as an NSIP, one can at least note that the various forms of development all fall within one of five 'fields'; namely energy, transport, water, waste water and waste. Thus, each of the 18 'types of project' falls within one of the five 'fields'.

The purpose of this article is to look firstly at what types of project are capable of amounting to an NSIP, before turning to consider the precise extent of development that is capable of being so regarded.

Types of project

PA 2008, s 14 (as amended) identifies the following 'types of project' as being nationally significant infrastructure projects, subject to the 'thresholds' identified in PA 2008, ss 15–30A:

- Energy
  - Generating stations (PA 2008, s 15)
  - Electric lines (PA 2008, s 16)
  - Underground gas storage facilities (PA 2008, s 17)
  - LNG facilities (PA 2008, s 18)
  - Gas reception facilities (PA 2008, s 19)
  - Gas transporter pipelines (PA 2008, s 20)
  - Other pipelines (PA 2008, s 21)
- Transport
  - Highways (PA 2008, s 22)
  - Airports (PA 2008, s 23)
  - Harbour facilities (PA 2008, s 24)

  - Railways (PA 2008, s 25)
  - Rail freight interchanges (PA 2008, s 26)
- Water
  - Dams and reservoirs (PA 2008, s 27)
  - Transfer of water resources (PA 2008, s 28)
  - Desalination plants (PA 2008, s 28A)
- Waste Water
  - Waste water treatment plants (PA 2008, s 29)
  - Infrastructure for the transfer or storage of waste water (PA 2008, s 29)
- Waste
  - Hazardous waste facilities (PA 2008, s 30)
  - Radioactive waste geological disposal facilities (PA 2008, s 30A).

These thresholds determine the scale of development that is deemed to be nationally significant and, therefore, within the ambit of the PA 2008. Thus the pre-existing consenting regimes still apply to projects below the relevant thresholds.

Most of the above provisions came into force on 1 March 2010, but some have later commencement dates and, indeed, some parts of certain sections are still not yet in force.

Statutory power to include/exclude development

It is important to note that, whilst the list provided at PA 2008, s 14(1) is expressed in exhaustive terms, the PA 2008 confers on the Secretary of State an express power both to add new types of development to that list and to remove existing ones from it (see PA 2008, s 14(3)). However, the power of the Secretary of State to amend the types of project that may be an NSIP is not without restriction. Only development connected with the five 'fields' of infrastructure project already identified (ie energy, transport, water, waste water and waste) may be added (PA 2008, s 14(5)(a) and (6)); furthermore the development must be one to be carried out entirely in England, its territorial waters, or a Renewable Energy Zone (except one where the Scottish Ministers have functions) (PA 2008, s 14(5)(b) and (7)). There is no corresponding power to add a new type of NSIP in Wales.

So far the PA 2008, s 14(3) power has only been exercised once; that being is relation to waste water infrastructure. The Infrastructure Planning (Waste Water Transfer and Storage) Order 2012 amended PA 2008, s 14 to create a new type of NSIP consisting of 'infrastructure for the transfer or storage of waste water' (amendment to PA 2008, s 14(1)(o)). The Order also created a 'threshold' for this new type of project by amending PA 2008, s 29 and made a 'supplementary provision' relating to compliance with pre-application requirements under the Act and certain Regulations.

Thresholds

When a particular development is of a type identified in PA 2008, s 14, the issue as to whether such development comprises an NSIP for the purposes of the PA 2008 turns on the application of the 'threshold criteria' set out in PA 2008, ss 15–30A. These criteria are, therefore, of critical importance in determining whether development requires development consent pursuant to the PA 2008 or is to be authorised under some other consenting regime.

The individual thresholds for particular types of project are considered in articles 15 to 23 of this work. What follows are some general points on the approach to thresholds.

Development forming part of an NSIP

The PA 2008 is designed to prevent a developer from artificially defining a project so as to fall below a relevant threshold; thereby avoiding the need to obtain development consent. PA 2008, s 31 states that 'Consent under this Act ('development consent') is required for development to the extent that the development is *or forms part of* a nationally significant infrastructure project' (emphasis added). As discussed above, whether a project is a nationally significant infrastructure project will depend both on the type of project and its relevant threshold. Clearly the words 'or forms part of' are intended to deal with the situation where a developer proposes to bring a project forward in phases with each phase falling below the relevant threshold, but the whole project falling above the relevant threshold. In such circumstances development consent would be required for each phase, as each would form 'part of' an NSIP.

This does raise the issue of what is meant by a 'project' in PA 2008, s 14. Whilst the term is familiar from European environmental law, it is not defined as such within the PA 2008. Much, however, hangs on the proper definition of the term. Clearly it might be possible to bring a development within the PA 2008 regime by claiming that it was an early phase of a much larger project or, alternatively, remove it from the regime by claiming that each phase was an entirely independent project.

The pragmatic solution to this issue may simply be that in most cases the thresholds are so low that nearly all developments within a particular type will be classed as nationally significant and there will be little opportunity for a coherent development below the threshold to be brought forward.

Identity of the applicant

For most types of project the relevant threshold is defined by reference to the scale or capacity of the proposed development. For some, however, it is the identity of the infrastructure provider that it critical. For example, PA 2008, s 20 makes the construction of a pipeline an NSIP, subject to certain thresholds, where is it is to be constructed by a 'gas transporter'. That term is defined by PA 2008, s 235 as having the same meaning as in Part 1 of the Gas Act 1986. A pipeline to be constructed other than by a gas transporter, however, is a different type of project and subject to different thresholds under PA 2008, s 21. This distinction would have implications for other provisions within the Act, such as PA 2008, s 156(3).

It is also worth noting that, whilst PA 2008, s 22(2)(a) relates to a highway for which the Secretary of State will be highway authority, the applicant for such a highway project may be someone other than the Secretary of State. Clearly, however, such a project could only be promoted with the consent of the Secretary of State. Where the applicant is a highway authority, PINS is likely to want to see an agreement under Highways Act 1980, s 6 (delegation of functions in relation to trunk roads).

The activity constituting the development

Each of the thresholds also has a term or terms describing the 'activity' that constitutes the development requiring development consent. In many cases this is simply 'construction or extension' – as in 'construction or extension of a generating station' (PA 2008, s 15) – but in other cases alternative terms are used, such as 'improvement', 'alteration' or 'installation'. These terms often reflect the language of the predecessor consenting regime, which will still apply to development below the relevant threshold. Thus PA 2008, s 16 relates to the 'installation' of an electric line above ground; reflecting the language of Electricity Act 1989, s 37.

As underground gas storage may take place in a depleted natural gas field, which is not constructed but is naturally occurring, PA 2008, s 17 makes it clear that the development would be 'starting to use' such a facility (PA 2008, s 17(2)(b)).

In each case it will be important to understand the relevant language and, where there is a choice of 'activity' – for example, the 'construction', 'improvement' or 'alteration' of a highway under PA 2008, s 22 – it will be important for the DCO and its supporting documents to be clear on what 'activity' and, therefore, what threshold applies.

Construction or alteration

In most instances it will be clear whether development is the 'construction' or 'alteration' of a project. However, there may be circumstances where the distinction is not so clear. At what point does the 'alteration' of (say) a gas reception facility under PA 2008, s 19 become so extensive that it is really the 'construction' of a new gas reception facility? Such questions will usually be a matter of fact and degree, but the issue may be an important one.

Taking the above example of a gas reception facility – 'construction' has a threshold of a maximum flow rate of 4.5 million standard cubic metres (mscm) per day, whereas 'alteration' has a threshold of an 'increase' of 4.5 mscm per day. Thus if a gas reception facility with an existing capacity of 3 mscm per day is completely rebuilt in phases with an ultimate capacity of 6 mscm per day, is such development an NSIP or not? The answer may be that, if the gas reception facility continued to operate at full capacity throughout the rebuilding, that is an alteration; but, if it closed down and was rebuilt, that is the construction of a new facility.

Capacity and throughput

PA 2008, s 23 defines the thresholds for airport-related development in terms of the 'construction' or 'alteration' that is 'expected' to be 'capable of providing services' that exceed certain levels of passenger or air transport movement thresholds; for example, an increase of 10 million passengers per year or 10,000 cargo air transport movements per year.

The issue of what is meant by 'expected' to be 'capable' of exceeding a certain threshold came into sharp relief in the context of a 2018 planning application by Stansted Airport to develop new taxiway links and aircraft stands that would increase the use and potential of the airport's single runway. It also applied to raise the planning cap on passenger throughput from 35 million to 43 million passengers per annum. An objector group (Stop Stansted Expansion) asked the Secretary of State to deem the project an NSIP on the basis that its throughput was 'capable' of exceeding the thresholds in PA 2008, s 23(5). When the Secretary of State declined, a member of the group brought a challenge by way of judicial review.

In *R (Ross) v Secretary of State for Transport* [2020] EWHC 226 (Admin), Dove J held (at [101]) that:

> 'The language of the statute in relation to whether the alteration will "increase by at least 10 million per year the number of passengers for whom the airport is capable of

providing air passenger transport services" requires the Defendant to form a judgment in relation to that question. In my view that judgment is to be formed by asking what increase in capacity could realistically be achieved, not what might technically or arithmetically be possible. It requires an analysis based on how the infrastructure is likely to perform, not a hypothetical approach assuming speculative figures in relation to each aspect of the calculation of capacity to show what might be possible rather than what is likely to occur in practice. I do not consider that the use of the wording "is capable" endorses the Claimants' contentions: it is important that these words are to be read in the context of the language of *section 23(4)* which speaks of the alteration being "expected to have the effect specified in subsection (5)". The use of the word "expected" is an important qualification which imports the requirement for an assessment which is grounded in the reality of the capacity which might be achieved, rather than one which takes a speculative arithmetical approach to all of the inputs to the calculation.'

The application for judicial review was, therefore, dismissed. In the event, the planning application was then refused by the local planning authority and the matter went to a planning appeal in 2021.

Extent of an NSIP

Whilst it may often prove straightforward to determine that certain parts of a development comprise an NSIP, or part of an NSIP, this will not always be the case. Specifically, it may be less than obvious whether development comprises part of the NSIP, or is simply 'associated development' within the meaning of PA 2008, s 115.

The PA 2008 draws a clear distinction between an NSIP for which development consent is required, and 'associated development' that may be included in a development consent order but does not have to be. PA 2008, s 115 recognises that these two elements of development are distinct, one from the another, whilst at the same time making clear that a development consent order may be granted in respect of both.

Articles 39 and 40 of this work deal with 'associated development' and 'associated development in Wales', but the issue of what is the NSIP and what is associated development is particularly pressing in Wales, where the types of 'associated development' that may be included in a DCO are more limited than in England (see PA 2008, s 115(4) and (4A)).

In England a number of confirmed DCOs do not draw a distinction between those parts of the project that are NSIP and those parts that are not, but others do. There does not appear to be any legal requirement to specify what part of a proposed development is NSIP and what part is not, so long as it is clear that at least some part of the proposed development is an NSIP or part of an NSIP (in other words, as long as it is clear that the proposed development does properly fall within the PA 2008 regime). There may be perfectly valid reasons for not wanting to specify what is NSIP and what is associated development, although as a matter of policy PINS does encourage applicants to make the distinction clear in Schedule 1 to any draft DCO.

Article 39

Associated Development in England

Alex Booth QC, ftb
Michael Humphries QC, ftb

Introduction

A development consent order may be granted not only in respect of development for which development consent is required (PA 2008, s 115(1)(a)) – that is, development which is or forms part of a nationally significant infrastructure project ('NSIP') as defined in PA 2008, ss 14–30 – but also in respect of certain other development known as 'associated development' ('AD') (PA 2008, s 115(1)(b)).

As to what comprises AD, PA 2008 itself provides only limited guidance. The term is defined as referring to development which is 'associated' with an NSIP (PA 2008, s 115(2)(a)), but which does not comprise construction/extension of one or more dwellings (PA 2008, s 115(2)(b)). In *R (Innovia Cellophane Ltd) v Infrastructure Planning Commission* [2011] EWHC 2883 (Admin), the High Court made clear that this exclusion of dwellings did not extend to temporary accommodation for workers.

Associated development can include development in England and in waters adjacent to England (PA 2008, s 115(3)). It can also include development in the field of energy in a Renewable Energy Zone, but not part of any Renewable Energy Zone in relation to which the Scottish Ministers have functions (PA 2008, s 115(3)). Associated development may not include development in Scotland or waters adjacent to Scotland. In Wales, an application for development consent may not include AD, save in respect of surface works, boreholes and pipes associated with underground gas storage by a gas transporter in natural porous strata (PA 2008, s 115(4)).

The remainder of this article is concerned with associated in England and waters adjacent to England; the position in Wales is the subject of article 40 of this work.

DCLG Guidance on associated development

In the DCLG Guidance on associated development (2013) the Secretary of State will decide on a case-by-case basis whether development is 'associated development'. The Secretary of State does, however, set out (paragraph 5) certain 'core principles' that will be applied in making any such decision:

- The definition of associated development (in PA 2008, s 115) *requires a direct relationship* between associated development and the principal development. Associated development should therefore either support the construction or operation of the principal development, or help address its impacts.
- Associated development *should not be an aim in itself* but should be subordinate to the principal development.
- Development *should not be treated as associated development* if it is *only necessary as a source of additional revenue* for the applicant, in order to cross-subsidise the cost of the principal

development. This does not mean that the applicant cannot cross-subsidise, but if part of a proposal is only necessary as a means of cross-subsidising the principal development then that part should not be treated as associated development.

- Associated development *should be proportionate to the nature and scale of the principal development.* However, this core principle should not be read as excluding associated infrastructure development (such as a network connection) that is on a larger scale than is necessary to serve the principal development if that associated infrastructure provides capacity that is likely to be required for another proposed major infrastructure project. When deciding whether it is appropriate for infrastructure which is on a larger scale than is necessary to serve a project to be treated as associated development, each application will have to be assessed on its own merits. For example, the Secretary of State will have regard to all relevant matters including whether a future application is proposed to be made by the same or related developer as the current application, the degree of physical proximity of the proposed application to the current application, and the time period in which a future application is proposed to be submitted.

This last point about development being associated with a future application is interesting and is further elaborated in footnote 3 in the DCLG Guidance as follows:

> '… in the case of an application for an offshore generating station, the Secretary of State may consider it appropriate for a degree of overcapacity to be provided in respect of the associated transmission infrastructure, so that the impacts of one or more other planned future projects which could make use of that infrastructure would be reduced by taking advantage of it. Applications that include elements designed for the basis of overcapacity would be expected to demonstrate the need for the overcapacity as well as fully assessing the environmental effects.'

Thus the four core principles in paragraph 5 of the DCLG Guidance are:

- there must be a 'direct' relationship between the NSIP and the AD;
- the AD should not be an aim in itself;
- the AD should not be included only to cross-subsidise the NSIP; and
- the AD should be 'proportionate' to the 'nature and scale' of the NSIP.

Some issues

What is beginning to emerge, however, is that there may not always be a clear line between that development which properly forms part of the NSIP itself and that which is AD. For example, are the internal roads within a proposed generating station site part of the NSIP or simply AD? This might not matter in England, where any AD can be included in an application for development consent, but it matters greatly in Wales, where such AD would have to be applied for by planning application. Indeed, even in England the distinction may matter as the Planning Inspectorate has started to request applicants to make clear in their DCO schedules what parts of the 'authorised development' are NSIP and what parts are AD. In this regard it is interesting to note that, whilst some approved DCOs have made this distinction, others have not. Whilst there does not appear to be any legal authority for the Planning Inspectorate's position on this point, it does appear to be developing as a policy position.

It is apparent, therefore, that some tension may exist between what is part of the NSIP and what is AD. Indeed, that tension may pull in different directions in England and in Wales. In

England, there may be a tendency to restrict the scope of the NSIP and enlarge that of AD. That would allow a developer to amend or supplement the AD by subsequent applications for planning permission; an avenue not available to development that is or forms part of an NSIP: see PA 2008, s 31. In Wales, by contrast, where AD is only available in the very limited circumstances of certain underground gas storage projects, there may be a tendency to widen the definition of the NSIP to include as much development as possible. Such a result is undoubtedly an unintended consequence of the Welsh devolution settlement, but is unwelcome nevertheless.

The DCLG Guidance on associated development (2013) does encourage applicants to include AD in a single application for development consent under the PA 2008, rather than applying for it via other routes (paragraph 8). That has clear merit in allowing the Examining Authority and Secretary of State to determine an application for the entire project and all its environmental effects; although such a solution is not, for the most part, available in Wales.

Examples of associated development

The DCLG Guidance on associated development (2013) sets out various examples of associated development, being (a) examples of general types of associated development (Annex A), and (b) examples of associated development specific to individual types of major infrastructure projects (Annex B).

However, the guidance identifies three important caveats to the examples provided, being:

- the annexes are not intended to be exhaustive;
- the annexes should not be read as a statement that the development in them should be treated as associated development as a matter of course: 'these lists should be read together with the core principles'; and
- the annexes should not be treated as an indication that the development in them is not an NSIP or an integral part of an NSIP for which development consent is required.

The annexes are, however, a useful starting point from which the core principles can be applied on a case-by-case basis as suggested by the Secretary of State.

Article 40

Associated Development in Wales

Alex Booth QC, ftb
Michael Humphries QC, ftb

Introduction

As compared to the situation in England, the position regarding what may lawfully comprise 'associated development' ('AD') in Wales is significantly more restricted.

As is the case with England, the statutory definition of development in Wales for which a development consent order may be granted is set out in PA 2008, s 115. However, the detail as to what can be considered AD in the two jurisdictions is governed by two different sub-sections: the relevant provisions for England being a combination of sub-ss (2)(c) and (3), with those for Wales being sub-ss (2)(c), (4) and (4A). PA 2008, s 115(4A) was introduced by the Wales Act 2017.

This article should, therefore, be read together with the more general article 39 of this work on 'associated development' in England.

The limits on 'associated development' in Wales

The PA 2008, s 115(4) criteria for including 'associated development' in an application for development consent in Wales are:

- the AD must be 'carried out wholly in Wales' (PA 2008, s 115(4)(a));
- the AD must be 'the carrying out or construction of surface work, boreholes or pipes' (PA 2008, s 115(4)(b));
- the NSIP with which the AD is associated must be development within PA 2008, s 17(3), that is, 'facilities for the storage of gas underground in natural porous strata' (PA 2008, s 115(4)(c)). [NB An application for development consent for an NSIP comprising the storage of gas underground in *cavities* (see PA 2008, s 17(6)) would not be able to include AD in Wales.] Furthermore the gas storage facility would still have to comply with the threshold in PA 2008, s 17(4); and
- once these criteria are met, the AD must comply with the normal rules as to what constitutes 'associated development'.

The PA 2008, s 115(4A)(a) criteria for including 'associated development' in an application for development consent in Wales are:

- the NSIP with which the AD is associated must be the construction or extension of a generating station (PA 2008, s 115(4A)(a)) that is expected to be within PA 2008, s 15(3A) or (3B);
- locationally, that generating station must be 'in Wales' (PA 2008, s 15(3A)) or 'in waters adjacent to Wales up to the seaward limits of the territorial sea or in the Welsh zone' (PA 2008, s 15(3B));

- if 'in Wales', the generating station must not generate electricity from wind and have a capacity of more than 350MW;
- if 'in waters adjacent to Wales', the generating station must have a capacity of more than 350MW;
- once these criteria are met, the AD must comply with the normal rules as to what constitutes 'associated development'.

The PA 2008, s 115(4A)(b) criteria for including 'associated development' in an application for development consent in Wales are:

- the NSIP with which the AD is associated must be the installation of an electric line that is or (when installed) is expected to be within PA 2008, s 14(1)(b); that is, an electric line above ground subject to the thresholds etc in PA 2008, s 16;
- once this criterion is met, the AD must comply with the normal rules as to what constitutes 'associated development'.

DCLG Guidance on associated development

In the DCLG Guidance on associated development (2013) the Secretary of State will decide on a case-by-case basis whether development is 'associated development'. The Secretary of State does, however, set out (paragraph 5) certain 'core principles' that will be applied in making any such decision.

Those core principles are discussed in some detail in article 39 of this work on associated development in England, but in broad terms they can be summarised as follows:

- there must be a 'direct' relationship between the NSIP and the AD;
- the AD should not be an aim in itself;
- the AD should not be included only to cross-subsidise the NSIP; and
- the AD should be 'proportionate' to the 'nature and scale' of the NSIP.

The DCLG Guidance on associated development (2013) also sets out various examples of associated development, being (a) examples of general types of associated development (Annex A), and (b) examples of associated development specific to individual types of major infrastructure projects (Annex B).

Some examples

A number of Welsh projects have had to grapple with the issue of what may be included as 'associated development' in Wales. Particular examples include:

- Brechfa Forest West DCO 2013; and
- Swansea Bay Tidal Lagoon DCO 2015.

Article 41

Cable Ducts for Future Projects

Hereward Phillpot QC, ftb
Michael Humphries QC, ftb

Introduction

This article concerns a specific issue that has arisen in relation to energy infrastructure projects, but has potential implications for other nationally significant infrastructure projects (NSIPs) because it concerns the approach to the question of what is 'associated development' (AD) under PA 2008, s 115.

The specific issue arises in circumstances where it is likely that future NSIP projects will need to lay electricity transmission cables along the same route proposed to be used for such cabling as part of an application for a development consent order (DCO). There are obvious practical advantages of installing the ducting for all of the cabling (that needed now, and that needed in the future) at the same time. As and when the future projects come to be implemented, all that would then be needed is the relatively quick and straightforward operation of pulling the cables through the ducts. Such an approach presents significant advantages both to the developer and those who might be affected by the works.

For the developer there is a saving in time and money, with one set of works to install the ducts rather than repeated works, and no need to either negotiate several sets of agreements or seek multiple orders for powers of compulsory acquisition. The process of implementing the future projects will also be quicker and easier.

Those who are affected by the works (particularly those who own or occupy the relevant land) are not subject to repeated disturbance by the developer's contractors, and productive use of the land can therefore be resumed and continued uninterrupted once the initial works are complete. The environmental effects arising from the more substantial engineering works involved in installing the ducts (traffic, noise, dust etc) only occur once, rather than repeatedly over a number of years.

In practical terms, it is therefore eminently desirable.

The issue is whether it is lawful and appropriate to include such works (and the powers of compulsory acquisition needed to implement them) in a DCO.

The legal issue

In order for such works to be included in a DCO, it must be shown that they are AD, and thus fall within PA 2008, s 115.

AD is defined by PA 2008, s 115(2) as development which is associated with the principal development (ie the NSIP for which development consent is required). In the case of an application for a DCO, the principal development will be the NSIP for which development consent is being sought at that time (as opposed to any potential future NSIP). Thus the additional ducting can only lawfully be approved if it is found to be 'associated with' the NSIP which is the subject of the application.

Guidance

DCLG has published 'Guidance on associated development applications for major infrastructure projects' (April 2013) ('the DCLG Guidance on associated development').

Paragraph 5 of the DCLG Guidance on associated development states that it is for the Secretary of State to decide, on a case-by-case basis, whether or not development should be treated as AD, and that in making the decision he will take into account four 'core principles'. Of particular relevance here are the following:

- Core principle (i) is that there must be a 'direct relationship' between the AD and the NSIP, and the AD should 'either support the construction or operation of the principal development, or help address its impacts'.
- Core principle (iv) is that the AD should be proportionate to the nature and scale of the NSIP. However, it is made clear that '... this core principle should not be read as excluding associated infrastructure development (such as a network connection) that is on a larger scale than is necessary to serve the principal development if that associated infrastructure provides capacity that is likely to be required for another proposed major infrastructure project'.
  - A footnote gives the following example: '... in the case of an application for an offshore generating station, the Secretary of State may consider it appropriate for a degree of overcapacity to be provided in respect of the associated transmission infrastructure, so that the impacts of one or more other planned future projects which could make use of that infrastructure would be reduced by taking advantage of it. Applications that include elements designed for the basis of overcapacity would be expected to demonstrate the need for the overcapacity as well as fully assessing the environmental effects.'
  - It is said that in assessing whether overcapacity should be treated as AD, the Secretary of State will have regard to all relevant matters including whether a future application is proposed to be made by the same or related developer as the current application, the degree of physical proximity of the proposed application to the current application, and the time period in which a future application is proposed to be submitted.

Thus, the DCLG Guidance on associated development explicitly contemplates an application for a DCO including a degree of 'overcapacity' in the associated transmission infrastructure, but it does not make clear whether the provision of separate additional ducting would constitute 'overcapacity' or the legal basis for concluding that such development was 'associated with' the NSIP for which development consent was being sought. That was left to the decision-making process.

The East Anglia One decision

The first application to tackle this issue was the East Anglia One Offshore Windfarm (EA One), submitted in November 2012 and determined in June 2014. As the name suggests, this was the first in what was intended to be a series of four applications for Offshore Generating Stations (the other three being referred to as EA Two, EA Three and EA Four) in the North Sea off the coast of Suffolk. An application in relation to EA Three was subsequently submitted in November 2015.

The AD for which development consent was sought in 2012 included not only the onshore transmission infrastructure for the EA One Windfarm, but also the laying of cable ducts for EA Three and EA Four alongside the ducts and cables for EA One.

One of the main controversial issues in the examination was whether this additional ducting was properly to be regarded as AD, and whether powers of compulsory acquisition should be granted to allow that part of the development to be implemented. The controversy was not as a result of any significant local objection to this aspect of the development. On the contrary, it had been included within the application in large part as a response to views expressed by local residents and businesses, and the local authority. The high profile given to the issue was as a result of the Examining authority quite properly approaching the matter on an inquisitorial basis and wanting to be satisfied that this was both lawful and justified.

The legal argument successfully employed on behalf of the promoter was that the additional ducting was properly treated as being associated with the EA One NSIP because it would help to address its *cumulative* impacts. These impacts included those likely to occur as result of the future works that would be associated with the EA Three and EA Four projects.

Thus the Examining authority was able to conclude that the ducts could properly be regarded as AD, applying the first of the core principles from the DCLG Guidance on associated development set out above (see paragraph 4.16 of the Examining authority's report).

By reference to the concept of 'overcapacity' in the DCLG Guidance on associated development, it was concluded that there is '… no distinction, in principle, between providing extra cable capacity, and providing additional duct capacity' (paragraph 5.41 of the Examining authority's report).

In addition, the Examining authority was satisfied that the factors identified in the fourth core principle pointed towards a conclusion that the ducts were AD:

> 'The development consent applications for east Anglia Three and Four would either be submitted by the same or by a related developer. A high degree of physical proximity would exist between the schemes. The onshore cable ducts to accommodate East Anglia Three and Four would be laid along the same route as the onshore cables for East Anglia One to connect to their respective converter stations adjacent to the East Anglia One converter station at Bramford. It is anticipated that the applications for development consent for East Anglia Three and Four would be made within a reasonable timescale. In particular at the ISH [HE-31] it was made clear that studies were well-advanced for the future wind farms.' (paragraph 4.13 of the Examining authority's report)

Ultimately, the Examining authority endorsed the promoter's submission that '… this is a paradigm case of the type of overcapacity provision that properly qualifies as associated development' (paragraph 5.46 of the Examining authority's report).

A requirement was imposed to secure the simultaneous installation of the ducts and cables (save in specified circumstances), thus ensuring that the advantages relied upon to justify the inclusion of the additional ducting in the DCO would be realised in practice.

Those conclusions cleared the way for the authorisation of the necessary powers of compulsory acquisition to be granted on the basis that the additional ducting was therefore 'development to which the development consent relates' and therefore PA 2008, s 122(2)(a) was engaged (see paragraph 5.116 of the Examining authority's report).

The Secretary of State endorsed both the conclusions and the reasoning of the Examining authority on these points (see paragraphs 4.4 and 4.74 of the decision letter dated 17 June 2014).

Conclusion

Although the issue has not yet been tested before the courts, the carefully reasoned decision in the EA One case seems likely to provide a reliable precedent for other promoters. It was, however, properly described as a 'paradigm case' because its facts were so clearly aligned with the DCLG Guidance on associated development. There will, no doubt, be other cases where the facts are less clear cut, and where the limits of this approach will fall to be tested.

Article 42

DCO Model Provisions

Michael Humphries QC, ftb

Introduction

Regulation 5(2)(b) of the Infrastructure Planning (Applications: Prescribed Forms and Procedure) Regulations 2009, SI 2009/2264 ('the APFP Regulations') requires that an application for an order granting development consent must be accompanied by 'the draft proposed order'.

It needs to be stressed that the drafting of a 'draft proposed order' is a very technical legal exercise and, as PINS Advice Note 13 (version 3) makes clear (para 2.8), 'Developers are strongly urged to take appropriate legal advice at all stages in the preparation and examination of a draft DCO'.

This article will examine the role of 'model provisions' in the drafting of a 'draft proposed order'.

The status of model provisions

PA 2008, s 38(1) (as originally enacted) allowed the Secretary of State by order to prescribe 'model provisions' for incorporation in a draft order accompanying an application for an order granting development consent. Furthermore, PA 2008, s 38(2) required the then IPC to 'have regard' to any such prescribed model provisions, although it was made clear (PA 2008, s 38(3)) that it was not mandatory for provisions included in a draft order to be in the prescribed form.

The Secretary of State exercised the power under PA 2008, s 38 in prescribing the Infrastructure Planning (Model Provisions) (England and Wales) Order 2009, SI 2009/2265 ('the Model Provisions Order').

The Explanatory Memorandum to the Model Provisions Order states (paragraph 7.8) that the order was 'intended to assist the applicant in preparing the draft proposed order, and to enable common issues across all or most applications to be addressed in a consistent manner'. The Government had consulted on a draft version of the order in 2009 and in the Explanatory Memorandum reported (paragraph 8.11) that 'The predominant view of respondents was that the model provisions were helpful, and would assist applicants when they come to formulate an application to the IPC'.

Despite this seeming endorsement of the role of model provisions, the Localism Act 2011 repealed PA 2008, s 38 with effect from 1 April 2012. Paragraph 1.2.9 of 'Statutory Instrument Practice' (November 2006) published by the Office of Public Sector Information observes that 'If an enabling Act, or the enabling section of it, is repealed, instruments made under it will lapse unless they are saved, i.e. continued in effect'. The Model Provisions Order does not appear to have been 'saved' and so should formally be regarded as having lapsed.

Despite this, it remains clear that PINS still wishes to be informed of any departures from the model provisions. Current guidance in PINS Advice Note 13 (version 3) is as follows (paras 2.12–2.13):

> 'Model provisions were intended as a guide for developers in drafting orders, rather than a rigid structure, but aided consistency, and assisted developers to draft a comprehensive set of lawful provisions.
>
> There is no longer a requirement to submit a tracked changed version of the draft DCO which compares the wording against The Infrastructure Planning (Model Provisions) (England and Wales) Order 2009.'

This last text replaced that in PINS Advice Note 13 (version 2), which said that:

> 'In the absence of relevant guidance published by DCLG, it would be helpful for the Planning Inspectorate to receive a track-change draft of the DCO showing any departures from the model provisions. The Planning Inspectorate would wish to receive such a track-change draft of the DCO both at the pre-application stage and with the formal submission of the application for development consent.'

Interestingly, although no longer a 'requirement', Examining Authorities still sometimes ask parties to a DCO Issue Specific Hearing why a model provision should, or should not, be followed. It is clear, therefore, that (for the moment, at least) the Model Provisions Order will continue to play some role in the PA 2008 regime.

For this reason, this article will continue to describe, in broad terms, the structure of the Model Provisions Order.

The structure of the Model Provisions Order

The Model Provisions Order contains four schedules comprising:

- general model provisions;
- model provisions for railways;
- model provisions for harbours; and
- model provisions in respect of requirements.

The Explanatory Memorandum to the Model Provisions Order states (paragraph 7.9) that 'The model provisions Order is constructed in such a way that promoters of nationally significant infrastructure projects only need look to the Schedule which is relevant to the infrastructure type'.

As will be seen in the text below, for most DCOs this statement goes too far, and those drafting a DCO are likely to have to look beyond the schedule relevant to any particular infrastructure type.

In that context, however, it is worth noting that the DCLG 'Application Form Guidance' (September 2008) states (paragraph 20) that the Explanatory Memorandum for a DCO 'should also clearly explain if and why any provisions in the draft order diverge from the model provisions in the Infrastructure Planning (Model Provisions) Order 2009'.

General model provisions

During consultation on the draft Model Provisions Order, some respondents requested that DCLG produce bespoke model provisions for each infrastructure type within PA 2008, ss 15–30.

Whilst the Explanatory Memorandum to the Model Provisions Order make it clear that DCLG considered doing this, it goes on to make clear (paragraph 8.12) that 'we found it impossible to fulfil all such requests, as many infrastructure types would only require "general" model provisions, or would need provisions that are so specific to the project in question that model provisions would not assist'.

Having referred to the model provisions for railways and harbours, the Explanatory Memorandum to the Model Provisions Order states (paragraph 7.10), therefore, that:

> 'We have not set out a complete set of model provisions for other NSIP types, since promoters of such projects are likely to need provisions which are bespoke to that project. However, Schedule 1 sets out a series of model provisions which may be relevant to a large number of infrastructure projects, which cover a number of issues common to large construction projects, such as the compulsory acquisition of land and stopping up of streets. In all cases, individual applicants will need to decide if they need to modify the model provisions for the purposes of their own draft development consent orders.'

Schedule 1 is not, therefore, put forward as a complete list of provisions likely to be relevant to all projects, but is clearly a menu of model provisions that may be relevant to any particular project and from which a promoter can select and, as appropriate, adapt and supplement DCO provisions.

Model provisions for railways

The Explanatory Memorandum to the Model Provisions Order states (paragraph 7.9) that:

> 'Schedule 2 sets out a complete set of model provisions to be used in nationally significant infrastructure projects (NSIP) relating to railways, and is based largely on the contents of the existing Transport and Works (Model Clauses for Railways and Tramways) Order 2006 (SI 2006/1954).'

Again, early experience seems to suggest that, far from regarding the Schedule 2 model provisions as a 'complete set', promoters are adapting and supplementing them.

The Doncaster and Ipswich Chord DCOs provide a helpful precedent for drafting detailed provisions in a rail DCO.

Model provisions for harbours

The Explanatory Memorandum to the Model Provisions Order further states (paragraph 7.9) that:

> 'Schedule 3 sets out a complete set of model provisions to be used in NSIP harbour projects, and is based on provisions stemming either from the Transport and Works (Model Clauses for Railways and Tramways) Order 2006, SI 2006/1954 or from one or more Harbour Revision Orders or Harbour Empowerment Orders.'

Again, as with Schedule 2 above, early experience seems to suggest that promoters are adapting and supplementing the Schedule 3 model provisions. Indeed, Part 2 of the Hinkley Point C (Nuclear Generating Station) Order 2013 is an example of a highly adapted use of some of the Schedule 3 model provisions.

Model provisions in respect of requirements

The Explanatory Memorandum to the Model Provisions Order further states (paragraph 7.11) that:

> 'The model provisions Order also includes (at Schedule 4) a series of model "requirements" (akin to planning conditions under existing regimes). We expect that applicants will include what they consider to be suitable requirements, in the draft proposed order they submit along with their application.'

Whilst the 'model provisions in respect of requirements' cover a broad range of issues, they will almost certainly need to be adapted and supplemented to meet the needs of any particular project.

PINS Advice Note 15 (version 2) states (para 15.2) that:

> 'The law and policy relating to planning conditions, imposed on planning permissions under the TCPA 1990, will generally apply when considering Requirements to be imposed in a DCO in relation to the terrestrial elements of a proposed NSIP. Requirements should therefore be precise, enforceable, necessary, relevant to the development, relevant to planning and reasonable in all other respects.'

The Advice Note also states (para 29.2) that:

> 'Whilst the law and policy relating to planning conditions does not necessarily apply to DCO Requirements relating to the offshore elements of an NSIP or to Deemed Marine Licence conditions, it is considered that similar principles should apply when drafting these (see paragraph 15.2).'

In essence, therefore, the drafting of requirements in a DCO should have regard to the model 'requirements' in the Model Provisions Order but, in adapting and supplementing them, should generally follow the advice in DLUHC's Planning Practice Guidance and circular 11/95 Annex A (model conditions). (Note that the other parts of circular 11/95 have been cancelled and replaced by the Planning Practice Guidance.)

The predecessor regimes as a basis for precedent

The Explanatory Memorandum to the Model Provisions Order appears to acknowledge, not surprisingly, that even the Model Provisions Order itself has borrowed from previous model clauses and, indeed, from actual clauses in orders made by the Secretary of State. This is helpful as in early DCO examinations the then Commissioners were often reluctant to recognise the value of draft DCO provisions adapted from other regimes. More recently, however, PINS appears to have accepted the assistance that may be derived from other regimes. PINS Advice Note 13 (version 3) states (para 2.15) that:

> 'Provisions used in "predecessor" regimes such as for Transport and Works Act Orders or Harbour Empowerment Orders may be helpful in the drafting of a DCO. Developers should satisfy themselves that the inclusion of particular wording is appropriate and relevant in all the circumstances of a given project. The relevant precedent and the rationale for including the particular wording of a provision will need to be set out and justified in the explanatory memorandum.'

There seems little doubt that provisions from previous orders, whether made under the Planning Act 2008 or otherwise, will continue to be a useful source of precedent in drafting DCO provisions. What is clear, however, is that PINS will expect the Explanatory Memorandum for any such draft DCO to set out and justify the proposed wording. Indeed, recent experience in examinations tends to indicate that Inspectors will not only seek an explanation for any departure from a model provision, but also, on occasion, an explanation for compliance with a model provision.

Drafting conventions for statutory instruments

If the 'draft proposed order' makes provision for: (a) the making of byelaws; (b) the creation of offences; (c) the application, modification or exclusion of a statutory provision; or (d) the making of amendments, repeals or revocations of statutory provisions of local application, then that 'draft proposed order' must be contained in a statutory instrument: see PA 2008, s 117(4). Experience so far with applications for development consent has shown that most DCOs will indeed need to 'apply, modify or exclude' statutory provisions and will, therefore, have to be made in the form of a statutory instrument.

An 'SI template' is available on the Office of Public Sector Information (OPSI) website, together with an 'SI template user manual'.

The Office of Parliamentary Counsel (OPC) has published 'Drafting Guidance' (June 2020) for the drafting of legislation that sets out a number of general drafting principles as well has detailed drafting guidance. Although this guidance is designed for members of OPC in the drafting of Bills, it is also clearly helpful for those drafting statutory instruments.

Conclusions

Although the Model Provisions Order has formally lapsed, it is clear that PINS continues to regard the model provisions as a helpful template and applicants need to be prepared, therefore, to justify departures from those provisions. As more DCOs are made, however, an expanding data base of acceptable provisions, for each NSIP type, will become available and, in these circumstances, it may be that the current standing of the model provisions will begin to fade.

Article 43

Modern Drafting Conventions

Michael Humphries QC, ftb

Introduction

Inspectors at DCO drafting Issue Specific Hearings have started to require promoters to adopt 'modern' drafting conventions for the wording of development consent orders. This has been reinforced by PINS Advice Note 15 (version 2) on Drafting Development Consent Orders, which gives the following advice (para 3.1):

> '... it is common for applicants to seek out and adopt drafting conventions from previously made DCOs. It may also assist applicants to consider the drafting conventions of made DCOs published by the same department as would authorise their DCO, which may help to identify that department's drafting preferences. However, applicants should note that policy does change and develop.'

It also states (para 3.3), in relation to drafting conventions, that 'Guidance is publicly available from the National Archives website and should be followed by applicants'. The reference to 'guidance publicly available from the National Archives website' refers to the Statutory Instrument Practice (5th edition) (2017) ('the SI Practice'). The Drafting Techniques Group of the Office of Parliamentary Counsel has also produced guidance in 'Office of Parliamentary Counsel – Drafting Guidance' (June 2020) ('the SI Drafting Guidance').

As well as looking at PINS Advice Note 15 (version 2), this article also identifies and discusses some of the advice in the SI Practice and the SI Drafting Guidance that may be particularly relevant to DCOs. This article does not seek to summarise all of the points made, or include all of the examples given, in the SI Practice and the SI Drafting Guidance, and it is also supplemented, where appropriate, with the author's own experience and views on good practice in 'modern' drafting.

PINS Advice Note 15

PINS Advice Note 15 (version 2) starts by emphasising the important of an Explanatory Memorandum that sets out a thorough justification of every Article and Requirement 'explaining why the inclusion of the power is appropriate in the specific case' and, helpfully, that 'The extent of justification should be proportionate to the degree of novelty and/ or controversy in relation to the inclusion of that particular power' (para 1.2). The Advice Note also makes clear (para 1.3) that:

> 'For each provision, the ExA is likely to want to be satisfied about certain matters, such as:
>
> - The source of the provision (whether it be a previous made DCO or Transport and Works Act Order, or a novel provision).
> - The section/ Schedule of the PA 2008 under which it is made.

- Why it is relevant to the Proposed Development.
- Why the Applicant considers it to be important/ essential to the delivery of the Proposed Development.'

The Advice Note recognises that DCOs may include text derived from earlier DCOs, but seeks an Explanatory Memorandum that explains 'why' particular working is relevant. Similarly, where a DCO includes language used in other statutory regimes (eg Transport and Works Act Orders), the use of such language should be explained and justified.

The expectation is, however, that 'A well-developed Explanatory Memorandum can potentially reduce the number of examination questions an ExA may need to ask about the draft provisions comprising the draft DCO' (para 1.4).

For 'drafting conventions', PINS Advice Note 15 (version 2) points, as stated above, to the SI Practice, but does emphasise the following:

> 'In particular applicants should:
>
> - provide footnotes in relation to statutory provisions referred to in the SI to provide the user of the SI with information about relevant amendments or extensions to, or applications of, enactments mentioned in the instrument;
> - use gender-neutral drafting (for example avoiding the use of "he" or "she" to refer to the Secretary of State or other persons, unless referring to a particular living individual);
> - provide an adequate preamble with recitation of powers;
> - avoid use of the words "shall" or "will" (because of ambiguity over whether they are an imperative or a statement of future intention);
> - avoid the word "may" (to avoid ambiguity over whether it is permissive or stating that it is uncertain whether something is to occur);
> - avoid archaisms (for example "therewith", "aforesaid");
> - not use obliques in operative text (because of ambiguity whether they signify "and" or "or");
> - spell out "metres", "millimetres" etc throughout (and not use "m", "mm" etc); and
> - if a paragraph is included in the Interpretation Article saying that distances, directions, lengths, areas etc are approximate, make sure that in the rest of the order the word "approximately" in conjunction with any of these dimensions does not appear.'

The Advice Note then sets out guidance on a range of drafting issues, including;

- Protective Provisions;
- References;
- Definitions;
- Footnotes;
- Schedules;
- Paragraphs;
- Numbering;
- Certification Articles;
- Preambles and explanatory notes;

- DCO revisions;
- Providing a DCO audit trail;
- Requirements – general considerations;
- Securing mitigation;
- Providing flexibility – approving and varying final details;
- Complying with Environmental Impact Assessment requirements;
- Discharging requirements;
- Environmental information for subsequent applications; and
- Defining "commencement" – advanced works and environmental protection.

This article will focus, however, on modern drafting conventions; that is, the language to use when drafting a DCO.

The SI Practice

The 4th edition of the SI Practice (2006) has an appendix (Appendix I) that was specifically devoted to 'Modernising SI drafting' and this contained helpful advice on modern drafting conventions. The current 5th edition of the SI Practice (2017) has a different focus and makes clear (para 1.1.4) that its purpose is more confined to the technical aspects of making a Statutory Instrument, including 'instruction on their required form and content'.

Some of the following guidance relates particularly to DCOs.

Preambles

The SI Practice makes clear (para 3.11.1) that – below the made, laid and coming into force dates and the table of contents (if used) – there needs to be a 'preamble' that should set out:

- the recitals of the enabling powers;
- the recital of any other matters upon which its validity depends; and
- the words of enactment.

Some DCOs provide a relatively short preamble, whereas others are much longer. Thus, for example, the preamble to the A1 Birtley to Coal House Development Consent Order 2021 simply states, as follows:

> 'The Secretary of State, having considered the representations made and not withdrawn, and the report of the Panel, has decided to make an Order granting development consent for the development described in the application with modifications which in the opinion of the Secretary of State do not make any substantial changes to the proposals comprised in the application.
>
> The Secretary of State, in exercise of the powers conferred by sections 114, 115(a), 117, 120 and 122 of, and paragraphs 1 to 3, 10 to 17, 19 to 23, 26, 33, 36 and 37 of Part 1 of Schedule 5(b) to, the 2008 Act, makes the following Order –'

Meanwhile, the preamble to the A38 Derby Junctions Development Consent Order 2021 runs to some seven paragraphs. Both are Highways England projects and both approaches are acceptable.

Interpretation provisions

Para 3.12.1 of the SI Practice states that, by convention, an interpretation will follow the provisions relating to citation, commencement and extent (or application) of the DCO (usually article 1), but the SI Practice defers giving detailed guidance on the appropriate use of the interpretation provision to (what is now) section 4.1 (Definitions) of the SI Drafting Guidance. It is also worth noting that definitions that are *only* used in a particular schedule (eg the Requirements schedule) will sometimes be defined in a paragraph in that schedule and not in the main body of the DCO.

Section 11 of the Interpretation Act 1978 provides the general proposition that, where an Act confers power to make subordinate legislation, expressions used in that legislation have, unless the contrary intention appears, the meaning which they bear in the Act. The SI Practice makes the point, therefore, that there is no need to repeat definitions used in the enabling Act. Having said that, the SI Practice also recognises that there may be circumstances where it would assist the reader of a statutory instrument to point out that a particular expression is defined in the enabling Act. This should be done by way of a footnote.

The SI Drafting Guidance

The SI Drafting Guidance relates to the drafting of Bills, rather than to Statutory Instruments, but gives more detailed and practical guidance on 'modern' drafting conventions.

This section of this article follows the broad structure of the SI Drafting Guidance but, again, simply identifies and adapts some points that may be particularly relevant to those drafting DCOs.

Telling the story

The SI Drafting Guidance makes a number of points about 'telling the story' including:

- *Find a logical order and structure* – The material in a DCO should be set out in a logical order, so that later propositions build on earlier ones. Re-ordering material can also help in reducing the need for extensive cross-referencing throughout the document.
- *Get to the point* – Get to the point as quickly as you can. Ideally the opening part of an article will contain the main proposition or at least give the reader some idea of what the article is about.
- *Keep propositions short* – Clarity is helped by the use of short sentences and it is usually best to stick to one idea per sentence. That said, there may be occasions with complex propositions where it is better to have a long sentence rather than a series of short sentences that then have to be put together again to make sense of the idea.
- *The medium is not the message* – A DCO should not draw more attention to its structure and mechanics than it needs to.
- *Tone* – The story must be told in a moderate level tone. The SI Drafting Guidance makes it clear that 'Legislation should speak firmly but not shout'.

Syntax

In relation to 'syntax' the SI Drafting Guidance includes the following advice:

- *Sentence structure* – Sentences should be simply and logically constructed. The classic structure is 'subject – verb – object'. If possible, avoid inserting words between the subject and the main verb.

- *Positive and negative* – Positive is often easier to understand than negative. Thus 'speak after the tone' is better than 'do not speak until you hear the tone'. Having said that, a prohibition may be better expressed in the negative; for example, 'do not walk on the grass'.
- *Active and passive* – The active voice is usually more readily understood than the passive. So, 'The relevant planning authority must give notice' is better than 'Notice must be given by the relevant planning authority'. An exception to this may be where the agent is unimportant, universal or unknown. Thus 'If a notice is given to the relevant planning authority …' is acceptable.
- *Verbs and nouns* – A verb is easier to understand than a noun; so prefer 'A person may apply' to 'A person may make an application'.
- '*Shall*' – Policy within the Office of Parliamentary Counsel is to avoid the use of the legislative 'shall', unless the context requires it (for example, inserting amending text into a DCO that already uses 'shall'). The fundamental objection to the use of the word 'shall' appears to be that it is imprecise and ambiguous, having different shades of meaning as a requirement to do something. Drafters should use the word 'must', if that is the particular meaning intended.

Vocabulary

Again, the SI Drafting Guidance has some helpful advice on good drafting:

- Which words to choose? – The SI Drafting Guidance urges those drafting to write in modern, standard English using vocabulary that reflects ordinary general usage. Thus avoid archaic language and other words or phrases that may give rise to difficulty. Equally, drafting should not be at the vanguard of linguistic development. The SI Drafting Guidance points specifically to the advice of Sir Ernest Gowers in 'The Complete Plain Words' on 'how best to convey our meaning without ambiguity and without giving unnecessary trouble to our readers':
  - use no more words than necessary;
  - use the most familiar words; and
  - use precise and concrete words rather than vague and abstract words.
- Use no more words than necessary – Drafters should prefer the single word to the 'roundabout phrase'; so, for example, consider using 'to' rather than 'for the purpose of', and using 'by' or 'under' rather than 'in accordance with'.
- Use the most familiar words – Do not use words that are not in modern standard English; so avoid 'hereafter' or 'thereby'. Also seek to avoid jargon, whether legal jargon or policy jargon, although technical legal expressions may sometimes be necessary.
- Use precise and concrete words – Drafters often intend words to have a broad meaning, such as 'affect' or 'in relation to', but if a more precise word can be used it is likely to get the meaning across more clearly.

Gender neutrality

There are two parts to gender neutral drafting, being:

- avoiding gender-specific pronouns (such as 'he') for a person who may be male or female; and

- avoiding nouns that appear to assume that a man or woman will perform a particular role (eg chairman).

Drafters should consider the following techniques for avoiding gender-specific pronouns:

- *Change the pronoun* – For example, consider making the noun plural and using the word 'they'.
- *Repeat the noun* – If the noun is 'person' then consider repeating the word 'person' rather than using 'he' or 'she' in subsequent references. If there is a long compound noun (eg 'the person who made the application'), consider using a defined term (eg 'the applicant').
- *Rephrase to avoid the need for a pronoun or noun* – Consider using the passive voice (despite earlier warnings); so use 'explaining why the requirement has not been discharged' rather than 'explaining why he has not discharged the requirement'. Also consider using 'who' instead of 'if he'; so 'a person who commits an offence' rather than 'if he commits an offence'; indeed, try generally to use impersonal constructions. Consider substituting 'the' or 'that' for a personal pronoun; thus 'the default' rather than 'his default'. It may also be possible to omit the pronoun altogether, as in 'circumstances that justify doing so' as opposed to 'circumstances that justify his doing so'. Indeed, it may be possible to omit the phrase with the pronoun; thus 'the Secretary of State may' rather than 'the Secretary of State may, if he thinks fit'.

Drafters should also avoid gender-specific nouns such as 'chairman'. The word 'chair' is now widely used, as are other gender-neutral expressions such as 'convenor' or 'president'. Some gender-specific words are now falling out of use, so that 'manager' would commonly be understood to refer to a man or woman and is, therefore, acceptable, as the term 'manageress' is increasingly redundant.

Numbers and dates

Cardinal numbers

The SI Drafting Guidance advises as follows:

- Figures (ie numerals) should be used for all numbers above 10.
- Figures should also be used for numbers up to and including 10 that relate to sums of money, ages, units of measurement or in quasi-mathematical contexts.
- In other context, whether numbers up to and including 10 are spelt out or expressed as figures should depend on what seems more natural or appropriate in the context.
- Drafters should avoid mixing words and figures for things of the same kind.

Ordinal numbers

Drafters should adopt the following advice:

- Ordinal numbers above 10th should *not* be spelt out.
- Whether ordinal numbers from 1st to 10th are spelt out should be decided in the light of what seems more natural.

Percentages

Drafters should use '%' rather than 'per cent'.

Dates

Numbers should be used *without* the endings –st, -nd, -rd and -th; thus 1 January 2016, not 1st January 2016.

Headings

Headings should give the reader an indication of the contents of that part of the DCO, individual article or schedule. Drafters should try to ensure that headings do not go into a second line. Headings should allow the reader to understand the overall structure of the DCO from just looking at the headings in the contents sheet.

Articles

Drafters should try to avoid articles having more than ten paragraphs, although this is a matter of judgement and will depend on context, including whether it would be inappropriate to break the article into two.

Within an article, the starting point is that each sentence in a paragraph (ie the sub-part of an article) should be a separate numbered provision, although there is no absolute rule against two sentences.

There are particular rules in the SI Drafting Guidance for formulae, method statements and tables that are less likely to be needed in DCOs and so are not summarised here.

Punctuating lists

Paragraphs containing lists that are linked by a conjunction (ie and / or) should end with commas. For example:

> 'This Act applies to–
>
> (a) cats,
>
> (b) dogs, and
>
> (c) rabbits.'

Whereas paragraphs that contain lists that are not linked by a conjunction should end in semi-colons. For example:

> 'The authority may require the applicant to supply any or all of the following–
>
> (a) a driving licence;
>
> (b) a passport;
>
> (c) a birth certificate.'

Conjunctions between paragraphs

'And' and 'or'

Ensure that it is clear whether paragraphs are intended to operate cumulatively, or instead as alternatives.

Often it will be sufficient to put the appropriate conjunction at the end of the penultimate paragraph and rely on the implication (in the absence of a contrary indication) that each of the preceding paragraphs is separated by the same conjunction.

However, this makes the reader wait until then to know whether the paragraphs are cumulative or alternative and may be unhelpful with a long list of paragraphs.

Do not mix conjunctions, ie put different conjunctions at the ends of different paragraphs in the same provision.

'Or'

'Or' can have an inclusive and an exclusive sense: so 'A or B' can mean 'A or B or both' or 'A or B but not both'. Reed Dickerson *Fundamentals of Legal Drafting* (Aspen Publishers, 1965) suggests that: 'Observation of legal usage suggests that in most cases "or"' 'is used in the inclusive rather than the exclusive sense'. This construction may be reinforced, or alternatively excluded, by the context.

The SI Drafting Guidance suggests that it may be tempting to omit 'or' from provisions in order to avoid any suggestion of exclusivity and perhaps to make it clear from the opening words what is intended. But where it is obvious from the context that the provisions would be read in an inclusive sense, it may be better from the point of view of clarity or consistency across the statute book to follow normal English and use 'or'.

Sometimes it will be desirable to spell out that both of two alternatives are a permissible option. For example, a provision allowing the imposition merely of a 'fine or a term of imprisonment' might be construed in favour of a defendant so as to exclude the imposition of both. So if both may be wanted, it is probably best to say so.

'And'

Similar issues can arise with 'and'. If, in the example above, the court were given power to order a fine and a term of imprisonment, would it have to do both? Again, though, the context will probably supply the answer.

Neither 'and' nor 'or'

It is possible to avoid a single conjunction by making it clear in the opening words whether the paragraphs are cumulative or alternative. Thus 'The undertaker must submit to the relevant planning authority [all] [at least one] of the following documents …'. This can be heavy-handed, however, in simple propositions when 'and' or 'or' may be better.

Schedules

Schedules are typically used for:

- technical provision that is unlikely to be of interest to many readers;
- lengthy material that is at something of a tangent to the main story;
- repeals;
- long series of minor textual amendments;
- large tables and very long lists.

For most DCOs, the list of Schedules is now fairly standardised, although some variation is still seen. Generally, the order of Schedules will reflect the order of the article that first refers to, or introduces, that Schedule.

Cross-references

Within an article it may be unnecessary to cross-refer to other parts of that article, as meaning may be clear from the order of the paragraphs or from the context or words used generally. Thus:

> '(1) An undertaker shall apply to the relevant planning authority to …
>
> (2) Any such application must …'

Needing to make forward references (ie to a concept not yet introduced) may indicate that the overall order of the provisions is not quite right. Again, this is not a hard and fast rule and forward sign-posting may be helpful.

The SI Drafting Guidance indicates that, on the whole, drafters should not use the words 'above' or 'below', although this may be necessary to achieve certainty.

Definitions

The SI Drafting Guidance now states that there are two main kinds of definition, being:

> '(1) Exhaustive definitions that *replace* the meaning that the defined term would otherwise have. It is usual to use "means" for this kind of definition.
>
> (2) Inclusive/exclusive definitions that *adapt* the meaning that the defined term would otherwise have by clarifying potential doubt or expanding or limiting the meaning. It is usual to use "includes/does not include" for this sort of definition.'

As a generality, a defined term should be given a 'label' that gives the reader some clue as to what it means; but be careful not to use bland terms or terms that may be confusing.

It is also important to be clear about the 'purpose' for which the definition applies. So expressions like 'In this Part …', 'In this Article …' or 'In this Schedule …' may be appropriate.

Bodies corporate

Statutory corporations and other bodies corporate should be treated as singular, rather than plural. Thus 'The Environment Agency has …', *not* 'The Environment Agency have …'.

Periods of time

The objective, when drafting in relation to periods of time, is to make it easy for the reader to understand when the period starts, the duration of the period and when the period ends. This is important because periods of time will often relate to the right to make an application or to enter an appeal.

Start of period

The expression 'beginning with [an event]' indicates that time runs from the date of that event. By contrast, the words 'from' and 'after' an event will usually be taken to mean that time runs from the day following the event. Because of the potential ambiguity with the words 'after' and 'from', it may be better to use the expression 'beginning with'. These terms were discussed in the context of the (then) wording of PA 2008, s 118 in *R (Blue Green London Plan) v Secretary of State for the Environment and Rural Affairs* [2015] EWHC 495 (Admin).

The period

The expression, 'a period of [XX] days' is often used, but the words 'a period of' do not really add anything and '[XX] days' may be sufficient.

It is sometimes necessary to use the expression 'working days' in order to exclude weekends and public holidays, in which case it is good practice to define the expression.

End of period

The expression 'before the end of [a period] beginning with [a date]' would allow an action to be taken at any time up to the end of the specified period, including before the period began. By contrast, the expression 'within [a period] from [a date]' would limit the taking of the action to the period specified. Often these expressions will be the same in practice, but this will not always be the case.

Words and phrases

The SI Drafting Guidance gives specific advice about 'modern' drafting conventions for a number of words or phrases commonly used in legislation. This advice has been adopted here with some adaptations to make it more relevant to the drafting of DCOs.

'affect'

The 'nothing in provision A affects provision B' formula is useful if you do not know all the effects that A might have on B, or where those effects would be too numerous to mention. But if you can identify what effect it is you have in mind, being specific may help the reader (so, for example, 'A does not limit B').

'any'

Beware of a proliferation of the use of 'any'. In many cases, 'a' or 'an' is just as good.

'Any' can be ambiguous. For example, 'The relevant planning authority must consult any parish council within which construction activities will be undertaken'. Does this mean any 'one' parish council or 'all' parish councils?

'Any' may, of course, be useful to emphasise that something is of universal application or without qualification (but consider whether emphasis is really needed).

'apart from'

For 'apart from', in the phrase 'apart from this section', consider 'but for' or 'leaving aside'.

However, the awkwardness here is not so much the words themselves as the task they impose on the reader – that of working out what the situation would be without the provision in question. It might be more helpful to expand on the thought and say what you have in mind.

'description'

This can seem rather vague and abstract; for example, 'development of a description specified in …'. Drafters might like to consider 'kind', 'class' or 'category' (or even 'sort'?).

'function'

Draft on the basis that the natural meaning of 'function' covers powers and duties. In *Hazell v Hammersmith and Fulham London Borough Council* [1992] 2 AC 1, Lord Templeman said that the word 'functions' in s 111 of the Local Government Act 1972 embraced 'all the duties and powers of a local authority; the sum total of the activities Parliament has entrusted to it'.

A definition to the effect that 'functions' includes powers and duties is generally unnecessary and unhelpful. If something further is needed, consider whether it is possible to get the point across more clearly.

'provide'

Where a DCO 'provides' for something, it effects or gives rise to that thing in law. So, for example, a DCO may give an undertaker power to enter an agreement with a street authority that will 'provide for the dedication of any new street as a public highway …'. The term is very useful because it does not require that the DCO should create it in any particular way. Sometimes 'make' or 'create' will allow for the same flexibility.

However, consider in any given case whether it is possible to be more precise. Will the DCO 'enable', 'authorise', 'require', 'set out' or 'stipulate' a particular result? A more immediate word may also be less legalistic.

'provision'

The word 'provisions' in a DCO may be a useful expression to refer to articles and schedules generally without having to specify which, although sometimes the word could be omitted without changing meaning.

Used in the expression 'make provision', the word is a useful generic phrase for what legislation does, but in some circumstances it can be legalistic and off-putting. It may be worth thinking about what the DCO actually does in the case you are concerned about: does it 'regulate', 'authorise' or 'require'?

It may be possible to avoid the word 'provision' completely. So, rather than 'This Part of this Schedule makes further provision about …', it might be better to say 'This Part of this Schedule contains more about …'.

'pursuant to'/'in pursuance of'

Where one thing follows directly from another, with no intervening cause or condition, 'pursuant to' can often be rendered as 'under'. Thus '… the provision of further information pursuant to paragraph …' could simply be '… the provision of further information under paragraph …'. The expression '… in accordance with' may also be appropriate in certain circumstances, as may 'as required by' or 'as authorised by'. In other cases 'because of' may work.

The same points may be made in relation to 'in pursuance of'.

'in relation to'/'in respect of'/'with respect to'/'as respects'

These phrases are all extremely useful, and sometimes essential, in that they do not require one to specify any particular relationship. 'In respect of' has been said to have 'the widest possible meaning of any expression intended to convey some connection or relation': see *Albon v Naza Motor Trading* [2007] EWHC 9 (Ch) at 27.

It is, though, tempting to use them in circumstances where a more precise relationship could be specified. In some circumstances 'in the case of', 'for', 'about', 'to' or 'as to' will do as well.

'subject to'

'Subject to' is not a very precise way of describing a relationship between two propositions. For example, this article 'is subject to' another article may not be easily understood and it may be better to describe the relationship between the two articles.

If you cannot conveniently describe the relationship, 'subject to' can sometimes be avoided. A signpost such as '(but see section x)' is suggested by the SI Drafting Guidance as possibly serving to alert the reader to the fact that there are qualifications without sounding as legalistic.

The relationship between the provisions may be particularly hard to follow if 'subject to' is at the beginning of the sentence. It may be better to start with the main proposition and then indicate that there is a qualification, perhaps in a second sentence.

'Subject to' is also not necessarily helpful if you cannot identify the provisions you are talking about. 'Subject to what follows' should be avoided unless it is abundantly obvious from the context exactly which of the following provisions are being referred to. Where there is any doubt, specify exactly which provisions you mean (or express the relationship in some other way).

It may be possible to dispense with 'subject to' altogether, especially if the qualifying proposition is close to the proposition it qualifies – in which case the reader may be expected to grasp the relationship between the two without extra help.

'such'

Avoid 'such' where possible. Often 'the' or 'a' will do just as well or the word can be omitted altogether. Thus '... at such locations within the Order limits as the undertaker reasonably requires' may be drafted as '... at the locations within the Order limits as the undertaker reasonably requires'.

'supplemental'/'supplementary'

There is no obvious difference in meaning between 'supplementary' and 'supplemental'. The SI Drafting Guidance says that drafters should prefer 'supplementary', as perhaps the more usual formulation.

'by virtue of'

Where a relationship is direct, there may be alternatives to the rather archaic 'by virtue of'.

Sometimes 'by' on its own is enough. Where one thing authorises or requires another, 'under' may be possible. Where one thing causes another, or makes it possible, try 'as a result of' or 'because of'.

That said, 'by virtue of' can be particularly useful for indirect relationships. For example, '... a power conferred by this Order may be exercised despite a provision made by, or by virtue of, a specified enactment ...'.

'where'/'if'

'Where' is useful for stating a case or a set of circumstances in which a later proposition applies. 'If' is used for stating a contingency.

So 'where' may be better for cases which inevitably will occur, 'if' for conditions which may or may not be satisfied.

There is, however, of course no clear-cut distinction and, in some cases, it may depend on the perspective from which you are looking at the situation.

'without prejudice'

Consider what the 'prejudice' might be and focus on that. So in the phrase 'Without prejudice to the generality of article 13 ...', if the fear is that the new provision might limit what article 13 says, perhaps use the drafting 'Without limiting article 13 ...'. If the fear is that the new provision might *affect* or *change* the way another provision operates, perhaps say that (but see *'affect'* above).

A phrase beginning without 'without prejudice to ...' can often be recast so as to start with the main proposition and then say how it relates to the other one.

Another way of avoiding 'without prejudice' is by 'in particular'. Thus rather than, '(b) without prejudice to the generality of (a) above, the undertaker may ...', it may be possible to draft in the form, '(b) in particular the undertaker may ...'.

Conclusions

This article is intended to give an overview of 'modern' drafting conventions, drawing on PINS Advice Note 15 (version 2), the SI Practice (2017) and the SI Drafting Guidance (2020). Clearly, other reference works exist on modern drafting conventions, including Michele Asprey's *Plain Language for Lawyers* (The Federation Press).

As more DCOs go through the examination process, drafting experience is continuing to develop and drafters will need to consider and adopt emerging best practice.

Article 44

Limits of Deviation

Richard Honey QC, ftb
Michael Humphries QC, ftb

Purpose of limits of deviation

Limits of Deviation (LODs) were first utilised in private Acts of Parliament and are still used in modern hybrid Acts that authorise particular infrastructure projects. In hybrid Acts, LODs are the limits within which lateral deviation in the construction of the works are allowed. Plans typically show the centre line of a linear work, such as a railway, and then show limits either side within which the powers to construct the work may be exercised.

LODs enable flexibility to deal with problems encountered during construction, such as engineering limitations or adverse ground conditions, as well as the inevitable differences that arise between what is shown on the plan and what is constructed in practice. Without this flexibility, there would be a risk that the works could not be constructed in practice, as they would be confined to the precise positions shown on the plans. The works can be constructed anywhere within the LOD.

In DCOs, the concept of the LOD needs to be distinguished from: (a) the 'Order limits', being the land shown on the works plans within which the authorised development may be carried out; and (b) the 'Order land', being the land shown on the land plans within which land may be acquired and which is identified in the Book of Reference. For the most part the powers granted under a DCO will be exercisable only within the Order limits, although there are cases where powers have been granted that could in principle be exercised outside a scheme's Order limits.

LODs, by contrast, have the function of setting a limit on where the authorised development, or more particularly an individual Work forming part of the authorised development, may be carried out. LODs are now used for most schemes, not only linear schemes such as railways or power lines, in order to provide the flexibility that most promoters want and many promoters need.

Horizontal and vertical limits of deviation

Horizontal limits of deviation are shown on the plans. Some DCOs, such as the Preesall Underground Gas Storage Facility Order 2015, only include horizontal or lateral limits of deviation, as shown on the plans.

Vertical limits of deviation tend to be defined in textual terms within the relevant article in the DCO, being a certain height above or below the level shown on a scaled section, although sometimes the vertical LOD is itself indicated on the section. It is often the case for major development works that a specific maximum height limit is set. This is especially relevant for the purposes of environmental impact assessment, in order to provide a 'Rochdale envelope' for assessment.

Downward vertical LODs are often unlimited. An unlimited downward vertical LOD will not usually have any environmental impact, but there will be cases where digging down could be problematic in some locations, as it might for example interfere with groundwater flows or buried archaeology. In such cases a limit on downward vertical deviation in some locations may be warranted.

Relevant statutory provisions

The PA 2008 does not have much to say about LODs. The phrase is mentioned in only a couple of places, where amendments are made to other legislation dealing with blight (see PA 2008, ss 175–176).

The Infrastructure Planning (Applications: Prescribed Forms and Procedure) Regulations 2009 provide in reg 5(2) that applications for DCOs must be accompanied by a works plan showing the proposed location or, for a linear scheme, the proposed route and alignment of the development and works, and the limits within which the development and works may be carried out and any limits of deviation provided for in the draft order.

Approach to drafting limits of deviation

It is in individual DCOs that the provisions on LODs are to be found. For example, the National Grid (Hinkley Point C Connection Project) Order 2016 defines the limits of deviation in Art 5. That article provides that, in carrying out the authorised development, the undertaker may:

(a) deviate laterally from the lines or situations of the authorised development shown on the Works Plans within the limits of deviation relating to a Work shown on those plans; and

(b) deviate vertically from the levels of the authorised development shown on the sections:

   (i) to any extent upwards not exceeding 4m in respect of the overhead lines;

   (ii) to any extent upwards not exceeding 10% of the maximum height in respect of structures such as substations and bridges; and

   (iii) to any extent downwards as may be found to be necessary or convenient.

Article 5 also provides specific limits for particular pylons. For example, in relation to one pylon it is provided that it must not deviate laterally in one direction at all from the position shown on the plans. This form of asymmetric LOD may be relevant in providing protection for a particular environmental receptor.

Article 3(2) provides that the authorised development must be constructed and installed in the lines and situations shown on the Works Plans listed in Schedule 2 and in accordance with the levels shown on the sections, subject to the limits of deviation in Art 5. There are also protective provisions in Art 51 that provide, for land at Bristol Port, that the lateral limits of deviation are confined to a maximum of 5m. Again, this form of non-standard LOD may be relevant in overcoming a particular issue.

The Network Rail (Tinsley Chord) Order 2015 is similar. Article 6 provides that in constructing or maintaining any of the scheduled works, the promoter may: (a) deviate laterally from the lines or situations shown on the works and land plan to the extent of the limits of deviation for that work; and (b) deviate vertically from the levels shown on the sections: (i) to any extent not exceeding 3m upwards; or (ii) to any extent downwards as may be found to be necessary or convenient. Article 6(2) contains a clarification that the points of commencement and termination of the works may deviate laterally.

Interestingly, in Art 13 of the Tinsley Chord Order the power to acquire land compulsorily is described as applying to 'land within the limits of deviation', rather than to 'the Order land', which is not a defined term. Furthermore, the term 'the Order limits' is defined as meaning 'any limits of deviation and any additional limits of land to be acquired or used which are shown on the works and land plan'. This Order, perhaps helpfully in the case of the particular project, thereby elides the concepts of the land to which the order powers relate with the LODs for particular works and the identification of the land to which the powers of compulsory purchase relate.

Variations in approach to drafting limits of deviation

LODs vary between orders, as can be seen. The upwards vertical LOD in the Able Marine Energy Park Development Consent Order 2014 and the Network Rail (Ipswich Chord) Order 2012 was, for example, 1m. The latter DCO also included a provision in Art 7(2) preventing any deviation which would reduce the headroom or clearance beneath any proposed bridge – or diminish the width of any walkway, staircase, flight of steps, carriageway, tunnel, footpath or cycleway – by more than 200mm from its dimension as shown on the design drawings. The M1 Junction 10a (Grade Separation) Order 2013 limited upward vertical deviation to 1.5m.

There are a variety of other variations, some examples of which are as follows.

The Norfolk County Council (Norwich Northern Distributor Road (A1067 to A47(T))) Order 2015 contained in Art 5 a table specifying different upwards vertical, downwards vertical and lateral limits of deviation for different works or groups of works. Permissible vertical deviation ranges from zero to 1m.

Article 3 of the Swansea Bay Tidal Generating Station Order 2015 provided that in constructing or maintaining the authorised development, the undertaker may: (a) deviate laterally from the lines or situations shown on the works plans within the limits of deviation, subject to maximum dimensions set out in a schedule; and (b) deviate vertically from the levels shown on works plans for specific works to any extent downwards as may be found necessary or convenient. In the schedule, a table provided maximum heights and dimensions for structures including the seawall, turbine housing, buildings and cranes.

Article 4 of the East Midlands Gateway Rail Freight Interchange and Highway Order 2016 contained provisions described as 'parameters of authorised development' rather than LODs. It provided that the authorised development is to be carried out within the parameters shown and described on the parameters plans, but went on to say that in carrying out the authorised development the undertaker may deviate laterally to the extent of LOD shown on the plans and vertically to 1.5m, save for some specific works which had 1.5m upwards and 2.5m downwards limits.

The North Blyth Biomass Power Station Order 2013 contained limits of lateral deviation shown on the plans for certain works but no textual provisions for limits other than a provision in Art 3(3) saying that the undertaker may deviate laterally from the lines or situations shown on the works plan within the limits of deviation.

Wind farms

The National Policy Statement for Renewable Energy Infrastructure (EN-3) supports micrositing for wind turbines and encourages the 'granting consents that allow for micrositing to be undertaken within a specified tolerance', to allow 'changes to be made to the precise location of infrastructure during the construction phase so that account can be taken of unforeseen circumstances' (para 2.6.146). The precise siting of turbines could influence effects on interests such as bats, peat resources, habitats, watercourses and the like.

For onshore wind, the NPS says (para 2.7.24) that:

> 'Whilst it is for the applicant to specify the level of tolerance they are seeking, a tolerance of between 30m and 50m of elements of the required infrastructure is typical. However, there may be some circumstances where the IPC considers that the micrositing tolerance requested by the applicant is too great, and that on the evidence of the EIA and its own assessment of the proposal, that it is necessary to restrict either the overall tolerance for the scheme or the tolerance of specific elements of the proposal. When making this judgement, the IPC should take into account the reason for the applicant having requested the micrositing.'

The Clocaenog Forest Wind Farm Order 2014, for example, contains a power (Art 6) for individual turbines to deviate laterally within LOD. There were separate restrictions in the Order that prevented turbines from being constructed within 50m of forest edges and watercourses. These provisions were intended to protect bats and also avoid run off into the watercourse (see report, 20 August 2015, para 6.0.22). Comparable provisions, including a limitation in relation to watercourses, were included in the Brechfa Forest West Wind Farm Order 2013.

Environmental impacts

The A19/A1058 Coast Road (Junction Improvement) Development Consent Order 2016 contained in Art 5 not only a limit on vertical deviation of a maximum of 0.5m upwards and 1m downwards, but also had the proviso that any deviation was only permitted if it is unlikely to give rise to any materially new or materially different environmental effects from those assessed in the environmental report.

The Thorpe Marsh Gas Pipeline Order 2016 contains limits of deviation in Art 6, which are defined laterally by limits shown on the plans and for vertical deviation are, with some specific exceptions, between 1.2m and 20m below the surface of the ground. Article 6(a) provides that certain works can deviate 'vertically only to the maximum extent assessed in the environmental statement' (see also report, 7 December 2015, para 9.2.23).

These provisions illustrate a tension between the natural desire of promoters to include a degree of flexibility in Orders to allow for design development and the equally natural desire of the Planning Inspectorate to ensure that the project, including its LODs, have been properly environmentally assessed.

Clearly, LODs are an important element of the parameters against which a project will undergo environmental impact assessment. The draft order, including plans, and the environmental assessment must be consistent. It will often be important to assess the reasonable worst case impacts of the authorised works being undertaken anywhere within their LODs, although in practice works will often be sited to avoid the worst impacts of the development.

Justification for the limits of deviation

Limits of deviation are not mandatory under the PA 2008. It is, however, usually a good idea to include limits of deviation. If they are to be included, as with other provisions of a DCO, they should be justified. The explanatory memorandum should explain why they are required, at least in general terms.

The Inspectorate has said that whether the deviation sought is acceptable is 'really a question of impacts, mitigation and merits which it will be for the ExA to take a view on' (register of advice, 18 April 2011, North Blyth Biomass).

It is good practice for applicants to produce reports to set out the rationale and justification for the LOD selected. This was done for example on the Willington C Gas Pipeline project, as an appendix to the environmental statement. The Willington C Gas Pipeline Order 2014 contained in Art 7 limits of deviation both laterally (by limits of deviation shown on the plans, 30m either side of the centre line) and vertically. The vertical deviation was defined generally as between 1.1m and 70m below the surface of the ground, but there was an upper limit of 2.8m in one location and specific height limits set out in a schedule for certain works.

A promoter will have to show that the limits of deviation are necessary and proportionate, especially if they are at the upper end of what is in practice adopted in DCOs. Examining Authorities have raised questions about LOD previously, during examination, including for example on the Thames Tideway Tunnel project and the National Grid North London Reinforcement project.

For schemes that are non-linear and involve little engineering work, there may be little justification for significant LOD. It is notable that the former Infrastructure Planning (Model Provisions) (England and Wales) Order 2009 included limits of deviation in the model provisions for railways but not the general model provisions.

In practice, how wide LODs will need to be is significantly influenced by how far advanced the design of the project is and how much has been done by way of site investigation and the like. It is advisable to err on the side of caution when setting LOD to allow flexibility to deal with the unexpected.

PINS Advice Note 9 (version 3) endorses the use of 'parameters' as a means of allowing flexibility within DCOs and in order to reflect the concept of the 'Rochdale Envelope'. The Advice Note states (para 5.5) that:

> 'An Applicant may choose to include parameters within the DCO as a practical way to address uncertainty and provide the required flexibility. Parameters can be secured within the DCO in a variety of ways; for example by inclusion within principal powers, by inclusion within schedules detailing the Authorised Development or by inclusion within Requirements. Applicants should take care to ensure that any flexibility sought in their DCO has been consistently and robustly assessed within their ES.'

In practice, LODs are often used to set coarse-grain limits to where 'Works' may be undertaken, with parameters – set by plans, sections or requirements – providing more fine-grain limits to the precise dimensions, location or orientation of buildings or other structures comprising any particular Work.

Article 45

Use of the Works

Richard Honey QC, ftb
Michael Humphries QC, ftb

The need for statutory authority

Authority is required not only for the construction of an infrastructure project but also for its use. Such authority can be express or implied from the statute that authorises the project. Some promoters may be authorised to operate a development, once constructed, under other legislation.

There will be a defence of statutory authority to a claim in nuisance where a statute authorises the user of land in a way that will inevitably involve a nuisance, even if every reasonable precaution is taken (see eg *Barr v Biffa* [2013] QB 455).

It was said by Lord Wilberforce in *Allen v Gulf Oil Refining* [1981] AC 1001 that 'where Parliament by express direction or by necessary implication has authorised the construction and use of an undertaking or works, that carries with it an authority to do what is authorised with immunity from any action based on nuisance'. The Act in that case provided 'authority to construct and operate a refinery upon the lands to be acquired'.

Dissenting in *Allen*, Lord Keith noted the approach of Lord Esher MR in *Altrincham Union Assessment Committee v Cheshire Lines Committee* (1885) 15 QBD 597 (at 603) to the construction of private legislation, 'which is obtained by persons for their own benefit', as being to 'construe more strictly provisions which they allege to be in their favour', 'because the persons who obtain a private Act ought to take care that it is so worded that that which they desire to obtain for themselves is plainly stated in it'.

In *Manchester Ship Canal v United Utilities* [2014] 1 WLR 2576, Lord Sumption said (para 2):

> 'A statutory right to commit what would otherwise be a tort may of course be implied. But since this necessarily involves an interference with the rights of others, the test has always been restrictive. The implication must be more than convenient or reasonable. It must be necessary. As a general rule, this will involve showing either that the existence of the power is necessarily implicit in the express terms of the statute, or else that the statutory purpose cannot be effectually achieved without the implication. In particular a right to commit what would otherwise be a tort may be implied if a statutory power is incapable of being exercised or a statutory duty is incapable of being performed without doing the act in question.'

Relevant provisions in the PA 2008

PA 2008, s 157 deals with the use of buildings in respect of which development consent is granted by a DCO. It provides that if development consent is granted for development that includes the erection, extension, alteration or re-erection of a building, the order granting consent may specify the purposes for which the building is authorised to be used. It goes on to provide that, if no purpose is so specified, the consent is taken to authorise the use of the building for the purpose for which it is designed.

Section 157 echoes the provision in the Town and Country Planning Act 1990, s 75 in relation to which there has been some case law (eg *Barnett v Secretary of State for Communities and Local Government* [2009] EWCA Civ 476). It should be noted that there is no equivalent provision for the use of works other than buildings.

There are some provisions of the PA 2008 which govern what DCOs can contain in relation to the operation or use of certain projects: operation of generating stations (PA 2008, s 140), keeping electric lines installed above ground (PA 2008, s 141), and use of underground gas storage facilities (PA 2008, s 142). Note that PA 2008, s 194 and Sch 9 also amend various other Acts to insert a power to override easements and other rights in relation to the use of land.

PA 2008, s 158, which provides statutory authority for carrying out development and doing anything else authorised by a DCO, is considered elsewhere in this work, as is PA 2008, s 152 which makes provision for compensation for the carrying out of the works.

Guidance on drafting DCOs

It will normally be the provisions of the DCO itself that confer the powers to use the works. PINS Advice Note 13 (April 2012) says that 'the description of the proposed development together with the provisions of the DCO (including requirements) will determine what is authorised to be carried out'. The advice note goes on to make the point that 'it is the responsibility of developers (not the Planning Inspectorate) to ensure that the draft order applied for would provide them with all the necessary powers and authorisations to implement and use their scheme'. As the document notes, 'clarity and precision in the description and drafting of the provisions can, for example, prevent future uncertainty over whether development and other activities are carried out within the terms of the order'.

The general model provisions in the former Infrastructure Planning (Model Provisions) (England and Wales) Order 2009 contained a grant of development consent in Art 2 together with a right in Art 3 to maintain the authorised project. This would probably have encompassed authority to use the works for the purpose for which they were authorised to be constructed under the DCO. In practice, many individual DCOs take a more explicit approach. The approach taken in relation to a range of different projects is considered below.

Gas storage

The Preesall Underground Gas Storage Facility Order 2015 contains in Art 3(1) the grant of consent not only for the carrying out of the development but also 'to use the authorised development for the purpose for which it is designed including use of the cavities to be created for the underground storage of gas'. This reflects PA 2008, s 120 and Sch 5, para 7 that expressly identifies 'The use of underground gas storage facilities' as a matter that may be included in a DCO as relating to, or to matters ancillary to, the development for which development consent is granted. Article 4 also includes the right to maintain the authorised development.

Rail freight interchange

The East Midlands Gateway Rail Freight Interchange and Highway Order 2016 includes the grant of development consent for carrying out the authorised development (Art 3) and the power to maintain (Art 6) but also includes in Art 5(1): 'the undertaker and any persons authorised by the undertaker may operate and use that part of the authorised development comprised in Works Nos 1 to 6 inclusive for the purposes of a rail freight terminal and warehousing and any purposes ancillary to those purposes'.

Harbour facilities

Article 11 of the Able Marine Energy Park Development Consent Order 2014 provides that 'the undertaker may from time to time within the area of jurisdiction provide and operate such harbour facilities, together with works ancillary to those facilities, as may be necessary or convenient for the construction of the authorised development or the operation of the undertaking'.

Rail

For rail projects, there tends to be a specific power to operate and use the relevant railway. For example, Art 34(1) of the Network Rail (Norton Bridge Area Improvements) Order 2014 provides that 'Network Rail may operate and use the railways and any other elements of the authorised development as a system, or part of a system, of transport for the carriage of passengers and goods'. Similar words are found in, for example, Art 27(1) of the Network Rail (Redditch Branch Enhancement) Order 2013. This is in addition to express provisions granting development consent and conferring power to maintain the authorised development.

Highways

Highway DCOs contain the grant of development consent and the power to maintain the development, but not express provisions empowering the use or operation of the relevant highway (see eg Arts 5–6 of the A14 Cambridge to Huntingdon Improvement Scheme Development Consent Order 2016 and Arts 3–4 of the Lancashire County Council (Torrisholme to the M6 Link (A683 Completion of Heysham to M6 Link Road)) Order 2013). As the highways will be owned and operated by highway authorities with pre-existing statutory powers, no additional power to use the new highway is it seems required.

Gas pipelines

In gas pipeline DCOs, there are provisions authorising the operation and use of the pipe: 'the undertaker may at any time operate and use the authorised development except to the extent that this Order or an agreement made under this Order provides otherwise' (see Art 4 of the Thorpe Marsh Gas Pipeline Order 2016 and Art 6 of the Willington C Gas Pipeline Order 2014).

Power generation facilities

The Brechfa Forest West Wind Farm Order 2013 contains the grant of development consent in Art 3 and the right to maintain in Art 5. Article 7 then provides: 'the undertaker is authorised to operate the generating station comprised in the authorised development'. The explanatory note to the DCO says that the 'Order grants development consent for, and authorises RWE

Npower Renewables Limited to construct, operate and maintain a wind electricity generating station'.

Similar wording is used in a range of other orders including the Ferrybridge Multifuel 2 Power Station Order 2015 (Art 6), the Swansea Bay Tidal Generating Station Order 2015 (Art 5), the North Killingholme (Generating Station) Order 2014 (Art 5), the North Blyth Biomass Power Station Order 2013 (Art 6), the Triton Knoll Offshore Wind Farm Order 2013 (Art 5), and the Rookery South (Resource Recovery Facility) Order 2013 (Art 6).

The Hinkley Point C (Nuclear Generating Station) Order 2013 contains the grant of development consent in Art 3 and the power to maintain the authorised project in Art 5. Article 6, headed 'authorisation of use', then provides: 'subject to the provisions of this Order and to the requirements the undertaker may operate and use the authorised project'. The same approach is taken in the Thames Water Utilities Limited (Thames Tideway Tunnel) Order 2014 (see Art 4).

Other power generation DCOs employ similar but slightly different wording:

- Article 7 of the Clocaenog Forest Wind Farm Order 2014 says 'the undertaker is authorised to operate and use the authorised development for generating electricity'.
- Article 6 of the Palm Paper Mill Generating Station Order 2016 provides that 'the undertaker may operate the generating station for which development consent is granted by this Order'.
- Article 5 of the Port Talbot Steelworks Generating Station Order 2015 provides that 'the undertaker is authorised to operate the generating station for which development consent is granted by this Order'.
- Article 5 of the Progress Power (Gas Fired Power Station) Order 2015 and of the Hirwaun Generating Station Order 2015 both provide that 'the undertaker is hereby authorised to operate the generating station comprised in the authorised development'.
- Article 5 of the Knottingley Power Plant Order 2015 provides that 'the undertaker is hereby authorised to operate the generating station and associated plant comprised in the authorised development'.

Overhead lines

In relation to overhead lines, Art 4(2) of the National Grid (North London Reinforcement Project) Order 2014 provides that 'the undertaker may install, and keep installed, above ground the electric lines included in the authorised development'. Article 4(2) of the National Grid (King's Lynn B Power Station Connection) Order 2013 similarly provides that 'the undertaker may install, and keep installed, above ground the electric line included in the authorised development'. In the National Grid (Hinkley Point C Connection Project) Order 2016 similar wording was removed by the Secretary of State from Art 3 of the draft Order as 'unnecessary given the terms of section 16 of the Planning Act 2016' (Secretary of State's decision letter para 143), although it is clear from PA 2008, Sch 5, para 6 that a DCO may include such a provision.

Landfill

Not all DCOs contain such express provisions relating to the use or operation of the project. The White Moss Landfill Order 2015 includes, in the definition of the project in paragraph 1 of Schedule 1, not only the 'construction of a new hazardous waste landfill facility' but also: 'the operation of a landfill gas collection and flare system, the operation of a leachate collection, treatment and lagoon system, the extraction, stockpiling and exportation of clay, mudstones, coal and other suitable materials including general fill materials and all other associated engineering works to construct the landfill phases'. Paragraph 2 then adds 'continuation of the filling with hazardous waste as shown on the works plan' and 'operation of the interceptor waste treatment facility for the treatment of waste'. This is an alternative means to seek to ensure that the use and operation of the project is expressly authorised by the DCO.

Article 46

Defence to Proceedings in Respect of Nuisance

James Pereira QC, ftb
Michael Humphries QC, ftb

Introduction

This chapter considers PA 2008, s 158. This section provides statutory authority for certain activities authorised by an order granting development consent, for the purpose of conferring a defence in civil or criminal proceedings in nuisance. Note that PA 2008, s 158 confers statutory authority rather than blanket immunity from actions in nuisance. It must therefore be read alongside relevant case law on the scope of the defence of statutory authority. It should also be read alongside PA 2008, s 152, which provides an entitlement to claim compensation where land has been injuriously affected by the carrying out of works. These and other matters are discussed in more detail below.

Statutory basis

PA 2008, s 158 provides as follows:

> '**Nuisance: statutory authority**
>
> (1) This subsection confers statutory authority for–
>
> (a) carrying out development for which consent is granted by an order granting development consent;
>
> (b) doing anything else authorised by an order granting development consent.
>
> (2) Statutory authority under subsection (1) is conferred only for the purpose of providing a defence in civil or criminal proceedings for nuisance.
>
> (3) Subsections (1) and (2) are subject to any contrary provision made in any particular case by an order granting development consent.'

The scope of PA 2008, s 158

The proceedings that fall within PA 2008, s 158(2)

The statutory authority is only conferred for the purpose of providing a defence in civil or criminal proceedings for nuisance: see PA 2008, s 158(2). Such proceedings would include private nuisance and public nuisance at common law.

The position in relation to statutory nuisance proceedings under the Environmental Protection Act 1990 is less clear. The Divisional Court in *Camden LBC v LUL* [2000] Env LR 369 (DC) at [25] has expressed the preliminary, non-binding, view on a similarly worded provision in Railways Act 1993, s 122(3) that it would apply to proceedings by way of an appeal against a statutory nuisance abatement notice served under Environmental Protection Act 1990, s 80 where that notice alleged a statutory nuisance amounting to a common law nuisance, but it would not apply where the notice alleged a statutory nuisance amounting to prejudice to health.

In the same case, the Divisional Court expressed the view that criminal proceedings for a nuisance order under Environmental Protection Act 1990, s 82 would be criminal proceedings for nuisance. Proceedings under section 82 are started by laying an information in the magistrates' court and are therefore criminal in nature: see *Botross v London Borough of Hammersmith and Fulham* [1995] Env LR 217. Consistent with this view, General Model Provision 7 ('GMP7') in the Infrastructure Planning (Model Provisions) (England and Wales) Order 2009 makes express provision for a defence to proceedings under Environmental Protection Act 1990, s 82 to be conferred upon a defendant in certain circumstances. This is addressed further below.

Activities that fall within PA 2008, s 158

The statutory authority extends to the carrying out of development for which consent is granted under the DCO (PA 2008, s 158(1)(a)), and to other activities (which need not amount to development) which are authorised by an order granting development consent (PA 2008, s 158(1)(b)). The defence therefore covers not only the construction of an NSIP, but also its operation. It could also extend to other activities that may be authorised by the NSIP, such as those associated with the lopping of trees or the carrying out of survey work.

The scope of a defence of statutory authority

It is important to note that the scope of the defence of statutory authority generally has been the subject of a number of court decisions which are therefore relevant to the scope of PA 2008, s 158.

A defence of statutory authority is only available where the nuisance created could not have been prevented by reasonable measures or due diligence by the perpetrator: see *Allen v Gulf Oil* [1981] AC 1001. It must be the inevitable result of carrying out the development or undertaking the activities in question: see *Managers of the Metropolitan Asylum District v Frederick Hill and Others* (1881) 6 App Cas 193 at 213. Hence where the nuisance has come about because of the negligence of the operator, the defence will not succeed.

Model provisions

As stated above, GMP7 makes express provision for a defence to proceedings for a nuisance order brought by an individual under Environmental Protection Act 1990, s 82 in certain circumstances. The relevant circumstances are as follows.

For proceedings in relation to a nuisance caused by the carrying out of development, the defendant must show that the nuisance:

- relates to premises used by the undertaker for the purposes of or in connection with the construction or maintenance of the authorised project and that the nuisance is attributable to the carrying out of the authorised project in accordance with a notice served under Control of Pollution Act 1974, s 60 (control of noise on construction site), or a consent given under s 61 (prior consent for work on construction site) or 65 (noise exceeding registered level); or
- is a consequence of the construction or maintenance of the authorised project and that it cannot reasonably be avoided.

For proceedings relating to nuisance caused by the operation of the project the defendant must show that the nuisance:

- relates to premises used by the undertaker for the purposes of or in connection with the use of the authorised project and that the nuisance is attributable to the use of the authorised project which is being used in accordance with a scheme of monitoring and attenuation of noise agreed with the Commission as described in requirement 25; or
- is a consequence of the use of the authorised project and that it cannot reasonably be avoided.

As a consequence of the above, GMP7 also disapplies certain statutory provisions where the consent relates to the use of premises by the undertaker for the purposes of or in connection with the construction or maintenance of the authorised project. These provisions are Control of Pollution Act 1974, s 61(9) (consent for work on construction site to include statement that it does not of itself constitute a defence to proceedings under Environmental Protection Act 1990, s 82) and Control of Pollution Act 1974, s 65(8) (corresponding provision in relation to consent for registered noise level to be exceeded).

Guidance

Paragraph 38 of the DCLG Application Form Guidance (2013), referring to Box 19 of the application form, advises that the applicant should refer to Environmental Protection Act 1990, s 79(1) in order to consider whether the development proposal would engage one or more of that section's issues relating to nuisance. If it does, the applicant's statement should set out its proposals for mitigating or limiting them.

Compensation

It is not the purpose of this work to give a detailed account of the law of compensation. Users of this Service who have a specific issue in relation to compensation should refer to a specialist text on this subject. This article does, however, give an overview of the entitlement to compensation arising under PA 2008, s 152.

Landowners whose ability to bring an action in nuisance has been curtailed by PA 2008, s 158 are provided with a right to claim compensation under PA 2008, s 152 subject to meeting the requirements of that provision. In simple terms, PA 2008, s 152 provides a right to compensation to any person whose land is injuriously affected by the carrying out of authorised works (see PA 2008, s 152(3)) or depreciated in value by physical factors caused by the use of the NSIP (see PA 2008, s 152(7)). Importantly, the right to compensation does not depend upon any land having been acquired by the use of compulsory purchase powers.

PA 2008, s 152(3) provides that if, by virtue of PA 2008, s 158 or an order granting development consent, there is a defence of statutory authority in civil or criminal proceedings for nuisance in respect of any authorised works, then:

> '(3) A person by whom or on whose behalf any authorised works are carried out must pay compensation to any person whose land is injuriously affected by the carrying out of the works.'

It is made clear that Compulsory Purchase Act 1965, s 10(2) (limitation on compensation) applies to PA 2008, s 152(3) as it applies to that section: see PA 2008, s 152(5). It is also made clear that Land Compensation Act 1973, Part 1 (compensation for depreciation of land value by physical factors caused by use of public works) applies in relation to authorised works as if: (a) references in that Part to any public works were to any authorised works; (b) references in that Part to the responsible authority were to the person for whose benefit the order granting development consent has effect for the time being; and (c) ss 1(6) and 17 of that Act were omitted: see PA 2008, s 152(7).

An order granting development consent may not include provision the effect of which is to remove or modify the application of any of PA 2008, s 152(1)–(7).

Compensation for injurious affection caused by the carrying out of authorised works

It seems likely from the wording of PA 2008, s 152(3) and (4) that the provision is to be applied in a similar manner to Compulsory Purchase Act 1965, s 10. However, by analogy with section 10, compensation would be payable where the following criteria are met:

- the loss has resulted from an act made lawful by the order granting development consent;
- the loss is such that in the absence of PA 2008, s 158 it would have given the landowner an entitlement to recover damages;
- the loss must arise from the physical interference with the land or with a right enjoyed with it, and must result in a depreciation of the value of the claimant's land; and
- the loss must arise from the execution of the authorised works and not from their use.

Note that under PA 2008, s 152(4) a dispute as to the principle or the amount of compensation may be referred to the Upper Tribunal (Lands Chamber).

Compensation for depreciation of land value caused by the use of public works

PA 2008, s 152(7) applies Land Compensation Act 1973, Part 1 with the modifications set out under s 152(7)(a)–(c) (above). The result is that a right to compensation exists where the following conditions are met:

- the value of the claimant's interest in land has been depreciated (Land Compensation Act 1973, s 1(1));
- the depreciation is caused by 'physical factors'. These are defined as noise, vibration, smell, fumes, smoke, artificial lighting and the discharge on to the land in respect of which the claim is made of any solid or liquid substance (Land Compensation Act 1973, s 1(1) and (2));
- the physical factors are caused directly by the use of the authorised works;
- the claimant has a qualifying interest (Land Compensation Act 1973, s 1(1)). [Reference should be made to Land Compensation Act 1973, s 2 for the specific statutory wording and requirements in relation to qualifying interests. Only an overview is given here.] This means that the claimant must have purchased his interest before the date on which the authorised works were first used, that in the case of a dwelling the claimant has a freehold interest or a tenancy with not less than three years unexpired term remaining at the date of the claim (and where the claimant is entitled to occupy the land he must do so as his residence), and that in the case of property that is not a dwelling, the claimant must be an owner occupier and the land must either be an agricultural unit or have an annual value which is less than the prescribed amount (Land Compensation Act 1973, s 2(1)–(6));

- the claimant has made his claim at the correct time and in the correct manner (see Land Compensation Act 1973, ss 3, 8, 10 and 19 in relation to the manner and timing of making a claim); and
- the compensation claimed exceeds £50 (Land Compensation Act 1973, s 7).

By PA 2008, s 152(7)(b) the compensation is payable by the person for whose benefit the order granting development consent has effect for the time being. Section 152(7)(b), therefore, modifies the effect of Land Compensation Act 1973, s 1(1) and (4).

Article 47

Streets

Rebecca Clutten, ftb
Michael Humphries QC, ftb

Street works

In order to construct and/or operate a development for which consent is being sought pursuant to the PA 2008, it will often be necessary for certain works to be undertaken in, on, under or over a street. This brings the PA 2008 regime into close contact with the provisions of the New Roads and Street Works Act 1991 (as amended) ('NRSWA 1991').

Where those works comprise or include:

- the placing of apparatus;
- inspecting, maintaining, adjusting, repairing, altering or renewing apparatus, changing the position of apparatus or removing it; or
- works required for or incidental to any such works (including, in particular, breaking up or opening the street, or any sewer, drain or tunnel under it, or tunnelling or boring under the street) (see NRSWA 1991, s 48(3)–(3A)),

they will constitute an offence unless the party undertaking the works has the benefit of either a street licence or statutory authority in respect of them (NRSWA 1991, s 51).

As such, it is best practice to include, within a development consent order, provisions that confer the requisite statutory authority.

The term 'street' with which this article is concerned has a wide definition, as set out in NRSWA 1991, s 48(1) which includes:

> '... the whole or any part of any of the following, irrespective of whether it is a thoroughfare–
>
> (a) any highway, road, lane, footway, alley or passage,
>
> (b) any square or court, and
>
> (c) any land laid out as a way whether it is for the time being formed as a way or not.
>
> Where a street passes over a bridge or through a tunnel, references in this Part to the street include that bridge or tunnel.'

The power to make provision for statutory authority to carry out street works in a development consent order is conferred by PA 2008, s 120(3) which provides that an order granting development consent may make provision relating to, or to matters ancillary to, the development for which consent is granted.

Particular matters for which provision may be made are identified in PA 2008, Sch 5, although that Schedule is not exclusive and provision may be made for other matters, provided that they can properly be regarded as ancillary (PA 2008, s 120(4)). Amongst other things, PA 2008, Sch 5 does nonetheless make provision for the:

- creation, suspension or extinguishment of, or interference with, interests in or rights over land;
- removal, disposal or re-siting of apparatus; and
- carrying out of civil engineering or other works (PA 2008, Sch 5, paras 2, 14 and 15),

all of which may be relevant to the exercise of street works powers.

No further guidance is given in Government Guidance or PINS Advice Notes about the inclusion of street works powers within development consent orders, although PINS Advice Note 13 does make clear (consistent with PA 2008, s 120 and Sch 5) that the draft order should include provisions 'giving the developer authority to take actions necessary for the project to be implemented satisfactorily'.

Although formally lapsed, the Infrastructure Planning (Model Provisions) (England and Wales) Order 2009 continues to provide useful drafting guidance for those wishing to include statutory authority for street works within their development consent order. The provisions of particular relevance include those set out in Model Provisions Schedule 1 at paragraphs 8 (Street works), 13 (Agreements with street authorities) and 16 (Authority to survey and investigate the land) and Schedule B (Streets subject to street works).

Paragraph 8 contains a useful reminder that those wishing to authorise street works that affect a trunk road (as defined in the Highways Act 1980) should not include them within their development consent order but should instead make a separate application for a licence under NRSWA 1991, s 50.

The grant of statutory authority to undertake street works pursuant to the development consent order will not relieve the undertaker of his obligations to comply with other provisions of Part III of the NRSWA 1991 (for example, in respect of the giving of notice of works to the street authority). As such, if any of those provisions would give rise to difficulties for the undertaker in the construction or operation of their nationally significant infrastructure project, then they will need to seek to disapply them within their order. An example of the disapplication of certain provisions of the NRSWA 1991 can be found within the Thames Water Utilities Limited (Thames Tideway Tunnel) Order 2014 (SI 2014/2384), art 10(4) and Sch 19, para 4).

The Thames Tideway Order is also notable as an example of a situation in which the applicant had sought to disapply the London Permit System (LoPS). LoPS is a scheme prepared in accordance with the Traffic Management Act 2004, and administered by Transport for London ('TfL') and the London local highway authorities, which makes provision for the co-ordination of works affecting the highway. In particular, it requires utilities and others seeking to undertake works affecting the highway to obtain a permit before carrying them out.

Although recognising that LoPS is generally regarded as a successful and well-managed scheme, the applicant was concerned about possible delays to their project if permits were not forthcoming in acceptably short timeframes, and so they sought to replace it with a bespoke scheme designed to meet the particular needs of their project. Although attempts were made to secure the agreement of TfL to the bespoke scheme, that agreement was not forthcoming prior to the issue of the Examining Authority's Report.

Whilst the Examining Authority shared some of the applicant's concerns about the suitability of the LoPS for nationally significant infrastructure projects on the scale of the proposed development, they nonetheless accepted TfL's submission that LoPS should be retained (subject to modification), to safeguard their position in the event that a bespoke scheme proved impossible to agree: see the Examining Authority's Report and Recommendation to the Secretaries of State at paragraphs 14.19–14.24.

As no bespoke agreement had been agreed by the time of the decision of the Secretaries of State, that recommendation was accepted and the development consent order was modified to provide for the application of LoPS in the absence of later agreement between the parties: see the Secretaries of State's decision letter at paragraph 83.

Stopping up and diversion of streets

In order to carry out street or other works, it may be necessary for streets to be stopped up or diverted, either on a permanent or temporary basis. As with authority for street works, provision should be made for this within the development consent order, pursuant to the power contained in PA 2008, s 120 and Sch 5.

Advice Note 13 specifically identifies stopping-up orders as amongst those that are to be included to give the developer 'authority to take actions necessary for the project to be implemented satisfactorily' (page 4), and paragraphs 9 and 11 of Schedule 1 to the Model Provisions provide guidance as to the appropriate drafting of such provisions.

Tolls / road user charging

Ordinarily, authorisation for the charging of 'tolls' in respect of a 'special road' is obtained by means of an order made pursuant to NRSWA 1991, s 6 and Sch 2. The order sets the period over which tolls may be charged, and their maximum amount, amongst other matters (see generally NRSWA 1991, ss 6–16).

Where it is proposed to levy a toll over a road – the construction, improvement or alteration of which requires development consent – no order may be obtained pursuant to NRSWA 1991, s 6 (see PA 2008, s 33(4)(g)) and, instead, provision to authorise the charging of tolls must be made by development consent order. This is the effect of PA 2008, s 144(1).

PA 2008, s 144(2) further provides that, where an order granting development consent includes provision authorising the charging of tolls in relation to a highway, that order is to be treated as a toll order for the purposes of NRSWA 1991 ss 7–18 and, as such, the development consent order will need to provide for all the matters specified in those provisions, including the maximum toll charge, the length of road in respect of which tolls are payable and any exemptions from the toll. PA 2008, s 144(2A), however, makes clear that this provision does not apply to an order that includes provision authorising other charges in respect of the 'use' or 'keeping' of motor vehicles on roads. Such other charges would include 'road user' charges to control, for example, the volume of traffic on a particular road.

The Silvertown Tunnel Order 2018 includes express power to charge not only for the use of the new road comprising the Silvertown Tunnel itself and its approaches, but also the existing road comprising the Blackwall Tunnel itself and its approaches. Part 5 of the Order (User Charging) sets out detailed provisions relating to 'The changing policy' (art 53), 'The power to charge for the use of the tunnels' (art 54), 'Payment and recovery of charges and penalty charges' (art 55), 'Penalty charges, examination of motor vehicles, etc' (art 56) and 'Application by TfL of charges levied' (art 57). Paragraph 14 of the Secretary of State's decision letter dealt with the issue of 'User charging' and accepted the lawfulness of the applicant, Transport for London, being able to charge for the use of both tunnels.

Article 48

Removal of other Consent Requirements

Michael Humphries QC, ftb
Daisy Noble, ftb

Introduction

In the 2007 White Paper 'Planning for a Sustainable Future', the Government identified one of the problems of the Town and Country Planning Act 1990 regime as being that:

> 'There are too many different and overlapping development consent regimes. A single project can require multiple permissions under several different regimes, particularly projects involving linked developments – for instance, where a port expansion needs road and rail links. Most of these different statutory consent processes have their own procedural rules and, while there are similarities, there are also some important differences. This can significantly increase the costs of applications and can act as a real barrier to bringing forward proposals and to participating in the debate about them.' (para 2.8(c))

In response to this problem, the Government proposed to:

> 'Streamline the procedures for infrastructure projects of national significance by rationalising the different development consent regimes and improving the inquiry procedures for all of them. This will harmonise requirements on developers *and, as far as possible, create a single application process for all of the development authorisations needed for nationally significant infrastructure projects.*' (emphasis added) (para 2.13(d))

The PA 2008 regime clearly aims to meet that objective by removing the requirement to obtain various permissions, consents and authorisations for development where development consent is required. PA 2008, s 33 sets out the effect of the requirement for development consent on various other consent regimes.

As the 2007 White Paper made clear, however, a single application process was only to be created 'as far as possible' and the reality is that the new regime is some way from being a complete 'one stop shop'. PA 2008, s 150, however, does provide a mechanism for including certain additional consents and authorisations within a DCO.

PA 2008, s 150

PA 2008, s 150 provides as follows:

> '(1) An order granting development consent may include provision the effect of which is to remove a requirement for a prescribed consent or authorisation granted, only if the relevant body had consented to the inclusion of the provision.
>
> (2) 'The relevant body' is the person of body which would otherwise be required to grant the prescribed consent or authorisation.'

The 'prescribed consents or authorisations' for the purposes of PA 2008, s 150 are set out at reg 5 of, and Schedule 2 to, the Infrastructure Planning (Interested Parties and Miscellaneous Prescribed Provisions) Regulations 2015, SI 2015/462 ('the 2015 Regulations'). Schedule 2 to the 2015 Regulations identifies a great number of 'other' consents and authorisations that may be brought within the 2008 Act regime. This schedule has effect from 6 April 2015.

It is important to note, however, that the effect of the provisions is to enable a DCO to contain provisions for removal of a prescribed consent or authorisation, only where the 'relevant body' that would otherwise be required to grant the prescribed consent or authorisation has consented to the inclusion of the provision.

The 'relevant bodies' under the Schedule

Schedule 2 has two parts. Part 1 relates to consents and authorisations in England and Wales, whereas Part 2 relates to consents and authorisations in Wales only.

Schedule 2, Part 1 provides as follows:

England and Wales

Column 1: Act	Column 2: Consent or Authorisation
Wildlife and Countryside Act 1981	A licence under section 16 (power to grant licences)
Gas Act 1986	A licence under section 7 (licensing of public gas transporters)
	A licence under section 7ZA (licences for operation of gas interconnectors)
	A licence under section 7A (licence of gas suppliers and gas shippers)
Electricity Act 1989	A licence under section 6 (licences authorising supply etc)
Land Drainage Act 1991	A consent under section 23 (prohibitions of obstructions etc in watercourses)
Water Resources Act 1991	A licence under section 24 (restrictions on abstraction)
	A licence under section 25 (restrictions on impounding)
	A consent under section 32 (restrictions on abstraction)
	A drought order under section 73 (drought orders)
	A drought permit under section 79A (drought permits)
	A consent under byelaws made under paragraphs 5, or 6 of Schedule 25 (byelaw-making powers of the appropriate agency)
	A consent under section 109 (structures in, over or under a main river)
Protection of Badgers Act 1992	A licence under section 10 (licences)
Petroleum Act 1998	A licence under section 3 (to search and bore for and get petroleum)

(continued)

Column 1: Act	Column 2: Consent or Authorisation
	An authorisation under section 14 (for the construction and use of pipelines)
Energy Act 2008	A licence under section 4 (importation and storage of combustible gas)
	A licence under section 18 (storage of carbon dioxide)
	An approval under section 46 (funded decommissioning programmes)
Nuclear Industries Security Regulations 2003	An approval under regulation 5 (submission and approval of first security plans)
	An approval under regulation 6 (replacement, amendment and revocation of approved security plans)
	An approval under regulation 8 (temporary security plans during building works etc)
Justification of Practices Involving Ionising Radiation Regulations 2004	A justification under regulation 9 (consideration of new practices)
	A review of a justification decision under regulation 10 (review of existing practices)
Conservation of Offshore Marine Habitats and Species Regulations 2017	A licence under regulation 55 (power to grant licences)
Persistent Organic Pollutants Regulations 2007	An authorisation under regulation 8 (derogation)
Conservation of Habitats and Species Regulations 2017	A licence under regulation 55 (licences for certain activities relating to animals or plants)
Environmental Permitting (England and Wales) Regulations 2016	An environmental permit or an exemption from the requirement for such a permit
Greenhouse Gas Emissions Trading Scheme Regulations 2012	A permit under Chapter 1 of Part 2 (permits)

Schedule 2, Part 2 provides as follows:

Wales

Column 1: Act	Column 2: Consent or Authorisation
Inclosure Act 1852	An order under section 14 (direction by order that village greens, etc, shall not be fenced)
Inclosure Act 1854	An order under section 5, 9 or 11 (exchanges etc, fencing etc)
Inclosure Act 1857	An order under section 1 (fences may be dispensed with)
Commons Act 1876	A consent or authorisation required under byelaws or regulations made pursuant to section 15 (owners may make byelaws)
Commons Act 1899	A consent or authorisation required under byelaws or regulations made pursuant to sections 1 and 10 (power for district council to make scheme for regulation of common; or provisions as to byelaws)

Column 1: Act	Column 2: Consent or Authorisation
Law of Property Act 1925	Imposition of limitations and conditions under section 193 (rights of public over commons and waste lands)
Coast Protection Act 1949	A consent under section 16 (consent of coast protection authority required to carrying out of coast protection work)
	A licence under section 18 (prohibition of excavation etc., of materials on or under the seashore)
National Parks and Access to the Countryside Act 1949	Authorisation under section 20 pursuant to byelaws (byelaws for protection of nature reserves)
Pipe-lines Act 1962	A consent under section 15 (power to place pipe-lines in streets)
Conservation of Seals Act 1970	A licence under section 10 (power to grant a licence)
Protection of Wrecks Act 1973	A licence under section 1 (protection of sites of historic wrecks consent or licence)
Health and Safety at Work Act 1974	Approval under section 16 (approval of codes of practice by the Executive)
Salmon and Freshwater Fisheries Act 1975	A confirmation or variation of an order under section 26 (limitation of fishing licences)
	A consent under section 30 (introduction of fish into inland waters)
Coity Wallia Commons Act 1976	A consent or Licence under section 6 or 10
Ancient Monuments and Archaeological Areas Act 1979	A consent under section 2 (control of works affecting scheduled monuments)
	A consent under section 3 (grant of scheduled monument consent by order of the Secretary of State)
Import of Live Fish (England and Wales) Act 1980	An order under section 1 (power to limit the import etc of fish and fish eggs)
Wildlife and Countryside Act 1981	A consent under section 28E (duties in relation to sites of special scientific interest)
	An order under section 53 (duty to keep definitive map and statement under continuous review)
Road Traffic Regulation Act 1984	An order for the regulation of traffic under section 1, 9, 14, 15 or 22BB (general provisions for traffic regulation: regulation in special cases)
Food and Environment Protection Act 1985	A licence under section 8 (licences)
Planning (Hazardous Substances) Act 1990	A consent under section 13 (application for hazardous substances consent without condition attached to previous consent)

(continued)

Column 1: Act	Column 2: Consent or Authorisation
	A consent under section 17 (revocation of hazardous substances consent on change of control of land)
	A consent under section 18 (determination of applications for continuation of hazardous substances consent)
Town and Country Planning Act 1990	A consent under section 198 (power to make tree preservation orders)
	A consent under section 221 (preservation of trees in conservation areas)
	An order under section 247 (highways affected by development: orders by Secretary of State)
	An order under section 257 (footpaths, bridleways and restricted byways affected by development: orders by other authorities)
Deer Act 1991	A licence under section 8 (exceptions for licensed persons)
Water Industry Act 1991	An order under section 110A (new connections with public sewers)
	A consent under section 118 (consent required for discharge of trade effluent into public sewer)
	A consent under section 166 (consents for certain discharges under section 165)
Water Resources Act 1991	A consent under section 164 (consents for certain discharges under section 163)
Clean Air Act 1993	Approval under section 4 (requirement that new furnaces shall be so far as practicable smokeless)
	Approval under section 6 (arrestment plant for new non-domestic furnaces)
	An exemption from operation of section 6 under section 7 (exemptions from section 6)
	Approval under section 8 (requirement to fit arrestment plant for burning solid fuel in other cases)
	Exemption under section 14 (height of chimneys for furnaces)
	Approval under section 15 (applications for approval of height of chimneys of furnaces)
	Approval of plans under section 16(2) (height of other chimneys)
	An exemption of fireplaces from the provisions of section 20 (prohibition on emission of smoke in smoke control area)
Countryside and Rights of Way Act 2000	A consent or authorisation required under byelaws pursuant to section 17 (byelaws)
	Directions under section 24, 25 or 26 (land management; Avoidance of risk of fire or of danger to the public; or Nature conservation and heritage preservation)
Control of Pesticide Regulations 1986	A consent under regulation 6 (consents)

Column 1: Act	Column 2: Consent or Authorisation
Hedgerows Regulations 1997	A consent under regulation 5 (removal of hedgerows)
Ionising Radiations Regulations 1999 [repealed and replaced by SI 2017/1075 from 1 January 2018]	Authorisation under regulation 5 (authorisation of specified practices)
Environmental Protection (Disposal of Polychlorinated Biphenyls and other Dangerous Substances) (England and Wales) Regulations 2000	A registration under regulation 9 (inventories of contaminated equipment)
Radiation (Emergency Preparedness and Public Information) Regulations 2019	Any assessment required under regulation 4 (hazard identification and risk evaluation)
	Any assessment required under regulation 5 (consequence assessment)
	Any assessment required under regulation 6 (review of hazard evaluation and consequence assessment)
Water Resources (Environmental Impact Assessment) (England and Wales) Regulations 2003	A consent under regulation 9 (restriction on abstracting or impounding water)
Environmental Permitting (England and Wales) Regulations 2016	A permit under regulation 13, where that function is exercisable by a local authority pursuant to regulations 32 or 33 (grant of an environmental permit)

Obtaining the consent of the relevant body

Experience is tending to demonstrate that the 'relevant bodies' are often reluctant to give up their consenting or authorising powers and that it is, in fact, proving difficult for promoters to include Schedule 1 consents and authorisations in a DCO.

PINS Advice Note 11 (version 4), 'Working with public bodies in the infrastructure planning process', provides the following guidance to promoters:

> 'Certain prescribed consents etc can be consented separately or included in a DCO. Section 150 of the PA 2008 provides that these consents can only be included in a DCO if the relevant consenting body agrees to their inclusion. *Applicants will need to engage early in the pre-application stage with consultees that have such consenting powers, so that it is clear by the time an application is submitted whether such consents are to be included in a draft DCO.*' (emphasis added)

Paragraph 27 of the DCLG 'Guidance on the pre-application process' (March 2015) provides the following advice to relevant consenting bodies and promoters:

> 'Where an applicant proposes to include non-planning consents within their Development Consent Order, the bodies that would normally be responsible for granting those consents should make every effort to facilitate this. They should only object to the inclusion of such non-planning consents with good reason, and after careful consideration of reasonable alternatives. It is therefore important that such bodies are consulted at an early stage.'

Expanding and improving the 'one stop shop' approach to consents

On 22 November 2012, DCLG published a consultation seeking views on proposals to expand and improve the 'one stop shop' approach for consents under the 2008 Act. In its response, published in March 2013, the Government announced its proposals to establish a 'Consents Service Unit' (CSU) within PINS and to make changes to streamline the Infrastructure Planning (Miscellaneous Prescribed Provisions) Regulations 2010 and the Infrastructure Planning (Applications: Prescribed Forms and Procedure) Regulations 2009.

In April 2013 the Government established a new 'Consents Service Unit' within PINS and, in its response to consultation document (Major infrastructure planning: expanding and improving the 'one stop shop' approach for consents – summary of responses and government response') is stated (paragraph 14) that:

> 'The Consents Service Unit, to be based in the Planning Inspectorate, will be operational from April 2013 and will offer a bespoke service to those developers that want to use it. It will provide a lead contact to work with the developer and relevant consenting bodies (with a strong emphasis on the pre-application stage), to coordinate a logical and systematic approach to the handling of 12 different consents which may be required in addition to development consent under the 2008 Act. These consents could be required during the construction phase and/or the operational phase. The aim is to ensure that, where possible, these are dealt with in parallel. The Unit's key role will be to facilitate effective and efficient decision-making, including identifying any process blockages and resource needs, and escalate such issues where necessary.'

In May 2013, PINS published the 'Consents Service Unit for Nationally Significant Infrastructure Projects – Prospectus for Developers' and a 'Frequently Asked Questions' document that both explain the workings of the CSU. The Prospectus for Developers was republished in July 2015.

Article 49

The Discharge of DCO Requirements

Michael Humphries QC, ftb

Introduction

PA 2008, s 120(1) provides that an order granting development consent may impose 'requirements' in connection with the development for which development consent is granted.

PA 2008, s 120 further provides that:

> '(2) The requirements may in particular include–
>
> (a) requirements corresponding to conditions which could have been imposed on the grant of any permission, consent or authorisation, or the giving of any notice, which (but for section 33(1)) would have been required for the development;
>
> (b) requirements to obtain the approval of the Secretary of State or any other person, so far as not within paragraph (a).'

This article considers the following matters in relation to the discharge of DCO requirements:

- drafting requirements to be discharged;
- the appropriate discharge authority;
- appealing the discharging authority's decision; and
- fees.

Drafting requirements to be discharged

Requirements are frequently drafted so as to require the submission of written details of an aspect of the development to a 'discharging authority' that then has the power to 'approve' or otherwise such details prior to development, or a stage of the development, commencing. Such pre-commencement requirements are commonplace as planning conditions and considerable judicial authority exists on their interpretation.

The DCO procedure does give the opportunity, however, to create bespoke requirements and definitions to suite the particular circumstances of a project. Three concepts will be considered:

- the definition of the term 'commence';
- the expression 'unless otherwise approved'; and
- non-material changes.

The definition of the term 'commence'

PA 2008, s 154(1) provides that development for which development consent is granted must be 'begun' before the end of 'the prescribed period' or such other period as is prescribed in the

DCO. The 'prescribed period' for these purposes is set down in Infrastructure Planning (Interested Parties and Miscellaneous Prescribed Provisions) Regulations 2015 ('the IPMPP Regs'), reg 6(1), which states that 'Development for which development consent is granted must be begun before the end of a period of five years beginning on the date on which the order granting development consent is made'. As to such other period that may be prescribed in a DCO, Model requirement 2 in Schedule 4 to the Infrastructure Planning (Model Provisions) (England and Wales) Order 2009 ('the Model Provisions Order') states that 'The authorised development must be *begun* within [insert number] years of the date of this Order' (emphasis added).

PA 2008, s 155(1) provides that development is 'begun' for these purposes on the earliest date on which 'any material operation' comprised in, or carried out for the purposes of, the development begins to be carried out, and the expression 'any material operation' means 'any operation except an operation of a prescribed description' (this being limited to the measuring or marking out of a proposed road – see IPMPP Regs, reg 7).

The Model Provisions Order, however, also makes extensive use of the term 'commence', such as in Model requirement 3 ('No authorised development shall commence until …'). However, this term is not defined in the Model Provisions Order, either in the General Model Provisions (Schedule 1) definitions or in the 'model requirements' (Schedule 4) definitions. Nor is the term defined in the 2008 Act itself. Thus if the term 'commence' is not to be given its 'ordinary meaning', it may be appropriate to define it in the DCO itself. Many DCOs do this by giving a restricted meaning to the term 'commence', such that some defined 'material operations' may start before the discharge of certain requirements.

In the Hinkley Point C nuclear generating station DCO (Schedule 2, paragraph 1 – interpretation) the term 'commencement' (and the words 'commence' and 'commenced') is defined as being 'the carrying out of a material operation, as defined in PA 2008, s 155 (which explains when development begins), comprised in or carried out for the purposes of the authorised project'.

In the Hinkley Point C Connection Project draft DCO (Schedule 3, paragraph 1 – interpretation) the term 'commence' was defined negatively so as to exclude certain activities that might otherwise have been captured by the ordinary meaning of the word.

The definition adopted was designed to allow the promoter to undertake certain identified preparatory and investigatory works before discharging the terms of any pre-commencement requirement.

PINS Advice Note 15 (version 2) states (paras 21.1 and 21.2) that:

> 'In some decisions the Secretary of State has removed definitions of "commence" and/or "preliminary works" which could have allowed for a range of site preparation works (such as demolition or de-vegetation) to take place before the relevant planning authority had approved details of measures to protect the environment under the Requirements.
>
> The definitions were removed because the Secretary of State considered them to be inappropriate, particularly where such advance works were themselves likely to have significant environmental effects, for example, in terms of noise or impacts on protected species or archaeological remains.'

It also, however, sets out 'good practice point 5', as follows:

> 'If applicants consider that such an approach is appropriate in the particular circumstances of their proposed NSIP, they should provide reasons in the Explanatory Memorandum.'

In *Tidal Lagoon (Swansea Bay) plc v Secretary of State for Business, Energy and Industrial Strategy* [2021] EWHC 3170 (Admin) the High Court considered the relationship between the terms 'begun' and 'material operation' in ss 154/155, and the concept of 'commence' in the Swansea Bay Tidal

Lagoon DCO that adopted a different definition of 'material operations'. The circumstances were such that it was agreed that the claimant had 'begun' a material operation within five years for the purposes of ss 154/155, but (because of the different definition in the DCO) had not 'commenced' a material operation within five years for the purposes of the DCO itself. The claimant sought a declaration that, as it had 'begun' the development for the purposes of s 154, the DCO remained extant and that it was entitled to apply to extend the period within which it could 'commence' the development pursuant to PA 2008, Sch 6. The Court held that the inclusion of a definition of the term 'commence' in the DCO impliedly excluded or modified, and thereby superseded, the statutory provisions in ss 154/155 and that the DCO was not, therefore, extant. The claimant has applied to the Court of Appeal for permission to appeal, but at the time of writing the above represents the law.

The expression 'unless otherwise approved'

Expressions such as 'unless otherwise approved' or 'save to the extent that revised plans [etc] have been submitted to and approved' have been relatively common in planning conditions and are similarly being proposed in DCO requirements.

In the Hinkley Point C nuclear power station DCO, requirement PW4 provides that:

> '(1) Buildings and structures comprising Works Nos … shall be carried out in accordance with the plans as set out in … of this Order, *save to the extent that revised plans* relating to the siting, scale or appearance *have been submitted to and approved by the local planning authority*.' (emphasis added)

In relation to planning conditions, the Courts have generally been reluctant to endorse expressions such as 'unless otherwise approved', as they may have the effect of allowing a form of development that was not assessed or permitted: see, for example, *Henry Boot Home Limited v Bassetlaw DC* [2002] EWCA Civ 983 at paras 51–54. Having said that, the Courts have accepted there may be some scope for non-material amendments to a permitted development.

In *R (Midcounties Co-operative Limited) v Wyre Forest DC* [2009] EWHC 964 (Admin), the Court considered a planning condition (condition 6) that set a retail floorspace limit but then stated 'unless otherwise agreed in writing with the Local Planning Authority' and a further condition (condition 4) that required 'strict compliance' with various plans and drawings 'unless other minor variations are agreed in writing after the date of this permission and before implementation with the Local Planning Authority'.

In relation to the condition 6 'tailpiece', the Court held (para 70) that:

> 'As I shall come to in connection with another condition, I accept the existence of a very limited power to make immaterial variations informally. But while the tailpiece in the condition in question could be applied in that way, it contains no words purporting to limits its application.'

In relation to condition 4, however, the Court held (para 79) that:

> 'I do not regard this tailpiece as unlawful. Its clear scope is to enable 'minor variations' to an obligation otherwise to develop 'in strict accordance' with plans and drawings. Both parts of the condition operate to limit the flexibility which the tailpiece provides.'

The Court added (para 81) that:

> 'In my judgement this scope covers at least those circumstances in which the change is immaterial in the sense that no reasonable local planning authority could refuse it,

> or take enforcement proceedings lawfully in respect of its implementation. I do not exclude other jurisprudential bases.'

There does appear to be, therefore, some limited flexibility for a planning condition to vary a permitted development. See also the approach of the Court in *R (Halebank PC) v Halton BC* [2012] EWHC 1889 (Admin) applying the approach in *Midcounties* and rejecting the approach taken by the deputy judge in *R (Warley) v Wealden DC* [2011] EWHC 2083 (Admin) (see paras 100–101).

In the Hinkley Point C nuclear generating station DCO, the applicant included a provision in the following terms (see Sch 2, para 1(4) (interpretation)):

> 'Where any requirement specifies "unless otherwise approved" by the discharging authority or requires the applicant to demonstrate the existence of exceptional circumstances such approval shall not be given or exceptional circumstances agreed except in relation to minor or immaterial changes where it has been demonstrated to the satisfaction of the discharging authority that the subject-matter of the approval sought or the undertaker's proposed response to exceptional circumstances is unlikely to give rise to any materially new or materially different environmental effects from those assessed in the Environmental Statement.'

This form of wording appears to be acceptable to the Secretary of State and may form a precedent for other DCOs.

PINS Advice Note 15 (version 2) states (para 17.4) that a 'tailpiece' requirement will not be acceptable if it allows the discharging authority 'to approve a change to the scope of the Authorised Development applied for and examined', thereby circumventing the statutory process for changes in PA 2008, s 153 and Sch 6.

Non-material changes

PA 2008, s 153, Sch 6, para 2 enables the Secretary of State to make certain changes to a DCO if the Secretary of State is satisfied that the change is not material. In deciding whether a change is material, the Secretary of State must have regard to the effect of the change, together with any previous changes made under paragraph 2, on the DCO as originally made. The power allows the Secretary of State to impose new requirements in connection with the development, as well as removing or altering existing requirements. The power in paragraph 2 may only be exercised on an application made to the Secretary of State made by, or on behalf of, the applicant or a successor in title of the applicant; a person with an interest in land; or, any other person for whose benefit the DCO has effect.

This approach broadly reflects that set out at Town and Country Planning Act 1990 ('TCPA 1990'), s 96A. That section allows a local planning authority to make 'non-material changes' to a planning permission. In principle, it would appear that this provision could be applied and adapted to permit a local planning authority to make non-material changes to the requirements under a DCO. PA 2008, s 120(5) allows a DCO to apply, modify or exclude a statutory provision which relates to a matter for which provision may be made in the order, although it would be a matter for the Secretary of State whether such a provision was necessary or appropriate.

The appropriate discharge authority

In the 'model requirements' at Schedule 4 to the Model Provisions Order, it is clearly contemplated that DCO requirements will be discharged by the (then) Infrastructure Planning Commission ('the IPC'), now the Planning Inspectorate. Model requirement 3, for example, states that: 'No [stage of the] authorised development shall commence until [for that stage] written details of the following have, after consultation with the relevant planning authority, been *submitted to and approved by the Commission*' (emphasis added).

Since the 'model requirements' were published in 2009, however, the IPC made it clear that it was not resourced to act as the 'discharge authority' for DCO requirements and PINS appears to be adopting the same position.

In January 2012 the IPC stated in a response in its website 'Register of Advice' that 'Generally discharges of requirements are dealt with by the relevant local authority or statutory undertaker rather than the IPC'. In its Advice Note 13 (version 3), PINS states (para 2.10) that 'The developer should seek to agree wording for proposed requirements with the body to whom details are to be submitted for subsequent approval, and in any event seek the local planning authority's views on proposed requirements as they will enforce any breach of the terms of any order granted'. This last advice appears to contemplate that the 'discharge authority' could be a body other than the local planning authority, although the local planning authority's role as consultee 'in any event' is emphasised, as is its role in enforcing any requirements.

This last point seems important. The PA 2008 makes a breach of the terms of a DCO a criminal offence (see PA 2008, s 161), but makes the relevant local planning authority responsible for the service of a notice of unauthorised development under PA 2008, s 169. It is likely, therefore, that in most cases the most appropriate discharge authority for a DCO requirement will be the relevant local planning authority. That is not to suggest that other bodies may not be the discharge authority in particular circumstances, but PINS is likely to need some convincing that a requirement should be discharged by one body, but enforced by another. Certainly the Secretary of State has shown no enthusiasm for taking on the role of discharge authority, although the Secretary of State could be asked to take on that role if particular circumstances indicated that it was appropriate.

Certainly the experience so far is that it is the relevant local planning authority which has been given responsibility for the discharge of DCO requirements.

Appealing the discharging authority's decision

Where conditional planning permission is granted under TCPA 1990, s 72, an applicant may appeal to the Secretary of State against a local planning authority's decision to 'refuse an application for any consent, agreement or approval of that authority required by a condition imposed on the grant of planning permission or grant it subject to conditions': see TCPA 1990, s 78(1)(b). Similarly, an applicant may appeal to the Secretary of State where the local planning authority has failed to determine such an application: see TCPA 1990, s 78(2). TCPA 1990, s 79 deals with the determination of appeals under TCPA 1990, s 78. Regulations and guidance set out the procedures to be followed in relation to such appeals.

No such equivalent procedure is prescribed under the Planning Act 2008 and neither is there a model provision in the Infrastructure Planning (Model Provisions) (England and Wales) Order 2009, SI 2009/2265 ('the Model Provisions Order'), that sets out a preferred appeal mechanism following refusal or conditional grant of an application under a DCO requirement.

In broad terms, there are two potential solutions to this issue, being:

- the application and adaptation of Part III of the TCPA 1990; and
- the creation of a bespoke system for the discharge of requirements.

The application and adaptation of Part III of the TCPA 1990

This solution simply seeks to incorporate, with any necessary modifications, the system for appealing planning conditions contained within Part III of the TCPA 1990. Typically, a DCO provision will simply allow an appeal against refusal, grant subject to conditions or non-determination of an application to discharge a DCO requirement to be made under Part III of the TCPA 1990 as if the requirement were a condition under TCPA 1990, s 78. An example of this approach may be found in the Preesall underground gas storage project DCO. In principle, this approach could allow some adaptation of the TCPA 1990 system by, for example, modifying timescales or other procedural steps. Any wholesale amendment of the TCPA 1990 system, however, is likely (in effect) to fall within the second of the above approaches.

The creation of a bespoke system for the discharge of requirements

An alternative approach seeks to create a bespoke system for the discharge of DCO requirements. This approach may be less straightforward, but does give the opportunity to tailor a system for the discharge of DCO requirements to the particular circumstances of the project. For example, it may be possible to create a 'fast track' written representations system with tight timescales for the exchange of representations and other procedural steps.

This approach has now become pretty much universal and is to be preferred.

PINS Advice Note 15 (version 2), section 19 contains specific guidance on the drafting of such provisions; and, indeed, Appendix 1 to the Advice Note contains PINS 'standard drafting' for such provisions.

Fees

As stated above, PA 2008 does not create a mechanism for the discharge of DCO requirements and so does not, therefore, specify any fee structure for local planning authorities acting as the discharge authority under any such requirements.

Three potential mechanism exist under which a fee structure may be identified, being:

- Planning Performance Agreements;
- Development consent obligations; and
- DCO provisions/schedules.

Planning Performance Agreements

Planning Performance Agreements (PPAs) between local planning authorities (LPAs) and applicants for major development projects have been around since 2007, following a Planning Advisory Service and ATLAS pilot project in 2006.

The online Planning Practice Guidance (Paragraph: 016 Reference ID: 20-016-20150326) states that:

> 'A planning performance agreement is a project management tool which the local planning authorities and applicants can use to agree timescales, actions and resources for handling particular applications. It should cover the pre-application and application

> stages but may also extend through to the post-application stage. Planning performance agreements can be particularly useful in setting out an efficient and transparent process for determining large and/or complex planning applications. They encourage joint working between the applicant and local planning authority, and can also help to bring together other parties such as statutory consultees. A planning performance agreement is agreed voluntarily between the applicant and the local planning authority prior to the application being submitted, and can be a useful focus of pre-application discussions about the issues that will need to be addressed.'

Such mechanisms are frequently used by promoters of large infrastructure projects to assist local planning authorities and others to process often large and complex projects both expeditiously and efficiently.

Development consent obligations

Development consent obligations are a form of Town and Country Planning Act 1990, s 106 planning obligation entered into in connection with an application (or proposed application) for an order granting development consent (see TCPA 1990, s 106(14)).

An appropriately drafted development consent obligation may present a further or alternative opportunity to set out a mechanism for the payment of fees to local planning authorities discharging DCO requirements. Indeed, the opportunity to submit a unilateral development consent obligation may be particularly attractive where a local planning authority is unable or unwilling to enter into a PPA. Such a mechanism may also be drafted so as to incentivise early decision making by the discharge authority.

A unilateral development consent obligation cannot, however, impose any positive obligation on a non-party. In other words, a unilateral development consent obligation cannot require a local planning authority to meet particular positive performance targets, although it may provide for payments based on a local planning authority meeting particular timescales for the determination of discharge applications.

DCO provisions/schedules

PA 2008, s 120(5)(d) provides that a DCO may include 'incidental, consequential, supplementary, transitional or transitory provisions and savings'. This power would appear to be wide enough to allow the DCO to make provision for payments to be made to local planning authorities discharging DCO requirements. Such a provision would appear to be 'incidental' or 'consequential' upon any DCO provision or requirement making a local planning authority the 'discharge authority' for a DCO requirement.

Article 50

The Relationship between Development Consent and Marine Licensing

Michael Humphries QC, ftb

Introduction

A number of Nationally Significant Infrastructure Projects (NSIPs) and associated development are proposed partly on land and partly within the UK marine licensing area, where development would normally require a marine licence granted by the Marine Management Organisation (MMO) or the Welsh Government Marine Consents Unit under Part 4 of the Marine and Coastal Access Act 2009 ('MCAA 2009'). PA 2008 allows a DCO to include a *deemed* marine licence, thereby removing the requirement to seek separate consent under the MCAA 2009. This article examines the relationship between development consent and marine licensing.

A general discussion of the role of the MMO within the PA 2008 regime is set out at Annex B (version 1) of PINS Advice Note 11 (version 4): working with public bodies in the infrastructure planning process.

Development within the UK marine licensing area

Part 4 of the MCAA 2009 sets up a regime for the licensing of 'licensable marine activities' within 'the UK marine licensing area': see MCAA 2009, ss 65 and 66. There is a long list of 'licensable marine activities' within MCAA 2009, s 66, which would encompass most forms of 'development' likely to be the subject-matter of an application for development consent. MCAA 2009, s 66(4) defines 'the UK marine licensing area' as consisting of 'the UK marine area' other than the Scottish inshore region. The term 'UK marine area' is itself defined in MCAA 2009, s 42 to include the area of sea within the seaward limits of the territorial sea adjacent to the United Kingdom, any area of sea within the limits of the 'exclusive economic zone', and the area of sea within the limits of the UK sector of the continental shelf. The term 'sea' is defined in MCAA 2009, s 42 to include any area submerged at mean high water spring tide. The 'Welsh Zone' is defined in Government of Wales Act 2006, s 158.

PA 2008, s 31 makes it clear that development consent is required for development to the extent that the development is, or forms part of, an NSIP. The classes of NSIP for which development consent is required are defined by PA 2008, ss 14–30 and, in many cases, include: (a) development in waters adjacent to England up to the limits of the territorial sea; (b) development in a Renewable Energy Zone (except the Welsh Zone or where the Scottish Ministers have functions); and (c) development in waters adjacent to Wales or in the Welsh Zone.

Furthermore, by PA 2008, s 115(1), development consent may also be granted for 'associated development' if it is to be carried out in England, waters adjacent to England up to the limits of the territorial sea, or in a Renewable Energy Zone (except where the Scottish Ministers have functions). Note that a DCO may include 'associated development' in waters adjacent to Wales where it is development associated with the construction or extension of a generating station and has a capacity of more than 350MW: see PA 2008, ss 115(4A)(a) and 15(3B).

Development consent may still be required, however, for development that would also be a 'licensable marine activity' under the MCAA 2009.

A deemed marine licence

PA 2008, s 149A provides that:

> '(1) An order granting development consent may include provision deeming a marine licence to have been issued under Part 4 of the Marine and Coastal Access Act 2009 (marine licensing) for any activity only if the activity is to be carried out wholly in one or more of the areas specified in subsection (2).
>
> (2) The areas are–
>
> (a) England,
>
> (b) waters adjacent to England up to the seaward limits of the territorial sea,
>
> (c) an exclusive economic zone, except any part of an exclusive economic zone in relation to which the Scottish Ministers have functions,
>
> (d) a Renewable Energy Zone, except any part of a Renewable Energy Zone in relation to which the Scottish Ministers have functions,
>
> (e) an area designated under section 1(7) of the Continental Shelf Act 1964, except any part of that area which is within a part of an exclusive economic zone or Renewable Energy Zone in relation to which the Scottish Ministers have functions.'

The PA 2008 does not, therefore, permit a DCO to grant a deemed marine licence in waters adjacent to Wales or in the Welsh Zone. Within those areas, marine licensing is undertaken by Natural Resources Wales on behalf of Welsh Ministers. For that reason, the rest of this article focuses on the relationship between DCOs and marine licensing in waters adjacent to England and Renewable Energy Zones.

Where PA 2008, s 149A 'deems' a marine licence to have been granted, the MMO will consider an application to vary that licence under MCAA 2009, s 72.

The role of the MMO in relation to applications for development consent

The MMO has an important role in relation to applications for development consent. This role is set out in MCAA 2009, s 23, which makes various amendments to PA 2008.

PA 2008, s 42 is amended to insert a new subsection (1)(aa) so that there is a duty to consult the MMO 'in any case where the proposed development would affect, or would be likely to affect, any of the areas specified in subsection (2)'. A new subsection (2) is then inserted, as follows:

> '(2) The areas are–
>
> (a) waters adjacent to England up to the seaward limits of the territorial sea,
>
> (b) an exclusive economic zone, except any part of an exclusive economic zone in relation to which the Scottish Ministers have functions,

(c) a Renewable Energy Zone, except any part of a Renewable Energy Zone in relation to which the Scottish Ministers have functions,

(d) an area designated under section 1(7) of the Continental Shelf Act 1964, except any part of that area which is within a part of an exclusive economic zone or Renewable Energy Zone in relation to which the Scottish Ministers have functions.'

For shorthand, these are simply referred to below as 'the s 42(2) areas'.

Thus the MMO's role as consultee extends beyond the circumstances where development is actually proposed within any of the s 42(2) areas and includes circumstances where the proposed development would affect, *or would be likely to affect*, any such area.

Interestingly, section 23(7) of the MCAA 2009 provides that the Secretary of State must give guidance to the MMO as to 'the kind of representations which may be made by the MMO' under (a) Chapter 2 of Part 5 of PA 2008 (pre-application procedure), or (b) Part 6 of that Act (deciding applications for orders granting development consent). This guidance was issued by Defra as 'Government guidance to the Marine Management Organisation (MMO) on its role in relation to applications, and proposed applications, to the Infrastructure Planning Commission (IPC) for development consent under the Planning Act 2008' (September 2010) ('the Defra guidance'). [NB This guidance does not appear to have been replaced, but it is now only available on the UK Government Web Archive.]

Paragraph 29 of the Defra guidance states that:

> 'The MMO is the UK Government's expert body on marine management and it is in this capacity that the MMO should contribute to proposed applications. Therefore, when the MMO is consulted it should limit its representations and comments on the proposed application to those matters that directly relate to its marine management role. A matter is directly related to the MMO's functions only insofar as the proposed development involves an activity or operation which the developer intends to carry out in an area, or likely to affect an area, mentioned above [that is, one of the section 42(2) areas]. It would, for example, be appropriate for the MMO to comment on any piers or jetties associated with an onshore power station development, as these may affect the areas specified in the MCA Act.'

Section 23 of the MCAA 2009 also amends PA 2008, s 56 (duty to notify persons of accepted applications) and PA 2008, s 102 (definition of 'interested party') to include reference to the MMO 'where the development for which the application seeks development consent would involve the carrying on of any activity' in one or more of the s 42(2) areas. Thus for the purposes of PA 2008, ss 56 and 102, the MMO's role is confined to circumstances where the 'activity' would actually be carried on within any of the s 42(2) areas.

By making the MMO an 'interested party' it is clearly contemplated that the MMO will be given the opportunity to play a role during the examination of any application for development consent. Paragraph 42 of the Defra guidance states that: 'The MMO will be invited to any specific issue hearings (see section 91 of the Planning Act) or open floor hearings (see section 93 of the Planning Act) where it can submit representations orally'.

Paragraph 43, however, puts this in context by making clear that: 'When the MMO attends a preliminary meeting or subsequent hearings or makes written representations to the IPC, the MMO should limit its representations on the application to those that directly relate to its marine management role, for example, as a licensing authority or marine planning authority'.

DCO 'requirements' and deemed marine licence 'conditions'

PA 2008, s 120 states that:

'(1) An order granting development consent may impose requirements in connection with the development for which consent is granted.

(2) The requirements may in particular include–

(a) requirements corresponding to conditions which could have been imposed on the grant of any permission, consent or authorisation, or giving of any notice, which (but for section 33(1)) would have been required for the development;

(b) requirements to obtain the approval of the Secretary of State or any other person, so far as not within paragraph (a).

(3) An order granting development consent may make provision relating to, or matters ancillary to, the development for which consent is granted.

(4) The provision that may be made under subsection (3) includes in particular provision for or relating to any of the matters listed in Part 1 of Schedule 5.'

The list of matters in Part 1 of Schedule 5 includes the following:

'30A Deeming a marine licence under Part 4 of the Marine and Coastal Access Act 2009 to have been given by the Secretary of State for activities specified in the order and subject to such conditions as may be specified in the order.

30B Deeming any such conditions to have been attached to the marine licence by the Secretary of State or the Welsh Ministers under that Part.'

There may be jurisdictional issues to resolve where part of a DCO 'Work' is on land and subject to 'requirements' to be discharged by the local planning authority, and part is in territorial waters and subject to 'conditions' on a 'deemed' marine licence to be discharged by the MMO. There are many examples of such projects in practice, including, for example, the Thames Water Utilities Limited (Thames Tideway Tunnel) Order 2014 (see deemed marine licence at Schedule 15).

Enforcement of 'conditions' in a deemed marine licence

DCO requirements are enforced under Part 8 of PA 2008. Deemed marine licence 'conditions', by contrast, are enforced under Part 4 of MCAA 2009.

PA 2008, s 160 makes it an offence to carry out, or cause to be carried out, development for which development consent is required at a time when no development consent is in force in respect of the development. PA 2008, s 161 creates a further offence where, without reasonable excuse, a person: (a) carries out, or causes to be carried out, development in breach of the terms of an order granting development consent; or (b) otherwise fails to comply with the terms of an order granting development consent. Thus, it would be an offence not to comply with a 'requirement' attached to a DCO.

In respect of a 'condition' attached to a deemed marine licence, however, PA 2008, s 149A(4) provides as follows:

'(4) A person who fails to comply with such a condition does not commit an offence under section 161 of this Act.'

This provision does not, however, prevent PA 2008, s 161 from being used to enforce any DCO requirement (as opposed to deemed marine licence condition) that happens to apply to the UK marine licensing area.

The enforcement provisions for marine licences are set out at MCAA 2009, Part 4, Chapter 3. Sections 85–89 set out provisions relating to offences where there has been failure to comply with a condition of a marine licence, and ss 90–92 set out provisions relating to enforcement notices where there has been failure to comply with a marine licence condition.

Paragraph 45 of the Defra guidance (above) states that:

> 'The MMO should prosecute any alleged offences in the marine area under the MCA Act, though it is open to bring legal proceedings for offences in the marine area under sections 160 or 161 of the Planning Act 2008 should this be deemed appropriate (for instance, where particular terms of a DCO do not flow into a deemed marine consent).'

Article 51

Protective Provisions

Richard Honey QC, ftb
Michael Humphries QC, ftb

The nature of protective provisions

Protective provisions are common in DCOs. They impose limitations on the exercise of the powers under the DCO, or give rights to people affected by the DCO, in order to reduce the potential adverse effect of the project. They are normally used to strike a balance in the overall public interest between the competing needs of public authorities and similar organisations that have an interest in the same land or infrastructure.

Protective provisions are usually put in place for those who operate other infrastructure of one sort or another which may be affected by a development, such as highways and rail authorities, electricity and water utilities, communications equipment operators and the like. Protective provisions may occasionally also extend to private parties who may be specially affected by a project.

The nature of protective provisions is such that they tend not only to place restrictions on the promoter's exercise of its powers but also include provisions requiring the protected party to perform functions. Examples of typical or notable protective provisions are given below.

The need for protective provisions

Those authorities at risk of being adversely affected by a project will normally object to the development, due to its effects on their interests, but express a willingness to withdraw the objection if sufficient safeguards can be put in place. It is normally possible to have such safeguards put in place through agreements between the parties, but often objectors will want them included in the DCO in order to provide greater assurance that they will be observed. Often considerable time is spent trying to resolve objections by way of the agreement of protective provisions.

The former Infrastructure Planning (Model Provisions) (England and Wales) Order 2009 included Schedule L into which protective provisions were to be inserted. Protective provisions need not, however, be included in every case. The Brechfa Forest West Wind Farm Order 2013 and the Palm Paper Mill Generating Station Order 2016, for example, do not contain any protective provisions.

Protective provisions at the pre-application stage

It is advisable if at all possible to negotiate and agree protective provisions with those affected by a project during the pre-application stage. This is not always possible, however. In such circumstances, PINS Advice Note 15 (version 2) recommends (para 4.1) that:

> 'Applicants are encouraged to agree Protective Provisions with the protected party(ies) prior to submitting the application for development consent. Where agreement on Protective Provisions has not been reached during the Preapplication stage, applicants should, as a minimum, submit with their application the standard Protective Provisions for all relevant protected parties with any amendments that the Applicant is seeking annotated with full justification included within the Explanatory Memorandum.'

Even if protective provisions are included in a draft DCO by agreement, the promoter will still need to satisfy the Examining Authority that they are necessary and appropriate.

Standard protective provisions

Some promoters, such as Network Rail, have their own standard protective provisions, which they include in DCOs that they promote. These contain protections for statutory undertakers and communications network operators. Additional or bespoke provisions are likely to be necessary in the particular circumstances of any case.

Network Rail also has standard protective provisions that it requires to be included in any DCO promoted by another party, which is likely to affect its railway undertaking. An example is the protective provisions included in the A160/A180 (Port of Immingham Improvement) Development Consent Order 2015. The provisions cover matters such as making the exercise of compulsory purchase powers subject to the consent of Network Rail, the approval of designs, carrying out protective works, and remedying harm done by the execution of the works.

PINS Advice Note 15 also recommends that, where protective provisions are drafted by others, the drafting is reviewed by the applicant to ensure the provisions 'appropriately align with the terminology and style of the draft DCO and are suitably drafted for use in an SI' (para 4.4).

Negotiating protective provisions post-examination

Negotiations on protective provisions may only be concluded during the course of the examination of a project. The final, agreed provisions will then have to be substituted for whatever had been included in the draft DCO, or inserted if nothing had been included.

In the case of the A14 Cambridge to Huntingdon Improvement DCO, it appears that negotiations between the parties broke down shortly before the Secretary of State's decision in relation to land drainage matters, so that both the land drainage consent dis-application and the related protective provisions were removed from the draft shortly before the DCO was made (decision letter, 11 May 2016). Ultimately, the A14 Cambridge to Huntingdon Improvement Scheme Development Consent Order 2016 contained protective provisions in Schedule 9 for the usual statutory undertakers, the Environment Agency, National Grid, Network Rail, Anglian Water, a pipeline operator, and the County Council in relation to watercourses.

For the Port Talbot Steelworks Generating Station Order 2015, proposed protective provisions included in the draft DCO, in favour of Associated British Ports ('ABP'), were omitted by the Secretary of State after the examination, as the promoter and ABP reached a separate agreement following the close of the examination (decision letter, 8 December 2015, para 4.11). There was therefore no longer any need for the provisions to be included in the order. There were, however, protective provisions in Schedule 4 in favour of Network Rail, Western Power Distribution, National Grid and Welsh Water.

Example protective provisions

An example of fairly extensive protective provisions is the Able Marine Energy Park Development Consent Order 2014, which contained protective provisions in Schedule 9. There were protective provisions in favour of the Humber Conservancy, the Environment Agency, the Highways Agency, Network Rail, National Grid, harbour authorities, a number of statutory undertakers, and some private companies. Examples include provisions that substitute rights had to be provided before existing rights were extinguished, and that junction improvements had to be made before any part of the development was implemented. As the Examining authority noted in its report, in this case 'it was evident from an early stage that the negotiation of protective provisions would be a complex and contested process' (report, 24 February 2013, para 19.15). Six versions of the protective provisions were provided during the examination.

Another example of protective provisions on a similar scale are those in the National Grid (Hinkley Point C Connection Project) Order 2016, which contained provisions in Schedule 15 to protect: electricity, gas, water and sewerage undertakers; operators of electronic communications code networks; highway authorities; Network Rail; First Corporate Shipping Limited in relation to its operation of the Bristol Port; the Environment Agency in relation to flood defence and drainage structures; RWE Generation UK plc in relation to its wharf and other facilities for the Aberthaw power station; and CLH Pipeline Systems Ltd in relation to its pipeline.

In the East Midlands Gateway Rail Freight Interchange and Highway Order 2016, Art 38 gave effect to protective provisions in Schedules 15 to 21. They include the provisions broadly summarised below:

- National Grid: rights in relation to apparatus in stopped-up streets, no acquisition of interests other than by agreement, no removal of apparatus until alternative apparatus has been constructed, alternative apparatus to be constructed as agreed with NG, rights for alternative apparatus to be no less favourable, protection of retained apparatus, payment of expenses, an indemnity, ground subsidence monitoring, co-ordination of works, alternative access, and arbitration.
- East Midlands Airport: compliance with the safeguarding strategy for the airport, production of a bird management plan to minimise any bird hazard impact, approval of any radio or solar equipment in the development, access, and arbitration.
- Severn Trent Water: compliance with the Construction Management Strategy for Safeguarding the Derwent Valley Aqueduct.
- Network Rail: limitation on use of certain powers except with the consent of NR, no acquisition of new rights except with the consent of NR, provision of plans for approval by NR, construction of protective works, making good damage, provision of access and information by both parties, alterations and additions to the works by NR, payment of costs and expenses, dealing with electromagnetic interference, and control over illumination.
- Highways England: approval of detailed design and works programme, approval of contractors, provision of security for the carrying out of the highway works, agreement of traffic management provisions, carrying out works to the satisfaction of HE, payment of costs and expenses, making good defects, insurance, indemnity, and warranties.
- Leicestershire County Council (as highways authority): approval of detailed design and works programme, maintenance, payment, indemnity, bond or alternative security, arbitration, protection of apparatus, satisfactory workmanship, traffic control, approval of contractors, inspection of works, and insurance.

- Tarmac: supply of detailed design information and works programme, not obstruct access to quarry / landfill / bagging plant, alteration of haul roads, payment of expenses, requirement to construct access for Tarmac before existing access is closed, reinstatement, and arbitration.

In the Thorpe Marsh Gas Pipeline Order 2016, Schedule 9 contains protective provisions for Network Rail and National Grid and then generic provisions for the protection of electricity, gas, water and sewerage statutory undertakers (Part 3) and for the protection of operators of electronic communications code networks (Part 4). The provisions of Part 3 include that no apparatus can be acquired other than by agreement, no apparatus can be removed without alternative apparatus being constructed and brought into operation, the imposition of requirements on carrying out of works, the payment of expenses, and making good and paying compensation for any damage done. The provisions of Part 4 include making good and paying compensation for any damage done.

Similar generic provisions are included in other DCOs, including for example Preesall Underground Gas Storage Facility Order 2015 and the A19/A1058 Coast Road (Junction Improvement) Development Consent Order 2016.

Examples of notable protective provisions include:

- Part 3 of Schedule 8 to the Preesall Underground Gas Storage Facility Order 2015, which protects Blackpool BC in relation to trams, including to protect access to tramway property, approval of plans, carrying out protective works, making good damage, paying expenses, an indemnity, and includes an arbitration provision.
- Part 3 of Schedule 13 to the Norfolk County Council (Norwich Northern Distributor Road (A1067 to A47(T))) Order 2015, which protects Anglian Water Services, including prevention of working within standard protection strips around pipes without agreement from AWS, no work to apparatus without all necessary consents being obtained, no acquisition of apparatus other than by agreement, alternative means of access, notification by the undertaker to AWS of the location of previously unmapped assets, and making good damage and paying reasonable compensation.
- Part 1 of Schedule 8 to Swansea Bay Tidal Generating Station Order 2015, which protects Associated British Ports, including preventing acquisition other than with consent of ABP, restriction on the exercise of some powers in respect of ABP's land, approval of plans and arrangements for the development, imposition of requirements by ABP to protect the harbour, remedy of any erosion or accumulation due to the construction of a tidal work, and an indemnity. There are also similar provisions in Part 2 for the benefit of the Neath Port Authority, and provisions in Part 8 for Swansea Council in relation to accumulation in the River Tawe.
- Part 3 of Schedule 10 to the Network Rail (Redditch Branch Enhancement) Order 2013, which protects the Canal and River Trust, including no interference with access to the Worcester and Birmingham Canal or the supply of water to or from the canal without the consent of the CRT, control over the discharge of water to the canal, pre-construction surveying of the canal, approval of plans, imposition of protective works, prevention of pollution, and an indemnity.
- Part 4 of Schedule 7 to the Network Rail (Ipswich Chord) Order 2012, which protects the Felixstowe Dock operators in relation to taking possession of or imposing speed restrictions on the railway, and Part 5 which protects the National Health Service in relation to making parking spaces available to the National Health Service Blood and Transplant authority.

Article 52

Ancillary Matters that may be Included in a DCO

Ned Westaway, ftb
Michael Humphries QC, ftb

Introduction

Whilst other parts of this work examine the scope of what may be included in a 'nationally significant infrastructure project' and 'associated development', this article considers the dividing line in PA 2008, Part 7 and Sch 5 between what other matters can and cannot be included in a DCO.

Express inclusions

A significant aim of the PA 2008 was to create a 'one-stop shop' for certain major infrastructure project consents. The regime created falls short of that. Nevertheless, a very considerable number of matters may be expressly included in a DCO.

PA 2008, s 120 states that:

> '(3) An order granting development consent may make provision relating to, or to matters ancillary to, the development for which consent is granted.
>
> (4) The provision that may be made under subsection (3) includes in particular provision for or relating to any of the matters listed in Part 1 of Schedule 5.'

The use of the word 'includes' in PA 2008, s 120(4) makes it clear that the items listed in PA 2008, Sch 5, Part 1 are not intended to be an exhaustive list of the matters for which provision may be made in a DCO. The scope of PA 2008, s 120(3) is sufficiently wide to allow a DCO to make provision for any matter, that is not otherwise excluded, so long as it relates to, or to matters ancillary to, the development for which development consent in granted. Thus, for example, PA 2008, Sch 5 says nothing about the temporary possession of land for construction or maintenance purposes and yet nearly every DCO so far made includes such provision by virtue of the wording of PA 2008, s 120(3). Nevertheless, PA 2008, Sch 5 does helpfully identify a very wide range of matters that may be included in a DCO.

One of the most significant matters that is expressly identified in PA 2008, Sch 5 is the acquisition of land, or rights over land, including Green Belt land (PA 2008, ss 122–134 and 147, Sch 5, paras 1, 2 and 8).

Also of note are:

- The carrying out of specified excavation, mining, quarrying or boring operations (PA 2008, Sch 5, para 4).
- The operation of a generating station (PA 2008, s 140, Sch 5, para 5).
- Keeping electric lines installed above ground (PA 2008, s 141, Sch 5, para 6).

- The use of underground gas storage facilities (PA 2008, s 142, Sch 5, para 7).
- The carrying out of surveys or taking of soil samples (PA 2008, Sch 5, para 12).
- The cutting down, uprooting, topping or lopping of trees or shrubs or cutting back their roots (although in Wales this requires the consent of the local planning authority) (PA 2008, Sch 5, para 13).
- The extinguishment or removal of statutory undertakers' rights and the removal, disposal or resiting of apparatus (PA 2008, s 138, Sch 5, para 14).
- The carrying out of civil engineering or other works (PA 2008, Sch 5, para 15).
- The diversion of watercourses (PA 2008, s 143, Sch 5, para 16).
- The extinguishment of diversion of highways or rights of way (PA 2008, s 136, Sch 5 para 17).
- The charging of tolls, fares (including penalty fares) and other charges (PA 2008, s 144, Sch 5, para 18).
- The designation, specification of traffic upon, appropriation or transfer of highways (PA 2008, Sch 5, paras 19–23).
- The operation and maintenance of a transport system (PA 2008, Sch 5, para 24).
- The entering into an agreement for the provision of police services (PA 2008, Sch 5, para 25).
- The authorisation of discharges of water into inland waters or underground strata (PA 2008, s 146, Sch 5, para 26).
- Deeming a marine licence under Part 4 of the Marine and Coastal Access Act 2009 and the imposition on 'conditions' on such licences (PA 2008, s 149A, Sch 5, paras 30A and 30B).
- The creation, or amendment of the powers and duties, of a harbour authority (PA 2008, s 145, Sch 5, paras 31 and 32, subject to the restriction in PA 2008, s 145(6)(b)).
- The making of byelaws by any person, and their enforcement (PA 2008, Sch 5, para 32A).
- The transfer of property, rights, liabilities, or functions (PA 2008, Sch 5, para 33).
- The transfer, leasing, suspension, discontinuance and revival of undertakings (PA 2008, Sch 5, para 34).
- The payment of contributions or compensation (PA 2008, Sch 5, paras 35 and 36).
- The submission of disputes to arbitration (PA 2008, Sch 5, para 37).
- The alteration of borrowing limits (PA 2008, Sch 5, para 38).

There is now a body of authorised DCOs where examples of the above provisions may be found. Many of them are also referred to in the (now lapsed) Infrastructure Planning (Model Provisions) (England and Wales) Order 2009.

There are some obvious restrictions on the inclusion of certain provisions. For example, a DCO may only include provisions relating to a harbour authority if the DCO application includes the construction or alteration of harbour facilities. As stated above, PA 2008, s 120(3) requires that any matter for which provision is to be made in a DCO must relate to, or be a matter ancillary to, the development for which consent is granted.

By PA 2008, s 150 (read together with the Infrastructure Planning (Interested Parties and Miscellaneous Prescribed Provisions) Regulations 2015) a DCO may include provisions removing the requirement for a range of further consents and authorisations, but only if the relevant consenting body agrees. There is also a restriction on a DCO permitting works (etc) on common land except in accordance with the compulsory acquisition provisions (which may involve special parliamentary procedure) in PA 2008, ss 132 and 133 (PA 2008, s 139).

Relating or ancillary

As stated above, the matters listed in PA 2008, Sch 5 are not exhaustive of what may be included in a DCO under PA 2008, s 120(3). It is therefore possible for a DCO to include other matters of a similar nature. This will comprise matters relating to, or matters ancillary to, the NSIP itself, such as operation and maintenance (see above), but also matters relating or ancillary to any associated development.

There is no guidance on what constitutes an 'ancillary' matter. However, 'ancillary' in the planning context is usually differentiated from 'primary'. In practice, this relies upon a subjective judgment as to type and scale, it is a test of functional relationship rather than extent (see *Main v Secretary of State for the Environment* (1998) 77 P&CR 300).

A good example of the extent of matters that may be regarded as relating to, or ancillary, is the inclusion in the Silvertown Tunnel Order 2018 of control and charging provisions for the *existing* Blackwall Tunnel. The Explanatory Memorandum explains that '[t]he implementation of user charging is critical to achieving the objectives of the Scheme, by acting as a demand management tool for traffic using the crossings' (para 3.3). The traffic flows on surrounding highway network will be changed by the construction and operation of the Silvertown Tunnel and, in that context, the ability to manage that network is seen as essential to the successful implementation of the Silvertown Tunnel itself. In that case, there was a clear functional link with the proposed development. Charging provisions may, however, not always be acceptable. The inclusion of provisions for the charging of tolls on highways is expressly provided for in PA 2008, s 144 and Sch 5, para 18.

Necessary or expedient to give full effect to DCO

An alternative justification for provisions in a DCO is PA 2008, s 120(5)(c) under which an order may include 'any provision that appears to the Secretary of State to be necessary or expedient for giving full effect to any other provision of the order'. This provides a useful reserve basis for a DCO to contain consequential provisions, for example a requirement for further consents or the making of TCPA 1990, s 106 agreements to secure the delivery of off-site benefits.

Protective provisions

DCOs routinely include provisions protecting the property or interests of any person affected, or potentially affected, by a scheme (PA 2008, Sch 5, para 10). They also may impose or exclude liability in respect of acts or omissions (PA 2008, Sch 5, para 11). Protective provisions are generally reserved for the protection of the property or other assets of statutory undertakers, such as National Grid, the Canal and River Trust or Communication Code operators.

Application, disapplication or modification of statutory provisions

A DCO may also make provision applying, modifying or excluding a statutory provision that relates to any matter in the order (PA 2008, s 120(5)(a)), or making such amendments, repeals or revocations of 'statutory provisions of local application' as appear to the Secretary of State to be necessary or expedient (PA 2008, s 120(5)(b)). It should be noted that, in broad terms, a statutory provision is 'modified' (PA 2008, s 120(5)(a)) where its application is changed in relation to a particular circumstance (eg in relation to a particular NSIP), whereas a statutory provision of local application may be 'amended' (PA 2008, s 120(5)(b)) by changing its wording for all purposes.

These provisions are based upon similar earlier powers for orders under Transport and Works Act 1992, s 5 and Harbours Act 1964, s 14. They apply to public or private Acts of Parliament, but will be of particular use in respect of private local Acts relating to infrastructure such as railways, that may preclude upgrades or other changes.

Incorporated into the PA 2008, however, the power in a DCO to apply, modify or exclude a statutory provision is of more general application and is not restricted to transport or harbour projects. That was the subject of some concerns during debate in the House of Lords. Responding to those concerns, the then Secretary of State, Lord Adonis, referred to 'a number of safeguards … to ensure that these essential powers are not used inappropriately or without proper scrutiny'. These were: (i) that the promoter of a DCO must include the legislation it is sought to alter in the application; (ii) the form of the draft order will be based on model provisions; (iii) there are limits on the creation of byelaws or criminal offences (but see below), (iv) a DCO may only be approved if it is in accordance the relevant NPS; and (iv) the Secretary of State may change the terms of a DCO if it would contravene EU law or Convention rights.

The (now lapsed) Infrastructure Planning (Model Provisions) (England and Wales) Order 2009 provided generic text in the general model provisions (Schedule 1) and the model provisions for railways (Schedule 2) for the application and modification of existing legislation. Also, model provision 54 of the model provisions for harbours (Schedule 3) provided as follows:

> '(1) Regulation 60 of the Conservation (Natural Habitats, &c.) Regulations 1994 (general development orders) ("the Habitats Regulations") shall not apply to any planning permission which relates to the works authorised by article 7 (subsidiary works) and which is granted by article 3(1) of the Town and Country Planning (General Permitted Development) Order 1995 for the class of development described as permitted development in Part 11 of Schedule 2 to that Order.
>
> (2) Paragraph (1) does not apply if and to the extent that those works–
>
> (a) do not form part of the plan and project which was subject to an appropriate assessment in accordance with regulation 48 of the Habitats Regulations (assessment of implications for European Site) in connection with the making of this Order; and
>
> (b) are not the subject of a further consent, permission or authorisation by a competent authority as defined in the Habitats Regulations.'

This gives a helpful example of the extent to which PA 2008, s 120(5)(a) may be used to disapply primary legislation in relation to particular 'Works' forming part of an NSIP. However, attempts to disapply statutory provisions in DCOs may well be controversial. Prospective applicants should identify any statutory modifications or exclusions sought early, and provide a clear and reasoned justification for them.

Certain statutory provisions may not be modified or excluded (PA 2008, s 151), these are:

- Any provision of the Nuclear Installations Act 1965.
- Liability for damage and injury due to escape of water from a reservoir constructed after 1930 under the Reservoirs Act 1975.

- Civil liability of water undertakers for escapes of water from pipes under the Water Industry Act 1991.
- Civil remedies for loss or damage due to water abstraction under the Water Resources Act 1991.

Byelaws and the creation of offences

By PA 2008, Sch 5, para 32A a DCO may include provision for the making of byelaws and their enforcement. A DCO may also create offences in connection with any of the following:

> '(a) non-payment of tolls, fares or other charges,
>
> (b) a person's failure to give the person's name or address in accordance with provision relating to penalty fares,
>
> (c) enforcement of byelaws, or
>
> (d) construction, improvement, maintenance or management of a harbour' (PA 2008, Sch 5, para 32B(1)).

Save for these limited examples, a DCO may not create, provide for the creation or alter powers in relation to the creation of offences (PA 2008, s 120(8)).

There are also controls on the severity of any offence thereby created, such that that offence may only be triable only summarily (ie in the magistrates' court) and the sentence is limited to a level 3 fine on the standard scale (currently £1,000) (PA 2008, Sch 5, para 32B(2)).

Article 53

Matters that may not be Included in a DCO

Hereward Phillpot QC, ftb
Michael Humphries QC, ftb

Introduction

PA 2008, s 120 identifies what may be included in an order granting development consent. PA 2008, s 120(9), however, provides as follows:

> 'To the extent that provision for or relating to a matter may be included in an order granting development consent, none of the following may include any such provision–
>
> (a) an order under section 14 or 16 of the Harbours Act 1964 (c 40) (orders in relation to harbours, docks and wharves);
>
> (b) an order under section 4(1) of the Gas Act 1965 (c 36) (order authorising storage of gas in underground strata);
>
> (c) an order under section 1 or 3 of the Transport and Works Act 1992 (c 42) (orders as to railways, tramways, inland waterways etc.).'

The effect of this provision

PA 2008, s 120(9) is not particularly clearly drafted, and (at least initially) this led to different suggested interpretations being advanced as to its meaning and effect.

In approaching its interpretation, it is important to bear in mind that PA 2008, s 120 is not itself concerned with the consenting of development, rather it is concerned only with the nature of the matters ancillary to development (see PA 2008, s 120(3)) which may or may not be authorised via orders under three separate statutory regimes that confer order-making powers.

Restrictions on the consenting of development are to be found elsewhere in the PA 2008. It is clear that once development consent has been granted under the PA 2008 authorising a particular associated development, that development cannot subsequently be authorised under any of these separate order-making powers. This is because PA 2008, s 115(5) applies PA 2008, s 33(2) to 'associated development' for which development consent exists. The effect is to remove jurisdiction for that development under those other statutory regimes.

This statutory restriction operates in one direction only. It prevents the granting of, say, a Harbour Empowerment Order (HEO) for an associated development *after* the grant of a Development Consent Order (DCO) authorising that development, but not before.

Although the matter has not been tested in the courts, it is suggested that the effect of PA 2008, s 120(9) is twofold:

1 Once a DCO has been granted, it operates to prevent the granting of an order under the other statutory regimes which varies the ancillary matters authorised in that DCO. Any such

variations would therefore need to be obtained via the procedure in the Infrastructure Planning (Changes to, and Revocation of, Development Consent Orders) Regulations 2011, SI 2011/2055.

2 It prevents promoters from obtaining consent for associated development in a DCO, but at the same time seeking authorisation for the necessary ancillary powers under a separate statutory regime. This supplementing of DCO powers via other statutory regimes is only permissible under PA 2008, s 120(9) where the provisions in question could not have been included in the DCO itself. Now that the former restriction on the creation of offences in a DCO has been revoked, there are likely to be few such provisions in practice.

Parallel applications

Subject to the important issue of relative timing, there is therefore nothing in PA 2008, s 120(9) which would prevent a promoter seeking an order under one of the other statutory regimes whilst at the same time seeking a DCO containing the same or similar provisions.

Neither PA 2008, s 115(5) nor s 120(9) prevents the relevant decision-maker from granting such an order in advance of the same development and ancillary matters being approved in a DCO. This remains the case even where an application has been made for the DCO in question.

This approach was used by EDF Energy in relation to the development of the Hinkley Point C new nuclear power station. EDF's proposal included the construction and operation of a large aggregates jetty (as associated development), to allow the import by sea of the majority of the aggregates needed to construct the power station. The early construction and availability of this jetty facility was considered likely to accelerate the construction of the power station itself, and to reduce its adverse effects, if and when that was authorised under the PA 2008. EDF therefore sought and obtained powers to construct and operate the jetty through an application for a HEO under the Harbours Act 1964 and a Transport and Works Act Order (TWAO) under the Transport and Works Act 1992. Essentially identical powers were sought and subsequently obtained in the DCO.

In advance of the public inquiry into the application for an HEO and a TWAO, the Department for Energy and Climate Change wrote to EDF asking for its views on whether PA 2008, s 120(9) caused any difficulties in reconciling the making of an HEO/TWAO with the existence of an application for a DCO which contains the same provisions. EDF responded to say that no such difficulties arose, for reasons which reflect the analysis set out above, and in due course the HEO and TWAO were both made and not challenged.

It should also be noted that, shortly after that public exchange of correspondence, the IPC published Annex B to its then Advice Note 11 (Working with Public Bodies), which confirmed that such an approach was legitimate. The same advice is now to be found in Annex B (version 1) to PINS Advice Note 11 (version 4).

Part 9

Compulsory Purchase

Article 54

Compulsory Purchase Powers in a DCO

Richard Honey QC, ftb
Michael Humphries QC, ftb

Introduction

A development consent order (DCO) under the PA 2008 can authorise the compulsory acquisition of land or of an interest in or right over land. DCOs are unusual in that they are a means by which even purely private developers may secure compulsory purchase powers. Before the PA 2008 this was not possible; save in the case of the privatised utility companies and under the Pipelines Act 1962.

Even so, the Government's policy position appears still to be that promoters should seek to acquire land by negotiation wherever practicable and that powers of compulsory acquisition should only be sought where attempts to acquire land or rights by agreement have failed.

In this article, as in DCOs themselves, references to acquiring a right over land include acquiring it by the creation of a new right as well as by the acquisition of an existing one (PA 2008, s 159(3)). Particular provision is made for the acquisition of rights in relation to underground gas storage facilities, which is dealt with in PA 2008, s 133. That section covers rights to store gas in underground gas storage facilities, to stop up a well, borehole or shaft, or prevent its use by another person, and rights of way over land.

Conditions for the exercise of compulsory purchase powers

There are important conditions attaching to the use of compulsory purchase powers through DCOs. First, a DCO can include provision authorising the compulsory acquisition of land only if the Secretary of State is satisfied that the land (PA 2008, s 122):

- is required for the development to which the development consent relates (PA 2008, s 122(2)(a));
- is required to facilitate that development (PA 2008, s 122(2)(b));
- is incidental to that development (PA 2008, s 122(2)(b)); or
- is replacement land which is to be given in exchange for the order land (PA 2008, s 122(2)(c)).

In relation to the concepts of 'facilitate' and 'incidental', PINS has said that PA 2008, s 122(2)(b) could encompass the acquisition of land for the construction of development (eg a gas pipeline) which was not authorised by the DCO but which would be authorised by a later consent (register of advice, 17 November 2011, North Killinghome Power Project). In this regard, see also footnote 3 at paragraph 5 of the DCLG Guidance on associated development.

These are wide powers of compulsory purchase that are likely to be sufficient for promoters in most, if not all, cases. The further removed the land is from actually being required for the development, however, the more difficult it is likely to be in practice to justify the acquisition of the land in question.

Secondly, a further important condition must be satisfied under PA 2008, s 122(3), namely that there is a 'compelling case in the public interest' for the land to be acquired compulsorily. Whilst this wording reflects a long-standing policy test and had appeared in various court decisions (see, for example, *De Rothschild v Secretary of State for Transport* (1989) 57 P&CR 330), it was not previously a statutory requirement; indeed, PA 2008, s 122 remains the only place where it does appear as a statutory requirement.

Thirdly, a DCO can only authorise compulsory acquisition of land if one of three further conditions is met (PA 2008, s 123). They are that:

- the application for the order included a request for compulsory acquisition of the land to be authorised (PA 2008, s 123(2));
- all persons with an interest in the land consent to the inclusion of the provision (PA 2008, s 123(3)); or
- the prescribed procedure has been followed in relation to the land (PA 2008, s 123(4)).

The third condition above is based on an equivalent provision in the Acquisition of Land Act 1981. It deals with 'additional land', that is land which it is proposed shall be subject to compulsory acquisition and which was not identified in the book of reference submitted with the application. The procedure for the purposes of PA 2008, s 123(4) is prescribed in the Infrastructure Planning (Compulsory Acquisition) Regulations 2010, SI 2010/104.

Justification for the exercise of compulsory purchase powers

As well as satisfying the fundamental conditions set out above, it is necessary to show that the compulsory purchase proposed is properly justified.

The DCLG 'Guidance related to procedures for the compulsory acquisition of land' (2013) ('DCLG Guidance on compulsory acquisition') explains what justification will be sought for a DCO authorising the compulsory acquisition of land, including factors to which the decision-maker must have regard (paragraphs 8–19). This includes that:

- all reasonable alternatives to compulsory acquisition (including modifications to the scheme) have been explored (paragraph 8);
- the proposed interference with the rights of those with an interest in the land is for a legitimate purpose and is necessary and proportionate (paragraph 8);
- the applicant must have a clear idea of how it intends to use the land to be acquired (paragraph 9);
- there is a reasonable prospect of the requisite funds becoming available (paragraph 9);
- the purposes for which an order authorises the compulsory acquisition of land are legitimate and sufficiently justify interfering with the human rights of those with an interest in the land affected (paragraph 10);
- the land to be acquired is no more than is reasonably required for the purposes of the development (paragraph 11(i));
- there is compelling evidence that the public benefits that would be derived from the compulsory acquisition will outweigh the private loss that would be suffered by those whose land is to be acquired (paragraph 12).

In determining where the balance of public interest lies, the DCLG Guidance on compulsory acquisition makes it clear (paragraph 14) that 'the Secretary of State will weigh up the public benefits that a scheme will bring against any private loss to those affected by compulsory acquisition.'

An applicant will also be required to provide a funding statement providing as much information as possible about the resource implications of both: (a) acquiring the land; and (b) implementing the project for which the land is required (paragraph 17).

Interestingly, the guidance does not say that the compulsory purchase of land is intended as a last resort in the event that attempts to acquire by agreement fail, as is stated for compulsory purchase orders generally in the MHCLG 'Guidance on Compulsory Purchase Process and the Crichel Down Rules' (2019).

Nonetheless, applicants should not underestimate how hard it can be to demonstrate that these policy tests are satisfied in practice. In some cases, such as the expansion of an airport or a harbour, it may not be too difficult to show that the particular land is required. Similarly, in the case of linear schemes such as road and rail routes, it may be easier to show that there are no alternatives but to acquire compulsorily the interests in land which have not been acquired by agreement in advance. In other cases, however, such as offsite ecological compensation works or landscape planting, it may be very hard to show that the particular land is required. The DCLG Guidance on compulsory acquisition states (paragraph 11(ii)) that the Secretary of State needs 'to be satisfied that the development *could only* be landscaped to a satisfactory standard if *the land in question* were to be compulsorily acquired' (emphasis added). This could be very hard to demonstrate in practice.

Types of land

There are various protective provisions in the Act for certain types of land, which are explained in turn below. It should be noted that the Growth and Infrastructure Act 2013 reduced the circumstances in which the special parliamentary procedure was to be engaged.

Statutory undertakers

PA 2008, s 127 provides protective provisions for the land of statutory undertakers which apply where land has been acquired, and is used, by a statutory undertaker for the purpose of its undertaking, and the undertaker makes a representation on the application. In those circumstances, PA 2008, s 127(2) provides that the DCO can only include provision authorising the compulsory acquisition of the undertaker's land where the Secretary of State is satisfied that the nature and situation of the land are such that either:

- it can be purchased and not replaced without serious detriment to the carrying on of the undertaking, or
- if purchased it can be replaced by other land belonging to, or available for acquisition by, the undertakers without serious detriment to the carrying on of the undertaking.

PA 2008, s 127(5) makes a similar provision in relation to the acquisition of a right over the undertaker's land.

PA 2008, s 138 relates to DCOs which authorise the acquisition of land in which there subsists a right vested in a statutory undertaker for carrying on their operations or where there is on, under or over the land apparatus of the undertaker. This encompasses statutory undertakers as defined in Part 11 of the Town and Country Planning Act 1990 and electronic communications code network operators. The DCO can include provision for the extinguishment of the relevant right, or the removal of the relevant apparatus, only if the Secretary of State is satisfied that this would be necessary for the purpose of carrying out the development to which the DCO relates.

The Growth and Infrastructure Act 2013 had the effect of removing the special parliamentary procedure in cases where a statutory undertaker or local authority holds land.

National Trust

PA 2008, s 130 applies to land belonging to the National Trust which is held by the Trust inalienably. It provides that to the extent that the DCO authorises the compulsory acquisition of such land it must be subject to special parliamentary procedure if a representation has been made by the Trust about the application objecting to the compulsory acquisition of land.

Commons, open spaces etc

Commons and open spaces are covered in PA 2008, ss 131–132, along with land forming part of a fuel or field garden allotment. PA 2008, s 131 relates to the acquisition of land and PA 2008, s 132 relates to the acquisition of rights over land. Under PA 2008, s 131 a DCO would be subject to special parliamentary procedure save in particular circumstances. Those circumstances are:

- replacement land has been or will be given in exchange for the order land and the replacement land has been or will be vested in the prospective seller and subject to the same rights, trusts and incidents as attach to the order land (PA 2008, s 131(4));
- for open space only, either there is no suitable land available to be given in exchange for the order land or any suitable land available to be given in exchange is available only at prohibitive cost, and it is strongly in the public interest for the development for which the order grants consent to be capable of being begun sooner than is likely to be possible if the order were to be subject (to any extent) to special parliamentary procedure (PA 2008, s 131(4A));
- for open space only, where the order land is being acquired for a temporary (although possibly long-lived) purpose (PA 2008, s 131(4B));
- where the order land does not exceed 200 sq m or is required for the widening or drainage of an existing highway, and the giving in exchange of other land is unnecessary, whether in the interests of the persons, if any, entitled to rights of common or other rights or in the interests of the public (PA 2008, s 131(5)).

PA 2008, s 132 sets out similar provisions in relation to the compulsory purchase of rights over land, although there are differences between the two provisions.

Green Belt

PA 2008, s 147 applies where the DCO includes the compulsory acquisition (or exchange or appropriation) of Green Belt land. It requires that the Secretary of State must notify the relevant local authorities of the proposed acquisition.

Notification requirements

For pre-application consultation, PA 2008, ss 42 and 44 apply to people who are owners, tenants or occupiers of affected land and people the promoter thinks would or might be entitled to make a claim for compensation under Compulsory Purchase Act 1965, s 10 or Land Compensation Act 1973, Part I. The same categories of persons must also be notified under PA 2008, ss 56 and 59.

Where a DCO is made which includes provision authorising the compulsory acquisition of land, PA 2008, s 134 requires that the promoter (known as a prospective purchaser) serve a 'compulsory acquisition notice' on owners, lessees and occupiers of the land that is to be acquired or to subject to rights being acquired. The persons who have to be served are those who would be qualifying persons for the purposes of Acquisition of Land Act 1981, s 12(1). The promoter also has to erect a compulsory acquisition notice on a conspicuous object or objects on or near the order land and, so far as practicable, keep it in place for six weeks, and publish a notice in one or more local newspapers.

PA 2008, s 134(7) explains that a compulsory acquisition notice is a notice in the prescribed form describing the order land (or the right if appropriate), stating that the DCO includes provision authorising the compulsory acquisition of land or a right over the land, where and when a copy of the order is available for inspection, and that a person aggrieved by the DCO may challenge it only in accordance with PA 2008, s 118. The form of notice is found in Schedule 1 to the Infrastructure Planning (Compulsory Acquisition) Regulations 2010.

Procedural requirements

There are various procedural provisions which apply to applications for a DCO where compulsory acquisition powers are sought. For example, the Infrastructure Planning (Applications: Prescribed Forms and Procedure) Regulations 2009, SI 2009/2264, require the provision with such applications of:

- a statement of reasons;
- a statement to indicate how the DCO is proposed to be funded;
- a land plan identifying land over which it is proposed to exercise powers of compulsory acquisition or any right to use land; and
- a book of reference.

There are also particular certification requirements in relation to PA 2008, s 56 (notification of an accepted application).

The DCLG Guidance on compulsory acquisition provides advice on what is required for the land plans, funding statement and the statement of reasons. The Inspectorate has said that it would be prepared to provide advice on the content of draft funding statements (register of advice, 25 October 2012, Thames Tideway Tunnel). Funding is likely to be more of an issue with DCOs than traditional compulsory purchase orders because the compulsory acquisition powers in a DCO are often given to purely private bodies and carry with them the liability to pay proper compensation for land and rights acquired.

The guidance also encourages the use of alternative dispute resolution techniques to resolve concerns about the compulsory acquisition of land, including both mediation and early neutral evaluation.

The 2013 version of the DCLG Guidance on compulsory acquisition omitted what was said in the February 2010 version to the effect that a promoter should be negotiating in parallel with the compulsory purchase process to acquire land by agreement. It is unlikely, however, that this omission was intended to signal a significant change of position on the part of the Government. The advice in the DCLG Guidance on compulsory acquisition remains (para 25) that 'Applicants should seek to acquire land by negotiation wherever practicable'.

PA 2008, s 106 provides that, in deciding an application for an order granting development consent, representations may be disregarded if they relate to compensation for compulsory acquisition of land or of an interest in or right over land.

The duration of a DCO authorising the compulsory acquisition of land is covered in PA 2008, s 154, which provides that steps in relation to the acquisition must be taken within the 'prescribed period' (ie five years – see Infrastructure Planning (Interested Parties etc) Regulations 2015, reg 6(2)) or such other period as is specified in the DCO.

PA 2008, s 175 extends the blight regime in the Town and Country Planning Act 1990 to include land identified in a DCO to be subject to compulsory acquisition.

Article 55

Incorporation of the Compulsory Purchase Code

Richard Honey QC, ftb
Michael Humphries QC, ftb

Introduction

Where compulsory acquisition powers are incorporated into a development consent order, it is necessary for them to rely on the mechanisms and processes set out in other legislation for their efficacy. The 'compulsory purchase code' is the name that is commonly given to the disparate group statutory provisions that relate to compulsory purchase, supplemented by case law.

Parts of the compulsory purchase code

In essence, there are four parts to the compulsory purchase code being:

- the statutory power authorising compulsory purchase;
- the procedure for seeking an 'order' by which a statutory power authorising compulsory purchase is applied to a particular parcel of land;
- the implementation of the 'order' (particularly in relation to entry on the land and the transfer of title); and
- compulsory purchase compensation.

The statutory power authorising compulsory purchase

In relation to the PA 2008, s 122 grants the statutory power to include provision authorising the compulsory acquisition of land in a DCO. Subject to the requirements of PA 2008, s 122, that power is, therefore, available to any person who may properly apply for a development consent order.

This makes the powers of compulsory purchase potentially available to a whole range of developers who would not otherwise have had direct access to such powers. This can be contrasted to the compulsory purchase powers available under other regimes where the power is normally only available to a clearly defined class of person; for example, the relevant local authority under Town and County Planning Act 1990, s 226 or the relevant highway authority under Highways Act 1980, s 239. No such limitations exist under the Planning Act 2008.

The procedure for seeking an 'order' by which a statutory power authorising compulsory purchase is applied to a particular parcel of land

The procedural requirements for making an application for development consent are set out in articles 36 and 37 of this work.

It is also worth reminding the reader, however, that the Infrastructure Planning (Compulsory Acquisition) Regulations 2010, SI 2010/104, set out various procedural requirements that relate particularly to the compulsory acquisition of 'additional land' that was not included in the Book of Reference.

The implementation of the 'order' (particularly in relation to entry on the land and the transfer of title)

PA 2008, s 125 relates to the application of certain other parts of the compulsory purchase code in a development consent order and, in particular, relating to the implementation of the compulsory purchase powers within a DCO. The section applies if a DCO includes provision authorising the compulsory acquisition of land. It provides that Part 1 of the Compulsory Purchase Act 1965 ('CPA 1965') (procedure for compulsory purchase) applies to the compulsory acquisition of land under the DCO as it applies to a compulsory purchase to which Part 2 of the Acquisition of Land Act 1981 applies, as if the DCO were a compulsory purchase order under the 1981 Act. The provisions of the CPA 1965 govern the procedures to be followed once the compulsory acquisition of land has been authorised in the DCO.

PA 2008, s 125 provides however that, subject to any contrary provisions made by the DCO, Part 1 of the CPA 1965 will have effect with the omission of s 4 (time limit for exercise of compulsory purchase powers), s 10 (compensation for injurious affection) and paragraph 3(3) of Schedule 3 (provision as to giving of bonds).

The effect of PA 2008, s 125 would also apply Part 1 of the CPA 1965 to any acquisition of land following the service of a blight notice on the grounds that the land is blighted because its compulsory purchase is proposed in an application for a DCO. PA 2008, s 175 amends the Town and Country Planning Act 1990 to apply the blight provisions to land in an application for a DCO or a DCO which is for compulsory acquisition and also land identified in national policy statements as suitable or potentially suitable for a development.

The procedures for implementing compulsory acquisition powers under a DCO are, therefore, the same as those for a compulsory purchase order, namely through Part 1 of the CPA 1965 and notices to treat and of entry. In addition, however, as is explained below, many DCOs also apply the Compulsory Purchase (Vesting Declarations) Act 1981. This creates an alternative means of implementing the compulsory purchase powers contained in a DCO and would allow the use of general vesting declarations.

Compulsory purchase compensation

Section 1 of the Land Compensation Act 1961 ('LCA 1961') provides as follows:

> 'Where by or under any statute (whether passed before or after the passing of this Act) land is authorised to be acquired compulsorily, any question of disputed compensation and, where any part of the land to be acquired is subject to a lease which comprises land not acquired, any question as to the apportionment of the rent payable under the lease, shall be referred to the [Upper Tribunal] and shall be determined by the Tribunal in accordance with the following provisions of this Act.'

Thus, where there is a dispute as to compensation, the compulsory purchase compensation provisions in the LCA 1961 are automatically applied to any compulsory purchase of land by the terms of s 1, unless specifically disapplied. The 'following provisions' of the LCA 1961 referred to in s 1 include the six rules for assessing compensation set out in LCA 1961, s 5, as follows:

> 'Compensation in respect of any compulsory acquisition shall be assessed in accordance with the following rules:
>
> (1) No allowance shall be made on account of the acquisition being compulsory:
>
> (2) The value of land shall, subject as hereinafter provided, be taken to be the amount which the land if sold in the open market by a willing seller might be expected to realise:
>
> (2A) The value of land referred to in rule (2) is to be assessed in the light of the no-scheme principle set out in section 6A:
>
> (3) The special suitability or adaptability of the land for any purpose shall not be taken into account if that purpose is a purpose to which it could be applied only in pursuance of statutory powers, or for which there is no market apart from the requirements of any authority possessing compulsory purchase powers:
>
> (4) Where the value of the land is increased by reason of the use thereof or of any premises thereon in a manner which could be restrained by any court, or is contrary to law, or is detrimental to the health of the occupants of the premises or to the public health, the amount of that increase shall not be taken into account:
>
> (5) Where land is, and but for the compulsory acquisition would continue to be, devoted to a purpose of such a nature that there is no general demand or market for land for that purpose, the compensation may, if the Upper Tribunal is satisfied that reinstatement in some other place is bona fide intended, be assessed on the basis of the reasonable cost of equivalent reinstatement:
>
> (6) The provisions of rule (2) shall not affect the assessment of compensation for disturbance or any other matter not directly based on the value of land:
>
> and the following provisions of this Part of this Act shall have effect with respect to the assessment.'

These rules form the starting point in most assessments of compulsory purchase compensation, although it needs to be recognised that the LCA 1961 contains a number of other important provisions relating to the assessment of compulsory purchase compensation.

Part 1 of the Land Compensation Act 1973 ('LCA 1973') (compensation for depreciation of land value by physical factors caused by use of public works) applies in relation to works authorised under a DCO, by means of PA 2008, s 152(7), as if references in the LCA 1973 to 'public works' were references to 'authorised works' in the DCO. Part 1 of the LCA 1973 is however applied with the omission of ss 1(6) and 17, which relate to statutory immunity from nuisance.

Compensation is payable pursuant to PA 2008, s 165(4), for damage caused to land or chattels in the exercise of a relevant right of entry, by the local authority that authorised the entry to any person suffering damage. In circumstances where a dispute about such compensation is referred to the Upper Tribunal (Lands Chamber) for determination, PA 2008, s 165(6) provides that the provisions of LCA 1961, s 4 apply (with any necessary modifications). LCA 1961, s 4 deals with the costs of Tribunal proceedings.

One important aspect of the compulsory purchase code that is amended by the PA 2008 is the disapplication of CPA 1965, s 10 (compensation for injurious affection) and its replacement by a bespoke provision. PA 2008, s 152 applies where a person affected by a DCO has no right to claim in nuisance (eg because of the provision in PA 2008, s 158 which gives a defence of statutory authority in civil or criminal proceedings for nuisance). PA 2008, s 152 gives a right to compensation for injurious affection in cases where a person would not be able to succeed in a claim for nuisance in respect of works authorised by the DCO.

PA 2008, s 152 applies if, by virtue of PA 2008, s 158 or the DCO itself, there is a defence of statutory authority in civil or criminal proceedings for nuisance in respect of any authorised works. It defines 'authorised works' as including both development for which consent is granted by the DCO and anything else authorised by the DCO. The substantive obligation is in PA 2008, s 152(3), which provides that the person by or on whose behalf any authorised works are carried out must pay compensation to any person whose land is injuriously affected by the carrying out of the works. PA 2008, s 152(8) provides that a DCO may not include provision the effect of which is to remove or modify the application of any of PA 2008, s 152(1)–(7), so that the provision is 'locked-in' to the DCO system.

The provision for compensation in PA 2008, s 152 effectively applies in lieu of CPA 1965, s 10. PA 2008, s 152(5) goes as far as to apply the limitation on compensation in CPA 1965, s 10(2) to compensation under PA 2008, s 152(3). Furthermore, PA 2008, s 152(6) applies to the construction of PA 2008, s 152(3) 'any rule or principle applied to the construction of section 10'. PA 2008, s 152(3) provides compensation where 'land is injuriously affected by the carrying out of the works'. CPA 1965, s 10, by contrast, provides compensation where a person's interest in land is injuriously affected by the execution of the works. It appears, therefore, that there is little difference between the ambit of the two provisions and that the intention is that the approach under CPA 1965, s 10 would apply to compensation for injurious affection under PA 2008, s 152.

Ability to modify or exclude a 'compensation provision'

It is important to note that the ability to 'modify' the application of a 'compensation provision', that is a provision in or made under an Act which relates to compulsory purchase compensation, is very limited by the terms of PA 2008, s 126 and can only be included to the extent necessary to apply the provision to the compulsory acquisition of land authorised by the order. Furthermore, a DCO may not include a provision the effect of which is to 'exclude' the application of a 'compensation provision'.

That said, there does appear to be some scope to introduce new provisions into a DCO relating to compulsory purchase compensation where the effect does not modify or exclude the application of an existing 'compensation provision' or, indeed, where it extends it.

Compulsory purchase provisions in DCOs

There are now large numbers of DCOs that have passed through the system and nearly all of those will include compulsory acquisition provisions. There is, therefore, a wealth of experience in drafting appropriate provisions. Set out below is simply a sample of interesting examples.

Taking first the Hinkley Point C (Nuclear Generating Station) Order 2013, SI 2013/648, the DCO makes various additional provision for the application of the compulsory purchase code. SI 2013/648, art 27(3), Sch 11 provides for the modification of compensation and compulsory purchase statutes to deal with the creation of new rights.

Article 29 provides for the application of the Compulsory Purchase (Vesting Declarations) Act 1981 to the DCO as if it were a compulsory purchase order, with certain modifications.

This enables the use of a general vesting declaration with DCOs, as opposed to notices to treat and of entry as would otherwise be the case.

Article 30 empowers the promoter to acquire only so much of, or such rights in, the subsoil of land as may be required, instead of acquiring the whole of the land. In such cases, Art 31 (considered below), applies where the promoter acquires a cellar, vault, arch or other construction forming part of a house, building or manufactory.

By contrast, in the Network Rail (North Doncaster Chord) Order 2012, SI 2012/2635, art 27 applies not only to subsoil but also to 'the airspace over the land' (see also eg the Lancashire County Council (Torrisholme to the M6 Link (A683 Completion of Heysham to M6 Link Road)) Order 2013, SI 2013/675, art 25).

Article 31 of the Hinkley Point C (Nuclear Generating Station) Order 2013 deals with the acquisition of part of certain properties. It applies in place of CPA 1965, s 8(1) (which would otherwise apply by virtue of PA 2008, s 125) where a notice to treat is served on the owner of land forming only part of a house, building or manufactory or of land consisting of a house with a park or garden, to enable the owner to serve a counter-notice within 21 days objecting to the acquisition but stating that the owner is willing and able to sell the whole of the land. Unless the promoter agrees to acquire the whole then the issue of whether the owner should be required to sell only the land subject to the notice to treat must be referred to the Lands Chamber of the Upper Tribunal for determination. On such a reference the test is whether the land subject to the notice to treat can be acquired without material detriment to the remainder of the land subject to the counter-notice, or, where the land subject to the notice to treat consists of a house with a park or garden, without material detriment to the remainder of the land subject to the counter-notice and without seriously affecting the amenity and convenience of the house. If so, then the owner is required to sell the land subject to the notice to treat. Where under this process a notice to treat is deemed to cover less land or more land than originally specified in the notice, the promoter has six weeks in which it can withdraw the notice. If it does, then it must pay the owner compensation for any loss or expense caused by the giving and withdrawing of the notice to treat. Article 31(10) provides that where the owner is required to sell only part of the land or property, compensation is payable by the promoter for severance.

In arts 33 and 34 relating to the temporary use of land for carrying out and maintaining the project, it is provided that CPA 1965, s 13 relating to refusal to give possession to the authority applies to the temporary use as it would to the compulsory acquisition of land under the DCO.

There are various provisions in the Hinkley Point C (Nuclear Generating Station) Order 2013 which confer on persons affected by the exercise of powers under the DCO an entitlement to compensation, to be determined under Part 1 of the LCA 1961 where it is disputed. These provisions cover for example:

- any person who suffers loss by the suspension or extinguishment of any private right of way under art 15 (permanent stopping up of streets);
- any person who suffers loss by the suspension of any private right of way under art 17 (temporary stopping up of streets);
- owners and occupiers of any building or land in relation to which rights under art 22 (protective work to buildings) have been exercised for any loss or damage arising to them by reason of the exercise of those rights;
- owners and occupiers of the relevant land for any loss or damage arising by reason of the exercise of the authority conferred by art 23 to survey and investigate land;
- any person who suffers loss by the extinguishment or suspension of any private right of way under art 28 (private rights of way);

- any person who is an owner or occupier of land appropriated under art 32(1) (rights under or over streets), without the promoter acquiring any part of that person's interest in the land, and who suffers loss as a result;
- owners and occupiers of land of which temporary possession is taken under art 33 (temporary use of land for carrying out authorised project) for any loss or damage arising from the exercise in relation to the land of any power conferred by art 33;
- owners and occupiers of land of which temporary possession is taken under art 34 (temporary use of land for maintaining authorised project) for any loss or damage arising from the exercise in relation to the land of the provisions of art 34;
- any person who suffers any loss or damage arising from unnecessary damage to any tree or shrub when carrying out felling or lopping trees under art 41;
- any person who suffers any loss or damage arising from unnecessary damage to any tree or shrub subject to a tree preservation order under art 42.

Moreover, the Lancashire County Council (Torrisholme to the M6 Link (A683 Completion of Heysham to M6 Link Road)) Order 2013, SI 2013/675, contains in art 18 powers temporarily to close, interfere with and undertake works in the Lancaster Canal. Article 18(7) provides that any person who suffers loss or damage as the result of either the suspension of any private right of navigation or any effect of the exercise of the art 18 powers on the functioning of any intake or discharge along the canal is entitled to compensation for such loss or damage.

Returning to the Network Rail (North Doncaster Chord) Order 2012, SI 2012/2635, art 41 of that DCO deals with the application of the Land Compensation Act 1973. It provides that regulations on the sound proofing of buildings affected by public works (eg the Noise Insulation (Railways and Other Guided Transport Systems) Regulations 1996, SI 1996/428 and the Noise Insulation Regulations 1975, SI 1975/1763) apply to the railway comprised in the authorised development under the DCO as if that railway was provided or used in the exercise of statutory powers.

Article 56

Extinguishment of Public Rights of Way

Alex Booth QC, ftb
Michael Humphries QC, ftb

Introduction

This article is concerned with the extinguishment of public rights of way and, in particular, PA 2008, ss 136 and 137.

PA 2008, s 136 provides that a DCO may extinguish public rights of way, subject to one of two criteria contained in PA 2008, s 136(1) being met to the satisfaction of the Secretary of State. PA 2008, s 136 is otherwise concerned with the procedure of extinguishment in circumstances where the land over which the right exists is authorised for acquisition by the DCO.

PA 2008, s 137 is a discrete provision, relating to the extinguishment of rights over land that accommodates either apparatus belonging to statutory undertakers, or apparatus operated in connection with an electronic communications code network.

To date, the extent to which the relevant provisions have been considered during the examination process is limited. Furthermore, no guidance has yet been issued which might indicate how the provisions are intended to operate.

General provision as to extinguishment

PA 2008, s 136(1) stipulates that a DCO may only extinguish a public right of way if the Secretary of States is satisfied either:

'(a) an alternative right of way has been or will be provided, or

(b) the provision of an alternative right of way is not required.'

The inclusion of a discretion for the Secretary of State to authorise the extinguishment of a public right of way without replacement, in the event of his/her concluding that such replacement is not required, would appear to provide potential for dispute. The exercise of such discretion would presumably be subject to regulation by the courts by means of judicial review, the period for challenge being limited to six weeks from the date of publication of the order granting development consent by virtue of Highways Act 1980, s 118(7).

In terms of the tests likely to be applied by the Secretary of State in this context, some limited assistance may be gained from decisions of the Courts in connection with Highways Act 1980, s 118. Sections 118(1) and (2) require respectively:

(i) that a highways authority, when considering whether to extinguish a public right of way, should determine whether 'it is expedient that the … way should be stopped upon on the ground that it is not needed for public use'; and

(ii) that the Secretary of State, when considering whether to confirm an order for extinguishment, should only do so having determined that 'it is expedient so to do having regard to the extent … that the path or way would … be likely to be used by the public, and having regard to the effect which the extinguishment or the right of way would have …'

The decisions of Phillips J in *R v Secretary of State ex parte Stewart* (1980) 39 P&CR 534 and Auld J in *R v Secretary of State ex parte Cheshire County Council* [1991] JPL 537 both offer some insight in this regard, though necessarily they are concerned with the statutory wording of Highways Act 1980, s 118 as opposed to PA 2008, s 136. In the former, and as regards the second of the two tests, Phillips J effectively concluded in *ex p Stewart* (p 541) that, where there was material demand for the route in question, it would not be 'expedient' to extinguish it.

However, the test in PA 2008, s 136(1)(b) is more broadly worded so as to suggest that a wide range of matters might be taken into consideration by the Secretary of State in the exercise of his discretion; such discretion to be exercised 'in the round'. At present, the extent to which the benefits of delivering the NSIP giving rise to the need for the extinguishment might fall to be considered in this context is unclear. However, it should be noted that, as regards development consented pursuant to the Town and Country Planning Act 1990 ('TCPA 1990'), s 247 of that Act confers on the Secretary of State a broad discretion to stop up/extinguish any right of way if it is considered 'necessary' to enable development to be carried out. Paragraph 7.15 of the Rights of Way Circular 1/09 speaks in terms of the decision-maker weighing up 'the advantages' of making an order to extinguish a right of way; such 'advantage' must necessarily include the benefit that the consented development would deliver.

As regards provision of alternative routes pursuant to PA 2008, s 136(1)(a), potentially problematic is the absence of any temporal requirement as to when a replacement right of way must take be provided. The reference to an alternative right that 'has been … provided' must of course relate to a right which has come into existence prior to the date of the Secretary of State's decision in respect of the application. However the reference to the Secretary of State being 'satisfied' that an alternative right 'will be provided', without any requirement as to the date by which such replacement provision must available, might be thought to leave some scope for dispute regarding the sufficiency of the replacement right of way.

The provision in practice

The Rookery South development consent order application provides a useful illustration of how the provision may be expected to work in practice.

In that instance the DCO sought (and ultimately published) provided for the extinguishment of two short sections of footpath: see article 11 of and Schedule 3 to the DCO. By way of mitigation, the promoters were also proposing to upgrade various existing routes, as well as to provide limited new stretches of footpath/cycleway; the improvements to be provided by, s 106 obligation. Notwithstanding that the proposed new provision did not in any sense 'replicate' the routes lost (which routes the Examining Panel observed were 'effectively short stubs and [did] not lead anywhere'), the Panel felt able to conclude (para 5.144) that: 'We are satisfied therefore that alternatives would be provided to enable these public rights of way to be extinguished'.

Accordingly, at least in this instance, the decision-maker did not consider that an 'alternative right of way' being provided pursuant to PA 2008, s 136(1)(a) need reflect or even approximate the route which it replaced. Rather, it was enough that an additional route was being provided. This is significant, in that in the ordinary course of events one might have expected a 'replacement' route to serve the same function as the route to be extinguished, on a 'like for like' basis.

Procedural requirements

Extinguishment where land acquired

PA 2008, s 136(2) and (3) is concerned with circumstances where the order granting development consent makes provision for the acquisition of land, compulsorily or by agreement, and the order extinguishes a right of way that is not a right enjoyed by vehicular traffic. PA 2008, s 136(3) proves in these circumstances that the order granting development consent may not provide for the right of way to be extinguished from a date which is earlier than that on which the order is 'published'.

It is worth pausing to consider the use of the word 'published' in this context. The term is used in a number of provisions within the PA 2008, but is not defined in PA 2008, s 235 or elsewhere. Its precise meaning in the context of PA 2008 is significant, if only because the six-week period within which judicial review proceedings must be brought in respect of legal challenge to the grant of a DCO pursuant to PA 2008, s 118(1), runs from the date on which the DCO or the statement of reasons in respect of it are 'published' (PA 2008, s 118(1)(b)).

In *R (Williams) v Secretary of State for Energy and Climate Change* [2015] EWHC 1202 (Admin), Lindblom J (as he then was) said (para 45) that:

> 'The way in which an order and the Secretary of State's statement of reasons for making it are to be "published" is not prescribed by section 118. But in my view the placing of the order on the Planning Inspectorate's infrastructure planning website ..., together with the Secretary of State's decision letter and the Examining Authority's report, and, on the same day, the notification of the interested parties, both by email and post, that this had been done, was enough to constitute publication of the order, and the reasons why it was made, within the meaning of section 118.'

Thus the date on which an order is 'published' on the PINS website would appear to be the correct date for the purposes of PA 2008, s 136(3) too.

Revival of right of way where acquisition of land abandoned

The remaining provisions of PA 2008, s 136 (s 136(4), (5) and (7)) relate to the circumstances where a public right of way has been extinguished by a DCO, but the anticipated acquisition of land over which the right formerly existed has not been completed. In these circumstances, where 'it appears to the Secretary of State that the proposal to acquire the land has been abandoned' (PA 2008, s 136(4)(b)), then the Secretary of State must make an order 'reviving' the extinguished right.

The provision is clearly intended to avoid the permanent loss to the public, of rights of way the extinguishment of which was not ultimately necessary – either because the NSIP was not constructed, or because it was constructed in such a way as did not require acquisition of the land over which the public rights historically ran.

It should be noted that PA 2008, s 136(7) expressly provides that the 'revival' of a right of way pursuant to PA 2008, s 136(5) is no bar to 'the making of a further order extinguishing the right of way'. The use of the term 'further order' suggests that this provision is not intended for some further extinguishment under the existing DCO, but rather either a fresh DCO or else another, wholly separate, order such as one sought pursuant to Highways Act 1980, s 118ZA.

Article 57

Temporary Possession

Michael Humphries QC, ftb
Richard Honey QC, ftb

Introduction

DCOs usually provide for the temporary possession of land for the purposes of the carrying out of the project or maintaining the project once completed. This is the case even though the PA 2008 contains no express power to take temporary possession. The power derives, however, from PA 2008, s 120(3) which provides that an order granting development consent may 'make provision relating to, or to matters ancillary to, the development for which development consent is granted'.

Where temporary possession is taken, it allows the undertaker to occupy and control the land to the exclusion of everyone else, including the landowner and any lessee. It authorises what would otherwise be a trespass. If the land were subject to a tenancy, taking temporary possession would have no direct legal effect on the operation of the tenancy, which would continue to apply to the land including obligations to pay rent; although such a tenant might seek to argue, as against its landlord, that the tenancy had become frustrated as the landlord was not providing vacant possession and, in any event, the tenant would have a claim in compensation for loss or damage against the person taking temporary possession.

Model articles granting temporary possession powers were included in Model Provisions 28 and 29 of the general model provisions of the (now lapsed) Infrastructure Planning (Model Provisions) (England and Wales) Order 2009 ('the Model Provisions Order'). Such powers have been included in most DCOs made to date and, indeed, the form of the relevant articles for both construction and maintenance is now reasonably well settled.

It is important to note that a power to take temporary possession is *not* the compulsory acquisition of that land or a right in that land, but simply a 'power' to enter on and take temporary possession of land for a specified purpose; in other words, the undertaker acquires no interest or right in the land itself.

Chapter 1 of Part 2 of the Neighbourhood Planning Act 2017 provides for a general power to take temporary possession of land, which will in due course apply instead of the bespoke provisions which have previously been included in DCOs. At the time of writing, these provisions have not been brought into force and it may be some time until they are commenced. The new provisions, and the position in the interim, are considered at the end of this section.

Temporary use of land for carrying out the authorised project

The first point to make is that the typical current form of an article granting temporary power of possession is different in a number of important respects from Model Provision 28 in the Model Provisions Order. The current preferred form has evolved over time in response to the needs of undertakers and experience. Having said that, there is no 'standard' template and such articles will continue to be adapted to the particular circumstances. What follows is an example of a recent temporary possession for construction article and then a brief commentary on its provisions.

Typical current drafting

Article 35 of the Great Yarmouth Third River Crossing DCO 2020 provides as follows:

> '(1) The undertaker may, in connection with the construction of the authorised development but subject to article 27(2) (time limit for exercise of powers to possess land temporarily or to acquire land compulsorily)–
>
> (a) enter on and take temporary possession of–
>
> (i) the land specified in columns (1) and (2) of Schedule 9 (land of which only temporary possession may be taken) for the purpose specified in relation to that land in column (3) of that Schedule relating to the part of the authorised development specified in column (4) of that Schedule; and
>
> (ii) any of the Order land in respect of which no notice of entry has been served under section 11(1) (powers of entry) of the 1965 Act (other than in connection with the acquisition of rights only) and no declaration has been made under section 4(2) (execution of declaration) of the 1981 Act;
>
> (b) remove any buildings and vegetation from the land referred to in sub-paragraphs (a)(i) to (ii);
>
> (c) construct temporary works (including the provisions of means of access) and buildings on the land referred to in sub-paragraphs (a)(i) to (ii); and
>
> (d) construct any works on the land referred to in sub-paragraphs (a)(i) to (ii) as are mentioned in Schedule 1 (authorised development).
>
> (2) Not less than 28 days before entering on and taking temporary possession of land under this article the undertaker must serve notice of the intended entry on the owners and occupiers of the land and that notice must state the works, facilities or other purpose for which the undertaker intends to take possession of the land.
>
> (3) The undertaker may not, without the agreement of the owners of the land, remain in possession of any land under this article–
>
> (a) in the case of any land specified in paragraph (1)(a)(i) after the end of the period of one year beginning with the date of completion of the part of the authorised development specified in relation to that land in column (4) of Schedule 9; or
>
> (b) in the case of any land referred to in paragraph (1)(a)(ii) after the end of the period of one year beginning with the date of completion of the works, use of facilities or other purpose for which temporary possession of the land was taken unless the undertaker has, by the end of that period, served a notice of entry under section 11 of the 1965 Act or made a declaration under section 4 of the 1981 Act in relation to that land.
>
> (4) Before giving up possession of land of which temporary possession has been taken under this article, the undertaker must remove all temporary works and restore the land to the reasonable satisfaction of the owners of the land; but the undertaker is not required to–
>
> (a) replace a building removed under this article;

(b) restore the land on which any permanent works have been constructed under paragraph (1)(d);

(c) remove any ground strengthening works which have been placed on the land to facilitate construction of the authorised development; or

(d) remove any measures installed over or around statutory undertakers' apparatus to protect that apparatus from the authorised development.

(5) Any person who suffers loss as a result of the suspension of any private right of navigation under this article is entitled to be paid compensation for such loss by the undertaker, to be determined, in case of dispute, under Part 1 (determination of questions of disputed compensation) of the 1961 Act.

(6) The undertaker must pay compensation to the owners and occupiers of land of which temporary possession is taken under this article for any loss or damage arising from the exercise in relation to the land of the provisions of this article.

(7) Any dispute as to a person's entitlement to compensation under paragraph (6), or as to the amount of the compensation, must be determined under Part 1 of the 1961 Act.

(8) Nothing in this article affects any liability to pay compensation under section 152 (compensation in case where no right to claim in nuisance) of the 2008 Act or under any other enactment in respect of loss or damage arising from the construction of any works, other than loss or damage for which compensation is payable under paragraph (6).

(9) Where the undertaker takes possession of land under this article, the undertaker is not required to acquire the land or any interest in it.

(10) Section 13(3) (refusal to give possession to acquiring authority) of the 1965 Act applies to the temporary use of land under this article to the same extent as it applies to the compulsory acquisition of land under this Order by virtue of section 125 (application of compulsory acquisition provisions) of the 2008 Act.'

Commentary

Article 35(1)

This is the principal power that grants the power to 'enter on and take possession of' the land, but also grants power to do related things whilst on the land, including the construction of certain 'temporary works' and, indeed, works comprised in the 'authorised development' itself (ie permanent works).

The power to enter on and take temporary possession of the land is divided into two parts. Article 35(1)(a)(i) relates solely to land in Schedule 9 to the Order – that is, land of which the undertaker may only take temporary possession and only for a purpose specified in that schedule. Such land it usually coloured separately on the relevant Land Plan to distinguish it from land where the land or rights in land may be acquired.

By contrast, the power in Article 35(1)(a)(ii) relates to any other part of the Order Land; in other words, it allows the undertaker to take temporary possession of land that is identified as land subject to compulsory acquisition of land or rights in land, but only where there has been no service of a notice to treat (other than for the compulsory acquisition of rights only) and no general vesting declaration in respect of the land. The purpose of this provision, which does not exist in Model Provision 28, is to allow the undertaker to take temporary possession of any land to construct the authorised development, but then only compulsorily acquire the land

and/or rights that are actually necessary for that development. This may be of assistance where the precise location or dimensions of a structure are not finally fixed until relatively late in the construction period. This approach is also 'proportionate', in that it means that the undertaker is able only to compulsorily acquire the actual land and rights required and is not forced to acquire more than is necessary 'just in case' it is needed.

Article 35(2)

This paragraph is very similar to the equivalent provision in Model Provision 28, although it is extended so that the notice of entry now has to state the purpose for which the undertaker is intending to take possession. This extended wording is, in effect, a consequence of Article 35(1)(a)(ii), discussed above. In Model Provision 28, temporary possession could only be taken for the purposes defined in Schedule 9 but, once that was extended to other land within the Order Limits, for which there is no stated purpose, the form of words in Article 35(2) became appropriate.

Article 35(3)

Here again, the wording in this sub-paragraph is extended in Article 35(3)(b) beyond that in Model Provision 28 to accommodate the effect of Article 35(1)(a)(ii). Article 35(3)(b) also has to reflect, however, the possibility that the undertaker may serve a notice to treat or general vesting declaration in respect of the land subject to temporary possession and so, where that has happened, does not require the undertaker to give up possession.

Article 35(4)

The sub-paragraph requires the undertaker to 'remove all temporary works and restore the land to the reasonable satisfaction of the owners of the land', subject to certain exceptions. The issue of what it would be 'reasonable' for landowners to be 'satisfied' with has not, as yet, come before the Courts in this context, but it is fraught with potential difficulty.

The equivalent provision to this in Model Provision 28 was very simple and required the undertaker to remove temporary works (because it only allowed for temporary works) and restore the land, although any building removed did not have to be replaced. That simple requirement does not really fit with the extended power in Article 35(1)(d), which allowed permanent works to be constructed on such land in certain circumstances.

Article 35(4)(c) is really a reflection of the equivalent provision in the Thames Tideway Tunnel DCO, where the Article 35 form of temporary possession article was first developed. For the Thames Tideway Tunnel project, it was necessary to undertake certain strengthening works to potentially unstable parts of the River Thames embankment during construction of the tunnel, but the undertaker had no further need for that land. The undertaker, therefore, carried out the strengthening works under a power of temporary possession, but then provided that it did not need to remove those works when it had carried out construction of the tunnel as this benefitted the embankment generally. Article 35(4)(c) has similar effect in respect of a river crossing project.

Article 35(5)

This is a specific provision relating to compensation relating to loss resulting from loss of navigation and is, therefore, specific to the circumstances of the Great Yarmouth Third River Crossing project.

Article 35(6)

This is the general 'compensation' sub-paragraph for loss or damage arising from the exercise of the temporary possession power and directly reflects the equivalent provision in Model Provision 28(5). The concept of 'loss or damage' is not defined in the legislation but will generally be interpreted widely so that landowners and occupiers are put in an equivalent position to what they would have been in if there had been no temporary possession.

Article 35(7)

This is a standard provision that makes it clear how any dispute as to compensation is to be determined and, again, reflects the equivalent provision in Model Provision 28.

Article 35(8)

This article, again, closely follows that in Model Provision 28; although Model Provision 28 refers to nothing in the article affecting any liability to pay compensation under Compulsory Purchase Act 1965 ('CPA 1965'), s 10(2), whereas Article 35(8) refers to PA 2008, s 152. This is, in effect, a distinction without any real difference as both of those provisions relate to compensation for injurious affection where no land is taken. On balance, however, the reference to PA 2008, s 152 is probably slightly clearer as it applies both CPA 1965, s 10(2) and Part 1 of the Land Compensation Act 1973 in the specific context of an order granting development consent.

Article 35(9)

This provision is in the same form as the equivalent sub-paragraph in Model Provision 28 and makes it clear that taking temporary possession of land does not mean that the undertaker is required to acquire the land or any interest in it.

Article 35(10)

This sub-paragraph mirrors the equivalent provision in Model Provision 28 and relates to the undertaker's ability to seek a warrant from a sheriff or enforcement officer to deliver possession where a landowner refuses to give possession under the article.

As mentioned above, it is perfectly acceptable to adapt this form of temporary possession article to reflect particular circumstances – and, for example, Article 35(5) has done exactly that to deal with potential compensation for any interruption to navigation; however, in general, Article 35 illustrates what has become a reasonably well-settled form of drafting.

Temporary use of land for maintaining authorised project

DCOs will also include a power of temporary possession to 'maintain' the authorised development for a period after it has first opened for use.

It is important to distinguish this power of temporary possession to 'maintain' from the permanent rights to maintain an authorised development that are often sought for projects such as overhead lines or cables. The permanent right to maintain (say) an overhead line is required because the undertaker will not have acquired the freehold of all the land over which the authorised development will be constructed; the undertaker will (typically) acquire a right to construct and keep the development on the land, but will also require a separate right to 'maintain' it in perpetuity. This right will, however, be within a defined corridor for a linear project that will (probably) not be as wide as the Order Limits that are required for construction.

This is very different from the power to take temporary possession for 'maintenance' of a project that is intended to allow the undertaker to maintain development during its early years and that may be undertaken anywhere within the Order Limits. This might be necessary where, for example, remedial maintenance of newly erected buildings or other structures needs to be undertaken on land that has not been acquired freehold. The temporary possession 'maintenance' power will typically relate to the whole of the land within the Order Limits, as did the original power to construct.

Again, the Great Yarmouth Third River Crossing DCO 2020 provides a helpful example of typical current drafting. In the case of this 'temporary possession' power, however, there is less divergence from the model provision (in this case, Model Provision 29).

Typical current drafting

Article 36 of the Great Yarmouth Third River Crossing DCO 2020 provides as follows:

> '(1) Subject to paragraph (3), at any time during the maintenance period relating to any of the authorised development, the undertaker may–
>
> (a) enter upon and take temporary possession of any land within the Order limits if possession is reasonably required for the purpose of maintaining the authorised development;
>
> (b) enter on any land within the Order limits for the purpose of gaining such access as is reasonably required for the purpose of maintaining the authorised development; and
>
> (c) construct such temporary works (including the provision of means of access) and buildings on the land as may be reasonably necessary for that purpose.
>
> (2) Paragraph (1) does not authorise the undertaker to take temporary possession of–
>
> (a) any house or garden belonging to a house; or
>
> (b) any building (other than a house) if it is for the time being occupied.
>
> (3) Not less than 28 days before entering upon and taking temporary possession of land under this article the undertaker must serve notice of the intended entry on the owners and occupiers of the land and that notice must state the purpose for which the undertaker intends to take possession of the land including the particulars of the part of the authorised development for which possession is to be taken.
>
> (4) The undertaker may only remain in possession of land under this article for so long as may be reasonably necessary to carry out the maintenance of the part of the authorised development for which possession of the land was taken.
>
> (5) Before giving up possession of land of which temporary possession has been taken under this article, the undertaker must remove all temporary works and restore the land to the reasonable satisfaction of the owners of the land.

(6) Any person who suffers loss as a result of the suspension of any private right of navigation under this article is entitled to be paid compensation for such loss by the undertaker, to be determined, in case of dispute, under Part 1 (determination of questions of disputed compensation) of the 1961 Act.

(7) The undertaker must pay compensation to the owners and occupiers of land of which temporary possession is taken under this article for any loss or damage arising from the exercise in relation to the land of the powers conferred by this article.

(8) Any dispute as to a person's entitlement to compensation under paragraph (7), or as to the amount of the compensation, must be determined under Part 1 of the 1961 Act.

(9) Nothing in this article affects any liability to pay compensation under section 152 (compensation in case where no right to claim in nuisance) of the 2008 Act or under any other enactment in respect of loss or damage arising from the execution of any works, other than loss or damage for which compensation is payable under paragraph (7).

(10) Where the undertaker takes possession of land under this article, the undertaker is not required to acquire the land or any interest in it.

(11) Section 13 (refusal to give possession to acquiring authority) of the 1965 Act applies to the temporary use of land under this article to the same extent as it applies to the compulsory acquisition of land under this Order by virtue of section 125 (application of compulsory acquisition provisions) of the 2008 Act.

(12) In this article "the maintenance period", in relation to any part of the authorised development, means the period of 5 years beginning with the date on which–

(a) that part of the authorised development is first opened for public use (where that part of the authorised development is intended to be used by the public); or

(b) in respect of any other part of the authorised development, that part is first brought into operational use by the undertaker.'

Commentary

Less commentary is required here because (a) the rationale for many of the provisions will have been explored above in relation to Article 35, and (b) there is less divergence from the model provision. Nevertheless, some general points can be made.

Article 36(1)

The power applies at any time within a specified 'maintenance period'. That period was defined in Model Provision 29 to be five years beginning with the date on which that part of the authorised development was 'opened for use'. Article 36(12) refines this, however, to 'first opened for public use' where intended for use by the public or, in other cases, 'first brought into operational use' by the undertaker.

This power allows the undertaker (a) to enter on and take temporary possession for maintaining the authorised development, (b) to enter on and take temporary possession to gain access to maintain, and (c) to construct temporary buildings for the same. It does not, however, allow permanent works to be undertaken on the temporary possession land, although such works may be undertaken on land acquired or where the necessary rights have been acquired.

Article 36(2)

The power does not apply to any house, or garden belonging to a house, or any other building which is occupied at the time. This reflects the wording in Model Provision 29.

Article 36(4)

The power to enter on and take temporary possession of any land within the Order Limits is only granted for 'so long as may be reasonably necessary' to carry out the maintenance of the relevant part of the authorised development.

Article 36(5)

Before giving up possession, the undertaker must remove all temporary works and restore the land to the reasonable satisfaction of the owner. Here there is no need, as with Article 35(4), to carve out exceptions for permanent works, because permanent works would not be allowed on the temporary possession land under this power.

The remaining provisions broadly reflect those in Article 35, with the exception of Article 36(12) (the maintenance period) which is discussed above.

Neighbourhood Planning Act 2017

Neighbourhood Planning Act 2017 ('NPA 2017'), ss 18–31 contain an entirely new statutory regime for the temporary possession of land. This regime is intended to apply instead of the bespoke provisions which have, to date, been included in DCOs. NPA 2017, s 18(3) provides that the power compulsorily to take temporary possession of land is, 'subject to any express provision in another Act', 'the only power under which a person may take temporary possession of land compulsorily'.

At the time of writing, these provisions of the NPA 2017 have not been brought into force. It is expected that regulations will be made under NPA 2017, s 29 before the provisions are commenced. Such regulations would have to be subject to a prior public consultation pursuant to NPA 2017, s 29(5). Moreover, under NPA 2017, s 44(2), such regulations would be subject to the affirmative resolution procedure in Parliament. For the moment, therefore, DCOs can continue to include temporary possession powers as they have done hitherto.

The main features of the regime in the NPA 2017

The power applies 'for purposes connected with the purposes for which [the authority] could acquire land compulsorily'. This appears to be presented as a secondary or ancillary power. It may potentially prevent the temporary use of land for the primary purposes of the project and, as such, not allow works for mitigation, ground strengthening and the like to be constructed and left on land where only temporary possession has been taken. If so, this would be a significant narrowing as against the existing powers. Where such works are to be undertaken, it may mean that the land has to be compulsorily acquired, unless it can be done by agreement.

The purposes for which temporary possession is required must be set out in the DCO for each parcel of land. This will require careful thought and drafting, as the use of authorised land is limited to that set out in the DCO. The DCO must contain authority for temporary possession and must identify the land subject to temporary possession. It will be possible to provide for temporary possession of land as well as, or instead of, permanent acquisition. Only inalienable National Trust land is subject to special parliamentary procedure.

Under NPA 2017, s 19(7), the DCO must specify the total period of time for which each parcel may be subject to temporary possession, but not the dates of any period of temporary possession.

The minimum notice period for taking temporary possession is increased by NPA 2017, s 20(3) to three months, from 14 or 28 days as currently applies. This is a significant reduction in the flexibility which has applied under DCOs before. The notice period can, however, be reduced by agreement.

Under NPA 2017, s 20(2), the notice must specify the period for which temporary possession is to be taken. This is a new requirement. It will not be easy to forecast for how long temporary possession will be required. It may be that undertakers will err on the side of caution and specify a longer rather than a shorter period. The statute does not impose a limit on the duration of temporary possession.

Important new counter-notice provisions are included in NPA 2017, s 21, allowing an owner or occupying leaseholder to serve a counter-notice within 28 days after notice of entry. There are two sorts of counter-notice. First, a time-limiting counter-notice under NPA 2017, s 21(2). For a dwelling, such a notice can seek to limit the period of temporary possession to 12 months. For other land, the limit is six years. Secondly, an occupying leaseholder can give notice under NPA 2017, s 21(3) that the undertaker may not take temporary possession. After a counter-notice is given, the undertaker then has 28 days to give notice of its decision.

First, for a time-limiting counter-notice under NPA 2017, s 21(2), the undertaker must accept the time limit, withdraw the proposed temporary possession, or acquire the land outright. Secondly, for an occupying leaseholder counter-notice under NPA 2017, s 21(3), the undertaker must either abandon the proposal or acquire the land outright. If the undertaker decides to acquire outright, NPA 2017, s 21(8) authorises compulsory acquisition, even if the DCO only provided for temporary possession. The possibility of such compulsory acquisitions may well need to be considered in examinations into DCOs, even though the land is only included in the DCO for temporary possession.

NPA 2017, s 28 includes new provisions to cover the impact of temporary possession on tenancies. A tenant is deemed to continue to occupy for the purposes of Part II of the Landlord and Tenant Act 1954 and is not to be treated as being in breach of any term of the tenancy, or associated obligation, to the extent that the person cannot reasonably comply with it as a result of the temporary possession.

NPA 2017, s 27(4) expressly limits the use of land to the purpose described in the authorising DCO. However, the undertaker is able to use the land as if it had acquired it and, for example, remove or erect buildings or other works and interfere with rights and interests (save for some protected rights).

Regulations are to be made to cover a number of matters, including the reinstatement of land and the resolution by an independent person of disputes about reinstatement.

Anyone with an interest in, or a right to occupy, the land will be entitled to compensation for any loss or injury sustained as a result of the temporary possession. This is a different formulation from that in the Model Provisions, which refers to loss or damage. NPA 2017, s 23(4) covers business use of land and provides that compensation is to include any loss sustained by reason of the disturbance of the business consequent upon having to quit. In estimating this compensation, particular matters have to be taken into account, including the period and terms of occupation reasonably expected to be available and the availability of other suitable land during the temporary possession period.

There is a new provision on limitation for compensation claims in NPA 2017, s 23(6), which provides that the cause of action accrues for limitation purposes on the last day of the temporary possession period. This would not appear to bar an earlier claim, as the right to compensation arises when any loss or injury is sustained.

There is a new requirement to pay interest under NPA 2017, s 23(7), but this only accrues from the last day of the loss or injury arising from the possession. There is also a new provision in NPA 2017, s 24 for advance payment of compensation for temporary possession. There is an obligation on a claimant to provide sufficient information, as well as the ability for the undertaker to request more information within 28 days. The advance payment must be 90% of the undertaker's estimate of compensation and must be made on the day on which possession is taken. Interest is payable on late advance payments and there is an obligation to make a further advance payment if a new estimate shows that the undertaker's original estimate was too low.

Article 58

Compulsory Purchase Compensation

Richard Honey QC, ftb
Michael Humphries QC, ftb

Introduction

PINS has made is consistently clear that it does not have a role in the determination of compulsory acquisition compensation, and it is clear that the quantum of compensation can have very little (if any) relevance within the examination of an application for development consent. Indeed, PA 2008, s 94(8)(d) makes it clear in terms that an Examining Authority may refuse to allow representations to be made at a hearing if it considers that the representations 'relate to compensation for compulsory acquisition of land or of an interest in or right over land'. This is then echoed in PA 2008, s 106(1)(c) that allows the Secretary of State to 'disregard' representations that relate to compensation for compulsory acquisition.

That said, there may be limited circumstances in which an Examining Authority may need to understand the broad principles relating to compensation for compulsory acquisition. This may arise, for example, in the context of a funding statement, and the policy requirement in the DCLG Guidance on compulsory acquisition (2013) states (para 18) that 'Applicants should be able to demonstrate that adequate funding is likely to be available to enable the compulsory acquisition within the statutory period following the order being made, and that the resource implications of a possible acquisition resulting from a blight notice have been taken account of'.

In that context, therefore, this article gives a broad overview of the law relating to compulsory purchase compensation.

An overview of compulsory purchase compensation under the PA 2008

Save in the case of CPA 1965, s 10, which is considered further below, the compensation provisions arising from a DCO are substantially the same as other similar orders, including compulsory purchase orders and Transport and Works Act orders. The text below gives a very brief overview of the compensation entitlements that arise and the main rules which apply to them.

Value of the land acquired

The principle underlying compensation for compulsory acquisition of land is that fair compensation should be given to the owner whose land has been taken. The aim is to provide a fair financial equivalent for the land taken. The owner is entitled to be compensated fairly and fully for his loss, but he is not entitled to receive more than fair compensation: see *Transport for London v Spirerose* [2009] 1 WLR 1797 at 1822C–D and *Waters v Welsh Development Agency* [2004] 1 WLR 1304 at 1306E, 1309B–D. Compensation cannot, and must not, exceed the owner's total loss, for, if it did, it would put an unfair burden on the public purse and it would transgress the principle of 'equivalence', which is at the root of statutory compensation, namely that the owner shall be paid neither less nor more than his loss (*Horn v Sunderland Corporation* [1941] 2 KB 26 at 49). A claimant is not entitled to receive more than fair compensation: a person is entitled to compensation for losses fairly attributable to the taking of his land, but not to any greater amount (*Director of Buildings and Lands v Shun Fung* [1995] 2 AC 111 at 125D).

The primary statutory rules for assessing compensation are found in Land Compensation Act 1961, s 5. Under s 5(2) of the LCA 1961 the value of land is taken to be the amount which the land if sold in the open market by a willing seller might be expected to realise. As to what the land might be expected to realise, this refers to the expectations of properly qualified persons who have taken pains to inform themselves of all the particulars ascertainable about the property, and its capabilities, and the demand for it (*Inland Revenue Commissioners v Clay* [1914] 3 KB 466 at 475). It must be assumed that the hypothetical vendor and purchaser did whatever reasonable people buying and selling such property would be likely to have done in real life; the hypothetical buyer is assumed to have behaved reasonably and made proper enquiries about the property and not to have appeared too eager to buy (*Ryde v London Regional Transport* [2004] RVR 60 at paras 18–19). So far as possible the assessment of compensation should reflect what would be likely to happen if the property were actually sold at the valuation date (*Waters* at p 1313C).

The principles applying to an open market valuation of land were summarised by Hoffmann LJ in *IRC v Gray* [1994] RVR 129 at 136:

> 'one assumes that the hypothetical vendor and purchaser did whatever reasonable people buying and selling such property would be likely to have done in real life. The hypothetical vendor is an anonymous but reasonable vendor, who goes about the sale as a prudent man of business, negotiating seriously without giving the impression of being either over-anxious or unduly reluctant. The hypothetical buyer is slightly less anonymous. He too is assumed to have behaved reasonably, making proper inquiries about the property and not appearing too eager to buy. But he also reflects reality in that he embodies whatever was actually the demand for that property at the relevant time. It cannot be too strongly emphasised that although the sale is hypothetical, there is nothing hypothetical about the open market in which it is supposed to have taken place. The concept of the open market involves assuming that the whole world was free to bid, and then forming a view about what in those circumstances would in real life have been the best price reasonably obtainable.'

The willing seller is a hypothetical character and the personal characteristics of the actual seller are not to be taken into account.

The starting point is that a search for the value of land at a particular date must take account of the attributes of the land at that date (*Spirerose* at p 1801G). As a generality, land is to be valued in the state in which it was in and in the circumstances prevailing at the valuation date. Where property is to be valued on an open market basis as at a certain date, no counter-factual assumptions should be made other than those which are inherent in the valuation exercise or those which are directed by statute (*Spirerose* at p 1814C). An interest in land is assumed to be sold in the state in which it existed as at the valuation date, taking into account any tenancies or restrictions to which it was subject. There are particular statutory rules and provisions arising from case-law (including *Pointe Gourde v Sub-Intendant of Crown Lands* [1947] AC 565) which require the effect on value of the scheme underlying the compulsory acquisition to be ignored in certain circumstances.

Where a DCO grants the power to create new rights in land it may need to apply parts of the statutory compensation code with necessary modifications: see, for example, Schedule 10 to the Lancashire County Council (Torrisholme to the M6 Link (A683 Completion of Heysham to M6 Link Road)) Order 2013.

Where temporary possession of land is taken, the promoter must pay compensation to the owners and occupiers of the land for any loss or damage arising from the exercise of the power. If the land is being used for the purposes of a business then the compensatable loss may properly reflect net profit which the business would have earned from its legitimate activities on the affected land, over the relevant period of temporary possession: see, by analogy, *Pennine Raceway Ltd v Kirklees MBC* [1984] RVR 85 and *Hobbs (Quarries) Ltd v Somerset CC* (1975) 30 P&CR 286. Where land is occupied by someone other than the owner, the relevant period would be from when temporary possession was taken until the earliest possible date on which the owner could have obtained possession of the land. The entitlement to compensation would be subject to the usual requirements of causation, remoteness and mitigation. The burden of proof to establish the loss or damage, and its quantum, would lie on the claimant.

LCA 1973, s 37 provides an avenue for compensation where a claimant has no compensatable interest in the land acquired. This would apply to persons in occupation under a licence, a tenancy at will, or holding over after a lease. LCA 1973, s 37 applies where a person is displaced from land in consequence of the acquisition of the land by an authority possessing compulsory purchase powers and he had no compensatable interest in the land but was in lawful possession of it. The displaced person is entitled to a disturbance payment.

Disturbance

LCA 1961 s 5(6) provides compensation for disturbance, known as Rule 6 compensation. This covers both the cost of being disturbed, or 'displaced', from the land, under the first limb, but also, under the second limb, any other matter not directly based on the value of the land. The second limb of Rule 6 was described as being potentially wide in *Ryde* (para 24). Consequential or economic losses other than those directly related to the value of the land itself are in principle recoverable as compensation under the second limb of Rule 6, including on the part of investment owners. A claim under Rule 6 may be made for consequential loss even it does not stem from a loss of occupation.

Any loss recoverable under Rule 6 must be a loss properly and actually incurred by a claimant. Moreover, such claims are subject in law to three particular tests. To be recoverable:

- there must be a causal connection between the compulsory acquisition and the loss (see *Shun Fung* at p 126A);
- the loss must be reasonably foreseeable and not too remote (see *Shun Fung* at p 126D–F); and
- the claimant must behave reasonably in taking steps to eliminate or reduce any loss (see *Shun Fung* at pp 126F–G, 127C–E, 138A, 138F).

It is the first of these, causation, which seems to give rise to most problems in practice. In *Wrexham Maelor BC v MacDougall* [1993] 2 EGLR 23 at 32J what was recoverable was described by the Court of Appeal as 'significant damage consequent upon the taking of his interest, other than costs and expenses, which is the natural and reasonable consequence of the taking of his interest and not too remote'. In *Shun Fung* it was said that 'there must be a causal connection between the resumption or acquisition and the loss in question' (at 126A).

Pre-possession losses may be claimed if they are due to the compulsory acquisition. They are only recoverable, however, where they are incurred in anticipation of the compulsory acquisition and because of the threat of compulsory acquisition (*Shun Fung* at 137H–138A). Save for the need to avoid double counting in relation to overlap with the value of the land, judged as at the valuation date, there is no difference in principle as to the recoverability of pre and post-possession losses.

A range of losses may be claimed under Rule 6. Lost profits arising from temporary or permanent loss of business as a result of a compulsory acquisition are generally recoverable. The expenses of removal to new premises are generally recoverable, including the costs of searching for and finding alternative premises, removal costs and the costs of setting-up the new premises. Consequential or economic losses, including taxation liabilities, are generally recoverable, subject to compliance with the three fundamental requirements for Rule 6 claims. The Court of Appeal in *Wrexham Maelor BC* recognised that claims for compensation for losses such as lost earnings or lost profits are not excluded in principle. Rule 6 also encompasses compensation for reasonable surveyor's, legal and other professional fees incurred as a direct consequence of the compulsory acquisition, and compensation for the personal time actually and reasonably spent by a claimant dealing with matters caused by the acquisition, and charged at a fair and reasonable hourly rate.

Severance and injurious affection

Where land is taken, a landowner may suffer loss by the detrimental effect of such acquisition on other land that he retains. CPA 1965, s 7 provides compensation for severance and injurious affection. Section 7 provides that, in assessing compensation for land taken, regard must be had to the damage to be sustained by the landowner through any injurious effect on that landowner's other land by reason of the exercise of the relevant statutory powers. This has been described as loss caused to the retained land by the works or use of the land acquired for the statutory purpose. Section 7 requires, in effect, that where a person's land is compulsorily acquired, if certain retained land suffers a diminution in value because of the project, then that diminution in value should be included in the compensation paid for the acquisition. Any loss of amenity which affects the value of the retained land could also give rise to a claim for compensation.

The main requirements in a claim for CPA 1965, s 7 compensation for injurious affection are:

- land must have been acquired compulsorily from the claimant;
- the harm must be caused by the exercise of the statutory powers;
- injurious affection can arise from both the execution and the use of the works or the land taken, and would include temporary loss during the execution of the works;
- there is no need for there to be an underlying right to claim in tort;
- injurious affection extends beyond matters that would normally be compensatable in tort, such as loss of privacy and general amenity;
- the injurious effect may arise from the works as a whole and not just from that part of the works on the land taken from the owner;
- compensation may (and ought to) be prospective, to include what is reasonably anticipated to happen as it must be claimed once and for all; and
- damage to purely personal rights unconnected with the land is not compensatable.

The 'other land' (the retained land) must be held with the land taken, but it need not be contiguous with or indeed part of the same title, or used in the same way or occupied by the same person, as the land taken. The two parcels of land must merely be owned by the same person and 'so near to each other, and so situated that the possession and control of each gives an enhanced value to all of them' (*Cowper Essex v Acton Local Board* (1889) 14 App Cas 153 at 167).

For there to be a claim for injurious affection under CPA 1965, s 7, the value of the owner's retained land must have been depreciated by injurious affection as a result of the construction or use of the scheme or the acquisition of land. CPA 1965, s 7 provides that compensation is payable for injury done 'by the exercise of the powers conferred by … the special Act'. The injury must be caused by the exercise of the relevant statutory powers. The measure of compensation is the diminution in value of the owner's retained land, and compensation is not to be measured by the costs the owner incurs to overcome the consequences of the construction or use of the scheme (*Cowper Essex* at pp 166, 178).

The provisions of PA 2008, s 152 are explained elsewhere in this work. The effect of PA 2008, s 152(3) is that the promoter must pay compensation to any person whose land is injuriously affected by the carrying out of the authorised works. The provision in CPA 1965, s 10(2) is to be applied and, furthermore, any rule or principle applied to the construction of CPA 1965, s 10 must also be applied to the construction of PA 2008, s 152(3). It appears that the effect of PA 2008, s 152 is intended to be equivalent to that of CPA 1965, s 10.

For PA 2008, s 152 to apply it is not necessary for a person to have had any land taken for the scheme. However, the land must be affected in a way that reduces its value and the injury can only arise from the carrying out of the works, not from the subsequent use of the works. Entitlement to compensation would be limited to cases where a person would have had a claim in tort but for the statutory authority conferred by the DCO. Entitlement only arises where a remedy would have been available in damages but for the defence of statutory authority.

The operation of CPA 1965, s 10 has become subject to a series of rules or conditions, known as the McCarthy rules after *Metropolitan Board of Works v McCarthy* (1874) LR 7 HL 243. The same rules would apply to a claim under PA 2008, s 152, pursuant to PA 2008, s 152(6). They are:

- the injurious affection must be the consequence of the lawful exercise of statutory powers;
- the injurious affection must be such that, if not done under statutory authority, would have given rise to a cause of action;
- compensation is payable only for damage to the claimant's land or interest in land; and
- compensation is payable in respect of only the execution of works and not their use.

These rules were summarised in *Clift v Welsh Office* [1999] 1 WLR 796 at 801B–C, with another point added: the compensation must be ascertainable in accordance with the general rules applicable to damages in tort. This includes the tortious requirements of foreseeability and directness of harm. The measure of damages is usually the diminution in the value of the interest in land affected, assessed at the date of the injury, for all the anticipated injury. The value of a claimant's interest in land must be affected by physical interference with some legal right, public or private, of which the claimant is entitled to make use in connection with his property (*McCarthy* at 253 and 256), irrespective of whether the damage was caused by permanent or temporary interference.

Damage arising from business lost by reason of an obstruction or interference making land less accessible or attractive to customers is recoverable, where such loss of business reduces the value of land (see *Wildtree Hotels v Harrow LBC* [2001] 2 AC 1). However, compensation is not available for personal losses, including lost business profits.

Another form of injurious affection compensation is provided under Part 1 of the LCA 1973, which is applied to works authorised under a DCO by PA 2008, s 152(7). Part 1 compensation is, in essence, compensation for depreciation of land value by physical factors caused by use of public works. Section 1 of the LCA 1973 provides that, where the value of an interest in land is depreciated by 'physical factors' caused by the use of public works then, subject to certain conditions, compensation is payable for that depreciation. In addition to compensation, reasonable valuation and legal expenses are also payable (LCA 1973, s 3(5)). The 'physical factors' are defined in LCA 1973, s 1(2) as noise, vibration, smell, fumes, smoke, artificial lighting and the discharge of any solid or liquid substance (eg dust). Noise is the most common physical factor in relation to which claims are made. The source of the physical factors must be situated on or in the public works the use of which is alleged to be their cause.

Part 1 claims may be made one year after the opening of the relevant public work. Compensation is assessed by reference to prices one year after opening, applying LCA 1961, s 5(2)–(4), less deduction for betterment. Reasonably expected intensification of the use of the works is taken into account. LCA 1973, s 9 makes similar provision to LCA 1973, s 1 but in circumstances where there are alterations to pre-existing public works (eg road widening).

Some additional points

In terms of procedure, the DCLG Guidance on compulsory acquisition (2013) says that promoters should seek to acquire land by negotiation wherever practicable (para 25). The guidance urges promoters to use alternative dispute resolution including in relation to agreeing the compensation payable for property acquired (para 27). Mediation and early neutral evaluation are mentioned.

It is also notable that the guidance suggests that, in order 'to alleviate concerns about future compensation entitlement', an applicant could enter into agreements with those whose land is to be acquired which guarantee a minimum compensation payment, if the project proceeds (para 30). This would be without prejudice to a claimant's ability to seek a higher level of compensation in the future. Such an approach may assist both in allowing those whose land is being acquired to plan for relocating or dealing with the acquisition, as well as reducing the objections which are made to DCOs on a protective basis.

Disputes about compensation which cannot be resolved must be referred to the Lands Chamber of the Upper Tribunal under the Tribunal Procedure (Upper Tribunal) (Lands Chamber) Rules 2010.

The DCLG guidance on compulsory acquisition also refers readers to (what is now) the MHCLG publication 'Guidance on Compulsory Purchase and the Crichel Down Rules' (2019).

More information on compensation for compulsory purchase can be found in Roots et al, *The Law of Compulsory Purchase* (4th edn, Bloomsbury Professional).

Article 59

A Good Practice Guide to Land Referencing and Compulsory Acquisition

Ashley Parry Jones, WSP
Vicky Bramhill, WSP

Introduction

Integral to the PA 2008 is a focus on those people that are affected by NSIPs, and ensuring their views are heard in the development of such projects. The PA 2008 regime requires certain persons to be identified through a process of 'diligent inquiry' so that they are adequately consulted about the proposals, their land interests and rights can be recorded and categorised in a Book of Reference, and they are appropriately notified as the project progresses. Whilst other consent methods, including compulsory purchase orders, similarly require diligent inquiry to identify interests impacted by compulsory purchase, the PA 2008 regime provides an additional emphasis on this at the early, statutory consultation stage, thereby creating a more proactive and inclusive process of engagement with potential interested parties and affected persons.

The categories of persons that require identification for the purposes of consultation and notification under sections 42 and 56 are set out in sections 44 and 57. This involves undertaking diligent inquiry to identify persons with an interest in land within what are identified as Categories 1, 2 and 3:

- Category 1 includes persons who are owners, lessees, tenants and occupiers of land within the proposed project development area (ie the 'Order Limits').
- Category 2 includes persons that are interested in the land or have the power to sell, convey or release the land within Order Limits.
- Category 3 includes persons that the applicant thinks, if the Order sought by the application were made and fully implemented, would or might be entitled to make a relevant claim for compensation under section 10 of the Compulsory Purchase Act 1965, Part 1 of the Land Compensation Act 1973 or section 152 of the PA 2008.

'Diligent inquiry', whilst legally required, is not defined in the PA 2008. As such, professional land referencing firms have developed their own methodologies for satisfying the 'diligent inquiry' requirement. Whilst the sources employed and data management techniques will vary between companies, best practice for diligent inquiry tends to follow the land referencing techniques set out below.

Diligent inquiry: an introduction to land referencing techniques

So, what is land referencing? Land referencing is a professional practice that dates to the development of the UK's canal network in the 18th century, through the railway boom in the 19th century, to modern-day requirements associated with obtaining powers to facilitate infrastructure and other development projects. It has evolved through the Standing Orders of the Houses of Commons and Lords for parliamentary Bills (which require land referencing for hybrid Bills like those for HS2) into other planning processes concerned with the acquisition of land or rights such as the Transport and Works Act, and today is well-understood in the infrastructure development industry as an essential part of the DCO process.

It is not always fully understood, however, exactly what the practice entails. Land referencing is the identification of all land and legal interests in land affected by an infrastructure proposal. In terms of the PA 2008, it is the completion of diligent inquiry to identify those categories of persons set out in sections 44 and 57. The identified parties are recorded by reference to spatial land parcels which are referred to throughout the Order and other submission documents, specifically the Order schedules, Land Plans, the Book of Reference, notices, and the Statement of Reasons. These parcels of land set the spatial scope of the powers sought and define precisely what powers are sought and where. These are the building blocks upon which a DCO rests and that much of the data 'refers' back to – hence the term 'land referencing'.

The basis of land referencing in the UK is that all land is owned by someone, from the centre of the earth to the heavens. Land referencers consider the spatial extents of ownership and occupation of each piece of land in a three-dimensional environment defined by its boundaries at the surface but taking into consideration subsoil interests, such as the criss-cross of tunnels beneath London, as well as floating ownership and rights above the surface, such as for bridges, skyscrapers and rights to light and air. All of these rights must be identified so those who hold them may be consulted and notified appropriately. There is no single source of data to identify these rights. In England and Wales, the Land Registry is a key data source but, as with other registries elsewhere, it records only freeholders, longer leases and certain charges. Furthermore, land ownership and occupation is constantly changing. Land referencing is the process of collecting and completing the full datasets necessary to support the statutory processes required to support planning applications.

There are, therefore, a number of steps that the land referencer must undertake.

Step 1. Identify your referencing limits

Referencing Limits (the boundary within which the project requires information about land interests) should be set to the widest extent that the prospective applicant considers may be within the Order Limits (covering Categories 1 and 2), or may have a relevant claim for compensation (Category 3). The Referencing Limits should be drawn to identify all legal interests (including freeholders, leaseholders, tenants, occupiers, rights, beneficiaries, mortgagees etc) of all land and property that may be affected by the project.

In practice, this means all the land that is going to be required for the principal works to be authorised, areas of land required for the provision of ancillary works or mitigation (for example, landscaping and habitat replacement), and all the land necessary to construct and maintain the works thereafter (for example, working sites, access / haul routes, welfare facilities, storage areas, subsidence, power supply, drainage, temporary access, etc). Special consideration should be given to any interference with public and private rights of way (no matter how fleeting that interference might be) as well as to watercourses. The Compulsory Purchase Act 1965, Land Compensation Act 1973 and PA 2008, s 152 further require consideration of those whose property values might be impacted by the construction and / or operation of the project. This means considering those affected by noise and vibration, air and light pollution, and the like. At the outset, these can be difficult to accurately gauge and so it is worth starting wide and narrowing the scope as the potential impacts are better understood.

This might require referencing a wider area to enable consideration of route alignment options, survey outcomes, design tweaks following consultation and ongoing design development.

These Limits can be refined inwards at a later date, but as a generality it is much easier to have wide Limits at the outset and consult more widely, rather than trying to push those Limits out later. There will be a balance to be struck with cost, but late additions to Limits can seriously compromise quality and programme (and hence cost) by requiring further targeted consultation when changes in the design fall beyond the scope of those people who have been referenced initially for consultation, or worse, all the way up to the preparation of the Order submission. If in doubt, promoters should set the scope of the land referencing exercise as wide as necessary, but not so wide as to cause unnecessary concern for landowners that will definitely not be required. The lead-in time for land referencing is such that late changes that bring more areas of land into scope are difficult to accommodate and can threaten either the programme or compliance with the requirements of the PA 2008 regime. Late changes should, therefore, be avoided or at least carefully managed.

Step 2. Desktop research: use a variety of data sources

Land referencers start with Land Registry enquiries. There are almost 30 million registered titles recorded by HM Land Registry, covering about 88% of all land in England and Wales. Land Registry titles provide information relating to registered freeholders, leaseholders, mortgage lenders, beneficiaries of rights and options, and other charges and restrictions on the land. Land referencers interrogate these titles, identify current beneficiaries of historic rights, and identify gaps requiring further investigation. They use other desktop sources to supplement and corroborate the registered information, such as records on electoral roll entries, beneficiaries of farming stewardship schemes, checks of current registered addresses with Companies House or the Charity Commission, and conduct online research and validation of addresses with Royal Mail.

The land is parcelled and referenced using land boundaries set out in the Land Registry records and validated against the most up-to-date Ordnance Survey base mapping data – using The General Boundary Rule, as included in Land Registration Act 2002, s 60. This can be as much an art as a science, knowing that mapping accuracy improves over time, but using geographic information systems ('GIS') to display and review information facilitates the production of an accurate mosaic of land boundaries against the most up-to-date base mapping.

Desktop sources are also used to identify special category land, defined as '… the land identified as forming part of a common, open space, National Trust land or fuel or field garden allotment …'. In this context:

- 'common' includes any land subject to be enclosed under the Inclosure Acts 1845 to 1882, and any town or village green;
- 'fuel or field garden allotment' means any allotment set out as a fuel allotment, or a field garden allotment, under an Inclosure Act; and
- 'open space' means any land laid out as a public garden, or used for the purposes of public recreation, or land being a disused burial ground.

Step 3. Request information from land interests

Whilst desktop sources will provide a good starting point for the land referencing process – and allow wider initial interrogation of land rights without causing unnecessary concern for landowners if the scope is then pulled in tighter – these publicly available data sources are not always current, accurate or complete. They also omit occupier information, including data about tenants, informal rights and licences to use land.

Land referencers will, therefore, contact all those parties with interests in land who have been identified through desktop research, as well seeking out and contacting those who may have interests in properties identified as lacking formally recorded information (such as those associated with any unregistered land). Sending letters to them by post establishes a first direct contact as part of the audit trail necessary to prove 'diligent inquiry'. However, because the postal addresses used may be sourced from Land Registry data, they may be out of date, there being no obligation to keep the address details recorded by Land Registry up to date. As a result, posting letters to addresses identified usefully tests the validity of this address data, which will later be required for the notifications which must be successfully served by post.

This initial correspondence will include questionnaires, referred to as Land Interest Questionnaires (LIQs) or Requests for Information (RFIs), confirming or seeking additional contact details and information about the recipient's interests in land. The questionnaires are provided with plans so the boundaries may be reviewed, amended or confirmed, thereby building a mosaic of land parcels. Specialist land referencing companies should be able to offer recipients options of questionnaire responses by both hard copy post and online, providing choices to maximise response rates.

These questionnaires may be followed up, either to chase the provision of a response, or to make further enquiries about any apparent anomalies in the data provided. At this stage, land referencers become detectives, chasing leads to unravel what may have become complex land ownership scenarios built up over time from historic records and agreements with successive changes that eventually lead to the correct persons recorded as the current interested parties. The land referencers will also make contact directly with major landowners in the area, such as local authorities, other significant local landowners and statutory undertakers to seek wider information about infrastructure, land uses, assets and apparatus.

The Planning Act 2008: Infrastructure Planning (Fees) Regulations 2010 guidance sets out that, where an applicant is refused information, they may submit a request to the Secretary of State who may then 'require' that the information be provided under PA 2008, s 52. A fee must be paid at the time any such request to the Secretary of State is made. Applicants are expected to act reasonably, first seeking to obtain relevant information directly before seeking authorisation under these provisions. Specifically, applicants should only submit requests for those aspects of information where they consider they have been unreasonably refused that information.

In practice, a requirement to provide information under PA 2008, s 52 is rarely used. Professional land referencers rely on robust land referencing methodologies and open and engaging approaches to their investigative interactions with affected parties. It is rare that these prove insufficient for obtaining information about interested parties. However, if a party is known to be withholding a significant amount of information that could result in the omission of other third parties from being identified and properly consulted, and this information cannot be obtained through any other method, the s 52 process remains a useful part of the land referencing methodology – if only as a potential available option to induce necessary cooperation.

Step 4. Site visits to verify information on the ground

Whilst improvements in the quality, availability and currency of aerial photography have been enormously helpful, site visits remain an essential element of a diligent inquiry methodology. Site visits are conducted to fully comprehend the land and recognise land interests on site, including tracks used by holders of private rights, land use and occupation, areas of boundary dispute and unregistered/unknown land. They may also be necessary to inform the land referencers exactly how to describe the land in the Book of Reference and notices. These visits will require consent from private landowners, something the land referencers should be able to negotiate. At this stage, it is important to verify any special category land, and mark these for the project's consideration so they may be avoided or carefully accommodated in the project design.

Where no questionnaires are returned, a 'diligent' approach requires that site visits are used to call on those land interests to request that they are completed and submitted in a timely manner, either by post or online, or offer support to complete the questionnaires. This often means that land referencers are the first real contact that an affected landowner will have with a project. It is therefore important that the land referencers, as project ambassadors, are suitably briefed so they can answer queries about a project, support and engage with anyone with concerns, possibly referring them to others in the project team to answer specific or more detailed concerns, whilst safely avoiding or managing any potential conflict or aggression issues that might arise.

Step 5. Further investigate gaps in data

Where there are gaps or uncertainties in the land referencing dataset, further investigations will be required. Depending on the nature of these gaps, additional efforts may be required which involve enquiries to other local landowners who may have knowledge of the area, or interrogation of local archives and records or other available local sources. Site notices can also be posted at locations where more information is required inviting anyone with relevant information to come forward and help ensure those who need to be informed of the project's potential impact are communicated with.

Step 6. Confirm and update information

Depending on the size of the project, the number of land interests involved, and the timeframes for land referencing, there can be a lag between the identification of some of the details about the land interests and those points in the programme when diligent inquiry is required to have been undertaken. This means there has been an opportunity for change to have occurred. To address this, prior to the key milestones of statutory consultation (under s 42) and acceptance notification (under s 56), land referencers will undertake a confirmation exercise to confirm or update the information they hold to ensure it is correct at the moment when it is needed. To do this, they may seek to refresh the Land Registry records to identify the changes that have happened since it was provided, as well as review and validate their desktop information, including checking correct addresses for the service of notices. They will also request all the parties identified to confirm that the information held about them and their property remains accurate and up to date. This last request will usually be conducted as a further mail shot encouraging a response but stating that, if no confirmation is received within a given timeframe, it will be assumed that the data held is correct.

Data management and protection

All the steps described above are essential elements of the necessary audit trail to demonstrate that the land referencing exercise has been carried out to the standards required by the PA 2008 regime. The Planning Inspectorate will ask for reassurance that evidence is available to demonstrate that a land referencing methodology that meets the standard has been employed, so the land referencers must be able to provide a detailed, project-specific methodology when this is asked for, usually alongside or soon after submission of a DCO application.

It is also essential that all the personal data collected in the course of the land referencing diligent inquiry exercise is processed securely and managed in accordance with the General

Data Protection Regulation (Council Regulation (EU) 2016/679 – retained EU legislation) (GDPR) and the Data Protection Act 2018. That means it must be collected and provided by the land referencers (the data processors) solely for the use by the client (the data controller) for their lawful purposes, which includes the development of a DCO application. It is necessary for the client to publish an information security policy that accommodates data processing of this nature. It may be reasonably expected that any professional service provider is able to demonstrate adherence to ISO27001, the international data security standard, for the manner in which they conduct their land referencing work.

Promoters are sometimes concerned that land referencing activities required to satisfy the PA 2008 (in particular, collecting and publishing personal data about those Category 1, 2 and 3 persons) are at odds with the GDPR requirement that data should not be shared. They may be reassured that responsible land referencing in line with GDPR will ensure the security of personal data (even if the data subjects would prefer the project not to), as long as the client can satisfy at least one of the lawful causes for processing personal data given in Article 6 of the GDPR – the development of a DCO application potentially satisfying at least one of these.

Best practice for the management of data is through a fully secure, password-protected and intelligent specialist database, integrated with a GIS, that ensures accuracy and currency of data as the design of the project develops. Storing all data centrally provides for a single source of truth without unnecessary duplication of data, maintains the information as safe and secure, and reduces paper records and the associated risk of theft or misplacement. It also enables secure data sharing across the project's multi-disciplinary teams, prompt and accurate responses to any GDPR-related requests, as well as providing consistency in the development of the DCO submission and supporting documents.

The ability to provide a compliant application from a single data source to satisfy the requirements of the PA 2008 is also matched by the ability to give access to the data to the client team, affected stakeholders and the Planning Inspectorate. Furthermore, libraries and other deposit locations may be relieved if they are not asked to make the required DCO application documentation available for public inspection if all the material may be provided online. Furthermore, the data contained in this documentation is additionally available in more accessible formats for virtual interrogation. Quick access to this data will also be of enormous benefit when fielding questions at Examination.

Completion of diligent inquiry

Once the above processes have been undertaken thoroughly and all data is validated and verified, the diligent inquiry process may be considered complete. Experience suggests that the process cannot be completed for even the smallest of schemes in under three months, given the essential participation of third parties, who may not exhibit the level of urgency necessary for a more accelerated project programme. However, for most projects, the time allowance for diligent inquiry, assuming a project scope that does not become appreciably wider, should be closer to six to nine months, allowing for full investigations and engagement with affected stakeholders. The data will be needed to consult under the requirements of s 42, and will need to be continually refined and kept up to date to complete the Land Plans and the Book of Reference, as well as the notices to interested parties required under s 56 once the application for a DCO is accepted by the Planning Inspectorate and, indeed, throughout the Examination.

Upon making a DCO application, as well as asking for an explanation of the land referencing methodology employed, the Planning Inspectorate will ask for an account for any differences between the data used for the s 42 consultation and the subsequent s 56 notices. Land referencers should anticipate this and, from the outset, maintain the records and audit trails necessary to fully answer these anticipated questions.

Production of the land plans and identification of compulsory acquisition requirements

Land plans set out the Order Limits and land required for compulsory acquisition or temporary use. Plots of land inside Order Limits are shown shaped according to the existing land ownership boundaries identified through the land referencing process, split and categorised according to the required compulsory acquisition powers set out in the Order. The DCO Examination process will require the Applicant to justify the compelling case in the public interest for the compulsory acquisition of every piece of land; this should be set out in the Statement of Reasons. Compulsory acquisition powers provided in the DCO tend to be defined in four main categories:

- permanent acquisition of land;
- permanent acquisition of rights;
- temporary possession of land; and
- temporary use of rights.

These four categories tend to be sufficient, but particularly complicated requirements might require additional categories.

When creating land plans, land referencers will require a preliminary design to set out the land requirements. The land referencers, together with their project team colleagues, should then ask themselves two questions:

Question 1: How much land do I need?

The following should be considered when including or excluding land within the Order Limits:

- Limit of Deviation and flexibility – Is the scheme design of sufficient detail to confirm the precise location of all works? What if new technologies emerge or the contractor identifies a better way of working? Might affording some flexibility make the scheme more efficient? Seek the maximum extent of land that may be required, but no more than can be justified for compulsory acquisition. It is possible to reduce the extent of compulsory acquisition as the design is developed; it is much more difficult to widen the Limits.
- Construction and maintenance – Have you considered the land required for compounds, storage, parking, loading / unloading, welfare facilities, etc? Do you need access to land outside the proposed fenceline to erect and maintain that fence? Where is the material to construct the scheme going to come from? Do you need to borrow pits?
- Access – It is best to assume that the project has no rights to access any land and, as a result, include all access arrangements within the Order Limits. Are you confident that your access requirements link up to the public highway (thereby ensuring no third party ransom strips)? Is the public road network up to the task? If there is a need for remote junction improvements to facilitate construction or over-sized vehicles, these should be included within the Order Limits.
- Utility diversions – Has land required for all water, power and gas supply and diversions been designed and included for both permanent and temporary works? If these are to be provided

by a third party, what reassurance have you that they will gain the necessary powers? Might it be better to secure these in the Order?

- Environmental mitigation – Are the areas of land for any environmental mitigations, plus the land required to build and maintain these mitigations, included within the Limits?
- Replacement land – Have you identified a requirement for special category land as part of the Order? If so, one of the options for achieving permission for this might be to identify and include appropriate replacement land within the Order Limits.
- 'Slivers' – Where the design minutely clips an adjacent third party's land, do you really need to make that encroachment? Could these 'slivers' of land be safely excluded to reduce the number of affected parties? Similarly, if you think you need to acquire an entire property, are you sure you have included its whole demise and not inadvertently omitted some small and, if left out, useless strip of land?

Question 2: What powers should be sought?

Consider the following when identifying which powers should be sought in the DCO for each plot:

- Seek the maximum power – To enable flexibility, it is advisable to seek the maximum power in the DCO required to achieve the outcome, so long as there is a compelling case in the public interest for the taking of such a power. It may possible to subsequently reduce the power sought in the DCO, possibly through the examination process, as the design is developed or objections resolved.
- Powers sought versus powers exercised – The Order should include the maximum appropriate type of power in a 'hierarchy' of powers (see above), but also enable the project to exercise lesser powers if it is later discovered that such powers are sufficient. If carefully drafted, DCOs may be able to provide for this hierarchy of powers. For instance, it may be discovered that land identified in the DCO for permanent acquisition is ultimately only needed for temporary possession and the DCO should be drafted to allow this lesser power to be exercised. Note, however, that land identified in a DCO for temporary possession only cannot later be served with a notice for (say) permanent acquisition.
- Practicalities of implementation – Consider how you intend to exercise any rights taken. Could you limit the powers, such as to air rights (for crane oversailing) or subsoil (for tunnelling)? How do you intend to maintain land required for essential mitigation? Is the acquisition of the land really required (with the responsibilities this entails) or would rights over the land be sufficient?
- Subsoil – The subsoil beneath publicly adopted roads normally belongs to those who own the properties on either side of the road (as per the *ad medium filum* rule). Referencers call these interests 'frontagers'. This means digging up a public road can involve the land referencing of many interests. The same applies to many rivers and streams. Soil nails and piling can only be driven into land over which the necessary powers are obtained. If any dewatering or settlement monitoring is required, the land plans should reflect this and the associated potential compensation claims must be recorded in the Book of Reference.
- Restrictive covenants – Perhaps the permanent acquisition of land can be limited by imposing restrictive rights on third parties to prevent certain activities, such as the interference with tunnels or cables.
- Three-dimensional environment – The rights sought may be further complicated when considered in a 3D context. A promoter may seek acquisition of land or rights in land at one

level (eg for a bridge structure) but only temporary possession below (eg if the bridge is to cross a river or railway that is not to be acquired, but over which temporary possession may be needed during construction). These instances may necessitate an illustrative explanation using insets on the plans, the development of a specific type of acquisition to be referenced in the plan key, careful definitions in the description in the Book of Reference, or a combination of any or all of these approaches.

- Exclusion of certain interests – It is possible to exclude the acquisition of interests even when the freehold or rights are required over the other interests in the land. This might be appropriate to exclude the assets of rights of tunnel owners, the Crown Estate or statutory undertakers. Again, this is possible through careful specification in the Book of Reference.

The Book of Reference

The plots referenced on the land plans and the associated land referencing information are compiled together into a Book of Reference, which ascribes the spatial plot number references used throughout the Order documents.

For a DCO, the Book of Reference is divided into five parts, as prescribed by Infrastructure Planning (Applications: Prescribed Forms and Procedures) Regulations 2009, reg 7(1):

- Part 1 lists the names and addresses of all Category 1 interests (owners, lessees, tenants and occupiers) and Category 2 interests (parties that have an interest in the land or who have the power to sell, convey or release the land within the Order Limits).
- Part 2 lists the names and addresses of all Category 3 interests (those with a potential relevant claim for compensation).
- Part 3 lists all parties entitled to enjoy easements or other private rights over land within the Order Limits.
- Part 4 lists all Crown interests in land within the Order Limits.
- Part 5 lists all special category land within the Order Limits.

A precedent has been developed in the formatting of these Books of Reference which are set out in tabular form and include an explanatory introduction, designed to direct the reader how to interact with what can be quite a lengthy and unwieldy reference document. Promoters may wish to publish the Book of Reference and other Order documentation in a more accessible format to render the suite of DCO documents more intuitive and user friendly. This capability is certainly possible and available. However, interactive formats are likely to remain supplemental to currently accepted formats until such time as the Infrastructure Planning (Applications: Prescribed Forms and Procedure) Regulations 2009 (as amended) are updated.

When developing a Book of Reference, there is best practice based on experience and precedent that should be considered:

- Data management and Book of Reference production – Use software that creates the Book of Reference directly from the central source of data used to hold the land referencing information rather than exporting it to another system and risk discrepancies being introduced in the transfer. This ensures currency and consistency of information and enables tracking of changes.
- Plot numbering strategy – Making the requirements of the users of the document the central consideration, use the most easily understood approach to numbering land plots on the land plans. Recent examples have included adding the land plan sheet number to prefix the plot

numbers (ie 08-01, denoting plot number 01 on sheet number 08). This approach has been found to be particularly useful on larger schemes. Smaller schemes will sometimes codify the freeholder of plots (eg 1, 1a, 1b, 2, 2a – whereby 1, 1a and 1b are owned by one party and 2 and 2a are owned by another). This can be a helpful representation of land ownership on the land plans, but it risks confusion in instances where landownership changes. Plots are often numbered and labelled sequentially from north-west to south-east, or along the route of a linear scheme. Whatever approach is employed, the references used must be unique and the logic consistently adhered to.

- <u>Descriptions</u> – Include reference to all existing and physical features within a plot, with particular attention to those that feature on the mapping. Descriptions should enable a reader to recognise the location of a plot in the absence of plans, with the area given in square metres.
- <u>Monitoring and managing change</u> – Ensure processes are put in place to enable regular updates of landownership data (which constantly changes) and track changes in the Book of Reference, as these will be required throughout the Examination and beyond.

Best practice and lessons learnt

Working to deliver land referencing services on 30+ DCOs (to the end of 2020), Ashley Parry Jones, Vicky Bramhill and the Planning Information Management team in WSP have gleaned a number of lessons learnt and explored areas of best practice. The most significant are shared here.

- *Programme sufficient time from design freeze to DCO deliverable*: The land referencing and legal teams can be challenged by project design freezes that have been permitted to melt, risking data inconsistencies and rushed updates and checks in final deliverables. Prudent applicants will attempt to maintain a programme that establishes early design freeze dates and will work with those who would be squeezed by any changes that are permitted, to mitigate their impacts.
- *Scope out, not in*: If changes are to be introduced, attempts should be made to drop elements of an initial scheme design, not introduce additional areas of land to the land referencing scope late in the programme, as these may prove difficult to accommodate to a compliant standard.
- *Manage data centrally, using a single source of common data*: In addition to satisfying GDPR guidance in how personal data should be managed, this enables quick turnarounds for additional drafts, mobilising and checking changes and ensuring consistency across DCO deliverables.
- *Adopt a 'one team' approach*: The development of DCOs is a complex, multidisciplinary effort. The most successful promoters facilitate collaboration in their supply chain.
- *Keep it simple*: Projects quickly become complex as more detail becomes available. However, plans and documents need to remain simple enough for landowners, stakeholders and the lay public to understand. Try to limit the number of different rights, powers and colours on plans to keep the documents simple and easy to understand for those who most need to use them.
- *Version control of the Order Limits*: Clearly defined responsibility should be assigned for the ownership and management of the Order Limits / red line boundary to help avoid inconsistencies across documents and to manage the resolution of any conflicting requirements.

- *Start the production of land plans as early as possible*: An early focus on the land plans can bring together disciplines across a project and help develop and share a clear, single picture of what the scheme is attempting to do, flushing out any conflicting requirements. There is usually a sufficient level of design detail available by the time the project reaches the Statutory Consultation stage to make good progress with the land plans.
- *Collaborative working sessions and workshops with land referencers, engineers, and environmental and legal teams are invaluable*: Reviewing land requirements in partnership across disciplines on a plot-by-plot basis ensures the satisfaction that the compelling case test can be met safely. These reviews may identify and resolve practical challenges, ransom strips and areas where compulsory powers could be constrained.
- *Consider the project's communications strategy in line with the land referencing methodology*: So far as the public are concerned, the land referencers and other consultants are all just part of the same project team. The response rate to land referencing enquiries, as well as wider public acceptance, is improved by allowing the land referencing exercise to be conducted as a strategic exchange of information. The required answers to the questions asked by land referencers can be facilitated by the provision of information, such as project explanatory leaflets or details of where to find additional information as part of the wider community engagement and consultation exercise.

Article 60

Special Categories of Land

Alex Booth QC, ftb

Introduction

The concept of 'Special Category Land' has a particular application for the purposes of the PA 2008. The premise is that certain categories of land should benefit from some degree of protection from compulsory purchase pursuant to powers contained in a development consent order ('DCO'). In this regard, the legislation provides variously in relation to these types of land, that either:

- compulsory acquisition is prohibited altogether (in the sense that the PA 2008 does not provide for it);
- the owner of land can require that authorisation of compulsory purchase powers be subject to Special Parliamentary Procedure ('SPP'); or
- the owner of land can require that authorisation of compulsory purchase powers be subject to SPP, unless certain statutory tests are met.

Relevant guidance is provided in the DCLG publication 'Planning Act 2008 Guidance related to procedures for the compulsory acquisition of land' (2013) ('the Guidance'), in particular in Appendices A and B.

Types of Special Category Land

The different types of land for which these special dispensations are made, and the key statutory provisions which govern them, are as follows:

- Crown Land (PA 2008, s 135).
- National Trust Land (PA 2008, s 130).
- Land belonging to Statutory Undertakers (PA 2008, s 127).
- Common Land, Open Space, and Fuel and Field Garden Allotments (PA 2008, ss 131 and 132).

In this regard, it should be noted that the provisions affording protection to Special Category Land in the PA 2008 were subject to significant amendment by the Growth and Infrastructure Act 2013 ('GIA 2013'). The GIA 2013 made various revisions to the original provisions, with the result that some of the protections previously afforded were 'rolled back'. This reflected concerns regarding the potential that the potential requirement for SPP had to cause delay to the consenting process.

In particular, by repealing PA 2008, s 128, the GIA 2013 removed the entitlement of Local Authorities to require SPP in the event of a DCO authorising the compulsory acquisition of land held by such authorities. In this respect, concerns had arisen following Central Bedfordshire

Council's decision to require SPP in relation to The Rookery South (Resource Recovery Facility) Development Consent Order 2011. In that instance the Examination was held between January and July 2011, and the DCO was made in November 2011. However, following the initiation of SPP, the DCO did not come into force until 2013.

Further, the repeal of s 128 also removed the entitlement of Statutory Undertakers to require SPP in respect of compulsory purchase powers relating to land which they had acquired for the purpose of their statutory undertaking. Again, by way of illustration, the Able Marine Energy Park Development Consent Order 2014 was subject to SPP following objection by Associated British Ports ('ABP'). In that matter, the Examination was held between May and November 2012 and the DCO then made in December 2013. However, the DCO did not come into force until 29 October 2014 following SPP.

Thus the protection now afforded to Special Category Land is somewhat reduced from that which the PA 2008 originally conferred.

The remainder of this article considers the different protections afforded to the different types of land.

Crown land

In respect of Crown land, the position is relatively straightforward. Crown land is defined in PA 2008, s 227(2) as land in which there is a Crown interest or a Duchy interest, which terms are defined in s 227(3) and (4) respectively. Section 135(1) of the PA 2008 serves to prohibit its compulsory acquisition, in that it directs that an interest in Crown land may only be acquired where (a) it is for the time being held by a party other than the Crown, and (b) the consent of the appropriate Crown authority has been secured. The expression '"appropriate Crown authority"' is defined in PA 2008, s 227(5) and the identity of that body will of course vary depending on by whom the Crown land is owned.

Section 135(2) of the PA 2008 further requires the consent of the appropriate Crown authority if a DCO is to include any other provision applying in relation to Crown land, or rights benefiting the Crown.

Accordingly, where any party promoting an application for development consent requires the use of or rights over Crown land, or proposes any other provision affecting Crown land, it is imperative that it approaches the appropriate Crown authority in order to secure its agreement.

Annex B of the Guidance is concerned with Crown land and specifically advocates that applicants should seek to obtain the consent of the Crown prior to submission of an application for development consent, to avoid the risk that consent may not have been secured by the date on which the application falls to be determined. It is noteworthy that many DCO decisions report Crown agreement only being secured very shortly before the expiry of the decision period, creating uncertainty for applicants as to whether the order will be made in the form sought (or, potentially, at all). As such, the advice that those promoting orders affecting Crown land should enter into the requisite discussions as early as possible should not be ignored.

A number of decisions have dealt with the status of 'escheat land', which is land that has passed to the Crown where no successor in title to it has been identified following the death of its owner. In the case of both the A19/A184 Testo's Junction Alteration Development Consent Order and the Southampton to London Pipeline Development Consent Order, the Examining Authorities and determining Secretaries of State accepted the views expressed by solicitors acting for the Crown (in letters submitted to the Examination) to the effect that escheat land should not be regarded as Crown Land for the purposes of section 135, at least where no acts of management have been undertaken in respect of it, and thus that no consent is required.

It is notable that, in 2018 correspondence to the Department for Business Energy and Industrial Strategy, submitted during the Examination held in respect of the Eggborough CCGT DCO, the Crown Estate disagreed with the view that PA 2008, s 135(1) only permits Crown land to be included within a DCO if its unconditional consent is obtained prior to the making of the DCO. It is not clear precisely what the intended meaning of the statement was – that is, whether the Crown Estates was disputing the need for its consent generally or, as seems more likely, the need to obtain its consent prior to the making of an order – but, in any event, the Examining Authority and the Secretary of State in that case both proceeded on the basis that the prior consent was indeed required.

National Trust land

As with Crown land, the position in respect of the National Trust is also relatively straightforward. Protection is afforded to land held 'inalienably' by the Trust, which PA 2008, s 130(4) defines as land belonging to the National Trust which is inalienable under either National Trust Act 1907, s 21 or National Trust Act 1939, s 8. National Trust land which is required for development and which is held inalienably must be subject to compulsory acquisition because, by definition, the National Trust is unable to dispose of it by agreement.

The effect of PA 2008, s 130(1)–(3) is however that, where land is held by the National Trust on this basis, then insofar as an application for development consent seeks to compulsorily acquire that land, it must be subject to SPP if the National Trust maintains an objection to the compulsory acquisition.

Once again, therefore, where an applicant requires National Trust land in order to deliver development, it is imperative for it to approach the National Trust at an early stage with a view to reaching agreement as to the necessary land. By way of example, in promoting the Southampton to London Pipeline Development Consent Order 2020, Esso obtained such agreement from the National Trust, having consulted the Trust regarding alternative routings for the pipeline in the vicinity of its property at Hinton Ampner. It was on this basis that the Trust did not object to the compulsory acquisition of its land and so SPP was not triggered. A similar result was achieved by Highways England in connection with the A303 Stonehenge Development Consent Order, where the National Trust's objection to the compulsory acquisition of its land was only withdrawn shortly before the end of the examination.

Note, however, that PA 2008, s 130 does *not* ordinarily confer the protection of SPP on National Trust land where an applicant seeks to acquire only rights over land, as distinct from the land itself. Only where s 132 makes such provision (see further below relating to rights over Common Land, Open Space, Fuel or Field Garden Allotments) will the acquisition of rights over National Trust land afford the opportunity for the National Trust to require SPP (PA 2008, s 130(3A)).

Statutory undertaker land

PA 2008, s 127 provides statutory undertakers with protection in relation to both the compulsory acquisition of land and the compulsory acquisition of new rights over land.

The protections do not, however, apply in relation to all land owned or used by such undertakers. In order to benefit from protection, s 127(1) provides that the relevant statutory undertaker must:

- have acquired the land concerned for the purpose of the undertaker's undertaking (s 121(1)(a)); and

- have made a representation about an application for an order granting development consent before completion of the Examination (with that representation not having been withdrawn) (s 121(1)(b));

Section 127(1)(c) further requires the Secretary of State to be satisfied that the land in question is either used for the purpose of the undertaker's undertaking, or that the interest is held for that purpose.

If the Secretary of State is satisfied in respect of these matters, then the protection afforded by s 127 is engaged.

First, this means that, by virtue of s 127(2) and (3), the DCO may only make provision for the authorisation of the compulsory acquisition of that land where the Secretary of State is satisfied its 'nature and situation' are such that it can be purchased and not replaced without serious detriment to the undertaker's undertaking or, if purchased, it can be replaced by other land belonging to or available for acquisition by the undertaker, without serious detriment to the undertaking.

Secondly, it means that, where an applicant seeks to acquire a right over a statutory undertaker's land, s 127(5) and (6) prohibits the creation of the new right unless the Secretary of State is satisfied that it can be purchased and not replaced without 'serious detriment' to the undertaker's undertaking, or any detriment to the carrying on of the undertaking, in consequence of the acquisition of the right, can be made good by the undertaker by the use of other land belonging to or available for acquisition by them.

The Guidance does not elaborate on the application of the statutory provisions. The general national policy guidance relating to compulsory acquisition, the MHCLG's 'Guidance on Compulsory purchase process and The Crichel Down Rules' (July 2019) ('the General CPO Guidance'), does, however, provide some limited guidance in respect of the application of Acquisition of Land Act 1981 ('ALA 1981'), s 16, which is in comparable terms to PA 2008, s 127.

In this regard, paragraph 229 of the General CPO Guidance states that, before making a representation, undertakers 'should take particular care over the status of the land which the acquiring authority propose to acquire, have regard to the provisions of the relevant act, and seek their own legal advice as may be necessary'. It goes on to give a practical example of where a statutory undertaker may not benefit from the protection of ALA 1981, s 16 (and thus also PA 2008, s 127), advising that although a gas transporter qualifies as a statutory undertaker, the protection afforded by s 16 of the ALA 1981 would not apply in relation to any non-operational land held by that undertaker, such as its administrative offices. In those circumstances, the General CPO Guidance notes, the land is not held for the purpose of the statutory provision; namely, the conveyance of gas through pipes to any premises or to a pipeline system operated by a gas transporter.

PA 2008, s 127(8) provides that the term 'statutory undertaker' has the same meaning as in ALA 1981, s 8, and that it should also include undertakers which are deemed to be statutory undertakers for the purposes of that Act, by virtue of another enactment, or which are statutory undertakers for the purposes of s 16(1) and (2) of that Act.

The definition in ALA 1981, s 8 provides that undertakers falling within the definition include:

- transport undertakings (such as rail, road, water transport);
- docks, harbours, piers or lighthouse undertakings;
- the Civil Aviation Authority and National Air Traffic Services; and
- universal postal service providers.

In general terms, both promoters of and objectors to applications for development consent are well advised to consider carefully whether any particular person or body is a statutory undertaker for the purposes of ALA 1981, s 8 (and consequently PA 2008, s 127), since many statutory undertakers are not listed within the provision itself, but are deemed to be such undertakers by virtue of other Acts. One such example of a body not listed within ALA 1981, s 8, but deemed to be a statutory undertaker for its purposes by virtue of another enactment, is National Grid Electricity Transmission plc.

Conversely, some statutory bodies may assume that they are statutory undertakers for the purposes of PA 2008, but may not in fact fall within the relevant statutory definition. By way of example, the Western Riverside Waste Authority ('WRWA') claimed the status of statutory undertaker in seeking to resist the compulsory acquisition of its land for the Riverside Energy Park Development Consent Order 2020, on the basis that its possession of docks and riparian rights meant that its undertaking was properly regarded as one of 'water transport'. The applicant disputed that the WRWA was in fact a statutory undertaker for the purposes of the PA 2008, noting that its undertaking was for a 'waste disposal' purpose, and not water transport, so that whilst a statutory body it was not a statutory undertaker.

Further in this context, in its report relating to the Wrexham Energy Centre Development Consent Order, the Examining Authority did not accept that a telecommunications provider, Fibrespeed, was a statutory undertaker for the purposes of s 127.

Statutory undertakers should consider making clear in their representations the basis upon which they maintain that they benefit from the protections afforded by s 127.

As noted above, the level of protection afforded to statutory undertakers has reduced following the coming into force of the GIA 2013, which removed the possibility of SPP in situations where a development consent order provided for the compulsory acquisition of land, or rights over land, held by a statutory undertaker for the purposes of their undertaking (formerly ss 128 and 129). SPP is now only potentially available where the undertaker's land otherwise falls within the remit of ss 131 and/or 132 (open space etc).

The importance of engaging with statutory undertakers and securing their agreement to the inclusion of their land was thrown into sharp relief in the report of the Examining Authority relating to the application for the development consent order at Manston Airport Development. In that case, the Examining Authority recommended the refusal of the applicant's request for compulsory acquisition of rights over the land of British Telecom and various gas and electricity undertakers in the absence of a statement from those parties confirming that the rights could be purchased without detriment to their undertakings. Although this approach was rejected in the decision of the Secretary of State (subsequently quashed on other grounds), the risk that another Examining Authority may take a similar approach cannot be discounted.

Common Land, Open Space, Fuel or Field Garden Allotments

Although grouped together for the purposes of this article, Common Land (which term also embraces town or village greens), Open Space, and Fuel or Field Garden Allotments all represent different and discrete land types. The relevant statutory definitions are those contained in ALA 1981, s 19 (which are adopted by ss 131(12) and 132(12)).

The protection afforded to this category is set out in two separate provisions, these being:

- PA 2008, s 131, which is concerned with the compulsory acquisition of land; and
- PA 2008, s 132, which is concerned with the acquisition of rights over land.

The following discussion primarily references s 131. The position regarding s 132 is all but identical, save where noted.

Procedure

Previously, PA 2008, s 131(3) directed that the compulsory acquisition of this type of special category land would be subject to SPP unless the Secretary of State certified that one or other of the 'excepting provisions' applied. In addition, PA 2008, s 131(6)–(10) provided for the Secretary of State to hold a Public Inquiry in respect of applications seeking such certification. However, the references to certification and the provisions relating to the holding of public inquiries for the purpose of determining such applications were repealed by the 2013 Act.

The procedure now applicable to consideration of powers to compulsorily acquire 'Open Space' was confirmed in correspondence from PINS to, what was then, DCLG dated 24 October 2014, with the position relating to 'Common Land' having been previously set out in 2013 correspondence between PINS and Defra. In essence, the current legislative position is as follows

- There is no longer any requirement for certification by the Secretary of State.
- There is no longer any provision for the holding of a separate Public Inquiry, discrete from the Examination, in respect of the matters raised by PA 2008, ss 131 and 132.
- Instead, for SPP to be avoided it is necessary only that the Secretary of State be satisfied as to the fact that one or more of the 'excepting provisions' applies, and that this be recorded in the DCO.
- In this regard, where the promoter of an application for development consent seeks to rely on an excepting provision, it must make its case within the context of the Examination, on which basis the Examining Authority will make a recommendation to the Secretary of State as a discrete issue in its report.

The PINS correspondence expressly advises applicants to provide sufficient information in the Statement of Reasons, submitted in support of an application, to enable an Examining Authority to make a positive recommendation to the Secretary of State.

Thus the 'streamlined' procedure is now employed, whereby all matters relevant to ss 131 and/or 132 are considered by the Examining Authority at the DCO examination and are then the subject of a decision by the determining Secretary of State.

Excepting provisions

The statutory presumption is that any acquisition of this category of land will trigger SPP unless an 'excepting provision' applies.

In the first instance, the excepting provisions are contained in PA 2008, s 131(4) and (5). These require either that:

- replacement land has been or will be given, and has been or will be vested in the seller, subject to the same rights, trusts and incidents (see 'Provision of replacement land' below), or
- the land is either less than 200 square metres in extent, or required for the widening or drainage of an existing highway or partly for the widening and partly for the drainage of such a highway, *and* its replacement is unnecessary (see 'Replacement land unnecessary' below).

Provision of replacement land

As to what will amount to 'replacement land', the definition is set out in PA 2008, s 131(12). Most significantly, the provision requires that such land will be:

- not less in area than the Order land; *and*
- no less advantageous to the persons, if any, entitled to rights of common or other rights, and to the public.

There are two issues which have proved to be a particular focus for debate in this context.

(a) Timing of provision

In light of the use of the term 'has been or will be given' in s 131(4), questions have been raised regarding the requirement as to timing of the provision of replacement land. In essence, does the replacement provision need to be made available before the Special Category Land vests in an undertaker, or is provision of replacement land at a later stage sufficient?

In this regard, and by way of example, Article 36 of the M20 Junction 10a Development Consent Order 2017 required only that a scheme and timetable for the replacement land be submitted and approved prior to the Special Category Land vesting in the undertaker. Such arrangement would provide welcome flexibility for a promoter, with the ability to delay delivery of replacement land until convenient. Significantly, however, it does not appear that in this case either the Examining Authority or the Secretary of State gave detailed consideration to the meaning of s 131 and how the requirement as to timing should be interpreted. As such, it is not recommended that promoters place great reliance on it by way of precedent.

The more orthodox position, and that adopted in the majority of DCOs, is for the order to provide for the acquisition of existing open space land only once a scheme for the provision of the replacement land as open space has actually been *implemented* to the satisfaction of the relevant body (often the local planning authority).

This position is also supported by case law which suggests that any 'delay' in provision of replacement land would not satisfy the terms of the statutory exemption. Hansard records that, when the Parliamentary Under-Secretary of State for Transport addressed the Public Bill Committee in connection with s 131 of the 2008 Act, he commented that the excepting provision relating to replacement land essentially replicated s 19 of the Acquisition of Land Act 1981. That provision was considered by Mr Justice Hutchison in *London Borough of Greenwich v Secretary of State* [1993] Env LR 344, in which the judge observed that he did not consider that 'delayed' provision of replacement land would satisfy the provision in the 1981 Act.

(b) Requirement that replacement provision be 'equally advantageous'

The decision in *Greenwich* also provides material guidance as to what is meant by the term 'equally advantageous' in the context of replacement land.

First, the judge ruled on the point of whether, for replacement land to satisfy the requirements of the statute, it must essentially 'replicate' the benefits afforded by the land to be acquired or, alternatively, whether it would be permissible to balance the loss of one type of benefit with the gain of another. In determining that the second, more flexible approach was appropriate, the judge essentially determined that all that was necessary was that the benefit to the public be broadly of the same character. By way of example, where the land to be acquired has provided an amenity for public recreation, it will be no answer that the replacement land, although providing an inferior recreational opportunity, comprises an area of enhanced ecological quality. The requirement as to equivalence of benefit would relate to the public recreational aspect of the land.

Secondly, a further point considered in the *Greenwich* decision was the date on which the 'equivalence of provision' fell to be assessed. The court found that the relevant comparison should be undertaken at the date of 'exchange'; the Secretary of State had to be satisfied that the two areas were equivalent at that point in time. However, in undertaking that exercise, the Secretary of State could have regard not only to the condition of the land in its form as at that date, but also to how that land could reasonably be expected to develop/be used in future years. This is consistent with the position as stated in the Guidance, which cross-refers at paragraph 45 to the General CPO Guidance. In this regard, paragraph 240 of the General CPO Guidance states that:

> 'the date upon which equality of advantage is to be assessed is the date of exchange … But the relevant Secretary of State may have regard to any prospects of improvement to the exchange land which exists at that date. Other issues may arise about the respective merits of an order and exchange land. The latter may not possess the same character and features as the order land, and it may not offer the same advantages, yet the advantages offered may be sufficient to provide an overall equality of advantage.'

Replacement land unnecessary

The application of the first part of this excepting provision – whether the land in question is either (a) less than 200 square metres in extent, or (b) required for the drainage or widening/partly for drainage and partly for widening of an existing highway – will involve questions of fact. The issue most likely to give rise to material dispute is whether the provision falls to be applied by reference to 'discrete plots' or instead the totality of the Special Category Land falling within a particular category (such as open space).

Section 131(5) describes the exception as applying to 'the order land', which term is in turn defined in s 131(12) as meaning 'the land authorised to be compulsorily acquired'. It is considered that the expression cannot sensibly be read as referring to the totality of the order land (ie all the land identified as being subject to compulsory acquisition); otherwise, the exceptions would rarely (if ever) apply. The better view is that the test will generally fall to be applied by reference to discrete plots. It is noted that this appears to have been the approach taken by the Secretary of State in the only order to have relied upon the s 131(5) exception to date, the A14 Cambridge to Huntingdon Improvement Scheme Development Consent Order 2016 ('the A14 DCO'). The preamble to the A14 DCO states:

> 'In accordance with section 131(5) of the 2008 Act, the Secretary of State is satisfied, having considered the report and recommendation of the Panel, that the parcels of common, open space or fuel or field garden allotment land comprised within the Order land are less than 200 square metres in extent individually, or that this land is required for the widening or drainage of an existing highway or partly for the widening and partly for the drainage of such a highway, and that the giving in exchange of other land is unnecessary, whether in the interests of the persons, if any, entitled to rights of common or other rights or in the interests of the public.'

Notwithstanding the above, it is conceivable that the Secretary of State (or the courts) may take a different view if they were persuaded that the plots had been drawn up so as to treat land that is, in function or ownership, a single parcel of land as being comprised in multiple plots, without proper justification and so as to allow reliance on this exception. Before placing reliance on this provision, applicants should therefore consider whether such an argument is capable of being advanced against their identification of the 'order land' for the purposes of applying the exception.

The second part of the excepting provision – that it is unnecessary to provide replacement land – requires a greater degree of judgement in its application. Some assistance can, however, be derived from the statutory language, which expressly requires that the judgement as to whether replacement land is unnecessary falls to be considered by reference to the interests of '"the persons, if any, entitled to rights of common or other rights or in the interests of the public'.

As noted above, the only development consent order in relation to which the s 131(5) exception has been applied was the A14 DCO. In that case, the Examining Authority and Secretary of State agreed with the applicant's view that replacement land was unnecessary, both in relation to a small area of common land acquired and in relation to a larger area of open space required, because:

- in the case of the common land, the area was a very small part of the overall common area (0.28%), and there were extensive recreational opportunities in the immediate area even if it were lost; and
- in the case of the open space, this again formed a very small part of a larger area of open space (a golf course), it was located on a boundary that did not form part of the fairways, and its loss would have no material adverse effect on the course.

It is to be noted that the s 131(5) exception is in materially the same terms as that contained in s 19(1)(b) of the 1981 Act, which provision is frequently relied upon but which has not been the subject of any authoritative case law.

Further exceptions

The exceptions discussed above are the only means by which an applicant can seek to avoid SPP in relation to the compulsory acquisition of Common Land or Fuel or Field Garden Allotments. However, the 2013 Act introduced two further exceptions in respect of land comprising solely Open Space.

In this regard, s 131(4A) provides that the SPP will not be necessary in circumstances where (a) the Secretary of State is satisfied that no suitable replacement land is available or else, to the extent there is such land, it is only available at prohibitive cost, *and* (b) there is strong public interest for the development for which the order grants consent to be begun sooner than SPP would allow.

Further, s 131(4B) provides that SPP will be unnecessary where the land is required only for a 'temporary (although possibly long-lived) purpose'.

The subsection (4A) test

As regards s 131(4A), there is limited guidance as to how the various elements of the statutory test fall to be applied. In particular, there is no statutory definition as to how the terms 'suitable', 'available', 'prohibitive cost', or 'public interest' should be understood in this particular context. However, material assistance can be obtained from the report dated 9 June 2014 ('the TWUL Report') prepared by the Inspector in relation to the Certification Application made in respect of the Thames Water Utilities Ltd (Thames Tideway Tunnel) Development Consent Order 2014. This report, prepared in respect of the only public inquiry held in relation to the ss 131 and 132 certification process before repeal of the provisions providing for that process, provides an in-depth analysis and application of the statutory provisions.

First, in this regard, both the Inspector and the Secretary of State were content to accept the approach of the applicant on whether or not any particular piece of land could be regarded as 'suitable' to serve as replacement land (see paras 261–268 of the TWUL Report in particular). The various matters to which consideration was given included:

- whether the land was within the same catchment area as the land to be acquired or within close proximity to the boundary of that catchment area;
- whether the land was at least the same size as the land to be acquired;
- whether the land was already in use as common, open space of allotment (which would preclude its serving as replacement land);
- whether the land was the location of essential infrastructure of community value – such as health, education or religious use – which could again preclude its consideration;
- whether the land was then occupied by an existing use which would itself need to be re-located; and
- whether the land had buildings upon it.

Clearly such a list is not prescriptive, and the question as to what considerations would be relevant in any particular instance will turn on the particular circumstances of any given application. However, the above list serves at least to provide an indication as to the type of matters to which regard should properly be had in this context.

As to whether land was properly regarded as being 'available', the issue was again one where the Inspector and the Secretary of State were content to accept the position adopted by the applicant (see paras 271–273 of the TWUL Report). This entailed consideration of various criteria, including:

- whether the land in question was on the market for sale;
- the ownership and occupation structure of the parties currently interested in the land;
- the issue of whether the land was, or was planned to be, in beneficial use; and
- the prospect of being able to conclude a voluntary sale without recourse to compulsory acquisition.

As regards the issue of 'prohibitive cost', both the Inspector and the Secretary of State once more accepted the approach adopted by the applicant. Such approach entailed introducing an objective test against which to measure the issue, by reference to the character of the proposed development and the additional land acquisition cost which would typically be entailed in acquiring land for that purpose, as compared to simply acquiring open space land.

In the case of the Thames Tideway Tunnel, the character of the proposed development was deemed to be 'industrial'. As such, the cost which a promoter of the development could be expected reasonably to incur in providing replacement land was identified as being the difference between the value of open space land and the value of industrial land in that location. To the extent that it would cost an applicant more than that uplift in value to acquire replacement land, then that cost was properly regarded as being prohibitive (see, in particular, paras 296–297 of the TWUL Report).

Lastly, in terms of 'public interest', it is of course important to pay close heed to the wording of the statute, noting that the emphasis is not on the public interest in the NSIP per se, but instead on the interest in its being brought forward urgently (or at least more quickly than it would be in the event of SPP). In the case of the Thames Tideway Tunnel, the applicant was able to point not only to the urgency/need for the project identified in the NPS, but also to matters such as the infraction proceedings brought by the European Commission against the UK Government in respect of breaches of the Urban Waste Water Treatment Directive, and the risk that further fines would be imposed.

The subsection (4B) test

This exception from the SPP requirement is potentially available in circumstances where existing open space land is to be permanently acquired, but only for a temporary purpose, such that the land could revert to open space land once the temporary use were concluded.

There is obviously scope for debate as to what period a Secretary of State might be prepared to accept in connection with the term 'temporary (although possibly long-lived) purpose', and there is little to be gleaned from the Parliamentary debate in respect of the provision. Notably, the Parliamentary Under-Secretary of State for Communities and Local Government, when discussing this clause in the Bill for the 2013 Act, observed that '"temporary" means that it is not for ever. There is a limit to the time, but it is not necessarily just a matter of months … although it will not be permanent'. The only helpful indication given was that the intention was to embed a significant degree of flexibility in the provision, to allow for the different circumstances applicable in the case of different developments. In this regard, the Under-Secretary of State observed that, 'As such purposes could vary considerably depending on the project concerned, we have not attempted to specify a time period for any temporary need of open space'.

In the absence of any more precise indication, the position is necessarily unclear. However, it arguably must be applicable in situations where the open space land is required for a longer period than could be secured using temporary possession powers, since otherwise it is difficult to see how compulsory acquisition of land permanently (as opposed to using temporary possession powers) could be justified. In this regard, provisions of the Neighbourhood Planning Act 2017 anticipate temporary possession being limited to periods of less than six years. As such, it is considered that there is scope to argue that the s 131(4B) exception will apply to uses lasting a considerable period of time.

This exception appears to have been relied upon only once, in relation to the M4 Motorway (Junctions 3 to 12) (Smart Motorway) Development Consent Order 2016. Neither the Examining Authority's report nor the Secretary of State's decision letter discuss the duration of the temporary uses being relied upon for the purposes of this exception, and the Book of Reference for the project (which may have described the nature of the temporary uses being carried on upon the affected plots) is no longer available on the National Infrastructure Planning website.

Article 61

The Land and Assets of Statutory Undertakers

Richard Honey QC, ftb

Introduction

This article considers the ways that the land and assets of statutory undertakers are protected under the PA 2008 regime. It considers first the relevant provisions in the Act. It then considers the arrangements that are commonly put in place for individual DCOs, in the form of protective provisions and side agreements.

Statutory provisions

The land and assets of statutory undertakers are provided with additional protections under the PA 2008. Three statutory provisions are relevant. Section 127 protects the land of statutory undertakers. Section 138 essentially protects the apparatus of statutory undertakers. Section 53(10) contains a protection for statutory undertakers in relation to rights of entry for surveying. The first two provisions are also considered in article 54 of this work.

PA 2008, s 127

Section 127 of the Act provides protection to land which has been acquired by statutory undertakers for the purposes of their undertaking. The protection is against both the compulsory acquisition of the land and the creation of new rights over the land. Section 127 is engaged where (a) a representation has been made (and not withdrawn) by a statutory undertaker about a DCO application before the completion of the examination of the application, and (b) the Secretary of State is satisfied that either the land is used for the purposes of carrying on the statutory undertaker's undertaking or an interest in the land is held by the undertaker for those purposes.

For the purposes of s 127, the Act adopts the definition of statutory undertakers set out in Acquisition of Land Act 1981 ('ALA 1981') s 8, plus statutory undertakers for the purposes of ALA 1981, s 16(1)–(2), and undertakers which are deemed to be statutory undertakers for the purposes of the ALA 1981 by virtue of another enactment.

Under s 127, protection is given against compulsory acquisition of the land and the creation of new rights over the land unless and to the extent that the Secretary of State is satisfied that certain statutory conditions are met.

In relation to the compulsory acquisition of the land, under s 127(3) the conditions are that the nature and situation of the land are such that either (a) it can be purchased and not replaced without 'serious detriment' to the carrying on of the undertaking, or (b) if purchased, it can be replaced by other land belonging to, or available for acquisition by, the undertakers without '''serious detriment' to the carrying on of the undertaking.

In relation to the creation of new rights over the land, under s 127(6) the conditions are that the nature and situation of the land are such that (a) the right can be purchased without 'serious detriment' to the carrying on of the undertaking, or (b) any resultant detriment to the carrying on of the undertaking can be made good by the undertakers by the use of other land belonging to or available for acquisition by them.

These provisions have a long pedigree in statute, echoing not only provisions in ALA 1981, s 16 but also, for example, the Pipe-lines Act 1962 and the Harbours Act 1964. The position of statutory undertakers in relation to compulsory acquisition is covered in the DCLG 'Guidance related to procedures for the compulsory acquisition of land' (2013), but this effectively just repeats the statutory provisions.

PA 2008, s 138

Section 138 provides protection against the extinguishment of rights, and the removal of apparatus, of statutory undertakers. The section applies where a DCO authorises the acquisition of land (compulsorily or by agreement) and either (a) there subsists over the land a relevant right, or (b) there is on, under or over the land, relevant apparatus.

For the purposes of s 138, the Act uses the definition of statutory undertakers set out in the Town and Country Planning Act 1990 ('the TCPA 1990'). This is different from the definition used for the purposes of PA 2008, s 127. Section 138(4B) provides that, in s 138, 'statutory undertakers' means persons who are, or are deemed to be, statutory undertakers for the purpose of any provision of Part 11 of the TCPA 1990. TCPA 1990, s 262(1) provides that 'statutory undertakers' means persons authorised by any enactment to carry on any railway, light railway, tramway, road transport, water transport, canal, inland navigation, dock, harbour, pier or lighthouse undertaking, or any undertaking for the supply of hydraulic power, and a relevant airport operator. Under TCPA 1990, s 262(3) the following are also deemed to be statutory undertakers: any gas transporter, water or sewerage undertaker, the Environment Agency, the Natural Resources Body for Wales, any universal postal service provider, the Civil Aviation Authority and a person who holds a licence under Transport Act 2000, Part I, Chapter I. Section 262(6) provides that a holder of a licence under Electricity Act 1989, s 6 shall also be deemed to be a statutory undertaker.

A 'relevant right' is a right of way, or a right of maintaining apparatus on the land, which is either (a) vested in or belongs to a statutory undertaker for the purpose of carrying on their undertaking, or (b) is conferred on an operator under the electronic communications code (s 138(2)).

'Relevant apparatus' covers both (a) apparatus vested in or belonging to statutory undertakers for the purpose of the carrying on of their undertaking, and (b) electronic communications apparatus kept installed for the purposes of an electronic communications code network (s 138(3)).

The substantive protection provided by s 138(4) is that a DCO can only include provision for the extinguishment of a 'relevant right', or the removal of 'relevant apparatus', if the Secretary of State is satisfied that it is 'necessary' for the purpose of carrying out the development to which the DCO relates.

PA 2008, s 53

Section 53 provides rights of entry for surveying land and other specified purposes. Section 53(10) provides that the authority of 'the appropriate Minister' is required for the carrying out of works to search and bore into the subsoil under s 53(3) where the land is held by statutory undertakers and they object to the proposed works on the ground that execution of the works would be seriously detrimental to the carrying-on of their undertaking. PINS Advice Note 5 (version 6) on rights of entry advises applicants for s 53 authorisations to contact the Planning Inspectorate before submitting their request where they have identified that the proposed request includes land held by statutory undertakers.

Protective provisions and agreements

Statutory undertakers do not usually have in-principle objections to DCOs, but they will often object to DCO proposals in order to ensure that their interests are adequately protected. Frequently this happens when the statutory undertaker has some existing apparatus that will be adversely affected by the DCO, either during construction or during operation.

Statutory undertakers will want to ensure that works are undertaken well away from their apparatus if possible. If work is to be undertaken in the vicinity of existing apparatus, a statutory undertaker will often require certain standards and practices to be observed to seek to protect the apparatus. It may well also want an indemnity, to ensure that it is protected if its apparatus is adversely affected.

If apparatus has to be removed or altered, the statutory undertaker will want to ensure that this only happens with its agreement, including as to timing and method, and usually that it carries out the works itself, subject to the promoter of the scheme reimbursing it.

These matters are normally addressed through 'protective provisions' contained in the DCO. This article considers how protective provisions deal with the land and assets of statutory undertakers.

PINS Advice Note 15 (version 2) on 'Drafting Development Consent Orders' expects the interests of statutory undertakers to be protected. It provides that, where an applicant is not proposing to include protective provisions for a statutory undertaker in the draft DCO, it needs 'to ensure that the consultation report explains why protective provisions for that statutory undertaker are not sought or required' (para 4.2).

The Southampton to London Pipeline Development Consent Order 2020 is a good example of how the interests of statutory undertakers are protected under the DCO regime, but only up to a point. The DCO sought to acquire land, interfere with interests and remove apparatus held by statutory undertakers. A significant number of statutory undertakers submitted representations in respect of the scheme. Negotiations continued throughout the examination about protective provisions. Some 10 statutory undertakers withdrew their objections by the end of the examination as a result, but six objections by statutory undertakers remained outstanding at the close of the examination. Both s 127 and s 138 were engaged. The Examining Authority report considered the objections of each statutory undertaker.

Affinity Water had an interest in 259 plots of land. It had concerns about the safeguarding of its water network and consequently sought consultation and agreement on the construction of the development in the vicinity of its apparatus. The applicant was seeking new rights over the land and contended that the proposed protective provisions would be adequate. The Examining Authority accepted that the proposed protective provisions were not worded as Affinity Water wanted, but were satisfied they would provide an appropriate form of protection.

Network Rail had an interest in 56 plots of land. The proposed pipeline would run under seven operational railway lines. Again, the content of the protective provisions was disputed but the Examining Authority concluded that they would provide an appropriate form of protection for Network Rail. Network Rail advanced its own version of the protective provisions it wished to see in the DCO. The Examining Authority considered the suggested wording and accepted some of the proposed changes and additions, but not all of them.

Thames Water had concerns about the impacts of the proposed works on its operations in relation to more than 50 plots of land. It objected to the wording of the DCO and sought a separate asset protection agreement. The Examining Authority decided that the protective provisions, which would apply in default of an agreement being concluded, meant there would not be serious detriment to the carrying on of Thames Water's undertaking.

Similarly, the promoter was attempting to negotiate an asset protection agreement with Southern Eastern Power Networks, but the agreement was not concluded at the end of the examination. The Examining Authority concluded that, in the absence of a completed agreement, the protective provisions in the DCO meant that there would not be serious detriment to the carrying on of the undertaking.

Overall, the Examining Authority concluded that the protective provisions in the recommended DCO would ensure that an appropriate degree of protection would be given to affected statutory undertakers, such that there would be no serious detriment to the carrying out of those companies' undertakings, and that the interference with apparatus and extinguishment of rights proposed would be necessary for the purposes of carrying out the development.

Following receipt of the Examining Authority's report, the Secretary of State for Business, Energy & Industrial Strategy consulted the statutory undertakers, where agreement had been outstanding at the close of the examination, about the status of their discussions. Network Rail and Affinity Water responded by stating that they had not reached agreement with the promoter and set out that their own suggested texts were necessary to protect their interests. Ultimately, however, the Secretary of State agreed with the Examining Authority's conclusions.

As will be apparent from this example, side agreements to protect the position of statutory undertakers are commonly entered into. They can, for example, be presented as asset protection agreements or construction liaison agreements.

In the case of the M42 Junction 6 Development Consent Order 2020, side agreements were reached with Severn Trent Water ('STW') and Cadent Gas. For STW, the Examining Authority decided that the protective provisions, taken with the proposed side agreement, would suffice to protect STW's interests. In the case of Cadent, the side agreement was completed after the close of the examination, but before the Secretary of State's decision.

Side agreements are often preferable to protective provisions in a DCO, as they can be negotiated and agreed between the promoter and statutory undertaker, without being constrained as to whether the provisions would be suitable to include in a DCO and without being subject to the supervision of the Examining Authority and the Secretary of State. If, however, agreement is not reached, a statutory undertaker can only ask for different protective provisions to be included in the DCO. It is usual, therefore, for statutory undertakers to seek both an agreement and improved protective provisions in parallel, unless and until agreement is reached.

If a side agreement is not reached, and a statutory undertaker is not content with the protective provisions offered, the ExA will consider whether the protective provisions need to be amended. They will be influenced in particular by whether there is precedent in other DCOs for the two forms of wording. A statutory undertaker arguing for a new form of protective provisions, against wording proposed by the promoter based on other DCOs, is unlikely to succeed.

When the ExA comes to consider the statutory tests in light of the promoter's proposed protective provisions, the tests are not that difficult to satisfy. In relation to s 127, it will often be hard for a statutory undertaker to demonstrate 'serious detriment to the carrying on of the undertaking'. A very substantial impact would be required to meet this high threshold. In relation to s 138, a promoter should be able to demonstrate that the extinguishment of the right or the removal of the apparatus is 'necessary' for the purpose of carrying out the development to which the DCO relates. Neither of these provisions provides very strong protection for statutory undertakers. It is unlikely that, if an Examining Authority is satisfied that the case for the DCO has otherwise been made out, it would uphold an objection by a statutory undertaker such as to lead to development consent being refused.

Part 10

Environmental Impact Assessment and Habitats Regulations Assessment

Article 62

The Status of European Union Law in the United Kingdom following its Withdrawal from the EU

Pavlos Eleftheriadis, ftb and Professor of Public Law, University of Oxford

Introduction

This article focuses on the status of European Union law in the United Kingdom following the UK's withdrawal from the EU. On leaving the European Union, the United Kingdom could in theory have chosen to repeal all of EU law. It did not do so. For reasons of convenience and continuity, it has chosen to follow much of it. The part of EU law that continues to have effect in the UK is now called 'EU retained law' and it is valid in the UK by way of the European Union (Withdrawal) Act 2018 ('EUWA 2018'). The legal landscape, however, is complex. The EUWA 2018 was enacted before it was known whether there would be a withdrawal agreement between the UK and the EU and it had planned for a clean break with EU law. As is well known, the negotiation of withdrawal was a difficult and protracted process. An EU-UK Withdrawal Agreement was finally agreed in the autumn of 2019. It was given effect in the UK by the European Union (Withdrawal Agreement) Act 2020 ('EUWAA 2020'). This Act provided for a transitional phase which was finally completed at 11 pm on 31 December 2020. Before the transition was over, the two parties agreed a Trade and Cooperation Agreement, which was itself given effect by the European Union (Future Relationship) Act 2020 ('EUFRA 2020'). As a result of these agreements, the relations between the UK and the EU are now a matter of international law as well as domestic law. They are, first, outlined in two separate treaties, the Withdrawal Agreement and the Trade and Cooperation Agreement. At the same time, these two Treaties take effect through domestic law and their particular role depends on the three incorporating statutes. Accordingly, there are three ways for EU law to be effective in post-withdrawal Britain: (a) EU law under the Withdrawal Agreement of 2019, (b) EU law following the Trade and Cooperation Agreement of 2020, and (c) as 'EU retained law', merely as a matter of domestic political choice. These are addressed in detail below.

Part A – The Withdrawal Agreement

After much controversy and political uncertainty, the negotiations resulted in the UK-EU Withdrawal Agreement ('WA') in late 2019; that is, the Agreement on the Withdrawal of the United Kingdom of Great Britain and Northern Ireland from the European Union and the European Atomic Energy Community (2019/C 384 I/01). The WA covers the following four general areas: citizens' rights (Part Two), separation matters (Part Three), financial matters (Part Five) and Northern Ireland (Protocol on Ireland/Northern Ireland). It applies to both phases of withdrawal and is still relevant after the end of the 'implementation period', something which matters especially for EU citizens' rights and Northern Ireland.

The WA was given domestic effect by EUWAA 2020, ss 5 and 6. Nevertheless, the EUWA 2018, as amended by the EUWAA 2020, remains the main mechanism for the incorporation of EU law after the end of the transition. The most important provisions of these Acts were commenced on 'implementation period completion day' ('IP completion day'), that is, by 11 pm on 31 December 2020; see the European Union (Withdrawal) Act 2018 and European Union (Withdrawal Agreement) Act 2020 (Commencement, Transitional and Savings Provisions) Regulations 2020, enacted on 21 December 2020.

Under the WA, the process of withdrawal would take place in two separate phases. The first phase was the transition or 'implementation period', where EU law applied in the United Kingdom as if it was a member. The second phase began at the end of the transition and is subject to both the WA and the subsequent Trade and Cooperation Agreement of 2020. It is important to note that, for all practical purposes, the UK was a member of the EU until the end of the 'implementation period'. Any vested rights that arose during that time are protected under the transitional arrangements of the WA. For example, under Article 92 of the WA, the EU institutions were competent to take measures against persons established in the United Kingdom in matters to do with state aid or competition law. Indeed, the Commission retains the power to take steps under the law of state aid for matters that took place before the end of the transition for a period of four years after the end of the transition (Article 93 of the WA).

Direct effect

The WA is intended to have direct effect. Article 4 of the WA provides that the 'provisions of this agreement and the provisions of Union law made applicable by this Agreement shall produce in respect of and in the United Kingdom the same legal effects as those which they produce within the Union and its Member States'. This provision means that the WA is supposed to enjoy direct effect and primacy in the United Kingdom. It is unlikely, however, that the WA will have material effects on infrastructure projects of planning and environmental matters, with the exception of Northern Ireland.

Northern Ireland

Under the Northern Ireland Protocol, the following domains of EU law still have effect in Northern Ireland and remain under the jurisdiction of the Court of Justice of the EU: customs and movement of goods (Article 5 of the Protocol); technical regulations, assessments, registrations, certificates, approvals and authorisations (Article 7 of the Protocol); VAT and excise (Article 8 of and Annex 3 to the Protocol); single electricity market (Article 9 of and Annex 4 to the Protocol); and state aid (Article 10 of and Annex 5 to the Protocol).

Article 12(4) of the Protocol states that, in relation to these provisions 'the institutions, bodies, offices, and agencies of the Union shall in relation to the United Kingdom and natural and legal persons residing or established in the territory of the United Kingdom have the powers conferred upon them by Union law'.

'Relevant separation agreement law'

Section 26(2) of the EUWAA 2020 creates the category of 'relevant separation agreement law' by inserting a new s 7C into the EUWA 2018. According to s 7C, 'relevant separation agreement law' means either some general parts of the EUWA 2018 itself or Part 3, or section 20, of the EUWAA 2020 (citizens' rights and financial provision), or any domestic law that relates to the WA. It covers therefore any secondary legislation made in order to give effect to the WA. Its interpretation must follow the WA in a special way, subject to EU law (under the general terms of the WA). The significance of the designation 'relevant separation agreement law' is that its application must be in line with the underlying WA. Any question as to the validity, meaning or effect of any relevant separation agreement law is to be decided 'in accordance with the withdrawal agreement, the EEA EFTA separation agreement and the Swiss citizens' rights agreement'.

Part B – The Trade and Cooperation Agreement

The second international treaty that determines the relations between the UK and the EU is the United Kingdom and European Union Trade and Cooperation Agreement('TCA'); that is, the Trade and Cooperation Agreement Between the European Union and the European Atomic Energy Community, of the One Part, and the United Kingdom of Great Britain and Northern Ireland, of the Other Part (OJ L444/14, 31.12.2020). The Agreement is accompanied by a Nuclear Cooperation Agreement (NCA) and a Security of Classified Information Agreement (SCIA), which are not addressed below.

The TCA was given effect in domestic law by way of the EUFRA 2020. This Act gave effect to specific provisions of the TCA but also created a requirement for domestic law to be applied in light of this Agreement. It also created a delegated power to make further provisions to give effect to the Agreement. The TCA is an international agreement establishing a Free Trade Zone and is therefore subject to the general conditions of the World Trade Organisation, of which both parties are members.

The TCA took effect provisionally on the expiry of the transition period at 11 pm on 31 December 2020. Its ratification by the EU was left to be completed at a later stage, so that the European Parliament would have a better chance to scrutinise and debate it. Ratification was completed on 29 April 2021, and the TCA took full legal effect from 1 May 2021. The TCA was not intended to be ratified by the member states. This was because it is not a mixed agreement.

The text of the TCA runs to about 1,500 pages. The TCA is divided into seven parts and has more than 40 annexes. The seven parts are:

(i) Common and Institutional Provisions (Articles 1–14);

(ii) Trade, Transport, Fisheries and Other Arrangements (Articles 15–521);

(iii) Law Enforcement and Judicial Cooperation (Articles 522–701);

(iv) Thematic Cooperation (Articles 702–707);

(v) Participation in Union Programmes (Articles 708–733);

(vi) Dispute Settlement and Horizontal Provisions (Articles 734–773); and

(vii) Final Provisions (Articles 774–783).

The TCA covers institutional provisions (setting up a partnership council and various committees of negotiation), trade and other economic aspects of the relationship (such as aviation, energy, environment, road transport, and social security), cooperation on law enforcement and criminal justice, health collaboration, participation in EU programmes, dispute settlement and final. It is envisaged that the TCA will be supplemented in due course by way of future bilateral agreements on other areas.

The nature of the TCA

The TCA is not a European Union Treaty. It was not concluded under the Article 50 process of withdrawal from the EU. It is a new international treaty between the EU and the UK, hence an 'external EU treaty' under Articles 216 and 217 of the Treaty on the Functioning of the European Union ('TFEU'). It is, therefore, a treaty of public international law between the European Union and a third country. The European Commission considers it an 'Association Agreement' under TFEU, Article 217, although nothing much turns on this designation.

Direct effect

The TCA is not intended to have direct effect. Article 5 on 'private rights' provides that:

> 'Without prejudice to Article SSC.67 of the Protocol on Social Security Coordination and with the exception, with regard to the Union, of Part Three of this Agreement, nothing in this Agreement or any supplementing agreement shall be construed as conferring rights or imposing obligations on persons other than those created between the Parties under public international law, nor as permitting this Agreement or any supplementing agreement to be directly invoked in the domestic legal systems of the Parties.'

It follows that the TCA does not intend to create directly effective rights to individuals. Whatever obligations the UK now has under that treaty, these are owed to the EU and not to individuals or corporations.

Interpretation

Article 4 specifies that the TCA and any supplementary agreement is to be interpreted 'in good faith in accordance with their ordinary meaning in their context and in light of the object and purpose of the agreement in accordance with customary rules of interpretation of public international law, including those codified in the Vienna Convention on the Law of Treaties, done at Vienna on 23 May 1969'. This article makes it clear that concepts that occur in European Union law (for example, 'waste', 'plans or programmes' or 'emissions', are not necessarily to be interpreted in light of European Union law or according to the case law of the Court of Justice. Their interpretation is now a matter of public international law, not European Union law. Of course, any usage in EU law will be a relevant consideration.

Article 4(2) states: 'For greater certainty, neither this Agreement nor any supplementing agreement establishes an obligation to interpret their provisions in accordance with the domestic law of either Party'. The term 'domestic law' should include all jurisdictions of the United Kingdom, as well as all jurisdictions of the member states of the EU. It is not technically correct to refer to EU law as 'domestic law' since EU law is not 'domestic law' of any jurisdiction, but is the law of an international organisation under the EU treaties. Nevertheless, read in light of the immediately preceding provision, the best interpretation of the phrase 'domestic law' in this context must be that it includes EU law.

Article 4(3) states that 'For greater certainty, an interpretation of this Agreement or any supplementing agreement given by the courts of either Party shall not be binding on the courts of the other Party'. It follows that interpretations of the TCA by the Court of Justice of the EU are not binding on the courts of the United Kingdom. This is to be contrasted, for example, to the solution adopted by the EU-Ukraine Association Agreement (the Association Agreement between the European Union and its Member States, of the one part, and Ukraine, of the other part, OJ, L161/3, 29.5.2014), where it is provided (Article 322) that, in cases of a dispute regarding regulatory approximation, an arbitration panel may refer the matter to the Court of Justice and that the ruling of the Court of Justice of the European Union is binding on the arbitration panel.

Secondary legislation

Sections 31 to 33 of the EUFRA 2020 create broad powers for ministers of the Crown to create further secondary legislation in order to give effect to the TCA. The precise content of these statutory instruments will be interpreted in light of the TCA. Under EUFRA 2020, s 31 a 'relevant national authority' in the United Kingdom (which includes a Minister of the Crown, a devolved authority or a Minister acting jointly with a devolved authority) has the power to make regulations that it considers necessary to implement or otherwise deal with matters relating to the TCA. Section 31(2) provides that regulations made under this power can do anything that an Act of Parliament can do, except impose or increase taxation, make retrospective provision, create a relevant criminal offence, amend, repeal or revoke the Human Rights Act 1998, or amend or repeal the Scotland Act 1998, the Government of Wales Act 2006 or the Northern Ireland Act 1998 (EUFRA 2020, s 31(4)). This is a very broad 'Henry VIII clause' which enables secondary legislation to repeal primary law. The rules about the procedure for making these regulations are set out in EUFRA 2020, Sch 5.

Governance and dispute settlement

The TCA sets out institutional and governance provisions. It establishes an EU-UK 'Partnership Council', which will supervise the implementation of the Agreement by the two sides. The Partnership Council is supported by various other committees.

Similar to the Joint Committee set up by the UK-EU Withdrawal Agreement, the Partnership Council is chaired by a UK Government Minister and European Commissioner. Decisions will be taken by mutual consent and will be binding on the two parties. The Partnership Council will meet at least once a year. The Partnership Council will oversee the attainment of the objectives of the Agreement and any supplementing agreement. Either party can refer any issue relating to the implementation or interpretation of the Agreement to the Partnership Council. It will have the power to adopt decisions and recommendations in relation to the application of the Agreement.

A general dispute settlement mechanism is detailed in Part Six of the TCA. The mechanism involves possible recourse to an independent arbitration panel, but not the CJEU. This mechanism does not apply to environmental and climate matters, which are covered by a special dispute settlement mechanism set out below.

Some environmental provisions

The TCA contains a number of provisions that are potentially relevant to environmental law and infrastructure planning. They are included in Part Two ('Trade, Transport, Fisheries and Other Arrangements') of the TCA and in particular in Title XI, 'Level Playing Field for Open and Fair Competition and Sustainable Development'. They include a chapter on 'Environment and Climate' (Articles 390–396), and a chapter on 'Other instruments for trade and sustainable development' (Articles 397–407). There is also a Title on Energy, which includes chapters on general provisions, electricity and gas, safe and sustainable energy, energy goods and raw materials and final provisions (Articles 299–331) and which is set to expire on 30 June 2026 unless renewed by the Partnership Council (Article 331).

The environment is an area where there appears to be a commitment to 'non-regression'. Nevertheless, the commitments made in the TCA are not unconditional and are put in language that gives the parties very wide discretion. Article 355(1) of Title XI on 'Level Playing Field for

Open and Fair Competition and Sustainable Development' sets out the general principle of the 'level playing field' establishing that the parties 'recognise that trade and investment between the Union and the United Kingdom under the terms set out in this Agreement require conditions that ensure a level playing field for open and fair competition between the parties and that ensure that trade and investment take place in a manner conducive to sustainable development'. Article 355(3) states that each party 'reaffirms its ambition of achieving economy-wide climate neutrality by 2050'.

Nevertheless, Article 356(1) recognises that both parties have wide discretion on these matters:

> 'The Parties affirm the right of each Party to set its policies and priorities in the areas covered by this Title, to determine the levels of protection it deems appropriate and to adopt or modify its law and policies in a manner consistent with each Party's international commitments, including its commitments under this Title'.

Similar expressions are repeated in the chapter on the environment. Article 391(1) provides that the Parties:

> 'affirm the right of each Party to set its policies and priorities in the areas covered by this Chapter, to determine the environmental levels of protection and climate level of protection it deems appropriate and to adopt or modify its law and policies in a manner consistent with each Party's international commitments, including those under this Chapter'.

Article 391(2) provides that the parties 'will not weaken or reduce' their levels of environmental protection that are in place at the end of the transition period, 'in a manner affecting trade or investment between the parties'. Article 391(3) gives the parties 'the right to exercise reasonable discretion and to make bona fide decisions regarding the allocation of environmental enforcement resources'. Article 393 introduces a requirement to respect 'internationally recognised environmental principles', set out in some detail.

All of these environmental provisions need to be read in light of Article 5 'Private rights' which, as we saw above, rules out direct effect. This means that the commitment to a 'level playing field' is a commitment made in international law between the two contracting parties: the EU and the UK. It is not meant to create rights in private persons. Hence the role of these provisions will be limited to informing the interpretation of the domestic law implementing the TCA, as well as to the special effects of EUFRA 2020, s 29 which is discussed below.

The ordinary provisions for dispute settlement, which are set out in Part Six of the TCA and provide for 'consultations' (Article 738), and an 'arbitration procedure' (Article 739) do not actually apply to the Title on level playing field (under Articles 735(2)(e) and 362). Article 357 of the Environment and Climate Chapter provides for a set of special procedures of dispute settlement in relation to this chapter. It provides (at Article 396) that, in the event of a dispute, the parties will have recourse only to a process of consultations, and of a 'panel of experts for non-regression areas' as further specified in Articles 408, 409 and 410.

A novel aspect of the agreement at Article 411 is what it calls a 'rebalancing mechanism' for the level playing field. In certain circumstances, both parties have the right 'to take countermeasures if they believe they are being damaged by measures taken by the other Party in subsidy policy, labour and social policy, or climate and environment policy', subject to arbitration. The mechanism provides that, if consultations between them are unsuccessful, either party can take unilateral temporary and proportionate 'rebalancing measures', based on 'reliable evidence' and not on 'conjecture or remote possibility'.

Domestic effect under EUFRA 2020, s 29

Section 29(1) of the EUFRA 2020 provides that the TCA has immediate domestic effect, even when it is not particularly implemented by domestic law:

> 'Existing domestic law has effect on and after the relevant day with such modifications as are required for the purposes of implementing in that law the Trade and Cooperation Agreement or the Security of Classified Information Agreement so far as the agreement concerned is not otherwise so implemented and so far as such implementation is necessary for the purposes of complying with the international obligations of the United Kingdom under the agreement.'

The term 'modifications' is defined very widely in s 29(4) as follows:

> '"modifications" does not include any modifications of the kind which would result in a public bill in Parliament containing them being treated as a hybrid bill;'

At s 37(1), 'modify' is defined as including 'amend, repeal or revoke (and related expressions are to be read accordingly)'.

It follows that this is an unusually open-ended provision. It appears to require that any 'existing domestic law' should be given effect subject to the requirements of the TCA if the agreement concerned is not otherwise implemented and if the 'implementation' of the TCA is 'necessary for the purposes of complying with the international obligations of the United Kingdom'. It is unclear how far this broad and unusual provision will have an impact on the law of the UK.

In March 2021 the Court of Appeal stepped in to offer a very useful interpretation of this provision in *Lipton v BA City Flyer Limited* [2021] EWCA Civ 454 in a case that concerned EU rules on the liability of airlines. Lord Justice Green observed (at para 75) that the TCA does not have direct effect, by virtue of Article 5 of the TCA. He then interpreted s 29 as meaning that, under domestic law, the TCA must be given effect, not by way of 'purposive interpretation' but by way of a much stronger obligation to give immediate effect:

> '78. The section 29 mechanism provides that domestic law (as defined) "has effect … with such modifications as are required for the purposes of implementing in that law the Trade and Cooperation Agreement". The phrase "has effect" is important. Parliament has mandated a test based upon the result or effect. The phrase "has" makes clear that this process of modification is automatic i.e. it occurs without the need for further intervention by Parliament. The concept of modification is interpreted broadly in section 37(1) to "include" (and therefore is not limited to) amendment, repeal or revocation. Section 29 is capable of achieving any one or more of these effects. This does not lay down a principle of purposive interpretation (such as is found in section 3 Human Rights Act) but amounts to a generic mechanism to achieve full implementation. It transposes the TCA into domestic law, implicitly changing domestic law in the process. Applying section 29 to domestic law on a particular issue now means what the TCA says it means, regardless of the language used."

The court also noted that s 29 applies on two conditions:

> '80. The process of automatic modification in section 29 is subject to two statutory clarifications. First, it applies only so far as necessary i.e. it does not modify a domestic law that, otherwise, is already consistent with the TCA. Secondly, it covers modifications "necessary for the purposes of complying with the international obligations of the

> United Kingdom under the agreement".This ensures that the construction of domestic law which best secures compliance by the United Kingdom with its international law obligations is to be applied. This is needed because under the TCA the parties bind themselves to a variety of international law obligations beyond the TCA itself.'

It follows that s 29 applies in three steps (see *Lipton*, para 82). First, one is to identify the relevant domestic law. Second, one is to ascertain whether the domestic law is the same as the corresponding provisions of the TCA. If it is, then under s 29(1), 'there is no need to apply the automatic read-across'. If there is 'inconsistency, daylight or a lacuna then the inconsistent or incomplete provision is amended or replaced, and the gap is plugged'.

Part C – 'EU retained law'

Most of EU law, however, is not covered by the WA or the TCA. It is given effect in the United Kingdom only as 'EU retained law', as set out in the EUWA 2018.

EU retained law

EU retained law is law that applied to the UK at the time of its full withdrawal from the EU (with the exception of the EU Charter of Fundamental Rights). All such law is protected from immediate demise on withdrawal by the EUWA 2018. According to EUWA 2018, s 6(7), retained EU law means:

> 'anything which, on or after exit day, continues to be, or forms part of, domestic law by virtue of section 2, 3 or 4 or subsection (3) or (6) above (as that body of law is added to or otherwise modified by or under this Act or by other domestic law from time to time);'

There are five categories of 'EU retained law'.

(i) 'EU-derived domestic legislation'

The first category concerns UK secondary legislation which had been enacted under the enabling provisions of the European Communities Act 1972. Under EUWA 2018, s 2, EU-derived domestic legislation is any primary legislation created in order to give effect to EU law obligations or secondary legislation made under the European Communities Act 1972, or 'relating otherwise to the EU or the EEA'. Strictly speaking, of course, there was no need to 'save' primary law, but the EUWA 2018 is doing so anyway.

EU-derived secondary legislation includes the Environmental Assessment of Plans and Programmes Regulations 2004, the Town and Country Planning (Environmental Impact Assessment) Regulations 2017 and the Conservation of Habitats and Species Regulations 2017. Such secondary legislation has now been amended by EU exit-related statutory instruments such as the Environmental Assessments and Miscellaneous Planning (Amendment) (EU Exit) Regulations 2018 (SI 2018/1232) and the Conservation of Habitats and Species (Amendment) (EU Exit) Regulations 2019 (SI 2019/579).

(ii) 'Direct EU legislation'

The second category concerns direct EU law that is given full effect. Of course, such law may be amended accordingly by the UK authorities (for example, removing the role of the Commission in the enforcement and implementation of the relevant rules). Under EUWA 2018, s 3, 'direct EU legislation, so far as operative immediately before exit day, forms part of domestic law on and after exit day'. Section 3(2)(a) specifies that direct EU legislation includes Regulations and Decisions but, importantly, not Directives. Section 5(4) explicitly excludes the Charter of Fundamental Rights from EU retained law.

Such direct EU legislation may, however, be modified by statutory instruments under the provisions of the EUWA 2018. So, for example, the EU Electricity Regulation (EU) 2019/943 on the internal market for electricity (recast) was amended for UK purposes by the Electricity and Gas (Amendment) (EU Exit) Regulations 2019 and various subsequent other statutory instruments. In most cases, practitioners will have to locate the statutory instrument that adapts EU law for the purposes of domestic use. This can be done by searching for the relevant statutory instrument by subject matter and the words 'EU Exit'.

(iii) 'Rights etc under section 2(1) of the ECA'

The third category concerns, in general, existing rights under EU law. Under EUWA 2018, s 4:

> '(1) Any rights, powers, liabilities, obligations, restrictions, remedies and procedures which, immediately before IP completion day–
>
> (a) are recognised and available in domestic law by virtue of section 2(1) of the European Communities Act 1972, and
>
> (b) are enforced, allowed and followed accordingly,
>
> continue on and after IP completion day to be recognised and available in domestic law (and to be enforced, allowed and followed accordingly).'

This provision effectively incorporates any remaining directly effective EU law into UK law (for example, Articles of the Treaty that have direct effect). This broad act of incorporation made it necessary for UK ministers to legislate to exclude various aspects of the Treaties from the status of 'EU retained law'. For example, the Freedom of Establishment and Free Movement of Services (EU Exit) Regulations 2019 removed Articles 49, 56 and 57 of the TFEU and Articles 36 and 37 of the EEA Agreement from retained EU law.

Section 4(2)(b) of the EUWA 2018 provides that any directly effective rights arising out of a directive will have effect if they are 'of a kind recognised by the European Court or any court or tribunal in the United Kingdom in a case before exit day (whether or not as an essential part of the decision of the case)'. It follows that rights arising out of directly effective directives continue to have direct effect under the EUWA 2018 if they had been recognised in a case of the Court of Justice of the EU.

(iv) 'Retained case law'

A fourth category concerns case law. Retained EU case law, according to EUWA 2018, s 6(7), includes 'any principles laid down by, and any decision of, the European Court, as they have effect in EU Law immediately before IP completion day'.

Section 6(3) provides that, although the Supreme Court of the UK is not 'bound' by any retained EU case law (s 6(4)), any question as to the validity, meaning or effect of any retained EU law is to be decided so far as this law is unmodified on or after the 'implementation period completion day', ie 31 December 2020, and so far as it is relevant to it (a) in accordance with any retained EU case law, and any general principles of EU law, and (b) having regard (among other things) to the limits, immediately before IP completion day, or EU competences.

However, the UK government has made use of the powers given to it under s 6(4)(ba) and (5A) by making the European Union (Withdrawal) Act 2018 (Relevant Court) (Retained EU Case Law) Regulations 2020 specifying that the Court of Appeal is also a 'relevant court' for the purposes of section 6, which means that it is not bound by retained EU case law. Under reg 4(2) of the 2020 Regulations, a 'relevant court is bound by retained EU case law so far as there is post-transition case law which modifies or applies that retained EU case law and which is binding on the relevant court'. Regulation 5 provides that '[i]n deciding whether to depart from any retained EU case law by virtue of section 6(4)(ba) of the EUWA 2018 and these Regulations, a relevant court must apply the same test as the Supreme Court would apply in deciding whether to depart from the case law of the Supreme Court'. Applying those principles in *Lipton*, Lord Justice Green said (para 83):

> '[...]
>
> vi) The meaning and effect of the measure should be determined by reference to case law of the CJEU made prior to 11 pm 31st December 2020.
>
> vii) General principles of EU Law from case law and as derived from the Charter of Fundamental Rights and the TFEU, are relevant to interpretation.
>
> viii) In construing and applying such a Regulation the Court can depart from any retained CJEU case law or any retained general principles. The Court is not bound by such principles and may depart from them if it considers it right to do so. It has not been necessary to do so in this case.'

In a case decided only a few days before *Lipton*, the Court of Appeal addressed itself on the conditions under which a 'relevant court' may depart from the Court of Justice's case law in *TuneIn v Warner Music* [2021] EWCA Civ 441. Arnold LJ said (para 75):

> 'In the domestic context both the House of Lords and the Supreme Court have consistently stated that this is a power to be exercised with great caution. As Lord Bingham of Cornhill said in *Horton v Sadler* [2006] UKHL 27, [2007] 1 AC 307 at [29] in a passage cited as continuing to be applicable by Lord Wilson in *Peninsula Securities Ltd v Dunnes Stores Ltd (Bangor) Ltd* [2020] UKSC 36, [2020] 3 WLR 521 at [49] (two decisions in which the power was exercised):
>
> > "Over the past 40 years the House has exercised its power to depart from its own precedent rarely and sparingly. It has never been thought enough to justify doing so that a later generation of Law Lords would have resolved an issue or formulated a principle differently from their predecessors".'

(v) 'Retained general principles of law'

The fifth category is the general principles of EU law. Section 6 of the EUWA 2018 provides that 'retained general principles of law' are relevant in the interpretation and application of EU retained law. These principles are defined in s 6(7) as:

> 'the general principles of EU law, as they have effect in EU law immediately before IP completion day and so far as they–
>
> (a) relate to anything to which section 2, 3 or 4 applies, and
>
> (b) are not excluded by section 5 or Schedule 1,
>
> (as those principles are modified by or under this Act or by other domestic law from time to time).'

Section 5(2) of the EUWA 2018 provides that the supremacy of EU law applies to any enactment or rule of EU law 'so far as relevant to the interpretation, disapplication or quashing of any enactment or rule of law passed or made before exit day'. In other words, supremacy is still a relevant principle for all EU retained law.

Conclusion

While the UK was a member of the EU, European law applied in a streamlined fashion, under the terms of the European Communities Act 1972. The withdrawal of the UK from the EU has resulted in a very complex legal framework. EU law will continue to apply to the UK through three different avenues: the Withdrawal Agreement and its implementation; the Trade and Cooperation Agreement and its implementation; and by way of the general provisions for EU retained law set out in the EUWA 2018. Much of EU law continues to apply in the UK in its new form as 'EU retained law', variously amended.

Article 63

EIA Screening

Rebecca Clutten, ftb
Michael Humphries QC, ftb

Introduction

This article discusses the process that developers are required to undertake to determine whether their proposed development requires environmental impact assessment ('EIA') in accordance with the Infrastructure Planning (Environmental Impact Assessment) Regulations 2017 ('the 2017 EIA Regulations'); a process known as 'screening'. It explains the principle of EIA screening; it sets out the procedural steps that an applicant is required to take, including identifying the documents that should accompany a screening request; it discusses some of the key legal principles relating to EIA screening; and it draws attention to guidance on the topic issued by Government and the Planning Inspectorate.

The 2017 EIA Regulations

Since 16 May 2017, EIA for nationally significant infrastructure projects has been governed by the 2017 EIA Regulations. These replaced the Infrastructure Planning (Environmental Impact Assessment) Regulations 2009 (as amended) ('the 2009 EIA Regulations').

It should be noted, however, that reg 37 of the 2017 EIA Regulations (revocation and transitional provisions) makes limited provision for the continuing effect of the 2009 EIA Regulations. Regulation 37(2) provides that the 2009 EIA Regulations will continue to apply where, prior to the commencement date of the 2017 EIA Regulations, either:

(a) the applicant has already submitted an environmental statement or updated environmental statement (as defined in 2009 EIA Regulations, reg 2(1)) in connection with an application for development consent;

(b) the applicant has requested a scoping or screening opinion as specified in the regulation (see 2017 EIA Regulations, reg 37(2)(a)(ii)–(iii)); this includes a request for a 'subsequent screening opinion' under 2009 EIA Regulations, reg 6(2)(a); or

(c) the Secretary of State has, by that time, initiated the making of a screening direction under 2009 EIA Regulations, reg 5(2)(b)(i).

There are likely now to be very few circumstances where the 2009 EIA Regulations will still apply. Where they do, however, PINS Advice Note 7 (version 7) advises (para 1.9) that 'version 5' of that Advice Note should be referred to.

The principle of EIA screening

Development which either:

(a) falls within a description of development contained within 2017 EIA Regulations, Sch 1 ('Schedule 1 development'); or

(b) falls within a description of development contained within 2017 EIA Regulations, Sch 2 and that would be likely to have significant effects on the environment by virtue of factors such as its nature, size or location ('Schedule 2 development'),

is known as 'EIA development' (2017 EIA Regulations, reg 3).

Consent cannot be granted for development that is EIA development unless an EIA has been carried out in respect of the development that is the subject of the application (2017 EIA Regulations, reg 4). The purpose of EIA screening is, therefore, to determine whether development for which a development consent order is being sought requires the carrying out of an EIA.

Screening pursuant to the 2017 EIA Regulations

The procedure for establishing whether development will require EIA is prescribed by 2017 EIA Regulations, reg 8.

Regulation 8 requires that, prior to the carrying out by an applicant of statutory consultation under PA 2008, s 42, a person who proposes to make an application for an order granting development consent must either:

(a) ask the Secretary of State to adopt a screening opinion in respect of the development to which the application relates; or

(b) notify the Secretary of State in writing that they propose to provide an environmental statement in respect of that development (2017 EIA Regulations, reg 8(1)).

As such, where an applicant is satisfied that the development for which they seek consent is EIA development, they will not need to undertake any further steps in respect of the screening process (beyond writing the letter described) and can proceed to undertake the required EIA. However, where it is less clear cut as to whether a given development is EIA development (or where it is considered that development does not meet that description), the making of a request for a screening opinion enables an applicant to obtain the Secretary of State's written view as to that matter, and potentially avoid having to undertake EIA if that view is favourable.

Although the only statutory requirement as to timing is that the request for a screening opinion should precede the PA 2008, s 42 consultation, DCLG Guidance on the pre-application process (2015) is that it should be made as early as possible in the process, to enable the environmental effects of the proposed development to be properly considered (para 90).

Where an applicant requests a screening opinion, it is required to provide certain specified information (2017 EIA Regulations, reg 8(3)). This information comprises:

(a) a plan sufficient to identify the land;

(b) a description of the development, including in particular:

- a description of the physical characteristics of the whole development and, where relevant, of demolition works;

- a description of the location of the development, with particular regard to the environmental sensitivity of geographical areas likely to be affected;

(c) a description of the aspects of the environment likely to be significantly affected by the development; and

(d) to the extent that the information is available, a description of any likely significant effects of the development on the environment resulting from:

- the expected residues and emissions and the production of waste, where relevant; and
- the use of natural resources, in particular soil, land, water and biodiversity.

In addition, an applicant may also provide details of any features of the proposed development and any measures envisaged to avoid or prevent what might otherwise have been significant adverse effects on the environment (2017 EIA Regulations, reg 8(5)).

The Planning Inspectorate has given more detailed advice as to the information it wishes to see provided alongside scoping requests in its Advice Note 7 (version 7). Insert 1 of the Advice Note states:

> 'The minimum information that Applicants must provide with a screening request is set out in the EIA Regulations in Regulation 8(3). This includes:
>
> - a plan sufficient to identify the land;
> - a description of the physical characteristics of the whole Proposed Development;
> - a description of the location and any sensitive areas likely to be affected;
> - a description of the aspects of the environment likely to be significantly affected;
> - information on the likely significant effects resulting from residues and emissions and the use of natural resources; and
> - details of any features of the Proposed Development and any measures envisaged to avoid or prevent what might otherwise have been a significant adverse effect on the environment.'

PINS Advice Note 7 (version 7) also identifies (para 3.11) the information that it wishes to see shown on 'the plan', and indicates (para 3.12) that, where practical, that information should be included on a single plan; where more than one plan is used, the plans should be at the same scale and an overview plan should be provided (as appropriate).

It is important that, in dealing with the description of the development and its possible effects on the environment, applicants should ensure that the information is set out with reference to the criteria in Schedule 3 to the EIA Regulations, these being:

- characteristics of the development;
- location of the development; and
- types and characteristics of the potential impacts.

The 2017 EIA Regulations, reg 8(3)(c) refers to the need for a description of 'the aspects of the environment' likely to be significantly affected by the development, and PINS Advice Note 7 (version 7) makes clear (para 3.14) that applicants should ensure that all aspects of the environment likely to be significantly affected by the development are addressed, and that PINS regards 'aspects' of the environment as meaning the relevant descriptions of the environment identified in accordance with the EIA Regulations.

Once a screening request has been made, the Secretary of State (or, as the case may be, the relevant authority) has an opportunity to consider whether they have been provided with sufficient information to enable them to adopt an opinion, and if not, to notify in writing the person making the request of the points on which they require additional information (see 2017 EIA Regulations, reg 8(7)).

The decision maker then has 21 days, from either receipt of the screening request or any further information requested by them, to then adopt a screening opinion, which must be sent to the applicant and (if the screening opinion has not come from him) the Secretary of State (2017 EIA Regulations, reg 8(8)).

In determining whether the development falls within the scope of either Schedule 1 or 2, and in particular whether any of the thresholds set out in either Schedule have been met, the decision maker must have regard to the description of development applied for – ie the development that is the subject of the application for development consent. However, the authorities are clear that, to the extent that the development subject of the application is part of a wider scheme, that wider scheme will need to be taken into account when determining (in the case of Schedule 2 development) whether the development is likely to have significant effects. In *R (Candlish) v Hastings BC* [2005] EWHC 1539 (Admin) this issue was determined in the context of the Town and Country Planning (Environmental Impact Assessment) Regulations 1999, but it is considered that the principle would apply equally to the DCO regime. This consideration is likely to arise in cases where aspects of the development are being consented as part of the Town and Country Planning regime, either in advance of or following submission of the development consent order.

Obligations on the decision maker as regards the screening opinion

Where the Secretary of State or the Examining Authority adopts a screening opinion, they must:

(a) state the main reasons for their conclusion, with reference to the relevant criteria listed in 2017 EIA Regulations, Sch 3; and

(b) if they have determined that the proposed development is not EIA development, state any features of the proposed development and measures envisaged to avoid or prevent what might otherwise have been significant adverse effects on the environment (2017 EIA Regulations, reg 8(9)).

Screening direction

In circumstances where either:

(a) an application for development consent was not preceded by a scoping opinion and was not accompanied by an environmental statement; or

(b) an application for development consent was the subject of a scoping opinion to the effect that the proposed development was not EIA development, but the Secretary of State considers that this opinion was formed without taking into account information that he considers material to that question,

then the Secretary of State may issue a 'screening direction' pursuant to 2017 EIA Regulations, reg 7. Such a direction states whether or not development (including any associated development) is EIA development, and is determinative of that question.

A screening direction may be made either of the Secretary of State's own volition or following a request made by him, at any time until a 'subsequent consent' is issued (2017 EIA Regulations, reg 7(2)). A subsequent consent is an approval given following an application made in pursuance of a requirement imposed by an order granting development consent, where that approval is required to be obtained before all or part of the development permitted by the consent may begin (ie an approval pursuant to some form of pre-commencement condition) (2017 EIA Regulations, reg 2(1)).

The Secretary of State has the power to request information in connection with a screening direction, and may in exceptional cases extend the period within which such a direction must be issued (2017 EIA Regulations, reg 7(5) and (6)).

Article 64

EIA Scoping

Hereward Phillpot QC, ftb
Michael Humphries QC, ftb

Introduction

The Infrastructure Planning (Environmental Impact Assessment) Regulations 2017, (the '2017 EIA Regulations'), reg 10 sets out the procedure for obtaining a written opinion as to the information to be provided in an environmental statement (ie a 'scoping opinion'). The procedure is only available to a person who proposes to make an application for a DCO (2017 EIA Regulations, reg 10(1)), or an application to discharge a requirement (2017 EIA Regulations, reg 10(2)).

The procedure is not, however, compulsory. Whilst it is, therefore, a matter of choice for applicants whether or not they apply for a scoping opinion, in practice almost all do. It is an important part of the Environmental Impact Assessment ('EIA') process and is regarded as good practice. The advantages are obvious, in that obtaining a scoping opinion helps to focus the process of environmental impact assessment and ensure that the concerns of key stakeholders are identified and addressed at an early stage. It also allows issues to be 'scoped out' of the EIA process at an early stage, which can save time and money. An effective scoping process also makes it less likely that the environmental statement ('ES') submitted with the application will be rejected as inadequate, or that requests will need to be made for additional information.

Under the previous 2009 EIA Regulations, there was no obligation to follow the advice given in the scoping opinion, although, for obvious enough reasons, most applicants chose to do so to reduce the prospect of their application being rejected. This was changed, however, in the 2017 EIA Regulations, and reg 14(3) now provides that, where a scoping opinion has been adopted, the ES must be based on the most recent scoping opinion adopted (so far as the proposed development remains materially the same as the proposed development which was subject to that opinion). The timing of any request for a scoping opinion has become a much more significant consideration as a result.

Procedural steps

The main procedural steps are the same whether the applicant is seeking a scoping opinion from the Secretary of State pursuant to 2017 EIA Regulations, reg 10(1), or from the authority responsible for the discharge of the requirement (the 'relevant authority') pursuant to 2017 EIA Regulations, reg 10(2).

Once a request has been made, the Secretary of State/relevant authority must consult the person who made the request and the 'consultation bodies' (2017 EIA Regulations, reg 10(6)). 2017 EIA Regulations, reg 3(1) defines 'the consultation bodies' as meaning:

> '(a) a body prescribed under section 42(1)(a) (duty to consult) and listed in column 1 of the table set out at Schedule 1 to the Infrastructure Planning (Applications: Prescribed Forms and Procedure) Regulations 2009 where the circumstances set out in column 2 are satisfied in respect of that body;

(b) each authority that is within section 43 (local authorities for the purposes of section 42(1)(b)); and

(c) if the land to which the application, or proposed application, relates or any part of that land is in Greater London, the Greater London Authority.'

If a consultation body fails to reply within 28 days of being consulted, the Secretary of State/relevant authority is entitled to assume it has no comments to make (2017 EIA Regulations, reg 10(11)).

Before adopting a scoping opinion, the Secretary of State/relevant authority must take into account: (a) any information provided about the proposed development; (b) the specific characteristics of the development; (c) the likely significant effects of the development on the environment; and (d) in the case of an application to discharge a requirement, the ES submitted with the original application (2017 EIA Regulations, reg 10(9)).

The Secretary of State/relevant authority must provide a scoping opinion within 42 days from receipt of the request. There are only two exceptions to this timescale. First, where additional information has been requested, the 42-day period runs from receipt of that additional information (2017 EIA Regulations, reg 10(6)). Secondly, where the request for a scoping opinion has been accompanied by a request for a screening opinion, the 42-day period runs from the date that the screening opinion was adopted (2017 EIA Regulations, reg 10(7) and (8)).

In practice, most applicants will undertake at least some form of informal consultation with the main consultation bodies before submitting a request to the Secretary of State. This allows their views to be considered and, where appropriate, reflected in the information accompanying the request and reduces the likelihood of significant dispute as to the appropriate scope of the EIA. As explained below, it is also important in enabling the applicant to satisfy the Secretary of State's expectations as to the information that ought to accompany a request for a scoping opinion, and to comply with the guidance issued by the Planning Inspectorate on his behalf.

Documents accompanying request

Where the request is to the Secretary of State in relation to a proposed application for a development consent order, the only obligatory requirements (2017 EIA Regulations, reg 10(3)) are:

- a plan sufficient to identify the land;
- a description of the proposed development, including its location and technical capacity;
- an explanation of the likely significant effects of the development on the environment; and
- such other information or representations as the person making the request may wish to provide or make.

Where the request is to a relevant authority in relation to the discharge of a requirement, in addition to the reference number of the DCO and a description of the proposed development, including its location and technical capacity, the applicant must (2017 EIA Regulations, reg 10(4)) also provide:

- an explanation of the likely effects on the environment which were not identified at the time the DCO was made; and
- such other information or representations as the person making the request may wish to provide or make.

In practice, there is generally a need to provide a substantial amount of information with the request in order to make it possible for the decision-maker to give an informed (and thus useful) scoping opinion. The precise level of information that ought to be provided will be a matter of judgment in each individual case, depending on the nature of the development and the area(s) where its effects might occur.

A common approach (and one recommended by the Planning Inspectorate – see below) is to submit a scoping report, which is structured in a similar way to an ES, explaining the nature and purpose of the proposed development, describing the receiving environment, setting out the proposed approach to the process of environmental impact assessment, and then identifying the scope of the proposed assessment on a topic-by-topic basis.

Form of scoping opinion

The structure that has generally been adopted by the Planning Inspectorate for its scoping opinions is to provide:

- an executive summary;
- an introductory section which identifies what the Secretary of State has done in order to satisfy the requirements of 2017 EIA Regulations, reg 10 and to inform the opinion;
- a description of the proposed development and the site and surroundings based on the information provided by the applicant, together with the Secretary of State's comments on that information to inform the process of environmental impact assessment;
- specific comments on the applicant's approach to EIA and the relevant topic areas set out in the applicant's scoping report; and
- a final section that does not formally comprise part of the scoping opinion, but responds to other issues the Secretary of State has identified which may help to inform the preparation of the application for the DCO. This might include information on additional procedural steps made necessary (or desirable) by the presence of protected habitats or species in the receiving environment, the need for information on other regulatory regimes etc.

Appended to the scoping opinion should be a list of consultees, copies of the responses received to consultation and general advice on the presentation of information in the ES.

Secretary of State not precluded from asking for further information

Obtaining a scoping opinion, and then undertaking the process of EIA in a way that reflects that opinion, does not guarantee that the resulting ES will be judged to be adequate. 2017 EIA Regulations, reg 10(10) makes explicit that neither the Secretary of State nor a relevant authority shall be precluded from asking for further information, notwithstanding what may have been said in the scoping opinion.

Guidance

The Department for Levelling Up, Housing and Communities (DLUHC) has not produced specific guidance on EIA scoping in the context of the PA 2008 regime, although the online Planning Practice Guidance for the TCPA 1990 regime does provide useful advice of wider application.

The Planning Inspectorate, however, has produced specific advice on the EIA scoping process for NSIPs in PINS Advice Note 7 (version 7).

Information requirements

PINS Advice Note 7 (version 7) provides (insert 2) the following guidance on information to be included in a scoping request:

> 'Although it is not a statutory requirement, the Planning Inspectorate suggests that Applicants provide their scoping request information in the form of a scoping report including simple paragraph numbering to aid referencing. The Planning Inspectorate recommends that the scoping report should include the following information:
>
> The Proposed Development
>
> - an explanation of the approach to addressing uncertainty where it remains in relation to elements of the Proposed Development eg design parameters;
> - referenced plans presented at an appropriate scale to convey clearly the information and all known features associated with the Proposed Development;
>
> EIA Approach and Topic Areas
>
> - an outline of the reasonable alternatives considered and the reasons for selecting the preferred option;
> - a summary table depicting each of the aspects and matters that are requested to be scoped out allowing for quick identification of issues;
> - a detailed description of the aspects and matters proposed to be scoped out of further assessment with a justification provided;
> - results of desktop and baseline studies where available and where relevant to the decision to scope in our out aspects or matters;
> - aspects and matters to be scoped in, the report should include details of the methods to be used to assess impacts and to determine significance of effect eg criteria for determining sensitivity and magnitude;
> - any avoidance or mitigation measures proposed, how they may be secured and the anticipated residual effects;
>
> Information Sources
>
> - references to any guidance and best practice to be relied upon;
> - evidence of agreements reached with consultation bodies (for example the statutory nature conservation bodies or local authorities); and
> - an outline of the structure of the proposed ES.'

Developers are advised (para 5.9) to consider the timing of any request carefully so as to obtain the most benefit from the process, waiting until there is sufficient certainty about the description of the scheme likely to have a significant environmental effect.

Further detailed guidance is provided for the justification that applicants are expected to supply to support the proposed scoping out of aspects or matters. This is set out in the form of nine questions that applicants should seek to answer (para 5.11). Although it would be open to an applicant not to provide answers to these questions, the Advice Note points out that including this information will increase the likelihood of PINS agreeing the 'scoping out' request (para 5.12), and that matters are not scoped out unless the scoping opinion confirms this (para 5.13).

PINS Advice Note 7 (version 7) also makes the point (para 5.14) that a completed transboundary screening matrix should also be provided to facilitate the Secretary of State's consideration under 2017 EIA Regulations, reg 32: see also PINS Advice Note 12, 'Transboundary Impacts' (version 6).

Procedural advice

Applicants are advised to undertake their own informal consultation with the prescribed consultation bodies prior to submitting their request to the Secretary of State, so as to inform the request that they make.

PINS Advice Note 7 (version 7) advises applicants (para 7.1) to give the Planning Inspectorate an early indication of the intention to make a request (preferably 'several months in advance') to ensure that 'sufficient resource is available to meet the required demand'. In addition, applicants are asked to provide an advance notification a minimum of ten working days ahead of seeking a scoping opinion, accompanied by a GIS shapefile to identify the land in question. This will enable the Planning Inspectorate to allocate resources and identify the prescribed consultation bodies.

PINS Advice Note 7 (version 7) also contains more detailed advice on referencing and administrative matters, which applicants should follow when preparing their requests.

Article 65

Preliminary Environmental Information

Cain Ormondroyd, ftb
Michael Humphries QC, ftb

Introduction

Where consent is sought for EIA development, the interaction between the Infrastructure Planning (Environmental Impact Assessment) Regulations 2017 ('the 2017 EIA Regulations') and the PA 2008 means that there is a legal requirement to consult on 'preliminary environmental information' ('PEI'). The provisions are inelegantly drafted. In order to understand the scope of this obligation and the level of information required in practice, it is necessary to have reference to DCLG guidance and PINS advice.

Consulting on PEI

Although technically the requirement to consult on PEI in the 2017 EIA Regulations is separate from the requirement to consult under PA 2008, ss 42 and 47, in practice the two will usually be undertaken at the same time.

Indeed, 2017 EIA Regulations, reg 12 provides that the statement of community consultation ('SoCC') required to be prepared by PA 2008, s 47 must state whether the development is EIA development. The implication of this is that the status of the development as EIA development must be resolved *before* formal pre-application consultation can begin. If the development is EIA development, which will nearly always be the case for an NSIP, the SoCC must also state 'how the applicant intends to publicise and consult on the preliminary environmental information'(2017 EIA Regulations, reg 12(1)(b)).

PINS Advice Note 7 (version 7) makes it clear (para 8.9) that:

> 'Applicants are not required to provide PEI when undertaking their formal consultation (although if they do so they must set out how it will be publicised and consulted on as part of this process). However, Applicants are encouraged to provide PEI to enable the statutory consultees to understand the environmental effects of the development and to inform the consultation. Provision of PEI may assist in the identification of potential issues, enabling these to be addressed at an earlier stage in the pre-application consultation process.'

In reality, local authorities, other prescribed consultation bodies, and indeed the public are likely to object strongly to PA 2008, ss 42 and 47 statutory consultation that does not include sufficient PEI to enable them to understand the effects of the development and make intelligible responses; and so the processes for PA 2008, ss 42 and 47 consultation and 2017 EIA Regulations consultation will need to be coordinated, but each will have to comply with its own legal requirements. Thus, PINS Advice Note 14 (version 3) states (para 3.26), in relation to a consultation report, that:

'Consultation undertaken as part of the EIA process is separate to that required under the PA 2008 eg statutory consultation on a Scoping Report following a Scoping Request to the Secretary of

State. Applicants may wish to draw attention to consultation responses received under the EIA process, but any reference to that consultation should be addressed separately from the statutory consultation carried out under the provisions of the PA 2008.'

PINS Advice Note 3 (version 7) helpfully explains the approach that will be taken by PINS, on behalf of the Secretary of State (SoS), when identifying consultation bodies to be notified and, where relevant, consulted on the scope of an environmental statement (ES) in accordance with the 2017 EIA Regulations.

What information must be included

PEI is defined in 2017 EIA Regulations, reg 12(2) as:

> 'information referred to in regulation 14(2) which–
>
> (a) has been compiled by the applicant; and
>
> (b) is reasonably required for the consultation bodies to develop an informed view of the likely significant environmental effects of the development (and of any associated development).'

2017 EIA Regulations, reg 14(2) sets out matters which must be included in the ES as a minimum.

PEI amounts to the 'reasonably required' information falling within 2017 EIA Regulations, reg 14(2) which 'has been' compiled.

The DCLG Guidance on the pre-application process (2015) states (para 93) that:

> 'For the pre-application consultation process, applicants are advised to include sufficient preliminary environmental information to enable consultees to develop an informed view of the project. The information required may be different for different types and sizes of projects. It may also vary depending on the audience of a particular consultation. The preliminary environmental information is not expected to replicate or be a draft of the environmental statement. However, if the applicant considers this to be appropriate (and more cost-effective), it can be presented in this way. The key issue is that the information presented must provide clarity to all consultees.'

In practical terms, the decision as to what to include will be shaped by the stage in the pre-application process at which the PEI is compiled. In this respect the applicant faces the familiar balancing exercise in consultation generally between consulting early enough so that the consultation exercise can be shown to be meaningful and late enough so that consultees can be sufficiently informed of the nature of the proposals to make useful comments.

The DCLG Guidance also warns (para 94) that, 'The Planning Inspectorate is unable to review draft preliminary environmental information documents, but encourages applicants to discuss their approach to preparing preliminary environmental information with them as part of their free pre-application service', but it then points to the advice in PINS Advice Note 7.

PINS Advice Note 7 (version 7) makes it clear (para 8.4) that there is no prescribed format as to what PEI should comprise, and it is not expected to replicate or be a draft of the ES. However, it also goes on to make the point that, if the applicant considers this to be appropriate (and more cost-effective), it can be presented in this way. A good PEI document is one that enables consultees (both specialist and non-specialist) to understand the likely environmental effects of the proposed development and helps to inform their consultation responses on the proposed development during the pre-application stage. Thus (para 8.5), the level of detail and type of PEI will vary depending on:

- at what stage in the design process the consultation is carried out;
- the target audience; and
- the complexity of the proposed development and the receiving environment.

The PINS Advice Note 7 (version 7) also advises (para 8.7) applicants to consider carefully whether publication of the PEI at a more advanced stage in the design process of the NSIP – where more detailed information is known about the proposed development and its environmental effects – would generate more detailed responses and so better inform the design of the Proposed Development and their EIA. This, it says, may provide a more effective consultation exercise.

The issue of what is adequate PEI is closely related to the broader issue of what is adequate consultation. This topic is considered in greater detail in article 31 of this work.

Article 66

Preparation of an Environmental Statement

Hereward Phillpot QC, ftb
Michael Humphries QC, ftb

Introduction

Regulation 11 of the Infrastructure Planning (Environmental Impact Assessment) Regulations 2017(the '2017 EIA Regulations'), sets out a procedure intended to facilitate the preparation of an environmental statement (ES).

Pursuant to 2017 EIA Regulations, reg 11(1) and (2), the procedure may be triggered by one of four possible events:

- the applicant notifying the Secretary of State under 2017 EIA Regulations, reg 8(1)(b) that it intends to provide an ES in respect of a proposed application for a development consent order (DCO);
- the applicant notifying the authority responsible for the discharge of a requirement on an existing DCO (the relevant authority) under 2017 EIA Regulations, reg 8(2)(b) that it intends to provide an updated ES in respect of a proposed application to discharge the requirement;
- the Secretary of State giving a screening opinion in respect of a proposed application for a DCO to the effect that the proposed development is EIA development; or
- the relevant authority giving a subsequent screening opinion to the effect that supplementary information is needed to enable it to determine an application to discharge a requirement.

The procedure itself is prescribed by 2017 EIA Regulations, reg 11(1), and involves a number of steps that the Secretary of State or the relevant authority, as the case may be, must follow.

The consultation bodies (defined in 2017 EIA Regulations, reg 3(1)) must be notified in writing of the name and address of the applicant, and of the duty imposed on those bodies by 2017 EIA Regulations, reg 11(3) to make information available to that person. The duty is subject to the exceptions from the duty to disclose environmental information under the Environmental Information Regulations 2004 or the equivalent Scottish legislation (2017 EIA Regulations, reg 11(4)).

The applicant must be notified in writing of the names and addresses of the bodies so notified.

The applicant must also be notified in writing of any person whom it considers: (a) to be, or to be likely to be, affected by or to have an interest in the proposed development; and (b) to be unlikely to become aware of the proposed development by means of the pre-application and application procedure in Part 5 of the Planning Act 2008 (ie pre-application consultation etc).

Preparation of ES

The law, guidance and good practice on the preparation of ES is extensive, and it would be unrealistic to seek to provide a comprehensive guide to those matters in this article. Instead, this article provides a brief overview of the key points, including those which have now been set down in the advice issued by PINS.

General case law

As the courts have become increasingly familiar with the process of EIA, so the potential pitfalls have become better mapped and understood, and the degree of risk associated with the process has reduced and become more readily manageable. A realistic and pragmatic approach to the process of EIA and the contents of ES has developed, recognising that there will often be room for legitimate disagreement as to the appropriate scope and content of an ES, without any issue of law arising.

The following key principles can be discerned:

- The ES does not have to contain every scrap of environmental information, and need only cover the main effects or likely significant effects. Excessive information can be a hindrance to good decision-making (see eg *R v Rochdale Metropolitan Borough Council, ex parte Milne* (2000) 81 P&CR 27; *R (Bedford) v London Borough of Islington* [2002] EWHC 2044 (Admin); *Derbyshire Waste Ltd v Blewett and Secretary of State for the Environment* [2004] EWCA Civ 1508).
- In the context of the 'standard of review' to be applied to adequacy of an environmental statement or environmental report, the High Court in *R (Spurrier and others) v Secretary of State for Transport* [2019] EWHC 1070 (Admin) at paras [419]–[432] held that 'the 'Blewett approach' is not a free-standing standard or principle: it is no more and no less than a practical application of conventional *Wednesbury* principles of judicial review. See also the treatment on this issue in the subsequent appeal to the Court of Appeal, *R (Hillingdon LBC and others) v Secretary of State for Transport* [2020] EWCA Civ 214 at paras 126–144.
- Where a project is to be approved in stages, with details of some matters reserved for approval at a later stage, the ES accompanying the application for the 'in principle' approval must allow the decision-maker to understand the likely significant effects of the project as a whole (see eg *R v London Borough of Bromley, ex parte Barker* [2006] UKHL 52).
- To enable this to be done, clear parameters will need to be established for the purpose of EIA, and secured in the approval so that the effects of the development as approved do not exceed those assessed (see *R v Rochdale Metropolitan Borough Council, ex parte Milne* (above)). This will often be an important issue with NSIPs, where much of the detail is likely to remain at large at the DCO stage. In this regard, further guidance has been issued by the Planning Inspectorate on how to deal with the resulting uncertainties (see below).
- Where a development is linked to a larger project, the ES for that development must consider the cumulative effects that are likely to arise as a result (see eg *R (Brown) v Carlisle City Council* [2010] EWCA Civ 523).
- It is important that members of the public do not have to engage in a 'paper chase' to piece together the ES, which must therefore be a properly integrated and accessible document accompanied by a non-technical summary (see *Berkeley v Secretary of State for the Environment* [2001] 2 AC 603).
- An ES will not be adequate if it lacks a key piece of information necessary to ascertain whether significant effects are likely. It is not acceptable to leave the gathering of that additional information until after consent has been granted (*R v Cornwall County Council, ex parte Hardy* [2001] Env LR 25). That is to be distinguished from situations where it is

possible to reach a conclusion on likely significant effects without certain information, but provision is made for that information to be gathered after permission is granted so as to inform mitigation measures etc (see eg *R (PPG 11 Ltd) v Dorset County Council* [2003] All ER (D) 68 (Jun)).

- Mitigation measures can be taken into account in determining likely significant effects, although these must be secured in any consent that is granted, and their likely effectiveness must be taken into account (see eg *R (PPG 11 Ltd) v Dorset County Council* (above)).
- A decision-maker is required to consider whether there is sufficient environmental information to enable an evaluation of the likely significant effects of a proposal and then make that evaluation. Furthermore, where the effects would be substantial, the decision-maker has no discretion to defer consideration of them until a subsequent application (see *Pearce v Secretary of State for Business, Energy and Industrial Strategy* [2021] EWHC 326 (Admin)).

Guidance

The PINS Advice Notes of most direct relevance here are: PINS Advice Note 3, 'EIA consultation and notification' (version 7); PINS Advice Note 7, 'Environmental Impact Assessment: Preliminary Environmental Information, Screening and Scoping' (version 7); PINS Advice Note 9, 'Rochdale Envelope' (version 3); PINS Advice Note 12, 'Transboundary Impacts and Process' (version 6); and also PINS Advice Note 17, 'Cumulative effects assessment' (version 2).

PINS Advice Note 3: EIA consultation and notification

PINS Advice Note 3 (version 7) sets out the approach to be taken by the Secretary of State when identifying consultation bodies to be notified under 2017 EIA Regulations, reg 11 and, where relevant, consulted on the scope of the ES under 2017 EIA Regulations, reg 10.

The Advice Note sets out in detail the approach that the Secretary of State will adopt when notifying and/or consulting:

- *Prescribed consultees* – This advice includes an overview of Schedule 2 to the Infrastructure Planning (Applications: Prescribed Forms and Procedure) Regulations 2009 ('the APFP Regulations') and advice on the application of the 'relevance test' and the 'circumstances test' under those regulations.
- *Section 43 local authorities* – This advice introduces the concept of categories 'A', 'B', 'C' and 'D' local authorities and points to further advice in PINS Advice Note 2.
- *Non-prescribed consultation bodies* – This advice introduces a number of bodies which are not defined as consultation bodies in the 2017 EIA Regulations, but have similar functions. These are listed at Table 3 in the Annex to PINS Advice Note 3 (version 7).

PINS Advice Note 7: Environmental Impact Assessment: Preliminary Environmental Information, Screening and Scoping

Advice Note 7 (version 7) explains when a nationally significant infrastructure project should be considered as Environmental Impact Assessment (EIA) development under the 2017 EIA Regulations. It details the procedural requirements that apply to NSIPs that are EIA development. This includes the role of preliminary environmental information; pre-application consultation requirements on applicants; notification and consultation requirements on the Secretary of State; and the procedures for screening and scoping developments.

Helpful practical advice on the production of Environmental Statements, including presentation techniques, is provided at Annex 1 to Advice Note 7 (version 7).

PINS Advice Note 9: Rochdale Envelope

The principles behind the use of the 'Rochdale envelope' are considered in Advice Note 9 (version 3) and, in relation to EIA, para 2.3 draws attention to some 'key propositions' from *R v Rochdale MBC ex parte Milne (No 2)* as follows:

- the assessment should be based on cautious 'worst case' approach:

  'such an approach will then feed through into the mitigation measures envisaged [...] It is important that these should be adequate to deal with the worst case, in order to optimise the effects of the development on the environment' (para 122 of the judgment);

- the level of information required should be:

  'sufficient information to enable "the main", or the "likely significant" effects on the environment to be assessed [...] and the mitigation measures to be described' (para 104 of the judgment); and

- the need for 'flexibility' should not be abused:

  'This does not give developers an excuse to provide inadequate descriptions of their projects. It will be for the authority responsible for issuing the development consent to decide whether it is satisfied, given the nature of the project in question, that it has "full knowledge" of its likely significant effects on the environment. If it considers that an unnecessary degree of flexibility, and hence uncertainty as to the likely significant environmental effects, has been incorporated into the description of the development, then it can require more detail, or refuse consent' (para 95 of the judgment).

There is an important point here. EIA is intended to identify the 'likely significant effects' of a development; this much is clear from the EIA Regulations themselves. The concept of a 'worst case' assessment is not a substitute for the concept of 'likely significant effects'; it is simply a recognition that 'flexibility' in what is permitted – such as by the use of a 'Rochdale envelope' – may require the 'likely significant effects' of a reasonable worst case form of the development to be assessed.

PINS Advice Note 9 (version 3) explains this further (para 4.13), where it states that:

> 'Where the Applicant chooses to follow a parameters-led assessment to establish the worst case scenario for the ES, they should ensure that the applicable parameters are explained and clearly set out in order to:
>
> - ensure that interactions [...] between aspect assessments [...] are taken into account relevant to the worst case scenario(s) established and that careful consideration is given to how these are assessed; and
> - ensure that the assessment of the worst case scenario(s) addresses impacts which may not be significant on their own but could become significant when they inter-relate with other impacts alone or cumulatively with impacts from other development (including those identified in other aspect assessments).'

Thus, it is the 'scenario' that is 'worst case'; not the 'significant effects'.

PINS Advice Note 12: Transboundary Impacts and Process

2017 EIA Regulations, reg 32 sets out the basis for statutory notification and consultation with a European Economic Area Member State ('EEA State'). This applies where the Secretary of State is of the view that an NSIP is likely to have significant effects on the environment in an EEA State; or where an EEA State that is likely to be significantly affected by an NSIP so requests. This duty applies until the decision on the DCO application is made.

In addition, there may be occasions for an applicant to consult directly with bodies in an EEA State. There are also opportunities for an EEA State to become involved in the examination of a DCO application.

PINS Advice Note 12 (version 6) sets out the procedures for transboundary notification and consultation in association with an application for a DCO under the PA 2008, where such development, in the view of the Secretary of State, has likely significant effects on the environment in an EEA State. It sets out how the obligations under 2017 EIA Regulations, reg 32 will be met, particularly in the light of the statutory timeframes as prescribed by the PA 2008. The applicant has no formal role under the 2017 EIA Regulations, reg 32 process, as the duties prescribed by 2017 EIA Regulations, reg 32 in notifying and consulting with an EEA State on potential transboundary impacts are the responsibility of the Secretary of State. However, when fulfilling these duties on behalf of the Secretary of State, PINS uses the information provided by the applicant to assist in determining the potential for likely significant effects on the environment in EEA States. To this end, PINS Advice Note 12 (version 6) provides that the applicant is requested to provide information to PINS to enable a view to be reached as to whether the development is likely to have significant transboundary effects on an EEA State. The Advice Note makes clear that information about the potential for transboundary effects should be provided by the applicant:

- with the scoping request, if a scoping opinion is requested by the applicant from the Secretary of State under 2017 EIA Regulations, reg 10, and
- with the DCO application, when submitted to the Secretary of State for acceptance.

PINS Advice Note 17: Cumulative effects assessment

The requirement for cumulative effects assessment (CEA) is set out in Articles 4(3) and 5(1) of the 2017 EIA Directive. With respect to applications for development consent under the PA 2008, the requirements of the Directive are implemented through 2017 EIA Regulations, regs 3 and 14 and Sch 4, para 5.

PINS Advice Note 17 (version 2) seeks to provide:

- a brief description of the legal context and obligations placed on an applicant, with respect to cumulative effects under national planning policy and the 2017 EIA Regulations;
- an overview of the CEA process that applicants may wish to adopt for NSIPs; and
- advice regarding a staged approach and the use of consistent template formats for documenting the CEA within an applicant's ES.

Article 67

Environmental Impact Assessment: Transboundary Consultation

Hereward Phillpot QC, ftb
Michael Humphries QC, ftb

Introduction

Despite withdrawal from the European Union, the United Kingdom is still a signatory to the United Nations Economic Commission for Europe (UNECE) Convention on Environmental Impact Assessment in a Transboundary Context (the 'Espoo Convention'). The United Kingdom is also still a signatory to the Convention on Access to Information, Public Participation in Decision-Making and Access to Justice in Environmental Matters (the 'Aarhus Convention') and its Protocol, which provide people with the rights to easily access information, to participate effectively in decision-making in environmental matters, and to seek justice if their rights are violated.

EU Directive 2011/92/EU (as amended) implemented the Espoo and Aarhus Conventions in the European Union. The Conventions, however, impose 'transboundary' obligations on the United Kingdom that are quite separate from its (former) membership of the European Union and the European Economic Area ('EEA'), and have, therefore, survived.

The law

The relevant law is to be found in reg 32 of the Infrastructure Planning (Environmental Impact Assessment) Regulations 2017 (the '2017 EIA Regulations'), which transposed the requirements of Article 7 of EU Directive 2011/92/EU (as amended by EU Directive 2014/52/EU) (the 'EIA Directive') into domestic law. Whilst the EIA Directive itself is not retained EU law, the 2017 EIA Regulations are domestic legislation and the provisions on transboundary effects continue to have effect (with amendments). Those amendments, made by the Environmental Assessment and Miscellaneous Planning (Amendment) (EU Exit) Regulations 2018, reflect the fact that, from the end of the 'Implementation Period' (31 December 2020), the United Kingdom is no longer a member of the EEA.

Regulation 32 of the 2017 EIA Regulations (as amended) provides:

> '**Development with significant transboundary effects**
>
> (1) This regulation applies where–
>
> (a) an event mentioned in regulation 6(2) occurs and the Secretary of State is of the view that the development is likely to have significant effects on the environment in an EEA State;
>
> (b) it otherwise comes to the attention of the Secretary of State that development proposed to be carried out in England, Wales or Scotland is the subject of an

application for EIA development made under these Regulations and the Secretary of State is of the view that such development is likely to have significant effects on the environment in an EEA State; or

(c) an EEA State likely to be significantly affected by such development so requests.

(2) Where this regulation applies, the Secretary of State must–

(a) send to the EEA State as soon as possible and no later than the date of publication in The London Gazette referred to in sub-paragraph (b), the particulars required by paragraph (3) and, if the Secretary of State thinks fit, the information referred to in paragraph (4);

(b) publish the information mentioned in sub-paragraph (a) in a notice placed in–

(i) the London Gazette, in relation to all proposed development; and

(ii) the Edinburgh Gazette, in relation to development proposed to be carried out in Scotland,

indicating the address where additional information is available; and

(c) give the EEA State a reasonable time in which to indicate whether it wishes to participate in the procedure for which these Regulations provide.

(3) The particulars mentioned in paragraph (2)(a) are–

(a) a description of the development, together with any available information on its possible significant effect on the environment in an EEA State; and

(b) information on the nature of the decision which may be taken.

(4) Where an EEA State indicates, in accordance with paragraph (2)(c), that it wishes to participate in the procedure for which these Regulations provide, the Secretary of State must as soon as possible send to that EEA State the following information–

(a) a copy of the application concerned;

(b) details of the authority responsible for deciding the application;

(c) a copy of any environmental statement in respect of the development to which that application relates; and

(d) relevant information regarding the procedure under these Regulations,

but only to the extent that such information has not been provided to the EEA State earlier in accordance with paragraph (2)(a).

(5) The Secretary of State must also ensure that the EEA State concerned is given an opportunity, before development consent for the development is granted, to forward to the Secretary of State, within a reasonable time, the opinions of its public and of the authorities which the EEA State designated to be consulted about the project on the information supplied.

(6) The Secretary of State must–

(a) enter into consultation with the EEA State concerned regarding, inter alia, the potential significant effects of the development on the environment of that EEA State and the measures envisaged to reduce or eliminate such effects; and

(b) determine in agreement with the EEA State a reasonable period of time for the duration of the consultation period.

> (7) Where an EEA State has been consulted in accordance with paragraph (6), on the determination of the application concerned the Secretary of State must inform the EEA State of the decision and must forward to it a copy of the decision notice referred to in regulation 30.'

Thus the transboundary consultation process can be triggered either by the Secretary of State reaching the view that the proposed development is likely to have significant effects on the environment in an EEA State, or as a result of a request from an EEA State. An example of the latter scenario occurred during the process of determining the application for the proposed new nuclear power station at Hinkley Point in Somerset, where the Austrian Government made a request following the close of the examination. The Austrian Government consulted its own people on the proposed application, and the views expressed in response were taken into account by the Secretary of State in reaching his decision.

All NSIPs that are EIA development will be screened by PINS on behalf of the Secretary of State on a case-by-case basis for likely significant effects on an EEA State.

In reaching a view on whether to initiate the process, the Secretary of State must decide whether significant environmental effects on EEA States are 'likely'.

The Court of Appeal has held that, for these purposes, 'likely' should be interpreted in the same way as it has been where it appears elsewhere in the (then) 2009 EIA Regulations and the (then) EIA Directive (*R (An Taisce) v (1) The Secretary of State for Energy and Climate Change (2) NNB Generation Company Limited* [2014] EWCA Civ 1111). An Taisce (The National Trust for Ireland) had argued that a significant adverse effect should be considered 'likely' if it cannot be excluded on the basis of objective evidence. This approach, mirroring that taken by the ECJ to the Habitats Directive in the *Waddenzee* case, was rejected by the Court of Appeal, which held that:

1 The words 'likely to have significant effects on the environment' must have the same meaning throughout the EIA Directive.

2 'Likely' for these purposes does not mean more probable than not.

3 There is a clear distinction between the Habitats Directive and the EIA Directive for these purposes.

4 The 'real risk' approach to likelihood that the domestic authorities have so far adopted when considering the EIA Directive embodies a precautionary approach.

5 Adopting An Taisce's suggested approach would be contrary to the objectives of the EIA Directive as the public and decision-makers would be likely to 'lose the wood for the trees', thereby causing the EIA process to become less effective as an aid to good environmental decision-making.

In deciding whether a project is 'likely' to have a significant adverse effect on the environment of an EEA State, the Secretary of State should therefore approach the question on the basis of whether this is a 'real risk' or a 'serious possibility'. This involves considering both the magnitude and complexity of the potential impact, and the probability of it occurring. The greater the potential impact, the lower will be the level of probability at which the competent authority will decide that it should be subject to the environmental impact assessment process (see *Miller v North Yorkshire CC* [2009] EWHC 2172 (Admin) per Hickinbottom J at paragraphs 31 and 32). The competent authority must therefore make a judgment, balancing the severity of any potential environmental harm against the probability of it occurring.

Once triggered, the process takes place in two stages. First, the paragraph (2) stage involves notification of the EEA State concerned, and providing it with an opportunity to consider whether it wishes to participate. For these purposes the EEA State need only be given relatively limited information about the project (paragraph (3)), although in practice it is likely that it would be provided with a copy of the environmental statement.

If the EEA State in question decides that it does not wish to participate, that is the end of the process. However, if it decides to participate it is then sent a copy of the application, the environmental statement and procedural information and given an opportunity to consult its public and provide their views to the Secretary of State (paragraphs (4) and (5)).

It is the EEA State concerned that must consult its public, and not the Secretary of State. The Secretary of State's role is confined to facilitating the process of consultation through notification and the provision of information, and then taking the results of that consultation into account in making his decision on the application. If the consultation process undertaken by the relevant EEA State is materially defective, however, there may be grounds on which the Secretary of State's ultimate decision could be challenged in the Courts.

Guidance

The Planning Inspectorate's guidance on the transboundary consultation process is contained in PINS Advice Note 12 (version 6), 'Transboundary impacts and process'.

In addition to providing an explanation of the legal background and the approach adopted by the Planning Inspectorate and the Government, PINS Advice Note 12 (version 6) also guides promoters on their role in making sure that the relevant information is available at the appropriate times.

Whilst it is important to read the Advice Note as a whole, the following specific guidance is given to applicants:

> '4.1.1 The Applicant has no formal role under the Regulation 32 process, as the duties prescribed by Regulation 32 in notifying and consulting with an EEA State(s) on potential transboundary impacts, lie with the Inspectorate, on behalf of the SoS as described above.
>
> 4.1.2 However, in fulfilling these duties, the Inspectorate uses the information provided by the Applicant to assist in determining the potential for likely significant effects on the environment in other EEA States. To this end, the Applicant is requested to provide information to the Inspectorate to enable a view to be reached as to whether the development is likely to have significant transboundary effects on other EEA States. Information about the potential for transboundary effects should be provided by the Applicant as part of:
>
> - The scoping request, if a scoping opinion is requested by the Applicant from the Inspectorate under Regulation 8 of the EIA Regulations, and
> - The suite of documents accompanying the application for development consent.
>
> 4.1.3 If such information is not provided voluntarily, or a clear and reasoned justification as to why it is not considered necessary, the Inspectorate may need to seek further information on which to determine whether or not there are likely to be significant effects on the environment in an EEA State, and will adopt a precautionary approach in doing so.'

PINS Advice Note 12 (version 6) also states (para 4.2.1) that, 'The Applicant may wish to consider whether to undertake their own consultation with governmental divisions and interest groups within relevant EEA State(s) and/or other relevant states (those that are parties to Espoo or Aarhus Conventions according to the UNECE website)'. And indeed (para 4.2.2) that, 'This could be informed by an Applicant's own research into environmental issues and may also be informed by the transboundary screening decisions issued by the Inspectorate'.

The Advice Note states (para 3.2.1) that PINS will identify the EEA States to be notified under reg 32 primarily on the basis of the type of NSIP, its location, and the nature of the receiving environment: criteria are given in the Annex to the Advice Note. However, it makes clear that PINS will exercise reasonable discretion to determine likely significant effects in an EEA State, based in part upon the information supplied by the applicant. In exercising this discretion and identifying that an NSIP is 'likely to have significant effects' on EEA States, this should be taken as meaning that in the view of the Secretary of State there is a possibility or real risk, embodying a precautionary approach, that the development will have an effect, and not that a development will definitely have an effect. Specific guidance is given in section 6 of PINS Advice Note 12 (version 6) on the approach to nuclear power stations.

Advice Note 12 also gives guidance on the approach to be taken to the timing of the different stages of the transboundary process.

Discussion

The profile of the issue of transboundary consultation has been raised as a result of the *An Taisce* litigation. It is also important to note that the Committee set up to monitor compliance with the obligations created by the original legal source of the transboundary consultation requirement – the Espoo Convention – has become increasingly active and interventionist.

Failure to undertake transboundary consultation where it ought to have taken place can therefore present a significant litigation risk.

Whilst the Court of Appeal in the *An Taisce* case rejected the argument that a significant transboundary effect was 'likely' for these purposes if it cannot be excluded on the basis of objective evidence, it did not entirely close the door on future litigation to determine what is in fact the correct approach to likelihood for the purposes of EIA. On the facts of that particular case it was successfully argued by the Secretary of State and the promoter that no matter how low the threshold might be set by the Court of Justice of the European Union (CJEU), the Secretary of State's decision would still be lawful. Once the Claimant's 'zero risk' approach had been rejected, it was therefore unnecessary to decide whether the 'real risk' approach might be overturned by the CJEU in order to dispose of the case.

However, at paragraph 33, Sullivan LJ said that if the Court of Appeal were a court of final appeal, and it was therefore necessary to apply the '*CILFIT* test':

> '… I could not say that I was convinced that the other Member States and the CJEU would necessarily conclude that the "real risk" approach is the correct approach to the likelihood of significant effects on the environment for the purposes of the EIA Directive.'

The '*CILFIT* test' is a reference to the case of *CILFIT (Srl) v Ministry of Health* (Case 283/81) [1982] ECR 3415, concerning the approach to be taken by a court of final appeal to the issue of whether or not a reference should be made to the European Court of Justice (CJEU). In the *CILFIT* case the CJEU said that the national court could only refrain from submitting a question of EU law to the CJEU if it is convinced that the correct application of EU law is so obvious as to leave no scope for any reasonable doubt as to the manner in which the question raised is to be resolved, and convinced that the matter would be equally obvious to the courts of the other Member States and the CJEU.

Sullivan LJ's comment seems to create room for future argument as to what the correct approach should be, albeit in another case with stronger facts.

The cautious approach espoused by the guidance would therefore seem prudent. In most cases, promoters ought not to have much to fear from the transboundary consultation process. If there is a real risk of significant adverse transboundary effects, the process of assessment and pre-application consultation itself may be complicated by the need to deal with another State, but if done properly it is likely to be less risky than the alternative.

Article 68

Habitats Regulations Assessment

Michael Humphries QC, ftb
Gregory Jones QC, ftb
Richard Honey QC, ftb

Introduction

This article gives a brief overview of when a nationally significant infrastructure project will require a Habitats Regulations Assessment ('HRA') under the Conservation of Habitats and Species Regulations 2017 ('the 2017 Habitats Regulations') and/or the Conservation of Offshore Marine Habitats and Species Regulations 2017 ('the 2017 Marine Habitats Regulations'). This article will focus, however, on the principles in the 2017 Habitats Regulations, unless otherwise stated.

The article should also be read in conjunction with articles 62 to 67 of this work that examine the EIA process, which will often overlap with assessment under the Habitats Regulations. However, it needs to be recognised that the EIA process is designed to *inform* a final decision on an application for development consent, whereas an assessment under the Habitats Regulations may, in certain circumstances, actually *determine* a final decision on such an application.

The legislative framework

The 2017 Habitats Regulations derive from both the EU Habitats Directive (92/43/EC) and the EU Birds Directive (92/43/EC), under which sites were designated as Special Areas of Conservation ('SACs') or Special Protection Areas ('SPAs') respectively. The 2017 Habitats Regulations (as amended) implemented the Directives and are 'EU derived domestic legislation' for the purposes of the European Union (Withdrawal) Act 2018 ('the EUWA 2018'). At this early stage in the new post-EU withdrawal regime it is not entirely clear whether (and, if so, to what extent) the Directives may give rise to directly effective rights or engage 'retained general principles of EU law' that are relevant to the interpretation of the 2017 Habitats Regulations.

Thus, the now familiar references in domestic case law to both the Directives and CJEU decisions have to be understood through the prism of 'retained EU law' as set out in the EUWA 2018. The issue of 'retained EU law' is dealt with in more detail in article 62 of this work.

What is clear, however, is that a domestic HRA must now be undertaken primarily within the framework of the 2017 Habitats Regulations and the 2017 Marine Habitats Regulations.

Within this overall context, however, it is important to note that the domestic Regulations retain many concepts from the EU Directives. Thus the 2017 Habitats Regulations retain the terms 'European Site' and 'European Marine Site' (reg 8), albeit with some amendment to reflect withdrawal from the European Union; and the concepts of 'competent authority' (reg 7) and 'appropriate authority' (reg 9 and reg 10) are also retained, again with some amendment.

Regulation 63(1) of the 2017 Habitats Regulations states as follows:

> '(1) A competent authority, before deciding to undertake, or give any consent, permission or other authorisation for, a plan or project which–
>
> (a) is likely to have a significant effect on a European site or a European offshore marine site (either alone or in combination with other plans or projects), and
>
> (b) is not directly connected with or necessary to the management of that site,
>
> must make an appropriate assessment of the implications of the plan or project for that site in view of that site's conservation objectives.'

Regulation 63 goes on to provide that a person applying for consent must provide such information as the 'competent authority' may reasonably require for the purposes of the assessment or to enable it to determine whether an appropriate assessment is required (reg 63(2)), and that the competent authority must for the purposes of the assessment consult the appropriate nature conservation authority (reg 63(3)) and, if appropriate, take the opinion of the general public (reg 63(4)).

This then leads to regulation 63(5), which provides as follows:

> '(5) In the light of the conclusions of the assessment, and subject to regulation 64, the competent authority may agree to the plan or project only after having ascertained that it will not adversely affect the integrity of the European site or the European offshore marine site (as the case may be).'

However, the words 'subject to regulation 64' contain an important exception to this prohibition on the grant of development consent. Regulation 64(1) sets this out in the following terms:

> '(1) If the competent authority is satisfied that, there being no alternative solutions, the plan or project must be carried out for imperative reasons of overriding public interest (which, subject to paragraph (2), may be of a social or economic nature), it may agree to the plan or project notwithstanding a negative assessment of the implications for the European site or the European offshore marine site (as the case may be).'

This, however, is itself subject to the proviso in regulation 64(2) that:

> '(2) Where the site concerned hosts a priority natural habitat type or a priority species, the reasons referred to in paragraph (1) must be either–
>
> (a) reasons relating to human health, public safety or beneficial consequences of primary importance to the environment; or
>
> (b) any other reasons which the competent authority, having due regard to the opinion of the appropriate authority, considers to be imperative reasons of overriding public interest.'

There is, however, a further final requirement in regulation 68, which states that:

> 'Where in accordance with regulation 64–
>
> (a) a plan or project is agreed to, notwithstanding a negative assessment of the implications for a European site or a European offshore marine site, or
>
> (b) a decision, or a consent, permission or other authorisation, is affirmed on review, notwithstanding such an assessment,
>
> the appropriate authority must secure that any necessary compensatory measures are taken to ensure that the overall coherence of Natura 2000 is protected.'

It is quite clear from the above that, in order to grant development consent for a nationally significant infrastructure project, the process of HRA follows a number of clearly identifiable stages:

- Determine whether the proposal is a 'plan or project'.
- Determine whether the plan or project is one that is likely to have a significant effect on a European site or a European offshore marine site.
- Undertake an 'appropriate assessment' of the implications of the plan or project for that site in view of that site's conservation objectives.
- Approve the plan or project only after having ascertained that it will not adversely affect the integrity of the European site or the European offshore marine site.
- There is an exception to this prohibition, however, where:
  - there are no alternative solutions; and
  - the plan or project must be carried out for imperative reasons of overriding public interest.
- This exception is restricted where the site concerned hosts a priority natural habitat type or a priority species, in which case certain additional 'reasons' must be demonstrated.
- Where the project is to be approved, necessary compensatory measures must be secured to ensure that the overall coherence of the network of European designated sites is protected.

The process of assessment under the 2017 Habitats Regulations

The (then) MHCLG published online guidance on 'Appropriate Assessment: Guidance on the use of Habitats Regulations Assessment' in July 2019. This guidance gives a helpful introduction to HRA and, in particular, on the implications of the 'People Over Wind' judgment for HRA screening.

Defra has also published online guidance on 'Habitats regulations assessments: protecting a European site – How a competent authority must decide if a plan or project proposal that affects a European site can go ahead' (February 2021). Although directed at 'competent authorities', this guidance is helpful for applicants too.

PINS Advice Note 10, 'Habitats Regulation Assessment' (version 8), gives advice for applicants in relation to the preparation of a report showing any European Site(s) or European Marine Site(s) that may be affected, together with sufficient information to enable the competent authority to make an Appropriate Assessment, if required. [NB PINS Advice Note 10 (version 8) has not been updated since the UK's withdrawal from the European Union and still refers to articles in the EU Habitats Directive, although the general advice remains sound.]

PINS Advice Note 10 (version 8) follows the European Commission's 'Methodological Guidance on the Provisions of Article 6(3) and (4) of the Habitats Directive' in breaking down the process down into four stages – screening, appropriate assessment, alternative solutions, and imperative reasons of overriding public interest ('IROPI') – and that approach is adopted here for consistency.

In relation to stages 3 and 4, it is noted that Defra has published guidance on 'Alternative solutions, imperative reasons of overriding public interest (IROPI) and compensatory measures' (2012).

Stage 1: Screening

Regulation 63(1) of the 2017 Habitats Regulations requires an appropriate assessment to be carried out where there is a plan or project, that is not connected to the management of the site, but is 'likely to have a significant effect' upon the site either individually or in combination.

On the question of what is a 'plan' or 'programme', the High Court in *R (Berks, Bucks and Oxon Wildlife Trust) v Secretary of State for Transport* [2019] EWHC 1786 (Admin) considered the issue of whether a decision by the Secretary of State on a preferred corridor for a new road between Oxford, Milton Keynes and Cambridge amounted to a 'plan' for the purposes of the Environmental Assessment of Plans and Programmes Regulations 2004 requiring Strategic Environmental Assessment ('SEA'), but also whether it was a 'plan' requiring 'appropriate assessment' for the purposes of art 6(3) of the Habitats Directive (ie reg 63(1) of the 2017 Habitats Regulations). For the reasons set out at paragraphs 41–47 of the decision in relation to SEA, the Court held that the decision was not a 'plan' for the purposes of art 6(3) either (para 69), but was 'a step taken in the course of the preparation of a project'.

On the related question of whether any plan or programme is likely to have a significant effect on a European Site, in *Sweetman v An Bord Pleanála* (Case C-258/11) [2013] 3 CMLR 16, the Advocate-General ('the AG') succinctly summed up her opinion in plain language that the purpose behind this stage was to require developers to ask the question 'should we bother to check' whether the plan or project adversely affects the integrity of the site? Stage 1 is therefore a preliminary stage.

When is an effect 'likely'? It does not have the same meaning as the English civil law test of 'more likely than not' (ie more than 50%). Applying the so-called 'precautionary approach', the courts have given the word 'likely' a much wider definition that an ordinary reading of the word might suggest. While to most it suggests an event that might well occur, cases such as *Landelijke Vereniging tot Behoud van de Waddenzee* (Case C-127/02) [2004] ECR I-7405 ('*Waddenzee*'), *R (Loader) v Secretary of State for Communities and Local Government* [2012] EWCA Civ 869 and *R (Bateman) v South Cambridgeshire DC* [2011] EWCA Civ 157 put it beyond doubt that the correct approach is to look for effects that 'such a risk exists if it cannot be excluded on the basis of objective information that the plan or project will have significant effects on the site concerned' and 'in the case of doubt about the absence of significant effects … an assessment must be carried out' (see *Waddenzee*, para 44). An effect is therefore likely where there is only a risk, or a mere possibility, of it occurring.

What is a 'significant effect'? To all intents and purposes, the definition of significant effects appeared settled after *Waddenzee*, which held that where 'a plan or project has an effect on that site but is not likely to undermine its conservation objectives, it cannot be considered likely to have a significant effect on the site concerned' (see para 47). *Waddenzee* continued at para 48 to say that where those objectives were undermined, it necessarily followed that there were significant effects. The focus therefore was clearly on the 'characteristics and specific environmental conditions of the site concerned by that plan or project' that went to the site's conservation objectives (also at para 48).

However, the *Sweetman* case, on one reading, modifies this approach. There, the AG's opinion was that 'significant' set a 'very low' de minimis threshold excluding only those sites that have 'no appreciable effect on the site'. That threshold 'operates as a trigger, in order to determine whether an appropriate assessment must be undertaken'. However, the AG also considered that the threshold was not so low as to not exclude plans or projects 'having any effect whatsoever on the site' so as not to prevent all activities on or near the site becoming 'impossible by reason of legislative overkill' (see paras 48 to 49).

Although the AG did not refer to *Waddenzee* in this part of her opinion, the Court did in its decision, albeit only to set out what was said in *Waddenzee*: 'Where a plan or project not directly connected with or necessary to the management of a site is likely to undermine the site's conservation objectives, it must be considered likely to have a significant effect on that site. The assessment of that risk must be made in the light of, in particular, the characteristics and specific environmental conditions of the site concerned by such a plan or project' (see para 30). It therefore seems that the better view is that the focus remains on the site's conservation objectives.

In *People Over Wind v Coillte Teoranta* (Case C-323/17) [2018] PTSR 1668, the CJEU held that, at the screening stage of deciding whether a development is like to have a significant effect on a designated site, mitigation measures (that is, measures intended to avoid or reduce the harmful effects of the development) cannot lawfully be taken into account. The reasoning included that taking account of mitigation presupposes that there will be likely significant effects on the site in question, so that the requirement for an appropriate assessment has been established. It was also pointed out that there are procedural safeguards applying to decision-making where appropriate assessment is required and these would be circumvented by using mitigation to avoid assessment. Moreover, mitigation measures must be directly linked to the likely impacts that have been identified in the appropriate assessment and so can only properly be defined once the impacts have been fully assessed. Pre-empting or second-guessing the outcome of the appropriate assessment by taking account of mitigation measures at the screening stage would be illegitimate.

The evidence base at Stage 1 screening

Regulation 63(2) of the 2017 Habitats Regulations places a mandatory requirement on a person applying for development consent to provide the appropriate authority with such information as may be required: (a) for the purposes of the appropriate assessment; or (b) to enable them to determine whether an appropriate assessment is required. If insufficient information is submitted for those purposes, the competent authority may, and most likely will, refuse to accept the application for a DCO.

It is therefore necessary to engage in a robust process of pre-application consultation with the relevant statutory nature conservation bodies to ensure that the potential impacts of the development have been identified and addressed in sufficient detail before submission. It is likely that this process will overlap with the consultation required for EIA purposes. It is also good practice to consult more widely.

It is noted here that practice in the UK in relation to the information to be provided at the screening stage goes beyond what would otherwise be thought to be required in light of the AG in *Sweetman* characterising the first stage as the 'should we bother to check?' stage. Instead, as PINS Advice Note 10 makes clear, the level of detail expected to accompany application is high. It advises that, if the applicant wishes to persuade the Secretary of State that Habitats Regulations Assessment ('HRA') is not needed, the information should be presented in the form of a 'No Significant Effects Report' (NSER), to meet the requirements of Infrastructure Planning (Applications: Prescribed Forms and Procedure) Regulations 2009, reg 5(2)(g). There is no prescribed format for the NSER, but the Advice Note explains that it should contain the information requested in Advice Note 10 and completed screening matrices (Annex 1). The NSER 'must be clear, be supported by sufficient information, and provide convincing reasons why the applicant has reached the view that there are no LSA and that AA will not be required'. It is therefore the case that a substantial amount of work may have to be undertaken prior to submission in order to clear this hurdle, notwithstanding that the European approach seems to contemplate a less exacting standard at this stage of the process.

PINS Advice Note 10 (version 8) lists the following as issues that developers should include in their stage 1 screening assessment or report:

- 'a detailed description of the development, processes, timings, and method of work proposed as part of the NSIP;
- details of the methodology used to determine which European sites should be included within the assessment. A definition of and justification for the scope of the assessment should be provided;

- a plan and description of the European site(s) potentially affected, including a description of all qualifying features (a copy of the site data sheet is useful to include);
- an appraisal of the potential effects resulting from the construction and operation of the project (e.g. noise) and the likely significant effect on the European site(s) and qualifying features (e.g. disturbance to bird species);
- an outline and interpretation of the baseline data collected to inform the findings;
- an appraisal of the effects of any other plans or projects which, in combination with the Proposed Development, might be likely to have a significant effect on the European site(s). The scope of that appraisal should be well-defined and agreed with the local authorities and SNCBs;
- an evaluation of the potential for the scheme to require other consents requiring consideration of LSE by different competent authorities (e.g. where a Marine Licence is required separate from development consent);
- a statement which specifies where the DCO boundary of the project overlaps into devolved administrations or other European Economic Area (EEA) States and map(s), as appropriate;
- a statement which identifies (with reasons) whether significant effects are considered to be likely in respect of European sites in devolved administrations or within other EEA States; and
- evidence (such as copies of correspondence or SoCG) of agreement between the Applicant and all relevant SNCBs (including those in devolved administrations) and/ or relevant bodies in other EEA States on the scope, methodologies, interpretation, and conclusions of the screening assessment.'

That screening report will have to come to one of two conclusions: (a) there is no potential likely significant effect on a site; or (b) an anticipated potential significant effect on a site exists.

Where screening concludes that there will be no potential likely significant effect on a site, it will be necessary to produce an NSER (as above). There is no template for this report, but it must make it clear what the developer's view is and contain sufficient information to enable the competent authority to reach its own (hopefully concurring) view.

Where screening concludes that there is an anticipated potential likely significant effect on a European site, alone or in combination with other projects, the applicant's HRA needs to move to Stage 2 (Appropriate assessment) of the HRA process.

The report on the outcome of screening assessment should clearly identify which European sites are being taken forward to Stage 2 (Appropriate assessment) and which have been screened out.

PINS has developed a set of matrices to assist the relevant Secretary of State, as competent authority, in fulfilling the requirements of the 2017 Habitats Regulations and the 2017 Marine Habitats Regulations, and those for Stage 1 (HRA screening) can be found at Appendix 1 to PINS Advice Note 10 (version 8).

Stage 2: Appropriate assessment

Having established that a plan or project is likely to have significant effects on the site, the next stage is to subject the plan or project to an 'appropriate assessment of its implications for the site in view of the site's conservation objectives'.

The question the appropriate assessment addresses is whether the plan or project will 'adversely affect the integrity of the site concerned'. It is not immediately clear from the English language version what that phrase means, and its interpretation was precisely the question the court considered in *Sweetman*.

The AG's opinion was that 'integrity' was directed at the 'essential unity' of the site (see paras 53 to 56). Adopting a purposive approach to interpretation, in making the determination as to whether integrity was affected, it was again necessary to focus on why the site was designated and what its conservation objectives were. If attributes of the site going to its designation and conservation objectives were adversely affected by the proposed plan or project, then so would be its integrity. Further, it was necessary to make the assessment on the basis of the precautionary principle – only if the appropriate authority were 'convinced' that the plan or project would not affect the integrity of the site could that finding properly be made (see para 51). On that basis, a temporary loss of part of the site, perhaps during construction works, is less likely to result in an adverse effect on integrity than a permanent loss.

The CJEU expressly adopted the AG's opinion in holding that the integrity of a site will not be adversely affected where the plan or project permits the 'lasting preservation of the constitutive characteristics of the site concerned that are connected to the presence of a natural habitat type whose preservation was the objective justifying the designation of that site …' (see para 39).

The CJEU emphasised (at para 40) that, having made that assessment, the precautionary principle required that authorisation could only be granted:

> 'on condition that the competent authorities – once all aspects of the plan or project have been identified which can, by themselves or in combination with other plans or projects, affect the conservation objectives of the site concerned, and in the light of the best scientific knowledge in the field – are certain that the plan or project will not have lasting adverse effects on the integrity of that site. That is so where no reasonable scientific doubt remains as to the absence of such effects.'

The CJEU made clear in *Grace v An Bord Pleanála* (Case C-164/17) [2018] Env LR 37 that integrity related to the preservation of the constitutive characteristics of the relevant site that are connected to the presence of a natural habitat type the preservation of which was the objective justifying the designation of the site. This case also made clear that compensating measures, such as habitat creation, cannot be taken into account in an appropriate assessment, as they are inherently uncertain. They can only be considered following stage 4, explained below.

In *Coöperatie Mobilisation for the Environment v College Van Gedeputeerde Staten Van Limburg* (Case C-293/17) [2019] Env LR 27, the CJEU held that a mitigation measure may be taken into consideration in the appropriate assessment only when it is sufficiently certain that a mitigation measure will make an effective contribution to avoiding harm to the integrity of the site concerned, by guaranteeing beyond all reasonable doubt that the project at issue will not adversely affect the integrity of the site. This means that an appropriate assessment is not to take into account the future benefits of mitigation measures if those benefits are uncertain, eg because the procedures needed to accomplish them have not yet been carried out or because the level of scientific knowledge does not allow them to be identified or quantified with certainty. This limits the extent to which mitigation measures can be taken into account in an appropriate assessment, by requiring a high degree of certainty that they will be effective.

In *Holohan v An Bord Pleanála* (Case C-461/17) [2019] PTSR 1054, the CJEU held that an appropriate assessment must cover all the habitat types and species for which the site is protected but must also identify and examine the implications of the project for species present on site for which the site has not been listed and habitats and species outside the site which could affect the conservation objectives of the site. It also held that the appropriate assessment must identify and assess all aspects of the project, save only for matters such as the siting of a compound where the conditions imposed were strict enough to guarantee that such elements would not adversely affect the integrity of the site.

Overall, it is now clear that a strict precautionary approach should be adopted to an appropriate assessment. It must be done in the light of the best scientific knowledge in the field, employing a high standard of investigation. The assessment cannot have lacunae and must contain up-to-date, complete, precise and definitive findings and conclusions capable of removing all reasonable scientific doubt as to the effects of the project on the site concerned. The authority must be certain and convinced that the project will not adversely affect the integrity of the site concerned. If doubt remains, consent must be refused.

The PINS Advice Note 10 (version 8) suggests that, as a minimum, the applicant's HRA report should contain:

- 'information identifying the qualifying features, conservation objectives and conservation status of each of the qualifying features that might be affected;
- evidence about the project's effects on the integrity of protected sites;
- a description of any mitigation measures proposed which avoid or reduce each effect, and any remaining residual effects;
- a schedule indicating the timing of mitigation measures in relation to the progress of the development;
- cross references to the relevant DCO requirements, development consent obligations and any other mechanisms proposed to secure these mitigation measures, and identification of any factors that might affect the certainty of their implementation;
- a statement as to which (if any) residual effects constitute an adverse effect on the integrity of European sites either alone or in combination with other plans or projects and therefore need to be included within the AA; and
- evidence to demonstrate that the Applicant has fully consulted and had regard to comments received by the relevant SNCBs during pre-application consultation.'

PINS has developed a further set of matrices to assist the relevant Secretary of State, as competent authority, in fulfilling the requirements on the 2017 Habitats Regulations and the 2017 Marine Habitats Regulations in relation to Stage 2 (HRA appropriate assessment), and those can be found at Appendix 2 to PINS Advice Note 10 (version 8).

The Court of Appeal decision in *R (on application of Mynnyd y Gwynt Ltd) v Secretary of State for Business, Energy and Industrial Strategy* [2018] EWCA Civ 231 is a salutary lesson in ensuring that the Secretary of State has been provided with sufficient information to grant an application. In that case, the proposed wind farm development site adjoined a Special Protection Area for which one of the conservation objectives was to support breeding Red Kite. The Secretary of State requested information from the applicant and the relevant conservation body, Natural Resources Wales, about Red Kite mortality from the wind farm in combination with other nearby wind farms. The applicant responded to the request only in part and the application was refused. The applicant challenged the refusal but the High Court and the Court of Appeal upheld the Secretary of State's decision. The judgment in the Court of Appeal includes a helpful discussion of the applicable law (paras 8–9), what is meant by 'information' within the meaning of reg 61(2) (para 29), the non-applicability of the concept of 'burden of proof' (para 31), whether 'certainty' is required by a decision-maker (para 34), and overall planning judgement (para 26).

Stage 3: Assessment of alternative solutions

Where, having carried out an appropriate assessment and come to the view that the integrity of the site will be adversely affected, authorisation can only be granted where a further assessment has been carried out and concluded that there are no alternative *solutions* to the proposed development (reg 64(1)), not just no alternative developments.

This is an onerous hurdle to clear and will require a detailed and thorough examination of alternative solutions to deliver the objectives of the project. That assessment will include considering, at a minimum, not going ahead with the project, as well as locating the project in other regions or even countries. It must be objectively demonstrated that there are no other feasible alternative solutions that will not affect the integrity of the site, and that the proposal is the least damaging of all the solutions as regards the integrity of the site and the habitats and species therein. The assessment of whether there are alternative sites must be based solely on ecological criteria; matters of economics and social policy are only considered at stage 4.

It is important to note, however, that the alternative solution must still meet the 'objective' of the plan or project, and a potential alternative that does not meet that objective may properly be rejected as not being an 'alternative solution': see *R (Hillingdon LBC and others) v Secretary of State for Transport* [2020] EWCA Civ 214 at paras [81]–[93].

Stage 4: Imperative reasons of overriding public interest ('IROPI')

If it is concluded that there are no alternative solutions, then development consent can only be granted if there are IROPI for granting consent. In such a case, compensatory measures must be taken.

Where the site hosts a protected species or habitat, IROPI must relate to human health, public safety or beneficial consequences of the development of primary importance to the environment or other reasons of IROPI where the advice of the European Commission has been sought and had regard to. In all other cases, this is unnecessary.

IROPI may be social or economic, but the use of the words 'imperative' and 'overriding' indicate that this too is a high threshold: the development must in essence be indispensable, and the *public* interest in it going ahead must clearly outweigh protecting the conservation objectives of the site.

Compensatory measures

Although not given as a separate stage 5 in the guidance, compensatory measures follow on from a finding that IROPI has been made out. Such measures will need to be agreed with the appropriate statutory nature conservation body and may well be both expensive and a cause of delay. Compensatory measures must protect the overall coherence of the network of European sites and may include extending sites or recreating sites elsewhere. It will usually be necessary, except where this is not possible, for compensatory measures to be delivered before the site is adversely affected. In framing compensatory measures, it should be borne in mind that these measures are to 'compensate'; they do not require more than is necessary to replace what is lost.

The issue of HRA compensatory measures is covered in more detail in article 69 of this work.

Consideration by the Courts

The EU Habitats Directive and the UK 2017 Habitats Regulations have been the subject matter of extensive judicial consideration over the years, and much of this learning was drawn together in the High Court and Court of Appeal decisions on the challenges to the Airports NPS; see *R (Spurrier and others) v Secretary of State for Transport* [2019] EWHC 1070 (Admin) and *R (Hillingdon LBC and others) v Secretary of State for Transport* [2020] EWCA Civ 214. In this regard, it needs to be borne in mind that, although the Court of Appeal's decision was reversed by the Supreme Court on climate change issues, it was not appealed on general Habitats Regulations and Strategic Environmental Assessment ('SEA') issues and, indeed, it endorses the High Court decision on these issues.

In this article on Habitats Regulations Assessment there are, perhaps, three aspects of the Court of Appeal's decision to emphasise:

- in determining whether there has been a breach of article 6(3) and (4) of the Directive, the standard of review is *Wednesbury* irrationality. *Wednesbury* irrationality is the normal standard of review in judicial review proceedings and it is appropriate to apply the same standard to rights under EU law (see paras 69, 74–80);
- in considering alternatives, the decision-maker is entitled to reject an alternative that does not meet the essential aims or objective of the policy (see paras 86–89, 93). In this case it was found that the expansion of Gatwick Airport did not meet the 'hub objective' of the Airports NPS (ie the objective of maintaining the UK's status as an international aviation hub) and that it was not, therefore, an 'alternative solution' within the meaning of article 6 of the Habitats Directive; and
- there is a distinction between the concept of 'alternative solutions' under the Habitats Directive and the concept of 'reasonable alternatives' under the SEA Directive (see paras 109, 111–119). This distinction reflects the different underlying purpose of each Directive. The purpose of the SEA Directive is to ensure the consideration of environmental information and to secure public participation in the formulation of plans and programmes, and as part of that it is necessary to identify all 'reasonable alternatives' so that consultees can make representations. By contrast, the Habitats Directive contains no corresponding duty to consult before concluding whether the requirements of article 6(4) (alternatives) have been met. Thus it may be appropriate to consult on a 'reasonable alternative' under the SEA Directive even if that alternative is not an 'alternative solution' that would meet the essential objective of the policy for the purposes of the Habitats Directive.

Article 69

A Practical Approach to Compensatory Measures

Caroline Daly, ftb

Introduction

The need for an NSIP to promote and secure compensatory measures arises where the project has not passed the 'integrity' test, and where the decision-maker is satisfied that there are both no alternative solutions and 'imperative reasons of overriding public interest' ('IROPI') for granting consent. The aim of compensatory measures is, as the name suggests, to compensate for a project that will give rise to significant adverse effects or where such effects cannot be ruled out. This article provides practical guidance regarding the location, nature and scope of compensatory measures. It uses Hornsea Project Three as a case study for a project in which compensatory measures were required.

Defra has published guidance on 'Habitats regulations assessments: protecting a European site' (2021), which covers compensatory measures in brief terms. The European Commission's Guidance entitled 'Managing Natura 2000 sites: The provisions of Article 6 of the "Habitats" Directive 92/43/EEC' (2018) also provides a more detailed guide to designing compensatory measures and their purpose.

The location, nature and scope of compensatory measures

Compensatory measures may be provided on the site affected by the project (see Case C-521/12 *Briels v Minister van Infrastructuur en Milieu*) or can involve an extension to a site, or the creation of a new site. The Defra Guidance states that, if the area providing compensatory measures is not within the site, it should become designated.

The ability to provide compensatory measures remote from the site affected by the project reflects the purpose of compensatory measures, which is to ensure that the overall coherence of Natura 2000 is protected (Habitats Regulations 2017, reg 68), as opposed to placing focus on the affected site alone.

The measures should be identified by considering: (a) the damage to the site in question, having regard to its conservation objectives and to the species and/or habitats negatively affected; (b) the contribution to the network of sites that will be lost through the damage to the site in question; and (c) how that loss can be offset.

It is important to stress the distinction between compensatory measures and mitigation measures. The purpose of mitigation measures is to to 'avoid' or 'reduce' any direct adverse effects that may be caused by a project in order to ensure that it does not adversely affect the integrity of a site, whereas compensatory measures 'compensate' for the negative effects of a project on a site and cannot be taken into account in the assessment of the implications of the project (Case C-164/17 *Grace and Sweetman v An Bord Pleanala*, para 47).

On several occasions, the CJEU has determined that measures characterised by applicants as mitigation were instead compensation. For example:

- In *Briels*, the CJEU determined that the creation of an area of equal or greater size of the same natural habitat type, molinia meadows, within the site was a compensatory measure in circumstances in which the pre-existing molinia meadows would be adversely affected by nitrogen deposition from a motorway-widening project. The provision of new habitat did not provide mitigation for the adverse effect, but instead compensated for it.
- In *Grace*, the relevant protected site provided a suitable habitat for hen harriers although the area suitable for providing for their needs fluctuated over time. A proposal for a wind farm on the site would result in some parts of it no longer being able to provide a suitable habitat for hen harriers. What was proposed was a dynamic management plan that sought to ensure that a part of the site that could provide suitable habitat would not be reduced and indeed may be enhanced. The CJEU held (at para 57) that:

  'where it is intended to carry out a project on a site designated for the protection and conservation of certain species, of which the area suitable for providing for the needs of a protected species fluctuates over time, and the temporary or permanent effect of that project will be that some parts of the site will no longer be able to provide a suitable habitat for the species in question, the fact that the project includes measures to ensure that, after an appropriate assessment of the implications of the project has been carried out and throughout the lifetime of the project, the part of the site that is in fact likely to provide a suitable habitat will not be reduced and indeed may be enhanced may not be taken into account for the purpose of the assessment that must be carried out in accordance with article 6(3) of the Directive to ensure that the project in question will not adversely affect the integrity of the site concerned; that fact falls to be considered, if need be, under article 6(4) of the Directive.'

When selecting compensatory measures, care must be taken to ensure that the measures go beyond the normal conservation measures required for the protection and management of sites. For example, a measure already included in a site management plan cannot also be relied upon as a compensatory measure. The Advocate General's opinion in *Briels* was that a compensatory measure must be 'specific to the plan or project and not part of a management or conservation plan to be carried out in any event' (para 49).

For an important discussion of these issues, see also the Court of Appeal decision in *Smyth v Secretary of State* [2015] EWCA Civ 174 at paras [64]–[77].

Case study: Hornsea Project Three

The Secretary of State granted development consent for Hornsea Project Three on 31 December 2020. It is one of the few DCO projects to date in which IROPI have been required for it to proceed and it, therefore, provides an insight into the approach to the identification of compensatory measures expected by the Secretary of State.

The project comprises an offshore wind farm of up to 2.4 GW with associated offshore and onshore development in the North Sea and in Norfolk. The determination of the application took some two and a half years from the date of application to a decision, with the delay attributable in large part to issues arising in respect of the Habitats Regulations Assessment.

The Secretary of State determined that he could not rule out an adverse effect on integrity on the kittiwake feature of the Flamborough and Filey Coast SPA due to the potential for collision mortality in combination with other plans or projects. The Secretary of State also determined that an adverse effect on integrity could not be ruled out in respect of the development alone or in combination with other projects and plans in relation to 'sandbanks slightly covered by sea water all the time', an Annex I qualifying feature of the North Norfolk Sandbanks and Saturn Reef SAC and the Wash and North Norfolk Coast SAC.

The compensatory measures accepted by the Secretary of State in respect of the kittiwakes consisted of the construction and maintenance of artificial nesting structures at English east coast location designed to increase the productivity of the kittiwake population. This followed the rejection by the Secretary of State of an alternative compensatory measure, which involved a programme of eradication of invasive mammalian predators. In agreement with Natural England and the RSPB, the Secretary of State considered that, whereas it was reasonable to conclude that a successful method of eradication could be developed, it was questionable whether predator eradication would result in an increase in the breeding productivity of kittiwake.

With regard to the sandbank habitats, the compensatory measures comprised the removal of lost and/or abandoned fishing gear from the habitats prior to the commencing of construction works, fishing gear awareness events and measures to facilitate the rapid recovery of lost fishing gear. Whereas the applicant's compensation strategy had proposed the restoration of blue mussel bed, the Secretary of State considered that this went beyond what was necessary as compensation, given that the impacts of the project were to the sandbank habitats and not the mussel bed.

From a procedural perspective, the Secretary of State's decision letter provides guidance as to the approach that should be taken by applicants to potential adverse impacts on the integrity of sites, pointing to an expectation that applicants and statutory nature conservation bodies will engage constructively during the pre-application period and provide all necessary evidence on these issues, including possible compensatory measures, for consideration during the examination.

Where an applicant does not agree with a statutory nature conservation body regarding significant adverse effects, the applicant should provide evidence of possible compensatory measures for consideration at the examination on a 'without prejudice' basis, even if it does not consider that such measures are required. The Examining Authority will be required to provide an opinion on the sufficiency of the proposed compensation, even if it considers that compensation is not required, in case the Secretary of State disagrees with that conclusion.

The preparation of evidence regarding compensatory measures on a without prejudice basis places a weighty burden on the applicant. On the other hand, the production of evidence at an early stage in the process is likely to speed up the Secretary of State's decision-making process following the completion of the Examining Authority's report.

Part 11

Other Application Documents

Article 70

Explanatory Memorandum

Richard Honey QC, ftb
Michael Humphries QC, ftb

Regulation 5(2) of the Infrastructure Planning (Applications: Prescribed Forms and Procedure) Regulations 2009 ('the APFP Regulations') requires an application for a DCO to be accompanied by 'an explanatory memorandum explaining the purpose and effect of provisions in the draft order'.

Explanatory notes or memoranda for legislative instruments are intended to describe in plain English the main effects of the instrument, to allow them to be quickly and easily understood by readers, especially those who are not legally qualified. An explanatory memorandum should also explain the purpose or objective of the instrument.

An explanatory memorandum for a DCO should fulfil this essential function, but also go further in order to meet the guidance and practice with which the Planning Inspectorate will expect compliance.

PINS Advice Note 15 (version 2) states (para 1.1) that:

> 'The Explanatory Memorandum is an aid to the Examining Authority (ExA), to Interested Parties and to the Secretary of State as decision-maker to help understand what is proposed in the draft Development Consent Order (DCO), why particular provisions have been included and from where the wording has been derived. The Explanatory Memorandum explains why draft DCO provisions have been tailored to meet the specific needs of a particular Nationally Significant Infrastructure Project (NSIP) (and may be required to address novel issues). It should also explain why the provisions are required, having regard to the scope and breadth of powers contained in the Planning Act 2008 (PA2008).'

An explanatory memorandum should be explanatory and uncontroversial. It is not intended to set out the case for the DCO. As it was put by Lord Steyn in relation to explanatory notes to Bills in *R (Westminster CC) v National Asylum Support Service* [2002] 1 WLR 2956:

> 'The notes are intended to be neutral in political tone: they aim to explain the effect of the text and not to justify it. The purpose is to help the reader to get his bearings and to ease the task of assimilating the law.'

It is possible for the courts to refer to an explanatory memorandum as an aid to construction, as part of giving the DCO an informed construction.

Pursuant to APFP Regulations, reg 5(2), an explanatory memorandum should be part of the application pack submitted with a DCO application. It is useful for the explanatory memorandum to contain overview information about the project. The Planning Inspectorate has advised on a draft explanatory memorandum at the pre-application stage (register of advice, 1 August 2014, Palm Paper CCGT 3):

> 'It would be very helpful if the applicant could include here a brief, user friendly description of the development for which consent is sought as well as referring to the

> technical description contained within the ES. The purpose of the EM is to explain the DCO and it would be helpful for readers to have a general over-view of the project at the beginning of this document.'

A DCO explanatory memorandum should explain the purpose and effect of the provisions in the DCO. This involves stating the reasons behind the drafting of specific provisions in the DCO, explaining why each provision is necessary, and identifying relevant precedents for the provisions.

PINS Advice Note 15 (version 2) also makes it clear that:

> 'A thorough justification should be provided in the Explanatory Memorandum for every Article and Requirement, explaining why the inclusion of the power is appropriate in the specific case. The extent of justification should be proportionate to the degree of novelty and/ or controversy in relation to the inclusion of that particular power.'

This last point is important as, clearly, the explanation in any explanatory memorandum needs to focus on assisting the ExA and Secretary of State with those aspects of any draft DCO that may require close scrutiny.

At one time, PINS required applicants to justify in an explanatory memorandum any departure from the (now lapsed) Infrastructure Planning (Model Provisions) Order 2009. This advice has now changed and PINS Advice Note 15 (version 2) says (para 1.3) that, 'There is no longer a requirement to submit a tracked changed version of the draft DCO which compares the wording against The Infrastructure Planning (Model Provisions) (England and Wales) Order 2009'. Having said that, PINS Advice Note 13 (version 3) does still say (para 2.27) that 'the explanatory memorandum should identify relevant precedents for any provisions'.

If a draft DCO includes wording derived from other made DCOs, the PINS Advice Note 15 (version 2) does state (para 1.5) that this should be explained in the explanatory memorandum. The explanatory memorandum should also explain why that particular wording is relevant to the proposed draft DCO – for example, detailing what is factually similar for both the relevant consented NSIP and the Proposed Development. In each case, it will be important that the ExA and Secretary of State understand why particular drafting is appropriate for the scheme applied for. Any divergence in wording from the consented DCO drafting should also be explained.

DCOs may also seek to rely on drafting found in other regimes, such as Transport and Works Act Orders. In such cases, however, 'the reasons for doing so and the relevance of this to the application should also be made clear in the Explanatory Memorandum': see PINS Advice Note 15 (version 2) at paragraph 1.6. A particular point to consider in this context is whether the particular proposed article is even within the powers that may be granted under the PA 2008. PINS Advice Note 13 (version 3) states (para 2.15) that:

> 'Provisions used in "predecessor" regimes such as for Transport and Works Act Orders or Harbour Empowerment Orders may be helpful in the drafting of a DCO. Developers should though satisfy themselves that the inclusion of particular wording is appropriate and relevant in all the circumstances of a given project. The relevant precedent and the rationale for including the particular wording of a provision will need to be set out and justified in the explanatory memorandum.'

If a DCO includes provisions which remove the need to obtain additional consents or authorisations under PA 2008, s 150, then PINS Advice Note 13 (version 3) says (para 2.24) that the explanatory memorandum should 'identify the authorisation, the reasons why the developer is following this route and should state how close the developer is to achieving the consent of the authority concerned'. PINS Advice Note 15 (version 2) also says (Good Practice Point 10, p 14) that the explanatory memorandum should contain 'a clear justification for the inclusion of such provisions in the particular circumstances'.

An explanatory memorandum should deal not only with the articles of the DCO but also explain the 'requirements' in the DCO. Where requirements include an authority as being responsible for discharging the requirement, the explanatory memorandum should confirm that the relevant authority has been consulted about, and is willing to assume, this role.

Moreover, for any requirements that include 'tailpiece' provisions, the explanatory memorandum should provide specific justification for needing the flexibility that such a provision would provide. PINS Advice Note 15 (version 2) states (para 17.1) that, 'Any provisions in the draft DCO that allow for flexibility must be thoroughly justified within the explanatory memorandum, and assessed within the ES'. Footnote 10 to the same passage states that the general approach to flexibility can be set out in other application documents and cross-referenced to the explanatory memorandum, where appropriate.

In practice, explanatory memoranda tend to be in the order of 30–50 pages long. They will usually have an introduction, a description of the project, a statement of the purpose of the DCO, and any description of ancillary or supplementary matters addressed in the DCO. The bulk of the explanatory memorandum is a detailed commentary on each of the articles of the DCO. Clearly, some articles will require more consideration than others.

The content of the schedules is usually explained in summary, but with a detailed commentary on the requirements and any unusual or particular provisions contained in the schedules, such as protective provisions for bodies specifically affected by the DCO. Sometimes, commentary on the schedules is integrated with commentary on the articles, rather than in a separate section, using the articles which make reference to the schedules.

Applicants should provide an updated explanatory memorandum with their last draft of the DCO before the end of the examination. The updated memorandum can respond to issues raised at the examination, where appropriate. For example, PINS Advice Note 15 recommends (Good Practice Point 1, p 9) that:

> 'Applicants should, in the Explanatory Memorandum submitted with the application, provide justification for any flexibility which allows details to be approved after the grant of development consent. Any relevant case law should be cited where it is relied upon.
>
> The updated Explanatory Memorandum which accompanies the Applicant's final draft DCO submitted towards the end of the Examination must include any further justification necessary for maintaining such flexibility in the light of the examination of the draft DCO and its Requirements, the views of the relevant local authorities and Interested Parties and the rationale for imposing the Requirement.'

There is, however, a clear carrot dangled before applicants, in that PINS Advice Note 15 (version 2) promises (para 1.4) that, 'A well-developed Explanatory Memorandum can potentially reduce the number of examination questions an ExA may need to ask about the draft provisions comprising the draft DCO'.

Article 71

Book of Reference

Richard Honey QC, ftb
Michael Humphries QC, ftb

Introduction

A DCO 'book of reference' is a schedule of parcels of land affected by an order, identifying persons with some connection to the land. A book of reference is not physically part of the DCO (ie it is not a schedule to the order itself), but is a separate document referred to in a DCO and thereby, in effect, incorporated within the terms of the DCO.

The book of reference to a DCO is important because the order will authorise the undertaker to acquire compulsorily the land and rights described in the book of reference and shown on the plans. Similarly, the undertaker may be authorised to remove or reposition apparatus belonging to statutory undertakers, which is described in the book of reference. For the order to work properly in practice, the book of reference needs to be accurate and complete. The book of reference also identifies particular categories of land, such as land forming part of a common, open space, or fuel or field garden allotment.

Where relevant, an application for a DCO should be accompanied by a book of reference (Infrastructure Planning (Applications: Prescribed Forms and Procedure) Regulations 2009, SI 2009/2264, reg 5(2)(d)).

Requirements

The requirements for a book of reference are specified in reg 7. It has to be in five parts, as follows:

(1) names and addresses for service of each person within Category 1 (owner, lessee, tenant or occupier) and Category 2 (person interested in the land or having power to sell, convey or release the land), as defined in the Planning Act 2008 ('PA 2008'), s 57, for any land to be subject to:

 (i) powers of compulsory acquisition;

 (ii) rights to use land; or

 (iii) rights to carry out protective works to buildings (eg underpinning or strengthening);

(2) names and addresses for service of each person within Category 3 in PA 2008, s 57 (persons who, after diligent enquiry, might be entitled to make a relevant claim if the development consent order were to be made and fully implemented);

(3) names of all those entitled to enjoy easements or other private rights over land (including private rights of navigation over water) to be extinguished, suspended or interfered with;

(4) the owner of any Crown interest in the land which is proposed to be used for the purposes of the order;

(5) land:

(i) the acquisition of which is subject to special parliamentary procedure;

(ii) which is special category land; and

(iii) which is replacement land for land being compulsorily acquired.

For each part of the book of reference, the area of the land in square metres should be stated for each plot of land within which it is intended that all or part of the proposed development and works shall be carried out.

It is important not to omit land that is to be compulsorily acquired from the book of reference, otherwise it may have to be dealt with as 'additional land' under the Infrastructure Planning (Compulsory Acquisition) Regulations 2010, SI 2010/104. Where land is being acquired by agreement, it would not need to be included in the book of reference unless, for example, there are restrictions on the title that need to be overcome. Having said that, undertakers often include land that is to be acquired by agreement to give protection against unknown third party rights or a landowner's failure or inability to complete a sale by agreement.

Guidance

Paragraph 50 of the DCLG Guidance on the pre-application process (2015) explains that:

> 'It is the applicant's responsibility to demonstrate at submission of the application that due diligence has been undertaken in identifying all land interests and applicants should make every reasonable effort to ensure that the Book of Reference (which records and categorises those land interests) is up to date at the time of submission.'

Annex D to the DCLG Guidance on compulsory acquisition (2013) contains specific guidance on the contents of a book of reference. Specific advice is also contained in paragraph 27 of the DCLG Application Form Guidance (June 2013).

As well as describing the various parts of a book of reference, Annex D to the DCLG Guidance on compulsory acquisition (2013) also makes some additional practical points, including:

- each part in the book of reference serves a different purpose and persons may need to be identified in one or more parts;
- applicants should not add any further (non-prescribed) parts to a book of reference;
- ambiguous descriptions should be avoided;
- where it is proposed to create and acquire new rights compulsorily, they should be clearly identified; and
- the book of reference should cross-refer to the relevant articles of the order.

The point that a person can be in more than one PA 2008, s 57 category, and listed in more than one part of the book of reference, is an important one to remember. Persons identified in Part 3 of the book of reference should generally also be recorded in Part 1, as persons within PA 2008, s 57 categories 1 or 2. If there is doubt whether a private right or easement qualifies for Part 1 it should be included in both Parts 1 and 3 so as to err on the side of caution. If a person is not identified in Part 1 of the book of reference then they would not be an affected person under PA 2008, s 92, and would not be notified under PA 2008, s 59, and so would be deprived of the opportunity to seek a compulsory acquisition hearing.

A book of reference may need to be updated before or during the course of an examination, because information changes or new persons are identified. The DCLG Guidance on the pre-application process (2015) states (paras 51–52) that:

> '... it is understood that land interests change over time and that new or additional interests may emerge after an applicant has concluded statutory consultation but just before an application is submitted. In such a situation, the applicant should provide a proportionate opportunity to any new person identified with a land interest to make their views known on the application. Where new interests in land are identified very shortly before the intended submission of an application, despite diligent efforts earlier in the process it may be difficult at that stage for applicants to consult and take account of any responses from those new interests before submitting their application as intended. If this situation arises applicants should be proactive and helpful in ensuring that the person understands how they can, if they so wish, engage with the process if the application is accepted for examination.
>
> Applicants should explain in the consultation report how they have dealt with any new interests in land emerging after conclusion of their statutory consultation having regard to their duties to consult and take account of any responses.'

An ExA will often seek schedules updating a book of reference during the course of an examination, with a final updated full book of reference (clean copy and track-changed copy) before the end of the examination.

Article 72

Funding Statement

James Pereira QC, ftb
Michael Humphries QC, ftb

The need for a funding statement

Where an applicant for development consent intends to apply for authorisation to compulsorily acquire land, interests in land or a right over land, he is required to provide with the application 'a statement to indicate how an order that contains the authorisation of compulsory acquisition is proposed to be funded': see Infrastructure Planning (Applications: Prescribed Forms and Procedures) Regulations 2009, SI 2009/2264, reg 5(1)(h) and DCLG Application Form Guidance (2013), paragraph 26. This statement is commonly referred to as a 'funding statement'.

A funding statement must also be produced where it is proposed to include a provision in the DCO to authorise the acquisition of land that was not shown in the book of reference submitted with the application and a person having an interest in the land does not consent to the inclusion of that provision: see Infrastructure Planning (Compulsory Acquisition) Regulations 2010, SI 2010/104, reg 5. The funding statement in such a case must relate to the funding of the acquisition proposed by the additional provision.

The contents of a funding statement

As to the contents of a funding statement, the DCLG Application Form Guidance (2013) explains (para 26) that it should contain:

> '... sufficient information to enable the Secretary of State to be satisfied that, if he was to grant the compulsory acquisition request, the proposed development is likely to be undertaken and not be prevented due to difficulties in sourcing and securing the necessary funding.'

A more detailed consideration of what a funding statement should contain is found later in this article.

The purpose of a funding statement

The 2009 version of the DCLG Application Form Guidance stated as follows (para 24) about the need for a funding statement:

> 'This is necessary because it is not appropriate for people's ownership of land, interest in land or rights over land to be compulsorily taken from them, if there is doubt as to whether the development will proceed after those rights, etc, have been taken away.'

This text does not exist in the equivalent paragraph 26 of the 2013 version of the Guidance.

The funding statement in the examination process

More detail on the approach that will be taken is given in the DCLG Guidance on compulsory acquisition (2013). This advises (paragraph 9) that:

> 'The applicant must have a clear idea of how they intend to use the land which they are proposing to acquire. They should also be able to demonstrate that there is a reasonable prospect of the requisite funds for acquisition becoming available. Otherwise, it will be difficult to show conclusively that the compulsory purchase of land meets the two conditions in section 122 ....'

In summary, the two conditions in PA 2008, s 122 referred to above are that the land is required for the development and that there is a compelling case in the public interest for the acquisition.

The resource implications of the proposed scheme are elaborated in the DCGL Guidance on compulsory acquisition (2013) in the following terms (paras 17–18):

> 'Any application for a consent order authorising compulsory acquisition must be accompanied by a statement explaining how it will be funded. This statement should provide as much information as possible about the resource implications of both acquiring the land and implementing the project for which the land is required. It may be that the project is not intended to be independently financially viable, or that the details cannot be finalised until there is certainty about the assembly of the necessary land. In such instances, the applicant should provide an indication of how any potential shortfalls are intended to be met. This should include the degree to which other bodies (public or private sector) have agreed to make financial contributions or to underwrite the scheme, and on what basis such contributions or underwriting is to be made.
>
> The timing of the availability of the funding is also likely to be a relevant factor. Regulation 3(2) of [the Infrastructure Planning (Miscellaneous Prescribed Provisions) Regulations 2010] allows for five years within which any notice to treat must be served beginning on the date on which the order granting development consent is made, though the Secretary of State does have the discretion to make a different provision in an order granting development consent. Applicants should be able to demonstrate that adequate funding is likely to be available to enable the promoter to carry out the compulsory acquisition within the statutory period following the order being made, and that the resource implications of a possible acquisition resulting from a blight notice have been taken account of.'

The guidance on funding in this context is very similar to that given at section 14 of the general MHCLG guidance on 'Compulsory purchase process and The Crichel Down Rules' (2019) in relation to compulsory acquisition under the Acquisition of Land Act 1981.

Practical issues and experience to date

The decisions and advice to date have highlighted a number of matters for consideration in this context. These are considered under the headings below.

Expect a high level of scrutiny, but note that the process is quite flexible

Applicants can expect that their funding statements and development consent obligations will be scrutinised very closely by ExAs. It is common for funding issues to be subject to extensive written questions and answers during the examination process, and also to be subject to oral examination at any compulsory acquisition hearing. They are also often closely examined by objectors, and so applicants need to be prepared.

Experience shows that the inquisitorial nature of the examination works well in this context. It should therefore be possible to ensure that all of the ExA's concerns have been addressed, whether by providing greater security or by explaining why such security is not appropriate in the particular case.

The inquisitorial nature of the process can sometimes be daunting for applicants who are used to an adversarial system, because of the more interventionist approach of the Inspectors during the examination. In particular, it is tempting to view questions from the Inspectors as indicating disapproval or criticism. This temptation should be resisted. While each matter must be judged on its merits, questions from Inspectors are just as likely to be motivated by their need to understand the applicant's position and to have matters explained and justified to them more clearly, as they are to be motivated by some underlying criticism of the applicant's case. As with all aspects of the examination process, it is therefore necessary to critically evaluate the questions being put and decide whether they require a change in the applicant's position or simply a better explanation of what that position is.

Inspectors are generally content to receive updated funding statements and to accommodate travelling drafts of any planning obligation that is being offered to provide the legal safeguards necessary. In this way the relevant documents can be drafted to reflect the issues raised during the examination. There should be no need to be in the dark about the issues by the end of the examination process.

On occasion, further information on funding has been sought by the Secretary of State following the close of an examination if funding has become a particular issue. That is obviously a proportionate approach to take where the alternative would be to refuse the application.

Matters to be covered in a funding statement

The DCLG Guidance on compulsory purchase indicates (paras 33–34) that the following should be addressed in the funding statement:

- The resource implications of the project, including:
  - acquiring the land;
  - implementing the project;
- The sources of funding;
- How potential shortfalls in funding are expected to be met;
- The basis upon which funding is being provided;
- The timing of available funding, in particular by reference to:
  - the time period for the exercise of powers of compulsory acquisition;
  - the possibility of a blight notice being served;
- Any uncertainties (e.g. around securing funding, or around the viability of the project), their implications, and how they are to be addressed.

In addition, the following points may be important:

- Contextual points about the standing of the Applicant, its parents, the importance of the project etc.
- Any points thought necessary to address particular funding concerns that have been raised during the application process, particularly where changes have not been made in response to issues raised by the Inspectorate.
- An explanation of how the funding is to be secured. Usually this will be an explanation of how the Town and Country Planning Act 1990, s 106 obligation which contains the necessary legal requirements for funding security will work.

The relevance of compensation

The extent to which the level of expected compensation is relevant to these issues is a moot point. Traditionally, it is said that matters of compensation are for the Upper Tribunal and not for the authority being asked to approve powers of compulsory acquisition. On the other hand, the level of expected compensation may be relevant to understanding whether the level of any funding is adequate to fund acquisitions.

PINS has shown itself willing to accept the proposition that a misunderstanding about the likely level of compensation required could undermine an applicant's arguments on whether there is a compelling case: see the Rookery South DCO ExA report at paragraph 7.98. Applicants are naturally – and quite properly – cautious about providing details of the amount of expected compensation. However, one way of dealing with this may for applicants to refer to the fact that expert advice has been taken on quantum, and that the level of funding for compensation that is available is considerably above the level so advised. In this way applicants are able to address this point without being over-exposed to examination of their precise compensation assessment, and while also giving comfort that any potential underestimate of liability is not a cause of concern: see, for example, the Galloper Wind farm Funding Statement at paragraph 4.15.

Single purpose corporate vehicles (SPVs) and parent companies

It is common for the funding statement submitted with the application to be quite light on detail. In particular, where an applicant is an SPV or subsidiary company with limited assets itself, the funding statement can be expected to refer to the financial standing of the parent(s). Usually such statements are superficially very impressive, because the parent company will often be a major corporate body of substance with a huge turnover. Nevertheless, the concern of PINS is to ensure that the 'particular' applicant has or will have the necessary funds. Accordingly, the examination of a funding statement of this sort will inevitably move on from these general statements to the particular issues surrounding the application and applicant in question and, indeed, to the detailed mechanisms by which funding security will be secured. Therefore, while there is often good sense in starting out in a fairly high-level way, such an approach may not stand up during the course of the examination process.

It is probably the case that publicly funded projects promoted by a public authority will get an easier ride. The notion of compulsory acquisition by a statutory body funded by the public purse is a more comfortable one than such acquisition by a private commercial body. Moreover, there is probably – rightly or wrongly – an implicit acceptance that that standing of a public authority and the public law principles which govern its conduct make it more accountable, and that when a public body says that it will commit funds to a project it will do just that.

Mechanism for securing the funding

The general guidance on the need for funding and the reasons for it has been referred to already. But what of the particular form or mechanism for securing funding in circumstances where there is doubt as to the particular applicants financial standing or the enforceability of any commitments to funding? The short answer is that each case will be judged on its own merits and the Secretary of State does not as yet have any best practice guidance to provide.

Experience of the examination process to date would suggest, however, that a development consent obligation will usually be required to ensure that the necessary funding will be in place before the project commences.

Applicants that are commercial enterprises, and in particular SPVs, can be expected to have to give consideration to the following being given by way of a planning obligation:

- Security for a particular, or minimum, sum of money for land acquisitions (which applicants usually see as preferable to an open-ended guarantee). It would be appropriate to time limit the duration of any security, provided the time limit is sufficiently lengthy to allow for disputes as to the amount of compensation payable. The type of security that will be provided (bond, bank guarantee, etc) should be specified.
- A power to approve the security, to be held by the local planning authority.
- A covenant not to exercise any powers of compulsory acquisition until the security in question has been approved.
- A covenant that the applicant will not place itself into voluntary liquidation.
- A covenant not to transfer the benefit of the DCO without first procuring equivalent obligations from the transferee. It may also be appropriate for the provisions of the DCO relating to the transfer of powers to third parties to make it clear that the transferee is under the same obligations as the (original) undertaker.

The need to demonstrate funding to meet compensation claims for severance, injurious affection and/or disturbance caused by the construction or operation of the project may well be challenging, as such compensation may be very difficult to quantify before a project has been implemented. Nevertheless, a funding statement should make it clear that such compensation has, at least, been considered where it might be relevant.

Although the DCLG Guidance on compulsory purchase also refers (para 33) to the need to identify the resource implications of 'implementing' the project, it is in the nature of large infrastructure projects that securing the necessary funding for their development in advance of the grant of development consent is often a wholly unrealistic expectation. Nevertheless, the funding statement should address the funding for the implementation of the scheme, even if it is necessary to do so at a relatively high level at the application stage. In some cases, more detail will be required.

Article 73

Statement of Reasons

Richard Honey QC, ftb
Michael Humphries QC, ftb

Regulation 5(2) of the Infrastructure Planning (Applications: Prescribed Forms and Procedure) Regulations 2009 requires an application for a DCO to be accompanied by a Statement of Reasons, if the proposed order would authorise the compulsory acquisition of land or an interest in land or right over land. The primary purpose of the Statement of Reasons is to set out the justification for the compulsory acquisition powers sought in the DCO.

The DCLG Guidance on compulsory acquisition (2013) says:

> 'The Statement of Reasons should seek to justify the compulsory acquisition sought, and explain in particular why in the applicant's opinion there is a compelling case in the public interest for it. This includes reasons for the creation of new rights.'

For compulsory acquisition to be justified, it must be expedient and necessary such that there is a compelling case in the public interest. A more detailed commentary on the conditions and justification for the exercise of compulsory purchase powers is found in articles 54 to 57 of this work.

In addition to what may properly be described as compulsory acquisition powers, Statements of Reasons will frequently also cover powers related to compulsory acquisition, such as a power of temporary possession and a power to 'extinguish' or 'override' existing rights.

As well as the overall justification for compulsory acquisition powers, the Statement of Reasons should contain a plot-by-plot justification for all of the compulsory acquisition authorised by the DCO. This should show that the land and rights being taken are necessary for the project, but are no more than is necessary to accomplish the objective of the DCO. For example, if a corridor of land is subject to compulsory acquisition for the construction of a linear project, such as with a transport or utilities DCO, the corridor should be no wider than is necessary.

In addition, the Statement of Reasons should explain matters which are important to the justification for compulsory acquisition. The explanation ought to be included in the Statement of Reasons, even if the detail is set out in other application documents. Matters of this sort include:

- alternatives, options assessment and design development (eg route selection), to show that the purpose of the compulsory acquisition could not be achieved by any other means;
- benefits of, and the need for, the project; and
- compliance with national policy.

There will also be important matters arising primarily in the context of compulsory acquisition which will need to be addressed in the Statement of Reasons. Such matters include:

- lack of physical or legal impediments to implementation of the project;
- availability of resources for the project;

- engagement with affected landowners and occupiers, including steps taken to acquire the land and rights by agreement;
- proportionality of the compulsory acquisition powers;
- justification for interference with the human rights of affected landowners and occupiers; and
- compliance with statutory procedures for compulsory acquisition.

The Statement of Reasons should be written in clear English, so that it can readily be understood by non-technical readers. The Statement of Reasons should be sent with a compulsory acquisition notice under PA 2008, s 134. The Statement of Reasons should be as comprehensive as possible. It should be read with other documents such as the book of reference, land plans and the funding statement. The explanatory memorandum for the DCO should also explain the compulsory acquisition provisions in the DCO.

The 2010 version of the DCLG Guidance on compulsory acquisition (now withdrawn) included, at Annex 2, a detailed list of the matters to be included in a Statement of Reasons. This list has been removed from the current DCLG Guidance on compulsory acquisition (2013), but similar guidance is set out in the general MHCLG guidance on the 'Compulsory purchase process and The Crichel Down Rules' (2019) relating to compulsory purchase orders. The MHCLG guidance states (section 196) that:

> 'The statement of reasons should include the following information:
>
> (i) a brief description of the order land and its location, topographical features and present use;
>
> (ii) an explanation of the use of the particular enabling power;
>
> (iii) an outline of the authority's purpose in seeking to acquire the land;
>
> (iv) a statement of the authority's justification for compulsory purchase, with regard to Article 1 of the First Protocol to the European Convention on Human Rights, and Article 8 if appropriate;
>
> (v) a statement justifying the extent of the scheme to be disregarded for the purposes of assessing compensation in the "no-scheme world";
>
> (vi) a description of the proposals for the use or development of the land;
>
> (vii) a statement about the planning position of the order site. See also Section 1: advice on section 226 of the Town and Country Planning Act 1990 for planning orders;
>
> (viii) information required in the light of government policy statements where orders are made in certain circumstances eg as stated in Section 5: local housing authorities for housing purposes where orders are made under the Housing Acts (including a statement as to unfitness where unfit buildings are being acquired under Part 9 of the Housing Act 1985);
>
> (ix) any special considerations affecting the order site eg ancient monument, listed building, conservation area, special category land, consecrated land, renewal area, etc;
>
> (x) if the mining code has been included, reasons for doing so;
>
> (xi) details of how the acquiring authority seeks to overcome any obstacle or prior consent needed before the order scheme can be implemented eg need for a waste management licence;

(xii) details of any views which may have been expressed by a government department about the proposed development of the order site;

(xiii) what steps the authority has taken to negotiate for the acquisition of the land by agreement;

(xiv) any other information which would be of interest to persons affected by the order eg proposals for rehousing displaced residents or for relocation of businesses;

(xv) details of any related order, application or appeal which may require a co-ordinated decision by the confirming minister eg an order made under other powers, a planning appeal/application, road closure, listed building; and

(xvi) if, in the event of an inquiry, the authority would intend to refer to or put in evidence any documents, including maps and plans, it would be helpful if the authority could provide a list of such documents, or at least a notice to explain that documents may be inspected at a stated time and place.'

Although needing some adaptation for an application under the PA 2008, this list provides a very helpful guide to the matters to be contained in a Statement of Reasons.

Other matters which are often addressed in Statements of Reasons include impacts on statutory undertakers, views expressed by Government bodies about the project, the land use and planning history of the land, economic impacts, environmental impacts, marine policy, national planning policy, and local planning policy.

Where parcels of land are in unknown ownership, this should be identified, together with an explanation of the land referencing and investigation undertaken to try to find the owner.

Where the applicant already owns some of the necessary land and rights, or has conditional contracts or options for their purchase, this is usually explained in the Statement of Reasons. This is, in part, to explain what might otherwise be thought an omission from compulsory acquisition but also to support the case for the compulsory acquisition of the remainder of the necessary land and rights.

There are some aspects of the justification which will require more attention than others. For example, demonstrating that the land and rights sought are no more than reasonably required, and that there are no reasonable alternatives to meet the same purpose, will not be straightforward in some cases. This will especially be the case where some design development remains to be undertaken or the DCO seeks to retain some flexibility in the development to be constructed.

Previous examples of Statements of Reasons have ranged from as little as, say, 15 pages up to almost 450 pages. The majority are in the order of 50 to 100 pages. An example of a long Statement of Reasons was that for the A14 Cambridge to Huntingdon improvement scheme, which contained appendices giving details of the purpose for which compulsory acquisition or temporary possession powers were sought in relation to each plot (160 pages) and the history of negotiations with landowners (170 pages). The approach taken was to seek to demonstrate that each parcel of land was necessary for the delivery of the project. It is right that a Statement of Reasons should contain a plot-by-plot justification for all of the compulsory acquisition authorised by the DCO.

Some Statements of Reasons contain or append a list of the application documents. This follows practice with compulsory purchase order statements of reasons. It is not necessary but may be helpful.

Article 74

Statutory Nuisance Statements

James Pereira QC, ftb

Introduction

Regulation 5(2)(f) of the Infrastructure Planning (Applications: Prescribed Forms and Procedure) Regulations 2009 provides that applications for development consent must be accompanied by 'a statement whether the proposal engages one or more of the matters set out in section 79(1) (statutory nuisances and inspections therefor) of the Environmental Protection Act 1990, and if so how the applicant proposes to mitigate or limit them'.

These statements are commonly referred to as 'statutory nuisance statements' and this article will briefly explore the requirements for such statements.

Context and importance

Part III of the Environmental Protection Act 1990 creates a regime for detecting, regulating and enforcing against certain kinds of nuisances from a variety of activities. These nuisances are known as statutory nuisances (because they are defined by statute). The local authority is usually the regulatory and enforcement body for statutory nuisances.

Section 79(1) of the Environmental Protection Act 1990 (referred to in reg 5(2)(f)) sets out categories of statutory nuisances, as follows:

> '...
>
> (a) any premises in such a state as to be prejudicial to health or a nuisance;
>
> (b) smoke emitted from premises so as to be prejudicial to health or a nuisance;
>
> (c) fumes or gases emitted from premises so as to be prejudicial to health or a nuisance;
>
> (d) any dust, steam, smell or other effluvia arising on industrial, trade or business premises and being prejudicial to health or a nuisance;
>
> (e) any accumulation or deposit which is prejudicial to health or a nuisance;
>
> (f) any animal kept in such a place or manner as to be prejudicial to health or a nuisance;
>
> (fa) any insects emanating from relevant industrial, trade or business premises and being prejudicial to health or a nuisance;
>
> (fb) artificial light emitted from premises so as to be prejudicial to health or a nuisance;
>
> (g) noise emitted from premises so as to be prejudicial to health or a nuisance;
>
> (ga) noise that is prejudicial to health or a nuisance and is emitted from or caused by a vehicle, machinery or equipment in a street or in Scotland, road;

(h) any other matter declared by any enactment to be a statutory nuisance;

...'

Normally, where the local authority detects a nuisance, it will serve an abatement notice requiring the nuisance to be restricted or abated. The notice can be appealed. Breach of the notice is a criminal offence.

However, in the context of DCOs there is limited scope for enforcing statutory nuisances because of the effect of PA 2008, s 158. Section 158(1) provides statutory authority for (a) carrying out development for which consent is granted by a development consent order, and (b) doing anything else authorised by an order granting development consent. Statutory authority is so granted for the purpose of conferring a defence in civil or criminal proceedings in nuisance (s 158(2)).

Given the restrictions created by s 158 on the enforcement of statutory nuisances, it is important for an Examining Authority to assess carefully the potential for statutory (and other) nuisances to arise. A statutory nuisance statement informs this assessment. It informs decisions on impacts and potential mitigation measures, and hence on the requirements that a Examining Authority might impose. It is normal for the assessment principles section of an NPS to make specific reference to nuisance and statutory nuisance; see, for example, the NPS for Energy EN-1 at paragraph 4.14.2, the Airports NPS at paragraphs 4.61 and 5.230, and the NPS for National Networks at paragraph 4.58.

Form and content of a statutory nuisance statement

As with other application documents, statutory nuisance statements should comply with the general guidance on the form, content and presentation, including in PINS Advice Note 6 (version 10): Preparation and submission of application documents.

There is no detailed guidance on the substantive content of a statutory nuisance statement. However, the following can be identified as good practice:

- *Preliminary*: apart from the normal heading, document referencing and contents section, the preliminary part of the document should identify other examination documents that are referenced in the statutory nuisance statement and also define key terms and abbreviations by reference to the common glossary of terms.
- *Executive summary*: an executive summary highlighting the main points is helpful.
- *Introduction*: this can set the context for the statement, refer to any relevant parts of the NPS that address statutory nuisance, and cross-refer to any relevant examination documents where the potential for statutory nuisances or their mitigation is addressed; this might, for example, include the construction management plan, or the environmental statement.
- *Statutory nuisances*: it is helpful to have a section setting out the relevant parts of the Environmental Protection Act 1990. The key provision will be section 79(1) which defines the categories of statutory nuisance. It may be that not all of the categories will be relevant to the particular project, and it is helpful to identify which are and which are not relevant.
- *Potential statutory nuisances*: having set the background in the earlier sections, the next section can assess the potential for each relevant statutory nuisance to arise. It is important to have all phases of the project in mind, from site preparation through to decommissioning and restoration (as appropriate). The assessment should:
  - identify when and how potential nuisances might arise, addressing issues such as the intensity, timing, frequency, geographical extent and duration of the impacts;

  - identify and discuss the mitigation measures that are proposed, and the means by which they are to be secured (for example, by specific requirements, through a construction management plan, and so on);
  - where these matters are assessed in other examination documents, cross-refer to these documents, and the relevant sections of them should be cross-referenced; and
  - pay particular attention to any context-specific matters that are known to be of importance (for example, particular kinds of impacts that are identified in the NPS).
- Note that reg 5(2)(f) uses the expression 'mitigate or limit'. This acknowledges that not all potential nuisances can be completely avoided. A transparent assessment will identify the extent to which controls under the DCO will either avoid or limit the occurrence of a potential nuisance.
- *Conclusion*: the statutory nuisance statement should end with short conclusions, ideally directed towards reinforcing the solutions offered by the proposed DCO to make the impacts acceptable.

Article 75

A Good Practice Guide to Planning Statements

Sean Bashforth, Quod

Introduction

Planning Statements are used by many DCO applicants to explain and justify their proposals and to demonstrate compliance with National Policy Statements and other policy. There is considerable variation in the use of the documents across NSIPs.

In this article we explore the use of Planning Statements in the DCO process and offer some guidance on their scope and how to make them as effective as possible.

Guidance

There is no statutory or official guidance which indicates that Planning Statements are either required or even a good idea. PINS Advice Note 6 (version 10) on the preparation and submission of application documents, for instance, only provides guidance on the scope and content of documents that are legally required to be submitted with a DCO, including an environmental statement, the draft Development Consent Order and certain plans and drawings etc.

Such lack of guidance is also apparent in national validation requirements for Town and Country Planning applications, albeit many local planning authority validation checklists indicate that they are required for major planning applications.

Whilst there is no requirement to submit a Planning Statement, they are undoubtedly good practice and, indeed, are submitted with most DCO applications.

Research

To inform this article, we have reviewed the role of Planning Statements in all DCOs determined during a two-year period up to February 2021. During that period, 28 DCOs were determined and all but five of those applications included a Planning Statement. Of those that did not, there was no correlation in type of project.

As might be expected, policy compliance and a project description were common elements of most of the Planning Statements, with commentary on the need for the project featuring in most, but commentary on the broader case only being evident in about a third of Planning Statements. Examination of the broad contents showed that Planning Statements varied in their approach, as follows (out of 23 Planning Statements):

- policy conformity – 23 (100%);
- project description – 22 (96%);

- need for the project – 18 (78%); and
- case for the scheme – 7 (30%).

Role of the Planning Statement

Carefully structured and objectively worded, the Planning Statement provides the opportunity for the applicant to tell its story and to bring the case together, in the context of planning policy.

The objective of a Planning Statement should be to inform, but also to influence, those interested in the project and, particularly, the Examining Authority and the decision maker. As the principal tests for a DCO decision set out in PA 2008, ss 104 and 105 are significantly concerned with policy compliance, the main role of the Planning Statement (to demonstrate policy compliance) is clear.

The Planning Statement should also anticipate and address key issues that decision makers will want to consider in the overall planning balance, taking into account feedback from consultation. Our research indicates that 78% of the Examining Authority's recommendation reports specifically refer to Planning Statements. Those that do not, however, will (hopefully) have been informed by them. Assisting the Examining Authority to consider policy compliance is clearly an important function of a Planning Statement.

Thus a core and distinct function of a Planning Statement is to analyse a project's compliance with relevant policy. This means that it must:

- provide a clear summary description of what the project is;
- describe what policy the project should be considered against; and
- analyse how the project performs against that policy framework, taking into account impacts and benefits and drawing on other application documents, where appropriate.

To do this effectively, the Planning Statement needs to work through the various assessment tests set in the NPSs and other policy – and to do that it needs to show a clear appreciation of the assessed effects of the project. The Planning Statement can therefore be seen as a central reference document in the DCO application, drawing together the key aspects of the project in the context of policy. Because of its broad scope, it needs to avoid directly duplicating other documents in the submission and use summary descriptions and explanations to clearly convey matters. Many statements use maps, diagrams, figures and appendices to aid communication, and authors should ensure that the body of the statement is not overburdened with detail or contextual information. Referencing to the source of material and assessments is key.

Content

Project descriptions

The Planning Statement should provide a clear explanation of what is proposed and why. It can provide an overview of the project and describe the principal components and their relationship with other parts of the project.

Project descriptions are typically included in several DCO application documents, including the description of the works in the draft DCO itself, design and access statements and the environmental statement. Each type of project description has a particular role to play. The Planning Statement should complement the technical and 'dry' descriptions in the draft DCO Schedule, and the more graphical description in design and access statements, and can provide a succinct description of those characteristics of the application which it is important to understand when judging the extent to which the application meets government objectives and policy requirements. Whilst not being the same, however, it is important to ensure that descriptions in different documents are consistent.

It is also helpful to use the Planning Statement to explain the way in which the application is structured. Some applications necessarily have a complex structure and the Planning Statement is the obvious place to explain what is being applied for and the status of the component parts of that application. Consequently, as well as a high-level project description, the Planning Statement should explain the following:

- which works fall within the NSIP or are Associated Development;
- the content of the application (sometimes in the form of an appended development specification); in other words, what and how much development is being applied for;
- the status of the submitted application drawings and documents – what is for approval and what is illustrative etc;
- any proposed parameters which the DCO proposes, both in terms of physical works and also commitments to operational limits which are to be controlled through requirements attached to the DCO; throughout, it should be made clear what is for approval and what is for information purposes only;
- the rationale for any flexibility being sought through any parameters, consistent with PINS Advice Note 9 (version 3) on the Rochdale Envelope; and
- the relationship between the main NSIP works, Associated Development any any other development that may have been brought forward separately; for example, enabling works that have been promoted in advance of the DCO or separate DCOs which are being promoted by others, such as new powerlines for a generating station project.

Policy compliance

As explained, this is a core function of the Planning Statement and early sections of the statement need to explain clearly the relevant provisions from National Policy Statements and other policy, including development plan policies, and explain what weight should be attached to them. As a starting principle, a relevant NPS will attract most weight where the decision is to be taken under section 104(3), but local plan policies may still be 'important and relevant' (s 104(2)(d)) and should, therefore, also be taken into account. Where decisions are to be taken under s 105, the weight to be attached to NPSs and local policy will be much more a matter of planning judgement for the decision maker.

Linear or very large projects may cross a number of local authority boundaries and the Planning Statement should provide plans (either for each authority or as composites) showing adopted and emerging policy maps to help the reader to clearly understand the local planning policy context.

Policy can be lengthy, however, and reciting more than key passages may unbalance the Statement. Appendices can be used, but the reader is more likely to be assisted by detailed referencing to the source documents.

Later chapters of Planning Statements should consider policy compliance on a topic-by-topic basis, starting with the principle of the development and then moving on to the key planning issues which the application raises. Individual topic areas, such as ecology and heritage, can overlap with environmental statement chapters, and it is important for the Planning Statement to focus on policy compliance taking into account the impacts identified in other documents.

Some topics may not have been considered elsewhere in the DCO application, particularly where they are mainly planning issues (for example, Green Belt, climate change and community impacts), and the Planning Statement has an important role to play in explaining how the proposals respond to relevant policy requirements for those issues.

Need and case for the scheme

As shown by the research, whilst it is common for Planning Statements to include sections on the need for the DCO project, it is less common for there to be specific sections for the overall case.

A clearly expressed 'case for the scheme' in the Planning Statement, including an explanation of why it is needed, what benefits it brings and how impacts have been minimised and mitigated, will help the Examiners to consider the overall planning balance.

At a planning or compulsory purchase inquiry a statement of case would help to fulfil this role. In the absence of a similar document in the DCO process, the Planning Statement, or even an entirely separate document called the 'Case for the Scheme', has a valuable role in justifying the overall DCO project and any related but separate development, and more specifically whether there is a compelling case in the public interest for land which requires compulsory acquisition. The case for the scheme, whether contained in a Planning Statement or in a document on its own, should always seek to advocate the scheme in a fair and balanced way.

Other matters

From experience and a review of statements prepared by others, the following are commonly included in Planning Statements:

- planning history, including extant consents for the site and how the proposals fit in with any relevant extant consents; and
- site selection/scheme development, to provide the justification for the location and scale and composition of what is proposed.

For large projects, this level of detail can sit best in appendices or separate documents, with the Planning Statement used to draw out key issues.

Relationship to other DCO documents

It is important to stress that there is no set template for a Planning Statement and it needs to be tailored to the project. Indeed, it may be appropriate to have a number of site-specific Planning Statements beneath an overarching one for the whole project if there are discrete Associated Development components which raise site-specific matters.

The scope of the Planning Statement needs to be considered early in the preparation of the DCO application documentation, to minimise overlap between documents and ensure that each document complements the others.

Early chapters or appendices of the Planning Statement describing policies can be prepared early to inform other documents (for example, the environmental statement), whilst later chapters will need to wait until other documents have been prepared so that impacts, mitigation / compensation and benefits can be summarised in the Planning Statement.

Overlap between documents can be avoided if each document has a clear purpose. Various points have been made above about how the Planning Statement differs from the environmental statement and design and access statement, and a clear distinction can be made with other documents too. Each has an important role, but it is the Planning Statement that brings the case together.

Article 76

Development Consent Obligations

Ned Westaway, ftb
Michael Humphries QC, ftb

Introduction

Agreements entered into pursuant to the Town and Country Planning Act 1990 (TCPA 1990), s 106 ('s 106 obligations'), are an established and valuable mechanism for securing off-site mitigation and/or benefits in connection with planning permissions.

PA 2008, s 174 made a number of amendments to TCPA 1990, ss 106, 106A and 106B, and introduced a new TCPA 1990, s 106C, enabling similar obligations to be made, modified and discharged in relation to DCOs. Such obligations are referred to in the PA 2008 as 'development consent obligations'. Their use is encouraged by a number of National Policy Statements and they have been widely used.

This article discusses how TCPA 1990, s 106 agreements have been accommodated within the PA 2008 regime and sets out some key considerations relevant to their use and enforcement.

Incorporation of TCPA 1990, s 106 obligations within DCO regime

By TCPA 1990, s 106(1A) 'the reference to development in subsection (1)(a) includes anything that constitutes development for the purposes of the Planning Act 2008'. This has the effect that TCPA 1990, s 106 obligations may restrict the ability of a scheme promoter to carry out development consent on his land in any specified way. The other obligations in TCPA 1990, s 106(1), such as requiring land to be used in a specified way or to pay a sum of money to a local planning authority, needed no amendment.

In all cases where a TCPA 1990, s 106 obligation is entered into in connection with an application for a DCO it is known as a 'development consent obligation' (TCPA 1990, s 106(14)). It is a requirement that a development consent obligation is entered into by deed and must contain a statement to the effect that it is a development consent obligation (TCPA 1990, s 106(9)(aa)).

There is nothing to prevent an applicant entering into an ordinary TCPA 1990, s 106 obligation with a local planning authority separately and / or ahead of a development consent application. For example, the Hinkley Point C (Nuclear Generating Station) Order was confirmed in the context of an existing site preparation TCPA 1990, s 106 agreement.

It will clearly be for the Secretary of State, in determining an application for development consent, to consider the adequacy or otherwise of any development consent obligation.

Modification and discharge

Applications to modify or discharge development consent obligations are made directly to the Secretary of State (TCPA 1990, s 106A(3) and (11)(aa)). By TCPA 1990, s 106A(4) a person against whom an obligation is enforceable may, following the 'relevant period' – that is, such period as may be 'prescribed' *or* the period of five years beginning with the date on which the obligation was entered into – apply to have the obligation modified or discharged.

In respect of TCPA 1990, s 106 obligations entered into on or before 6 April 2010, Town and Country Planning (Modification and Discharge of Planning Obligations) Regulations 1992, reg 2A 'prescribes' a 'relevant period' in England only of one month beginning with 28 February 2013. There are unlikely to have been many, if any, development consent obligations entered into before 6 April 2010 and so, for all practical purposes, an application to modify or discharge a development consent obligation under TCPA 1990, s 106A(4) may not now be made until five years after it was entered into.

There is no 'merits' appeal against the Secretary of State's decision; however, by TCPA 1990, s 106C, a challenge by way of judicial review may be brought against any determination that is otherwise than in accordance with the modification or discharge sought, or any non-determination. The claim for judicial review must be filed before six weeks after the date of notification, or in the case of non-determination, a prescribed period (which has yet to be prescribed).

No secondary legislation has yet been brought forward that might help clarify the procedural expectations and set out requirements for applications to modify or discharge development consent obligations. It is likely that the spirit of the Town and Country Planning (Modification and Discharge of Planning Obligations) Regulations 1992 will apply.

Law and guidance on the use of development consent obligations

A number of National Policy Statements make express reference to the use of planning obligations. For example, the Overarching National Policy Statement for Energy (EN-1) encourages the use of planning obligations where appropriate to provide nature conservation enhancement, mitigation and/or compensation around a development site (see eg paras 5.3.15 and 5.3.17).

The National Planning Policy Framework ('NPPF') and Planning Practice Guidance ('PPG') on TCPA 1990, s 106 obligations will also be relevant. Paragraph 56 of the NPPF (2019) provides that TCPA 1990, s 106 obligations should only be sought where they meet the following tests:

- necessary to make the development acceptable in planning terms;
- directly related to the development; and
- fairly and reasonably related in scale and kind to the development.

In the context of planning permissions, these tests are put on a statutory footing by Community Infrastructure Levy Regulations 2010, reg 122(2). That provision does not apply to development consent obligations although, in practice, the Secretary of State is highly unlikely to have regard to a development consent obligation as a reason for granting development unless it meets the tests. It is therefore important that development consent obligations are carefully considered and framed.

An issue can also arise as to the enforceability of obligations. Unless the party entering into the obligation has control of the land to which the obligation relates it will not be enforceable and is likely to be rejected (see *PNH (Properties) Ltd v SSCLG* [2012] EWHC 1998 (Admin)). A DCO example is the National Grid (North London Reinforcement Project) Order 2014, where although the DCO was made, no weight was given to given to a fund proposed by a TCPA 1990, s 106 obligation to provide enhancements to land outside of the applicant's control.

The issue may be avoided by including a requirement in DCOs that land outside the applicant's control be bound by appropriate obligations before development (or the relevant part of development) can commence. For planning permissions, such an approach has been established, in particular by the Arsenal Stadium development, which has lent its name to the technique (ie 'Arsenal' conditions). It is particularly useful for NSIPs where a degree of land assembly is often necessary. Art 60 of the Thames Water Utilities Limited (Thames Tideway Tunnel) Order 2014 is an example of the application of the 'Arsenal' approach for DCOs.

Enforcement of development consent obligations

Development consent obligations are registered as local land charges (TCPA 1990, s 106(11)) and bind successors in title (TCPA 1990, s 106(3)(b)).

A development consent obligation is enforceable by the local planning authority to which it applies. It will become binding upon the making of a DCO and its enforceability will not depend upon its general reasonableness, connection with the development or whether it meets any of the policy tests set out above (see eg *R (Millgate Developments Ltd) v Wokingham BC* [2011] EWCA Civ 1062; [2012] JPL 258).

TCPA 1990, s 106 provides three ways by which a requirement in an obligation may be enforced:

- by injunction (TCPA 1990, s 106(5)),
- by entry onto land to carry out operations and recovery of expenses (TCPA 1990, s 106(6)), or
- by charging the land (TCPA 1990, s 106(11)).

Part 12

Pre-examination, Examination and Post-examination

Article 77

Timescales for Pre-examination, Examination and Post-examination Procedures

Isabella Tafur, ftb
Michael Humphries QC, ftb

Introduction

One of the guiding principles behind the development consent regime was a need to improve the efficiency of the planning process for dealing with major infrastructure projects, which was too slow and complicated: see Planning for a Sustainable Future, White Paper 2007, paragraph 1.20. The Government considered that prolonged procedures increased costs, resulted in years of blight for individuals and communities and put the country's economic and environmental well-being at risk. As a consequence, the PA 2008 regime contains a prescribed timetable to facilitate faster decision-making.

This article examines the individual elements within the overall prescribed timetable and considers how the timetable is performing in practice.

Acceptance of an application

The timing of any application for development consent under the PA 2008 is, obviously, within the control of the applicant. However, it is from the date of application that the prescribed timetable applies.

The Secretary of State must decide whether or not to accept the application (PA 2008, s 55) within 28 days from the day after the receipt of an application purporting to be an application for development consent under PA 2008, s 37.

The Secretary of State must notify the applicant of its decision of whether it has accepted the application (PA 2008, s 55(6) and (7)). Although there is no prescribed time period for such notification, experience suggests that PINS will notify the applicant promptly.

Notification of acceptance

If the application has been accepted, the applicant must then notify certain persons – as set out in PA 2008, s 56(2) and Infrastructure Planning (Applications: Prescribed Forms and Procedure) Regulations 2009 ('the APFP Regulations'), Sch 1 – in accordance with reg 8 of the APFP Regulations. The notice of acceptance under PA 2008, s 56(2) must also notify such persons of the deadline for making representations to the Secretary of State of their interest in, or objection, to the application (PA 2008, s 56(4)).

The deadline for making representations under PA 2008, s 56(4) must not be earlier than the period of 28 days that begins with the day after the day on which the person receives the notice (PA 2008, s 56(5)). The applicant must also publicise the application in the manner prescribed by reg 9 the APFP Regulations.

Pursuant to PA 2008, s 56, the applicant must certify to the Secretary of State that it has complied with the notification and publication requirements in PA 2008, s 56. This certificate must be in the form prescribed by the APFP Regulations (set out in Sch 3 to those Regulations), and must be sent to the Secretary of State within 10 *working* days from the deadline set for the making of representations (reg 10 of the APFP Regulations). Note this is the only reference to 'working days'; all other statutory deadlines under the PA 2008 and the APFP Regulations are calendar days. At the same time, if the application includes a request to authorise compulsory purchase powers, the applicant must send the Secretary of State a notice of the affected persons (PA 2008, s 59 and reg 10 of the APFP Regulations): see, for example, the North London Reinforcement Project application for an example of PINS's approach of where all persons under PA 2008, s 56(2) had not been correctly notified.

Initial assessment and preliminary meeting

The Examining Authority must make an initial assessment of the principal issues arising on the application within 21 days from the day after the applicant notified the relevant persons of the acceptance of the application under PA 2008, s 56.

Having made the initial assessment, the Examining Authority must hold a preliminary meeting (PA 2008, s 88), to which it must invite the applicant, interested parties (PA 2008, s 102), statutory parties (PA 2008, s 88(3A)) and each local authority (PA 2008, s 88A). It may also invite other persons.

There is no prescribed timeframe during which the preliminary meeting must be held. This is significant and gives PINS the opportunity to set the date of the preliminary meeting with a view to allowing adequate preparation time for the examination of a complex or controversial application.

At the preliminary meeting, or as soon as practicable thereafter, the Examining Authority must set a timetable for the examination of the application (Infrastructure Planning (Examination Procedure) Rules 2010, SI 2010/103, reg 8). The timetable must set out, *inter alia*, the date by which representations must be received by the Examining Authority; the period within which the Examining Authority will ask questions in writing and seek further written information; the period within which the applicant will have the opportunity to comment in writing on the relevant representations and any responses to written questions; the period within which the applicant and any interested party must agree a statement of common ground and the date of any issue specific hearing.

Examination

The day after the preliminary meeting (or the last day of the preliminary meeting, if it runs over more than one day) is the start date for the examination of the application. The Examining Authority must complete the examination of the application within six months of the start date (PA 2008, s 98).

The Examining Authority must report to the Secretary of State within three months of the deadline for completion of the examination (or, if it completed the examination earlier than that, within three months of completing the examination) (PA 2008, s 98(3)).

There is a power for the Secretary of State to extend this time limit in PA 2008, s 98(4), provided he notifies all interested parties of the new deadline, and publicised the new deadline in the manner he considers appropriate. The Secretary of State must also make a statement to the Houses of Parliament, announcing the new deadline: see the Able Marine Energy Park application for an example of the Secretary of State extending the three-month period for making a decision.

Decision

The Secretary of State must then decide an application within three months from the date on which he received the Examining Authority's report (PA 2008, s 107).

The Secretary of State has a power to extend that time limit, pursuant to PA 2008, s 107(3), provided he notifies interested parties of his decision, publicises the new deadline and announces the new deadline to the Houses of Parliament.

Summary of experience

Set out at Table 1 below is a summary of the times within which the various procedural steps have been taken for the first 25 projects that reached the PA 2008, s 55 decision stage (whether to accept the application).

A number of themes emerge:

- the range of periods from acceptance of the application to preliminary meeting is quite wide at 98 days (Redditch Branch Enhancement Scheme and Stafford Area Improvements Norton Bridge Railway) to 215 (North London Electricity Line Reinforcement where there has been a procedural error in the PA 2008, s 56(2) notices – although the typical range is about 100 days to 130 days.
- there appears to be some correlation, although not a particularly strong one, between the length of period from acceptance of the application to preliminary meeting and whether the Examining Authority is a Panel or a single appointed person;
- the range of period from application to decision is relatively constant at between 14 and 18 months (excluding projects that have gone to Special Parliamentary Procedure) and that even for the largest projects, including the Thanes Tideway Tunnel (18 months).

Table 1

PROJECT	APPLICATION	SECTION 55 DECISION	PRELIMINARY MEETING [days after s 55 decision]	REPORT [days after s 55 decision]	DECISION	TOTAL (MONTHS) [days after s 55 decision]	COMMENTS
Overhead electricity line to connect Maesgwyn Wind Farm	3.8.10	31.8.10	N/A				Application not accepted
Rookery South Energy from Waste Generating Station	5.8.10	26.8.10	17.1.11 [144 days]	N/A IPC made the decision	13.10.11	14 [413 days]	DCO only published on 26.3.13 following SPP
Brig y Cwm Energy from Waste Generating Station	31.12.10	26.1.11	7.6.11 [132 days]	N/A			Application withdrawn following refusal to allow amendment
North Doncaster Rail Chord	22.6.11	19.7.11	16.11.11 [120 days]	31.7.12 [378 days]	16.10.12	16 [455 days]	
Ipswich Rail Chord	29.6.11	21.7.11	9.11.11 [111 days]	12.6.12 [327 days]	5.9.12	15 [412 days]	
Kentish Flats Extension	14.10.11	10.11.11	22.2.12 [104 days]	29.11.12 [385 days]	19.2.13	16 [467 days]	
Hinkley Power Station	31.10.11	24.11.11	21.3.12 [118 days]	19.12.12 [391 days]	19.3.13	17 [481 days]	
Brechfa Forest West Wind Farm	4.11.11	30.11.11	13.3.12 [104 days]	12.12.12 [378 days]	12.3.13	16 [468 days]	
Galloper Offshore Wind Farm	21.11.11	19.12.11	29.5.12 [162 days]	27.2.13 [436 days]	24.5.2013	18 [522 days]	

PROJECT	APPLICATION	SECTION 55 DECISION	PRELIMINARY MEETING [days after s 55 decision]	REPORT [days after s 55 decision]	DECISION	TOTAL (MONTHS) [days after s 55 decision]	COMMENTS
Preesall Saltfield Underground Gas Storage	1.12.11	23.12.11	24.4.12 [123 days]	22.1.13 [396 days]	9.4.2013	16 [473 days]	
Heysham to M6 Link Road	6.12.11	23.12.11	3.4.12 [102 days]	19.12.12 [362 days]	19.3.13	15 [452 days]	
Able Marine Energy Park	19.12.11	12.1.12	24.5.12 [133 days]	25.2.13 [410 days]	18.12.13	23 [707 days]	DCO delayed due to SPP
Triton Knoll Offshore Wind Farm	31.1.12	23.2.12	23.7.12 [151 days]	17.4.13 [419 days]	11.7.13	16 [505 days]	
East Northants Resource Management Facility	14.3.12	11.4.12	26.7.12 [106 days]	22.4.13 [376 days]	11.7.13	13 [457 days]	
Port Blyth New Biomass Plant	15.3.12	11.4.12	2.8.12 [113 days]	2.5.13 [386 days]	24.7.13	15 [470 days]	
M1 Junction 10a Grade Separation – Luton	29.6.12	27.7.12	15.11.12 [111 days]	13.8.13 [382 days]	30.10.13	15 [461 days]	
Roosecote Biomass Power Station	3.7.12	31.7.12	N/A				Application withdrawn
Kings Lynn B Connection Project	27.7.12	21.8.12	11.1.13 [143 days]	10.10.13 [415 days]	18.12.13	16 [485 days]	
Fieldes Lock – Rail linked power station	14.8.12	7.9.12					Application withdrawn

(continued)

Table 1 ***(Continued)***

PROJECT	APPLICATION	SECTION 55 DECISION	PRELIMINARY MEETING [days after s 55 decision]	REPORT [days after s 55 decision]	DECISION	TOTAL (MONTHS) [days after s 55 decision]	COMMENTS
North London (Electricity Line) Reinforcement	30.8.12	27.9.12	30.4.13 [215 days]	23.1.14 [483 days]	16.4.14	18 [567 days]	Preliminary meeting postponed after it became apparent that the applicant had not fully complied with its obligation under PA 2008, s 56(2) to notify certain persons of the application.
Redditch Branch Enhancement Scheme	4.9.12	1.10.12	7.1.13 [98 days]	2.8.13 [305 days]	31.10.13	13 [369 days]	
East Anglia ONE Offshore Windfarm	21.11.12	14.12.12	25.6.13 [193 days]	18.3.14 [459 days]	17.6.14	18 [551 days]	
Stafford Area Improvements Norton Bridge Railway	19.12.12	10.1.13	18.4.13 [98 days]	3.1.14 [358 days]	31.3.14	15 [446 days]	
Daventry International Rail Freight Terminal	22.2.13	20.3.13	8.7.2013 [110 days]	7.4.14 [383 days]	3.10.14	18 [563 days]	Re-submitted application following non-acceptance of application on 29.11.12
Thames Tideway Tunnel	28.2.13	27.3.13	12.9.13 [170 days]	12.6.14 [442 days]	12.9.14	17 [535 days]	

From experience, it is also possible to give some broad indications of the likely timetable for an examination. Table 2 below sets out a typical timetable. This can be helpful in identifying potential peak periods of activity.

Table 2

EVENT	APPROX PERIOD AFTER PRELIMINARY MEETING
PRELIMINARY MEETING	0
Notice of procedural decisions following Preliminary Meeting (incl Timetable for examination; ExA's first written questions; Note of Preliminary Meeting)	1–2 weeks
Deadline for receipt of Responses to ExA's first written questions; Written representations; Local Impact Reports	5–6 weeks
Deadline for receipt of Comments on relevant / written reps Comments on LIRs Comments on responses to ExA's first written questions	9–10 weeks
ExA's second written questions	11–12 weeks
Deadline for receipt of Responses to ExA's second written questions	15–16 weeks
Deadline for receipt of Comments on responses to ExA's second written questions	17–18 weeks
Issue specific hearings Compulsory acquisition hearings Open floor hearings	A few days within range of (say) 12–20 weeks
CLOSE OF EXAMINATION	24 weeks

Article 78

Acceptance of an Application

Isabella Tafur, ftb
Michael Humphries QC, ftb

Following the lengthy pre-submission stage, the submission of a DCO application is something of a milestone for every applicant. After the inevitable flurry of activity in submitting the application documents, the next stage requires the applicant to wait for up to 28 days to learn whether the Secretary of State will accept the application.

PA 2008, s 55 – decisions on whether to accept an application

Pursuant to PA 2008, s 55 the Secretary of State must make a decision on whether to accept the application within 28 days, beginning with the day after the application is received.

The Secretary of State may only accept the application if he is satisfied of four things, being;

(a) that the application is for an order granting development consent (PA 2008, s 55(3)(a));

(b) that development consent is required for any of the development to which the application relates (PA 2008, s 55(3)(c));

(c) that the applicant has complied with the pre-application procedure in Chapter 2 of Part 5 of the Act (PA 2008, s 55(3)(e)) and

(d) that the application (including its accompanying documentation) is of a standard that the Secretary of State considers 'satisfactory' (PA 2008, s 55(3)(f)).

This last requirement – that the Secretary of State be satisfied that the application is satisfactory – was introduced by an amendment to the PA 2008 made by the Localism Act 2011.

In deciding whether the applicant has complied with the pre-application procedure under PA 2008, s 55(3)(c), the Secretary of State must have regard to the applicant's consultation report (PA 2008, s 55(4)(a)); the 'adequacy of consultation' representation from local authority consultees who have been consulted pursuant to PA 2008, s 42(1)(b) (PA 2008, s 55(4)(b)) and the extent to which the applicant has had regard to guidance on pre-application procedure issued by the Secretary of State (PA 2008, s 55(4)(c)).

In deciding whether the application is 'satisfactory' under PA 2008, s 55(3)(f), the Secretary of State must have regard to the extent to which the application complies with the requirements in PA 2008, s 37(3) (form and contents of the application) and any standards set under PA 2008, s 37(5) (PA 2008, s 55(5A)). Prior to the amendments made by the Localism Act 2011, an application could only be accepted if it complied with the requirements in PA 2008, s 37(3) and the standards set under PA 2008, s 37(5). The Localism Act 2011 has relaxed that requirement, such that the Secretary of State can now accept an application even if those requirements have not been met, provided that he has regard to those requirements in reaching his decision about whether the application is 'satisfactory'.

The Secretary of State must notify the applicant whether he accepts the application or not (PA 2008, s 55(6) and (7)). If he does not consider that the application can be accepted, then he must also provide his reasons for that view. PA 2008, s 55 contemplates that the applicant may modify the application in response to a negative decision from the Secretary of State, and provides that, in such event, the decision as to whether to accept the modified application should be determined in the same way as the original application (PA 2008, s 55(8)). Any challenge to a refusal to accept an application has to be made by judicial review pursuant to PA 2008, s 118(3).

Notification of an accepted application

On the acceptance of an application, the applicant must notify prescribed persons of that acceptance pursuant to PA 2008, s 56. Regulation 8 of and Schedule 1 to the Infrastructure Planning (Applications: Prescribed Forms and Procedure) Regulations 2009 ('APFP Regulations') set out the persons to be notified, and the information to be included in the notification.

At the same time as it notifies prescribed persons under PA 2008, s 56, the applicant must send a copy of the PA 2008, s 56 notice to those persons who were notified to the applicant as persons whom the Secretary of State considered would be, or would be likely to be, affected by or have an interest in the proposed development and who would be unlikely to have become aware of the proposed development through the pre-submission consultation and publicity (Infrastructure Planning (Environmental Impact Assessment) Regulations 2017 ('the EIA Regulations 2017'), reg 16(2)(a)). The Secretary of State must also send to the 'consultation bodies' (as defined in EIA Regulations 2017, reg 3) a copy of the accepted application, a map showing the location of the proposed development and a copy of the Environmental Statement (EIA Regulations 2017, reg 16(2)(b)).

The applicant must also publish a notice of the acceptance in accordance with APFP Regulations, reg 9.

Acceptance checklist

PINS uses a non-statutory checklist to assist in and inform its decision as to whether to accept an application. The checklist is included as PINS Advice Note 6 (version 10), Appendix 3. The checklist is in tabular form, with the requirements for acceptance and relevant statutory references in the left-hand column and notes in the right-hand column directing the approach the Planning Inspectorate should take in considering each requirement. For example, headed 'Section 42: Duty to consult' the application checklist asks, 'Did the applicant consult the applicable persons set out in s 42 of the PA 2008 about the proposed application?'; and then lists five categories of s 42 person.

Whilst applicants are advised in paragraph 17.1 of PINS Advice Note 6 (version 10) that they may find it helpful to refer to the checklist in preparing their applications, they are also warned that completion of the checklist by the applicant itself should not be seen as a guarantee that the application will be accepted. Even so, many applicants do complete the form in order to assist the Examining Authority and direct it to the relevant sections of the application documentation.

Even though applicants make every effort to ensure that their applications comply with all relevant formalities and requirements, inevitably things will sometimes go wrong. In such cases, the question will be whether the Secretary of State considers that the application is, nonetheless, 'satisfactory'. There is little in the way of guidance as to how the Secretary of State will determine that question and it is, therefore, useful to consider other application checklists in order to gauge the Secretary of State's likely approach to irregularities in the application documents.

In the Glyn Rhonwy Pumped Storage DCO application, the Examining Authority noted in the application checklist that the Works Plans did not indicate any limits of deviation, but considered that the limits of deviation would be unlikely to have a bearing on the pre-application consultations and concluded that they were sufficient for acceptance.

In respect of the North London Heat and Power Project DCO, the Examining authority noted in the acceptance checklist some inconsistencies regarding consultation, in that a number of consultees listed in the Consultation Report had been excluded from the Book of Reference without justification. It also expressed concern over the lack of precision in the upper limit of generating capacity in the application documents including the draft DCO, which referred to an upper capacity of 'around 70 megawatts'. Notwithstanding these concerns, the Secretary of State found that the application was satisfactory and simply issued advice pursuant to PA 2008, s 51 to the applicant on how to rectify the concerns that it had expressed.

In the Hirwaun Power Station application checklist, the Examining authority noted that two required consultees did not appear to have been consulted, and that 'a small number of precautionary ones' were also missing without explanation. There were also three inconsistencies between the Book of Reference, the Explanatory Memorandum and the Consultation Report, but the Secretary of State considered that the application was 'satisfactory' nonetheless, and that all of the matters identified in the checklist were capable of being addressed during the examination of the application.

It would appear, therefore, that the Secretary of State will consider an application 'satisfactory' where an error is capable of being corrected in the post-acceptance period and where there is no substantial prejudice to another party.

Article 79

Notifying Persons of Accepted Application and Relevant Representations

Hereward Phillpot QC, ftb
Michael Humphries QC, ftb

Notifying persons of accepted application

PA 2008, s 56(2) places a duty on the applicant to give notice of the application to certain individuals and organisations.

The form and content of the notice

The notice must include the information prescribed by Infrastructure Planning (Applications: Prescribed Forms and Procedure) Regulations 2009, ('the APFP Regulations'), reg 8(2): see PA 2008, s 56(3).

The applicant must make available to each person required to be notified a copy of the application and certain prescribed documents: see PA 2008, ss 56(6)(b), 37(3)(d) and APFP Regulations, reg 6.

Who must be notified?

Notification must be given to 'such persons as may be prescribed' (PA 2008, s 56(2)(a)), the identity of 'such persons' to be determined by reference to APFP Regulations, reg 8(1), Sch 1. APFP Regulations, Sch 1, Column 1 provides a list of statutory bodies, and Column 3 identifies the circumstances in which each of those bodies must be notified. For example, Natural England must be notified in the case of all applications likely to affect land in England.

Notification must also be given to the Marine Management Organisation ('MMO') where the proposed development involves activity within its jurisdiction (PA 2008, s 56(2)(aa), (2A)), each local authority that is within PA 2008, s 56A (PA 2008, s 56(2)(b)), the Greater London Authority ('GLA') where the application site (or part of it) is within Greater London (PA 2008, s 56(2)(c)), and each person who is within one or more of the categories set out in PA 2008, s 57 (PA 2008, s 56(2)(d)).

PA 2008, s 57 identifies three categories of person. Those who the applicant knows, after making 'diligent inquiry', have a legal interest in, and/or are occupiers of, land forming all or part of the application site, fall within 'Category 1': see PA 2008, s 57(1). Those known to have an interest in, or the power to sell and convey or release, such land, fall within 'Category 2': see PA 2008, s 57(2). Category 3 is less straightforward and comprises those that the applicant thinks would or might be entitled to 'make a relevant claim' if the order were to be made and fully implemented: see PA 2008, s 57(4)–(6). A 'relevant claim' for these purposes is defined by subsection (6) as one under Compulsory Purchase Act 1965, s 10 (compensation where satisfaction not made for the taking, or injurious affection, of land subject to compulsory purchase), Land Compensation

Act 1973, Part 1 (compensation for depreciation of land value by physical works caused by use of public works), or PA 2008, s 152(3) (a claim by a person whose land is injuriously affected by the carrying out of works authorised by the DCO).

Publicity

In addition to the requirement to notify certain persons, the applicant must also publicise the application in the prescribed manner: see PA 2008, s 56(7). APFP Regulations, reg 9 stipulates that this is to be done by way of a notice containing specified details, published in the same way as a proposed application and also displayed at or near to the site.

Deadline for receipt of relevant representations

The applicant's notice must also identify the deadline for receipt by the Secretary of State of representations giving notice of the person's interest in, or objection to, the application: see section 56(4). The minimum period that must be allowed is 28 days beginning with the day after that on which the person receives the notice: see PA 2008, s 56(5). The same minimum period has been prescribed for the purposes of the publicity notice under PA 2008, s 56(7): see PA 2008, s 56(8) and APFP Regulations, reg 9(3).

PA 2008, s 102(2)/(4) definitions of 'representation' and 'relevant representation'

PA 2008, s 102(1) defines who will qualify as an 'interested party' for the purposes of the examination into the application and, in addition to the applicant, comprises those falling into one of the three categories identified in PA 2008, s 57 (above), the MMO (where relevant), the local authorities and the GLA (where relevant), and anyone who has 'made a relevant representation'.

This is important as, once a person has acquired the status of an 'interested party', such a person also acquires certain rights before, during and after the examination process. These include the right to be invited to a preliminary meeting; the right to require, and be heard at, an open-floor hearing; the right to be heard at an Issue Specific Hearing, if one is held; the right to be notified of when the Examining Authority has completed its examination; and the right to be notified of the decision: see paragraph 16 of the CLG Guidance on the examination of applications (March 2015).

A 'representation' for these purposes is defined inclusively, so as to include evidence: see PA 2008, s 102(2). A 'relevant representation', by contrast, is one that satisfies all of the following requirements (PA 2008, s 102(4)):

- it is a representation about the application;
- it is made to the Secretary of State in the prescribed form and manner;
- it is received by the Secretary of State no later than the s 56 deadline that applies to the person making it;
- it contains material 'of a prescribed description'; and
- it does not contain:
  - material about compensation for compulsory acquisition;

- material about the merits of policy in NPSs; or
- material that is vexatious or frivolous.

The DCLG Guidance on the examination of applications (2015) states (para 27) that:

> 'In certain cases it may be difficult to determine whether a request is frivolous or vexatious. In such borderline cases, the benefit of the doubt will be given to the party making the representation. Any subsequent examination of the representation, at a hearing for example, would then provide an opportunity for the person or party making the representation to amplify and clarify it. If it then emerged that the representation did not merit any further serious consideration, the Examining Authority could decide to give it little weight.'

That would appear to be sensible and pragmatic advice.

The Infrastructure Planning (Interested Parties and Miscellaneous Prescribed Provisions) Regulations 2015 ('the Interested Parties Regulations') prescribe the form and manner in which relevant representations must be made. Interested Parties Regulations, reg 4 requires relevant representations to be in the form of a 'registration form', and that it include certain basic information about the person registering (for example, name, address and telephone number of the person registering), as well as 'an outline of the principal submissions which the person registering intends to make in respect of the application' (Interested Parties Regulations, reg 4(2)(b)).

Guidance on what is meant by an 'outline of the principal submissions' is to be found at paragraphs 23–24 of the DCLG Guidance on the examination of applications (2015). A person's relevant representation does not need to set out in full the arguments which the person intends to make during the examination, but it should contain sufficient information to enable the Examining Authority to understand which aspects of the application the person supports or objects to, and the reasons why. This will help the Examining Authority identify the main issues likely to feature in the examination, guide its structure and programme, and suggest where interested parties with similar cases might consider collaborating to present a joint case.

The guidance also suggests that this process of considering the relevant representations will help the Examining Authority to see whether there are any relevant issues at risk of not being properly covered, and how to remedy this. In practice this is unlikely to arise very often, as the prolonged and detailed pre-application process should ensure that all of the potentially important issues are flushed out in advance of the application being made.

Infrastructure Planning (Examination Procedure) Rules 2010

Rule 3 – relevant representations

Further provision in relation to relevant representations is made in the Infrastructure Planning (Examination Procedure) Rules 2010 ('the Examination Procedure Rules'), r 3.

Those making relevant representations must ensure that they are received by the Examining Authority by the later of the dates specified in the notices required by PA 2008, s 56(4), (8). Any written comment on relevant representations that are made must be received either by the date on which the preliminary meeting is held, or, if later, the date specified in the timetable set by the Examining Authority pursuant to Examination Procedure Rules, r 8.

The Examining Authority can ask for further information about matters contained in a relevant representation, or a comment made in respect of such a representation, and set a date by which such information must be provided.

All relevant representations and comments must be made available by the Examining Authority as soon as practicable after receipt, in accordance with Examination Procedure Rules, r 21. This involves publishing the material on the PINS website (https://infrastructure.planninginspectorate.gov.uk/) and making hard copies available for inspection and copying – see Examination Procedure Rules, r 21(2).

Time periods

Later representations

The examination process involves a series of stages at which further representations will be sought by the Examining Authority from interested parties. At the preliminary meeting, or as soon as practicable thereafter, the Examining Authority will publish a timetable in accordance with Examination Procedure Rules, r 8. That timetable will set a date for the making of written representations, for the Examining Authority to ask questions in writing about any matter contained in the application, in relevant representations, written representations, or anything else it considers relevant, and for the applicant and interested parties to comment in writing on any relevant or written representations or responses provided to written questions.

The timetable will tend to evolve during the course of the examination, with further deadlines being set for additional rounds of questions and comments, hearings and written representations. In order to keep the examination to time, these deadlines are generally fairly tight, and a great deal of effort is required in order adequately to deal with the multiple (and often complex) matters of law and evidence arising in the limited time available.

Examination Procedure Rules, r 23 – allowing extra time

The Examining Authority does have the power to allow extra time for the taking of any step which may or must be taken under Examination Procedure Rules, r 23.

Whilst this is a power exercised from time to time, the Examining Authority is generally reluctant to allow more time unless there are very good reasons for doing so and it would not put at risk the prospects of finishing the examination on time. Generalised pleas for more time, because of the very significant administrative and cost burdens involved in sticking to the tight timetables needed to complete the examination on time, are likely to be refused.

Article 80

Interested Parties

Hereward Phillpot QC, ftb
Michael Humphries QC, ftb

Introduction

The main participants in an examination held under the PA 2008 are those who have, or acquire, the status of 'interested parties'. Designation as an interested party carries with it important consequences in terms of notification, the right to make and receive representations, and the right to require and to participate in hearings.

PA 2008, s 102

PA 2008, s 102(1) defines who is or may become an 'interested party' for the purposes of the examination of any individual application.

The applicant and the local authority in whose area the land is located are automatically accorded the status of interested parties (PA 2008, s 102(1)(a), (c) and (8)). In addition, the Marine Management Organisation and the Greater London Authority are automatically given the status of interested parties where the development proposed falls within their respective areas of jurisdiction (PA 2008, s 102(1)(ba) and (d)).

Other persons can become interested parties in the following ways:

- By reason of being notified of the application in accordance with PA 2008, s 56(2)(a) (PA 2008, s 102(1)(aa)).
- By reason of a decision by the Examining Authority under PA 2008, s 102A that the person is within one of the categories set out in PA 2008, s 102B (PA 2008, s 102(1)(ab) – see below).
- In the case of 'statutory parties' (see PA 2008, s 88(3)(c) and below) and local authorities within PA 2008, s 88A, by notifying the Examining Authority of a desire to become an interested party following the preliminary meeting (PA 2008, s 102(1)(ca)).
- By making a relevant representation PA 2008, (s 102(1)(e)) (see PA 2008, s 102(4) for the definition of a 'relevant representation').

PINS Advice Note 8.2 (version 2) gives helpful advice on 'How to register to participate in an Examination'.

Once a person has become an interested party, he may choose to relinquish that status by notifying the Examining Authority to that effect (PA 2008, s 102(1ZA)). For example, various interested parties wrote to the Examining Authority to relinquish their status during the examination into the East Northants Research Management Facility.

PA 2008, ss 102A and 102B

The purpose of PA 2008, ss 102A and 102B is to enable the Examining Authority to accord interested party status to those who should have been, but were not, notified of the acceptance of the application under PA 2008, s 56 (and thus acquired interested party status via that route).

PA 2008, s 102A allows for those who consider themselves to be in this position to ask the Examining Authority to become interested parties. On receipt of a request which meets the requirements set out in PA 2008, s 102A(1), the Examining Authority must decide whether the person is within one or more of the categories set out in PA 2008, s 102B. If it is satisfied to that effect, it must then notify that person and the applicant that the person has become an interested party (PA 2008, s 102A(3)).

There are four requirements which PA 2008, s 102A(1) sets before the obligation under subsection (2) arises:

- the person must have made a request to the Examining Authority to become an interested party;
- the request must state that the person claims to be within one or more of the categories in PA 2008, s 102B;
- the person must not have been notified of the acceptance of the application in accordance with PA 2008, s 56(2)(d); and
- the applicant must have issued a PA 2008, s 58 certificate in relation to the application (certifying compliance with the PA 2008, s 56 requirement to notify persons of the accepted application).

PA 2008, s 102B identifies three categories of person, corresponding to the categories of person who should have been notified under PA 2008, s 56(2)(d).

Infrastructure Planning (Interested Parties and Miscellaneous Prescribed Provisions) Regulations 2015

As explained above, PA 2008, s 102(1)(ca) provides that a 'statutory party' (PA 2008, s 88(3)(c)) may become an interested party on notifying the Examining Authority (PA 2008, s 89(2A)(b)). PA 2008, s 88(3A) provides that a 'statutory party' means a person specified in, or of a description specified in, regulations made by the Secretary of State.

The Infrastructure Planning (Interested Parties and Miscellaneous Prescribed Provisions) Regulations 2015 contain a schedule of persons specified as 'statutory parties' for the purposes of PA 2008, s 88(3A). Regulation 3 provides that the persons specified for these purposes are:

- those listed in Column 1 of the Schedule to the Regulations in the circumstances specified in Column 2 to that Schedule [NB this is subject to certain parties marked with an asterisk (*) not being 'statutory parties' in respect of projects in England]; and
- any affected person.

Column 1 lists various persons, and Column 2 lists the circumstances in which those persons are deemed to be statutory parties. So, for example, the Welsh Ministers are a statutory party for all applications likely to affect land in Wales, and the Health and Safety Executive is a statutory party for all applications.

PA 2008, s 59(4) states that 'A person is an "affected person" for the purposes of this section if the applicant, after making diligent inquiry, knows that the person is interested in the land to which the compulsory acquisition request relates or any part of that land'; and PA 2008, s 59(2) provides that the applicant must give the Secretary of State a notice specifying the name of each 'affected person'.

All 'affected persons' may, therefore, become 'interested parties', and have all the entitlements associated with that status. In addition, they may also request that a compulsory acquisition hearing be held to consider the issues arising in connection with the proposed compulsory acquisition of land.

Status of 'interested parties' in the examination process

The Act provides interested parties with a particular status in the examination process. In particular:

- Interested parties must be invited to the preliminary meeting (PA 2008, s 88(3)(b)) and have a right to participate in that meeting (PA 2008, s 88(4)(a)).
- Procedural decisions made by the Examining Authority must be notified to all interested parties (PA 2008, s 89(2A) and (4)).
- In determining whether a hearing should be held, the Examining Authority is required to ensure that 'an interested party has a fair chance to put the party's case' (PA 2008, s 91(1)(b)), and hence interested parties have a special status when considering the fairness of the examination procedure.
- Interested parties are entitled to make oral representations at hearings (PA 2008, s 91(3)).
- Interested parties are entitled to require to be heard at an open floor hearing (PA 2008, s 93(1)) and to make oral representations about the application at that hearing (PA 2008, s 93(3)).
- Notification of, and participation in, site visits is limited to interested parties (Infrastructure Planning (Examination Procedure) Rules 2010, r 16); see eg the invitation to interested parties to make submissions on locations for the site visit at the Galloper Offshore Windfarm examination.
- The Secretary of State must notify interested parties of the deadline for the decision on the application, and of any changes to that deadline (PA 2008, s 98).

Participation by those who are not interested parties

The Examining Authority retains a discretion to allow participation in the examination by those who are not interested parties. It is a discretion that has already been exercised in a number of examinations, including those into the Triton Knoll Offshore Wind Farm and Preesall Saltfield Underground Gas Storage proposals.

The DCLG Guidance for the examination of applications for development consent (March 2015) states (para 34) as follows about the exercise of that discretion:

> 'It is for the Examining Authority to decide whether to allow persons other than those categorised as interested parties to participate in the examination of the application, including expert witnesses. But where a request is received from an interested party to

> allow an expert witness to take part in the examination of the application, the Secretary of State considers that this should be given serious consideration, in the interests of informed decision making.'

This needs to be read and understood together with paragraph 20 of the DCLG Guidance, which states that, where an interested party wishes to take part in an oral hearing, they may appoint a representative, including a legal representative, to speak on their behalf at the hearing.

In practice, the nature and format of issue-specific hearings often make it necessary for the panel's questions to be answered by more than one person. For example, a question might require both the explanation of a point of law, or DCO drafting, and the giving of expert evidence on the practicalities lying behind that point. Participants at issue-specific hearings sometimes therefore adopt an approach whereby questions are dealt with by a rotating cast of individuals from within the team. Lawyers cannot give evidence, and whilst they can relay instructions to the panel in response to questions, it will often be much more sensible and efficient simply to ask the relevant member of the team to deal with a point. That should not require an application for the Examining Authority's consent on each occasion, and a pragmatic approach seems to have been adopted in hearings so far.

Article 81

Local Impact Reports

Hereward Phillpot QC, ftb
Michael Humphries QC, ftb

PA 2008, s 60

PA 2008, s 60 provides that certain local authorities are to be invited to produce a 'Local Impact Report' (LIR) in order to inform the examination of the likely impact of the proposed development on that authority's area. In some cases the invitation to produce such a report will be made to a number of different authorities who may choose to co-operate to produce a combined LIR. There is no obligation on an authority that receives such an invitation to produce an LIR, but it is strongly encouraged to do so: see PINS Advice Note 1 (version 2): Local Impact Reports.

The Act defines an LIR as follows: 'a report in writing giving details of the likely impact of the proposed development on the authority's area (or any part of that area)' (PA 2008, s 60(3)).

PA 2008, s 104(2)(b) imposes an obligation upon the Secretary of State to have regard to any LIR submitted to him within the relevant time limit.

Procedural requirements and timescales

The invitation to produce an LIR is triggered by a notice given by the Secretary of State (PA 2008, s 60(2)), which must also specify the deadline for receipt of the LIR (PA 2008, s 60(5)). The Secretary of State must give the requisite notice once the application has been accepted and he has received a PA 2008, s 58 certificate (certifying compliance with the requirements of PA 2008, s 56) and (where it applies) notification under PA 2008, s 59.

PINS Advice Note 1 (version 2) explains that the Examining Authority will take account of the complexity of the application and other relevant matters, and also the overall timescale set by the Act for examining the application. In practice, this last factor means that the deadline set by the notice is likely to be quite short.

The deadline for receipt of the LIR will be one of the items included amongst the procedural decisions made following the preliminary meeting, together with the period within which Interested Parties (including the applicant) will have the opportunity to make written comments on any LIRs that are submitted.

Authorities are advised in PINS Advice Note 1 (version 2) not to wait until the deadline has been set before commencing the preparation of their LIR, because of the scale of the task and the limited time likely to be available between notification and expiry of the deadline. The consultation and pre-application periods are likely to be the most appropriate time to commence the evaluation of impacts and gathering of material. The LIR can then be compiled once the application has been accepted and the invitation to submit an LIR has been received. The Examining Authority may agree to an extension of time for an authority to complete its LIR, but this is likely to be a discretion exercised only rarely, and then only to allow a limited additional period of time.

Authorities should also take account of the other deadlines that are likely to be looming for them at this stage of the examination, such as those for production of Statements of Common Ground and written representations.

PA 2008, s 56A identifies which adjoining authorities (unitary authorities, lower-tier district councils and upper-tier county councils), in addition to the authority (or authorities) within whose area the development is to be located, are to be invited to submit an LIR. In respect of offshore proposals, it may be the case that there are no local authorities who would be invited to produce an LIR, although in those circumstances the nearest local authority has sometimes voluntarily produced an LIR in any event.

Contents and style of an LIR

Provided that the LIR satisfies the statutory definition, the precise style and content of the document is a matter of choice for each individual authority.

Contents

Paragraphs 45 and 46 of the DCLG Guidance on the pre-application process (2015) contain brief guidance on LIRs and make it clear that they 'allow local authorities to set out details of their views on the likely effect of the development on the local area and community'. The DCLG Guidance on the examination of applications for development consent (2015) gives further guidance (paras 52–57) and makes two important points (para 54), being:

1 There is no need for the LIR to replicate the Environmental Impact Assessment produced by the applicant. This is of great practical significance because of the highly complex and technical nature of such assessments, and the length of the Environmental Statements to which the assessment process leads.

2 The LIR should be distinguished from any representation a local authority may choose to make in respect of the merits of an application. Again, this is a significant point because maintaining that distinction should make the task of producing the LIR more manageable, and help the authority to focus on the proper role of that document.

More detailed guidance on the contents of an LIR is available in PINS Advice Note 1 (version 2), which contains the following very helpful list of topics that may be of assistance in compiling the LIR:

1 Site description and surroundings/location.

2 Details of the proposal.

3 Relevant planning history and any issues arising.

4 Relevant development plan policies, supplementary planning guidance or documents, development briefs or approved master-plans and an appraisal of their relationship and relevance to the proposals.

5 Relevant development proposals under consideration or granted permission but not commenced or completed.

6 Local area characteristics such as urban and landscape qualities and nature conservation sites.

7 Local transport patterns and issues.

8 Site and area constraints.

9 Designated sites.

10 Socio-economic and community matters.

11 Consideration of the impact of the proposed articles and requirements within the draft Order (such as the scheme) in respect of all of the above.

12 DCO obligations and their impact on the local authority's area.

Both the (withdrawn) DCLG Guidance and the current PINS Advice Note stress the importance of using the LIR to provide local knowledge and experience, and evidence of local concerns and issues to the Examining Authority. Examples given in PINS Advice Note 1 (version 2) include local evidence of flooding, local social or economic issues or local knowledge of travel patterns to community facilities. This should ensure that local issues which might not otherwise come to the attention of the examination are properly taken into account.

PINS Advice Note 1 (version 2) indicates that LIRs are also expected to contain the local authority's appraisal of the proposed development's compliance with local policy and guidance. This may well be a material consideration, but it must also be remembered that the development plan has no particular status in decision-making under the PA 2008.

PINS Advice Note 1 (version 2) encourages local authorities to give their views on the relative importance of different social, environmental or economic issues and the impact of the scheme on them, on the basis that they are well placed to appreciate the impacts of proposals, for example in terms of employment, local services, associated development, or DCO obligations under PA 2008, s 174.

National Policy Statements (NPSs) may also be helpful to local authorities in preparing their LIRs as a guide to matters of local impact that are likely to be relevant to the determination of an application. However, local authorities are advised by PINS Advice Note 1 that there is no need for them to undertake an assessment of compliance with an NPS as this would duplicate the Examining Authority's role.

PINS Advice Note 1 (version 2) also suggests that where an NPS is locationally specific, the local authority should consider those local impacts of a development proposal which would not have been considered at the national policy development stage. In such instances there may be local impacts on sensitive receptors not apparent at the NPS stage, stemming from, for example, the particular layout, design, scale, appearance, or access arrangements of the scheme.

An important task for local authorities in compiling the LIR is to consider in detail the impact of the proposed DCO articles, requirements and DCO obligations, and any changes or additions which the local authority consider to be needed. These matters are likely to be the focus of much of the Examining Authority's attention during the course of the examination, and it is essential that local authorities get to grips with the detail of these matters at the earliest opportunity. By doing so, they will also help to ensure that their LIR and written representations are properly focused, and maximise the prospects of influencing the Secretary of State's decision.

Style

PINS Advice Note 1 (version 2) suggests that the LIR should consist of a statement of positive, neutral and negative local impacts, but it does not need to contain a balancing exercise between positives and negatives, as that is a matter for the Examining Authority; nor does it need to take the form of a formal committee report.

Emerging good practice

It is inevitable that the approach taken to the production of the LIR will differ from authority to authority and from project to project. Much may depend on the scale and complexity of the individual proposal, and the extent to which it has been possible to agree statements of common ground with the applicant.

For example, in the Hinkley Point C examination, the two District Councils and the County Council produced a joint LIR. The LIR was a very substantial document, supported by detailed appendices, but its nature and scale were not dictated simply by the complex nature and scale of the development to be assessed and the fact that it involved multiple sites in a number of quite different locations. In that case there had been a failure to agree much in the way of common ground in advance of the production of the LIR, and the impacts were in dispute between the authorities and the applicant.

The overall structure of the LIR in that case was as follows:

1 An Executive Summary, identifying the structure and role of the LIR, its contents and the key impacts identified.

2 A main LIR, divided into three parts:

   a Site-related matters.

   b Topic-based matters.

   c Community/area-based matters.

3 A set of Appendices, comprising:

   a Figures.

   b Topic papers (the evidence and supporting data said to justify the impacts articulated in the main LIR).

   c A list of documents used in compiling the LIR.

   d Preliminary comments on draft requirements.

Whilst the contents and focus of the LIR were the subject of lengthy and detailed criticism by the applicant during the examination process, the broad structure adopted may nevertheless offer some assistance for other authorities dealing with large and complicated applications.

Article 82

Initial Assessment of Issues

Isabella Tafur, ftb
Michael Humphries QC, ftb

Introduction

While it is for the Examining Authority to decide how to examine an application, in making any decision about how the application will be examined, it must comply with the provisions in Part 6 of the PA 2008. Pursuant to PA 2008, s 88, the examining authority must make an initial assessment of the principal issues arising on the application prior to the Preliminary Meeting.

Initial assessment of the principal issues

In making its initial assessment of the principal issues, the Examining Authority will have regard to the application documents and is also likely to take into account the relevant representations received from interested parties: see para 38 of the DCLG Guidance on the examination of applications for development consent (2015).

Rule 5 of the Infrastructure Planning (Examination Procedure) Rules 2010 requires the Examining Authority to make the initial assessment of issues within 21 days from the day after the deadline for the receipt of representations by the Secretary of State (as specified by the applicant in its PA 2008, s 56 notification letter).

Notification of the initial assessment

Having made the initial assessment of principal issues, the Examining Authority will hold a Preliminary Meeting. Rule 6 of the Infrastructure Planning (Examination Procedure) Rules 2010 requires the Examining Authority to give notice of that Meeting, and to notify all those invited of the matters to be discussed at the Preliminary Meeting. This is done by a 'Rule 6 letter'.

The Examining Authority's initial assessment of principal issues will often be listed as Appendix C to the Rule 6 letter. The Examining Authority makes it clear that it is not a comprehensive or exclusive list of all relevant matters, as it will have regard to all the important and relevant matters raised during the examination. This last point is important, as the list of principal issues will not preclude parties from raising other issues, nor the Examining Authority from considering them during the examination.

The initial assessment of principal issues will also usually then form an agenda item at the Preliminary Meeting allowing parties the opportunity to comment on the initial assessment list and raise potential additional issues. PINS Advice Note 8.3 (version 4) gives advice on 'Influencing how an application is examined: the Preliminary Meeting'.

Following the Preliminary Meeting the Examining Authority will set out the timetable for the examination: see Rule 8 of the Infrastructure Planning (Examination Procedure) Rules 2010. This is usually done by issuing a 'Rule 8 letter' a few days after the close of the Preliminary Meeting. The Rule 8 letter will also contain the Examining Authority's list of principal issues or refer back to the initial assessment of principal issues if the list has not changed.

Conclusion

Given the relatively short time-scales for responding to written questions during the examination period, the initial assessment of principal matters can provide applicants and interested parties with a useful steer in identifying areas in which further work could usefully be focused.

Examples of initial assessments

Typically, the list of principal issues will include numbered headings, with bullet point issues below. These can be very detailed. The list of principal issues below, from the East Anglia ONE North offshore windfarm 'Rule 6 letter' (Annex C) (July 2020), identifies the following 'Initial Assessment of Principal Issues':

> **'East Anglia ONE North offshore windfarm**
>
> **1. Aviation**
>
> - Civil and Ministry of Defence (MoD) radar and aviation operations.
> - Maintenance of safe air navigation during construction and operation.
>
> **2. Biodiversity, Ecology and Natural Environment**
>
> - Potential effects on the ecological value of species and habitats in the marine and terrestrial environment, including protected species.
> - Implications for the integrity of designated sites, including:
>   - internationally designated sites, in particular European sites and European marine sites;
>   - nationally designated sites, such as Sites of Special Scientific Interest (SSSIs), Areas of Outstanding Natural Beauty (AONBs) and Marine Conservation Zones;
>   - regionally and locally designated sites, such as County Wildlife Sites;
>   - ancient woodlands and protected trees; and
>   - habitats of nature conservation importance.
> - Potential cumulative and in-combination impacts.
> - Adequacy and security of mitigation measures, including timing and seasonal effects.
> - Adequacy and security of monitoring commitments.
> - Potential ecological effects outside of the UK and its territorial waters.

3. Compulsory Acquisition (CA), Temporary Possession (TP) and other Land or Rights Considerations

- The CA and TP case, including:
  - Project funding; and
  - Guarantees.
- Objections to it.
- Human rights considerations.

4. Construction

- Temporary work sites and storage.
- Exclusion zones including highway management arrangements.
- Cable laying and foundation installation.
- Construction phasing and timetable (including linkage to local highway management).
- Waste (onshore) and management of contaminated land.

5. Draft Development Consent Order (dDCO)

- Relevant definitions.
- The structure of the dDCO.
- The appropriateness of proposed requirements.
- Application and modification of legislative provisions.
- Relationships with other projects and consents.
- Deemed Marine Licence matters.
- Dispute resolution measures.

6. Electricity Connections, Infrastructure and other users

- The onshore connection point.
- Relationship with and implications for other major projects including East Anglia TWO, Sizewell C, Sizewell A decommissioning, Sizewell B operation and decommissioning and other transmission and interconnector projects.
- Implications for the electricity and gas transmission and distribution systems.
- Oil and gas activities.
- Marine aggregate activities.
- Unexploded ordnance.

7. Environmental Statement General

- Approaches to the identification of significance and risk.
- Site and route selection and alternatives.

8. Flood Risk, Water Quality and Resources

- Flood risk including site drainage and surface water flooding.
- The physical, biological or chemical character of surface water or groundwater.
- The Water Framework Directive.

9. Historic Environment

- Effects on the onshore terrestrial historic environment including geoarchaeology, buried archaeology and setting of designated assets
- Effects on the intertidal terrestrial historic environment
- Effects on the inshore marine historic environment.
- Effects on the offshore marine historic environment.
- Future archaeological investigation, monitoring and supervision.

10. Land Use

- Effects of the proposal on agricultural land and farming operations.
- Soil quality.
- Residential amenity.
- Recreational opportunities.

11. Landscape and Visual Impact

- Adequacy of assessment methodology and approach.
- Extent of study area.
- Impact on landscape character.
- Effectiveness of mitigation, specifically substation design and planting (to include growth rates and security within the DCO).
- Cumulative effects of substation infrastructure.

12. Marine and Coastal Physical Processes

- Scouring and scour protection, sand wave effects, other deposition and reef formation.
- Effects on the coast (wave climate, deposition, erosion and flooding).
- Climate change effects.
- Marine water and sediment quality including management of waste, debris and potential contaminants in marine sediments.
- Impact of landfall location on cliff stability.

13. Marine Effects

- Maintenance of safe marine navigation during construction and operation.
- Changes to bathymetry including deposition and other changes to vessel channels and safe operating distances.
- Other offshore interests and transboundary issues.
- Impacts on fishing and fisheries.

14. Nuisance and other Public Health Effects

- Construction, maintenance and decommissioning noise effects on marine and terrestrial environments.
- Operational noise and vibration effects on marine and terrestrial environments
- Air quality during construction and impact on the Air Quality Management Area (AQMA).
- Light pollution.
- Electric and Magnetic Fields (EMFs).
- Compliance with regulatory policy and guidelines.
- Impact on human health.

15. Other Projects and Proposals

- Interface with East Anglia TWO.
- Nuclear power operation, development and planning.
- The effects of the application on other constructed and proposed major projects nearby including offshore wind farms.
- Cumulative and in-combination effects with other major projects and proposals.
- The effects of other major projects on the application

16. Project Description and Site Selection

- Nature of the proposal in terms of the 'Rochdale' envelope.
- Design considerations.
- Assessment of alternatives.
- Need for the development.

17. Seascape, Landscape and Visual Amenity

- Adequacy of assessment methodology and approach.
- Extent of study area.
- Approach to Rochdale Envelope in respect of offshore platforms, including substations, together with dDCO drafting.
- Cumulative effects with other nearby Offshore Wind Farms (OWFs).
- Effect on Suffolk Coast and Heaths AONB.

18. Socio Economic Effects

- Effect on tourism in respect of the potential landscape and visual effect of the proposal, both on and offshore including during construction and operation.
- Effect of the project on the availability of tourism accommodation, particularly during the construction period.
- Effect on jobs and skills, during construction and operation.
- The potential for any 'edu-tourism' effect.

- Localised spatial effects of tourism arising from the onshore substation development.
- Distinctions and divergence between the conclusions reached in studies submitted as supporting evidence by the Applicant and the DMO (Suffolk Destination Management Organisation).

19. Transportation and Traffic

- Traffic generation, traffic management and highway safety.
- Effects on the Public Rights of Way (PROW) network including temporary and permanent diversion and/or stopping up.
- Implications for the Sizewell evacuation route.'

An Examining Authority's 'Initial Assessment of Principal Issues' will often be less detailed than this, but such a list of issues is a helpful indication of where the inspectors' minds are focusing and should, therefore, help parties with preparation for the Examination. It is important to bear in mind, however, that the Examining Authority will not feel constrained by this 'initial assessment' if other issues arise.

Article 83

Preliminary Meetings and Conduct of the Examination

Hereward Phillpot QC, ftb
Michael Humphries QC, ftb

Introduction

The focus of this article is on preliminary meetings and decisions made by the Examining Authority as to the conduct of the examination. Articles 84 to 88 of this work provide a more in-depth consideration of specific issues related to the conduct of the examination (for example, the various different types of hearings, written representations, and statements of common ground).

In order to understand how preliminary meetings fit into the examination process, how they are conducted, and their significance, it is first necessary to consider the relevant parts of the PA 2008 and then the procedural rules. Against that background, this article then considers the available guidance and advice, before identifying some further practical considerations for those attending preliminary meetings.

PA 2008

The conduct of examinations under the PA 2008 is a matter for the discretion of the Examining Authority, subject to complying with the provisions of Chapter 4 of Part 6 of the PA 2008 ('Chapter 4'), and any procedural rules made under PA 2008, s 97 (see PA 2008, s 87). The provisions of Chapter 4 guide and constrain the Examining Authority's discretion in a number of important ways, giving effect to the underlying legislative intention to create a faster and more streamlined process for the examination of applications.

Preliminary meetings

One of the specific requirements of Chapter 4 is that, following the Examining Authority's initial assessment of the principal issues arising on the application, it must hold what is known as a 'preliminary meeting' (PA 2008, s 88(2)).

The initial assessment of the issues must be undertaken within the period of 21 days that begins with the notified deadline for receipt of representations – see rule 5 of the Infrastructure Planning (Examination Procedure) Rules 2010 ('the Examination Procedure Rules').

The Examining Authority's initial assessment of principal issues is examined in article 82 of this work and so is only addressed relatively briefly here. In short, the assessment is informed not only by the Examining Authority's preliminary examination of the application documents, but also by any relevant representations received. This makes it essential that interested parties take care to ensure that their relevant representations are sufficiently clear, detailed and persuasive to influence the Examining Authority's decisions about the conduct of the examination (eg if a party wishes to try and persuade the Examining Authority that their issues (or at least some of them) are sufficiently weighty and complex to justify the need for an Issue Specific Hearing).

Those invited to the preliminary meeting must include:

- the applicant;
- each other interested party;
- each statutory party; and
- each local authority that is within PA 2008, s 88A.

Statutory parties are identified in reg 3 of, and Sch 1 to, the Infrastructure Planning (Interested Parties and Miscellaneous Prescribed Provisions) Regulations 2015 ('the 2015 Regulations'). They include bodies such as the Canal & River Trust, the Environment Agency, Historic England and Natural England.

The Examining Authority is free to invite others to the preliminary meeting if it considers that to be appropriate. It may also hold other meetings at other times (PA 2008, s 88(5)).

The purposes of the preliminary meeting are prescribed by PA 2008, s 88(4), albeit in fairly broad terms:

- To enable invitees present at the meeting to make representations to the Examining Authority about how the application should be examined.
- To discuss any other matter that the examining authority wishes to discuss.
- Any other purpose that may be specified in rules under PA 2008, s 97 [the Examination Procedure Rules do not specify any other purpose for the preliminary meeting].

In the light of the discussion at the preliminary meeting, the Examining Authority must make such procedural decisions (ie decisions about how the application is to be examined) as it thinks appropriate. The decisions may be made at the preliminary meeting itself, or afterwards, but the Examining Authority must then inform interested parties, statutory parties and local authorities within PA 2008, s 88A of those decisions (PA 2008, s 89(2A) and (4)).

The Examining Authority also has a general discretion to make procedural decisions at other times, pursuant to PA 2008, s 89(3).

Conduct of the examination

An examination will normally take the form of a combination of written representations and hearings, but it is primarily a written process. This stems from PA 2008, s 90(1), which provides as a starting point that:

> 'The Examining authority's examination of the application is to take the form of consideration of written representations about the application.'

This general rule is then made subject to a number of exceptions:

- The first is that PA 2008, ss 91 to 93 include requirements for a hearing to be held in certain circumstances. Hearings and other meetings forming part of the examination are generally held in public.

- The second is that the Examining Authority is given a general discretion under PA 2008, s 89(2) to decide that any part of the examination is to take a form that is *neither* consideration of written representations *nor* consideration of oral representations made at a hearing. No further assistance is offered either by the Examination Procedure Rules or in guidance as to what form this element of an examination might take if it involves neither written nor oral representations. It may simply be intended to provide flexibility to cover, for example, the consideration of audio-visual recordings.

PA 2008, s 91 makes provision for hearings into specific issues (known as 'Issue Specific Hearings' ('ISHs'). It is for the Examining Authority to decide if an ISH is necessary in relation to a particular issue, and it must make that decision in accordance with the following criteria in PA 2008, s 91(1):

> '… in order to ensure–
>
> (a) adequate examination of the issue, or
>
> (b) that an interested party has a fair chance to put the party's case.'

Whilst PA 2008, s 91(4) enables an Examining Authority sitting as a Panel to hold concurrent hearings into different issues, so far this power has not been exercised. It is not difficult to see why, given the practical difficulties and scope for potential unfairness that would arise where interested parties wish to be represented at both hearings.

It is normal for there to be at least some ISHs during the course of an examination, but these will generally be one-day hearings and, in most cases, there would be no more than a handful of ISHs over the course of the six-month examination. More complex examinations may involve more ISHs, sometimes with the same issue being dealt with in multiple hearings taking place at different stages of the examination. For example, the Thames Tideway Tunnel examination involved 16 ISHs (together with 20 compulsory acquisition hearings and 10 open floor hearings), and the National Grid Richborough Connection Project examination involved three sets of hearings interspersed throughout the examination to consider one issue (impact on South East Water's planned new reservoir). By contrast, the examination into National Grid's application for the Yorkshire and Humber CCS Pipeline Project involved only four ISHs, most of which did not extend beyond the lunch adjournment.

PA 2008, s 92 makes provision for compulsory acquisition hearings, which must be held where compulsory acquisition powers are included within the draft order and an affected person notifies the Secretary of State within the deadline that it wishes such a hearing to be held.

PA 2008, s 93 makes provision for open floor hearings. Like compulsory acquisition hearings, these must be held where an interested party notifies the Examining Authority that it wishes to be heard at such a hearing within the deadline (PA 2008, s 93(1)–(2)).

The power to make procedural rules regulating the examination of applications is bestowed upon the Lord Chancellor by PA 2008, s 97 (subject to a specific exception for gas or oil pipelines that cross from England or Wales into Scotland, where the power lies with the Secretary of State (PA 2008, s 97(1)). The current procedural rules are contained in the Examination Procedure Rules.

The beginning and end of the timetable for the examination is set by PA 2008, s 98, which imposes a duty on the Examining Authority to complete the examination within six months beginning with the day after the 'start day'. PA 2008, s 98(2) provides that the 'start day' is the day after the preliminary meeting is held.

This is important because, once the six-month period has started, it is very difficult to pause. The discretion to set a new deadline for the end of the examination lies with the Secretary of State, not the Examining Authority; and, if it is to be exercised, the Secretary of State is required to make a statement to Parliament announcing the new date (PA 2008, s 98(8)). In practice, extensions have been relatively infrequent and a very good reason would be needed to persuade the Secretary of State that one is appropriate. For example, a request for an extension made by the applicant in the Thames Tideway Tunnel examination was rejected by the Secretary of State, even though it was entirely unopposed and had been welcomed by the Examining Authority itself. However, extensions of time have been granted in a limited number of other cases (see, for example, the East Anglia ONE North / East Anglia TWO offshore windfarms examination, where the examination was extended for three months).

As a result, it is important for applicants to ensure, ahead of the preliminary meeting, that the application is ready for examination, and that they do not need any more time in order, for example, to make and consult about changes to the application. If more time is needed, it may be appropriate to seek to delay the preliminary meeting and hence the start of the examination.

The DCLG Guidance on examination (2015) acknowledges (para 45) that such a delay, whilst rare, may be appropriate in some circumstances. If necessary, it should be kept to the minimum period necessary, and the Secretary of State's expectation is that Examining Authorities will not normally agree to postpone the start of the examination for longer than three months.

The PA 2008 also makes provision for the Examining Authority to appoint expert 'assessors' to assist them in their examination (PA 2008, s 100), and to appoint a barrister or solicitor to provide legal advice and assistance (including oral questioning) (PA 2008, s 101). This latter power has been exercised, albeit only rarely. Both leading and junior counsel were appointed to assist the Examining Authority during the Thames Tideway Tunnel examination by providing advice and undertaking cross-examination of witnesses. In most cases, however, the Examining Authority undertake the examination without the appointment of either assessors or lawyers.

Procedural rules

The Examination Procedure Rules provide more detail as to the procedure for, and conduct of, both the preliminary meeting and the examination in general.

The preliminary meeting

Rule 6 of the Examination Procedure Rules requires at least 21 days' notice to be given of the date, time and place of the preliminary meeting. This notice is commonly known as the 'rule 6 letter', and will include:

- a list of the matters to be discussed at the preliminary meeting; and
- the draft examination timetable.

It is for the Examining Authority to determine what is discussed at the preliminary meeting, and how much time will be allocated for each matter (rule 7).

As soon as practicable after the preliminary meeting the Examining Authority must prepare a note of the meeting and make it available to all interested parties and those who attended the meeting itself.

Conduct of the examination

The timetable for the examination is set by the Examining Authority, either at the preliminary meeting or as soon as practicable after it has ended. Rule 8 of the Examination Procedure Rules requires the following matters (amongst others) to be specified in that timetable:

- the date for receipt of written representations;
- the timing of any written questions from the Examining Authority;
- the timing of any opportunity for the applicant and other interested parties to comment on relevant and written representations, and responses to written questions received by the Examining Authority;
- the timing of statements of common ground;
- the date for any interested party to give notice of a wish to be heard at an open floor hearing;
- the date for any affected person to give notice of a wish to be heard at a compulsory acquisition hearing;
- the date of any ISH; and
- the date for receipt of any local impact report.

This initial timetable is commonly varied during the course of the examination, most often by the addition of further ISHs. Although the discretion to vary the timetable given by rule 8(3) is expressed in broad terms, in practice most Examining Authorities are very reluctant to extend deadlines that have been set or to defer or rearrange hearings identified in the initial timetable. This seems to be a result of the pressure imposed by the six-month deadline, rather than any specific concern for the potential impact (or lack of impact) on any other party to the examination. The reluctance to make even relatively minor adjustments to the timetable can cause practical problems, for applicants in particular, if, for example, their advocate or witnesses are unavailable for the date(s) set for hearings.

Rules 9 to 13 of the Examination Procedure Rules contain various requirements as to giving notice of: procedural decisions; the making of written representations; the appointment of assessors and lawyers; and hearings.

Procedure at hearings is governed by rule 14, which is examined in more detail in articles 85 to 87 of this work that relate to the different types of hearing. In brief, it provides that the Examining Authority determines the procedure at the hearing and then sets out a series of specific rules, as summarised below:

- At the start of the hearing the Examining Authority identifies:
  - the matters to be considered;
  - the persons entitled to make oral representations; and
  - the persons permitted to make oral representations.

  In practice, this is generally done by way of the publication of a written agenda for each hearing, a week or so in advance of the hearing.
- Oral representations must be based on either the relevant or written representations that have been made. In other words, oral representations should not be used to introduce new issues (subject to the discretion allowed in rule 14(4)). The practical policing of this rule is not always straightforward, because simply repeating what has been said in writing is of little utility or purpose, and there can be a fine line between elaborating upon or explaining an objection and introducing points not previously canvassed in writing.

- Oral questioning of witnesses is undertaken by the Examining Authority, and not those representing interested parties, except where the Examining Authority decides that this would be necessary in order to ensure:
  - adequate testing of any representation; or
  - that the party in question has a fair chance to put its case.

  Cross-examination by advocates representing the parties is, therefore, the exception rather than the rule. There have been a number of instances where this has been allowed (eg Navitus Bay, Thames Tideway Tunnel and Manston Airport), but generally speaking it tends to be a less effective tool in hearings under the PA 2008 than it is in public inquiries. There are perhaps two main reasons.

  Firstly, the time allowed for such questioning in what tends to be a packed agenda is often very limited (see rule 14(6), which allows the Examining Authority to bring questioning to an end if it is imperilling the timetable). Advocates are thus constrained in their ability to develop points and to set the ground for key questions.

  Secondly, unlike a public inquiry, the end of the oral examination of a witness's evidence does not mark the end of their ability to give further evidence. ISHs will be followed by multiple opportunities to submit further written evidence and representations on issues covered during the hearing itself. Unhelpful answers given in oral evidence can therefore be qualified and/or supplemented or otherwise addressed by further written submissions prepared with the benefit of more time and consideration. Any damage done by an advocate in the limited time allowed during the hearing is thus easier to repair.

The Examining Authority is able to undertake unaccompanied site inspections without notice, but must give notice to all interested parties when it proposes to undertake an accompanied site visit (rule 16).

DCLG/PINS Guidance

DCLG has published non-statutory guidance on the examination process. The most recent guidance is contained in 'Planning Act 2008: Guidance for the examination of applications for development consent' (March 2015) ('the DCLG Guidance on examinations').

PINS has also published its own advice in the following Advice Notes:

- PINS Advice Note 8.3: Influencing how an application is Examined: the Preliminary Meeting (version 4);
- PINS Advice Note 8.4: The Examination (version 6);
- PINS Advice Note 8.5: The Examination: hearings and site inspections (version 4); and
- PINS Advice Note 8.6: Virtual examination events (version 1).

The preliminary meeting

The key points to note from the DCLG Guidance on examinations (2015) and the PINS Advice Notes are as follows:

- The meeting can be used to get a better understanding of the approach to take in examining the issues, but will not discuss the merits of the application or involve a substantive discussion on a particular issue (DCLG Guidance, para 41).

- Investing time ahead of the examination to identify issues and work out how best to consider them is vital to ensuring an effective and efficient examination process (DCLG Guidance, para 42).
- Ahead of the meeting the Examining Authority will circulate its own initial assessment of what are the principal issues, but this is not definitive. It can also identify those issues which it considers either do not need to be considered, or at least not in great detail, during the examination process (DCLG Guidance, para 43).
- PINS Advice Note 8.3 (version 4) includes helpful practical guidance for those unfamiliar with the process, including as to the layout of the room (theatre-style), seating arrangements, microphones etc. It also explains the availability of an audio recording of the meeting itself (a feature of all hearings conducted during the examination), and warns against attempts to use the meeting for making political statements or debating the merits of the application.

Conduct of the examination

The DCLG Guidance on examinations (2015) and the PINS Advice Notes provide advice on all aspects of the examination, and this is covered in articles 84 to 87 of this work on particular types of hearings and statements of common ground. Those points are not repeated here.

Further practical points about preliminary meetings

Applicants and interested parties objecting to the application will generally approach the preliminary meeting and the associated procedural decisions with quite different objectives in mind.

For an applicant, the objective might be summarised as seeking a quiet and uneventful examination, with as few hearings as possible. Hearings are inherently less easy to control than the process of written representations, particularly in terms of what witnesses for the applicant might say in response to questions. The decision to hold an ISH, in and of itself, suggests that the Examining Authority considers that an issue is not straightforward and that written representations alone will not suffice to get to the bottom of it.

For an objecting interested party, this means that an important objective will generally be to try and secure an ISH (preferably more than one) at which its concerns can be more fully explained and explored. To that end, it may well wish to make the issues seem as complex and fraught with difficulty as possible. Even if the interested party is ultimately seeking only some adjustment to the draft order and/or protective provisions, there is much to be gained, in terms of negotiating leverage, from applying pressure on the time and resources of the applicant during the examination process.

For all parties, however, attendance at the preliminary meeting is important because this is the first opportunity to see the individuals who make up the Examining Authority and to try and discern, from what they say (and how they say it), any signals as to their initial reaction to the application, the representations submitted and the issues arising. Sometimes these signals are subtle, sometimes unmistakeable.

Article 84

Statements of Common Ground

James Pereira QC, ftb
Michael Humphries QC, ftb

Introduction

Paragraph 58 of the DCLG Guidance for the examination of applications for development consent (2015) ('DCLG Guidance on examinations') describes a statement of common ground in the following way:

> 'A statement of common ground is a written statement prepared jointly by the applicant and another party or parties, setting out any matters on which they agree. As well as identifying matters which are not in real dispute, it may also be useful for a statement to identify areas where agreement has not been reached. The statement should include references to show where those matters are dealt with in the written representations or other documentary evidence.'

Statements of common ground are given legislative recognition in rule 8 of the Infrastructure Planning (Examination Procedure) Rules 2010, which provides that among the matters to be included in the timetable which is set at, or shortly after, the Preliminary Meeting on the DCO application is the period within which the applicant and any interested party must agree a statement of common ground.

The purpose of a statement of common ground

Statements of common ground are useful documents to assist the parties and the Examining Authority in identifying and understanding what are the issues of dispute and what are the issues that are agreed between the parties to the statement. This is useful to ensure that the evidence and the examination focus on the material differences between the parties. The effective use of such statements is expected to lead to a more efficient examination process.

The form and content of a statement of common ground

A statement of common ground is a written statement prepared jointly by the parties to the statement. It will usually be signed by a representative from each party. It is possible for the parties to an examination to enter into more than one statement of common ground, and for there to be different statements of common ground between different parties.

The content of a statement of common ground will depend upon the subject-matter of the statement, which in turn will depend upon the issues raised by the particular application. Paragraphs 61 and 62 of the DCLG Guidance on examinations (2015) advise as follows:

> 'The statement should be clear about the basic information on which the parties have agreed, such as the precise nature of the proposed infrastructure, a description of the

site and its planning history. Effective cross-referencing of other application documents should be used in order to avoid duplication between documents and keep the volume of examination material to the necessary minimum.

In addition to basic information agreement can often be reached on technical matters and topics that rely on basic statistical data. For example, the evidence to be submitted on traffic flows. Ideally, agreement should also be sought before the examination commences about any requirements (i.e. conditions) that should be attached to a Development Consent Order if granted.'

The following points should be noted:

- It would be usual for there to be statements of common ground between the applicant for the DCO and the main statutory parties who are relevant to the application. This might include, for example, bodies such as the local planning authority, the local highway authority, the Environment Agency, Natural England, Natural Resources Wales, Historic England and, where appropriate, the Marine Management Organisation.
- Cross-referencing to other documents that are before the Examining Authority, or annexing documents that support propositions in the statement of common ground, can be a useful means of increasing the weight that such documents carry. It also helps the reader of the statement to understand the basis of the agreement (or disagreement), which in turn will help to shape the examination process.
- Statements of common ground are often made on a topic or issue basis. For example, in any one application there may be a statement of common ground setting out a general description of the project, another statement of common ground on pre-application procedures, another on noise impacts, another on nature conservation matters, and so on.
- In cases where the statement of common ground concerns matters of expert evidence and opinion, it is good practice for it to be signed by the parties' relevant experts, and for it to carry an appropriate experts' declaration. This will assist the examining authority in assessing the weight to be given to the statement, and will help it decide who to question about the statement, should questioning be necessary.

The timing of a statement of common ground

It is usual for the Examining Authority to set a deadline for the submission of statements of common ground in the formal 'Rule 8 letter' which is sent out following a Preliminary Meeting. However, the early submission of statements of common ground is encouraged, and applicants are advised that they need not wait until the start of the examination period to prepare or submit statements of common ground. The DCLG Guidance on examinations (2015) gives particular encouragement to reaching agreement about any requirements (ie conditions) that should be attached to a development consent order if granted before the examination commences.

Preparing a statement of common ground

There is no set way of preparing a statement of common ground. Paragraph 63 of the DCLG Guidance on examinations (2015) advises as follows:

'How such agreement is reached will vary depending on the nature and complexity of the application and the matters at issue. Where there are only two or three major parties involved and the issues are fairly straightforward, the Examining Authority is likely to expect the parties to have considered producing a statement of common ground containing agreed facts or setting out those areas where agreement will not be reached. For more complex applications it is likely that the Examining Authority will expect the applicant to agree a number of statements of common ground with different parties, each focused on separate aspects of the application.'

It is to be remembered that the parties are expected to co-operate with the examination process, and hence in the preparation of statements of common ground. Where the statements involve matters of expert opinion, any experts involved in preparing the statement of common ground should do so in accordance with their overriding duty to the Examining Authority.

The effect of a statement of common ground

It is important to recognise that the Examining Authority is not bound to accept the contents of a statement of common ground, nor are participants in the examination process who are not parties to the statement. Parties to statements of common ground therefore need to be prepared to answer questions on the contents of the statement and to justify the agreement reached.

As paragraph 64 of the DCLG Guidance on examinations (2015) makes clear:

> '... the duty of the Examining Authority is not simply to accept the statement of common ground or to react to the evidence presented. The role of the Examining Authority is to ensure that all aspects of any given matter are explored thoroughly, especially with regard to the matters fundamental to the decision, rather than simply accepting the statement of common ground without question.
>
> Consequently, the Examining Authority should probe the evidence thoroughly if their judgement or professional expertise indicates that either:
>
> - all of the evidence necessary for a soundly reasoned decision has not been put before them, or
> - that a material part of the evidence in front of them has not been adequately tested.'

However, it is important that any questioning or challenge to the statement of common ground from the Examining Authority is conducted fairly. It is good practice to ensure that fair, advanced, warning is given by the Examining Authority of any questioning or examination of matters that are agreed in the statement of common ground. In extreme cases, where the parties have proceeded on the basis that an issue is agreed but the decision-maker goes back on that agreement in its decision without giving fair warning to the parties, and without allowing them to comment, the courts may be prepared to quash the decision as being procedurally unfair: see *Edward Ware New Homes v Secretary of State for Transport, Local Government and the Regions* [2003] EWCA Civ 566, where an Inspector's decision letter following a planning appeal was quashed because he had reached a contrary view on an issue which was agreed in the statement of common ground between the parties at the inquiry, and which had not been treated as controversial at the inquiry, without giving the parties the opportunity to comment first.

Article 85

Issue Specific Hearings

Hereward Phillpot QC, ftb
Michael Humphries QC, ftb

Introduction

Issue Specific Hearings ('ISHs') have a very important role in the examination of applications, but it is important to understand how they fit into what is an essentially written process. Whilst, under the Town and Country Planning Act 1990 regime, a planning inquiry will form the centrepiece of the process of gathering, reviewing and testing evidence, a PA 2008 examination is often said to be primarily a written process.

That is not to say that ISHs are unimportant, because they should be arranged only if the Examining Authority concludes they are needed to get to the bottom of important issues that it cannot resolve satisfactorily on the basis of the written material, or to enable a party to have a fair chance to put its case. However, the format and approach can lead to some frustration for those who are more familiar with an inquiry-based system of scrutiny. It is important, therefore, not to focus too heavily on the ISH as representing the main opportunity to make your case, to the detriment of making your written submissions as clear, effective and persuasive as possible.

The conduct of ISHs will naturally vary to some extent depending on the individual case, the personalities and approach of those involved (both members of the Examining Authority and advocates), and the nature of the issues being examined. Nevertheless, some essential common characteristics can be identified, and are important in terms of what to expect and how to participate effectively. These are explained below.

Good practice in this field is evolving, but after more than 10 years of examinations it is becoming clearer what tends to work well and what does not. This article summarises the formal requirements governing the conduct of ISHs, and the available advice and guidance, before offering some thoughts on good practice based on experience of the system so far.

Requirements

PA 2008

PA 2008, s 91 makes provision for ISHs. It is for the Examining Authority to decide if an ISH is necessary in relation to a particular issue, and it must make that decision in accordance with the following criteria in PA 2008, s 91(1):

> '... in order to ensure–
>
> (a) adequate examination of the issue, or
>
> (b) that an interested party has a fair chance to put the party's case.'

The purpose of an ISH is to enable the Examining Authority to receive oral representations about the issue (PA 2008, s 91(2)). An ISH must be held in public (PA 2008, s 94(2)(a)).

At the ISH, each interested party is entitled, subject to the Examining Authority's powers of control over the conduct of the hearing, to make oral representations about the issue (PA 2008, s 91(3)).

The Examining Authority has discretion as to how the ISH is to be conducted, including whether to allow cross-examination and, if so, on what matters, and the time allowed for making representations and for any cross-examination (PA 2008, s 94(3) and (4)). That discretion is subject to any rules made under PA 2008, s 97, and to PA 2008, s 94(6) which states that the Examining Authority's powers 'may not be exercised so as to deprive the person entitled [to make oral representations] of all benefit of the entitlement'. So far, there has been no case law on what might constitute depriving an interested party of 'all benefit' of the entitlement to make oral representations.

The presumption is that all oral questioning of those making representations at an ISH should be undertaken by the Examining Authority, except where it thinks that cross-examination by another person is necessary to ensure adequate testing of any representations, or that a person has a fair chance to put their case (PA 2008, s 94(7)).

The Examining Authority may refuse to allow representations that it considers: to be irrelevant, vexatious or frivolous; to relate to the merits of policy in an NPS; to repeat other representations made (in any form); or to relate to compensation for compulsory acquisition (PA 2008, s 94(8)).

There is a power to exclude those who behave in a disruptive manner, or to make their continued participation subject to conditions (PA 2008, s 95(1)).

Procedural rules

The Infrastructure Planning (Examination Procedure) Rules 2010 ('the Examination Procedure Rules') make further provision governing the conduct of hearings, including ISHs.

Rule 14(2) of the Examination Procedure Rules obliges the Examining Authority to identify at the start of the hearing the matters to be considered. In practice, this is invariably supplemented by means of the circulation of a written agenda in advance, so that participants have a reasonable opportunity to prepare.

Any oral representations must be based on either the relevant or written representations made by the party in question, although the Examining Authority retains a discretion to allow interested parties to refer to other issues that it considers relevant to the examination, whether these were raised in the relevant or written representations (and regardless of whether they were identified by the Examining Authority at the start of the hearing) (rule 14(4)).

Rule 14(5) reflects the presumption against cross-examination by interested parties in PA 2008, s 94(7), but this is supplemented in the rules by the following:

> 'The Examining authority may refuse to permit the oral questioning of persons giving evidence, or may require such questioning to cease, if it appears to the Examining authority that permitting such questioning or allowing it to continue (as the case may be) would have the effect that the timetable referred to in rule 8 could not be met.'

Rule 8 of the Examination Procedure Rules refers to the timetable for the examination set by the Examining Authority at the preliminary meeting, or as soon as practicable after the end of that meeting.

This sets up an interesting tension in terms of ensuring that interested parties have a fair hearing. Cross-examination by interested parties will only be allowed (rule 14(5)) where the Examining Authority has concluded that it:

> 'is necessary to ensure–
>
> (a) adequate testing of any representation; or
>
> (b) that [the interested party] has a fair chance to put [its] case.'

Hence, rule 14(6) contemplates a situation whereby an Examining Authority decides that, without cross-examination, an interested party would not have a fair chance to put its case, and/or a representation would not be adequately tested, but nevertheless prevents it from happening. It is easy to see how, in those circumstances, the interested party might feel aggrieved at the overall fairness of the procedure, and may well wish to consider options for legal challenge.

Guidance and advice

DCLG Guidance for the examination of applications for development consent (2015) ('DCLG Guidance on examinations') includes some limited guidance on the conduct of ISHs.

Although hearings will normally take place during the working day and early evenings, the DCLG Guidance on examinations (2015) does provide that the Examining Authority may exceptionally hold hearings late in the evening or at weekends (para 81). So far, the author is not aware of any ISHs taking place at the weekend but there have been at least some ISHs that have gone on beyond 9pm (eg at the examination into the Thames Tideway Tunnel).

Paragraphs 90 to 102 of the DCLG Guidance on examinations (2015) provide guidance on the procedure to be followed at hearings, including ISHs. It is important to read this part of the DCLG Guidance as a whole and in context, but the main points can be summarised as follows:

- In most cases the applicant will give evidence first, and will have the final right of reply.
- The Examining Authority must be even-handed in allocating time for the making of oral submissions, to ensure that reasonable time is allowed.
- Where a number of those attending the hearing are likely to wish to repeat others' representations, the Examining Authority will encourage them to work together to agree a spokesperson to put forward a case on everyone's behalf.
- Questioning by the Examining Authority is intended to probe, test and assess the evidence. It should be truth-seeking, but the approach should not be aggressively adversarial.
- The Examining Authority will formulate its questions in light of discussions with interested parties, most likely at the preliminary meeting.
- Where an interested party is permitted to cross-examine another, there is no presumption that reciprocal rights will apply.
- If an interested party is aggrieved by a rejection of their request to be allowed to cross-examine, they may challenge the Examining Authority's decision by way of a claim for judicial review (note, however, the provisions of PA 2008, s 118(7) as to the timing of legal challenges, which is considered in article 97 of this work).

- In addition to bringing cross-examination to an end where continuation could jeopardise the timetable, the Examining Authority may also do so if the questioning 'becomes aggressively adversarial'. No guidance is offered as to what might constitute 'aggressively' adversarial cross-examination (adversarial cross-examination does not, in itself, appear to be regarded as problematic).
- There is no automatic right for an interested party to call witnesses to corroborate their evidence, but they can be helpful in ensuring adequate and proper examination of the issues and may provide a fairer chance to some interested parties to make their case. Examining Authorities should not, therefore, unreasonably deny applications for a witness to take part in the examination.
- Hearings can be recorded and filmed using electronic and social media, provided it is done reasonably and does not disrupt proceedings.

PINS Advice Note 8.5 (version 4) also provides some useful practical guidance in relation to ISHs (at paras 3.1 to 3.3 and 5.1 to 10.1). In the main, it covers the same ground as the DCLG Guidance, but it does add more detailed guidance on the following points:

- The layout of the room for an ISH, and seating.
- Recording of the hearing for the public record.
- Practical arrangements for registering an intention to speak in advance.
- Catering for those with specific needs in relation to the venue of the hearing (eg accessibility).
- Discouraging the submission of written comments at the hearing.

Note also that, following the need for social distancing as a consequence of the Covid-19 pandemic, PINS also introduced specific advice on 'Virtual examination events': see PINS Advice Note 8.6 (version 1).

Good practice

The nature and format of an ISH, and its role within the overall examination, impose certain constraints on participants. It is important to understand these, and their implications in terms of what constitutes good practice.

The constraints and associated challenges arise as a result of three main factors:

(1) Time is limited. Most ISHs will be one day in length, with even a two-day ISH being relatively unusual. The sitting day will generally start at 10am, with short mid-morning and mid-afternoon breaks and an hour for lunch, and will finish at around 5pm. There may be a number of interested parties who wish to speak on any agenda item, and agendas can be lengthy. This inevitably limits how much time each individual speaker will be allowed on each item.

(2) The agenda and thus focus of the discussion is controlled by the Examining Authority. The Examining Authority will often decide to hold an ISH because it wishes to have an opportunity to probe further into certain issues and evidence – it is not an opportunity for interested parties to present their cases on matters not on the agenda.

(3) The ISH is not intended to be used to introduce new evidence and issues. Participants should refer to and rely upon the evidence and written submissions that are already before the

Examining Authority. The existing evidence and submissions will generally be voluminous, and will have developed through the different stages of the examination process, including the submission of written representations, answers to written questions and responses to representations and answers submitted by others. Relevant material will therefore be scattered across numerous different documents, and piecing all of this together in a coherent way can be challenging.

Against that background, the author's suggestions as to what constitutes good practice are organised into four themes: be prepared, be organised, be succinct, and be helpful.

Be prepared

Study the agenda

Some agendas are more detailed than others. Preparation is easier and more effective where the Examining Authority has circulated a detailed agenda, with specific issues and focused questions identified for examination. Participants can then work out what they wish to say about each item, without having to spend time (and money) on unnecessary work preparing to deal with any and every issue that might come up under a particular broad heading.

Where the agenda is less detailed, with broad headings identified rather than detailed and specific issues, it can be helpful to look at the Examining Authority's written questions and the written submissions of the main interested parties on that topic, and seek to identify those points likely to be raised. Preparation can then focus on preparing what should be said on each of those points. That process can be worthwhile even if the agenda is detailed, because the Examining Authority's concerns and views tend to be revealed by the written questions they ask, and reviewing the representations of interested parties helps in preparing responses to points that they may raise on the day.

Identify speakers and support speakers

If you have a team of speakers (because there are witnesses to speak on certain issues), a key task will be identifying who within your team will take the lead on any particular agenda item, and who needs to be available and ready to speak on specific sub-issues, depending on where discussion leads.

This is more than simply avoiding an awkward silence and confusion when the Examining Authority seeks your view; it is also about ensuring that responsibility for preparing and delivering the response is clearly allocated in advance. Nothing sharpens the mind quite like knowing that you will be the one on the spot.

Some issues will be suitable for submission by advocates on the basis of instruction, but others may require evidence from suitably expert and experienced witnesses. It will be important, ahead of the ISH, to identify where that is the case, and thus which experts need to attend and be ready to speak.

On the day, each member of the team who speaks will need to identify themselves before they do so, in order that those listening to the audio recording can understand who said what. In addition, it is helpful to provide the Examining Authority and other participants with a typed list of speakers, together with their qualifications and the topics that they will address.

Identify where additional evidence/information is needed

Preparing for an ISH can lead to the identification of areas where it would be advantageous to submit further evidence or information.

In an examination, such opportunities are limited, and only occur at those stages that are provided for by the timetable. The ISH is not itself an opportunity to submit that evidence or information, but it can sometimes be used to create an opportunity for its submission. For example, part of the response to a particular agenda item may be to offer to provide the Examining Authority with a written submission or note on a specific point as part of the written summary of submissions made at the ISH. Examining Authorities often welcome such offers.

Prepare a speaking note

While each member of the team who has been given a speaking role will no doubt wish to prepare their own personal speaking note, it can be helpful to have a common shared speaking note to co-ordinate the individual contributions.

For example, the shared speaking note can identify the following for each agenda item:

- Lead speaker and support speakers.
- Main issues and sub-issues.
- Summary of the response to be given on each main issue and sub-issue.
- Key document references within the examination library.

Be organised

Document management

In a public inquiry the evidence and documents tend to be available and referred to in hard copy format, often stored in boxes on and around a large table or tables for the Inspector, advocates and witnesses. ISHs are different.

The Examining Authority may well have a small sample of key documents or plans in hard copy with them in the room, but mostly they will work from the electronic versions of the documents. When they need to look at a document, they will ask for it to be displayed on their screens and on the large screen behind them visible to those in attendance at the ISH.

Participants at the ISH will generally not have space for much in the way of hard copy documentation (let alone sufficient boxes to accommodate the voluminous material that they may need to have available). There will often be, at most, one or two chairs available at the table for each participant, with no tables available for those sitting behind in a support role and/or preparing to take their turn at the table on a particular issue.

The inevitable consequence of these constraints is that participants need to work primarily from the electronic document library. There should be space for a limited number of files of key documents in hard copy on the table, but there is unlikely to be much more.

All members of the team need to think through the practical implications of these constraints in advance, and how best to adapt to them.

If submissions or oral evidence on a particular topic will require people to look at a particular document, make sure that the examination library reference number of that document is identified and preferably provided at the start of the day to the individual tasked with putting the relevant documents on to the screens used by the Examining Authority. This will make for a quicker and smoother presentation, and avoid precious time being wasted while documents are located.

Typically, Examining Authorities will not allow new documents to be introduced during an ISH, although exceptions are sometimes allowed where other parties are not disadvantaged.

Be succinct

Consider how many agenda items there are, and what that means for the time that will be available for each one. Also consider how many of those invited to attend are likely to be represented, and the nature and extent of their likely participation. Will they be represented by an advocate? Do they have particular expertise and knowledge that will make them an important participant in the discussion of some agenda items (eg the Environment Agency on flooding issues)? This will enable a broad understanding of how much time you might realistically be allowed to provide your own contribution. It will often be limited to five minutes or less for each participant per agenda item.

There may be some items where longer is allowed but, as a general rule, speakers need to keep what they say reasonably brief and to the point.

Experienced advocates and witnesses should have a fairly well-developed idea of how long it will take them to deliver oral representations based on their notes. For those who are new to the experience, it can often take longer than they anticipate – particularly if their progress is interrupted by the need to respond to interventions by the Examining Authority. Timed rehearsal can help.

Be helpful

The main purpose of an ISH is generally to help the Examining Authority in its investigation and consideration of the issues arising. It is the Examining Authority's hearing, and they will expect participants to help them to get the information they consider that they need and have not been able to extract from the written exchanges.

The Examining Authority has a job to do. It is demanding and time consuming and, before any judgments can be made in their report to the Secretary of State about the issues in dispute, it is necessary for them to understand (and summarise in writing, with references) the key points relied on by each side and the relevant evidence. Many issues will require consideration of what should be included within the Development Consent Order (whether in terms of the description of particular works, requirements and/or protective provisions). Keep that in mind when preparing oral presentations and in drafting the written summary that is submitted after the ISH. For example, if you want a concern to be reflected in the order, it will be important (indeed, essential) to provide a suitable form of words that could be added to the order to address the point.

An ISH is also a valuable opportunity for applicants and other interested parties to obtain a clearer sense of what is on the Examining Authority's mind(s), and a more detailed understanding of what they are particularly interested in and concerned about, and why. Picking up and responding to these signals is essential to effective participation in the examination process overall. This is not just a matter of courtesy and good practice, it is also important in maximising your prospects of persuading the Examining Authority of the merits of your position.

Article 86

Compulsory Acquisition Hearings

Richard Honey, ftb
Michael Humphries QC, ftb

Introduction

PA 2008, s 92 imposes a duty on an Examining Authority to hold a compulsory acquisition hearing (CAH) where one is duly requested by an 'affected person'; that is, a person with an interest in land. This is in contrast to the holding of an Issue Specific Hearing, which is at the discretion of an Examining Authority.

Requiring a compulsory acquisition hearing

Where an application for a development consent order (DCO) includes a request for authorisation of compulsory acquisition of land or an interest in or right over land, the Examining Authority 'must' fix, and cause each 'affected person' to be informed of, the deadline by which an affected person must notify the Secretary of State that the person wishes a CAH to be held (PA 2008, s 92(2)).

PA 2008, s 92(5) defines an 'affected person' by reference to PA 2008, s 59(4) which states that 'A person is an affected person … if the applicant, after making diligent inquiry, knows that the person is interested in the land to which the compulsory acquisition request relates or any part of that land'.

At, or as soon as practical after the end of, the Preliminary Meeting for an examination held pursuant to PA 2008, s 88, rule 8 of the Infrastructure Planning (Examination Procedure) Rules 2010 ('the Examination Procedure Rules') requires the Examining Authority to set the timetable for the examination of the application, including '(g) the date by which any affected person must notify the Examining authority or their wish to be heard at a compulsory acquisition hearing'. This timetable is set out in what is generally known as the Examining Authority's Rule 8 letter. Rule 13 of the Examination Procedure Rules provides that at least 21 days' notice must be given of a deadline for an affected person to give notice requesting a CAH.

If any such a request for a CAH is duly made by an 'affected person', then PA 2008, s 92(3) provides that a CAH 'must' be held. The Examination Procedure Rules also provide that at least 21 days' notice must be given to an affected person of the date, time and place of the CAH itself (rule 13(3)). In practice, considerably more notice is likely to be given.

Arrangements for a compulsory acquisition hearing

The Preliminary Meeting held under rule 7 will usually consider, where necessary, how CAHs are to be arranged and timetabled, prior to the timetable actually being issued. Even before then, it is normal for persons to have indicated in their relevant representations whether they qualify as an affected person and whether they would like a CAH to be held.

It is possible for the Examining Authority to consider all compulsory acquisition requests relating to the same application at the same CAH, although it can also convene separate CAHs (rule 15(2)).

The conduct of a compulsory acquisition hearing

It is for the Examining Authority to decide how a CAH is to be conducted (PA 2008, s 94(3)). Within that context, however, both the applicant and each affected person are 'entitled' to make oral representations about the compulsory acquisition of land at a CAH (PA 2008, s 92(4)).

The DCLG Guidance for the examination of applications for development consent (2015) ('DCLG Guidance on examinations') states that a CAH is intended to consider the issues arising in connection with the authorisation of the compulsory acquisition of land (para 31). It also says that affected persons 'may make oral representations about the compulsory acquisition requests' (para 87) and that 'a key matter to be considered will be whether there is a compelling case in the public interest for the compulsory acquisition of land' (para 91).

The general provisions in relation to hearings at a DCO examination are found in PA 2008, ss 94, 95 and 95A. A hearing must be in public (PA 2008, s 94(2)). The Examining Authority has the power to decide how the hearing is to be conducted. PA 2008, s 94(4) states that it is for the authority to decide whether a person making oral representations may be questioned, and the matters on which they may be questioned, as well as the amount of time for making representations and asking questions. PA 2008, s 94(7) goes on to provide that the Examining Authority must apply the principle that any oral questioning should be undertaken by the Examining Authority itself, except where the it thinks that oral questioning by another person is necessary in order to ensure 'adequate testing of any representations' or 'that a person has a fair chance to put the person's case'. The Examining Authority can refuse to allow representations to be made at a hearing for a number of reasons, including that they relate to compensation for compulsory acquisition of land or of an interest in or right over land (PA 2008, s 94(8)).

The Examination Procedure Rules set more detailed rules for the conduct of hearings. Rule 14(2) obliges the Examining Authority to identify at the start of any hearing the matters to be considered at the hearing and any matters on which they require further explanation. Rule 14(3) provides that oral representations must be based on representations submitted in writing earlier in the process, but rule 14(4) allows other issues to be referred to. Rule 14(9) entitles an affected person to be represented by any other person at a hearing.

The DCLG Guidance on examinations (2015) provides that hearings should be 'carried out as efficiently as possible, whilst remaining fair to all parties and thorough in their examination of evidence' (para 90). In relation to compulsory acquisition, it is likely that the Examining Authority will allow more latitude to objectors than in other types of hearings, as they are subject to appropriation of land or rights against their will.

The DCLG Guidance on examinations (2015) provides that the examining authority 'will probe, test and assess the evidence through direct questioning of persons making oral representations' (para 96). The Examining Authority is able to appoint a barrister or solicitor itself to test evidence through oral questioning. The DCLG Guidance also says that the Examining authority may allow cross-examination 'where it considers that this is necessary to ensure the adequate testing of any representations, or where it considers that it is necessary to allow an interested party a fair chance to put their case' (para 98) and goes on to say that the authority 'will ensure that parties are not denied the opportunity to ask questions where the answers are required in order to complete their cases' (para 99).

It is possible for the Examining Authority to allow witnesses to be called at CAHs. The DCLG Guidance explains that although there is no automatic right to call witnesses, the authority has the discretion to allow this to be done either by the authority of its own volition or upon the request of a party (para 101).

Whilst PA 2008, s 92 entitles certain parties to make 'oral representations' and PA 2008, s 94 places limits on the questioning of a person making oral representations other, that is, than by the Examining Authority itself, experience so far suggests that Examining Authorities do on occasion conduct CAHs in a reasonably formal way and, indeed, have allowed cross-examination of witnesses.

By contrast, other CAHs have been structured more like other hearings, that is, with an agenda of issues to be addressed in turn and very much led by the Inspector(s).

Perhaps the underlying message here is that the procedural rules are sufficiently flexible to allow a range of responses appropriate to the particular circumstances.

Article 87

Open Floor Hearings

Hereward Phillpot QC, ftb
Michael Humphries QC, ftb

Introduction

PA 2008, s 93 establishes a duty on the Examining Authority to cause an open floor hearing (OFH) to be held where one is duly requested by an interested party (IP). The purpose of an OFH is to hear, first hand, from IPs about their thoughts on the proposed development.

The Examining Authority must first fix and inform IPs of a deadline by which they must notify the Secretary of State of their wish to be heard at an OFH (PA 2008, s 93(1)). Where at least one notification has been received in time, the Examining Authority is obliged to cause an OFH to be held (PA 2008, s 93(2)), at which each IP is entitled to make oral representations about the application.

The deadline for the purposes of PA 2008, s 93(1) must be at least 21 days after the date on which notice of the deadline is given (Infrastructure Planning (Examination Procedure) Rules 2010 ('the Examination Procedure Rules'), r 13(1)). The Examining Authority must notify all IPs of the date of any OFH as soon as practicable after the expiry of the deadline (r 13(3)).

Procedural rules

The Examination Procedure Rules do not make very detailed provision for the procedure to be adopted at hearings, leaving the precise procedure to the discretion of the Examining Authority. They do, however, set some important ground rules, which apply to both OFHs and issue specific hearings (ISHs).

The Examining Authority shall determine the procedure at the hearing (rule 14(1)), identifying at the start of the hearing the matters to be considered, and any matters where it requires further explanation from IPs (rule 14(2)). That does not prevent additional matters being referred to during the hearing, subject to the Examining Authority's discretion as to how the hearing is to be conducted (rule 14(4)).

Any oral representations must be based on either the relevant or written representations made by or on behalf of the IP (rule 14(3)).

The Examining Authority may proceed with the OFH even if the IP who requested it does not attend (rule 14(7)).

DCLG Guidance and PINS Advice

The guidance on hearings (including OFHs) is provided in the DCLG Guidance on the examination of applications for development consent (2015).

The DCLG Guidance explains that, subject to the Examining Authority's powers of control over the conduct of the hearing, all IPs will have an opportunity to make oral representations about the application (para 89). However, it also underlines the point that it is for the Examining Authority to determine how the hearing is conducted, including the amount of time to be allowed for the making of a person's representations. The Examining Authority is expected generally to use its powers to ensure that hearings are carried out 'as efficiently as possible, whilst remaining fair to all parties and thorough in their examination of evidence' (para 90). In practice the emphasis has tended to be on efficiency and expedition, not only to keep the examination timetable on track, but also to try to make time for all IPs to have their say. IPs will generally be reminded that the process is primarily a written one, and that there is no need to repeat points that have already been made in writing.

Those with similar interests, who are likely to submit similar evidence, are encouraged to work to agree upon a spokesperson to put forward a joint case. Repetition of points is strongly discouraged (paras 24 and 95).

PINS Advice Note 8.5 (version 4) states (para 2.1) that OFHs tend to have a community focus and are an opportunity for individuals and community groups to speak directly to the Examining Authority. For larger projects that may be spread over a wider area, there may be more than one open floor hearing, held in different locations. However, as the name suggests they are open to any IP to attend and are not about a particular location or topic.

The Advice Note also makes the point (para 2.2) that there is usually no agenda for these hearings, but that (para 2.3), to ensure that everyone has a chance to speak, the Examining Authority might set a time limit for each person and may ask questions based on what has been said.

Practice at OFHs

The following points can be made about the emerging practice at OFHs:

- PINS makes audio recordings of the hearings, and these recordings (together with written summaries) are made available on the PINS website. Listening to these recordings provides an invaluable insight into how an OFH is likely to be conducted.
- The Examining Authority does not generally allow IPs to use the OFH as an opportunity to question the applicant.
- Responses by the applicant to points made by IPs at OFHs will generally be expected to be provided in writing in due course (sometimes alongside responses made to written representations).
- Therefore, whilst a representative of the applicant will usually be in attendance, this may well not be the applicant's advocate.
- If large numbers of IPs register a wish to speak at an OFH, then the time available for each IP will be correspondingly limited (for example, in some of the OFHs held in relation to EDF's application for its new nuclear power station at Hinkley Point in Somerset, a limit of three minutes per person was adopted). Objectors should therefore be aware that mass participation in an OFH may ultimately be counter-productive.
- Although there can be a temptation on the part of applicants to view OFHs as little more than an opportunity for objectors to let off steam (akin to hearing from members of the public in a planning inquiry under Town and Country Planning Act 1990, s 78), this would be a mistake. The Examining Authority appears to be very conscious of the additional burden placed upon its shoulders by the inquisitorial nature of the examination system and will tend

to pick up and pursue any apparently well-founded concerns raised by IPs. Applicants should therefore take care to note what is said at OFHs, particularly by members of the Examining Authority in response to concerns that are aired before them. In particular:

- Do the members of the Examining Authority appear to be interested in and/or sympathetic to particular points raised by IPs?
- What questions do the members of the Examining Authority ask IPs, and what (if any) further details emerge in answer to those questions?
- Are any reassurances given to IPs that particular issues that are raised will be a focus of later hearings (eg on requirements)?

Meritorious concerns raised by IPs at an OFH will generally be revisited by the Examining Authority at the relevant moment in ISHs later in the examination, and/or in written questions. A well-advised applicant will therefore pay heed to these advanced indications and prepare its responses accordingly.

Article 88

Site Inspections

Gregory Jones QC, ftb
Michael Humphries QC, ftb

Introduction

Site inspections are invariably carried out in respect of all planning appeals to the Planning Inspectorate whether the appeals are by way of written representations, hearings or public inquiry conducted under the Town and Country Planning Act 1990 (as amended) (TCPA 1990). Accordingly, whilst there is no direct case authority on the conduct of site inspections carried out by the Examining Authority under the PA 2008 or the Infrastructure Planning (Examination Procedure) Rules 2010 ('the Examination Procedure Rules') in respect of NSIPs, there is an established body of case law on the conduct of site inspections by planning inspectors.

In its Procedural Guide on Planning Appeals England (March 2021), PINS sets out general guidance on site inspections as they relate to applications and appeals under the Town and Country Planning Act 1990. Section 11 of PINS Advice Note 8.5 (version 4) contains specific advice on site inspections, as follows:

> '11.1 To fully understand the proposed development and the Examination of the application, the Examining Authority will visit the site of the proposed development.
>
> **Unaccompanied site inspections**
>
> 11.2 If the Examining Authority is able to view the site from public land, they are likely to carry out site inspection(s) without the company of any Interested Parties. After the unaccompanied site inspection(s) have taken place, a note of the date, time and location visited will be published on the relevant project page of the National Infrastructure Planning website.
>
> **Accompanied site inspections**
>
> 11.3 If the Examining Authority requires access to private land or require Interested Parties to be present at the visit to guide them or point out certain features, an accompanied visit will be arranged. The applicant is likely to be present and other Interested Parties may attend.
>
> 11.4 For practical reasons the number of attendees may be limited. Ultimately attendance is at the discretion of the Examining Authority and dependant on the landowner granting access. The Examining Authority will invite Interested Parties to indicate if they wish to attend the accompanied site inspection in advance. All requests to participate should be received by the deadline(s) specified in the Examination Timetable.
>
> **Notification of site inspections**
>
> 11.5 The notification will typically contain information about where and when the site visit will start from, any health and safety considerations, an itinerary for the day and travel arrangements.

> 11.6 Where a site inspection includes multiple sites (for example for a linear project such as a pipeline, railway or road) a minibus or similar may be provided to transport Interested Parties. In each case you should read the notification and speak to the case team if you have any questions about the arrangements.
>
> **Conduct at site inspections**
>
> 11.7 As with hearings, the conduct and timings of the site inspections are at the discretion of the Examining Authority. Unlike hearings, site inspections are not an opportunity for anyone to approach the Examining Authority and discuss the proposed development or its merits. The Examining Authority may, however, wish to ask parties to point out features of the site for the purpose of factual clarification.'

Helpful guidance on site inspections in the context of Town and Country Planning Act 1990 appeals is also contained in section D8 of the PINS 'Procedural Guide: Planning appeals – England' (March 2021).

Unaccompanied site inspections

It is common practice for the persons appointed to examine applications for development consent to make a site visit to familiarise themselves with the proposed development area: see paragraph 103 of the DCLG Guidance for the examination of applications for development consent (2015) ('DCLG Guidance on examinations').

Rule 16(1) of the Examination Procedure Rules provides that the Examining Authority may make an unaccompanied inspection of an application site before, or during the examination, without giving notice to the persons entitled to take part in the examination.

Such inspections are commonly known as an 'unaccompanied site inspection'. They frequently take place in ordinary planning appeals whether they are conducted by written representations, hearing or public inquiry.

The Examining Authority must ensure that it acts fairly and lawfully in the conduct of any site visits. Accordingly, the Examining Authority should, as matter of good practice, let the parties know what the Examining Authority has seen on the unaccompanied site visit. The best way to do this is to make a written record of the unaccompanied site visit available to the parties – it can be put on the hearing website – describing anything which it saw on the site visit which it considers might be of potential relevance to determination of the application. This allows the parties an opportunity to make representation about anything which the Examining Authority has seen.

In *R (London Borough of Haringey) v Secretary of State for Communities and Local Government, O.A Kwateng (Ebenezer Community Learning Centre)* [2008] EWHC 1201 (Admin), a planning inspector on a site inspection had observed that neighbouring buildings were being used for educational purposes and relied upon that fact in arriving at his decision to grant planning permission. The High Court quashed his decision, holding not only that it was unfair not to raise this new matter with the parties and allow them a fair opportunity to make representations upon it, but also because it subsequently proved that he had made an error of fact in assuming that the educational use was lawful or had been tolerated by the local planning authority. The same principles would appear to apply to a site inspection under the PA 2008.

An unaccompanied site visit might require the Examining Authority to gain access to the site from the owner of the site. The Examining Authority should be wary of engaging in any conversation other than normal pleasantries and certainly not discuss matters relating to the application with, or in the presence of, the owner or his representatives (see *Wilkson Properties Ltd v Royal Borough of Kensington and Chelsea* [2010] EWHC 3274; [2011] JPL 1083).

Accompanied site inspections

Rule 16(2) of the Examination Procedure Rules allows the Examining Authority 'before the completion of its examination of the application or specified matters, inspect any site to which the application or specified matters relate in the company of any interested party or their representative.' This power is more widely drafted than the power to carry out an unaccompanied site visit under rule 16(1). The former is restricted to an inspection of the application site, the latter permits the Examining Authority to conduct an accompanied site inspection to 'any site' to which 'the application or specified matters relate.' This may, for example, allow the Examining Authority, where such issues are relevant, to inspect sites which are said to be comparable sites, or alternatives sites, or sites which are said to be impacted by the proposed development.

It is important to note that rule 16(2) of the Examination Procedure Rules grants a power; it does not impose an obligation. Having said that, where a decision maker has a power, it has a corresponding duty to consider whether to exercise it (see eg *Stovin v Wise* [1996] 3 WLR 388). Thus, an Examining Authority is obliged, at least, to consider any request by an interested party to conduct an accompanied inspection at any such site coming within rule 16(2) of the Examination Procedure Rules. It is for the Examining Authority to determine whether such an inspection is required.

Sometimes landowners are reluctant to allow opposing parties to accompany inspectors on site visits. There are, indeed, instances where planning inspectors considering applications under the TCPA 1990 have gone on site inspections where third parties have been excluded from attending by the land owner. Such approach is said not to be unfair where the local planning authority that has refused to grant planning permission is also present on the site visit to represent the 'opposition side'. This view is open to considerable doubt.

In applications under the PA 2008, however, the role of the local planning authority is quite different and an Examining Authority should be extremely wary of conducting an accompanied site inspection where a particular party has been refused access by the landowner. An Examining Authority could refuse a request for an accompanied site inspection under rule 16(2) of the Examination Procedure Rules. This may not be a significant problem where the site in question is the application site because the Examining Authority has the power to go on an unaccompanied site inspection under rule 16(1) of the Examination Procedure Rules. However, the Examining Authority has no power to go on an unaccompanied site inspection of any site that is not part of the application site. In practice, a landowner who is a party to the proceedings would be well advised not to refuse access to the representatives of an opposing party, since the absence of an accompanied site inspection on their land is likely to tell against the landowner's case whether it be as a promoter or as objector to the NSIP application.

Not surprisingly, rule 16(3) of the Examination Procedure Rules provides that where the Examining Authority intends to make an accompanied site inspection 'it must notify all interested parties of the date, time and place at which it proposes to make the inspection.' However, rule 16(4) of the Examination Procedure Rules provides that the Examining Authority 'shall not be bound to defer an [accompanied site] inspection … *where an interested party is neither present nor represented at the time appointed*' (emphasis added). However, this does not mean that the Examining Authority can fix the time of the accompanied site visit without regard for the availability of the interested parties. Like any decision it must be exercised fairly and in a way which would not unfairly cause prejudice to any particular party.

Paragraph 105 of the DCLG Guidance on examinations (2015) makes clear that, 'The Examining Authority will refuse to hear evidence or other submissions during any accompanied visit. It is acceptable, however, for people to draw their attention to particular features of the site and its surroundings'. If something arises at the site inspection which is relevant and which has not been addressed at the hearing, the Examining Authority should, depending on the circumstances, either reopen the hearing or invite the matter to be addressed by the parties in writing, rather than discussing the matter with the representatives of the parties who happened to be at the site inspection (see *R (London Borough of Haringey) v Secretary of State for Communities and Local Government, O.A Kwateng (Ebenezer Community Learning Centre)* (above).

In *Fox v Secretary of State for the Environment* [1993] JPL 448 an inspector who travelled to a site inspection in a car with one of the parties was criticised by the High Court, as was the inspector who went for a drink with both parties and then stayed behind to finish his drink with the local planning authority witness when the applicant had finished up and left (*Cotterell v Secretary of State for the Environment* [1991] JPL 1155). In both cases the decisions were not quashed because the other party had known what had happened and agreed or waived his right to object. Nonetheless, it is not conduct to be encouraged, and the issue of apparent bias will be considered very carefully.

By contrast, it is respectfully suggested that the courts in England and Wales are unlikely to follow the approach recently adopted by the High Court of Northern Ireland in *Alternative A5 Alliance's Application for Judicial Review* [2013] NIQB 30, which found that there was no apparent bias where inspectors, on more than one occasion, rode in cars with officers employed in the promotion of a road scheme without notifying objectors or, still less, getting their consent.

Article 89

Procedures following Completion of Examination

Isabella Tafur, ftb
Michael Humphries QC, ftb

Introduction

The examination of a DCO application must be completed within six months from the day after the preliminary meeting. When the Examining Authority has completed its examination, it must inform each of the interested parties of that fact (PA 2008, s 99).

The focus of this article is on the procedure following completion of the examination.

Reporting to the Secretary of State

Within three months from the deadline for completion of the examination, or, if the examination closed earlier, within three months from the date of its closure, the Examining Authority must make a report to the Secretary of State, setting out its findings and conclusions in respect of the application, and its recommendation as to the decision to be made (PA 2008, s 98(3); Infrastructure Planning (Examination Procedure) Rules 2010 ('the Examination Procedure Rules'), rule 19).

There is no statutory provision governing the form of the Examining Authority's report. However, reports generally provide a file reference at the outset (summarising the dates on which the application was made, received and accepted; the dates on which the examination commenced and closed and a brief summary of the development), followed by a summary of the Examining Authority's recommendation and the main body of the report. With certain minor variations, the main body of the reports often follow a format such as this: introduction, main features of the proposal, legal and policy context, findings and conclusions on main issues, overall conclusion and recommendation on the case for development consent, compulsory acquisition, the development consent order, overall conclusions and recommendation.

Extending the deadline for the report

The period for making the report can be extended by the Secretary of State, who is empowered pursuant to PA 2008, s 98(4) to set a later date for any of the deadlines set out in PA 2008, s 98. The same deadline may be extended more than once, and can be extended even after the deadline has already passed (PA 2008, s 98(5)).

Where the power of extension is exercised, the Secretary of State must notify each interested party of the new deadline, must publicise a new deadline in such a manner as he thinks appropriate and must make a statement (either written or oral) to the House of Parliament of which he is a member, announcing the new deadline.

The Secretary of State's decision

Having received the report from the Examining Authority, the Secretary of State must make a decision on the application within three months of its receipt – or within three months of the deadline under PA 2008, s 98(3) – whichever is the earlier date (PA 2008, s 107(1)).

If the Secretary of State differs from the Examining Authority on any matter of fact mentioned in, or appearing to the Secretary of State to be material to, a conclusion reached by the Examining Authority, or if he takes into account new evidence or new matters of fact, and is for that reason disposed to disagree with a recommendation made by the Examining Authority, he must not come to a decision at variance with the recommendation without first notifying all interested parties of his disagreement with the Examining Authority and the reasons for it, and giving them an opportunity to make representations in writing in respect of any new evidence or new matter of fact (Examination Procedure Rules, rule 19(3)).

Extending the deadline for the decision

Similar to the power of extension under PA 2008, s 98(4), the Secretary of State is also empowered to extend the deadline for making his decision, pursuant to PA 2008, s 107(3). Again, he can extend a deadline more than once, and may extend it even after the date for the deadline has passed. If the deadline is extended, the Secretary of State must make a statement (either written or oral) to the House of Parliament of which he is a member, and must publish that statement in such a form and manner as he considers appropriate.

Experience so far

The power to extend the deadline for the Examining Authority to provide a report to the Secretary of State (PA 2008, s 98(4)) has not, so far as the authors are aware, been exercised in any of the DCO applications examined to date. By contrast, the power to extend the deadline for the Secretary of State to make a decision has been exercised on a number of occasions.

Article 90

Decision-making where an NPS 'has effect'

James Pereira QC, ftb
Michael Humphries QC, ftb

Introduction

Part 6 of the PA 2008 makes separate provision for the approach to decision-making in relation to an application for an order granting development consent depending on whether or not there is a relevant National Policy Statement ('NPS') that 'has effect' in relation to development of the description to which the application relates.

Section 104 of the PA 2008 applies where an NPS 'has effect' in relation to development of the description to which the application relates (PA 2008, s 104(1)).

The structure of PA 2008, s 104

PA 2008, s 104 contains three distinct parts:

(1) A list of matters to which the Secretary of State must 'have regard' when making a decision. This list is set out in PA 2008, s 104(2).

(2) A legal presumption in favour of the determination of an application 'in accordance with' a relevant NPS, subject to certain defined exceptions. This is found in PA 2008, s 104(3).

(3) A list of exceptions to the presumption in favour of determining an application in accordance with a relevant NPS. This list is found in PA 2008, s 104(4) to (8). In relation to these exceptions, PA 2008, s 104(9) makes it clear that the fact that a relevant NPS identifies a location as suitable (or potentially suitable) for a particular description of development does not prevent one or more of subsections (4) to (8) from applying.

Each of these three aspects of PA 2008, s 104 is considered below.

Matters to which the Secretary of State must have regard

PA 2008, s 104(2) contains a list of matters to which the Secretary of State must have regard in deciding an application for an order granting development consent.

These are:

- Any national policy statement which 'has effect' in relation to development of the description to which the application relates. This is called a 'relevant national policy statement': PA 2008, s 104(2)(a). There may be more than one relevant NPS for any given application. The expression 'has effect' is discussed further below.
- The appropriate marine policy documents (if any), determined in accordance with Marine and Coastal Access Act 2009, s 59: PA 2008, s 104(2)(aa). Marine policy documents are

policy documents applying to decisions that affect all or part of a UK marine area. Marine and Coastal Access Act 2009, s 59 sets out the criteria by which the appropriate marine policy documents for decision-making are to be identified.

- Any local impact report within the meaning given by PA 2008, s 60(3) which has been submitted to the Secretary of State before the deadline specified in a notice under PA 2008, s 60(2): PA 2008, s 104(2)(b). Local impact reports are discussed in article 81 of this work.
- Any matters prescribed in relation to development of the description to which the application relates: PA 2008, s 104(2)(c). The Infrastructure Planning (Decisions) Regulations 2010 (as amended) prescribe certain matters for the purposes of PA 2008, s 104(2)(c) as follows:
  - *Listed buildings, conservation areas and scheduled monuments* – Regulation 3 imposes duties similar to those which apply to determinations under the Town and Country Planning Acts.
  - *Deemed consents under the Marine and Coastal Access Act 2009* – Regulation 3A applies where a deemed marine licence has been applied for, and requires the Secretary of State to have regard to:
    - the need to protect the environment;
    - the need to protect human health; and
    - the need to prevent interference with legitimate uses of the sea.
  - *Hazardous substances* – Regulation 6 provides that, where the development would involve the presence of certain hazardous substances, the Secretary of State must have regard to:
    - any current or contemplated use of the land to which the application relates;
    - the way in which other land in the vicinity is being used or is likely to be used; and
    - any planning permission or development consent that has been granted for development of that other land in the vicinity.
  - *Biological diversity* – Regulation 7 requires the Secretary of State to have regard to the UN Environmental Programme Convention on Biological Diversity of 1992 (and, in Scotland, to any strategy designated under Nature Conservation (Scotland) Act 2004, s 2(1)).
- Any other matters which the Secretary of State regards as both important and relevant to his decision: PA 2008, s 104(2)(d). This provision gives the Secretary of State a general discretion to take into account other relevant matters, provided they are regarded as sufficiently important to consider as part of the determination.

The presumption in favour of an NPS

PA 2008, s 104(3) provides that the Secretary of State 'must' decide an application 'in accordance with' any 'relevant national policy statement', except to the extent that one or more of subsections (4) to (8) applies. By PA 2008, s 104(2)(a), any national policy statement which 'has effect' in relation to development of the description to which the application relates is a 'relevant national policy statement'.

The expression 'has effect' is worthy of some consideration. An NPS may not 'have effect' in relation to all forms of development to which it seemingly relates. Thus, NPS EN-1 states (para 1.4.5) that 'Insofar as this NPS has effect in relation to applications for development of new nuclear power stations, it only has effect in relation to applications for development of new nuclear power stations on sites listed in EN-6'.

As to the words 'in accordance with', it is clear that this means in accordance with any relevant NPS judged as a whole. In *R (Spurrier and others) v Secretary of State for Transport* [2019] EWHC 1070 (Admin) at [329], the Divisional Court held (original emphasis) that:

> 'Section 104(3) provides that "the Secretary of State must decide [an application for a DCO] *in accordance with* any relevant [NPS] ..."... The italicised phrase appears, analogously, in section 38(6) of the Planning and Compulsory Purchase Act 2004, which requires an application for planning permission to be determined "in accordance with the [development] plan ...". Just as that means "in accordance with the development plan *judged as whole*", as [Counsel for the Secretary of State] rightly submits, section 104(3) requires an application for a DCO to be decided in accordance with any relevant NPS *judged as a whole*, recognising that the statement's policies (or their application) may pull in different directions and that, for example, a breach of a single policy does not carry the consequence that the proposal fails to accord with the NPS (paragraph 4(2) of the Secretary of State's written submissions, citing *R v Rochdale Metropolitan Borough Council ex parte Milne* [2000] EWHC 650 (Admin); [2001] Env LR 22).'

On the similar presumption in the Planning and Compulsory Purchase Act 2004, s 38(6), the Supreme Court has said in *Suffolk Coastal District Council v Hopkins Homes Ltd* [2017] UKSC 37 at [8] (citing an earlier case):

> 'It has introduced a requirement with which the decision-maker must comply, namely the recognition of the priority to be given to the development plan. It has thus introduced a potential ground on which the decision-maker could be faulted were he to fail to give effect to that requirement. But beyond that it still leaves the assessment of the facts and the weighing of the considerations in the hands of the decision-maker.'

The weight to be given to particular considerations within an NPS is, therefore, a matter of planning judgement for the Secretary of State in the particular circumstances of the case: see also *R (Scarisbrick) v Secretary of State for Communities and Local Government* [2017] EWCA Civ 787 at [31] – a decision in the context of the NPS on hazardous waste infrastructure. See also article 23 of this work, which considers this decision.

Exceptions to the presumption in favour of a relevant NPS

The presumption in favour of any relevant NPS does not apply 'to the extent that one or more of subsections (4) to (8) applies': PA 2008, s 104(3).

Subsections (4) to (8) apply if the Secretary of State is satisfied that:

- Deciding the application in accordance with any relevant NPS would lead to the UK being in breach of any of its international obligations: PA 2008, s 104(4).
- Deciding the application in accordance with any relevant NPS would lead to the Secretary of State being in breach of any duty imposed on the Secretary of State by or under any enactment: PA 2008, s 104(5).
- Deciding the application in accordance with any relevant NPS would be unlawful by virtue of any enactment: PA 2008, s 104(6).
- The adverse impact of the proposed development would outweigh its benefits: PA 2008, s 104(7).
- Any condition prescribed for deciding an application otherwise than in accordance with an NPS is met: PA 2008, s 104(8).

The words 'to the extent that' in PA 2008, s 104(3) seem to suggest that the presumption in favour of granting consent applies even where one or more of the circumstances in subsections (4) to (8) is engaged to some extent; there being a balancing exercise. Thus, in relation to subsection (7), it may be that the 'impact' of the proposed development marginally outweighs its 'benefits', but that this harm is itself outweighed by the 'need' for the development established through the NPS.

In this regard, it is now clear that national 'need' as established through an NPS is a material consideration to be weighed against any adverse impact of the proposed development in undertaking a PA 2008, s 104(7) balancing exercise. Thus, in *R (Thames Blue Green Economy) v Secretary of State for Environment, Food and Rural Affairs* [2015] EWCA Civ 876, the Court of Appeal held at [16] that:

> 'Section 104(7) allows the Secretary of State to bring into consideration the statement of national need, which appears from a National Policy Statement, as against particular detriments which may be identified in the process of examining the application for a specific development consent order in specific circumstances and to weigh them against each other: it allows for the possibility that the local and particular detriments may be so great as to outweigh in the particular circumstances of a specific application a national need reflected in the National Policy Statement.'

The Court of Appeal in *R (ClientEarth) v Secretary of State for Business, Energy and Industrial Strategy and Drax Power Ltd* [2021] EWCA Civ 43 gave detailed guidance on the application of the s 104(3) and (7) balance at [104]–[109], as follows:

> '104. First, the purpose of the balancing exercise in section 104(7) is to establish whether an exception should be made to the requirement in section 104(3) that an application for development consent must be decided "in accordance with any relevant national policy statement". The exercise involves a straightforward balance, setting "adverse impact" against "benefits". It is not expressed as excluding considerations arising from national policy itself. It does not restrain the Secretary of State from bringing into account, and giving due weight to, the need for a particular type of infrastructure as recognised in a national policy statement, and setting it against any harm the development would cause (see the judgment of Sales LJ in *Thames Blue Green Economy Ltd*, at paragraph 16).
>
> 105. Secondly, however, as [Counsel] submitted, section 104(7) may not be used to circumvent other provisions in the statutory scheme, including section 106(1)(b), which enables the Secretary of State, when deciding an application for development consent, to "disregard representations" relating to "the merits of policy set out in a national policy statement". It does not provide a means of challenging such policy, or of anticipating a review under section 6, which is the process for accommodating changes of circumstances after designation (see *Spurrier*, at paragraphs 106 to 110).
>
> 106. Thirdly, in this case the Secretary of State identified her task under section 104(7) in … the decision letter. She did so accurately by setting out the provisions of both subsection (3) of section 104 and subsection (7), and directing herself that she would "need to consider the impacts of any proposed development and weigh these against the benefits of any scheme".
>
> 107. Fourthly, the Secretary of State concluded …, on the basis of her earlier conclusions …, that the proposed development was "in accordance with EN-1", having satisfied herself that it "should benefit from [the policy presumption in favour of granting consent for energy NSIPs in EN-1] because there are no more specific and more relevant NPS policies which clearly indicate that consent should be refused" and that "therefore the Development accords with relevant NPSs". This was a lawful conclusion.

108. Fifthly, the Secretary of State undertook the balancing exercise under section 104(7) ..., concluding ... that "[on] balance ... the benefits of the Development outweigh its adverse effects". This too was a lawful conclusion. There is nothing illogical or unlawful in recognising the general policy that greenhouse gas emissions are "not reasons to prohibit the consenting of projects", but considering whether to "give greater weight to GHG emissions in the context of the Drax application" and deciding not to do so. In undertaking the section 104(7) balance, this was perfectly appropriate.

109. Sixthly, there is no question of the Secretary of State having fettered herself in striking the section 104(7) balance, either by proceeding as if she had to adhere slavishly to the policies in EN-1 and EN-2, including the policies on need and on greenhouse gas emissions, or in any other way. She took those policies into account. But she did not regard herself as unable to give such weight to the proposal's compliance with them as she thought was right in the circumstances. In weighing the adverse effect of greenhouse gas emissions ..., she took account of "the Government's policy and legislative framework for delivering a net zero economy by 2050". She acknowledged that she was free to "depart from the NPS policies and give greater weight to GHG emissions" in this case, but decided not to do so. I do not read her reference to there being "no compelling reason" as setting some unduly onerous test. She was merely expressing a lawful planning judgment on the facts of the case – as she also did on the question of need ..., where she recognised that there were "strong arguments" weighing in favour of granting consent for a development of this capacity, because of its "contribution to meeting the need case set out in the NPSs".'

Decisions where there is a section 35 direction

A further point of some importance is whether an application for development consent for a project below the PA 2008 thresholds, but where a direction has been made under PA 2008, s 35, can be determined under PA 2008, s 104 or whether it must be made under s 105.

This issue is considered in article 25 of this work on s 35 directions, but now appears to be as set out in the judgment of the High Court in *EFW Group Ltd v Secretary of State for Business, Energy and Industrial Strategy* [2021] EWHC 2697 (Admin) where it was held at [60] that:

> 'The question arises as to whether or not the section 35 direction which was made in relation to [the project] has the effect of bringing it within the scope of the decision-making framework pursuant to section 104. In my view it does not. I am unable to accept the submission that the terms of section 35(1) have the effect of turning a project or development which does not fall within the definition of NSIPs provided within sections 14 and 15 of the 2008 Act into a project which has such a designation. The words "be treated as development for which development consent is required" simply have the effect of making the proposed development subject to the decision-making framework contained within the provisions of the 2008 Act. They do not change the understanding of the proposal as not being within the definition of an NSIP, any more than they change the physical nature of what is comprised within the development. More particularly, they cannot have the effect of altering the scope of an NPS which has been drafted specifically to apply only to those projects that are within the definition of an NSIP.'

The Claimant in that case was refused permission to appeal to the Court of Appeal and the correct position is, therefore, as set out in the *EFW Group* decision; in other words, that a section 35 direction does not bring an application within the ambit of section 104.

Article 91

Decision-making where there is no NPS

Hereward Phillpot QC, ftb
Michael Humphries QC, ftb

Introduction

Part 6 of the PA 2008 makes separate provision for the approach to decision-making in relation to an application for an order granting development consent depending on whether or not there is a relevant National Policy Statement ('NPS') in relation to development of the description to which the application relates.

Section 105 of the PA 2008 applies in relation to an application for development consent if PA 2008, s 104 does not apply; in other words, if no NPS 'has effect' in relation to development of the description to which the application relates.

The structure of PA 2008, s 105

PA 2008, s 105(2) provides that, in deciding an application to which PA 2008, s 104 does not apply, the Secretary of State must have regard to:

(a) any local impact report submitted within the specified deadline;

(b) any matters prescribed in relation to development of the description to which the application relates; and

(c) any other matters which the Secretary of State thinks are both important and relevant to the Secretary of State's decision.

This is a materially different and less prescriptive approach than that provided for by PA 2008, s 104. The most obvious difference, clearly, is that there is no equivalent in PA 2008, s 105 to the PA 2008, s 104(3) duty to decide the application in a particular way (ie in accordance with the NPS unless …). Nevertheless, an application determined under PA 2008, s 105 may still have regard to an NPS where the Secretary of State considers it both important and relevant to the decision. This might be the case, for example, where an application for development consent was made in relation to airport-related development that was not the Heathrow Northwest Runway identified in the Airports NPS.

The Infrastructure Planning (Decisions) Regulations 2010 set out the prescribed matters for the purposes of PA 2008, s 105(2)(b). The prescribed matters are as follows:

- *Listed buildings, conservation areas and scheduled monuments* – Regulation 3 imposes duties similar to those which apply to determinations under the Town and Country Planning Acts.
- *Deemed consents under the Marine and Coastal Access Act 2009* – Regulation 3A applies where a deemed marine licence has been applied for, and requires the Secretary of State to have regard to:
  - the need to protect the environment;

  - the need to protect human health; and
  - the need to prevent interference with legitimate uses of the sea.
- *Hazardous substances* – Regulation 6 provides that, where the development would involve the presence of certain hazardous substances, the Secretary of State must have regard to:
  - any current or contemplated use of the land to which the application relates;
  - the way in which other land in the vicinity is being used or is likely to be used; and
  - any planning permission or development consent that has been granted for development of that other land in the vicinity.
- *Biological diversity* – Regulation 7 requires the Secretary of State to have regard to the UN Environmental Programme Convention on Biological Diversity of 1992 (and, in Scotland, to any strategy designated under Nature Conservation (Scotland) Act 2004, s 2(1)).

In the usual way, the requirements which govern applications for EIA development – such as the prohibition on granting consent without consideration of environmental information (reg 3 of the Infrastructure Planning (Environmental Impact Assessment) Regulations 2009) – will apply to decisions made under PA 2008, s 105. The difference is that there will be no NPS to provide guidance on how the environmental impacts should be treated for the purposes of decision-making.

The same would be true for any application which engages the provisions of the Conservation of Habitats and Species Regulations 2010, or other similar statutory regimes of relevance to applications for development consent.

Likewise, the statutory tests for authorising compulsory acquisition (PA 2008, s 122) and the relevant guidance (DCLG, Planning Act 2008: Guidance related to procedures for the compulsory acquisition of land, September 2013) are the same whether or not there is a relevant NPS in place, and are dealt with elsewhere in this book. However, in practical terms it is likely to be somewhat harder to satisfy those tests, because of the requirement to establish need and to deal with potential alternatives in the absence of an NPS which makes provision for these matters.

Decision making under s 105

In *R (David Gate) v The Secretary of State for Transport* [2013] EWHC 2937 (Admin), Turner J dismissed an application for judicial review of the decision by the Secretary of State to make the Lancashire County Council (Torrisholme to the M6 Link (A683 Completion of Heysham to M6 Link Road)) Order 2013.

This was a decision made before the National Networks NPS was designated and, hence, was made under PA 2008, s 105. One of the grounds of challenge was that the Secretary of State had erred in basing his decision, at least in part, in reliance upon various NPSs which were said not to be material to the type of development under consideration.

Dismissing this ground of challenge, Turner J referred to PA 2008, s 105(2)(c) and said (paragraphs 56–58) that:

> 'It must follow, and common sense would in any event dictate, that the decision maker is not precluded from taking into account matters incorporated within national policy statements which are not directly applicable to the development so long as he considers that they are both important and relevant to his decision.
>
> The Examining Authority in this case specifically and accurately noted both the absence of a directly applicable national policy statement and the requirement to have

regard to important and relevant matters under section 105. He went on to refer to the national policy statements in respect of ports and of nuclear power generation in this specific context. Heysham is a port and the site of two nuclear power stations. There is a possibility that a third may be constructed here.

Against this background, it is clear that the Examining Authority was fully aware of the fact that the national policy statements had no direct application to this project. No objection could reasonably have been taken if the defendant had simply articulated matters relevant to Heysham's status as a port and site of nuclear power generation without reference to national policy statements and the fact that national policy statements were referred to does not vitiate the relevance of the matters which they contain. Once the matters are correctly categorised as relevant then it is a matter for the defendant to determine what weight to give them subject to the very limited constraints of judicial review. …'

There are perhaps three main points to take from this:

- the NPS taken into account by the Secretary of State under PA 2008, s 105(2)(c) was 'relevant' to the Secretary of State's decision;
- if something is 'relevant', the weight to attach to it (and hence whether it is 'important' under PA 2008, s 105(2)(c)) is a matter of planning judgment for the Secretary of State; and
- an NPS dealing with a different type of development can be relevant and important in appropriate circumstances.

Decision making under both ss 104 and 105

The language of s 105 – this section applies in relation to an application for development consent if s 104 does not apply in relation to that application – appears to suggest that those two sections are 'mutually exclusive' in relation to any single application.

That, indeed, was what had been widely understood to be the position until the decision in *EFW Group Limited v Secretary of State for Business, Energy and Industrial Strategy* [2021] EWHC 2697 (Admin), where the High Court held the opposite. This decision arose out of a single application by EFW Group for one generating station project that was acknowledged to be an NSIP ('the K3 Project') and another adjoining generating station project that fell below the s 15 threshold, but which had a s 35 direction ('the WKN Project'). The examination had proceeded on the basis that s 104 applied to the K3 Project and s 105 applied to the WKN Project, and recommended approval for the first and refusal for the second.

The Secretary of State disagreed with the Examining Authority and found that ss 104 and 105 were 'mutually exclusive' and so decided the application solely under s 104, but still granted development consent for the K3 Project and refused the WKN Project. EFW Group challenged the decision, accepting that the decision was correctly made under just s 104, but arguing that the s 104 presumption had not been properly applied to the WKN Project. In the High Court the Secretary of State reversed his position and argued that the Examining Authority was right to consider the application under both ss 104 and 105.

The High Court upheld the Secretary of State's revised position and concluded as follows:

'57. In my view the ExA was correct in his approach to sections 104 and 105 of the 2008 Act in the context of the present proposals. Clearly there is no dispute, firstly, that it is possible to include more than one project or development within the same application for a DCO and, secondly, that the K3 Project was one for which

> the NPS had effect, and therefore to which section 104 applied. Whilst I can see the force in the submissions of the claimant in relation to the use of the word "application" in both sections 104 and 105, the use of this word needs to be understood in the context of the statutory framework as a whole.
>
> 58. To suggest that by incorporating a project in respect of which the NPS has no effect within an application for a separate free-standing project which does fall within the scope of an NPS it is possible effectively to enlarge the scope of the NPS so as to include a project to which it was not designed to apply would clearly run contrary to the overall statutory scheme. That overall statutory scheme places the NPS at the heart of the decision-making process, and prescribes specific procedures, including endorsement by Parliament, prior to its designation. The contents of the NPS cannot be questioned in the decision-making process: so much is made clear in sections such as section 106(1) which applies in the decision-making context, and which entitles the defendant to disregard representations which "relate to the merits of policy set out in a national policy statement". Similar provisions are contained in section 87(3) respecting like representations to the ExA, and section 94(8) in relation to like representations made at hearings. It would be inconsistent with the centrality of the NPS within the statutory decision-making framework for its scope to be enlarged and its provisions bypassed by the manner in which an application has been formulated.

Thus the decision turned upon whether the Energy NPSs applied to a project below the s 15 thresholds for a generating station. As mentioned in article 90 of this work on decision-making where an NPS has effect, the Court also held that a section 35 direction for the WKN Project did not mean it had to be treated as an NSIP such that the Energy NPSs would 'have effect'. The claimant was refused permission to appeal to the Court of Appeal and the correct position is, therefore, that ss 104 and 105 are not 'mutually exclusive' and a single application may be decided under both.

Some additional points

There have been relatively few NSIPs promoted in the absence of a relevant NPS, although there clearly have been a number.

The application for a Tidal Lagoon at Swansea Bay is an example of an application that was approved by the Secretary of State for Energy and Climate Change in June 2015, even though this was not a technology covered by the Energy NPSs. The Energy NPSs were, however, treated as being important and relevant to the decision because they established a national need for the development of new nationally significant electricity generating and network infrastructure (see the Secretary of State's decision letter at paragraphs 11–12). It was not therefore necessary for the applicant to establish the need for the proposed development from first principles in a policy vacuum. As this was a Welsh case, the Welsh Government's guidance in 'Planning Policy Wales' was also taken into account, alongside local development plan policy.

Within England, paragraph 5 of the National Planning Policy Framework (2019) (NPPF) states that:

> 'The Framework does not contain specific policies for nationally significant infrastructure projects. These are determined in accordance with the decision-making framework in the Planning Act 2008 (as amended) and relevant national policy statements for major infrastructure, as well as any other matters that are relevant (*which may include the National Planning Policy Framework*).' (emphasis added)

Thus, as well as NPSs, other planning policy may also be taken into account as important and relevant under PA 2008, s 105.

Part 13

Correction of Errors, Changes and Revocation

Article 92

Correction of Errors in Development Consent Decisions

Isabella Tafur, ftb
Michael Humphries QC, ftb

Introduction

Pursuant to PA 2008, s 119, Sch 4, the Secretary of State may correct certain errors in development consent decisions. The documents that can be corrected are:

(a) where development consent has been granted, errors in the development consent order; and

(b) where development consent has been refused, errors in the refusal letter.

The Act, however, only allows corrections to 'correctable errors'. These are defined as errors or omissions that are part of the document recording the decision, but are *not* part of the statement of reasons for the decision (PA 2008, Sch 4, para 1(3)). Any error in the statement of reasons for the decision cannot, therefore, be corrected. Furthermore, there is no power of correction in relation to DCO provisions included pursuant to PA 2008, Sch 5, paras 30A and 30B which relate to deemed marine licences (see PA 2008, Sch 4, para 1(11)).

Where the development consent order was required to be contained in a statutory instrument, the correction of any error/omission must also be made by an order contained in a statutory instrument (PA 2008, Sch 4, para 1(8)). As soon as possible after the instrument containing the order is made, the Secretary of State must deposit a copy of it in the office of the Clerk of the Parliaments (PA 2008, Sch 4, para 1(10)).

Conditions

The Secretary of State may only correct an error or omission if the following conditions are satisfied:

(a) the Secretary of State has received a written request to correct the error/omission from any person before the end of the relevant period (PA 2008, Sch 4, para 1(5)(a)); or

(b) the Secretary of State has sent a statement in writing to the applicant, explaining the error/omission and stating that the Secretary of State is considering making the correction before the end of the relevant period (PA 2008, Sch 4, para 1(5)(b)).

The 'relevant' periods are:

(a) if development consent has been granted, the Secretary of State will only have the power to correct an error if the request is received/statement is sent before the expiry of six weeks, beginning with the day on which the order was published, or, if later, the day on which the statement of reasons for making the order was published (PA 2008, Sch 4, para 1(6)(a) and s 118(1)(b)); or

(b) if development consent is refused, the Secretary of State will only have the power to correct an error if the request is received/statement is sent before the expiry of six weeks, beginning with the day on which the statement of reasons for refusal is published (PA 2008, Sch 4, para 1(6)(b) and s 118(1)(b)).

Furthermore, the Secretary of State must inform each relevant local planning authority that the request has been made/statement has been sent (PA 2008, Sch 4, para 1(7)).

Correction notices

If a written request has been received or a statement sent, the Secretary of State must issue a correction notice (PA 2008, Sch 4, para 2(1)). The correction notice must be served as soon as practicable after making the correction or deciding not to make the correction (PA 2008, Sch 4, para 2(2)). The notice must specify the correction of the error/omission or give notice of the decision not to correct the error/omission, and it must be given to the applicant, each local planning authority for all (or any part) of the area in which the development is situated, and to the person who requested the correction (PA 2008, Sch 4, para 2(3)). The Secretary of State may also give to the notice to other persons, but is not obliged to do so (PA 2008, Sch 4, para 2(4)).

Effect of a correction

If a correction is made to a decision, the original decision (whether the development consent order or the refusal of development consent) remains in force, but is treated as corrected by the terms specified in the correction notice (PA 2008, Sch 4, para 3(1)). The correction takes effect from the date when the 'correction notice' is issued or, if the correction is required to be made by statutory instrument, the date specified in the 'correction order'. The correction is required to be contained in a a statutory instrument (ie a correction order) in the circumstances identified in PA 2008, Sch 4, para 1(8); namely, where the original DCO was required to be in a statutory instrument (see PA 2008, s 117).

Where a correction is not made, the original decision continues to have full force and effect (PA 2008, Sch 4, para 3(2)).

Examples of correction notices / orders

There are now many examples of 'correction notices' and 'correction orders' made by the Secretary of State pursuant to PA 2008, Sch 4. Examples in 2020 alone include:

- Riverside Energy Park (Correction) Order 2020;
- Reinforcement to the North Shropshire Electricity Distribution Network (Correction) Order 2020;
- A303 (Amesbury to Berwick Down) Development Consent (Correction) Order 2020;
- A63 Castle Street Improvement – Hull (Correction) Order 2020;
- West Midlands Rail Freight Interchange (Correction) Order 2020; and
- Lake Lothing (Lowestoft) Third Crossing (Correction) Order 2020.

A variety of reasons are given for the need to make the above corrections.

Relationship with other provisions

It is worth noting the relationship between the power to correct errors (in PA 2008, Sch 4) and the power to make changes to, and revocation of, development consent orders (in PA 2008, Sch 6, para 3) provides that the Secretary of State may by order make a change to, or revoke, a development consent order without an application being made if he is satisfied that:

(a) the development consent order contains a significant error; and

(b) it would *not* be appropriate for the error to be corrected by means of the power conferred by PA 2008, Sch 4, para 1 (see above) or by PA 2008, Sch 6, para 2 (non-material changes).

It is not entirely clear in what circumstances it would not be 'appropriate' for an error to be corrected under PA 2008, Sch 4, para 1 or PA 2008, Sch 6, para 2, but it might still be appropriate to change a development consent order under PA 2008, Sch 6.

Note also the relationship between PA 2008, Sch 4 and PA 2008, s 161 (breach of terms of order granting development consent). PA 2008, s 161(3) provides that it is a defence for a person charged with an offence under PA 2008, s 161(1) to prove that:

(a) the breach or failure to comply occurred only because of an error or omission in the order; and

(b) a correction notice specifying the correction of the error or omission has been issued under PA 2008, Sch 4, para 2.

Conclusion

Errors and omissions in development consent orders, and in notices refusing development consent, can, in certain circumstances, be corrected. Any person may request such a correction, or the Secretary of State may unilaterally decide to make a correction, within the statutory period during which a legal challenge can be made to a decision to grant or refuse an application for development consent.

Article 93

Changes to, and Revocation of, Development Consent Orders

Isabella Tafur, ftb
Michael Humphries QC, ftb

Introduction

Once a development consent order has been made, the Secretary of State may make changes to, or indeed revoke, the DCO pursuant to PA 2008, s 153, Sch 6. This is distinct from the Secretary of State's power to 'correct' an error in a DCO under PA 2008, s 119, Sch 4 (see article 92 of this work).

PA 2008, Sch 6, para 2 authorises the Secretary of State to make non-material changes to a DCO, and PA 2008, Sch 6, para 3 authorises the making of material changes to, and the revocation of, DCOs. The power to make material changes under para 3 includes a power to require the removal or alteration of buildings or works; require the discontinuance of a use of land; impose specified requirements in connection with the continuance of a use of land; impose new requirements in connection with the relevant development and to remove or alter existing requirements (PA 2008, Sch 6, para 5). Material changes to a DCO can only be made within four years of the date on which the development was substantially complete (PA 2008, Sch 6, para 5), but this time limit does not prevent the Secretary of State from revoking a DCO or making changes to the requirements on a DCO at any time.

The procedure for applying for changes to be made to DCOs and the consultation requirements in respect of such applications are set out in the Infrastructure Planning (Changes to, and Revocation of, Development Consent Orders) Regulations 2011 ('the Changes Regulations'). Guidance on applications to change or revoke a development consent order is set out in the DCLG Guidance on changes to development consent orders (2015).

Non-material changes to a DCO

Under PA 2008, Sch 6, para 2 the Secretary of State may make non-material changes to a DCO. This includes a power to impose new requirements or to remove or alter existing requirements on a DCO but it does not authorise the making of any changes to a deemed marine licence under the Marine and Coastal Access Act 2009. It will be for the Secretary of State to decide whether the proposed change is material, having regard to the effect of the change, together with any previous non-material changes, on the DCO as originally made.

The DCLG Guidance on changes (2015) provides advice on the types of change that are likely to be material. It explains that changes should be treated as material if they would require an updated ES to take account of new, or materially different, likely significant effects on the environment or if they are likely to invoke the need for a Habitats Regulations Assessment or the need for a new or additional licence in respect of a European Protected Species. Equally, a change should be treated as material if it would authorise the compulsory acquisition of any land or interest in land and the potential impact of the proposed changes on local people will be a consideration in determining whether a change is material.

An application for the making of a non-material change to a DCO can be made by the person who applied for the DCO or a successor in title; any person with an interest in the land to which the DCO relates or any other person for whose benefit the DCO has effect. The application must be made in accordance with the requirements of reg 4 of the Changes Regulations and must be accompanied by a consultation and publicity statement. The fee for making such an application is currently £6,891 (reg 5 of the Changes Regulations).

Pursuant to reg 6 of the Changes Regulations, the applicant must publish a notice of the application explaining its main elements, in a local newspaper for at least two successive weeks and in any other publication necessary to ensure that notice of the application is given in the vicinity of the land. The publication must include details of how to respond to the publicity and must allow at least 28 days for responses to be made.

The applicant must send a copy of the notice to each person for whose benefit the DCO has effect, each person who was notified of the original application under PA 2008, s 56, and any other person who may be directly affected by the proposed change (reg 7 of the Changes Regulations), unless the Secretary of State has given written consent that the applicant need not consult any such persons. If the Secretary of State authorises the applicant not to consult any such person, he must publish his reasons for doing so on its website.

There is no statutory timetable for making the decision in respect of a non-material change. However, the DCLG Guidance on changes (2015) explains (para 37) that where the applicant has complied with all necessary procedural requirements and has provided all the information and documents necessary for a decision to be made, a decision should normally be expected within 6 weeks of the closing date for responses to publicity and consultation.

If the change is made to the DCO, the Secretary of State must notify its decision to the applicant, any person consulted about the application and any person who made a relevant representation in response to the publicity or consultation exercises (reg 8 of the Changes Regulations).

Material changes to, and revocation of, a DCO

Pursuant to PA 2008, Sch 6, para 3 the Secretary of State may make changes to, or revoke a DCO, either on receipt of an application or, in certain circumstances, without any application being made.

An application may be made by the original applicant or a successor in title; a person with an interest in the land; or any other person for whose benefit the DCO has effect. A local planning authority ('LPA') can also make such an application provided the Secretary of State is satisfied that the DCO authorised development wholly or partly in the area of that LPA, the development has been begun but been abandoned and the amenity of other land in the LPA's area or an adjoining area is adversely affected by the condition of the land.

The power can only be exercised without any application if the Secretary of State is satisfied (PA 2008, Sch 6, para 3(3)) that the DCO contains a significant error and that it would not be appropriate for the error to be corrected under PA 2008, Sch 4 (correction of errors) or PA 2008, Sch 6, para 2 (non-material changes). The power may also be exercised by the Secretary of State without an application being made if the Secretary of State is satisfied (PA 2008, Sch 6, para 3(7)) that, if the development were carried out in accordance with the DCO, there would be a contravention of relevant retained EU law or a Convention right (ie a right within the meaning of the Human Rights Act 1998), or there are other exceptional circumstances that make it appropriate to exercise the power.

The applicant must consult those persons prescribed by reg 10 of the Changes Regulations in respect of a proposed application under this provision and must allow a period of at least 28 days for representations to be made. Prior to carrying out that consultation exercise, the applicant must notify the Secretary of State of the proposed application (reg 12 of the Changes Regulations). Unless the applicant has the written consent of the Secretary of State to dispense with any of these requirements, a notice of the proposed application must also be published in one or more local newspapers for at least two successive weeks, as well as once in the London Gazette and, if land in Scotland is affected, the Edinburgh Gazette. If the proposed application relates to offshore development, a notice must be published once in Lloyd's List and once in an appropriate fishing trade journal (reg 14 of the Changes Regulations). A notice must also be displaced on the land, or as close to it as is reasonably practicable. Once the application has been made, notice must be given to persons prescribed by reg 19 of the Changes Regulations and a notice must be published again in the relevant newspapers etc., in accordance with reg 14.

The application must contain the information prescribed by reg 16 of the Changes Regulations and must be accompanied, among other things, by a statement as to whether the application involves EIA development and by a consultation report. Unless the application is made by the LPA, a fee of £6,750 is payable on the making of the application, with further fees payable at pre-examination and examination stages (reg 18 of and Sch 2 to the Changes Regulations).

The Secretary of State may refuse to determine an application for a change to a DCO. In particular, the Secretary of State may exercise this power if it is considered that the development that would be authorised as a result of the change should properly be the subject of a new application for a DCO.

In some cases, the Secretary of State may decide that it is not necessary for an Examining body to examine the application, in which case he must notify the applicant and all those who had made relevant representations of this decision and publish the reasons for the decision on the website, allowing a period of at least 28 days for representations to be made (regs 21A and 21B of the Changes Regulations).

By reg 17 of the Changes Regulations, an application under this section will be treated as a 'subsequent application' for the purposes of reg 3 (prohibition on granting consent without consideration of environmental information), reg 6 (procedure for establishing whether environmental impact assessment is required), reg 8 (application for a scoping opinion), reg 18 (subsequent application for EIA development) and reg 19 (subsequent application not complying with EIA requirements) of the Infrastructure Planning (EIA) Regulations 2009.

Regulations 22–41 of the Changes Regulations set down the procedures for the appointment of the Examining body and the conduct of the examination, which are akin to the procedures for the examination of a DCO. Where an Examining body has been appointed to examine the application, it must complete its examination within 4 months of the start day (ie the day of the preliminary meeting) (reg 42 of the Changes Regulations) and report to the Secretary of State within two months of the completion of the examination (reg 43 of the Changes Regulations). The Secretary of State must decide the application within two months of receiving the report from the Examining body, or within two months of the deadline for receiving that report, whichever is the earliest (reg 49 of the Changes Regulations). If the Secretary of State has determined the application without examination by an Examining body, then it must determine the application within two months of issuing the notification under reg 21A that such examination was not necessary.

Where a material change is made to a DCO, the DCO will continue in force and the change will take effect from the date on which the Secretary of State gives notice of his decision or, if the change to the DCO is required to be made by a statutory instrument, the date specified in the order making the change. If a DCO is revoked, the revocation takes effect on the date specified in the order making the revocation or, where there is no date specified, the date on which the order making the revocation is made (reg 53 of the Changes Regulations).

Where the change or revocation to a DCO is made by the Secretary of State without any application, the procedure set out in Part 3 of the Changes Regulations applies. This requires the Secretary of State to give notice to prescribed persons of his intention to consider making such an order and to publish a notice in relevant newspapers etc. in accordance with the requirements in reg 14 of the Changes Regulations. Once the decision has been made, the Secretary of State must notify the persons prescribed by reg 58 of the Changes Regulations.

Compensation

Where a material change is made to a DCO, or a DCO is revoked, any person who has incurred expenditure in carrying out work (ie in the preparation of plans or other similar matters of preparatory work) which is rendered abortive by the change or revocation can claim compensation from the Secretary of State, as can any person who has otherwise sustained any loss or damage which is directly attributable to the change or revocation (PA 2008, Sch 6, para 6). However, no compensation is payable in respect of any works done before the DCO was made or in respect of any other loss or damage arising out of anything done or omitted to be done before the DCO was made (other than loss or damage consisting of the depreciation of the value of an interest in land).

Any claim for compensation must be made in accordance with reg 61 of the Changes Regulations and must be made within 12 months of the notification of the Secretary of State's decision to make the change or revoke the DCO under reg 50 or 57. Any dispute as to the compensation payable will be referred to the Upper Tribunal for determination.

Part 14

Legal Challenges

Article 94

Legal Challenge to Grant of Development Consent

Richard Honey QC, ftb
Michael Humphries QC, ftb

Introduction

A legal challenge to the grant of development consent is by way of judicial review. The normal principles and procedures of judicial review generally apply, subject to the provisions of PA 2008, s 118. In particular, there is a six-week time limit for bringing judicial review proceedings.

PA 2008, s 118(1)

PA 2008, s 118 governs legal challenges relating to applications for orders granting development consent. Section 118(1) (as amended) provides that:

> 'A court may entertain proceedings for questioning an order granting development consent only if
>
> (a) the proceedings are brought by a claim for judicial review, and
>
> (b) the claim form is filed before the end of the period of 6 weeks beginning with the day after–
>
> (i) the day on which the order is published, or,
>
> (ii) if later, the day on which the statement of reasons for making the order is published.'

This six-week time limit was unusual when the Act was introduced, but it is now the standard time limit for judicial review of planning decisions given the change made in July 2013 by the Civil Procedure (Amendment No 4) Rules 2013.

The requirement to 'publish' the order is contained in PA 2008, s 117. The order must be published 'in such manner as the Secretary of State thinks appropriate' (PA 2008, s 117(3)), unless the order:

- makes by-laws,
- introduces offences,
- applies, modifies or excludes a statutory provision, or
- amends, repeals or revokes a statutory provision of local application,

in which case it must be contained in a statutory instrument (PA 2008, s 117(4)). Statutory instruments are officially published by Her Majesty's Stationery Office (HMSO) on the website of The National Archives (www.legislation.gov.uk), where new statutory instruments are listed by publication date.

The requirement to 'publish' a statement of reasons for a decision to grant development consent is contained in PA 2008, s 116. The statement must again be published 'in such manner as the Secretary of State thinks appropriate' (PA 2008, s 116(3)).

Typically an Order granting development consent and the Secretary of State's statement of reasons for making the Order will be published simultaneously on the Planning Inspectorate's website (infrastructure.planninginspectorate.gov.uk).

In *R (Williams) v Secretary of State for Energy and Climate Change* [2015] EWHC 1202 (Admin), Lindblom J (as he then was) said (para 45) that:

> 'The way in which an order and the Secretary of State's statement of reasons for making it are to be "published" is not prescribed by section 118. But in my view the placing of the order on the Planning Inspectorate's infrastructure planning website ..., together with the Secretary of State's decision letter and the Examining Authority's report, and, on the same day, the notification of the interested parties, both by email and post, that this had been done, was enough to constitute publication of the order, and the reasons why it was made, within the meaning of section 118.'

In the case of Rookery South, where there was the special parliamentary procedure to be followed subsequent to the panel's decision, the Inspectorate advised that 'in cases where special parliamentary procedure applies, the publication of the order, for the purposes of PA 2008, s 118, will follow the special parliamentary procedure' (register of advice, 18 November 2011, Rookery South Energy from Waste Generating Station).

Date from which time runs

Section 118 (as amended by the Criminal Justice and Courts Act 2015) sets out details of the date from which the six-week time limit runs in each given circumstances (see PA 2008, s 118(1)–(7) inclusive).

It should be noted that in the section as originally enacted, time ran from the day beginning with the event specified in PA 2008, s 118(1)–(7) and, in the case of PA 2008, s 118(1), from the day on which the order was published or, if later the day of which the statement of reasons for making the order was published. The words 'beginning with' in PA 2008, s 118 contrasted with the word 'from' which is used in r 54.5 of the Civil Procedure Rules (CPR) for judicial reviews generally. This led to two challenges to the Thames Tideway Tunnel DCO being held to be out of time when the applicants calculated the six weeks from the day after the publication of the DCO and their applications for judicial review were dismissed: see *R (Blue Green London Plan and LB Southwark) v Secretary of State for Environment, Food and Rural Affairs* [2015] EWHC 495 (Admin).

Following the decision in these challenges, the wording of PA 2008, s 118(1) was amended so as to provide that a challenge by way of judicial review must be made within the period of six weeks 'beginning with *the day after*' (emphasis added) the publication of the DCO and Statement of Reasons.

For example: if an Order and statement of reasons were published on 5 January, the first day of the six weeks would be 6 January, and the time for challenge would expire on 17 February.

Accuracy is vital, bearing in mind the inability of the court to extend time where there is a statutory time limit (see below).

The time limit of six weeks is set by statute

The time limit of six weeks for challenges to the grant of development consent is one set by statute (ie by the terms of PA 2008, s 118 and not by the Civil Procedure Rules) and thus it is important to note that the court has no power or discretion to extend it: see *Mucelli v Government of Albania* [2009] 1 WLR 276.

Procedural issues

Promptness

Apart from the six-week time limit, the requirement for promptness in CPR r 54.5(1)(a) appears not to apply to judicial reviews within the scope of PA 2008, s 118, because r 54.5(3) states that the rule does not apply when any other enactment specifies a shorter time limit for making a claim for judicial review; PA 2008, s 118 would be such an enactment.

Although the requirement for promptness in the CPR would appear not to apply to judicial reviews brought under PA 2008, s 118, the 'undue delay' provision in Senior Courts Act 1981, s 31(6) would still apply. Senior Courts Act 1981, s 31(6) provides that, where the High Court considers that there has been undue delay in making an application for judicial review, the court may refuse to grant permission or relief, if it considers that the granting of the relief sought would be likely to cause substantial hardship to, or substantially prejudice the rights of, any person, or would be detrimental to good administration. Senior Courts Act 1981, s 31(7) says that this provision is 'without prejudice to any enactment or rule of court which has the effect of limiting the time within which an application for judicial review may be made'. Accordingly, 'undue delay' together with one of the harms identified in Senior Courts Act 1981, s 31(6) (substantial hardship, substantial prejudice of rights, or detriment to good administration) would allow a court to refuse permission or relief, even where a claim was brought within six weeks. It is, however, unlikely that, save in exceptional circumstances, a court would regard six weeks for bringing a claim as representing 'undue delay'. Nonetheless, potential claimants would need to bear this in mind and could not simply wait until the end of the six-week period to bring a claim.

Pre-action protocol for judicial review

The courts will normally expect the Pre-Action Protocol for Judicial Review produced under the CPR to be followed before proceedings are commenced. However, the abridged time limit under PA 2008, s 118 (six weeks instead of three months) may make full compliance with the pre-action protocol difficult. The Pre-Action Protocol for Judicial Review (17 September 2019) states (para 6) that:

> 'This protocol will not be appropriate in very urgent cases. In this sort of case, a claim should be made immediately. … Even in very urgent cases, it is good practice to alert the defendant by telephone and to send by email (or fax) to the defendant the draft Claim Form which the claimant intends to issue. A claimant is also normally required to notify a defendant when an interim order is being sought.'

In practice, however, claimants and respondents ought to try to comply with the pre-action protocol, although the normal periods for compliance may have to be abridged.

There are two main stages under the pre-action protocol. First, the claimant sends a letter before claim which should identify the issues in dispute and establish whether litigation can be avoided. A standard form letter before claim is included in Annex A to the protocol. The letter should contain the date and details of the decision being challenged and a clear summary of the facts on which the claim is based. It should also contain the details of any relevant information that the claimant is seeking and an explanation of why this is considered relevant. The second stage is the letter of response, sent by the proposed defendant and any interested parties, following the standard form set out in Annex B to the protocol. The letter should be sent within 14 days, or, if this is not possible, then the defendant should send an interim response and propose a reasonable extension of time. If the claim is being conceded in full, in part or not at all, the reply should say so in clear and unambiguous terms. Where appropriate the letter should contain a fuller explanation of the decision being challenged, deal with any points of dispute, and enclose any relevant documents.

Alternative dispute resolution

In applications for judicial review, there is generally an encouragement by the courts to consider alternative dispute resolution: see eg *R (Cowl) v Plymouth City Council (Practice Note)* [2002] 1 WLR 803 and the pre-action protocol. However, given the nature of the grant of development consent by means of a DCO, the ability to use ADR in this context is likely to be limited.

Standing

To be able to bring a claim for judicial review, a claimant must have a sufficient interest in the matter to which the claim relates. Standing is a ground on which both permission and substantive relief may be refused, but the test at the permission stage is lower, essentially to exclude troublemakers. The importance and merits of the claim can alter the degree of standing required. A 'sufficient interest' has been given a wide and flexible interpretation by the courts. In planning and environmental cases, a reasonably low threshold is usually applied, including those with a general interest in the issue to be determined. Representative and campaign groups would usually be regarded as having sufficient standing.

Significant planning cases

The Planning Liaison Judge may categorise a Planning Court claim as 'significant' (CPR PD54D, para 3.1). The criteria for so categorising a claim are set out in paragraph 3.2 of CPR PD54D and include claims that relate to commercial or other developments which have 'significant economic impact', either at a local level or beyond their immediate locality, claims that raise important points of law, and also claims that generate significant public interest. A number of PA 2008 challenges to DCOs or NPSs have been designated as 'significant', reflecting their importance. Paragraph 3.4 of CPR PD54D sets down shorter target timescales for 'significant' planning cases. Where appropriate, a party will normally request that a s 118 challenge is categorised as 'significant' in its application for permission to bring judicial review.

Claim form

A judicial review claim is commenced using the Part 8 claim procedure. The claim form should be accompanied by a detailed statement of the claimant's grounds, a statement of the facts relied on, and any applications, eg for directions. The claim form must be served within seven days from issue, and an acknowledgement of service filed by the defendant and interested parties within 21 days of service, including a statement of grounds for contesting the claim.

Permission to bring an application for judicial review

There is a permission stage in all applications for judicial reviews that will apply also to challenges to the making of a DCOs under PA 2008, s 118(1). It is necessary for a claimant to secure permission from the court to bring an application for judicial review. This is usually considered first by a judge on the papers. At the 'permission stage' the court will consider the merits of the claim against the relevant test: whether the claim discloses an arguable case. Permission should not be granted for judicial review claims that are misguided complaints of administrative error. The purpose of the permission stage is to protect public authorities against weak and vexatious claims. The court will make an order giving or refusing permission, and giving any directions. Permission may be granted with conditions or only on certain of the grounds sought.

If permission is refused it is possible then to renew the application for permission at an oral hearing before a single judge, usually listed for 30 minutes. If permission is refused after an oral hearing then a right of appeal lies to the Court of Appeal. Sometimes, in urgent or complex cases, a judge will order a permission hearing without a paper decision being reached, or that there be a rolled-up hearing, where permission and the substantive case are considered at the same hearing. In July 2013 the CPR were changed to remove the right to reconsideration at a hearing of the refusal of permission in cases where the application was certified as totally without merit by the judge considering the application on the papers.

As far as the costs of the permission stage are concerned, a successful defendant should be entitled to recover the cost for its acknowledgement of service, including the preparation of summary grounds of resistance, but not of any pre-action correspondence (see *R (Mount Cook) v Westminster CC* [2004] 2 P&CR 22 at para 76(1) and *R (Ewing) v Office of the Deputy Prime Minister* [2006] 1 WLR 1260 at 1267A–B). Defendants are not generally entitled to their costs of attending any oral permission hearing, but may be awarded them in certain circumstances as an exception.

Grounds for judicial review

If permission is granted, the defendant and any interested parties must within 35 days serve detailed grounds for contesting the claim and any written evidence. Skeleton arguments must be filed and served before the hearing. The court's permission is required if a claimant seeks to rely on grounds other than those for which he has been given permission to proceed. Where justified by urgency, for example where a development needs to commence, it is possible to seek to have the hearing expedited. If a claim is commenced in, or transferred to, an Administrative Court location outside London it is likely that the claim will be heard more quickly.

The grounds of challenge to the grant of consent are likely often to feature issues of European law, for example arising in connection with the EIA Directive, the Birds Directive or the Habitats Directive. It is also inevitable that some challenges will seek to rely on human rights issues, such as Articles 6 (fair hearing) and 8 (home and family life) and Article 1 of the First Protocol (property). There may also be arguments in relation to statutory duties such as the public sector equality duty in Equality Act 2010, s 149, breach of which would give rise to grounds for judicial review.

Otherwise, grounds of judicial review of the grant of development consent will be the same as for any judicial review. These will include: error of law; excess of power, ie going beyond the powers conferred by statute; jurisdictional error; unauthorised delegation; acting as if discretion is fettered; over-rigid adherence to policy or rules; irrelevant considerations taken in to account, or a refusal to take in to account relevant considerations; irrationality; acting in bad faith; failure to observe procedural rules; procedural unfairness; breach of right to a fair hearing; actual or apparent bias; failure to give adequate reasons; misinterpretation of policy; fundamental error of fact; lack of evidence for a conclusion; proportionality; failure properly to consult; and, breach of a substantive or procedural legitimate expectation.

The ambit of judicial review is quite limited and so gives defendants a fair degree of protection from challenges. The merits of the decision cannot be considered. Matters of judgment are the exclusive province of the decision-maker. The assessment of facts and weighing of considerations is in the hands of the decision-maker alone and the court has no power to intervene. A decision-maker is entitled to attach what weight it pleases to relevant considerations, and the courts will not entertain a submission that undue weight was given to one consideration or too little weight was given to another. If a matter would not have caused the decision-maker to reach a different conclusion then it is irrelevant whether it was taken in to account; and, if a judge is uncertain whether a matter would have made a difference to a decision then he cannot conclude that the decision was invalid. Where there is a factual error which is insignificant or insubstantial then the relevant decision will not be quashed. Where it can be shown that notwithstanding any error the decision-maker would have reached the same decision on the other factors stated, the court will not interfere.

Other issues during conduct of proceedings

Orders for disclosure against a respondent can be made, but disclosure is not required. Such orders are fairly rare, since questions of fact play much less part in judicial review proceedings than in other cases and since the decision and the basis for it is usually clearly evidenced (eg by a panel report). However, there has been a trend towards increasing disclosure in judicial review cases. The Secretary of State will normally hold the relevant documents that are not already in the public domain, such as those relating to Ministerial consideration of whether or not to grant a DCO. Traditionally there has been a duty of candour on public authorities voluntarily to provide full and frank disclosure of relevant material to a challenger. Lord Donaldson MR said in *R v Lancashire CC ex p Huddleston* [1986] 2 All ER 941 that judicial review was 'a process which falls to be conducted with all the cards face upwards on the table and the vast majority of the cards will start in the authority's hands'. The courts have made it clear that the duty of candour is a very high and important duty to assist the court with full and accurate explanations of all the facts relevant to the issues the court must decide. An authority should explain fully what it has done and why it has done it, so far as is necessary fairly to meet the challenge made. The duty of candour had perhaps not been working so well in recent years. But following the decisions in *Tweed v Parades Commission* [2007] 1 AC 650, *R (Al-Sweady) v Secretary of State for Defence* [2009] EWHC 2387 (Admin) and *R (Shoesmith) v Ofsted* [2010] EWHC 852 (Admin), it is increasingly common for a defendant to provide something like disclosure.

Cross-examination is unusual in judicial review proceedings (see eg *R (Bancoult) v Secretary of State for Foreign and Commonwealth Affairs* [2012] EWHC 2115 (Admin)). Cross-examination is exceptional because the primary facts are often not in dispute, or at least those asserted by the defendant are undisputed, and the authority may normally be relied upon to disclose relevant documents pursuant to its duty of candour. But the court retains a discretion to permit cross-examination and should do so if it is necessary for the claim to be, and be seen to be, determined fairly and justly.

Remedies

The remedy sought in judicial review is likely to be the quashing of the DCO. It may also be that a declaration is sought as to what the correct legal position is on some issue. In judicial review, all remedies are discretionary, so even where a decision has been held by the court to be unlawful it may be that it is not quashed. However, discretion must be exercised judicially and, in most cases in which a decision has been found to be flawed, it would not be a proper exercise of discretion to refuse to quash it (*R (Edwards) v Environment Agency* [2008] UKHL 22 at para 63).

Costs

In relation to costs of judicial reviews generally, Part 45 of the CPR now provides a regime of fixed costs in claims to which the Aarhus Convention applies. This is likely to cover most if not all challenges to DCOs, depending on the actual grounds of challenge, as the Aarhus Convention applies to environmental matters generally. CPR rr 45.41 to 45.44 enable a claimant to tick a box on the claim form to seek costs protection, which will apply unless it is successfully challenged by a defendant. The only ground for challenging the application of this fixed costs regime is that the claim is not one within the ambit of the Aarhus Convention. Where the rules apply, the total costs recoverable from a claimant are limited to £5,000 (individual) or £10,000 (others) and the costs recoverable by a claimant are limited to £35,000.

Otherwise, there remains an ability for a claimant to apply for a protective costs order in accordance with the principles set out in *R (Corner House Research) v Secretary of State for Trade and Industry* [2005] EWCA Civ 192. The basic guidelines for the award of a PCO are:

- the issues raised are of general public importance;
- the public interest requires that those issues be resolved;
- the claimant has no private interest in the outcome;
- having regard to the financial resources and the costs, it is fair and just to make the order; and
- if the order is not made, the claimant will probably discontinue the proceedings and will be acting reasonably in so doing.

It was also said that if the claimant's lawyers were acting *pro bono* then it would be likely to enhance the merits of the application. These conditions have been applied flexibly in subsequent cases.

Where the grant of development consent is challenged, the promoter will be an interested party. A promoter is entitled to, and in practice is likely to, participate in the judicial review in order to seek to uphold the DCO. The Secretary of State, represented usually by the Treasury Solicitor, will be the defendant. As such, the role of a promoter is somewhat limited. It is unlikely that a third party in such a judicial review would be awarded their costs if the challenge is dismissed (see *Bolton MDC v Secretary of State for the Environment (Costs)* [1995] 1 WLR 1176), although two sets of costs are awarded in some cases.

Article 95

Legal Challenge to Refusal of Development Consent

Richard Honey QC, ftb
Michael Humphries QC, ftb

Introduction

A legal challenge to the refusal of development consent is by way of judicial review. The normal principles and procedures of judicial review generally apply, subject to the provisions of PA 2008, s 118. In particular, there is a six-week time limit for bringing judicial review proceedings.

The main principles and procedural provisions relating to judicial review are considered in article 94 of this work. Those principles and procedural provisions, however, also apply to the challenge of a refusal of an application for development consent, subject to some key differences that are considered below.

PA 2008, s 118(2)

PA 2008, s 118 governs legal challenges relating to the refusal of development consent. Section 118(2) (as amended) provides that:

> 'A court may entertain proceedings for questioning a refusal of development consent only if–
>
> (a) the proceedings are brought by a claim for judicial review, and
>
> (b) the claim form is filed before the end of the period of 6 weeks beginning with the day after the day on which the statement of reasons for the refusal is published.'

This six-week time limit was unusual when the Act was introduced, but it is now the standard time limit for judicial review of planning decisions, given the change made in July 2013 by the Civil Procedure (Amendment No 4) Rules 2013.

The requirement to 'publish' a statement of reasons for a decision to refuse development consent is contained in PA 2008, s 116. The statement must be published 'in such manner as the Secretary of State thinks appropriate' (PA 2008, s 116(3)).

Procedural issues

Standing

A promoter bringing such a judicial review would have no problem establishing standing. The decision would be defended by the Secretary of State. It is unlikely that an objector to the DCO would actively participate in the judicial review, although that would in practice depend on the circumstances of each case and the grounds of challenge.

Grounds for judicial review

As to grounds of judicial review, a promoter might be arguing that there has been an error of law in the sense that a legal test has been misconstrued and applied more rigorously than it ought to have been. It is, however, more likely that a promoter would be challenging on the grounds for example of: over-rigid adherence to policy or rules; irrelevant considerations taken in to account, or a refusal to take in to account relevant considerations; irrationality; failure to observe procedural rules; procedural unfairness; failure to give adequate reasons; misinterpretation of policy; fundamental error of fact; and, lack of evidence for a conclusion. Other grounds may of course be applicable in particular cases.

Other issues during conduct of proceedings

Where a DCO has been refused contrary to the recommendation of a panel's report, the promoter is likely to wish to secure, by way of disclosure, all documents evidencing the consideration of the application by the Minister and his advisers. This could be secured under the duty of candour or by way of an application for specific disclosure, if necessary.

Remedy

The remedy sought in judicial review is likely to be the quashing of the Secretary of State's decision to refuse consent. If the challenge is successful, the Secretary of State will then have to re-decide the application. Where the error of law lies with the Examining Authority, it may be advisable to seek an order that the report should be quashed as well, but that is unlikely to be necessary. It has been held in relation to comparable decisions that where a decision is quashed then 'the Secretary of State had to start again de novo with a clean sheet' (*Kingswood v Secretary of State for the Environment* (1989) 57 P&CR 153 at 162). The Judge in *Kingswood* went on to conclude that 'there can be no doubt that the Secretary of State must consider the matter de novo in circumstances where a decision is quashed' (p 163). It may also be that a declaration is sought as to what the legal position is.

Costs

In relation to costs it is possible that a promoter would be able to take advantage of the fixed costs regime in Part 45 of the CPR. Although it will depend on the precise grounds of challenge, it is entirely possible that such a challenge would be a claim to which the Aarhus Convention would apply. Where the rules apply, however, the total costs recoverable from a claimant are limited to £5,000 (individual) or £10,000 (others), and the costs recoverable by a claimant are limited to £35,000.

The availability of the £10,000 cap means, however, that a promoter might be tempted to launch a judicial review with limited prospects of success, knowing that costs exposure would be limited if the case were lost. Given how much would have been invested by a promoter in taking a DCO application through examination, some promoters might see the limited further expense of a judicial review as being a worthwhile risk, even if there were only very limited prospects of success.

Generally

The first judicial review by a promoter of a refusal of development consent was in relation to the Preesall Underground Gas Storage DCO: see *R (Halite Energy Group Ltd) v Secretary of State for Energy and Climate Change* [2014] EWHC 17 (Admin). The challenge was successful and led to the redetermination and, ultimately, to the grant of development consent for the project.

Article 96

Legal Challenge to Decision not to Accept Application

Richard Honey QC, ftb
Michael Humphries QC, ftb

Introduction

A legal challenge to a decision not to accept an application would be by way of judicial review. The normal principles and procedures of judicial review generally apply, subject to the provisions of PA 2008, s 118. In particular, there is a six-week time limit for bringing judicial review proceedings.

The main principles and procedural provisions relating to judicial review are considered in article 94 of this work. Those principles and procedural provisions, however, also apply to a challenge to a decision not to accept an application for development consent; subject to some key differences that are considered below.

PA 2008, s 118(3)

PA 2008, s 118 governs legal challenges relating to a decision not to accept an application. Section 118(3) (as amended) provides that:

> 'A court may entertain proceedings for questioning a decision of the Secretary of State under section 55 not to accept an application for an order granting development consent only if
>
> (a) the proceedings are brought by a claim for judicial review, and
>
> (b) the claim form is filed before the end of the period of 6 weeks beginning with the day after the day on which the Secretary of State notifies the applicant as required by subsection (7) of that section.'

This six-week time limit was unusual when the Act was introduced, but it is now the standard time limit for judicial review of planning decisions given the change made in July 2013 by the Civil Procedure (Amendment No 4) Rules 2013.

PA 2008, s 55 provides that the Secretary of State has 28 days after receipt of what purports to be an application for a development consent order to decide whether or not to accept the application. PA 2008, s 55(7) provides that, if the Secretary of State is of the view that the application cannot be accepted, he must notify the applicant of that and the reasons for it. This is the start date for the six-week period.

Procedural issues

Standing

A promoter bringing such a judicial review would have no problem establishing standing and the Planning Inspectorate's decision not to accept an application would be defended by the relevant Secretary of State. It is unlikely that an objector to the DCO would actively participate in the judicial review, although that would in practice depend on the circumstances of each case and the grounds of challenge. If, for example, the applicant was not accepted on grounds relating to adequacy of consultation, it is not inconceivable that a local authority that had given an adverse 'adequacy of consultation representation' (see PA 2008, s 55(4)(b) and (5)) might wish to participate in the judicial review.

Grounds for judicial review

PA 2008, s 55(3) provides that the Secretary of State may accept an application only if he concludes:

(a) that it is an application for an order granting development consent,

(c) that development consent is required for any of the development to which the application relates,

(e) that the applicant has, in relation to a proposed application that has become the application, complied with Chapter 2 of Part 5 (pre-application procedure), and

(f) that the application (including accompaniments) is of a standard that the Secretary of State considers satisfactory.

[NB other parts of PA 2008, s 55(3) were repealed by the Localism Act 2011.]

In relation to PA 2008, s 55(3)(e) above (that is, pre-application procedure), PA 2008, s 55(4) identifies a number of matters to which the Secretary of State must 'have regard' when reaching his conclusion, being:

(a) the consultation report received under PA 2008, s 37(3)(c),

(b) any adequacy of consultation representation received by the Secretary of State from a local authority consultee, and

(c) the extent to which the applicant has had regard to any guidance issued under PA 2008, s 50.

In relation to PA 2008, s 55(3)(f) above (that is, whether the application is of a 'satisfactory' standard), PA 2008, s 55(5A) identifies a number of further matters to which the Secretary of State must 'have regard' when reaching his conclusion, being the extent to which:

(a) the application complies with the requirements in PA 2008, s 37(3) (form and contents of application) and any standards set under PA 2008, s 37(5), and

(b) any applicable guidance given under PA 2008, s 37(4) has been followed in relation to the application.

It can be readily seen, therefore, that inherent in any decision not to accept an application under PA 2008, s 55 are a number of judgments by the Secretary of State that are susceptible to scrutiny in any application for judicial review. The Inspectorate could, for example, misunderstand or misinterpret one of the matters in PA 2008, s 55(3), including, for example, whether the pre-application procedures have been properly complied with.

PA 2008, s 55(3)(f) (application of a 'satisfactory' standard) was a matter added to PA 2008, s 55(3) on 1 April 2012 by the Localism Act 2011. This appears to be an additional matter to those in PA 2008, s 55(3)(a), (c) and (e), rather than a standard against which those other matters should be tested. Thus it would appear that, even if an application is of a standard that the Secretary of State considers 'satisfactory' (PA 2008, s 55(3)(f)), he must still be satisfied that it has also 'complied' with Chapter 2 of Part 5 of the Act (PA 2008, s 55(3)(e)). This understanding of how PA 2008, s 55(3) operates has not, however, been tested in the courts.

The reasons given pursuant to PA 2008, s 55(7) could also be inadequate, although reasons challenges often simply result in the reasons being 'corrected'.

Beyond such grounds focused on the requirements of PA 2008, s 55 itself, all the other usual grounds for judicial review would apply. Having said that, however, a challenge alleging that a decision not to accept an application on the basis of 'irrationality' would be likely to struggle to succeed. For a conclusion to be irrational or perverse, it must be one that that no reasonable person in the position of the Secretary of State, properly directing himself on the relevant material, could have reached (*Seddon v Secretary of State for the Environment* (1981) 42 P&CR 26). The courts have made it clear that they will require 'something overwhelming' from a claimant before allowing a challenge of this sort (*Associated Provincial Picture Houses v Wednesbury Corporation* [1948] 1 KB 223 at 230; see also 233–234). A claimant alleging that the Inspectorate has reached a *Wednesbury* unreasonable conclusion on a matter of judgment faces a particularly daunting task: see, for example, *R (Newsmith Stainless Ltd) v Secretary of State for the Environment, Transport and the Regions* [2001] EWHC Admin 74 at para 8.

PA 2008, s 55(4)(c) required the Secretary of State to have regard, in reaching the conclusion in PA 2008, s 55(3)(e) (pre-application procedures), to the extent to which the applicant has had regard to any guidance issued by the Secretary of State under PA 2008, s 50. Clearly if an applicant had correctly followed DCLG Guidance on an issue on which its application was later not accepted under PA 2008, s 55, that could raise issues of legitimate expectation: see eg *R v North and East Devon Health Authority, ex parte Coughlan* [2001] QB 213 and *Nadarajah & Abdi v Secretary of State for the Home Office* [2005] EWCA Civ 1363.

Other issues during conduct of proceedings

Where a decision has been made not to accept an application, the promoter is likely to wish to secure by way of disclosure all documents evidencing the consideration of the application by the Inspectorate, including the PA 2008, s 55 application checklist. This is likely to contain more detailed reasons than those set out pursuant to PA 2008, s 55(7). This could be secured under the duty of candour or by way of an application for specific disclosure, if necessary.

Generally

Although PA 2008, s 118(3) applies to a decision not to accept an application, it does not apply to a decision to accept an application. Such a challenge would be caught by PA 2008, s 118(7) which applies to 'proceedings for questioning anything else done, or omitted to be done, by the Secretary of State in relation to an application for an order granting development consent'.

As a decision under PA 2008, s 55 is a procedural decision, rather than a substantive decision, and some at least of the impediments to acceptance could be cured by an applicant supplying further or different information, it is a decision which might lead to a different outcome if taken a second time in different circumstances. It is not therefore a final decision in one sense, in that the Inspectorate could change its mind in the light of further information. This seems also to be the intention of PA 2008, s 55(8) that provides that 'If in response the applicant modifies (or further modifies) the application, subsections (2) to (7) then apply to the application as modified'.

This is, therefore, one area of judicial review in connection with the PA 2008 where both the pre-action protocol and alternative dispute resolution might have an important role in removing to reducing the need for judicial review. If errors are pointed out to, and accepted by, the Planning Inspectorate and/or the applicant, then there may be scope to re-submit or modify the application so that the re-submitted or modified application could be accepted.

The position with the Daventry International Rail Freight Terminal application, which was not accepted by the Inspectorate due to non-compliance with PA 2008, s 55(3)(e) and (f), is illustrated by the meeting note published on the register of advice (5 December 2012) and subsequent correspondence (19 December 2012). Following the Planning Inspectorate's decision not to accept, a meeting was held between the Planning Inspectorate and the promoter to agree the way forward; this led to an acceptable re-submission of the application. In the letter dated 28 November 2012 containing the notification of the decision not to accept the application, the Inspectorate had stated:

> 'We would also encourage you to meet with us so we can advise how best to address the issues to help facilitate a new application at the earliest opportunity.'

PINS Advice Note 6 (version 10 makes it very clear (para 1.3), however, that:

> 'Applicants are strongly encouraged to hold pre-application discussions with the Planning Inspectorate about how their application information should be prepared and submitted well in advance of formal submission. The Planning Inspectorate's pre-application service for Applicants "Prospectus for Applicants" is available on the National Infrastructure Planning website Prospectus for Applicants page.'

It is clearly in applicants' interests to engage with PINS before making any application, in order to remove, or at least reduce, the risk of an application not being accepted.

Article 97

Legal Challenge to Other Action of Secretary of State

Alex Booth QC, ftb
Michael Humphries QC, ftb

Introduction

PA 2008, s 118 deals with legal challenges to applications for orders granting development consent. Its purpose is, in effect, to regulate the timescales within which a challenge by way of judicial review may be brought against a decision of the Secretary of State in relation to an application for an order granting development consent. PA 2008, s 118 identifies six specific 'decisions' to which its provisions relate and then provides a general provision covering anything else done, or omitted to be done, by the Secretary of State. This general provision does not cover challenges to national policy statements, which are specifically dealt with under PA 2008, s 13.

The specific 'decisions' covered by PA 2008, s 118 comprise:

- an order granting development consent (PA 2008, s 118(1));
- a refusal of development consent (PA 2008, s 118(2));
- a decision under PA 2008, s 55 *not* to accept an application for an order granting development (PA 2008, s 118(3));
- a decision under PA 2008, Sch 4, para 1 in relation to an error or omission in a decision document (PA 2008, s 118(4));
- a decision under PA 2008, Sch 6, para 2(1) to make a change to an order granting development consent (PA 2008, s 118(5)); and
- a decision under PA 2008, Sch 6, para 3(1) to make a change to, or revoke, an order granting development consent (PA 2008, s 118(6)).

In the case of each of these specific decisions, a challenge may *only* be brought by way of judicial review where the claim form is filed before the end of the period of six weeks 'beginning with the day after' the date of an event identified in the individual provision.

The PA 2008 recognises, however, that there could be other decisions of the Secretary of State, or the Examining Authority on behalf of the Secretary of State, which do not fall within the above six cases and where a legal challenge could otherwise be brought under the normal judicial review timescales. As stated above, to deal with this eventuality the Act provides a general provision covering 'anything else done, or omitted to be done, by the Secretary of State' (PA 2008, s 118(7)). This article examines this general provision.

As yet, of the various applications for judicial review that have lodged in respect of the development consent process, none have been brought pursuant to the general provision under PA 2008, s 118(7).

PA 2008, s 118(7)

PA 2008, s 118(7) (as amended) provides as follows:

> 'A court may entertain proceedings for questioning anything else done, or omitted to be done, by the Secretary of State in relation to an application for an order granting development consent only if–
>
> (a) the proceedings are brought by a claim for judicial review, and
>
> (b) the claim form is filed before the end of the period of 6 weeks beginning with the day after the relevant day.'

It is important to note that a court may entertain proceedings for questions anything else done, or omitted to be done, 'only' if brought by judicial review before the end of six weeks beginning with the day after the 'relevant day'. The effect of PA 2008, s 118(7) is, therefore, to 'oust' any other avenue of legal challenge and impose a strict six-week time limit.

It is also important to note that PA 2008, s 118(7) is directed to anything done, or omitted to be done, 'in relation to an application' for development consent. It is not absolutely clear, therefore, whether it covers an act or omission of the Secretary of State during the pre-application procedures under the 2008 Act. Certainly the point did not appear to have been raised be the defendant in the *Innovia Cellophane Ltd* challenge to the (former) Infrastructure Planning Commission's grant of PA 2008, s 53 authorisation in respect of the then proposed Hinkley Point C application for development consent: see *R (Innovia Cellophane Ltd) v Infrastructure Planning Commission* [2011] EWHC 2883 (Admin).

Within six weeks 'beginning with' the 'relevant day'

The period within which a claim may be brought is identified as 'beginning with the day after the relevant day' (PA 2008, s 118(7)(b)). The 'relevant day' is itself defined (PA 2008, s 118(8)) as meaning the day on which:

- the application for development consent is withdrawn;
- the order granting development consent or the statement of reasons in respect of that order is 'published', whichever is the later;
- the statement of reasons for refusing to grant development consent is 'published'.

The first of these potential starting dates envisages a scenario in which an applicant for development consent has withdrawn its application, but a person still wishes to challenge a decision of the Secretary of State. Whilst it is not immediately obvious why a person might still wish to challenge a decision of the Secretary of State after an application for a development consent order has been withdrawn, it might be relevant, for example, where the Secretary of State had authorised entry on land by the promoter of a project under PA 2008, s 53 before the application for development consent had been withdrawn. Such a claim would allow a landowner to challenge a 'redundant' PA 2008, s 53 authorisation.

It is worth noting that this 'withdrawn' application scenario provides the only opportunity for a challenge to be brought in respect of a decision of the Secretary of State prior to either the publication of the order or, alternatively, the publication of the statement of reasons for its refusal.

Thus the effect of PA 2008, s 118 in general, and PA 2008, s 118(7) in particular, is that a legal challenge may not be brought in respect of a decision of the Secretary of State from the making of the application until the grant or refusal of consent (subject to the 'withdrawn' application point). Thus a challenge may not be brought to any procedural decision taken during the examination of an application for development consent. The absence of any means of challenge during an examination may, however, mean storing up trouble for later in the process. Indeed, an applicant may even recognise that a particular act or omission by the Examining Authority, on behalf of the Secretary of State, at an early stage in the examination process could afford potential claimants with a fertile ground of challenge, but then be left waiting until the order is granted to see whether a challenge is indeed brought. Thus there is a risk that considerable resources may be expended during the remainder of the examination and ultimately be wasted.

A further point to consider within the context of timing, concerns the second of the start dates identified above, and the fact that the claim form may only be filed during the period of six weeks 'beginning with the day after' the 'publication' of a development consent order.

The requirement to 'publish' the order is contained in PA 2008, s 117. The order must be published 'in such manner as the Secretary of State thinks appropriate' (PA 2008, s 117(3)), unless the order:

- makes by-laws,
- introduces offences,
- applies, modifies or excludes a statutory provision, or
- amends, repeals or revokes a statutory provision of local application,

in which case it must be contained in a statutory instrument (PA 2008, s 117(4)). Statutory instruments are officially published by Her Majesty's Stationery Office (HMSO) on the website of The National Archives (www.legislation.gov.uk), where new statutory instruments they are listed by publication date.

The requirement to 'publish' a statement of reasons for a decision to grant development consent is contained in PA 2008, s 116. The statement must again be published 'in such manner as the Secretary of State thinks appropriate' (PA 2008, s 116(3)).

Typically, an Order granting development consent and the Secretary of State's statement of reasons for making the Order will be published simultaneously on the Planning Inspectorate's website (https://infrastructure.planninginspectorate.gov.uk).

In *R (Williams) v Secretary of State for Energy and Climate Change* [2015] EWHC 1202 (Admin), Lindblom J (as he then was) said (para 45) that:

> 'The way in which an order and the Secretary of State's statement of reasons for making it are to be "published" is not prescribed by section 118. But in my view the placing of the order on the Planning Inspectorate's infrastructure planning website …, together with the Secretary of State's decision letter and the Examining Authority's report, and, on the same day, the notification of the interested parties, both by email and post, that this has been done, was enough to constitute publication of the order, and the reasons why it was made, within the meaning of section 118.'

The requirement to 'publish' a statement of reasons for a decision to refuse development consent is contained in PA 2008, s 116. The statement must be published 'in such manner as the Secretary of State thinks appropriate' (PA 2008, s 116(3)).

The effect of PA 2008, s 118 delaying legal challenge until the 'publication' of a development consent order can be seen in relation to FCC Environmental Ltd (formerly Waste Recycling Group Ltd) in respect of its PA 2008, s 118(1) claim for judicial review of the development consent order granted to Covanta Rookery South Ltd for a resource recovery facility in Bedfordshire.

In that instance, the Infrastructure Planning Commission issued its statement of reasons for the grant of development consent on 13 October 2011 and made a draft DCO on 22 November 2011. The draft was placed before Parliament on 29 November that year, but thereafter underwent special parliamentary procedure. The DCO was then 'published' on 26 March 2013, and it was only at that stage that judicial review proceedings were, or indeed could be, lodged.

Matters for challenge

There are a limited number of matters which might conceivably form the basis of a challenge pursuant to PA 2008, s 118(7), since in most cases proceedings are likely to be brought either pursuant to PA 2008, s 118(1) (challenge to order granting development consent) or PA 2008, s 118(2) (challenge to refusal of development consent). Although as yet there is no legal authority upon the point, such would appear to be the case even if the substance of a complaint related to a procedural decision of the Secretary of State during the examination period. Thus a decision in respect of an application made by an objector that an examination should be suspended pursuant to reg 17 of the Infrastructure Planning (Environmental Impact Assessment) Regulations 2009, SI 2009/2263, on the basis of the inadequacy of an environmental statement, might well still be made under PA 2008, s 118(1) if development consent were granted; notwithstanding it was a procedural decision on which the claim was founded.

As such, it is only certain discrete actions of the Secretary of State that would fall to be challenged pursuant to PA 2008, s 118(7) such as, by way of example, the decision to issue a certificate pursuant to PA 2008, s 127(2) approving the compulsory acquisition of land held by a statutory undertaker.

In such an instance, the subject-matter of the challenge would not comprise part of the decision reached in respect of the DCO application itself, but would instead comprise an associated but distinct determination. In this example, PA 2008, s 118(7) would be relevant, as a challenge to the decision to issue/refuse certification for compulsory purchase pursuant to PA 2008, s 127 would not comprise 'proceedings for questioning an order granting development consent' under PA 2008, s 118(1).

It may be that the full scope of PA 2008, s 118(7) will only become apparent as the provision is tested in the courts. For the present, however, it would appear that it will have only limited application.

Part 15

Enforcement

Article 98

Enforcement under the Planning Act 2008

Michael Humphries QC, ftb

Introduction

PA 2008, Part 8 sets up the system of 'enforcement' under the Act for: (a) development without development consent; and (b) breach of the terms of an order granting development consent. It is worth noting at the outset that the PA 2008 enforcement system is radically different from that under the Town and Country Planning Act 1990.

In broad terms, the PA 2008 creates two criminal offences:

(a) the carrying out of development for which development consent is required without first obtaining without development consent (PA 2008, s 160); and

(b) the carrying out of development in breach of the terms of a DCO or otherwise failing to comply with the terms of a DCO (PA 2008, s 161).

Only where a person has been found guilty of an offence under either of these provisions may a local planning authority serve a 'notice of unauthorised development' requiring 'steps' to be carried out to rectify the position. This is in sharp contrast to the Town and Country Planning Act 1990 regime where breaches of planning control are first made subject to civil enforcement and only then, in certain circumstances, made the subject-matter of an offence. A local planning authority may, however, apply to the High Court for an injunction to restrain any actual or apprehended activity that would be an offence under PA 2008, s 160 or 161.

This article will consider:

- offences;
- notices of unauthorised development; and
- injunctions.

Offences

PA 2008, ss 160 and 161

PA 2008, Part 8 creates two primary offences, those being under PA 2008, ss 160 and 161.

PA 2008, s 160

PA 2008, s 160 provides that:

> '(1) A person commits an offence if the person carries out, or causes to be carried out, development for which development consent is required at a time when no development consent is in force in respect of the development.'

A person guilty of an offence under this section is liable on summary conviction, or on conviction on indictment, to a fine: see PA 2008, s 160(2).

The reference in PA 2008, s 160(1) to development for which development consent is 'required' relates directly to PA 2008, s 31 and the requirement for development consent for 'development' to the extent that such development 'is or forms part of a nationally significant infrastructure project'. This again relates back to PA 2008, s 14, which defines the term 'nationally significant infrastructure project', and the various thresholds in PA 2008, ss 15–30.

It seems unlikely that an infrastructure developer would deliberately carry out development requiring development consent without first having obtained a DCO and so offences are likely to fall within two broad categories, being:

- development thought to be within PA 2008 regime that extends physically or functionally beyond that actually granted by a DCO; or
- development thought to be outside the PA 2008 regime that has breached some NSIP threshold.

In relation to the first of these categories, it is clearly within the power of the promoter to ensure that any DCO is drafted so as to grant the necessary consent to carry out the development. It is for this reason that 'parameters' and the concept of the 'Rochdale envelope' are so important.

In relation to the second category above, it will be particularly important for any developer proposing an infrastructure project to ascertain with some certainty whether such project falls within the scope of the PA 2008, as any error of understanding could result in a criminal conviction. Such an error may be made, for example, where what is being proposed is an 'alteration' to an existing infrastructure development, that alteration itself falling above a relevant threshold. An offence will be committed under this section notwithstanding that planning permission, or other consent, may have been granted for the development by a local planning authority or other decision-maker acting under the same error of understanding.

Clearly the criminal law standard of proof (ie beyond reasonable doubt) will apply to any proceedings under PA 2008, s 160.

PA 2008, s 161

PA 2008, s 161 provides that:

> '(1) A person commits an offence if without reasonable excuse the person–
>
> (a) carries out, or causes to be carried out, development in breach of the terms of an order granting development consent, or
>
> (b) otherwise fails to comply with the terms of an order granting development consent.'

Again, a person guilty of an offence under this section is liable on summary conviction, or on conviction on indictment, to a fine: see PA 2008, s 160(2).

It is important to note that, by virtue of s PA 2008, ss 161(2) and 149A(4), a person who fails to comply with a 'condition' under a deemed 'marine licence' does not commit an offence under PA 2008, s 161, although breach of requirement for, or conditions of, a marine licence would be an offence under Marine and Coastal Access Act 2009, s 85.

The offence under PA 2008, s 161 may be committed where a person either: (a) carries out development in 'breach' of the terms of an order (PA 2008, s 161(1)(a)); or (b) 'fails to comply with the terms' of an order (PA 2008, s 161(1)(b)). In this context, the expression 'the terms of an order' would appear to comprise the articles in the body of the DCO, the contents of its schedules (including any plans) and, in particular, its 'requirements'.

PA 2008, s 161(1)(a) appears to contemplate the person committing the offence undertaking some positive action in 'carrying out development' in breach of the terms of a DCO which does exist for the project. This offence can be distinguished, therefore, from that under PA 2008, s 160 where the carrying out of development is at a time where there is no DCO for that project. An offence under this provision might comprise, for example, the carrying out of development in breach of a requirement first to submit details for approval by the local planning authority.

By contrast, PA 2008, s 161(1)(b) does not require the person committing the offence to be 'carrying out development' and so would be particularly relevant during the operational stages of any project. An offence under this provision might comprise, for example, operating the project in breach of any requirement relating to hours of operation.

The offence created under PA 2008, s 161 does introduce the potential defence of 'reasonable excuse', which was absent from PA 2008, s 160. The term 'reasonable excuse', which also appears in PA 2008, ss 53(6) and 168, is not defined in PA 2008, although it is a concept that occurs in other legislation. In such circumstances, it would appear that the words should be given their ordinary meaning and that an 'excuse' (in other words, an explanation for not complying with the terms of a DCO) will have to be advanced by a defendant, which will have to be judged 'reasonable' in considering whether an offence has been committed under PA 2008, s 161.

PA 2008, s 161(3) also makes it a defence under PA 2008, s 161 to prove that: (a) the breach or failure to comply occurred only because of 'an error or omission in the order'; and (b) a 'correction notice' specifying the correction of the error or omission has been issued under PA 2008, Sch 4, para 2.

Clearly, as with an offence under PA 2008, s 160, the criminal law standard of proof (ie beyond reasonable doubt) will apply to any proceedings under PA 2008, s 161.

Time limits

PA 2008, s 162 sets certain time limits for charging a person with an offence under PA 2008, ss 160 and 161. PA 2008, s 162(1) provides that a person may not be charged with an offence under PA 2008, s 160 or 161 after the end of:

- the 'relevant four-year period'; or
- in certain circumstances, the 'extended period'.

The four-year period

PA 2008, s 162(2) provides that:

> 'The "relevant 4-year period" means–
>
> (a) in the case of an offence under section 160, the period of 4 years beginning with the date on which the development was substantially completed;

(b) in the case of an offence under section 161, the period of 4 years beginning with the later of–

(i) the date on which the development was substantially completed, and

(ii) the date on which the breach or failure to comply occurred.'

The term 'substantially completed' in PA 2008, s 162(2) reflects the same language as Town and Country Planning Act 1990, s 171B, and the case law that has developed under that section is likely to be highly material in relation to PA 2008, s 162(2).

The extended period

The 'extended period' applies where an information notice has been served under PA 2008, s 167 (see below) or an injunction applied for under PA 2008, s 171 (see below): see PA 2008, s 162(3). In such circumstances, PA 2008, s 162(4) provides that the four-year period runs from:

- the date of service of any information notice;
- the date of any application for an injunction; or
- the later of those dates, if both apply.

The relevant local planning authority

For the purposes of PA 2008, Part 8, the term 'the relevant local planning authority' in relation to any land is defined by PA 2008, s 173 as the local planning authority for the area in which the land is situated.

Where, however, there is both a district planning authority and a county planning authority for an area then:

- if the 'relevant development' (see PA 2008, s 173(6)) is the construction or alteration of a hazardous waste facility within PA 2008, s 14(1)(p), the relevant local planning authority is the county planning authority (PA 2008, s 173(4)); and
- in any other case, the relevant local planning authority is the district planning authority (PA 2008, s 173(5)).

Rights of entry

PA 2008, s 163 provides a right to enter land 'without warrant' if the 'relevant local planning authority' 'has reasonable grounds for suspecting' that an offence under PA 2008, s 160 or 161 'is being, or has been, committed' on or in respect of the land.

The person authorised to enter the land under PA 2008, s 163 may 'at any reasonable hour' enter the land for the purpose of 'ascertaining whether' an offence under PA 2008, s 160 or 161 has been, or is being, committed on the land: see PA 2008, s 163(2); although the person may only enter a building occupied as a dwelling on the giving of 24 hours' notice to the occupier of the building: see PA 2008, s 163(3).

This power clearly relates to any offence under PA 2008, s 160 or 161 that 'is being, or has been' committed; but not to 'apprehended' future offences. To the extent, therefore, that PA 2008, s 171 allows a local planning authority to apply for an injunction to restrain an 'apprehended' 'prohibited activity' (ie an anticipated future offence under PA 2008, s 160 or 161), PA 2008, s 163 would not give the relevant local planning authority power to enter the land.

PA 2008, s 164 gives the relevant local planning authority power to enter land 'under warrant' where: (a) admission to the land has been refused, or a refusal is reasonably apprehended; or (b) the case is one of urgency.

PA 2008, s 165 set out various supplementary provisions relating to the rights of entry under PA 2008, ss 163 and 164, including in relation to matters such as the wilful obstruction of a person exercising a right of entry as above, and compensation for damage caused to the land and chattels in the exercise of any such right of entry.

Information notices

An 'information notice' may be served under PA 2008, s 167 where it appears to 'the relevant local planning authority' that an offence under PA 2008, s 160 or 161 'may have been committed on or in respect of the land'.

This power clearly relates to offences that 'may have' been committed (ie 'past' offences), rather than anticipated future offences under PA 2008, s 160 or 161. As with the right to enter under PA 2008, s 163, therefore, to the extent that PA 2008, s 171 allows a local planning authority to apply for an injunction to restrain an 'apprehended' 'prohibited activity' (ie an anticipated future offence), PA 2008, s 167 would not allow the relevant local planning authority to require the giving of information to that 'apprehended' activity.

By virtue of PA 2008, s 167(2), such a notice may only be served by 'the relevant local planning authority' and, by PA 2008, s 167(3), may only be served on any person who: (a) is the owner or occupier of the land or has any other interest in it; or (b) is carrying out operations on the land or is using it for any purpose. Thus the power is wide enough to require information from contractors or others carrying out development.

An information notice may require (PA 2008, s 167(4)) the person served to give:

- information about any operations being carried out in, on, over or under the land, any use of the land and any other activities being carried out in, on, over or under the land; and
- information about the provisions of any order granting development consent for development of the land.

Notices of unauthorised development

PA 2008, s 169 provides for the relevant local planning authority to serve a 'notice of unauthorised development' where a person is found guilty of an offence under PA 2008, s 160 or 161.

The first thing to note is that such a notice can only *follow* successful criminal proceedings under PA 2008, s 160 or 161; a notice under PA 2008, s 169 cannot be served in advance of, or in parallel with, such proceedings. This is in sharp contrast with the approach under the Town and Country Planning Act 1990 where civil enforcement precedes any criminal proceedings.

Where the offence in respect of which a person has been found guilty is under PA 2008, s 160, then the relevant local planning authority may serve a notice of unauthorised development on the person under PA 2008, s 169(2), requiring such 'steps' as may be specified in the notice to be taken:

- to remove the development; and
- to restore the land on which the development has been carried out to its condition before the development was carried out.

The notice of unauthorised development must specify the period within which any 'steps' are required to be taken and may specify different periods for different steps: see PA 2008, s 169(5).

Where the offence in respect of which a person has been found guilty is under PA 2008, s 161, then the relevant local planning authority may serve a notice of unauthorised development on the person under PA 2008, s 169(4), requiring the person to remedy the breach or failure to comply.

Although PA 2008, s 169(4) does not refer to 'steps' required to be taken to remedy the breach or failure to comply, and therefore it is not clear whether PA 2008, s 169(5) applies, it would appear prudent to set out in the notice any period, or periods, within which the person is to remedy the breach or failure to comply.

PA 2008, s 170 sets out various matters relating to the execution of works required by notice of unauthorised development, including in relation to liability for expenses incurred in complying with any such notice (PA 2008, s 170(2)).

Injunctions

A 'local planning authority' may apply to the High Court or the county court for an injunction pursuant to PA 2008, s 171 if it considers it 'necessary or expedient' for any 'actual or apprehended prohibited activity' to be restrained by injunction.

For these purposes a 'prohibited activity' means an activity that constitutes an offence under PA 2008, s 160 or 161 in relation to land in the area of the local planning authority: see PA 2008, s 171(2).

PA 2008, s 171 makes it clear that an application for an injunction may be brought by 'a local planning authority' for the land in respect of which the 'prohibited activity' has taken place; thus the exercise of the power is not restricted to the 'relevant local planning authority' under PA 2008, s 173. Consequently, for land where there is both a district planning authority and a county planning authority, it would appear that either may make an application for an injunction under PA 2008, s 171.

It is important to note that a local planning authority may apply for an injunction under PA 2008, s 171 for any 'actual' or 'apprehended' prohibited activity. An 'actual' prohibited activity is clearly one that has occurred or is occurring. The term 'apprehended' is not one that is defined in PA 2008 but, given its ordinary meaning, an 'apprehended' prohibited activity is clearly one that is reasonably anticipated. Indeed, as injunctions are not granted lightly by the High Court or the county court, one might expect a local planning authority to have to demonstrate fairly clear grounds for 'apprehending' that an offence is likely to be committed under PA 2008, s 160 or 161.

On an application under PA 2008, s 171 the court may grant such an injunction as it 'thinks fit' for the purpose of restraining the prohibited activity: see PA 2008, s 171(3).

Part 16

Miscellaneous Issues

Article 99

Amendments to a DCO Application

Isabella Tafur, ftb
Michael Humphries QC, ftb

Introduction

Circumstances may arise in which an application for a development consent order requires amendment after it has been accepted by the Secretary of State. This article examines the extent to which is it possible to amend a DCO application post-acceptance and the policy guidance for doing so.

PA 2008, s 114

PA 2008, s 114(1) provides that, when the Secretary of State has decided an application for an order granting development consent, he or she must either:

- make the order granting development consent; or
- refuse development consent.

PA 2008, s 114(1) is not explicit on the point as to whether the Secretary of State can make the order 'with or without modifications', but there is nothing in PA 2008, s 114(1) to limit the Secretary of State's power to make such order as he thinks fit.

PA 2008, s 114(2) empowers the Secretary of State to make provision regulating the procedure to be followed if he proposes to make an order granting development consent in terms which are materially different from those proposed in the application. No such 'provision' has so far been made by regulation or otherwise, save in relation to compulsory acquisition by the Infrastructure Planning (Compulsory Acquisition) Regulations 2010. However, there is nothing in PA 2008, s 114(2) that 'requires' the Secretary of State to make provision for any particular procedure if he proposed to make an order granting development consent on terms materially different from those proposed in the application.

In practice, therefore, it is clear that PA 2008, s 114 does allow the Secretary of State to make an order granting development consent on terms materially different from those applied for. This view appears to be entirely consistent with the so-called 'Bob Neill letter'.

On 28 November 2011 the then Secretary of State, Bob Neill MP, wrote to Sir Michael Pitt on the scope of PA 2008, s 114 in the context of the Brig y Cwm application. He set out the Government's position as follows:

> 'My Department has received representation questioning whether section 114(1) empowers the decision-maker to make a development consent order in different terms from that applied for. This was the subject of an amendment laid at the Lord Report stage of the Localism Bill, and in response, Earl Attlee confirmed the Government's view, that section 114(1) clearly places the responsibility for making a development

consent order on the decision-maker, and does not limit the terms in which it can be made. If follows from this that the decision-maker has them power under section 114(1) to make a development consent order which is different from that originally applied for, and that no regulations are needed under section 114(2) in order to do so.

The power to make regulations in section 114(2) is unconnected, and has no bearing on the extent of the s 114(1) power. Section 114(2) merely provides the Secretary of State with a power to make regulations about how material changes should be dealt with, if he thinks it appropriate to do so.'

Examination Procedure Rules

Infrastructure Planning (Examination Procedure) Rules 2010, r 2 makes it absolutely clear that amendments can be made to an application post-acceptance, by defining 'application' in the following way:

> 'an application for development consent under section 37 (application for orders granting development consent) and includes–
>
> (a) part of an application;
>
> (b) any accompanying documents and further representations made by the applicant; and
>
> (c) *any amendments made to the application*.' (emphasis added)

Guidance on making a change to a DCO application

In the Bob Neill letter, the Secretary of State also commented that:

> 'This power provided by section 114(1) is, of course, limited in a number of ways. If the Examining Authority decides to consider material changes to an application as part of the examination, the Examining Authority will need to act reasonably, and in accordance with the principles of natural justice. In particular the principles arising from the *Wheatcroft* case must be fully addressed, which essentially require that anyone affected by amended proposals must have a fair opportunity to have their views heard and properly taken into account regarding them.
>
> … Depending on the circumstances, in accordance with the principles set out in *Wheatcroft*, the Examining Authority may need to:
>
> - extend the examination using the power in section 98(4) of the Act to consult interested parties on the effect of the proposed amendments, and allow time to consider any amendments accepted for examination
> - take into account what publicity (if any) the promoter has carried out to ensure people who are not interested parties have an opportunity to make representations
> - use the general power to control the examination of an application in section 87(1) of the 2008 Act to make changes to the timetable to allow for representations to be made regarding any such amendments
> - exercise its discretion under rules 10(3) and 14(10) of the Infrastructure Planning (Examination Procedure) Rules 2010 to permit representations to be made by people who are not interested parties in cases where it is appropriate to do so.'

DCLG Guidance for the examination of applications for development consent (2015) gives the following guidance (paras 109–115) on changing a draft development consent order post-acceptance:

> 'It is expected that applications will be as well prepared as possible prior to submission and an application will not be accepted if it is not of a satisfactory standard. However, the Government recognises that there are occasions when applicants may need to make material changes to a proposal after an application has been accepted for examination. Reasons for this could include, for example, regulatory changes, technical developments or the discovery of previously unknown factors arising from representations received after acceptance or examination submissions.
>
> However, if it is determined that a proposed change is of such a degree that it constitutes a materially different project then the applicant will need to determine how best to proceed. The applicant may decide to withdraw their existing application and restart the pre-application process or continue with their application in its original form or they may decide to submit an alternative proposal for change. It should be noted that the Examining Authority will not be able to indicate what degree of change would be acceptable in advance of the applicant submitting a proposed change.
>
> It is important for all parties to remember that it is for the applicant to decide whether or not to propose a change to a proposal during the examination. Other parties can highlight those areas where they think a proposal should be changed during their discussion with the applicant in the pre-application period and also in their written representations.
>
> Before proposing a change, applicants should carefully consider the impact that it will have on any non-planning permits which they are seeking alongside their Development Consent Order. A change in the Development Consent Order may mean that it is not possible to issue these non-planning permits to the same timescale as the Development Consent Order.
>
> In considering a proposed material change to an application and before making a procedural decision about whether and how to examine the changed application, the Examining Authority will need to ensure it is able to act reasonably and fairly, in accordance with the principles of natural justice and in doing so, there will be a number of factors to consider such as:
>
> - whether the application (as changed) is still of a sufficient standard for examination;
> - whether sufficient consultation on the changed application can be undertaken to allow for the examination to be completed within the statutory timetable of 6 months; and
> - whether any other procedural requirements can still be met.
>
> It is expected that applicants will discuss the implications of any changes they wish to make with relevant statutory consultees and notify the Examining Authority at the earliest opportunity. This should allow the Examining Authority to accommodate any appropriate consultation on the change within the six month examination period.
>
> If an applicant seeks to introduce a material change during the final stages of the examination period, it is unlikely to be accepted on the basis that the application cannot be examined within the statutory timetable without breaching the principles of fairness and reasonableness.'

The DCLG Guidance has now been supplemented by PINS Advice Note 16 (version 2) on 'How to request a change which may be material'. The Advice Note states (preamble) that:

> 'This advice note is intended to build on the Examination Guidance and establish a structured approach to provide greater certainty for applicants when making a request for a material change, as well as explaining the implications of doing so. This note is relevant to the Pre-examination and Examination stages since these are the only times when a request to make a material change to an application can be considered by the appointed ExA.'

And later (para 1.3) that:

> 'The justification for making a material change after an application has been accepted for examination must be robust and there should be good reasons as to why the matters driving the change were not identified and dealt with proactively at the pre-application stage. Before an applicant makes a material change request it should carefully consider how it will impact upon the other interested parties and the examination timetable.'

Within that context, the Advice Note covers the following issues:

- what constitutes a material change;
- key steps in requesting a potential material change to an application;
- information required with a material change request;
- the role of the Examining Authority; and
- timing implications.

These points are not summarised here but, before making any application to make a material change to an application after it has been accepted for examination, it will be important to consider carefully the information that PINS will require in support of any such application. In this regard, PINS Advice Note 16 (version 2) states (Figure 3) that the following information will be required:

> '1. A clear description of the proposed change, including any new/altered works and any new/altered ancillary matters.
>
> 2. A statement setting out the rationale and pressing need for making the change with reference to Examination Guidance, any relevant National Policy Statement(s) as appropriate and any other important and relevant matters.
>
> 3. A full schedule … of all application documents and plans listing consequential revisions to each document and plan or a "no change" annotation. The schedule should include an update of any consents/licences required and whether (given the proposed change to the application) there will be any impediment to securing the consents/licences before the Examination is concluded.
>
> 4. A track changed version of the draft DCO showing each proposed change, and a track changed revised draft Explanatory Memorandum. If drafting changes have been made to the draft DCO during the course of the Examination, applicants should check with the ExA which version of the draft DCO and draft Explanatory Memorandum should be used for this purpose.
>
> 5. If the proposed change involves changes to the Order land …, confirmation that the Infrastructure Planning (Compulsory Acquisition) Regulations 2010 (the CA Regulations) are not engaged including if appropriate a copy of the

consent obtained from persons with an interest in the additional land. If the CA Regulations are engaged applicants must provide the information prescribed by Regulation 5 of the CA Regulations … and should clarify how it is considered that the procedural requirements of the CA Regulations can be met within the statutory six month Examination stage.

6. If the proposed change results in any new or different likely significant environmental effects, provision of other environmental information and confirmation that:

   A. the effects have been adequately assessed and that the environmental information has been subject to publicity. Whilst not statutorily required, the publicity should reflect the requirements of The Infrastructure Planning (Environmental Impact Assessment) Regulations 2017 (the EIA Regulations) and applicants should also submit copies of any representations received in response to this publicity with the change request.

   B. any consultation bodies who might have an interest in the proposed changes have been consulted (reflecting the requirements of the EIA Regulations). It is recommended that applicants submit copies of any responses received from consultation bodies with the change request. Applicants should identify those consultation bodies who were consulted on the proposed changes but NOT on the original application.

7. Where (proportionate) additional non-statutory consultation has been carried out (either voluntarily or at the direction of the ExA) a Consultation Statement confirming who has been consulted in relation to the proposed change should be submitted. Copies of any consultation responses received by the applicant should also be included with any request, as an annex.'

However, the preamble to PINS Advice Note 16 (version 2) makes an important point that should be carefully considered by all applicants:

> 'A material change request made in the final few weeks of the examination is unlikely to be accepted by the ExA, and its report and recommendation will be made on the basis of the application as it stands at the time of Examination close.'

Article 100

Costs in DCO Examinations

Douglas Edwards QC, ftb
Michael Humphries QC, ftb

Introduction

At the conclusion of the examination process, it may be that one or more of the interested parties, affected persons or indeed any other person who takes part in an examination wishes to claim the costs, or some of the costs, that they incurred in that process from another person. This article considers the power to make an order for costs, the procedure for applying for costs, the approach that will be taken to such applications, and also gives some examples of situations where costs awards may be appropriate.

DCLG published guidance on 'Awards of costs: examination of applications for development consent orders' in July 2013.

It is important to note that the Planning Practice Guidance ('PPG') advice on costs applies to the 'Planning Acts' (see PPG Paragraph: 029 Reference ID: 16-029-20140306), but these are defined *not* to include the PA 2008 (TCPA 1990, s 336). Thus the PPG advice on costs is not directly applicable to applications under the PA 2008.

The power to award costs

PA 2008, s 95(4) applies Local Government Act 1972, s 250(5) to the examination by an Examining Authority ('ExA') of an application for a development consent order. It consequently gives an ExA the power to award costs in the same way that an Inspector may award costs at a planning inquiry.

Procedure for claiming costs

Who can apply?

Standing to apply for costs is broad; any party who took part in the examination can apply. That includes interested parties under PA 2008, s 102, affected persons under PA 2008, s 59, additional affected persons and additional interested parties under reg 2 of the Infrastructure Planning (Compulsory Acquisition) Regulations 2010, and any other person who took part in the examination. The use of the term 'party' in this article refers to all such categories of person.

Time limits

An application for costs must be made within 28 days of the ExA giving notice that it has completed its examination. Failure to apply within 28 days will usually result in the ExA refusing to consider the application, unless good reason can be shown for applying late. It is therefore always best practice to apply within the 28 days.

In the event that the examination comes to an early end, perhaps because the application for development consent is withdrawn or because the examination is cancelled, the 28-day period begins to run from the date on which the ExA gives notification of that withdrawal or the cancellation.

Procedure

In either case, the application for costs should be made in writing to the Planning Inspectorate at Temple Quay House, 2 The Square, Temple Quay, Bristol, BS1 6PN. There is no particular format for the application, but it should set out the broad nature of the costs claimed, the basis on which costs are sought (ie the conduct complained of) and should explain how costs have been incurred as a result of that conduct.

The costs application will be assessed by the same ExA that considered the main application for development consent, but as the costs decision is made after the conclusion of the examination it is obviously made separately and a party who, for instance, unsuccessfully opposes development consent, may still be awarded their costs.

Upon receipt of an application for costs, the ExA will first contact the parties against whom costs are sought and require them to respond within a set period of time. It will then invite final comments from the party who applied for costs, again within a set period of time. The ExA will then take all of these submissions into account in reaching a decision.

Assessment of costs

Beyond determining whether an award of costs will be full or partial (see below), the ExA's decision will not settle the amount of costs that should be paid. Therefore, when a party receives a full or partial costs award, the next step will be for that party to contact the paying party and attempt to agree the costs payable.

If the parties cannot agree, then the matter will require detailed assessment by a Costs Officer of the Senior Court Costs Office at Thomas More Building, Royal Courts of Justice, Strand, London WC2A 2LL and on 020 7947 6000. Part 47 of the Civil Procedure Rules and its accompanying Practice Direction will apply to any detailed assessment.

Given the various stages in the process it will therefore be appreciated that the final costs decision may come some time after the completion of the examination, and indeed after the initial costs application.

Enforcement

It is to be hoped that matters do not reach this stage, but if after having received a costs award and having the amount of those costs determined by agreement or on detailed assessment, those costs are not then paid, the costs award can be enforced through the courts. Part 70 of the Civil Procedure Rules and its accompanying Practice Direction will apply.

Approach taken to applications for costs

Principles applied

The starting point of any assessment of costs is that, unlike in most litigation, in the ordinary course of events all parties should bear their own costs. An award of costs must therefore be seen as being out of the ordinary, and should be made against this background.

An ExA is most likely to award costs where the following three conditions are satisfied:

- first, the application for costs has been made in a timely manner within 28 days of the completion of the examination;
- secondly, the party from whom costs are sought has acted unreasonably; and
- thirdly, that unreasonable behaviour has caused, in whole or in part, the party seeking their costs to incur wasted or otherwise unnecessary expenditure.

As is therefore apparent, the key issue will be whether the other party acted unreasonably. The courts have been clear that in the context of cost awards, 'unreasonable' is to be given its ordinary English meaning.

Although the costs awarded can only relate to those incurred in the examination itself, the conduct complained of can relate to the pre-examination period or indeed even to the period before the application for development consent was submitted. The key is that the conduct caused costs to be incurred in the examination.

Examples of 'unreasonable' conduct

The list of unreasonable conduct is never closed, but common examples of procedure related behaviour that may be found an award of costs include:

- submitting documents late;
- failing to cooperate or to respond to reasonable requests in a timely fashion;
- submitting new or substantial evidence late, especially where this then requires other parties to submit further evidence in response;
- failing to agree on a statement of common ground or factual matters where this increases the amount of work other parties have to complete on other documents;
- withdrawing evidence at a late stage, especially where other parties have prepared on the basis of the withdrawn documents;
- failing to appear at a hearing or a site visit; and
- withdrawing the development consent application itself where no material change in circumstance can be identified to justify such a course of action, unless other exceptional circumstances can be shown.

Examples of substantive unreasonable behaviour could include:

- submitting a development consent application that is plainly contrary to policy (ie the content of a National Policy Statement);
- making submissions, or acting, contrary to established case law;

- pursuing objections that fail to accord proper weight to policy statements and which fail to provide objective evidence in support of the objection; and
- a local authority requiring the development consent applicant to enter into an obligation which fails to comply with paragraph 56 of the National Planning Policy Framework (2019), or an applicant failing to enter into such an obligation where the ExA considers it necessary.

Compulsory acquisition

An exception to the need to show unreasonable behaviour occurs in development consent applications where the applicant seeks authorisation to compulsorily acquire land. Here an objector will be entitled to costs if they:

(a) maintain their objection throughout the process prior to the Secretary of State's decision (or withdrawal of the application for development consent and/or compulsory acquisition powers);

(b) participate in the examination by way of representations; and

(c) have their objection upheld by the Secretary of State, either through the wholesale refusal of development consent or by way of a development consent order that does not include compulsory acquisition powers (or if the applicant withdraws their request as in (a) above).

If an objector is unsuccessful under (c), they may still be entitled to costs if they can show unreasonable behaviour in the normal way. Partial success in an objection to compulsory acquisition (i.e. through the exclusion of only some land from the Order) will usually be met with a partial award of costs.

Different time limits also apply in this case. The application for costs should be made within 28 days of notification of the Secretary of State's decision, or withdrawal of the application.

Basis of assessment

Where an ExA decides to make an award of costs, it has two options available: a full award, or a partial award.

- A full award will provide for the payment of all of a party's necessary and reasonable costs incurred in its taking part in the examination, including preparation for and involvement in the examination, and the costs of applying for costs.
- A partial award by contrast will award a party its necessary and reasonable costs insofar as they relate to the unreasonable conduct of another, or to a specific part of the examination.

What is included within recoverable costs?

A party may have to incur costs for a number of reasons, including: obtaining professional advice or representation; drafting; document preparation; travel; and accommodation. So long as the unreasonable behaviour can be shown to have caused those costs to be incurred, those costs are, in principle, and subject to their being necessary and reasonable, recoverable.

Appendix

Planning Act 2008

Planning Act 2008 c. 29

An Act to establish the Infrastructure Planning Commission and make provision about its functions; to make provision about, and about matters ancillary to, the authorisation of projects for the development of nationally significant infrastructure; to make provision about town and country planning; to make provision about the imposition of a Community Infrastructure Levy; and for connected purposes.

[26th November 2008]

BE IT ENACTED by the Queen's most Excellent Majesty, by and with the advice and consent of the Lords Spiritual and Temporal, and Commons, in this present Parliament assembled, and by the authority of the same, as follows:—

Part 1 [Infrastructure planning: fees][1]

1–3 ...

Repealed by Localism Act 2011, ss 128(2), 237, Sch 13, paras 1, 2, Sch 25, Pt 20 as from 1 April 2012.

1 Words substituted by Localism Act 2011, s 128(2), Sch 13, paras 1, 3(1), (5) (15 January 2012 for the purpose of conferring power on the Secretary of State to make regulations or rules; 1 April 2012 otherwise).

4 Fees

(1) The Secretary of State may make regulations providing for the [charging of fees by the Secretary of State in connection with the performance of any of the Secretary of State's major-infrastructure functions][1].

(2) Regulations under subsection (1) may in particular make provision—

(a) about when a fee (including a supplementary fee) may, and may not, be charged;

(b) about the amount which may be charged;

(c) about what may, and may not, be taken into account in calculating the amount charged;

(d) about who is liable to pay a fee charged;

(e) about when a fee charged is payable;

(f) about the recovery of fees charged;

(g) about waiver, reduction or repayment of fees;

(h) about the effect of paying or failing to pay fees charged;

(i) for the supply of information for any purpose of the regulations.

(3) The regulations may provide for the amounts of fees to be calculated by reference to costs [incurred by the Secretary of State][2]—

(a) in the performance of any of [the Secretary of State's major-infrastructure functions][3], and

(b) in doing anything which is calculated to facilitate, or is conducive or incidental to, the performance of any of [the Secretary of State's major-infrastructure functions][3].

[(4) In this section 'the Secretary of State's major-infrastructure functions' means—

(a) the Secretary of State's functions under Parts 2 to 8 and under Part 12 so far as applying for the purposes of those Parts,

(b) the giving of advice to which section 51 applies, and

(c) the Secretary of State's functions, in relation to proposed applications for orders granting development consent, under statutory provisions implementing—

(i) Council Directive 85/337/EC on the assessment of the effects of certain public and private projects on the environment, as amended from time to time, or

(ii) provisions of an EU instrument which from time to time replace provisions of that Directive.

(5) In subsection (4)(c) 'statutory provision' means a provision of an Act or of an instrument made under an Act.][4]

1 Words substituted by Localism Act 2011, s 128(2), Sch 13, paras 1, 3(1), (2) (15 January 2012 for the purpose of conferring power on the Secretary of State to make regulations or rules; 1 April 2012 otherwise).
2 Words substituted by Localism Act 2011, s 128(2), Sch 13, paras 1, 3(1), (3)(a) (15 January 2012 for the purpose of conferring power on the Secretary of State to make regulations or rules; 1 April 2012 otherwise).
3 Words substituted by Localism Act 2011, s 128(2), Sch 13, paras 1, 3(1), (3)(b) (15 January 2012 for the purpose of conferring power on the Secretary of State to make regulations or rules; 1 April 2012 otherwise).
4 Inserted by Localism Act 2011, s 128(2), Sch 13, paras 1, 3(1), (4) (15 January 2012 for the purpose of conferring power on the Secretary of State to make regulations or rules; 1 April 2012 otherwise).

Part 2 National policy statements

5 National policy statements

(1) The Secretary of State may designate a statement as a national policy statement for the purposes of this Act if the statement—

(a) is issued by the Secretary of State, and

(b) sets out national policy in relation to one or more specified descriptions of development.

(2) In this Act 'national policy statement' means a statement designated under subsection (1) as a national policy statement for the purposes of this Act.

(3) Before designating a statement as a national policy statement for the purposes of this Act the Secretary of State must carry out an appraisal of the sustainability of the policy set out in the statement.

(4) A statement may be designated as a national policy statement for the purposes of this Act only if the consultation and publicity requirements set out in section 7, and the parliamentary requirements set out in section 9, have been complied with in relation to it [and—][1]

[(a) the consideration period for the statement has expired without the House of Commons resolving during that period that the statement should not be proceeded with, or

(b) the statement has been approved by resolution of the House of Commons—

(i) after being laid before Parliament under section 9(8), and

(ii) before the end of the consideration period.][1]

[(4A) In subsection (4) 'the consideration period', in relation to a statement, means the period of 21 sitting days beginning with the first sitting day after the day on which the statement is laid before Parliament under section 9(8), and here 'sitting day' means a day on which the House of Commons sits.][2]

(5) The policy set out in a national policy statement may in particular—

(a) set out, in relation to a specified description of development, the amount, type or size of development of that description which is appropriate nationally or for a specified area;

(b) set out criteria to be applied in deciding whether a location is suitable (or potentially suitable) for a specified description of development;

(c) set out the relative weight to be given to specified criteria;

(d) identify one or more locations as suitable (or potentially suitable) or unsuitable for a specified description of development;

(e) identify one or more statutory undertakers as appropriate persons to carry out a specified description of development;

(f) set out circumstances in which it is appropriate for a specified type of action to be taken to mitigate the impact of a specified description of development.

(6) If a national policy statement sets out policy in relation to a particular description of development, the statement must set out criteria to be taken into account in the design of that description of development.

(7) A national policy statement must give reasons for the policy set out in the statement.

(8) The reasons must (in particular) include an explanation of how the policy set out in the statement takes account of Government policy relating to the mitigation of, and adaptation to, climate change.

(9) The Secretary of State must—

(a) arrange for the publication of a national policy statement[.]

[...][3]

(10) In this section 'statutory undertakers' means persons who are, or are deemed to be, statutory undertakers for the purposes of any provision of Part 11 of TCPA 1990.

1 Inserted by Localism Act 2011, s 130(1), (2) (1 April 2012).
2 Inserted by Localism Act 2011, s 130(1), (3) (1 April 2012).
3 Repealed by Localism Act 2011, ss 130(1), (4), 237, Sch 25, Pt 20 (1 April 2012).

6 Review

(1) The Secretary of State must review each national policy statement whenever the Secretary of State thinks it appropriate to do so.

(2) A review may relate to all or part of a national policy statement.

(3) In deciding when to review a national policy statement the Secretary of State must consider whether—

(a) since the time when the statement was first published or (if later) last reviewed, there has been a significant change in any circumstances on the basis of which any of the policy set out in the statement was decided,

(b) the change was not anticipated at that time, and

(c) if the change had been anticipated at that time, any of the policy set out in the statement would have been materially different.

(4) In deciding when to review part of a national policy statement ('the relevant part') the Secretary of State must consider whether—

(a) since the time when the relevant part was first published or (if later) last reviewed, there has been a significant change in any circumstances on the basis of which any of the policy set out in the relevant part was decided,

(b) the change was not anticipated at that time, and

(c) if the change had been anticipated at that time, any of the policy set out in the relevant part would have been materially different.

(5) After completing a review of all or part of a national policy statement the Secretary of State must do one of the following—

(a) amend the statement;

(b) withdraw the statement's designation as a national policy statement;

(c) leave the statement as it is.

(6) Before amending a national policy statement the Secretary of State must carry out an appraisal of the sustainability of the policy set out in the proposed amendment.

(7) The Secretary of State may amend a national policy statement only if the consultation and publicity requirements set out in section 7, and the parliamentary requirements set out in section 9, have been complied with in relation to the proposed amendment [and—][1]

[(a) the consideration period for the amendment has expired without the House of Commons resolving during that period that the amendment should not be proceeded with, or

(b) the amendment has been approved by resolution of the House of Commons—

(i) after being laid before Parliament under section 9(8), and

(ii) before the end of the consideration period.][1]

[(7A) In subsection (7) 'the consideration period', in relation to an amendment, means the period of 21 sitting days beginning with the first sitting day after the day on which the amendment is laid before Parliament under section 9(8), and here 'sitting day' means a day on which the House of Commons sits.][2]

(8) Subsections (6) [to (7A)][3] do not apply if the Secretary of State thinks that the proposed amendment (taken with any other proposed amendments) does not materially affect the policy as set out in the national policy statement.

(9) If the Secretary of State amends a national policy statement, the Secretary of State must—

(a) arrange for the amendment, or the statement as amended, to be published, and

(b) lay the amendment, or the statement as amended, before Parliament.

1 Inserted by Localism Act 2011, s 130(1), (5) (1 April 2012).
2 Inserted by Localism Act 2011, s 130(1), (6) (1 April 2012).
3 Words substituted by Localism Act 2011, s 130(1), (7) (1 April 2012).

[6A Interpretation of sections 5(4) and 6(7)

(1) This section applies for the purposes of section 5(4) and 6(7).

(2) The consultation and publicity requirements set out in section 7 are to be treated as having been complied with in relation to a statement or proposed amendment ('the final proposal') if—

(a) they have been complied with in relation to a different statement or proposed amendment ('the earlier proposal'),

(b) the final proposal is a modified version of the earlier proposal, and

(c) the Secretary of State thinks that the modifications do not materially affect the policy as set out in the earlier proposal.

(3) The consultation and publicity requirements set out in section 7 are also to be treated as having been complied with in relation to a statement or proposed amendment ('the final proposal') if—

(a) they have been complied with—

(i) in relation to a different statement or proposed amendment ('the earlier proposal'), and

(ii) in relation to modifications of the earlier proposal ('the main modifications'),

(b) the final proposal is a modified version of the earlier proposal, and

(c) there are no modifications other than the main modifications or, where the modifications include modifications other than the main modifications, the Secretary of State thinks that those other modifications do not materially affect the policy as set out in the earlier proposal modified by the main modifications.

(4) If section 9(8) has been complied with in relation to a statement or proposed amendment ('the final proposal'), the parliamentary requirements set out in section 9(2) to (7) are to be treated as having been complied with in relation to the final proposal where—

(a) the final proposal is not the same as what was laid under section 9(2), but

(b) those requirements have been complied with in relation to what was laid under section 9(2).

(5) Ignore any corrections of clerical or typographical errors in what was laid under section 9(8).][1]

1 Inserted by Localism Act 2011, s 130(1), (8) (1 April 2012).

[6B Extension of consideration period under section 5(4A) or 6(7A)

(1) The Secretary of State may—

(a) in relation to a proposed national policy statement, extend the period mentioned in section 5(4A), or

(b) in relation to a proposed amendment of a national policy statement, extend the period mentioned in section 6(7A),

by 21 sitting days or less.

(2) The Secretary of State does that by laying before the House of Commons a statement—

(a) indicating that the period is to be extended, and

(b) setting out the length of the extension.

(3) The statement under subsection (2) must be laid before the period would have expired without the extension.

(4) The Secretary of State must publish the statement under subsection (2) in a way the Secretary of State thinks appropriate.

(5) The period may be extended more than once.][1]

1 Inserted by Localism Act 2011, s 130(1), (8) (1 April 2012).

7 Consultation and publicity

(1) This section sets out the consultation and publicity requirements referred to in sections 5(4) and 6(7).

(2) The Secretary of State must carry out such consultation, and arrange for such publicity, as the Secretary of State thinks appropriate in relation to the proposal.

This is subject to subsections (4) and (5).

(3) In this section 'the proposal' means—

(a) the statement that the Secretary of State proposes to designate as a national policy statement for the purposes of this Act, or

(b) (as the case may be) the proposed amendment.

(4) The Secretary of State must consult such persons, and such descriptions of persons, as may be prescribed.

(5) If the policy set out in the proposal identifies one or more locations as suitable (or potentially suitable) for a specified description of development, the Secretary of State must ensure that appropriate steps are taken to publicise the proposal.

(6) The Secretary of State must have regard to the responses to the consultation and publicity in deciding whether to proceed with the proposal.

8 Consultation on publicity requirements

(1) In deciding what steps are appropriate for the purposes of section 7(5), the Secretary of State must consult—

(a) each local authority that is within subsection (2)[, (3) or (3A)][1], and

(b) the Greater London Authority, if any of the locations concerned is in Greater London.

(2) A local authority is within this subsection if any of the locations concerned is in the authority's area.

(3) A local authority ('A') is within this subsection if—

(a) any of the locations concerned is in the area of another local authority ('B'), [...][2]

[(aa) B is a unitary council or a lower-tier district council, and][2]

(b) any part of the boundary of A's area is also a part of the boundary of B's area.

[(3A) If any of the locations concerned is in the area of an upper-tier county council ('C'), a local authority ('D') is within this subsection if—

(a) D is not a lower-tier district council, and

(b) any part of the boundary of D's area is also part of the boundary of C's area.][3]

(4) In this section 'local authority' means—

(a) a county council, or district council, in England;

(b) a London borough council;

(c) the Common Council of the City of London;

(d) the Council of the Isles of Scilly;

(e) a county council, or county borough council, in Wales;

(f) a council constituted under section 2 of the Local Government etc. (Scotland) Act 1994 (c. 39);

(g) a National Park authority;

(h) the Broads Authority.

[(5) In this section—

'lower-tier district council' means a district council in England for an area for which there is a county council;

'unitary council' means a local authority that is not an upper-tier county council, a lower-tier district council, a National Park authority or the Broads Authority;

'upper-tier county council' means a county council in England for each part of whose area there is a district council.][4]

1 Words substituted by Localism Act 2011, s 130(1), (9) (1 April 2012).
2 Inserted by Localism Act 2011, s 130(1), (10) (1 April 2012).
3 Inserted by Localism Act 2011, s 130(1), (11) (1 April 2012).
4 Inserted by Localism Act 2011, s 130(1), (12) (1 April 2012).

9 Parliamentary requirements

(1) This section sets out the parliamentary requirements referred to in sections 5(4) and 6(7).

(2) The Secretary of State must lay the proposal before Parliament.

(3) In this section 'the proposal' means—

(a) the statement that the Secretary of State proposes to designate as a national policy statement for the purposes of this Act, or

(b) (as the case may be) the proposed amendment.

(4) Subsection (5) applies if, during the relevant period—

(a) either House of Parliament makes a resolution with regard to the proposal, or

(b) a committee of either House of Parliament makes recommendations with regard to the proposal.

(5) The Secretary of State must lay before Parliament a statement setting out the Secretary of State's response to the resolution or recommendations.

(6) The relevant period is the period specified by the Secretary of State in relation to the proposal.

(7) The Secretary of State must specify the relevant period in relation to the proposal on or before the day on which the proposal is laid before Parliament under subsection (2).

[(8) After the end of the relevant period, but not before the Secretary of State complies with subsection (5) if it applies, the Secretary of State must lay the proposal before Parliament.

(9) If after subsection (8) has been complied with—

(a) something other than what was laid under subsection (8) becomes the proposal, or

(b) what was laid under subsection (8) remains the proposal, or again becomes the proposal, despite the condition in section 5(4)(a) not having been met in relation to it,

subsection (8) must be complied with anew.

(10) For the purposes of subsection (9)(a) and (b) ignore any proposal to correct clerical or typographical errors in what was laid under subsection (8).][1]

1 Inserted by Localism Act 2011, s 130(1), (13) (1 April 2012).

10 Sustainable development

(1) This section applies to the Secretary of State's functions under sections 5 and 6.

(2) The Secretary of State must, in exercising those functions, do so with the objective of contributing to the achievement of sustainable development.

(3) For the purposes of subsection (2) the Secretary of State must (in particular) have regard to the desirability of—

(a) mitigating, and adapting to, climate change;

(b) achieving good design.

11 Suspension pending review

(1) This section applies if the Secretary of State thinks that the condition in subsection (2) or (3) is met.

(2) The condition is that—

(a) since the time when a national policy statement was first published or (if later) last reviewed, there has been a significant change in any circumstances on the basis of which any of the policy set out in the statement was decided,

(b) the change was not anticipated at that time, and

(c) if the change had been anticipated at that time, any of the policy set out in the statement would have been materially different.

(3) The condition is that—

(a) since the time when part of a national policy statement ('the relevant part') was first published or (if later) last reviewed, there has been a significant change in any circumstances on the basis of which any of the policy set out in the relevant part was decided,

(b) the change was not anticipated at that time, and

(c) if the change had been anticipated at that time, any of the policy set out in the relevant part would have been materially different.

(4) The Secretary of State may suspend the operation of all or any part of the national policy statement until a review of the statement or the relevant part has been completed.

(5) If the Secretary of State does so, the designation as a national policy statement of the statement or (as the case may be) the part of the statement that has been suspended is treated as having been withdrawn until the day on which the Secretary of State complies with section 6(5) in relation to the review.

12 …

Repealed by Localism Act 2011, s 237, Sch 25, Pt 20 as from 1 April 2012.

13 Legal challenges relating to national policy statements

(1) A court may entertain proceedings for questioning a national policy statement or anything done, or omitted to be done, by the Secretary of State in the course of preparing such a statement only if—

(a) the proceedings are brought by a claim for judicial review, and

(b) the claim form is filed [before the end of][1] the period of 6 weeks beginning with [the day after][2]—

(i) the day on which the statement is designated as a national policy statement for the purposes of this Act, or

(ii) (if later) the day on which the statement is published.

(2) A court may entertain proceedings for questioning a decision of the Secretary of State not to carry out a review of all or part of a national policy statement only if—

(a) the proceedings are brought by a claim for judicial review, and

(b) the claim form is filed [before the end of][1] the period of 6 weeks beginning with [the day after][2] the day of the decision not to carry out the review.

(3) A court may entertain proceedings for questioning a decision of the Secretary of State to carry out a review of all or part of a national policy statement only if—

(a) the proceedings are brought by a claim for judicial review, and

(b) the claim form is filed [before the end of][1] the period of 6 weeks beginning with [the day after][2] the day on which the Secretary of State complies with section 6(5) in relation to the review concerned.

(4) A court may entertain proceedings for questioning anything done, or omitted to be done, by the Secretary of State in the course of carrying out a review of all or part of a national policy statement only if—

(a) the proceedings are brought by a claim for judicial review, and

(b) the claim form is filed [before the end of][1] the period of 6 weeks beginning with [the day after][2] the day on which the Secretary of State complies with section 6(5) in relation to the review concerned.

(5) A court may entertain proceedings for questioning anything done by the Secretary of State under section 6(5) after completing a review of all or part of a national policy statement only if—

(a) the proceedings are brought by a claim for judicial review, and

(b) the claim form is filed [before the end of][1] the period of 6 weeks beginning with [the day after][2] the day on which the thing concerned is done.

(6) A court may entertain proceedings for questioning a decision of the Secretary of State as to whether or not to suspend the operation of all or part of a national policy statement under section 11 only if—

(a) the proceedings are brought by a claim for judicial review, and

(b) the claim form is filed [before the end of][1] the period of 6 weeks beginning with [the day after][2] the day of the decision.

1 Words substituted by Criminal Justice and Courts Act 2015, s 92(3)(a) (13 April 2015).
2 Words inserted by Criminal Justice and Courts Act 2015, s 92(3)(b) (13 April 2015).

Part 3 Nationally significant infrastructure projects

General

14 Nationally significant infrastructure projects: general

(1) In this Act 'nationally significant infrastructure project' means a project which consists of any of the following—

(a) the construction or extension of a generating station;

(b) the installation of an electric line above ground;

(c) development relating to underground gas storage facilities;

(d) the construction or alteration of an LNG facility;

(e) the construction or alteration of a gas reception facility;

(f) the construction of a pipe-line by a gas transporter;

(g) the construction of a pipe-line other than by a gas transporter;

(h) highway-related development;

(i) airport-related development;

(j) the construction or alteration of harbour facilities;

(k) the construction or alteration of a railway;

(l) the construction or alteration of a rail freight interchange;

(m) the construction or alteration of a dam or reservoir;

(n) development relating to the transfer of water resources;

[(na) the construction or alteration of a desalination plant;][1]

(o) the construction or alteration of a waste water treatment plant [or of infrastructure for the transfer or storage of waste water][2];

(p) the construction or alteration of a hazardous waste facility;

[(q) development relating to a radioactive waste geological disposal facility.][3]

(2) Subsection (1) is subject to sections 15 to [30A][4].

(3) The Secretary of State may by order—

(a) amend subsection (1) to add a new type of project or vary or remove an existing type of project;

(b) make further provision, or amend or repeal existing provision, about the types of project which are, and are not, within subsection (1).

(4) An order under subsection (3)(b) may amend this Act.

(5) The power conferred by subsection (3) may be exercised to add a new type of project to subsection (1) only if—

(a) a project of the new type is a project for the carrying out of works in one or more of the fields specified in subsection (6), and

(b) the works are to be carried out wholly in one or more of the areas specified in subsection (7).

(6) The fields are—

(a) energy;

(b) transport;

(c) water;

(d) waste water;

(e) waste.

(7) The areas are—

(a) England;

(b) waters adjacent to England up to the seaward limits of the territorial sea;

(c) in the case of a project for the carrying out of works in the field of energy, a Renewable Energy Zone, except any part of a Renewable Energy Zone in relation to which the Scottish Ministers have functions.

1 Inserted by Infrastructure Planning (Water Resources) (England) Order 2019, SI 2019/12, art 2(1), (2) (9 January 2019).
2 Words inserted by Infrastructure Planning (Waste Water Transfer and Storage) Order 2012, SI 2012/1645, art 2(1), (2) (23 June 2012: insertion has effect subject to supplementary provision specified in SI 2012/1645, art 3).
3 Inserted by Infrastructure Planning (Radioactive Waste Geological Disposal Facilities) Order 2015, SI 2015/949, art 2(1), (2)(a) (27 March 2015).
4 Word substituted by Infrastructure Planning (Radioactive Waste Geological Disposal Facilities) Order 2015, SI 2015/949, art 2(1), (2)(b) (27 March 2015).

Energy

15 Generating stations

(1) The construction or extension of a generating station is within section 14(1)(a) only if the generating station is or (when constructed or extended) is expected to be within subsection (2)[, (3), (3A) or (3B)][1].

(2) A generating station is within this subsection if—

(a) it is in England [...][2],

[(aa) it does not generate electricity from wind,][3]

(b) it is not an offshore generating station, and

(c) its capacity is more than 50 megawatts.

(3) A generating station is within this subsection if—

(a) it is an offshore generating station, and

(b) its capacity is more than 100 megawatts.

[(3A) A generating station is within this subsection if—

(a) it is in Wales,

(b) it does not generate electricity from wind, and

(c) its capacity is more than 350 megawatts.

(3B) A generating station is within this subsection if—

(a) it is in waters adjacent to Wales up to the seaward limits of the territorial sea, or in the Welsh zone, and

(b) its capacity is more than 350 megawatts.][4]

[(3C) To the extent that an exempt electricity storage facility forms part of a generating station (or is expected to do so, when the generating station is constructed or extended), any capacity provided by the facility is to be disregarded for the purposes of determining whether the generating station is within subsection (2), (3), (3A) or (3B).

(3D) The construction or extension of a generating station is not within section 14(1)(a) to the extent that the generating station comprises or (when constructed or extended) is expected to comprise an exempt electricity storage facility.][5]

(4) An 'offshore' generating station is a generating station that is—

(a) in waters in or adjacent to England [...][2] up to the seaward limits of the territorial sea, or

(b) in a Renewable Energy Zone, except [the Welsh zone or][6] any part of a Renewable Energy Zone in relation to which the Scottish Ministers have functions.

['Welsh zone' has the meaning given in section 158 of the Government of Wales Act 2006.][4]

[(6) In this section—

'electricity storage facility' means a facility which generates electricity from energy that—

(a) was converted from electricity by that facility, and

(b) is stored within that facility for the purpose of its future reconversion into electricity;

'exempt electricity storage facility' means an electricity storage facility which is not a pumped hydroelectric storage facility;

'pumped hydroelectric storage facility' means an electricity storage facility that stores the gravitational potential energy of water that has been pumped to a higher level so that its return to a lower level can be used to generate electricity.][5]

1 Substituted by Wales Act 2017, s 39(1), (2) (1 April 2018).
2 Repealed by Wales Act 2017, s 39(1), (3), (5)(a) (1 April 2018).
3 Inserted by Infrastructure Planning (Onshore Wind Generating Stations) Order 2016, SI 2016/306, art 3 (5 March 2016).
4 Inserted by Wales Act 2017, s 39(1), (4), (6) (31 March 2017).
5 Inserted by Infrastructure Planning (Electricity Storage Facilities) Order 2020, SI 2020/1218, art 3 (2 December 2020).
6 Inserted by Wales Act 2017, s 39(1), (5)(b) (1 April 2018).

16 Electric lines

(1) The installation of an electric line above ground is within section 14(1)(b) only if (when installed) the electric line will be—

(a) wholly in England,

(b) wholly in Wales,

(c) partly in England and partly in Wales, or

(d) partly in England and partly in Scotland, subject to subsection (2).

(2) In the case of an electric line falling within subsection (1)(d), the installation of the line above ground is within section 14(1)(b) only to the extent that (when installed) the line will be in England.

(3) The installation of an electric line above ground is not within section 14(1)(b)—

(a) if the nominal voltage of the line is expected to be less than 132 kilovolts, [...][1]

[(aa) if the length of the line (when installed) will be less than two kilometres,

(ab) if—

(i) the line will replace an existing line,

(ii) the nominal voltage of the line is expected to be greater than the nominal voltage of the existing line (but see subsection (3A)),

(iii) the height above the surface of the ground of any support for the line will not exceed the height of the highest existing support or support which is being replaced by more than 10 per cent, and

(iv) where the line is to be installed in a different position from the existing line, the distance between any new support and the existing line will not exceed 60 metres and the existing line will be removed within twelve months from the date on which the installation of the line which replaces it is complete,][2]

(b) to the extent that (when installed) the line will be within premises in the occupation or control of the person responsible for its installation[, or][3]

[(c) if section 37(1) of the Electricity Act 1989 (consent required for overhead lines) does not apply to it by virtue of the Overhead Lines (Exemption) (England and Wales) Regulations 2009 (S.I. 2009/640), as amended by the Overhead Lines (Exempt Installations) (Consequential Provisions) Order 2010.][3]

[(3A) Paragraph (ab)(ii) of subsection (3) (condition that nominal voltage of line expected to be greater than nominal voltage of existing line) does not apply if any part of the line (when installed) will be within a European site or an SSSI.][2]

[(3B) The installation of an electric line above ground is not within section 14(1)(b) if the line is associated with the construction or extension of a devolved Welsh generating station granted planning permission or consented to on or after the day on which section 39 of the Wales Act 2017 comes into force and the nominal voltage of the line is expected to be no greater than 132 kilovolts.

(3C) 'Devolved Welsh generating station' means a generating station that—

(a) is in Wales and—

(i) generates electricity from wind, or

(ii) has a capacity of 350 megawatts or less; or

(b) is in waters adjacent to Wales up to the seaward limits of the territorial sea or in the Welsh zone and has a capacity of 350 megawatts or less.

(3D) 'Welsh zone' has the meaning given in section 158 of the Government of Wales Act 2006.]

[(4) In this section—

'European site' has the same meaning as in [the Conservation of Habitats and Species Regulations 2017 (S.I. 2017/1012)][5];

'existing line' means an electric line which—

(a) has been installed or is kept installed above ground in accordance with a consent granted under section 37(1) of the Electricity Act 1989 or an order granting development consent; or

(b) has been installed above ground and is an electric line to which section 37(1) of the Electricity Act 1989 does not apply by virtue of—

(i) paragraph 5(4) or (5) of Schedule 17 to that Act, or

(ii) the Overhead Lines (Exemption) (England and Wales) Regulations 2009 (S.I. 2009/640), as amended by the Overhead Lines (Exempt Installations) (Consequential Provisions) Order 2010;

'premises' includes any land, building or structure;

'SSSI' means a site of special scientific interest notified under sections 28 to 28D of the Wildlife and Countryside Act 1981.][6]

1 Word repealed by Overhead Lines (Exempt Installations) Order 2010, SI 2010/277, art 2(a) (1 March 2010).
2 Inserted by Planning Act 2008 (Nationally Significant Infrastructure Projects) (Electric Lines) Order 2013, SI 2013/1479, art 2(a), (b) (18 June 2013).
3 Inserted by Overhead Lines (Exempt Installations) Order 2010, SI 2010/277, art 2(b) (1 March 2010).
4 Inserted by Wales Act 2017, s 42(4) (31 March 2017).
5 Substituted by Conservation of Habitats and Species Regulations 2017, SI 2017/1012, reg 139, Sch 6, para 6 (30 November 2017).
6 Substituted by Planning Act 2008 (Nationally Significant Infrastructure Projects) (Electric Lines) Order 2013, SI 2013/1479, art 2(c) (18 June 2013).

17 Underground gas storage facilities

(1) Development relating to underground gas storage facilities is within section 14(1)(c) only if the development is within subsection (2), (3) or (5).

(2) Development is within this subsection if—

(a) it is the carrying out of operations for the purpose of creating underground gas storage facilities in England, or

(b) it is starting to use underground gas storage facilities in England,

and the condition in subsection (4) is met in relation to the facilities.

(3) Development is within this subsection if—

(a) it is starting to use underground gas storage facilities in Wales,

(b) the facilities are facilities for the storage of gas underground in natural porous strata,

(c) the proposed developer is a gas transporter, and

(d) the condition in subsection (4) is met in relation to the facilities.

(4) The condition is that—

(a) the working capacity of the facilities is expected to be at least 43 million standard cubic metres, or

(b) the maximum flow rate of the facilities is expected to be at least 4.5 million standard cubic metres per day.

(5) Development is within this subsection if—

(a) it is the carrying out of operations for the purpose of altering underground gas storage facilities in England, and

(b) the effect of the alteration is expected to be—

(i) to increase by at least 43 million standard cubic metres the working capacity of the facilities, or

(ii) to increase by at least 4.5 million standard cubic metres per day the maximum flow rate of the facilities.

(6) 'Underground gas storage facilities' means facilities for the storage of gas underground in cavities or in porous strata.

(7) In this section—

'maximum flow rate', in relation to underground gas storage facilities, means the maximum rate at which gas is able to flow out of the facilities, on the assumption that—

(a) the facilities are filled to maximum capacity, and

(b) the rate is measured after any processing of gas required on its recovery from storage;

'working capacity', in relation to underground gas storage facilities, means the capacity of the facilities for storage of gas underground, ignoring any capacity for storage of cushion gas.

(8) In subsection (7) 'cushion gas' means gas which is kept in underground gas storage facilities for the purpose of enabling other gas stored there to be recovered from storage.

18 LNG facilities

(1) The construction of an LNG facility is within section 14(1)(d) only if (when constructed) the facility will be in England and—

(a) the storage capacity of the facility is expected to be at least 43 million standard cubic metres, or

(b) the maximum flow rate of the facility is expected to be at least 4.5 million standard cubic metres per day.

(2) The alteration of an LNG facility is within section 14(1)(d) only if the facility is in England and the effect of the alteration is expected to be—

(a) to increase by at least 43 million standard cubic metres the storage capacity of the facility, or

(b) to increase by at least 4.5 million standard cubic metres per day the maximum flow rate of the facility.

(3) 'LNG facility' means a facility for—

(a) the reception of liquid natural gas from outside England,

(b) the storage of liquid natural gas, and

(c) the regasification of liquid natural gas.

(4) In this section—

'maximum flow rate', in relation to a facility, means the maximum rate at which gas is able to flow out of the facility, on the assumption that—

(a) the facility is filled to maximum capacity, and

(b) the rate is measured after regasification of the liquid natural gas and any other processing required on the recovery of the gas from storage;

'storage capacity' means the capacity of the facility for storage of liquid natural gas.

(5) The storage capacity of an LNG facility is to be measured as if the gas were stored in regasified form.

19 Gas reception facilities

(1) The construction of a gas reception facility is within section 14(1)(e) only if (when constructed)—

(a) the facility will be in England and will be within subsection (4), and

(b) the maximum flow rate of the facility is expected to be at least 4.5 million standard cubic metres per day.

(2) The alteration of a gas reception facility is within section 14(1)(e) only if—

(a) the facility is in England and is within subsection (4), and

(b) the effect of the alteration is expected to be to increase by at least 4.5 million standard cubic metres per day the maximum flow rate of the facility.

(3) 'Gas reception facility' means a facility for—

(a) the reception of natural gas in gaseous form from outside England, and

(b) the handling of natural gas (other than its storage).

(4) A gas reception facility is within this subsection if—

(a) the gas handled by the facility does not originate in England, Wales or Scotland,

(b) the gas does not arrive at the facility from Scotland or Wales, and

(c) the gas has not already been handled at another facility after its arrival in England.

(5) 'Maximum flow rate' means the maximum rate at which gas is able to flow out of the facility.

20 Gas transporter pipe-lines

(1) The construction of a pipe-line by a gas transporter is within section 14(1)(f) only if (when constructed) each of the conditions in subsections (2) to (5) is expected to be met in relation to the pipe-line.

(2) The pipe-line must be wholly or partly in England.

(3) Either—

(a) the pipe-line must be more than 800 millimetres in diameter and more than 40 kilometres in length, or

(b) the construction of the pipe-line must be likely to have a significant effect on the environment.

(4) The pipe-line must have a design operating pressure of more than 7 bar gauge.

(5) The pipe-line must convey gas for supply (directly or indirectly) to at least 50,000 customers, or potential customers, of one or more gas suppliers.

(6) In the case of a pipe-line that (when constructed) will be only partly in England, the construction of the pipe-line is within section 14(1)(f) only to the extent that the pipe-line will (when constructed) be in England.

(7) 'Gas supplier' has the same meaning as in Part 1 of the Gas Act 1986 (c. 44) (see section 7A(11) of that Act).

21 Other pipe-lines

(1) The construction of a pipe-line other than by a gas transporter is within section 14(1)(g) only if (when constructed) the pipe-line is expected to be—

(a) a cross-country pipe-line,

(b) a pipe-line the construction of which would (but for section 33(1) of this Act) require authorisation under section 1(1) of the Pipe-lines Act 1962 (c. 58) (cross-country pipe-lines not to be constructed without authorisation), and

(c) within subsection (2).

(2) A pipe-line is within this subsection if one end of it is in England or Wales and—

(a) the other end of it is in England or Wales, or

(b) it is an oil or gas pipe-line and the other end of it is in Scotland.

(3) For the purposes of section 14(1)(g) and the previous provisions of this section, the construction of a diversion to a pipe-line is treated as the construction of a separate pipe-line.

(4) But if—

(a) the pipe-line to be diverted is itself a nationally significant pipe-line, and

(b) the length of the pipe-line which is to be diverted has not been constructed,

the construction of the diversion is treated as the construction of a cross-country pipe-line, whatever the length of the diversion.

(5) For the purposes of subsection (4), a pipe-line is a nationally significant pipe-line if—

(a) development consent is required for its construction by virtue of section 14(1)(g), and has been granted, or

(b) its construction has been authorised by a pipe-line construction authorisation under section 1(1) of the Pipe-lines Act 1962 (c. 58).

(6) 'Diversion' means a lateral diversion of a length of a pipe-line (whether or not that pipe-line has been constructed) where the diversion is beyond the permitted limits.

(7) The permitted limits are the limits of lateral diversion permitted by any of the following granted in respect of the construction of the pipe-line—

(a) development consent;

(b) authorisation under the Pipe-lines Act 1962;

(c) planning permission.

Transport

[22 Highways

(1) Highway-related development is within section 14(1)(h) only if the development is—

(a) construction of a highway in a case within subsection (2),

(b) alteration of a highway in a case within subsection (3), or

(c) improvement of a highway in a case within subsection (5).

(2) Construction of a highway is within this subsection only if—

(a) the highway will (when constructed) be wholly in England,

(b) the Secretary of State [or a strategic highways company][1] will be the highway authority for the highway, and

(c) the area of development is greater than the relevant limit set out in subsection (4).

(3) Alteration of a highway is within this subsection only if—

(a) the highway is wholly in England,

(b) the Secretary of State [or a strategic highways company][1] is the highway authority for the highway, and

(c) the area of development is greater than the relevant limit set out in subsection (4).

(4) For the purposes of subsections (2)(c) and (3)(c) the relevant limit —

(a) in relation to the construction or alteration of a motorway, is 15 hectares,

(b) in relation to the construction or alteration of a highway, other than a motorway, where the speed limit for any class of vehicle is expected to be 50 miles per hour or greater, is 12.5 hectares, and

(c) in relation to the construction or alteration of any other highway is 7.5 hectares.

(5) Improvement of a highway is within this subsection only if—

(a) the highway is wholly in England,

(b) the Secretary of State [or a strategic highways company][1] is the highway authority for the highway, and

(c) the improvement is likely to have a significant effect on the environment.

(6) Highway-related development does not fall within section 14(1)(h) if—

(a) an order mentioned in section 33(4) has been made in relation to the development before 1 March 2010,

(b) a further order is needed in relation to the development, and

(c) not more than 7 years have elapsed since the making of the earlier order.

(7) Alteration of a highway is not within section 14(1)(h) if

(a) planning permission has been granted for a development,

(b) the alteration is necessary as a result of the development, and

(c) the developer has asked for the alteration to be made to the highway.

(8) Alteration of a highway is not within section 14(1)(h) if—

(a) an order mentioned in section 33(4) has been made in relation to local highway works,

(b) the alteration is necessary as a result of the local highway works, and

(c) the local highway authority responsible for the local highway works has asked for the alteration to be made to the highway.

(9) In this section—

'area of development'—

(a) in relation to construction of a highway, means the land on which the highway is to be constructed and any adjoining land expected to be used in connection with its construction;

(b) in relation to alteration of a highway, means the land on which the part of the highway to be altered is situated and any adjoining land expected to be used in connection with its alteration;

'local highway authority' has the meaning given by section 329(1) of the Highways Act 1980;

'local highway works' means works carried out by or on behalf of a local highway authority in relation to a highway for which it is the highway authority (and the local highway authority is referred to in this section as 'responsible' for those works);

'motorway' means a highway which is a special road in accordance with section 16 of the Highways Act 1980;

['strategic highways company' means a company for the time being appointed under Part 1 of the Infrastructure Act 2015.][1]][2]

1 Words inserted by Infrastructure Act 2015, s 1(6), Sch 1, para 153 (12 February 2015).
2 Substituted by Highway and Railway (Nationally Significant Infrastructure Project) Order 2013, SI 2013/1883, art 3 (25 July 2013).

23 Airports

(1) Airport-related development is within section 14(1)(i) only if the development is—

(a) the construction of an airport in a case within subsection (2),

(b) the alteration of an airport in a case within subsection (4), or

(c) an increase in the permitted use of an airport in a case within subsection (7).

(2) Construction of an airport is within this subsection only if (when constructed) the airport—

(a) will be in England or in English waters, and

(b) is expected to be capable of providing services which meet the requirements of subsection (3).

(3) Services meet the requirements of this subsection if they are—

(a) air passenger transport services for at least 10 million passengers per year, or

(b) air cargo transport services for at least 10,000 air transport movements of cargo aircraft per year.

(4) Alteration of an airport is within this subsection only if—

(a) the airport is in England or in English waters, and

(b) the alteration is expected to have the effect specified in subsection (5).

(5) The effect is—

(a) to increase by at least 10 million per year the number of passengers for whom the airport is capable of providing air passenger transport services, or

(b) to increase by at least 10,000 per year the number of air transport movements of cargo aircraft for which the airport is capable of providing air cargo transport services.

(6) 'Alteration', in relation to an airport, includes the construction, extension or alteration of—

(a) a runway at the airport,

(b) a building at the airport, or

(c) a radar or radio mast, antenna or other apparatus at the airport.

(7) An increase in the permitted use of an airport is within this subsection only if—

(a) the airport is in England or in English waters, and

(b) the increase is within subsection (8).

(8) An increase is within this subsection if—

(a) it is an increase of at least 10 million per year in the number of passengers for whom the airport is permitted to provide air passenger transport services, or

(b) it is an increase of at least 10,000 per year in the number of air transport movements of cargo aircraft for which the airport is permitted to provide air cargo transport services.

(9) In this section—

'air cargo transport services' means services for the carriage by air of cargo;

'air passenger transport services' means services for the carriage by air of passengers;

'air transport movement' means a landing or take-off of an aircraft;

'cargo' includes mail;

'cargo aircraft' means an aircraft which is—

(a) designed to transport cargo but not passengers, and

(b) engaged in the transport of cargo on commercial terms;

'English waters' means waters adjacent to England up to the seaward limits of the territorial sea;

'permitted' means permitted by planning permission or development consent.

24 Harbour facilities

(1) The construction of harbour facilities is within section 14(1)(j) only if (when constructed) the harbour facilities—

[(a) will be—

(i) wholly or partly in England or in waters adjacent to England up to the seaward limits of the territorial sea, or

(ii) wholly in Wales or in waters adjacent to Wales up to the seaward limits of the territorial sea and will be, or will form part of, a reserved trust port, and][1]

(b) are expected to be capable of handling the embarkation or disembarkation of at least the relevant quantity of material per year.

(2) The alteration of harbour facilities is within section 14(1)(j) only if—

[(a) the harbour facilities are—

(i) wholly or partly in England or in waters adjacent to England up to the seaward limits of the territorial sea, or

(ii) wholly in Wales or in waters adjacent to Wales up to the seaward limits of the territorial sea and are, or form part of, a reserved trust port, and][1]

(b) the effect of the alteration is expected to be to increase by at least the relevant quantity per year the quantity of material the embarkation or disembarkation of which the facilities are capable of handling.

(3) 'The relevant quantity' is—

(a) in the case of facilities for container ships, 500,000 TEU;

(b) in the case of facilities for ro-ro ships, 250,000 units;

(c) in the case of facilities for cargo ships of any other description, 5 million tonnes;

(d) in the case of facilities for more than one of the types of ships mentioned in paragraphs (a) to (c), an equivalent quantity of material.

(4) For the purposes of subsection (3)(d), facilities are capable of handling an equivalent quantity of material if the sum of the relevant fractions is one or more.

(5) The relevant fractions are—

(a) to the extent that the facilities are for container ships—

x / 500,000

where x is the number of TEU that the facilities are capable of handling;

(b) to the extent that the facilities are for ro-ro ships—

y / 250,000

where y is the number of units that the facilities are capable of handling;

(c) to the extent that the facilities are for cargo ships of any other description—

z / 5,000,000

where z is the number of tonnes of material that the facilities are capable of handling.

(6) In this section—

'cargo ship' means a ship which is used for carrying cargo;

'container ship' means a cargo ship which carries all or most of its cargo in containers;

['reserved trust port' has the meaning given in section 32 of the Wales Act 2017;][2]

'ro-ro ship' means a ship which is used for carrying wheeled cargo;

'TEU' means a twenty-foot equivalent unit;

'unit' in relation to a ro-ro ship means any item of wheeled cargo (whether or not self-propelled).

1 Substituted by Wales Act 2017, s 33(1), (2), (3) (1 April 2018).
2 Inserted by Wales Act 2017, s 33(1), (4) (1 April 2018).

25 Railways

(1) Construction of a railway is within section 14(1)(k) only if—

(a) the railway will (when constructed) be wholly in England,

(b) the railway will (when constructed) be part of a network operated by an approved operator,

[(ba) the railway will (when constructed) include a stretch of track that—

(i) is a continuous length of more than 2 kilometres, and

(ii) is not on land that was operational land of a railway undertaker immediately before the construction work began or is on land that was acquired at an earlier date for the purpose of constructing the railway,][1]

and

(c) the construction of the railway is not permitted development.

(2) Alteration of a railway is within section 14(1)(k) only if—

(a) the part of the railway to be altered is wholly in England,

(b) the railway is part of a network operated by an approved operator,

[(ba) the alteration of the railway will include laying a stretch of track that—

(i) is a continuous length of more than 2 kilometres, and

(ii) is not on land that was operational land of a railway undertaker immediately before the alteration work began or is on land that was acquired at an earlier date for the purpose of the alteration,][1]

and

(c) the alteration of the railway is not permitted development.

[(2A) Construction or alteration of a railway is not within section 14(1)(k) to the extent that it takes place on the operational land of a railway undertaker unless that land was acquired for the purpose of the construction or alteration.][1]

(3) Construction or alteration of a railway is not within section 14(1)(k) to the extent that the railway forms part (or will when constructed form part) of a rail freight interchange.

(4) 'Approved operator' means a person who meets the conditions in subsections (5) and (6).

(5) The condition is that the person must be—

(a) a person who is authorised to be the operator of a network by a licence granted under section 8 of the Railways Act 1993 (c. 43) (licences for operation of railway assets), or

(b) a wholly-owned subsidiary of a company which is such a person.

(6) The condition is that the person is designated, or is of a description designated, in an order made by the Secretary of State.

(7) In this section—

'network' has the meaning given by section 83(1) of the Railways Act 1993 (c. 43);

['operational land' has the same meaning as in the TCPA 1990;][1]

'permitted development' means development in relation to which planning permission is granted by article 3 of the Town and Country Planning (General Permitted Development) Order 1995;

['railway undertaker' has the same meaning as in Part 17 of Schedule 2 to the Town and Country Planning (General Permitted Development) Order 1995;][1]

'wholly-owned subsidiary' has the same meaning as in the Companies Act 2006 (c. 46) (see section 1159 of that Act).

(8) [In the definition of 'permitted development' in subsection (7), the reference][2] to the Town and Country Planning (General Permitted Development) Order 1995 is to that Order as it has effect immediately before the day on which this section comes fully into force.

1 Inserted by Highway and Railway (Nationally Significant Infrastructure Project) Order 2013, SI 2013/1883, art 4(1)–(5).
2 Substituted by Highway and Railway (Nationally Significant Infrastructure Project) Order 2013, SI 2013/1883, art 4(1), (6).

26 Rail freight interchanges

(1) The construction of a rail freight interchange is within section 14(1)(l) only if (when constructed) each of the conditions in subsections (3) to (7) is expected to be met in relation to it.

(2) The alteration of a rail freight interchange is within section 14(1)(l) only if—

(a) following the alteration, each of the conditions in subsections (3)(a) and (4) to (7) is expected to be met in relation to it, and

(b) the alteration is expected to have the effect specified in subsection (8).

(3) The land on which the rail freight interchange is situated must—

(a) be in England, and

(b) be at least 60 hectares in area.

(4) The rail freight interchange must be capable of handling—

(a) consignments of goods from more than one consignor and to more than one consignee, and

(b) at least 4 goods trains per day.

(5) The rail freight interchange must be part of the railway network in England.

(6) The rail freight interchange must include warehouses to which goods can be delivered from the railway network in England either directly or by means of another form of transport.

(7) The rail freight interchange must not be part of a military establishment.

(8) The effect referred to in subsection (2)(b) is to increase by at least 60 hectares the area of the land on which the rail freight interchange is situated.

(9) In this section—

'goods train' means a train that (ignoring any locomotive) consists of items of rolling stock designed to carry goods;

'military establishment' means an establishment intended for use for naval, military or air force purposes or for the purposes of the Department of the Secretary of State responsible for defence.

(10) The following terms have the meanings given by section 83(1) of the Railways Act 1993—

'network';

'rolling stock';

'train'.

Water

27 Dams and reservoirs

(1) The construction of a dam or reservoir is within section 14(1)(m) only if—

(a) the dam or reservoir (when constructed) will be in England,

(b) the construction will be carried out by one or more water undertakers, and

[(c) it is expected that—

(i) the volume of water to be held back by the dam or stored in the reservoir will exceed 30 million cubic metres, or

(ii) the deployable output of the dam or reservoir will exceed 80 million litres per day.][1]

(2) The alteration of a dam or reservoir is within section 14(1)(m) only if—

(a) the dam or reservoir is in England,

(b) the alteration will be carried out by one or more water undertakers, and

[(c) it is expected that—

(i) the additional volume of water to be held back by the dam or stored in the reservoir as a result of the alteration will exceed 30 million cubic metres, or

(ii) the additional deployable output of the dam or reservoir as a result of the alteration will exceed 80 million litres per day.][1]

(3) 'Water undertaker' means a company appointed as a water undertaker under the Water Industry Act 1991 (c. 56).

1 Substituted by Infrastructure Planning (Water Resources) (England) Order 2019, SI 2019/12, art 2(1), (3) (9 January 2019).

28 Transfer of water resources

(1) Development relating to the transfer of water resources is within section 14(1)(n) only if—

(a) the development will be carried out in England by one or more water undertakers,

[(b) it is expected that—

(i) the deployable output of the facility to be constructed as a result of the development will exceed 80 million litres per day, or

(ii) the additional deployable output of the facility to be altered as a result of the development will exceed 80 million litres per day,]

(c) the development will enable the transfer of water resources—

(i) between river basins in England,

(ii) between water undertakers' areas in England, or

(iii) between a river basin in England and a water undertaker's area in England, and

(d) the development does not relate to the transfer of drinking water.

(2) In this section—

'river basin' means an area of land drained by a river and its tributaries;

'water undertaker' means a company appointed as a water undertaker under the Water Industry Act 1991;

'water undertaker's area' means the area for which a water undertaker is appointed under that Act.

1 Substituted by Infrastructure Planning (Water Resources) (England) Order 2019, SI 2019/12, art 2(1), (4) (9 January 2019).

[28A Desalination plants

(1) The construction of a desalination plant is within section 14(1)(na) only if—

(a) the desalination plant (when constructed) will be in England or in waters adjacent to England up to the seaward limits of the territorial sea,

(b) the construction will be carried out by one or more water undertakers, and

(c) the deployable output of the desalination plant is expected to exceed 80 million litres per day.

(2) The alteration of a desalination plant is within section 14(1)(na) only if—

(a) the desalination plant is in England or in waters adjacent to England up to the seaward limits of the territorial sea,

(b) the alteration will be carried out by one or more water undertakers, and

(c) the additional deployable output of the desalination plant as a result of the alteration is expected to exceed 80 million litres per day.

(3) 'Water undertaker' means a company appointed as a water undertaker under the Water Industry Act 1991.][1]

1 Inserted by Infrastructure Planning (Water Resources) (England) Order 2019, SI 2019/12, art 2(1), (5) (9 January 2019).

Waste water

29 Waste water treatment plants

(1) The construction of a waste water treatment plant is within section 14(1)(o) only if the treatment plant (when constructed)—

(a) will be in England, and

(b) is expected to have a capacity exceeding a population equivalent of 500,000.

[(1A) The construction of infrastructure for the transfer or storage of waste water is within section 14(1)(o) only if —

(a) the works will be carried out wholly in England and the infrastructure will (when constructed) be wholly in England,

(b) the main purpose of the infrastructure will be—

(i) the transfer of waste water for treatment, or

(ii) the storage of waste water prior to treatment,

or both, and

(c) the infrastructure is expected to have a capacity for the storage of waste water exceeding 350,000 cubic metres.][1]

(2) The alteration of a waste water treatment plant is within section 14(1)(o) only if—

(a) the treatment plant is in England, and

(b) the effect of the alteration is expected to be to increase by more than a population equivalent of 500,000 the capacity of the plant.

[(2A) The alteration of infrastructure for the transfer or storage of waste water is within section 14(1)(o) only if—

(a) the works will be carried out wholly in England and the part of the infrastructure to be altered is wholly in England,

(b) the main purpose of the infrastructure is —

(i) the transfer of waste water for treatment, or

(ii) the storage of waste water prior to treatment,

or both, and

(c) the effect of the alteration is expected to be to increase the capacity of the infrastructure for the storage of waste water by more than 350,000 cubic metres.][1]

(3) 'Waste water' includes domestic waste water, industrial waste water and urban waste water.

(4) The following terms have the meanings given by regulation 2(1) of the Urban Waste Water Treatment (England and Wales) Regulations 1994 (S.I. 1994/2841)—

'domestic waste water';

'industrial waste water';

'population equivalent';

'urban waste water'.

1 Inserted by Infrastructure Planning (Waste Water Transfer and Storage) Order 2012, SI 2012/1645, art 2(1), (3) (23 June 2012: insertions have effect subject to supplementary provision specified in SI 2012/1645, art 3).

Waste

30 Hazardous waste facilities

(1) The construction of a hazardous waste facility is within section 14(1)(p) only if—

(a) the facility (when constructed) will be in England,

(b) the main purpose of the facility is expected to be the final disposal or recovery of hazardous waste, and

(c) the facility is expected to have the capacity specified in subsection (2).

(2) The capacity is—

(a) in the case of the disposal of hazardous waste by landfill or in a deep storage facility, more than 100,000 tonnes per year;

(b) in any other case, more than 30,000 tonnes per year.

(3) The alteration of a hazardous waste facility is within section 14(1)(p) only if—

(a) the facility is in England,

(b) the main purpose of the facility is the final disposal or recovery of hazardous waste, and

(c) the alteration is expected to have the effect specified in subsection (4).

(4) The effect is—

(a) in the case of the disposal of hazardous waste by landfill or in a deep storage facility, to increase by more than 100,000 tonnes per year the capacity of the facility;

(b) in any other case, to increase by more than 30,000 tonnes per year the capacity of the facility.

(5) The following terms have the same meanings as in the Hazardous Waste (England and Wales) Regulations 2005 (S.I. 2005/894) (see regulation 5 of those regulations)—

'disposal';

'hazardous waste';

'recovery'.

(6) 'Deep storage facility' means a facility for the storage of waste underground in a deep geological cavity.

[30A Radioactive waste geological disposal facilities

(1) A radioactive waste geological disposal facility means a facility which meets the conditions in subsection (2).

(2) The conditions are that—

(a) the main purpose of the facility is expected to be the final disposal of radioactive waste,

(b) the part of the facility where radioactive waste is to be disposed of is expected to be constructed at a depth of at least 200 metres beneath the surface of the ground or seabed, and

(c) the natural environment which surrounds the facility is expected to act, in combination with any engineered measures, to inhibit the transit of radionuclides from the part of the facility where radioactive waste is to be disposed of to the surface.

(3) Development is within section 14(1)(q) only if the development is within subsection (4) or (6) of this section.

(4) Development is within this subsection if—

(a) it is the construction of one or more boreholes, and the carrying out of any associated excavation, construction or building work,

(b) the borehole or boreholes will be constructed, and any associated excavation, construction or building work will be carried out, in England or waters adjacent to England up to the seaward limits of the territorial sea, and

(c) the conditions in subsection (5) are met in relation to each borehole.

(5) The conditions are that—

(a) the borehole is expected to be constructed to a depth of at least 150 metres beneath the surface of the ground or seabed, and

(b) the main purpose of constructing the borehole is to obtain information, data or samples to determine the suitability of a site for the construction or use of a radioactive waste geological disposal facility.

(6) Development is within this subsection if—

(a) it is the construction of a radioactive waste geological disposal facility, and

(b) the facility (when constructed) will be in England or waters adjacent to England up to the seaward limits of the territorial sea.

(7) In this section—

'disposal' in relation to radioactive waste means emplacement in an appropriate facility without the intention to retrieve;

'radioactive waste' has the same meaning as in [the Environmental Permitting (England and Wales) Regulations 2016 (SI 2016/1154)][1] (see paragraph 3(1) of Part 2 of Schedule 23 to those regulations).][2]

1 Words substituted by Environmental Permitting (England and Wales) Regulations 2016, SI 2016/1154, reg 75, Sch 29, Pt 1, para 17 (1 January 2017).

2 Inserted by Infrastructure Planning (Radioactive Waste Geological Disposal Facilities) Order 2015, SI 2015/949, art 2(1), (3) (27 March 2015).

Part 4 Requirement for development consent

31 When development consent is required

Consent under this Act ('development consent') is required for development to the extent that the development is or forms part of a nationally significant infrastructure project.

32 Meaning of 'development'

(1) In this Act (except in Part 11) 'development' has the same meaning as it has in TCPA 1990.

This is subject to subsections (2) and (3).

(2) For the purposes of this Act (except Part 11)—

(a) the conversion of a generating station with a view to its being fuelled by crude liquid petroleum, a petroleum product or natural gas is treated as a material change in the use of the generating station;

(b) starting to use a cavity or strata for the underground storage of gas is treated as a material change in the use of the cavity or strata;

(c) an increase in the permitted use of an airport is treated as a material change in the use of the airport.

(3) For the purposes of this Act (except Part 11) the following works are taken to be development (to the extent that they would not be otherwise)—

(a) works for the demolition of a listed building or its alteration or extension in a manner which would affect its character as a building of special architectural or historic interest;

(b) demolition of a building in a conservation area;

(c) works resulting in the demolition or destruction of or any damage to a scheduled monument;

(d) works for the purpose of removing or repairing a scheduled monument or any part of it;

(e) works for the purpose of making any alterations or additions to a scheduled monument;

(f) flooding or tipping operations on land in, on or under which there is a scheduled monument.

(4) In this section—

'conservation area' has the meaning given by section 91(1) of the Listed Buildings Act;

'flooding operations' has the meaning given by section 61(1) of the Ancient Monuments and Archaeological Areas Act 1979 (c. 46);

'listed building' has the meaning given by section 1(5) of the Listed Buildings Act;

'permitted' means permitted by planning permission or development consent;

'petroleum products' has the meaning given by section 21 of the Energy Act 1976 (c. 76);

'scheduled monument' has the meaning given by section 1(11) of the Ancient Monuments and Archaeological Areas Act 1979 (c. 46);

'tipping operations' has the meaning given by section 61(1) of that Act.

33 Effect of requirement for development consent on other consent regimes

(1) To the extent that development consent is required for development, none of the following is required to be obtained for the development or given in relation to it—

(a) planning permission;

(b) consent under section 10(1), 11(1) or 12(1) of the Green Belt (London and Home Counties) Act 1938 (c. xciii) (erection of buildings and construction of sewer main pipes, watercourses and electric lines etc. on Green Belt land);

(c) a pipe-line construction authorisation under section 1(1) of the Pipe-lines Act 1962 (c. 58) (authorisation for construction of cross-country pipe-lines);

(d) authorisation by an order under section 4(1) of the Gas Act 1965 (c. 36) (storage of gas in underground strata);

[...][1]

(f) to the extent that the development relates to land in England, consent under section 2(3) or 3 of the Ancient Monuments and Archaeological Areas Act 1979;

(g) to the extent that the development relates to land in England, notice under section 35 of the Ancient Monuments and Archaeological Areas Act 1979;

(h) consent under section 36 or 37 of the Electricity Act 1989 (c. 29) (construction etc. of generating stations and installation of overhead lines);

(i) to the extent that the development relates to land in England, consent under section 8(1), (2) or (3) of the Listed Buildings Act;

(j) to the extent that the development relates to land in England, consent under section 74(1) of the Listed Buildings Act.

(2) To the extent that development consent is required for development, the development may not be authorised by any of the following—

(a) an order under section 14 or 16 of the Harbours Act 1964 (c. 40) (orders in relation to harbours, docks and wharves);

(b) an order under section 4(1) of the Gas Act 1965 (order authorising storage of gas in underground strata);

(c) an order under section 1 or 3 of the Transport and Works Act 1992 (c. 42) (orders as to railways, tramways, inland waterways etc.).

(3) Subsection (2) is subject to section 34.

(4) If development consent is required for the construction, improvement or alteration of a highway, none of the following may be made or confirmed in relation to the highway or in connection with the construction, improvement or alteration of the highway—

(a) an order under section 10 of the Highways Act 1980 (c. 66) (general provisions as to trunk roads) directing that the highway should become a trunk road;

(b) an order under section 14 of that Act (supplementary orders relating to trunk roads and classified roads);

(c) a scheme under section 16 of that Act (schemes authorising the provision of special roads);

(d) an order under section 18 of that Act (supplementary orders relating to special roads);

(e) an order or scheme under section 106 of that Act (orders and schemes providing for construction of bridges over or tunnels under navigable waters);

(f) an order under section 108 or 110 of that Act (orders authorising the diversion of navigable and non-navigable watercourses);

(g) an order under section 6 of the New Roads and Street Works Act 1991 (c. 22) (toll orders).

[(5) The Secretary of State may by order—

(a) amend subsection (1) or (2)—

(i) to add or remove a type of consent, or

(ii) to vary the cases in relation to which a type of consent is within that subsection;

(b) make further provision, or amend or repeal provision, about—

(i) the types of consent that are, and are not, within subsection (1) or (2), or

(ii) the cases in relation to which a type of consent is, or is not, within either of those subsections.

(6) In this section 'consent' means—

(a) a consent or authorisation that is required, under legislation, to be obtained for development,

(b) a consent, or authorisation, that—

(i) may authorise development, and

(ii) is given under legislation, or

(c) a notice that is required by legislation to be given in relation to development.

(7) In subsection (6) 'legislation' means an Act or an instrument made under an Act.

(8) An order under subsection (5) may not affect—

(a) a requirement for a devolved consent to be obtained for, or given in relation to, development, or

(b) whether development may be authorised by a devolved consent.

(9) A consent is 'devolved' for the purposes of subsection (8) if—

(a) provision for the consent would be within the legislative competence of the National Assembly for Wales if the provision were contained in an Act of the Assembly,

(b) provision for the consent is, or could be, made by the Welsh Ministers in an instrument made under an Act,

(c) the consent is not within subsection (6)(c) and the Welsh Ministers have a power or duty—

(i) to decide, or give directions as to how to decide, whether the consent is given,

(ii) to decide, or give directions as to how to decide, some or all of the terms on which the consent is given, or

(iii) to revoke or vary the consent, or

(d) the consent is within subsection (6)(c) and the notice has to be given to the Welsh Ministers or otherwise brought to their attention.

(10) An order under subsection (5)(b) may amend this Act.][2]

1 Repealed by Growth and Infrastructure Act 2013, s 18(3)(a) (25 June 2013).
2 Inserted by Localism Act 2011, s 131(1), (2) (1 April 2012).

34 Welsh offshore generating stations

(1) Section 33(2) does not prevent an order under section 3 of the Transport and Works Act 1992 (c. 42) from authorising the carrying out of works consisting of the construction or extension of a generating station that is or (when constructed or extended) will be a Welsh offshore generating station.

(2) A 'Welsh offshore generating station' is a generating station that is in waters in or adjacent to Wales up to the seaward limits of the territorial sea.

(3) If, by virtue of subsection (1), an order under section 3 of the Transport and Works Act 1992 authorises the carrying out of any works, development consent is treated as not being required for the carrying out of those works.

[35 Directions in relation to projects of national significance

(1) The Secretary of State may give a direction for development to be treated as development for which development consent is required.

This is subject to the following provisions of this section and section 35ZA.

(2) The Secretary of State may give a direction under subsection (1) only if—

(a) the development is or forms part of—

(i) a project (or proposed project) in the field of energy, transport, water, waste water or waste, or

(ii) a business or commercial project (or proposed project) of a prescribed description,

(b) the development will (when completed) be wholly in one or more of the areas specified in subsection (3), and

(c) the Secretary of State thinks the project (or proposed project) is of national significance, either by itself or when considered with—

(i) in a case within paragraph (a)(i), one or more other projects (or proposed projects) in the same field;

(ii) in a case within paragraph (a)(ii), one or more other business or commercial projects (or proposed projects) of a description prescribed under paragraph (a)(ii).

(3) The areas are—

(a) England or waters adjacent to England up to the seaward limits of the territorial sea;

(b) in the case of a project for the carrying out of works in the field of energy, a Renewable Energy Zone, except any part of a Renewable Energy Zone in relation to which the Scottish Ministers have functions.

(4) The Secretary of State may give a direction under subsection (1) only with the consent of the Mayor of London if—

(a) all or part of the development is or will be in Greater London, and

(b) the development is or forms part of a business or commercial project (or proposed project) of a description prescribed under subsection (2)(a)(ii).

(5) Regulations under subsection (2)(a)(ii) may not prescribe a description of project which includes the construction of one or more dwellings.][1]

1 Sections 35 and 35ZA substituted for s 35 by Growth and Infrastructure Act 2013, s 26(1), (2) (25 April 2013).

[35ZA Directions under sections 35: procedural matters

(1) The power in section 35(1) to give a direction in a case within section 35(2)(a)(i) (projects in the field of energy etc) is exercisable only in response to a qualifying request if no application for a consent or authorisation mentioned in section 33(1) or (2) has been made in relation to the development to which the request relates.

(2) The power in section 35(1) to give a direction in a case within section 35(2)(a)(ii) (business or commercial projects of prescribed description) is exercisable only in response to a qualifying request made by one or more of the following—

(a) a person who proposes to carry out any of the development to which the request relates;

(b) a person who has applied, or proposes to apply, for a consent or authorisation mentioned in section 33(1) or (2) in relation to any of that development;

(c) a person who, if a direction under section 35(1) is given in relation to that development, proposes to apply for an order granting development consent for any of that development.

(3) If the Secretary of State gives a direction under section 35(1) in relation to development, the Secretary of State may—

(a) if an application for a consent or authorisation mentioned in section 33(1) or (2) has been made in relation to the development, direct the application to be treated as an application for an order granting development consent;

(b) if a person proposes to make an application for such a consent or authorisation in relation to the development, direct the proposed application to be treated as a proposed application for development consent.

(4) A direction under section 35(1), or subsection (3) of this section, may be given so as to apply for specified purposes or generally.

(5) A direction under subsection (3) may provide for specified provisions of or made under this or any other Act—

(a) to have effect in relation to the application, or proposed application, with any specified modifications, or

(b) to be treated as having been complied with in relation to the application or proposed application.

(6) If the Secretary of State gives a direction under subsection (3), the relevant authority must refer the application, or proposed application, to the Secretary of State instead of dealing with it themselves.

(7) If the Secretary of State is considering whether to give a direction under subsection (3), the Secretary of State may direct the relevant authority to take no further action in relation to the application, or proposed application, until the Secretary of State has decided whether to give the direction.

(8) The Secretary of State may require an authority within subsection (9) to provide any information required by the Secretary of State for the purpose of enabling the Secretary of State to decide—

(a) whether to give a direction under section 35(1), and

(b) the terms in which such a direction should be given.

(9) An authority is within this subsection if an application for a consent or authorisation mentioned in section 33(1) or (2) in relation to the development has been, or may be, made to it.

(10) If the Secretary of State decides to give a direction under section 35(1), the Secretary of State must give reasons for the decision.

(11) In this section—

'qualifying request' means a written request, for a direction under section 35(1) or subsection (3) of this section, that—

(a) specifies the development to which it relates, and

(b) explains why the conditions in section 35(2)(a) and (b) are met in relation to the development;

'relevant authority'—

(a) in relation to an application for a consent or authorisation mentioned in section 33(1) or (2) that has been made, means the authority to which the application was made, and

(b) in relation to such an application that a person proposes to make, means the authority to which the person proposes to make the application.][1]

1 Sections 35 and 35ZA substituted for s 35 by Growth and Infrastructure Act 2013, s 26(1), (2) (25 April 2013).

[35A Timetable for deciding request for direction under section 35

(1) This section applies if the Secretary of State receives a qualifying request from a person ('R').

(2) The Secretary of State must make a decision on the qualifying request before the primary deadline, subject to subsection (3).

(3) Subsection (2) does not apply if, before the primary deadline, the Secretary of State asks R to provide the Secretary of State with information for the purpose of enabling the Secretary of State to decide—

(a) whether to give the direction requested, and

(b) the terms in which it should be given.

(4) If R—

(a) is asked under subsection (3) to provide information, and

(b) provides the information sought within the period of 14 days beginning with the day on which R is asked to do so,

the Secretary of State must make a decision on the qualifying request before the end of the period of 28 days beginning with the day the Secretary of State receives the information.

(5) In this section—

'the primary deadline' means the end of the period of 28 days beginning with the day on which the Secretary of State receives the qualifying request;

'qualifying request' has the meaning given by [section 35ZA(11)][1].][2]

1 Word substituted by Growth and Infrastructure Act 2013, s 26(1), (3) (25 April 2013).
2 Inserted by Localism Act 2011, s 132(10) (1 April 2012).

36 Amendments consequential on development consent regime

Schedule 2 makes amendments consequential on the development consent regime.

Part 5 Applications for orders granting development consent

Chapter 1 Applications

37 Applications for orders granting development consent

(1) An order granting development consent may be made only if an application is made for it.

(2) An application for an order granting development consent must be made to the [Secretary of State][1].

(3) An application for an order granting development consent must[, so far as necessary to secure that the application (including accompaniments) is of a standard that the Secretary of State considers satisfactory][2] —

(a) specify the development to which it relates,

(b) be made in the prescribed form,

(c) be accompanied by the consultation report, and

(d) be accompanied by documents and information of a prescribed description.

(4) The [Secretary of State][1] may give guidance about how the requirements under subsection (3) are to be complied with.

(5) The [Secretary of State][1] may set standards for—

(a) the preparation of a document required by subsection (3)(d);

(b) the coverage in such a document of a matter falling to be dealt with in it;

(c) all or any of the collection, sources, verification, processing and presentation of information required by subsection (3)(d).

(6) The [Secretary of State][1] must publish, in such manner as [the Secretary of State][3] thinks appropriate, any guidance given under subsection (4) and any standards set under subsection (5).

(7) In subsection (3)(c) 'the consultation report' means a report giving details of—

(a) what has been done in compliance with sections 42, 47 and 48 in relation to a proposed application that has become the application,

(b) any relevant responses, and

(c) the account taken of any relevant responses.

(8) In subsection (7) 'relevant response' has the meaning given by section 49(3).

1 Word substituted by Localism Act 2011, s 128(2), Sch 13, paras 1, 5(1), (2) (1 April 2012).
2 Words inserted by Localism Act 2011, s 137(1), (5) (1 April 2012).
3 Word substituted by Localism Act 2011, s 128(2), Sch 13, paras 1, 5(1), (3) (1 April 2012).

38 ...

Repealed by Localism Act 2011, ss 128(2), 237, Sch 13, paras 1, 6, Sch 25, Pt 20 as from 1 April 2012.

39 Register of applications

(1) The [Secretary of State][1] is to maintain a register of applications received by [the Secretary of State][2] for orders granting development consent ('the register').

(2) Where the [Secretary of State][1] receives an application for an order granting development consent, [the Secretary of State][2] must cause details of the application to be entered in the register.

(3) The [Secretary of State][1] must publish the register or make arrangements for inspection of the register by the public.

(4) The [Secretary of State][1] must make arrangements for inspection by the public of—

(a) applications received by the [Secretary of State][1] for orders granting development consent,

(b) consultation reports received by the [Secretary of State][1] under section 37(3)(c), and

(c) accompanying documents and information received by the [Secretary of State][1] under section 37(3)(d).

1 Word substituted by Localism Act 2011, s 128(2), Sch 13, paras 1, 7(1), (2) (1 April 2012).
2 Word substituted by Localism Act 2011, s 128(2), Sch 13, paras 1, 7(1), (3) (1 April 2012).

40 Applications by the Crown for orders granting development consent

(1) This section applies to an application for an order granting development consent made by or on behalf of the Crown.

(2) The Secretary of State may by regulations modify or exclude any statutory provision relating to—

(a) the procedure to be followed before such an application is made;

(b) the making of such an application;

(c) the decision-making process for such an application.

(3) A statutory provision is a provision contained in or having effect under this Act or any other enactment.

Chapter 2 Pre-application procedure

41 Chapter applies before application is made

(1) This Chapter applies where a person ('the applicant') proposes to make an application for an order granting development consent.

(2) In the following provisions of this Chapter—

'the proposed application' means the proposed application mentioned in subsection (1);

'the land' means the land to which the proposed application relates or any part of that land;

'the proposed development' means the development for which the proposed application (if made) would seek development consent.

42 Duty to consult

[(1)][1] The applicant must consult the following about the proposed application—

(a) such persons as may be prescribed,

[(aa) the Marine Management Organisation, in any case where the proposed development would affect, or would be likely to affect, any of the areas specified in subsection (2),][2]

(b) each local authority that is within section 43,

(c) the Greater London Authority if the land is in Greater London, and

(d) each person who is within one or more of the categories set out in section 44.

[(2) The areas are—

(a) waters in or adjacent to England up to the seaward limits of the territorial sea;

(b) an exclusive economic zone, except any part of an exclusive economic zone in relation to which the Scottish Ministers have functions;

(c) a Renewable Energy Zone, except any part of a Renewable Energy Zone in relation to which the Scottish Ministers have functions;

(d) an area designated under section 1(7) of the Continental Shelf Act 1964, except any part of that area which is within a part of an exclusive economic zone or Renewable Energy Zone in relation to which the Scottish Ministers have functions.][2]

1 Existing s 42 renumbered as s 42(1) by Marine and Coastal Access Act 2009, s 23(1), (2)(a) (1 April 2010).
2 Inserted by Marine and Coastal Access Act 2009, s 23(1), (2)(b), (c) (1 April 2010).

43 [Local authorities for purposes of section 42(1)(b)][1]

(1) A local authority is within this section if the land is in the authority's area.

(2) A local authority ('A') is within this section if—

(a) the land is in the area of another local authority ('B'),

[(aa) B is a unitary council or a lower-tier district council,][2] and

(b) any part of the boundary of A's area is also a part of the boundary of B's area.

[(2A) If the land is in the area of an upper-tier county council ('C'), a local authority ('D') is within this section if—

(a) D is not a lower-tier district council, and

(b) any part of the boundary of D's area is also part of the boundary of C's area.][3]

[(3) In this section—

'local authority' means—

(a) a county council, or district council, in England;

(b) a London borough council;

(c) the Common Council of the City of London;

(d) the Council of the Isles of Scilly;

(e) a county council, or county borough council, in Wales;

(f) a council constituted under section 2 of the Local Government etc (Scotland) Act 1994;

(g) a National Park authority;

(h) the Broads Authority;

'lower-tier district council' means a district council in England for an area for which there is a county council;

'unitary council' means a local authority that is not an upper-tier county council, a lower-tier district council, a National Park authority or the Broads Authority;

'upper-tier county council' means a county council in England for each part of whose area there is a district council.][4]

1 Heading substituted by Marine and Coastal Access Act 2009, s 23(1), (3)(a) (1 April 2010).
2 Inserted by Localism Act 2011, s 133(1), (2) (1 April 2012).
3 Inserted by Localism Act 2011, s 133(1), (3) (1 April 2012).
4 Substituted by Localism Act 2011, s 133(1), (4) (1 April 2012).

44 [Categories for purposes of section 42(1)(d)][1]

(1) A person is within Category 1 if the applicant, after making diligent inquiry, knows that the person is an owner, lessee, tenant (whatever the tenancy period) or occupier of the land.

(2) A person is within Category 2 if the applicant, after making diligent inquiry, knows that the person—

(a) is interested in the land, or

(b) has power—

(i) to sell and convey the land, or

(ii) to release the land.

(3) An expression, other than 'the land', that appears in subsection (2) of this section and also in section 5(1) of the Compulsory Purchase Act 1965 (c. 56) has in subsection (2) the meaning that it has in section 5(1) of that Act.

(4) A person is within Category 3 if the applicant thinks that, if the order sought by the proposed application were to be made and fully implemented, the person would or might be entitled—

(a) as a result of the implementing of the order,

(b) as a result of the order having been implemented, or

(c) as a result of use of the land once the order has been implemented,

to make a relevant claim.

This is subject to subsection (5).

(5) A person is within Category 3 only if the person is known to the applicant after making diligent inquiry.

(6) In subsection (4) 'relevant claim' means—

(a) a claim under section 10 of the Compulsory Purchase Act 1965 (c. 56) (compensation where satisfaction not made for the taking, or injurious affection, of land subject to compulsory purchase);

(b) a claim under Part 1 of the Land Compensation Act 1973 (c. 26) (compensation for depreciation of land value by physical factors caused by use of public works) [;][2]

[(c) a claim under section 152(3).][2]

1 Heading substituted by Marine and Coastal Access Act 2009, s 23(1), (3)(b) (1 April 2010).
2 Inserted by Localism Act 2011, s 135(1), (8) (1 April 2012).

45 Timetable for consultation under section 42

(1) The applicant must, when consulting a person under section 42, notify the person of the deadline for the receipt by the applicant of the person's response to the consultation.

(2) A deadline notified under subsection (1) must not be earlier than the end of the period of 28 days that begins with the day after the day on which the person receives the consultation documents.

(3) In subsection (2) 'the consultation documents' means the documents supplied to the person by the applicant for the purpose of consulting the person.

46 Duty to notify [Secretary of State][1] of proposed application

(1) The applicant must supply the [Secretary of State][2] with such information in relation to the proposed application as the applicant would supply to the [Secretary of State][2] for the purpose of complying with section 42 if the applicant were required by that section to consult the [Secretary of State][2] about the proposed application.

(2) The applicant must comply with subsection (1) on or before commencing consultation under section 42.

1 Word substituted by Localism Act 2011, s 128(2), Sch 13, paras 1, 8(1), (3) (1 April 2012).
2 Word substituted by Localism Act 2011, s 128(2), Sch 13, paras 1, 8(1), (2) (1 April 2012).

47 Duty to consult local community

(1) The applicant must prepare a statement setting out how the applicant proposes to consult, about the proposed application, people living in the vicinity of the land.

(2) Before preparing the statement, the applicant must consult each local authority that is within section 43(1) about what is to be in the statement.

(3) The deadline for the receipt by the applicant of a local authority's response to consultation under subsection (2) is the end of the period of 28 days that begins with the day after the day on which the local authority receives the consultation documents.

(4) In subsection (3) 'the consultation documents' means the documents supplied to the local authority by the applicant for the purpose of consulting the local authority under subsection (2).

(5) In preparing the statement, the applicant must have regard to any response to consultation under subsection (2) that is received by the applicant before the deadline imposed by subsection (3).

(6) Once the applicant has prepared the statement, the applicant [must—][1]

[(za) make the statement available for inspection by the public in a way that is reasonably convenient for people living in the vicinity of the land,][1]

(a) [publish,][2] in a newspaper circulating in the vicinity of the land[, a notice stating where and when the statement can be inspected][3], and

(b) [publish the statement in such manner][4] as may be prescribed.

(7) The applicant must carry out consultation in accordance with the proposals set out in the statement.

1 Words and para (za) substituted for words by Localism Act 2011, s 134(a) (1 April 2012).
2 Word inserted by Localism Act 2011, s 134(b)(i) (1 April 2012).
3 Words inserted by Localism Act 2011, s 134(b)(ii) (1 April 2012).
4 Words substituted by Localism Act 2011, s 134(c) (1 April 2012).

48 Duty to publicise

(1) The applicant must publicise the proposed application in the prescribed manner.

(2) Regulations made for the purposes of subsection (1) must, in particular, make provision for publicity under subsection (1) to include a deadline for receipt by the applicant of responses to the publicity.

49 Duty to take account of responses to consultation and publicity

(1) Subsection (2) applies where the applicant—

(a) has complied with sections 42, 47 and 48, and

(b) proposes to go ahead with making an application for an order granting development consent (whether or not in the same terms as the proposed application).

(2) The applicant must, when deciding whether the application that the applicant is actually to make should be in the same terms as the proposed application, have regard to any relevant responses.

(3) In subsection (2) 'relevant response' means—

(a) a response from a person consulted under section 42 that is received by the applicant before the deadline imposed by section 45 in that person's case,

(b) a response to consultation under section 47(7) that is received by the applicant before any applicable deadline imposed in accordance with the statement prepared under section 47, or

(c) a response to publicity under section 48 that is received by the applicant before the deadline imposed in accordance with section 48(2) in relation to that publicity.

50 Guidance about pre-application procedure

(1) Guidance may be issued about how to comply with the requirements of this Chapter.

(2) Guidance under this section may be issued by [...][1] the Secretary of State.

(3) The applicant must have regard to any guidance under this section.

1 Words repealed by Localism Act 2011, ss 128(2), 237, Sch 13, paras 1, 9, Sch 25, Pt 20 (1 April 2012).

Chapter 3 Assistance for applicants and others

51 Advice for potential applicants and others

(1) [This section applies to advice][1] about—

(a) applying for an order granting development consent;

(b) making representations about an application, or a proposed application, for such an order.

[(3) The Secretary of State may by regulations make provision about the giving of advice to which this section applies.

(4) In particular, regulations under subsection (3) may make provision that has the effect that—

(a) a request for advice made by an applicant, potential applicant or other person, or

(b) advice given to an applicant, potential applicant or other person,

must be, or may be, disclosed by the Secretary of State to other persons or to the public generally.][2]

1 Words substituted by Localism Act 2011, s 128(2), Sch 13, paras 1, 10(1), (2) (15 January 2012 for the purpose of conferring power on the Secretary of State to make regulations or rules; 1 April 2012 otherwise).

2 Section 51(3)–(4) substituted for s 51(2)–(4) by Localism Act 2011, s 128(2), Sch 13, paras 1, 10(1), (3) (15 January 2012 for the purpose of conferring power on the Secretary of State to make regulations or rules; 1 April 2012 otherwise).

52 Obtaining information about interests in land

(1) Where a person is applying, or proposes to apply, for an order granting development consent, [subsections (2) and (2A) apply][1] for the purpose of enabling the person ('the applicant') to comply with provisions of, or made under, Chapter 2 of this Part or Chapter 1 of Part 6.

(2) The [Secretary of State][2] may authorise the applicant to serve a notice on a person mentioned in subsection (3) requiring the person ('the recipient') to give to the applicant in writing the name and address of any person the recipient believes is one or more of the following—

(a) an owner, lessee, tenant (whatever the tenancy period) or occupier of the land;

(b) a person interested in the land;

(c) a person having power—

(i) to sell and convey the land, or

(ii) to release the land.

[(2A) The Secretary of State may authorise the applicant to serve a notice on a person mentioned in subsection (3) requiring the person ('the recipient') to give to the applicant in writing the name and address of any person the recipient believes is a person who, if the order sought by the application or proposed application were to be made and fully implemented, would or might be entitled—

(a) as a result of the implementing of the order,

(b) as a result of the order having been implemented, or

(c) as a result of the use of the land once the order has been implemented,

to make a relevant claim.][3]

(3) The persons are—

(a) an occupier of the land;

(b) a person who has an interest in the land as freeholder, mortgagee or lessee;

(c) a person who directly or indirectly receives rent for the land;

(d) a person who, in pursuance of an agreement between that person and a person interested in the land, is authorised to manage the land or to arrange for the letting of it.

(4) A notice under subsection (2) [or (2A)][4] must—

(a) be in writing,

(b) state that the [Secretary of State][2] has authorised the applicant to serve the notice,

(c) specify or describe the land to which the application, or proposed application, relates,

(d) specify the deadline by which the recipient must give the required information to the applicant, and

(e) draw attention to the provisions in subsections (6) to (9).

(5) A deadline specified under subsection (4)(d) in a notice must not be earlier than the end of the 14 days beginning with the day after the day on which the notice is served on the recipient of the notice.

[(5A) A notice under subsection (2A) must explain the circumstances in which a person would or might be entitled as mentioned in that subsection.][5]

(6) A person commits an offence if the person fails without reasonable excuse to comply with a notice under subsection (2) [or (2A)][4] served on the person.

(7) A person commits an offence if, in response to a notice under subsection (2) [or (2A)][4] served on the person—

(a) the person gives information which is false in a material particular, and

(b) when the person does so, the person knows or ought reasonably to know that the information is false.

(8) If an offence under this section committed by a body corporate is proved to have been committed with the consent or connivance of, or to be attributable to any neglect on the part of—

(a) a director, manager, secretary or other similar officer of the body,

(b) a person purporting to act in any such capacity, or

(c) in a case where the affairs of the body are managed by its members, a member of the body,

that person, as well as the body, is guilty of that offence and liable to be proceeded against accordingly.

(9) A person guilty of an offence under this section is liable on summary conviction to a fine not exceeding level 5 on the standard scale.

(10) In subsections [(2) to (3)][6] 'the land' means—

(a) the land to which the application, or proposed application, relates, or

(b) any part of that land.

(11) Any other expression that appears in either of paragraphs (b) and (c) of subsection (2) and also in section 5(1) of the Compulsory Purchase Act 1965 (c. 56) has in those paragraphs the meaning that it has in section 5(1) of that Act.

[(12) In subsection (3) as it applies for the purposes of subsection (2A) 'the land' also includes any relevant affected land (see subsection (13)).

(13) Where the applicant believes that, if the order sought by the application or proposed application were to be made and fully implemented, there would or might be persons entitled—

(a) as a result of the implementing of the order,

(b) as a result of the order having been implemented, or

(c) as a result of the use of the land once the order has been implemented,

to make a relevant claim in respect of any land or in respect of an interest in any land, that land is 'relevant affected land' for the purposes of subsection (12).

(14) In this section 'relevant claim' means—

(a) a claim under section 10 of the Compulsory Purchase Act 1965 (compensation where satisfaction not made for compulsory purchase of land or not made for injurious affection resulting from compulsory purchase);

(b) a claim under Part 1 of the Land Compensation Act 1973 (compensation for depreciation of land value by physical factors caused by use of public works);

(c) a claim under section 152(3).][7]

1 Words substituted by Localism Act 2011, s 135(1), (2) (1 April 2012).
2 Word substituted by Localism Act 2011, s 128(2), Sch 13, paras 1, 11 (1 April 2012).
3 Inserted by Localism Act 2011, s 135(1), (3) (1 April 2012).
4 Words inserted by Localism Act 2011, s 135(1), (4) (1 April 2012).
5 Inserted by Localism Act 2011, s 135(1), (5) (1 April 2012).
6 Words substituted by Localism Act 2011, s 135(1), (6) (1 April 2012).
7 Inserted by Localism Act 2011, s 135(1), (7) (1 April 2012).

53 Rights of entry

(1) Any person duly authorised in writing by the [Secretary of State][1] may at any reasonable time enter any land for the purpose of surveying and taking levels of it[, or in order to facilitate compliance with the provisions mentioned in subsection (1A),][2] in connection with—

(a) an application for an order granting development consent, whether in relation to that or any other land, that has been accepted by the [Secretary of State][1],

(b) a proposed application for an order granting development consent, or

(c) an order granting development consent that includes provision authorising the compulsory acquisition of that land or of an interest in it or right over it.

[(1A) Those provisions are any provision of or made under an Act for the purpose of implementing—

(a) Council Directive 85/337/EEC of 27 June 1985 on the assessment of the effects of certain public and private projects on the environment, as amended from time to time,

(b) Council Directive 92/43/EC of 21 May 1992 on the conservation of natural habitats and of wild fauna and flora, as amended from time to time, or

(c) any EU instrument from time to time replacing all or any part of either of those Directives.][3]

(2) Authorisation may be given by the [Secretary of State][1] under subsection (1)(b) in relation to any land only if it appears to the [Secretary of State][1] that—

(a) the proposed applicant is considering a distinct project of real substance genuinely requiring entry onto the land[.][4]

[...][4]

(3) Subject to subsections (9) and (10), power conferred by subsection (1) to survey land includes power to search and bore for the purpose of ascertaining the nature of the subsoil or the presence of minerals or other matter in it.

[(3A) Power conferred by subsection (1) for the purpose of complying with the provisions mentioned in subsection (1A) includes power to take, and process, samples of or from any of the following found on, in or over the land—

(a) water,

(b) air,

(c) soil or rock,

(d) its flora,

(e) bodily excretions, or dead bodies, of non-human creatures, or

(f) any non-living thing present as a result of human action.][5]

(4) A person authorised under subsection (1) to enter any land—

(a) must, if so required, produce evidence of the person's authority, and state the purpose of the person's entry, before so entering,

(b) may not demand admission as of right to any land which is occupied unless 14 days' notice of the intended entry has been given to the occupier, and

(c) must comply with any other conditions subject to which the [Secretary of State's][6] authorisation is given.

(5) A person commits an offence if the person wilfully obstructs a person acting in the exercise of power under subsection (1).

(6) A person guilty of an offence under subsection (5) is liable on summary conviction to a fine not exceeding level 3 on the standard scale.

(7) Where any damage is caused to land or chattels—

(a) in the exercise of a right of entry conferred under subsection (1), or

(b) in the making of any survey for the purpose of which any such right of entry has been conferred,

compensation may be recovered by any person suffering the damage from the person exercising the right of entry.

(8) Any question of disputed compensation under subsection (7) must be referred to and determined by the [Upper Tribunal][7].

(9) No person may carry out under subsection (1) any works authorised by virtue of subsection (3) unless notice of the person's intention to do so was included in the notice required by subsection (4)(b).

(10) The authority of the appropriate Minister is required for the carrying out under subsection (1) of works authorised by virtue of subsection (3) if—

(a) the land in question is held by statutory undertakers, and

(b) they object to the proposed works on the ground that execution of the works would be seriously detrimental to the carrying-on of their undertaking.

(11) In subsection (10)—

'the appropriate Minister' means—

(a) in the case of land in Wales held by water or sewerage undertakers, the Welsh Ministers, and

(b) in any other case, the Secretary of State;

'statutory undertakers' means persons who are, or who are deemed to be, statutory undertakers for the purposes of any provision of Part 11 of TCPA 1990.

1 Word substituted by Localism Act 2011, s 128(2), Sch 13, paras 1, 12(1), (2) (1 April 2012).
2 Words inserted by Localism Act 2011, s 136(1), (2) (1 April 2012).
3 Inserted by Localism Act 2011, s 136(1), (3) (1 April 2012).
4 Repealed by Localism Act 2011, s 237, Sch 25, Pt 20 (1 April 2012).
5 Inserted by Localism Act 2011, s 136(1), (5) (1 April 2012).
6 Word substituted by Localism Act 2011, s 128(2), Sch 13, paras 1, 12(1), (3) (1 April 2012).
7 Words substituted by Transfer of Tribunal Functions (Lands Tribunal and Miscellaneous Amendments) Order 2009, SI 2009/1307, art 5(1), (2), Sch 1, paras 291, 292 (1 October 2009: substitution came into force on 1 June 2009 but could not take effect until the commencement of Planning Act 2008, s 53(8) on 1 October 2009).

54 Rights of entry: Crown land

(1) Subsections (1) [to (3A)][1] of section 53 apply to Crown land subject to subsections (2) and (3) of this section.

(2) A person must not enter Crown land unless the person ('P') has the permission of—

(a) a person appearing to P to be entitled to give it, or

(b) the appropriate Crown authority.

(3) In section 53(3), the words 'Subject to subsections (9) and (10)' must be ignored.

(4) Subsections (4) to (6) and (9) to (11) of section 53 do not apply to anything done by virtue of subsections (1) to (3) of this section.

1 Words substituted by Localism Act 2011, s 136(1), (6) (1 April 2012).

Part 6 Deciding applications for orders granting development consent

Chapter 1 Handling of application by Commission

55 Acceptance of applications

(1) The following provisions of this section apply where the [Secretary of State][1] receives an application that purports to be an application for an order granting development consent.

(2) The [Secretary of State][1] must, by the end of the period of 28 days beginning with the day after the day on which [the Secretary of State][2] receives the application, decide whether or not to accept the application.

(3) The [Secretary of State][1] may accept the application only if the [Secretary of State][1] concludes—

(a) that it is an application for an order granting development consent,

[...][3]

(c) that development consent is required for any of the development to which the application relates,

[...][3]

(e) that the applicant has, in relation to a proposed application that has become the application, complied with Chapter 2 of Part 5 (pre-application procedure)[, and][4]

[(f) that the application (including accompaniments) is of a standard that the Secretary of State considers satisfactory.][4]

(4) The [Secretary of State][1], when deciding whether [the Secretary of State][2] may reach the conclusion in subsection (3)(e), must have regard to—

(a) the consultation report received under section 37(3)(c),

(b) any adequacy of consultation representation received by [the Secretary of State][2] from a local authority consultee, and

(c) the extent to which the applicant has had regard to any guidance issued under section 50.

(5) In subsection (4)—

'local authority consultee' means—

(a) a local authority consulted under [section 42(1)(b)][5] about a proposed application that has become the application, or

(b) the Greater London Authority if consulted under [section 42(1)(c)][6] about that proposed application;

'adequacy of consultation representation' means a representation about whether the applicant complied, in relation to that proposed application, with the applicant's duties under sections 42, 47 and 48.

[(5A) The Secretary of State, when deciding whether the Secretary of State may reach the conclusion in subsection (3)(f), must have regard to the extent to which—

(a) the application complies with the requirements in section 37(3) (form and contents of application) and any standards set under section 37(5), and

(b) any applicable guidance given under section 37(4) has been followed in relation to the application.][7]

(6) If the [Secretary of State][1] accepts the application, [the Secretary of State][2] must notify the applicant of the acceptance.

(7) If the [Secretary of State][1] is of the view that [the application cannot be accepted, the Secretary of State][8] must—

(a) notify that view to the applicant, and

(b) notify the applicant of [the Secretary of State's][9] reasons for that view.

(8) If in response the applicant modifies (or further modifies) the application, subsections (2) to (7) then apply in relation to the application as modified.

1 Word substituted by Localism Act 2011, s 128(2), Sch 13, paras 1, 13(1), (2) (1 April 2012).
2 Word substituted by Localism Act 2011, s 128(2), Sch 13, paras 1, 13(1), (3) (1 April 2012).
3 Repealed by Localism Act 2011, s 237, Sch 25, Pt 21 (1 April 2012).
4 Inserted by Localism Act 2011, s 137(1), (3) (1 April 2012).
5 Words substituted by Marine and Coastal Access Act 2009, s 23(1), (4)(a) (1 April 2010).
6 Words substituted by Marine and Coastal Access Act 2009, s 23(1), (4)(b) (1 April 2010).
7 Inserted by Localism Act 2011, s 137(1), (4) (1 April 2012).
8 Words substituted by Localism Act 2011, s 128(2), Sch 13, paras 1, 13(1), (4)(a) (1 April 2012).
9 Word substituted by Localism Act 2011, s 128(2), Sch 13, paras 1, 13(1), (4)(b) (1 April 2012).

56 Notifying persons of accepted application

(1) Subsections (2), (6) and (7) apply where the [Secretary of State][1] accepts an application for an order granting development consent.

(2) The applicant must give notice of the application to—

(a) such persons as may be prescribed,

[(aa) the Marine Management Organisation, in any case where the development for which the application seeks development consent would involve the carrying on of any activity in one or more of the areas specified in subsection (2A),][2]

[(b) each local authority that is within section 56A,][3]

(c) the Greater London Authority if the land to which the application relates, or any part of it, is in Greater London, and

(d) each person who is within one or more of the categories set out in section 57.

[(2A) The areas are—

(a) waters in or adjacent to England up to the seaward limits of the territorial sea;

(b) an exclusive economic zone, except any part of an exclusive economic zone in relation to which the Scottish Ministers have functions;

(c) a Renewable Energy Zone, except any part of a Renewable Energy Zone in relation to which the Scottish Ministers have functions;

(d) an area designated under section 1(7) of the Continental Shelf Act 1964, except any part of that area which is within a part of an exclusive economic zone or Renewable Energy Zone in relation to which the Scottish Ministers have functions.][4]

(3) Notice under subsection (2) must be in such form and contain such matter, and be given in such manner, as may be prescribed.

(4) The applicant must, when giving notice to a person under subsection (2), notify the person of the deadline for receipt by the [Secretary of State][1] of representations giving notice of the person's interest in, or objection to, the application.

(5) A deadline notified under subsection (4) must not be earlier than the end of the period of 28 days that begins with the day after the day on which the person receives the notice.

(6) The applicant must make available, to each person to whom notice is given under subsection (2), a copy of—

(a) the application, and

(b) the documents and information that were required by section 37(3)(d) to accompany the application.

(7) The applicant must publicise the application in the prescribed manner.

(8) Regulations made for the purposes of subsection (7) must, in particular, make provision for publicity under subsection (7) to include a deadline for receipt by the [Secretary of State][1] of representations giving notice of persons' interests in, or objections to, the application.

(9) A deadline specified in accordance with subsection (8) does not apply to a person to whom notice is given under subsection (2).

1 Word substituted by Localism Act 2011, s 128(2), Sch 13, paras 1, 14 (1 April 2012).
2 Inserted by Marine and Coastal Access Act 2009, s 23(1), (5)(a) (1 April 2010).
3 Substituted by Localism Act 2011, s 138(1), (2) (1 April 2012).
4 Inserted by Marine and Coastal Access Act 2009, s 23(1), (5)(b) (1 April 2010).

[56A Local authorities for the purposes of sections 56(2)(b) and 60(2)(a)

(1) A local authority is within this section if the land is in the authority's area.

(2) A local authority ('A') is within this section if—

(a) the land is in the area of another local authority ('B'),

(b) B is a unitary council or a lower-tier district council, and

(c) any part of the boundary of A's area is also a part of the boundary of B's area.

(3) If the land is in the area of an upper-tier county council ('C'), a local authority ('D') is within this section if—

(a) D is not a lower-tier district council, and

(b) any part of the boundary of D's area is also part of the boundary of C's area.

(4) In this section—

'the land' means the land to which the application concerned relates or any part of that land;

'local authority' has the meaning given in section 102(8);

'lower-tier district council' means a district council in England for an area for which there is a county council;

'unitary council' means a local authority that is not an upper-tier county council, a lower-tier district council, a National Park authority or the Broads Authority;

'upper-tier county council' means a county council in England for each part of whose area there is a district council.][1]

1 Inserted by Localism Act 2011, s 138(1), (3) (1 April 2012).

57 Categories for purposes of section 56(2)(d)

(1) A person is within Category 1 if the applicant, after making diligent inquiry, knows that the person is an owner, lessee, tenant (whatever the tenancy period) or occupier of the land.

(2) A person is within Category 2 if the applicant, after making diligent inquiry, knows that the person—

(a) is interested in the land, or

(b) has power—

(i) to sell and convey the land, or

(ii) to release the land.

(3) An expression, other than 'the land', that appears in subsection (2) of this section and also in section 5(1) of the Compulsory Purchase Act 1965 (c. 56) has in subsection (2) the meaning that it has in section 5(1) of that Act.

(4) A person is within Category 3 if the applicant thinks that, if the order sought by the application were to be made and fully implemented, the person would or might be entitled—

(a) as a result of the implementing of the order,

(b) as a result of the order having been implemented, or

(c) as a result of use of the land once the order has been implemented,

to make a relevant claim.

This is subject to subsection (5).

(5) A person is within Category 3 only if the person is known to the applicant after making diligent inquiry.

(6) In subsection (4) 'relevant claim' means—

(a) a claim under section 10 of the Compulsory Purchase Act 1965 (compensation where satisfaction not made for the taking, or injurious affection, of land subject to compulsory purchase);

(b) a claim under Part 1 of the Land Compensation Act 1973 (c. 26) (compensation for depreciation of land value by physical factors caused by use of public works) [;][1]

[(c) a claim under section 152(3).][1]

(7) In this section 'the land' means the land to which the application relates or any part of that land.

1 Inserted by Localism Act 2011, s 135(1), (9) (1 April 2012).

58 Certifying compliance with section 56

(1) Subsection (2) applies where—

(a) the [Secretary of State][1] has accepted an application for an order granting development consent, and

(b) the applicant has complied with section 56 in relation to the application.

(2) The applicant must, in such form and manner as may be prescribed, certify to the [Secretary of State][1] that the applicant has complied with section 56 in relation to the application.

(3) A person commits an offence if the person issues a certificate which—

(a) purports to be a certificate under subsection (2), and

(b) contains a statement which the person knows to be false or misleading in a material particular.

(4) A person commits an offence if the person recklessly issues a certificate which—

(a) purports to be a certificate under subsection (2), and

(b) contains a statement which is false or misleading in a material particular.

(5) A person guilty of an offence under this section is liable on summary conviction to a fine not exceeding level 5 on the standard scale.

(6) A magistrates' court may try an information relating to an offence under this section whenever laid.

(7) Section 127 of the Magistrates' Courts Act 1980 (c. 43) has effect subject to subsection (6) of this section.

1 Word substituted by Localism Act 2011, s 128(2), Sch 13, paras 1, 15 (1 April 2012).

59 Notice of persons interested in land to which compulsory acquisition request relates

(1) This section applies where—

(a) the [Secretary of State][1] has accepted an application for an order granting development consent, and

(b) the application includes a request for an order granting development consent to authorise compulsory acquisition of land or of an interest in or right over land (a 'compulsory acquisition request').

(2) The applicant must give to the [Secretary of State][1] a notice specifying the names, and such other information as may be prescribed, of each affected person.

(3) Notice under subsection (2) must be given in such form and manner as may be prescribed.

(4) A person is an 'affected person' for the purposes of this section if the applicant, after making diligent inquiry, knows that the person is interested in the land to which the compulsory acquisition request relates or any part of that land.

1 Word substituted by Localism Act 2011, s 128(2), Sch 13, paras 1, 16 (1 April 2012).

60 Local impact reports

(1) Subsection (2) applies where the [Secretary of State][1] —

(a) has accepted an application for an order granting development consent, and

(b) has received—

(i) a certificate under section 58(2) in relation to the application, and

(ii) where section 59 applies, a notice under that section in relation to the application.

(2) The [Secretary of State][1] must give notice in writing to each of the following, inviting them to submit a local impact report [to the Secretary of State][2] —

[(a) each local authority that is within section 56A, and][3]

(b) the Greater London Authority if the land to which the application relates, or any part of it, is in Greater London.

(3) A 'local impact report' is a report in writing giving details of the likely impact of the proposed development on the authority's area (or any part of that area).

(4) 'The proposed development' is the development for which the application seeks development consent.

(5) A notice under subsection (2) must specify the deadline for receipt by the [Secretary of State][1] of the local impact report.

1 Word substituted by Localism Act 2011, s 128(2), Sch 13, paras 1, 17(1), (2) (1 April 2012).
2 Words substituted by Localism Act 2011, s 128(2), Sch 13, paras 1, 17(1), (3) (1 April 2012).
3 Substituted by Localism Act 2011, s 138(1), (4) (1 April 2012).

61 Initial choice of Panel or single [appointed person][1]

[(1) Subsection (2) applies where the Secretary of State has accepted an application for an order granting development consent.][2]

[(2) The Secretary of State must decide whether the application—

(a) is to be handled by a Panel under Chapter 2, or

(b) is to be handled by a single appointed person under Chapter 3.

(3) The Secretary of State must publish the criteria that are to be applied in making decisions under subsection (2).][3]

1 Word substituted by Localism Act 2011, s 128(2), Sch 13, paras 1, 18(1), (4) (1 April 2012).
2 Substituted by Infrastructure Act 2015, s 26 (12 April 2015).
3 Section 61(2)–(3) substituted for s 61(2)–(5) by Localism Act 2011, s 128(2), Sch 13, paras 1, 18(1), (3) (1 April 2012).

62 Switching from single [appointed person][1] to Panel

(1) Subsection (2) applies where an application for an order granting development consent is being handled by a single [appointed person][1] under Chapter 3.

[(2) The Secretary of State may decide that the application should instead be handled by a Panel under Chapter 2.

(3) The Secretary of State must publish the criteria that are to be applied in making decisions under subsection (2).][2]

1 Word substituted by Localism Act 2011, s 128(2), Sch 13, paras 1, 19(1), (2) (1 April 2012).
2 Section 62(2)–(3) substituted for s 62(2)–(5) by Localism Act 2011, s 128(2), Sch 13, paras 1, 19(1), (3) (1 April 2012).

63 …

Repealed by Localism Act 2011, ss 128(2), 237, Sch 13, paras 1, 20, Sch 25, Pt 20 (1 April 2012).

Chapter 2 The Panel procedure

Panels

64 Panel for each application to be handled under this Chapter

(1) This Chapter applies where—

(a) the [Secretary of State][1] accepts an application for an order granting development consent, and

(b) under section 61(2) or 62(2), it is decided that the application is to be handled by a Panel under this Chapter.

(2) There is to be a Panel (referred to in this Chapter as 'the Panel') to handle the application.

1 Word substituted by Localism Act 2011, s 128(2), Sch 13, paras 1, 21 (1 April 2012).

65 Appointment of members, and lead member, of Panel

[(1) The Secretary of State must appoint—

(a) [two,][1] three, four or five persons to be members of the Panel, and

(b) one of those persons to chair the Panel.][2]

(2) In this Chapter 'the lead member' means the person who for the time being is appointed to chair the Panel.

[…][3]

1 Word inserted by Infrastructure Act 2015, s 27(1) (5 April 2017).
2 Substituted by Localism Act 2011, s 128(2), Sch 13, paras 1, 22(1), (2) (1 April 2012).
3 Repealed by Localism Act 2011, ss 128(2), 237, Sch 13, paras 1, 22(1), (3), Sch 25, Pt 20 (1 April 2012).

66 Ceasing to be member, or lead member, of Panel

[...][1]

(2) The person appointed to be the lead member ceases to hold that office if the person ceases to be a member of the Panel.

(3) A person may resign from membership of the Panel by giving notice in writing to the [Secretary of State][2].

(4) The lead member may resign that office, without also resigning from membership of the Panel, by giving notice in writing to the [Secretary of State][2].

(5) The [Secretary of State][3] —

(a) may remove a person ('the Panel member') from membership of the Panel if the [Secretary of State][4] is satisfied that the Panel member is unable, unwilling or unfit to perform the duties of Panel membership;

(b) may remove the lead member from that office, without also removing the lead member from membership of the Panel, if the [Secretary of State][4] is satisfied that the lead member is unable, unwilling or unfit to perform the duties of the office.

1 Repealed by Localism Act 2011, ss 128(2), 237, Sch 13, paras 1, 23(1), (2), Sch 25, Pt 20 (1 April 2012).
2 Word substituted by Localism Act 2011, s 128(2), Sch 13, paras 1, 23(1), (3) (1 April 2012).
3 Words substituted by Localism Act 2011, s 128(2), Sch 13, paras 1, 23(1), (4)(a) (1 April 2012).
4 Word substituted by Localism Act 2011, s 128(2), Sch 13, paras 1, 23(1), (4)(b) (1 April 2012).

67 ...

Repealed by Localism Act 2011, ss 128(2), 237, Sch 13, paras 1, 24, Sch 25, Pt 20 (1 April 2012).

68 Additional appointments to Panel

(1) Subsections (2) and (3) apply at any time after the initial members of the Panel have been appointed under section 65(1)(a).

[(2) The Secretary of State may appoint a person to be a member of the Panel, but this power may not be exercised so as to cause the Panel to have more than five members.][1]

(3) If at any time the Panel has only [...][2] a single member, it is the duty of the [Secretary of State][3] to ensure that the power under subsection (2) is exercised so as to secure that the Panel again has at least [two][4] members.

(4) A person appointed under subsection (2) becomes a member of the Panel in addition to any person who is otherwise a member of the Panel.

[...][5]

1 Substituted by Localism Act 2011, s 128(2), Sch 13, paras 1, 25(1), (2) (1 April 2012).
2 Words repealed by Infrastructure Act 2015, s 27(2)(a) (5 April 2017).
3 Words substituted by Localism Act 2011, s 128(2), Sch 13, paras 1, 25(1), (3) (1 April 2012).
4 Word substituted by Infrastructure Act 2015, s 27(2)(b) (5 April 2017).
5 Repealed by Localism Act 2011, ss 128(2), 237, Sch 13, paras 1, 25(1), (4), Sch 25, Pt 20 (1 April 2012).

69 Replacement of lead member of Panel

(1) Subsection (2) applies where a person ceases to hold the office of lead member.

(2) The [Secretary of State][1] must appoint a member of the Panel to chair the Panel.

(3) A person may be appointed under subsection (2) even though that person was not a member of the Panel when the vacancy arose.

[…][2]

1 Words substituted by Localism Act 2011, s 128(2), Sch 13, paras 1, 26(1), (2) (1 April 2012).
2 Repealed by Localism Act 2011, ss 128(2), 237, Sch 13, paras 1, 26(1), (3), Sch 25, Pt 20 (1 April 2012).

70 …

Repealed by Localism Act 2011, ss 128(2), 237, Sch 13, paras 1, 27, Sch 25, Pt 20 (1 April 2012).

71 Supplementary provision where Panel replaces single [appointed person][1]

(1) Subsections (2) and (3) apply where this Chapter applies as the result of a decision under section 62(2).

(2) [An appointed person][2]—

(a) may be appointed under section 65(1)(a) or 68(2) as a member of the Panel, and

(b) if a member of the Panel, may be appointed under section 65(1)(b) or 69(2) to chair the Panel.

(3) The Panel may, so far as it thinks appropriate, decide to treat things done by or in relation to [an appointed person][3] in proceedings under Chapter 3 on the application as done by or in relation to the Panel.

(4) Where the Panel makes a decision under subsection (3), the lead member is under a duty to ensure that the membership of the Panel has the necessary knowledge of the proceedings under Chapter 3 on the application.

[(5) In this section 'appointed person' means a person appointed to handle the application under Chapter 3.][4]

1 Word substituted by Localism Act 2011, s 128(2), Sch 13, paras 1, 28(1), (5) (1 April 2012).
2 Words substituted by Localism Act 2011, s 128(2), Sch 13, paras 1, 28(1), (2) (1 April 2012).
3 Words substituted by Localism Act 2011, s 128(2), Sch 13, paras 1, 28(1), (3) (1 April 2012).
4 Inserted by Localism Act 2011, s 128(2), Sch 13, paras 1, 28(1), (4) (1 April 2012).

72 Panel ceasing to have any members

(1) If the Panel ceases to have any members, a new Panel must be constituted under section 65(1).

(2) At times after the new Panel has been constituted (but subject to the further application of this subsection in the event that the new Panel ceases to have any members), references in this Chapter to the Panel are to be read as references to the new Panel.

(3) The new Panel may, so far as it thinks appropriate, decide to treat things—

(a) done by or in relation to a previous Panel appointed to handle the application, or

(b) treated under section 71(3) as done by or in relation to a previous Panel appointed to handle the application,

as done by or in relation to the new Panel.

(4) Where the Panel makes a decision under subsection (3), the lead member is under a duty to ensure that the membership of the Panel has the necessary knowledge of the proceedings on the application up until the reconstitution of the Panel.

(5) The power under section 68(2) is not exercisable at times when the Panel has no members.

73 Consequences of changes in Panel

(1) The Panel's continuing identity is to be taken not to be affected by—

(a) any change in the membership of the Panel;

(b) the Panel's coming to have only [...][1] a single member;

(c) any change in the lead member;

(d) a vacancy in that office.

(2) When there is a change in the membership of the Panel, the lead member is under a duty to ensure that the membership of the Panel after the change has the necessary knowledge of the proceedings on the application up until the change.

(3) Subsection (2) does not apply where the change occurs as a result of the Panel being reconstituted as required by section 72(1).

1 Words repealed by Infrastructure Act 2015, s 27(3) (5 April 2017).

Panel's role in relation to application

74 Panel to decide, or make recommendation in respect of, application

[...][1]

(2) [The Panel][2] has the functions of—

(a) examining the application, and

(b) making a report to the Secretary of State on the application setting out—

(i) the Panel's findings and conclusions in respect of the application, and

(ii) the Panel's recommendation as to the decision to be made on the application.

(3) The Panel's functions under this section are to be carried out in accordance with Chapter 4.

[...][1]

1 Repealed by Localism Act 2011, ss 128(2), 237, Sch 13, paras 1, 29(1), (2), (4), Sch 25, Pt 20 (1 April 2012).
2 Words substituted by Localism Act 2011, s 128(2), Sch 13, paras 1, 29(3) (1 April 2012).

75 Decision-making by the Panel

[(A1) If the members of a Panel with two members disagree as to a proposed decision by the Panel, the view of the lead member is to prevail.][1]

(1) The making of a decision by [a Panel with three or more members][2] requires the agreement of a majority of its members.

(2) The lead member has a second (or casting) vote in the event that the number of members of the Panel agreeing to a proposed decision is the same as the number of members not so agreeing.

1 Inserted by Infrastructure Act 2015, s 27(4)(a) (5 April 2017).
2 Words substituted by Infrastructure Act 2015, s 27(4)(b) (5 April 2017).

76 Allocation within Panel of Panel's functions

(1) This section applies in relation to the Panel's examination of the application.

(2) The Panel, as an alternative to itself undertaking a part of the examination, may allocate the undertaking of that part to any one or more of the members of the Panel.

(3) Where there is an allocation under subsection (2)—

(a) anything that under Chapter 4 is required or authorised to be done by or to the Panel in connection with the allocated part of the examination may be done by or to the member or members concerned (or by or to the Panel), and

(b) findings and conclusions of the member or members concerned in respect of the matters allocated are to be taken to be the Panel's.

(4) Subsection (3)(b) has effect subject to any decision of the Panel, made on the occasion of making the allocation or earlier, as to the status of any such findings or conclusions.

(5) Where there is an allocation under subsection (2) to two or more of the members of the Panel, the making of a decision by the members concerned requires the agreement of all of them.

77 Exercise of Panel's powers for examining application

(1) In this section 'procedural power' means any power conferred on the Panel for the purposes of its examination of the application.

(2) A procedural power, as well as being exercisable by the Panel itself, is also (subject to subsection (3)) exercisable by any one or more of the members of the Panel.

(3) The Panel may decide to restrict or prohibit the exercise of a procedural power otherwise than by the Panel itself.

(4) Subsection (2)—

(a) applies whether or not there is an allocation under section 76(2), and

(b) where there is such an allocation, is in addition to section 76(3)(a).

(5) Subsection (3) does not authorise curtailment of a power conferred by section 76(3)(a).

Chapter 3 The [single appointed person][1] procedure

The single [appointed person][1]

78 Single [appointed person][1] to handle application

(1) This Chapter applies where—

(a) the [Secretary of State][2] accepts an application for an order granting development consent, and

(b) under section 61(2), it is decided that the application is to be handled by a single [appointed person][3] under this Chapter.

(2) In this Chapter 'the single [appointed person][4], means the person who is appointed to handle the application under this Chapter.

1 Word substituted by Localism Act 2011, s 128(2), Sch 13, paras 1, 30(1), (5), (6) (1 April 2012).
2 Word substituted by Localism Act 2011, s 128(2), Sch 13, paras 1, 30(1), (2) (1 April 2012).
3 Word substituted by Localism Act 2011, s 128(2), Sch 13, paras 1, 30(1), (3) (1 April 2012).
4 Word substituted by Localism Act 2011, s 128(2), Sch 13, paras 1, 30(1), (4) (1 April 2012).

[79 Appointment of single appointed person

The Secretary of State must appoint a person to handle the application.][1]

1 Substituted by Localism Act 2011, s 128(2), Sch 13, paras 1, 31 (1 April 2012).

80 Ceasing to be the single [appointed person][1]

[...][2]

(2) A person may resign from being the single [appointed person][3] by giving notice in writing to the [Secretary of State][4].

(3) The [Secretary of State][5] may remove a person ('the appointee') from being the single [appointed person][6] [if the Secretary of State][7] is satisfied that the appointee is unable, unwilling or unfit to perform the duties of the single [appointed person][6].

1 Word substituted by Localism Act 2011, s 128(2), Sch 13, paras 1, 32(1), (5) (1 April 2012).
2 Repealed by Localism Act 2011, ss 128(2), 237, Sch 13, paras 1, 32(1), (2), Sch 25, Pt 20 (1 April 2012).
3 Word substituted by Localism Act 2011, s 128(2), Sch 13, paras 1, 32(1), (3)(a) (1 April 2012).
4 Word substituted by Localism Act 2011, s 128(2), Sch 13, paras 1, 32(1), (3)(b) (1 April 2012).
5 Words substituted by Localism Act 2011, s 128(2), Sch 13, paras 1, 32(1), (4)(a) (1 April 2012).
6 Word substituted by Localism Act 2011, s 128(2), Sch 13, paras 1, 32(1), (4)(b) (1 April 2012).
7 Words substituted by Localism Act 2011, s 128(2), Sch 13, paras 1, 32(1), (4)(c) (1 April 2012).

81 ...

Repealed by Localism Act 2011, ss 128(2), 237, Sch 13, paras 1, 33, Sch 25, Pt 20 (1 April 2012).

82 Appointment of replacement single [appointed person][1]

(1) Where a person ceases to be the single [appointed person][1], a new appointment of a person to handle the application must be made under section 79.

(2) Where that happens, the new single [appointed person][1] may, so far as may be appropriate, decide to treat things done by or in relation to any previous single [appointed person][1] as done by or in relation to the new single [appointed person][1].

(3) Where the single [appointed person][1] makes a decision under subsection (2), the single [appointed person][1] is under a duty to acquire the necessary knowledge of the previous proceedings on the application.

1 Words substituted by Localism Act 2011, s 128(2), Sch 13, paras 1, 34 (1 April 2012).

Single [appointed person][1]'s role in relation to application

83 Single [appointed person][1] to examine and report on application

(1) The single [appointed person][1] has the functions of—

(a) examining the application, and

(b) making a report [to the Secretary of State][2] on the application setting out—

(i) the single [appointed person][1]'s findings and conclusions in respect of the application, and

(ii) the single [appointed person][1]'s recommendation as to the decision to be made on the application.

[...][3]

(3) The single [appointed person][1]'s functions under subsection (1) are to be carried out in accordance with Chapter 4.

[...][3]

1 Words substituted by Localism Act 2011, s 128(2), Sch 13, paras 1, 35(1), (2) (1 April 2012).
2 Words inserted by Localism Act 2011, s 128(2), Sch 13, paras 1, 35(1), (3) (1 April 2012).
3 Repealed by Localism Act 2011, ss 128(2), 237, Sch 13, paras 1, 35(1), (4), (5), Sch 25, Pt 20 (1 April 2012).

Commission's role in respect of application

84–85 ...

Repealed by Localism Act 2011, ss 128(2), 237, Sch 13, paras 1, 36, Sch 25, Pt 20 (1 April 2012).

Chapter 4 Examination of applications under Chapter 2 or 3

86 Chapter applies to examination by Panel or single [appointed person][1]

(1) This Chapter applies—

(a) in relation to the examination of an application by a Panel under Chapter 2, and

(b) in relation to the examination of an application by a single [appointed person][1] under Chapter 3.

(2) In this Chapter as it applies in relation to the examination of an application by a Panel under Chapter 2, 'the Examining authority' means the Panel.

(3) In this Chapter as it applies in relation to the examination of an application by a single [appointed person][1] under Chapter 3, 'the Examining authority' means the single [appointed person][1].

1 Word substituted by Localism Act 2011, s 128(2), Sch 13, paras 1, 37 (1 April 2012).

87 Examining authority to control examination of application

(1) It is for the Examining authority to decide how to examine the application.

(2) The Examining authority, in making any decision about how the application is to be examined, must—

(a) comply with—

(i) the following provisions of this Chapter, and

(ii) any rules made under section 97[.][1]

[...][1]

(3) The Examining authority may in examining the application disregard representations if the Examining authority considers that the representations—

(a) are vexatious or frivolous,

(b) relate to the merits of policy set out in a national policy statement, or

(c) relate to compensation for compulsory acquisition of land or of an interest in or right over land.

1 Repealed by Localism Act 2011, ss 128(2), 237, Sch 13, paras 1, 38, Sch 25, Pt 20 (1 April 2012).

88 Initial assessment of issues, and preliminary meeting

(1) The Examining authority must make such an initial assessment of the principal issues arising on the application as the Examining authority thinks appropriate.

(2) After making that assessment, the Examining authority must hold a meeting.

(3) The Examining authority must invite to the meeting—

(a) the applicant, [...][1]

(b) each other interested party,

[(c) each statutory party, and

(d) each local authority that is within section 88A,][2]

whether or not the Examining authority is required by rules under section 97, or chooses, also to invite other persons.

[(3A) In subsection (3)(c) 'statutory party' means a person specified in, or of a description specified in, regulations made by the Secretary of State.][3]

(4) The purposes of the meeting are—

(a) to enable invitees present at the meeting to make representations to the Examining authority about how the application should be examined,

(b) to discuss any other matter that the Examining authority wishes to discuss, and

(c) any other purpose that may be specified in rules under section 97.

(5) Subsections (2) to (4) do not prevent the Examining authority holding other meetings.

(6) Rules under section 97—

(a) may (in particular) make provision supplementing subsections (1) to (4), and

(b) must make provision as to when the assessment under subsection (1) is to be made and as to when the meeting required by subsection (2) is to be held.

1 Word repealed by Localism Act 2011, s 138(1), (5)(a) (15 January 2012 for the purpose of conferring power on the Secretary of State to make regulations; 1 April 2012 otherwise).
2 Inserted by Localism Act 2011, s 138(1), (5)(b) (15 January 2012 for the purpose of conferring power on the Secretary of State to make regulations; 1 April 2012 otherwise).
3 Inserted by Localism Act 2011, s 138(1), (5)(c) (15 January 2012 for the purpose of conferring power on the Secretary of State to make regulations; 1 April 2012 otherwise).

[88A Local authorities for the purposes of section 88(3)(d)

(1) A local authority ('A') is within this section if—

(a) the land is in the area of another local authority ('B'),

(b) B is a unitary council or a lower-tier district council, and

(c) any part of the boundary of A's area is also a part of the boundary of B's area.

(2) If the land is in the area of an upper-tier county council ('C'), a local authority ('D') is within this section if—

(a) D is not a lower-tier district council, and

(b) any part of the boundary of D's area is also part of the boundary of C's area.

(3) In this section—

'the land' means the land to which the application relates or any part of that land;

'local authority' has the meaning given in section 102(8);

'lower-tier district council' means a district council in England for an area for which there is a county council;

'unitary council' means a local authority that is not an upper-tier county council, a lower-tier district council, a National Park authority or the Broads Authority;

'upper-tier county council' means a county council in England for each part of whose area there is a district council.][1]

1 Inserted by Localism Act 2011, s 138(1), (6) (1 April 2012).

89 Examining authority's decisions about how application is to be examined

(1) The Examining authority must in the light of the discussion at the meeting held under section 88(2) make such procedural decisions as the Examining authority thinks appropriate.

(2) The decisions required by subsection (1) may be made at or after the meeting.

[(2A) Upon making the decisions required by subsection (1), the Examining authority must inform each person mentioned in section 88(3)(c) and (d)—

(a) of those decisions, and

(b) that the person may notify the Examining authority in writing that the person is to become an interested party.][1]

(3) The Examining authority may make procedural decisions otherwise than as required by subsection (1), and may do so at any time before or after the meeting.

(4) The Examining authority must inform each interested party of any procedural decision made by the Examining authority.

(5) In this section 'procedural decision' means a decision about how the application is to be examined.

1 Inserted by Localism Act 2011, s 138(1), (7) (1 April 2012).

90 Written representations

(1) The Examining authority's examination of the application is to take the form of consideration of written representations about the application.

(2) Subsection (1) has effect subject to—

(a) any requirement under section 91, 92 or 93 to cause a hearing to be held, and

(b) any decision by the Examining authority that any part of the examination is to take a form that is neither—

(i) consideration of written representations, nor

(ii) consideration of oral representations made at a hearing.

(3) Rules under section 97 may (in particular) specify written representations about the application which are to be, or which may be or may not be, considered under subsection (1).

91 Hearings about specific issues

(1) Subsections (2) and (3) apply where the Examining authority decides that it is necessary for the Examining authority's examination of the application to include the consideration of oral representations about a particular issue made at a hearing in order to ensure—

(a) adequate examination of the issue, or

(b) that an interested party has a fair chance to put the party's case.

(2) The Examining authority must cause a hearing to be held for the purpose of receiving oral representations about the issue.

(3) At the hearing, each interested party is entitled (subject to the Examining authority's powers of control over the conduct of the hearing) to make oral representations about the issue.

(4) Where the Examining authority is a Panel acting under Chapter 2, any two or more hearings under subsection (2) may be held concurrently.

92 Compulsory acquisition hearings

(1) This section applies where the application includes a request for an order granting development consent to authorise compulsory acquisition of land or of an interest in or right over land (a 'compulsory acquisition request').

(2) The Examining authority must fix, and cause each affected person to be informed of, the deadline by which an affected person must notify the [Secretary of State][1] that the person wishes a compulsory acquisition hearing to be held.

(3) If the [Secretary of State][1] receives notification from at least one affected person before the deadline, the Examining authority must cause a compulsory acquisition hearing to be held.

(4) At a compulsory acquisition hearing, the following are entitled (subject to the Examining authority's powers of control over the conduct of the hearing) to make oral representations about the compulsory acquisition request—

(a) the applicant;

(b) each affected person.

(5) A person is an 'affected person' for the purposes of this section if the person's name has been given to the [Secretary of State][1] in a notice under section 59.

1 Word substituted by Localism Act 2011, s 128(2), Sch 13, paras 1, 39 (1 April 2012).

93 Open-floor hearings

(1) The Examining authority must fix, and cause the interested parties to be informed of, the deadline by which an interested party must notify the [Secretary of State][1] of the party's wish to be heard at an open-floor hearing.

(2) If the [Secretary of State][1] receives notification from at least one interested party before the deadline, the Examining authority must cause an open-floor hearing to be held.

(3) At an open-floor hearing, each interested party is entitled (subject to the Examining authority's powers of control over the conduct of the hearing) to make oral representations about the application.

1 Word substituted by Localism Act 2011, s 128(2), Sch 13, paras 1, 40 (1 April 2012).

94 Hearings: general provisions

(1) The following provisions of this section apply—

(a) to a hearing under section 91(2),

(b) to a compulsory acquisition hearing (see section 92), and

(c) to an open-floor hearing (see section 93).

(2) The hearing—

(a) must be in public, and

(b) must be presided over by one or more of the members of the Panel or (as the case may be) the single [appointed person][1].

(3) It is for the Examining authority to decide how the hearing is to be conducted.

(4) In particular, it is for the Examining authority to decide—

(a) whether a person making oral representations at the hearing may be questioned at the hearing by another person and, if so, the matters to which the questioning may relate;

(b) the amount of time to be allowed at the hearing—

(i) for the making of a person's representations (including representations made in exercise of an entitlement under section 91(3), 92(4) or 93(3)), or

(ii) for any questioning by another person.

(5) The Examining authority's powers under subsections (3) and (4) are subject to—

(a) subsection (2), and

(b) any rules made under section 97.

(6) Although the Examining authority's powers under subsections (3) and (4) may be exercised for the purpose of controlling exercise of an entitlement under section 91(3), 92(4) or 93(3), those powers may not be exercised so as to deprive the person entitled of all benefit of the entitlement.

(7) In making decisions under subsection (4)(a), the Examining authority must apply the principle that any oral questioning of a person making representations at a hearing (whether the applicant or any other person) should be undertaken by the Examining authority except where the Examining authority thinks that oral questioning by another person is necessary in order to ensure—

(a) adequate testing of any representations, or

(b) that a person has a fair chance to put the person's case.

(8) The Examining authority may refuse to allow representations to be made at the hearing (including representations made in exercise of an entitlement under section 91(3), 92(4) or 93(3)) if the Examining authority considers that the representations—

(a) are irrelevant, vexatious or frivolous,

(b) relate to the merits of policy set out in a national policy statement,

(c) repeat other representations already made (in any form and by any person), or

(d) relate to compensation for compulsory acquisition of land or of an interest in or right over land.

1 Word substituted by Localism Act 2011, s 128(2), Sch 13, paras 1, 41 (1 April 2012).

95 Hearings: disruption, supervision and costs

(1) Where an interested party or any other person behaves in a disruptive manner at a hearing, the Examining authority may decide to do any one or more of the following—

(a) exclude the person from all, or part, of the remainder of the hearing;

(b) allow the person to continue to attend the hearing only if the person complies with conditions specified by the Examining authority;

(c) exclude the person from other hearings;

(d) direct that the person is allowed to attend other hearings only if the person complies with conditions specified by the Examining authority.

(2) In this section 'hearing' means—

(a) a preliminary meeting under section 88,

(b) a hearing under section 91(2),

(c) a compulsory acquisition hearing (see section 92),

(d) an open-floor hearing (see section 93),

(e) any other meeting or hearing that the Examining authority causes to be held for the purposes of the Examining authority's examination of the application, or

(f) a site visit.

[...][1]

(4) Subsection (5) of section 250 of the Local Government Act 1972 (c. 70) (provisions about costs applying where Minister causes a local inquiry to be held) applies in relation to the Examining authority's examination of the application as it applies in relation to an inquiry under that section, but with references to the Minister causing the inquiry to be held being read as references to the Examining authority.

This is subject to subsection (5) of this section.

(5) Subsections (6) to (8) of section 210 of the Local Government (Scotland) Act 1973 (c. 65) (provisions about expenses applying where Minister causes a local inquiry to be held) apply in relation to the Examining authority's examination of the application in so far as relating to a hearing held in Scotland as they apply in relation to an inquiry under that section, but with references to the Minister causing the inquiry to be held being read as references to the Examining authority.

1 Repealed by Public Bodies (Abolition of Administrative Justice and Tribunals Council) Order 2013, SI 2013/2042, art 2(2), Schedule, para 40(a) (19 August 2013).

[95A Hearings: defence and national security

(1) Subsection (2) applies if the Secretary of State is satisfied that if all or part of the Examining Authority's examination of the application takes the form of a meeting or hearing—

(a) the making of particular oral representations at such a meeting or hearing would be likely to result in the disclosure of information as to defence or national security, and

(b) the public disclosure of that information would be contrary to the national interest.

(2) The Secretary of State may direct that representations of a description specified in the direction may be made only to persons of a description so specified (instead of being made in public).

(3) If the Secretary of State gives a direction under subsection (2), the Attorney General or (where the representations are to be made in Scotland) the Advocate General for Scotland may appoint a person (an 'appointed representative') to represent the interests of an interested party who (by virtue of the direction) is prevented from being present when the representations are made.

(4) Rules under section 97 may (in particular) make provision as to the functions of an appointed representative.

(5) The Secretary of State may direct a person (a 'responsible person') to pay the fees and expenses of an appointed representative if the Secretary of State thinks that the responsible person is interested in a meeting or hearing in relation to any representations that are the subject of a direction under subsection (2).

(6) Subsections (7) and (8) apply if the Secretary of State gives a direction under subsection (5).

(7) If the appointed representative and the responsible person are unable to agree the amount of the fees and expenses, the amount must be determined by the Secretary of State.

(8) The Secretary of State must cause the amount agreed between the appointed representative and the responsible person, or determined by the Secretary of State, to be certified.

(9) An amount so certified is recoverable from the responsible person as a civil debt.

(10) In this section 'representations' includes evidence.][1]

1 Inserted by Localism Act 2011, s 128(2), Sch 13, paras 1, 42 (15 January 2012).

96 Representations not made orally may be made in writing

(1) Subsection (2) applies where—

(a) a person asks the Examining authority to be allowed to make oral representations about the application at a hearing,

(b) the person does not (for whatever reason) make the representations orally at a hearing,

(c) written representations from the person are received by the [Secretary of State][1] before the Examining authority completes the Examining authority's examination of the application, and

(d) the written representations state that they are ones that the person asked to be allowed to, but did not, make orally at a hearing.

(2) The Examining authority must consider the written representations as part of the Examining authority's examination of the application, subject to section 87(3).

1 Word substituted by Localism Act 2011, s 128(2), Sch 13, paras 1, 43 (1 April 2012).

97 Procedure rules

(1) The Lord Chancellor or (if subsection (2) applies) the Secretary of State […][1] may make rules regulating the procedure to be followed in connection with the Examining authority's examination of the application.

(2) This subsection applies if the development to which the application relates (or part of the development) is the construction (other than by a gas transporter) of an oil or gas cross-country pipe-line—

(a) one end of which is in England or Wales, and

(b) the other end of which is in Scotland.

(3) Rules under subsection (1) may make provision for or in connection with authorising the Examining authority, alone or with others, to enter onto land, including land owned or occupied otherwise than by the applicant, for the purpose of inspecting the land as part of the Examining authority's examination of the application.

(4) Rules under subsection (1) may regulate procedure in connection with matters preparatory to the Examining authority's examination of the application, and in connection with matters subsequent to the examination, as well as in connection with the conduct of the examination.

(5) Power under this section to make rules includes power to make different provision for different purposes.

(6) Power under this section to make rules is exercisable by statutory instrument.

(7) A statutory instrument containing rules under this section is subject to annulment pursuant to a resolution of either House of Parliament.

1 Words repealed by Public Bodies (Abolition of Administrative Justice and Tribunals Council) Order 2013, SI 2013/2042, art 2(2), Schedule, para 40(b) (19 August 2013).

98 Timetable for examining, and reporting on, application

(1) The Examining authority is under a duty to complete the Examining authority's examination of the application by the end of the period of 6 months beginning with the day after the start day.

(2) The start day is the day on which the meeting required by section 88 is held or, if that meeting is held on two or more days, the later or latest of those days.

(3) [The Examining authority is under a duty to make its report under section 74(2)(b) or 83(1)(b)][1] by the end of the period of 3 months [beginning with—

(a) the deadline for completion of its examination of the application, or

(b) (if earlier) the end of the day on which it completes the examination.][2]

(4) The [Secretary of State][3] may set a date for a deadline under this section that is later than the date for the time being set.

(5) The power under subsection (4) may be exercised—

(a) more than once in relation to the same deadline;

(b) after the date for the time being set for the deadline.

[(6) Subsections (7) and (8) apply where the power under subsection (4) is exercised.

(7) The Secretary of State must—

(a) notify each interested party of the new deadline, and

(b) publicise the new deadline in such manner as the Secretary of State thinks appropriate.

(8) The Secretary of State exercising the power must make a statement, to the House of Parliament of which that Secretary of State is a member, announcing the new deadline.

(9) A statement under subsection (8) may be written or oral.][4]

1 Words substituted by Localism Act 2011, s 128(2), Sch 13, paras 1, 44(1), (2) (1 April 2012).
2 Words and (a) and (b) substituted for words by Localism Act 2011, s 139(1), (2) (1 April 2012).
3 Words substituted by Localism Act 2011, s 128(2), Sch 13, paras 1, 44(1), (3) (1 April 2012).
4 Section 98(6)–(9) substituted for s 98(6) by Localism Act 2011, s 128(2), Sch 13, paras 1, 44(1), (4) (1 April 2012).

99 Completion of Examining authority's examination of application

When the Examining authority has completed its examination of the application, it must inform each of the interested parties of that fact.

100 Assessors

(1) The [Secretary of State][1] may, at the request of the Examining authority, appoint a person to act as an assessor to assist the Examining authority in the Examining authority's examination of the application.

(2) A person may be appointed as an assessor only if it appears to the [Secretary of State][2] that the person has expertise that makes the person a suitable person to provide assistance to the Examining authority.

1 Words substituted by Localism Act 2011, s 128(2), Sch 13, paras 1, 45(1), (2) (1 April 2012).
2 Words substituted by Localism Act 2011, s 128(2), Sch 13, paras 1, 45(1), (3) (1 April 2012).

101 Legal advice and assistance

(1) The [Secretary of State][1] may, at the request of the Examining authority, appoint a barrister, solicitor or advocate to provide legal advice and assistance to the Examining authority in connection with its examination of the application.

(2) The assistance that may be given by a person appointed under subsection (1) includes carrying out on behalf of the Examining authority any oral questioning of a person making representations at a hearing.

1 Words substituted by Localism Act 2011, s 128(2), Sch 13, paras 1, 46 (1 April 2012).

102 Interpretation of Chapter 4: 'interested party' and other expressions

(1) For the purposes of this Chapter, a person is an 'interested party' if—

(a) the person is the applicant,

[(aa) the person has been notified of the acceptance of the application in accordance with section 56(2)(d),

(ab) the Examining authority has under section 102A decided that it considers that the person is within one or more of the categories set out in section 102B,][1] [(ba) the person is the Marine Management Organisation and the development for which the application seeks development consent would involve the carrying on of any activity in one or more of the areas specified in subsection (1A),][2]

[(c) the person is a local authority in whose area the land is located,

(ca) the person—

(i) is mentioned in section 88(3)(c) or (d), and

(ii) has notified the Examining authority as mentioned in section 89(2A)(b),][3]

(d) the person is the Greater London Authority and the land is in Greater London, or

(e) the person has made a relevant representation.

[(1ZA) But a person ceases to be an 'interested party' for the purposes of this Chapter upon notifying the Examining authority in writing that the person no longer wishes to be an interested party.][4]

[(1A) The areas are—

(a) waters in or adjacent to England up to the seaward limits of the territorial sea;

(b) an exclusive economic zone, except any part of an exclusive economic zone in relation to which the Scottish Ministers have functions;

(c) a Renewable Energy Zone, except any part of a Renewable Energy Zone in relation to which the Scottish Ministers have functions;

(d) an area designated under section 1(7) of the Continental Shelf Act 1964, except any part of that area which is within a part of an exclusive economic zone or Renewable Energy Zone in relation to which the Scottish Ministers have functions.][5]

(2) In this Chapter 'representation' includes evidence, and references to the making of a representation include the giving of evidence.

[...][6]

(4) A representation is a relevant representation for the purposes of subsection (1) to the extent that—

(a) it is a representation about the application,

(b) it is made to the [Secretary of State][7] in the prescribed form and manner,

(c) it is received by the [Secretary of State][7] no later than the deadline that applies under section 56 to the person making it,

(d) it contains material of a prescribed description, and

(e) it does not contain—

(i) material about compensation for compulsory acquisition of land or of an interest in or right over land,

(ii) material about the merits of policy set out in a national policy statement, or

(iii) material that is vexatious or frivolous.

[...][6]

(8) In [subsection (1)(c)][8] 'local authority' means—

(a) a county council, or district council, in England;

(b) a London borough council;

(c) the Common Council of the City of London;

(d) the Council of the Isles of Scilly;

(e) a county council, or county borough council, in Wales;

(f) a council constituted under section 2 of the Local Government etc. (Scotland) Act 1994 (c. 39);

(g) a National Park authority;

(h) the Broads Authority.

(9) In this section 'the land' means the land to which the application relates or any part of that land.

1 Section 102(1)(aa) and (ab) substituted for s 102(1)(b) by Localism Act 2011, s 138(1), (8)(a) (1 April 2012).
2 Inserted by Marine and Coastal Access Act 2009, s 23(1), (6)(a) (1 April 2010).
3 Section 102(1)(c) and (ca) substituted for s 102(1)(c) by Localism Act 2011, s 138(1), (8)(b) (1 April 2012).
4 Inserted by Localism Act 2011, s 138(1), (8)(c) (1 April 2012).
5 Inserted by Marine and Coastal Access Act 2009, s 23(1), (6)(b) (1 April 2010).
6 Repealed by Localism Act 2011, ss 138(1), (8)(d), (e), 237, Sch 25, Pt 21 (1 April 2012).
7 Word substituted by Localism Act 2011, s 128(2), Sch 13, paras 1, 47 (1 April 2012).
8 Words substituted by Localism Act 2011, s 138(1), (8)(f) (1 April 2012).

[102A Persons in certain categories may ask to become interested parties etc

(1) Subsection (2) applies if—

(a) a person makes a request to the Examining authority to become an interested party,

(b) the request states that the person claims to be within one or more of the categories set out in section 102B,

(c) the person has not been notified of the acceptance of the application in accordance with section 56(2)(d), and

(d) the applicant has issued a certificate under section 58 in relation to the application.

(2) The Examining authority must decide whether it considers that the person is within one or more of the categories set out in section 102B.

(3) If the Examining authority decides that it considers that the person is within one or more of the categories set out in section 102B, the Examining authority must notify the person, and the applicant, that the person has become an interested party under section 102(1)(ab).

(4) If the Examining authority thinks that a person might successfully make a request mentioned in subsection (1)(a), the Examining authority may inform the person about becoming an interested party under section 102(1)(ab).

But the Examining authority is under no obligation to make enquiries in order to discover persons who might make such a request.][1]

1 Inserted by Localism Act 2011, s 138(1), (9) (1 April 2012).

[102B Categories for the purposes of section 102A

(1) A person is within Category 1 if the person is an owner, lessee, tenant (whatever the tenancy period) or occupier of the land.

(2) A person is within Category 2 if the person—

(a) is interested in the land, or

(b) has power—

(i) to sell and convey the land, or

(ii) to release the land.

(3) An expression, other than 'the land', that appears in subsection (2) of this section and also in section 5(1) of the Compulsory Purchase Act 1965 has in subsection (2) the meaning that it has in section 5(1) of that Act.

(4) A person is within Category 3 if, should the order sought by the application be made and fully implemented, the person would or might be entitled—

(a) as a result of the implementing of the order,

(b) as a result of the order having been implemented, or

(c) as a result of use of the land once the order has been implemented,

to make a relevant claim.

(5) In subsection (4) 'relevant claim' means—

(a) a claim under section 10 of the Compulsory Purchase Act 1965 (compensation where satisfaction not made for the taking, or injurious affection, of land subject to compulsory purchase);

(b) a claim under Part 1 of the Land Compensation Act 1973 (compensation for depreciation of land value by physical factors caused by use of public works);

(c) a claim under section 152(3).

(6) In this section 'the land' means the land to which the application relates or any part of that land.][1]

1 Inserted by Localism Act 2011, s 138(1), (9) (1 April 2012).

Chapter 5 Decisions on applications

103 [Secretary of State is to decide applications][1]

(1) The Secretary of State has the function of deciding an application for an order granting development consent[.][2]

[…][2]

[…][3]

1 Heading substituted by Localism Act 2011, s 128(2), Sch 13, paras 1, 48(1), (4) (1 April 2012).
2 Word and s 103(1)(a)–(b) repealed by Localism Act 2011, ss 128(2), 237, Sch 13, paras 1, 48(1), (2), Sch 25, Pt 20 (1 April 2012).
3 Repealed by Localism Act 2011, ss 128(2), 237, Sch 13, paras 1, 48(1), (3), Sch 25, Pt 20 (1 April 2012).

104 [Decisions in cases where national policy statement has effect][1]

(1) This section applies in relation to an application for an order granting development consent if [a national policy statement has effect in relation to development of the description to which the application relates][2].

(2) In deciding the application the [Secretary of State][3] must have regard to—

(a) any national policy statement which has effect in relation to development of the description to which the application relates (a 'relevant national policy statement'),

[(aa) the appropriate marine policy documents (if any), determined in accordance with section 59 of the Marine and Coastal Access Act 2009,][4]

(b) any local impact report (within the meaning given by section 60(3)) submitted to the [Secretary of State][5] before the deadline specified in a notice under section 60(2),

(c) any matters prescribed in relation to development of the description to which the application relates, and

(d) any other matters which the [Secretary of State][3] thinks are both important and relevant to [the Secretary of State's][6] decision.

(3) The [Secretary of State][7] must decide the application in accordance with any relevant national policy statement, except to the extent that one or more of subsections (4) to (8) applies.

(4) This subsection applies if the [Secretary of State][7] is satisfied that deciding the application in accordance with any relevant national policy statement would lead to the United Kingdom being in breach of any of its international obligations.

(5) This subsection applies if the [Secretary of State is][8] satisfied that deciding the application in accordance with any relevant national policy statement would lead to the [Secretary of State being in breach of any duty imposed on the Secretary of State][9] by or under any enactment.

(6) This subsection applies if the [Secretary of State][10] is satisfied that deciding the application in accordance with any relevant national policy statement would be unlawful by virtue of any enactment.

(7) This subsection applies if the [Secretary of State][10] is satisfied that the adverse impact of the proposed development would outweigh its benefits.

(8) This subsection applies if the [Secretary of State][10] is satisfied that any condition prescribed for deciding an application otherwise than in accordance with a national policy statement is met.

(9) For the avoidance of doubt, the fact that any relevant national policy statement identifies a location as suitable (or potentially suitable) for a particular description of development does not prevent one or more of subsections (4) to (8) from applying.

1 Heading substituted by Localism Act 2011, s 128(2), Sch 13, paras 1, 49(1), (7) (1 April 2012).
2 Words substituted by Localism Act 2011, s 128(2), Sch 13, paras 1, 49(1), (2) (1 April 2012).
3 Words substituted by Localism Act 2011, s 128(2), Sch 13, paras 1, 49(1), (3)(a) (1 April 2012).

4 Inserted by Marine and Coastal Access Act 2009, s 58(5) (12 November 2010).
5 Word substituted by Localism Act 2011, s 128(2), Sch 13, paras 1, 49(1), (3)(b) (1 April 2012).
6 Word substituted by Localism Act 2011, s 128(2), Sch 13, paras 1, 49(1), (3)(c) (1 April 2012).
7 Words substituted by Localism Act 2011, s 128(2), Sch 13, paras 1, 49(1), (4) (1 April 2012).
8 Words substituted by Localism Act 2011, s 128(2), Sch 13, paras 1, 49(1), (5)(a) (1 April 2012).
9 Words substituted by Localism Act 2011, s 128(2), Sch 13, paras 1, 49(1), (5)(b) (1 April 2012).
10 Words substituted by Localism Act 2011, s 128(2), Sch 13, paras 1, 49(1), (6) (1 April 2012).

105 [Decisions in cases where no national policy statement has effect][1]

(1) This section applies in relation to an application for an order granting development consent [if section 104 does not apply in relation to the application][2].

(2) In deciding the application the Secretary of State must have regard to—

(a) any local impact report (within the meaning given by section 60(3)) submitted to the [Secretary of State][3] before the deadline specified in a notice under section 60(2),

(b) any matters prescribed in relation to development of the description to which the application relates, and

(c) any other matters which the Secretary of State thinks are both important and relevant to the Secretary of State's decision.

1 Heading substituted by Localism Act 2011, s 128(2), Sch 13, paras 1, 50(1), (4) (1 April 2012).
2 Words substituted by Localism Act 2011, s 128(2), Sch 13, paras 1, 50(1), (2) (1 April 2012).
3 Word substituted by Localism Act 2011, s 128(2), Sch 13, paras 1, 50(1), (3) (1 April 2012).

106 Matters that may be disregarded when deciding application

(1) In deciding an application for an order granting development consent, the [Secretary of State][1] may disregard representations if the [Secretary of State][1] considers that the representations—

(a) are vexatious or frivolous,

(b) relate to the merits of policy set out in a national policy statement, or

(c) relate to compensation for compulsory acquisition of land or of an interest in or right over land.

(2) In this section 'representation' includes evidence.

1 Words substituted by Localism Act 2011, s 128(2), Sch 13, paras 1, 51 (1 April 2012).

107 Timetable for decisions

(1) The [Secretary of State][1] is under a duty to decide an application for an order granting development consent by the end of the period of 3 months beginning [with—

(a) the][2] [deadline under section 98(3)][3][, or

(b) (if earlier) the end of the day on which the Secretary of State receives a report on the application under section 74(2)(b) or 83(1)(b).][4]

[...][5]

(3) The [Secretary of State][6] may set a date for the deadline under subsection (1) that is later than the date for the time being set.

[...][5]

(5) The power under subsection (3) may be exercised—

(a) more than once in relation to the same deadline;

(b) after the date for the time being set for the deadline.

[(6) Subsection (7) applies where the power under subsection (3) is exercised.

(7) The Secretary of State exercising the power must make a statement, to the House of Parliament of which that Secretary of State is a member, announcing the new deadline.

(8) A statement under subsection (7) must be published in such form and manner as the Secretary of State considers appropriate.

(8A) A statement under subsection (7) may be written or oral.][7]

1 Words substituted by Localism Act 2011, s 128(2), Sch 13, paras 1, 52(1), (2)(a) (1 April 2012).
2 Words substituted by Localism Act 2011, s 139(1), (3)(a) (1 April 2012).
3 Words substituted by Localism Act 2011, s 128(2), Sch 13, paras 1, 52(1), (2)(b) (1 April 2012).
4 Word and a new s 107(1)(b) inserted by Localism Act 2011, s 139(1), (3)(b) (1 April 2012).
5 Repealed by Localism Act 2011, ss 128(2), 237, Sch 13, paras 1, 52(1), (3), (5), Sch 25, Pt 20 (1 April 2012).
6 Words substituted by Localism Act 2011, s 128(2), Sch 13, paras 1, 52(1), (4) (1 April 2012).
7 Section 107(6)–(8A) substituted for s 107(6)–(9) by Localism Act 2011, s 128(2), Sch 13, paras 1, 52(1), (6) (1 April 2012).

Chapter 6 Suspension of decision-making process

108 Suspension during review of national policy statement

(1) This section applies where—

(a) an application is made for an order granting development consent for development of a description in relation to which a national policy statement has effect, and

(b) the Secretary of State thinks that, as a result of a change in circumstances since the national policy statement was first published or (if later) the statement or any part of it was last reviewed, all or part of the statement should be reviewed before the application is decided.

(2) The Secretary of State may direct that, until the review has been completed and the Secretary of State has complied with section 6(5) in relation to the review, [examination of the application by a Panel under Chapter 2, or a single appointed person under Chapter 3, is suspended (if not already completed).][1]

1 Words substituted by Localism Act 2011, s 128(2), Sch 13, paras 1, 53 (1 April 2012).

Chapter 7 Intervention by Secretary of State

109–113 ...

Repealed by Localism Act 2011, ss 128(2), 237, Sch 13, paras 1, 54, Sch 25, Pt 20 (1 April 2012).

Chapter 8 Grant or refusal

114 Grant or refusal of development consent

(1) When [the Secretary of State][1] has decided an application for an order granting development consent, the [Secretary of State][2] must either—

(a) make an order granting development consent, or

(b) refuse development consent.

(2) The Secretary of State may by regulations make provision regulating the procedure to be followed if the [Secretary of State][3] proposes to make an order granting development consent on terms which are materially different from those proposed in the application.

1 Word substituted by Localism Act 2011, s 128(2), Sch 13, paras 1, 55(1), (2)(a) (1 April 2012).
2 Words substituted by Localism Act 2011, s 128(2), Sch 13, paras 1, 55(1), (2)(b) (1 April 2012).
3 Words substituted by Localism Act 2011, s 128(2), Sch 13, paras 1, 55(1), (3) (1 April 2012).

115 Development for which development consent may be granted

(1) Development consent may be granted for development which is—

(a) development for which development consent is required, or

(b) associated development[, or

(c) related housing development.][1]

(2) 'Associated development' means development which—

(a) is associated with the development within subsection (1)(a) (or any part of it),

(b) [does not consist of or include][2] the construction or extension of one or more dwellings, and

(c) is within subsection (3)[, (4) or (4A)][3].

(3) Development is within this subsection if it is to be carried out wholly in one or more of the following areas—

(a) England;

(b) waters adjacent to England up to the seaward limits of the territorial sea;

(c) in the case of development in the field of energy, a Renewable Energy Zone, except any part of a Renewable Energy Zone in relation to which the Scottish Ministers have functions.

(4) Development is within this subsection if—

(a) it is to be carried out wholly in Wales,

(b) it is the carrying out or construction of surface works, boreholes or pipes, and

(c) the development within subsection (1)(a) with which it is associated is development within section 17(3).

[(4A) Development is within this subsection if the development within subsection (1)(a) with which it is associated is—

(a) the construction or extension of a generating station that is or (when constructed or extended) is expected to be within section 15(3A) or (3B), or

(b) the installation of an electric line that is or (when installed) is expected to be within section 14(1)(b).][4]

[(4B) 'Related housing development' means development which—

(a) consists of or includes the construction or extension of one or more dwellings,

(b) is on the same site as, or is next to or close to, any part of the development within subsection (1)(a), or is otherwise associated with that development (or any part of it),

(c) is to be carried out wholly in England, and

(d) meets the condition in subsection (4C).

(4C) Development meets the condition in this subsection if the development within subsection (1)(a) to which it is related is to be carried out in one or more of the following areas—

(a) England;

(b) waters adjacent to England up to the seaward limits of the territorial sea.][1]

(5) To the extent that development consent is granted for associated development [or related housing development][1], section 33 applies to the development as it applies to development for which development consent is required.

[...][5]

[(7) The Secretary of State, in deciding an application for an order granting development consent for development that includes related housing development, must take into account any matters set out in guidance published by the Secretary of State.][1]

1 Inserted by Housing and Planning Act 2016, s 160(1), (2), (4), (5), (6) (6 April 2017).
2 Substituted by Housing and Planning Act 2016, s 160(1), (3) (6 April 2017).
3 Words substituted by Wales Act 2017, s 43(1), (2) (31 March 2017).
4 Inserted by Wales Act 2017, s 43(1), (3) (31 March 2017).
5 Repealed by Localism Act 2011, ss 128(2), 237, Sch 13, paras 1, 56, Sch 25, Pt 20 (1 April 2012).

116 Reasons for decision to grant or refuse development consent

(1) The [Secretary of State][1] must prepare a statement of [the Secretary of State's][2] reasons for deciding to—

(a) make an order granting development consent, or

(b) refuse development consent.

(2) The [Secretary of State][3] must provide a copy of the statement to each person who is an interested party in relation to the application for the purposes of Chapter 4 (see section 102).

(3) The [Secretary of State][4] must publish the statement in such manner as [the Secretary of State][5] thinks appropriate.

[...][6]

1 Words substituted by Localism Act 2011, s 128(2), Sch 13, paras 1, 57(1), (2)(a) (1 April 2012).
2 Word substituted by Localism Act 2011, s 128(2), Sch 13, paras 1, 57(1), (2)(b) (1 April 2012).
3 Words substituted by Localism Act 2011, s 128(2), Sch 13, paras 1, 57(1), (3) (1 April 2012).
4 Words substituted by Localism Act 2011, s 128(2), Sch 13, paras 1, 57(1), (4)(a) (1 April 2012).
5 Words substituted by Localism Act 2011, s 128(2), Sch 13, paras 1, 57(1), (4)(b) (1 April 2012).
6 Repealed by Localism Act 2011, ss 128(2), 237, Sch 13, paras 1, 57(1), (5), Sch 25, Pt 20 (1 April 2012).

117 Orders granting development consent: formalities

(1) This section applies in relation to an order granting development consent.

[...][1]

(3) Except in a case within subsection (4), the [Secretary of State][2] must publish the order in such manner as [the Secretary of State][3] thinks appropriate.

[(4) If the order includes provision—

(a) made under section 120(3) for or relating to any of the matters listed in paragraphs 32A and 32B of Schedule 5, or

(b) made in the exercise of any of the powers conferred by section 120(5)(a) or (b),

the order must be contained in a statutory instrument.][4]

[...][1]

(6) As soon as practicable after the instrument [containing the order is made, the Secretary of State][5] must deposit in the office of the Clerk of the Parliaments a copy of—

(a) the instrument,

(b) the latest version of any plan supplied by the applicant in connection with the application for the order contained in the instrument, and

(c) the statement of reasons prepared under section 116(1).

[...][6]

1 Repealed by Localism Act 2011, ss 128(2), 237, Sch 13, paras 1, 58(1), (2), Sch 25, Pt 20 (1 April 2012).
2 Words substituted by Localism Act 2011, s 128(2), Sch 13, paras 1, 58(1), (3)(a) (1 April 2012).
3 Words substituted by Localism Act 2011, s 128(2), Sch 13, paras 1, 58(1), (3)(b) (1 April 2012).
4 Substituted by Localism Act 2011, s 128(2), Sch 13, paras 1, 58(1), (4) (1 April 2012).
5 Words substituted by Localism Act 2011, s 128(2), Sch 13, paras 1, 58(1), (5) (1 April 2012).
6 Repealed by Localism Act 2011, ss 128(2), 237, Sch 13, paras 1, 58(1), (6), Sch 25, Pt 20 (1 April 2012).

Chapter 9 Legal challenges

118 Legal challenges relating to applications for orders granting development consent

(1) A court may entertain proceedings for questioning an order granting development consent only if—

(a) the proceedings are brought by a claim for judicial review, and

(b) the claim form is filed [before the end of][1] the period of 6 weeks beginning with [the day after][2]—

(i) the day on which the order is published, or

(ii) if later, the day on which the statement of reasons for making the order is published.

(2) A court may entertain proceedings for questioning a refusal of development consent only if—

(a) the proceedings are brought by a claim for judicial review, and

(b) the claim form is filed [before the end of][1] the period of 6 weeks beginning with [the day after][2] the day on which the statement of reasons for the refusal is published.

(3) A court may entertain proceedings for questioning a decision of the [Secretary of State][3] under section 55 not to accept an application for an order granting development consent only if—

(a) the proceedings are brought by a claim for judicial review, and

(b) the claim form is filed [before the end of][1] the period of 6 weeks beginning with [the day after][2] the day on which the [Secretary of State][3] notifies the applicant as required by subsection (7) of that section.

(4) A court may entertain proceedings for questioning a decision under paragraph 1 of Schedule 4 in relation to an error or omission in a decision document only if—

(a) the proceedings are brought by a claim for judicial review, and

(b) the claim form is filed [before the end of][1] the period of 6 weeks beginning with the day [after the day][2] on which a correction notice in respect of the error or omission is issued under paragraph 2 of that Schedule or, if the correction is required to be made by order contained in a statutory instrument, the day [after the day][2] on which the order is published.

(5) A court may entertain proceedings for questioning a decision under paragraph 2(1) of Schedule 6 to make a change to an order granting development consent only if—

(a) the proceedings are brought by a claim for judicial review, and

(b) the claim form is filed [before the end of][1] the period of 6 weeks beginning with the day [after the day][2] on which notice of the change is given under paragraph 2(12)(b) of that Schedule or, if the change to the order is required to be made by order contained in a statutory instrument, the day [after the day][2] on which the order making the change is published.

(6) A court may entertain proceedings for questioning a decision under paragraph 3(1) of Schedule 6 to make a change to, or revoke, an order granting development consent only if—

(a) the proceedings are brought by a claim for judicial review, and

(b) the claim form is filed [before the end of][1] the period of 6 weeks beginning with the day [after the day][2] on which notice of the change or revocation is given under paragraph 4(6) of that Schedule or, if the change or revocation is required to be made by order contained in a statutory instrument, the day [after the day][2] on which the order making the change or revocation is published.

(7) A court may entertain proceedings for questioning anything else done, or omitted to be done, by the Secretary of State [...][4] in relation to an application for an order granting development consent only if—

(a) the proceedings are brought by a claim for judicial review, and

(b) the claim form is filed [before the end of][1] the period of 6 weeks beginning with [the day after][2] the relevant day.

(8) 'The relevant day', in relation to an application for an order granting development consent, means the day on which—

(a) the application is withdrawn,

(b) the order granting development consent is published or (if later) the statement of reasons for making the order is published, or

(c) the statement of reasons for the refusal of development consent is published.

(9) Subsections (7) and (8) do not apply in relation to—

(a) a failure to decide an application for an order granting development consent, or

(b) anything which delays (or is likely to delay) the decision on such an application.

1 Words substituted by Criminal Justice and Courts Act 2015, s 92(4)(a)(i), (b)(i), (c)(i) (13 April 2015).
2 Words inserted by Criminal Justice and Courts Act 2015, s 92(4)(a)(ii), (b)(ii), (c)(ii) (13 April 2015).
3 Word substituted by Localism Act 2011, s 128(2), Sch 13, paras 1, 59(1), (2) (1 April 2012).
4 Words repealed by Localism Act 2011, ss 128(2), 237, Sch 13, paras 1, 59(1), (3), Sch 25, Pt 20 (1 April 2012).

Chapter 10 Correction of errors

119 Correction of errors in development consent decisions

Schedule 4 (correction of errors in development consent decisions) has effect.

Part 7 Orders granting development consent

Chapter 1 Content of orders

General

120 What may be included in order granting development consent

(1) An order granting development consent may impose requirements in connection with the development for which consent is granted.

(2) The requirements may in particular include[—][1]

[(a)][1] requirements corresponding to conditions which could have been imposed on the grant of any permission, consent or authorisation, or the giving of any notice, which (but for section 33(1)) would have been required for the development[;][2]

[(b) requirements to obtain the approval of the Secretary of State or any other person, so far as not within paragraph (a).][2]

(3) An order granting development consent may make provision relating to, or to matters ancillary to, the development for which consent is granted.

(4) The provision that may be made under subsection (3) includes in particular provision for or relating to any of the matters listed in Part 1 of Schedule 5.

(5) An order granting development consent may—

(a) apply, modify or exclude a statutory provision which relates to any matter for which provision may be made in the order;

(b) make such amendments, repeals or revocations of statutory provisions of local application as appear to the [Secretary of State][3] to be necessary or expedient in consequence of a provision of the order or in connection with the order;

(c) include any provision that appears to the [Secretary of State][3] to be necessary or expedient for giving full effect to any other provision of the order;

(d) include incidental, consequential, supplementary, transitional or transitory provisions and savings.

(6) In subsection (5) 'statutory provision' means a provision of an Act or of an instrument made under an Act.

(7) Subsections (3) to (6) are subject to subsection (8) and the following provisions of this Chapter.

[(8) With the exception of provision made under subsection (3) for or relating to any of the matters listed in paragraph 32B of Schedule 5, an order granting development consent may not include—

(a) provision creating offences,

(b) provision conferring power to create offences, or

(c) provision changing an existing power to create offences.][4]

(9) To the extent that provision for or relating to a matter may be included in an order granting development consent, none of the following may include any such provision—

(a) an order under section 14 or 16 of the Harbours Act 1964 (c. 40) (orders in relation to harbours, docks and wharves);

(b) an order under section 4(1) of the Gas Act 1965 (c. 36) (order authorising storage of gas in underground strata);

(c) an order under section 1 or 3 of the Transport and Works Act 1992 (c. 42) (orders as to railways, tramways, inland waterways etc.).

1 Existing text renumbered as s 120(2)(a) inserted by Localism Act 2011, s 140(a) (1 April 2012).
2 Inserted by Localism Act 2011, s 140(b) (1 April 2012).
3 Words substituted by Localism Act 2011, s 128(2), Sch 13, paras 1, 60(1), (2) (1 April 2012).
4 Substituted by Localism Act 2011, s 128(2), Sch 13, paras 1, 60(1), (3) (1 April 2012).

121 ...

Repealed by Localism Act 2011, ss 128(2), 237, Sch 13, paras 1, 61, Sch 25, Pt 20 (1 April 2012).

Compulsory acquisition

122 Purpose for which compulsory acquisition may be authorised

(1) An order granting development consent may include provision authorising the compulsory acquisition of land only if the [Secretary of State][1] is satisfied that the conditions in subsections (2) and (3) are met.

(2) The condition is that the land—

(a) is required for the development to which the development consent relates,

(b) is required to facilitate or is incidental to that development, or

(c) is replacement land which is to be given in exchange for the order land under section 131 or 132.

(3) The condition is that there is a compelling case in the public interest for the land to be acquired compulsorily.

1 Words substituted by Localism Act 2011, s 128(2), Sch 13, paras 1, 62 (1 April 2012).

123 Land to which authorisation of compulsory acquisition can relate

(1) An order granting development consent may include provision authorising the compulsory acquisition of land only if the [Secretary of State][1] is satisfied that one of the conditions in subsections (2) to (4) is met.

(2) The condition is that the application for the order included a request for compulsory acquisition of the land to be authorised.

(3) The condition is that all persons with an interest in the land consent to the inclusion of the provision.

(4) The condition is that the prescribed procedure has been followed in relation to the land.

1 Words substituted by Localism Act 2011, s 128(2), Sch 13, paras 1, 62 (1 April 2012).

124 ...

Repealed by Localism Act 2011, ss 128(2), 237, Sch 13, paras 1, 63, Sch 25, Pt 20 (1 April 2012).

125 Application of compulsory acquisition provisions

(1) This section applies if an order granting development consent includes provision authorising the compulsory acquisition of land.

(2) Part 1 of the Compulsory Purchase Act 1965 (c. 56) (procedure for compulsory purchase) applies to the compulsory acquisition of land under the order—

(a) as it applies to a compulsory purchase to which Part 2 of the Acquisition of Land Act 1981 (c. 67) applies, and

(b) as if the order were a compulsory purchase order under that Act.

(3) Part 1 of the Compulsory Purchase Act 1965, as applied by subsection (2), has effect with the omission of the following provisions—

(a) section 4 (time limit for exercise of compulsory purchase powers);

(b) section 10 (compensation for injurious affection);

(c) [...][1].

(4) In so far as the order includes provision authorising the compulsory acquisition of land in Scotland—

(a) subsections (2) and (3) do not apply, and

(b) the Acquisition of Land (Authorisation Procedure) (Scotland) Act 1947 (c. 42) ('the 1947 Act') applies to the compulsory acquisition of that land under the order as if the order were a compulsory purchase order as defined in section 1(1) of that Act.

(5) The 1947 Act, as applied by subsection (4), has effect with the omission of the following provisions—

(a) Parts 2 and 3 of the First Schedule (compulsory purchase by Ministers and special provisions as to certain descriptions of land);

(b) section 116 of the Lands Clauses Consolidation (Scotland) Act 1845 (c. 19) (time limit for exercise of compulsory purchase powers) (that section being incorporated into the 1947 Act by paragraph 1 of the Second Schedule to the 1947 Act).

(6) Subsections (2) to (5) are subject to any contrary provision made by the order granting development consent.

1 Repealed by Housing and Planning Act 2016, s 190, Sch 16, para 17 (13 July 2016).

126 Compensation for compulsory acquisition

(1) This section applies in relation to an order granting development consent which includes provision authorising the compulsory acquisition of land.

(2) The order may not include provision the effect of which is to modify the application of a compensation provision, except to the extent necessary to apply the provision to the compulsory acquisition of land authorised by the order.

(3) The order may not include provision the effect of which is to exclude the application of a compensation provision.

(4) A compensation provision is a provision of or made under an Act which relates to compensation for the compulsory acquisition of land.

127 Statutory undertakers' land

(1) This section applies in relation to land ('statutory undertakers' land') if—

(a) the land has been acquired by statutory undertakers for the purposes of their undertaking,

(b) a representation has been made about an application for an order granting development consent before the completion of the examination of the application, and the representation has not been withdrawn, and

(c) as a result of the representation the [Secretary of State][1] is satisfied that—

(i) the land is used for the purposes of carrying on the statutory undertakers' undertaking, or

(ii) an interest in the land is held for those purposes.

(2) An order granting development consent may include provision authorising the compulsory acquisition of statutory undertakers' land only to the extent that the [Secretary of State is satisfied of the matters set out in subsection (3).][2]

(3) The matters are that the nature and situation of the land are such that—

(a) it can be purchased and not replaced without serious detriment to the carrying on of the undertaking, or

(b) if purchased it can be replaced by other land belonging to, or available for acquisition by, the undertakers without serious detriment to the carrying on of the undertaking.

(4) Subsections (2) and (3) do not apply in a case within subsection (5).

(5) An order granting development consent may include provision authorising the compulsory acquisition of a right over statutory undertakers' land by the creation of a new right over land only to the extent that the [Secretary of State is satisfied of the matters set out in subsection (6).][2]

(6) The matters are that the nature and situation of the land are such that—

(a) the right can be purchased without serious detriment to the carrying on of the undertaking, or

(b) any detriment to the carrying on of the undertaking, in consequence of the acquisition of the right, can be made good by the undertakers by the use of other land belonging to or available for acquisition by them.

[…][3]

(8) In this section—

'statutory undertakers' has the meaning given by section 8 of the Acquisition of Land Act 1981 (c. 67) and also includes the undertakers—

(a) which are deemed to be statutory undertakers for the purposes of that Act, by virtue of another enactment;

(b) which are statutory undertakers for the purposes of section 16(1) and (2) of that Act (see section 16(3) of that Act).

(9) In the application of this section to a statutory undertaker which is a health service body (as defined in section 60(7) of the National Health Service and Community Care Act 1990 (c. 19)), references to land acquired or available for acquisition by the statutory undertakers are to be construed as references to land acquired or available for acquisition by the Secretary of State for use or occupation by the body.

1 Words substituted by Localism Act 2011, s 128(2), Sch 13, paras 1, 64(1), (2) (1 April 2012).
2 Words substituted by Growth and Infrastructure Act 2013, s 23(1), (2)(a), (b) (25 June 2013).
3 Repealed by Growth and Infrastructure Act 2013, s 23(1), (2)(c) (25 June 2013).

128, 129 …

Repealed by Growth and Infrastructure Act 2013, s 24(1) (25 June 2013).

130 National Trust land

(1) This section applies to land belonging to the National Trust which is held by the Trust inalienably.

(2) An order granting development consent is subject to special parliamentary procedure, to the extent that the order authorises the compulsory acquisition of land to which this section applies, if the condition in subsection (3) is met.

(3) The condition is that—

(a) a representation has been made by the National Trust about the application for the order granting development consent before the completion of the examination of the application,

[(aa) the representation contains an objection to the compulsory acquisition of the land,][1] and

(b) the [objection][2] has not been withdrawn.

[(3A) In a case to which this section applies and to which section 131 or 132 also applies, special parliamentary procedure—

(a) may be required by subsection (2) whether or not also required by section 131(3) or 132(2), and

(b) may be required by section 131(3) or 132(2) whether or not also required by subsection (2).][3]

(4) In this section 'held inalienably', in relation to land belonging to the National Trust, means that the land is inalienable under section 21 of the National Trust Act 1907 (c. cxxxvi) or section 8 of the National Trust Act 1939 (c. lxxxvi).

(5) In this section 'the National Trust' means the National Trust for Places of Historic Interest or Natural Beauty incorporated by the National Trust Act 1907 (c. cxxxvi).

1 Inserted by Localism Act 2011, s 141(1), (3)(a) (1 April 2012).
2 Word substituted by Localism Act 2011, s 141(1), (3)(b) (1 April 2012).
3 Inserted by Growth and Infrastructure Act 2013, s 24(5) (25 June 2013).

131 Commons, open spaces etc: compulsory acquisition of land

(1) This section applies to any land forming part of a common, open space or fuel or field garden allotment.

(2) This section does not apply in a case to which section 132 applies.

(3) An order granting development consent is subject to special parliamentary procedure, to the extent that the order authorises the compulsory acquisition of land to which this section applies, [unless—

(a) the Secretary of State is satisfied that one of subsections (4) to (5) applies, and

(b) that fact, and the subsection concerned, are recorded in the order or otherwise in the instrument or other document containing the order.][1]

(4) This subsection applies if—

(a) replacement land has been or will be given in exchange for the order land, and

(b) the replacement land has been or will be vested in the prospective seller and subject to the same rights, trusts and incidents as attach to the order land.

[(4A) This subsection applies if—

(a) the order land is, or forms part of, an open space,

(b) none of the order land is of any of the other descriptions in subsection (1),

(c) either—

(i) there is no suitable land available to be given in exchange for the order land, or

(ii) any suitable land available to be given in exchange is available only at prohibitive cost, and

(d) it is strongly in the public interest for the development for which the order grants consent to be capable of being begun sooner than is likely to be possible if the order were to be subject (to any extent) to special parliamentary procedure.

(4B) This subsection applies if—

(a) the order land is, or forms part of, an open space,

(b) none of the order land is of any of the other descriptions in subsection (1), and

(c) the order land is being acquired for a temporary (although possibly long-lived) purpose.][2]

(5) This subsection applies if—

(a) the order land does not exceed 200 square metres in extent or is required for the widening or drainage of an existing highway or partly for the widening and partly for the drainage of such a highway, and

(b) the giving in exchange of other land is unnecessary, whether in the interests of the persons, if any, entitled to rights of common or other rights or in the interests of the public.

[...][3]

(11) If an order granting development consent authorises the compulsory acquisition of land to which this section applies, it may include provision—

(a) for vesting replacement land given in exchange as mentioned in subsection (4)(a) in the prospective seller and subject to the rights, trusts and incidents mentioned in subsection (4)(b), and

(b) for discharging the order land from all rights, trusts and incidents to which it is subject.

(12) In this section—

'common', 'fuel or field garden allotment' and 'open space' have the same meanings as in section 19 of the Acquisition of Land Act 1981 (c. 67);

'the order land' means the land authorised to be compulsorily acquired;

'the prospective seller' means the person or persons in whom the order land is vested;

'replacement land' means land which is not less in area than the order land and which is no less advantageous to the persons, if any, entitled to rights of common or other rights, and to the public.

1 Words substituted by Growth and Infrastructure Act 2013, s 24(2)(a) (25 June 2013).
2 Inserted by Growth and Infrastructure Act 2013, s 24(2)(b) (25 June 2013).
3 Repealed by Growth and Infrastructure Act 2013, s 24(2)(c) (25 June 2013).

132 Commons, open spaces etc: compulsory acquisition of rights over land

(1) This section applies to any land forming part of a common, open space or fuel or field garden allotment.

(2) An order granting development consent is subject to special parliamentary procedure, to the extent that the order authorises the compulsory acquisition of a right over land to which this section applies by the creation of a new right over land, [unless—

(a) the Secretary of State is satisfied that one of subsections (3) to (5) applies, and

(b) that fact, and the subsection concerned, are recorded in the order or otherwise in the instrument or other document containing the order.][1]

(3) This subsection applies if the order land, when burdened with the order right, will be no less advantageous than it was before to the following persons—

(a) the persons in whom it is vested,

(b) other persons, if any, entitled to rights of common or other rights, and

(c) the public.

(4) This subsection applies if—

(a) replacement land has been or will be given in exchange for the order right, and

(b) the replacement land has been or will be vested in the persons in whom the order land is vested and subject to the same rights, trusts and incidents as attach to the order land (ignoring the order granting development consent).

[(4A) This subsection applies if—

(a) the order land is, or forms part of, an open space,

(b) none of the order land is of any of the other descriptions in subsection (1),

(c) either—

(i) there is no suitable land available to be given in exchange for the order right, or

(ii) any suitable land available to be given in exchange is available only at prohibitive cost, and

(d) it is strongly in the public interest for the development for which the order grants consent to be capable of being begun sooner than is likely to be possible if the order were to be subject (to any extent) to special parliamentary procedure.

(4B) This subsection applies if—

(a) the order land is, or forms part of, an open space,

(b) none of the order land is of any of the other descriptions in subsection (1), and

(c) the order right is being acquired for a temporary (although possibly long-lived) purpose.][2]

(5) This subsection applies if—

(a) the order land does not exceed 200 square metres in extent or the order right is required in connection with the widening or drainage of an existing highway or in connection partly with the widening and partly with the drainage of such a highway, and

(b) the giving of other land in exchange for the order right is unnecessary, whether in the interests of the persons, if any, entitled to rights of common or other rights or in the interests of the public.

[…][3]

(11) If an order granting development consent authorises the compulsory acquisition of a right over land to which this section applies by the creation of a new right over land, it may include provision—

(a) for vesting replacement land given in exchange as mentioned in subsection (4)(a) in the persons in whom the order land is vested and subject to the rights, trusts and incidents mentioned in subsection (4)(b), and

(b) for discharging the order land from all rights, trusts and incidents to which it has previously been subject so far as their continuance would be inconsistent with the exercise of the order right.

(12) In this section—

'common', 'fuel or field garden allotment' and 'open space' have the same meanings as in section 19 of the Acquisition of Land Act 1981 (c. 67);

'the order land' means the land to which this section applies over which the order right is to be exercisable;

'the order right' means the right authorised to be compulsorily acquired;

'replacement land' means land which will be adequate to compensate the following persons for the disadvantages which result from the compulsory acquisition of the order right—

(a) the persons in whom the order land is vested,

(b) the persons, if any, entitled to rights of common or other rights over the order land, and

(c) the public.

1 Words substituted by Growth and Infrastructure Act 2013, s 24(3)(a) (25 June 2013).
2 Inserted by Growth and Infrastructure Act 2013, s 24(3)(b) (25 June 2013).
3 Repealed by Growth and Infrastructure Act 2013, s 24(3)(c) (25 June 2013).

133 Rights in connection with underground gas storage facilities

(1) This section applies if—

(a) the development to which an order granting development consent relates is development within section 14(1)(c), and

(b) the order authorises the compulsory acquisition of one or more rights within subsection (2).

(2) The rights are—

(a) a right to store gas in underground gas storage facilities;

(b) a right to stop up a well, borehole or shaft, or prevent its use by another person;

(c) a right of way over land.

(3) If the right within subsection (2) is an existing right to store gas in underground gas storage facilities, this Act has effect in relation to the compulsory acquisition of the right with the omission of section 131.

(4) If the order authorises the compulsory acquisition of the right by the creation of a new right within subsection (2), this Act has effect in relation to the compulsory acquisition of the right with the omission of sections 127 to 132.

134 Notice of authorisation of compulsory acquisition

(1) This section applies if—

(a) an order is made granting development consent, and

(b) the order includes provision authorising the compulsory acquisition of land.

(2) In this section—

'the order land' means—

(a) in a case where the order granting development consent authorises the compulsory acquisition of a right over land by the creation of a new right, the land over which the right is to be exercisable;

(b) in any other case where the order granting development consent authorises the compulsory acquisition of land, the land authorised to be compulsorily acquired;

'the prospective purchaser' means—

(a) in a case where the order granting development consent authorises the compulsory acquisition of a right over land by the creation of a new right, the person for whose benefit the order authorises the creation of the right;

(b) in any other case where the order granting development consent authorises the compulsory acquisition of land, the person authorised by the order to compulsorily acquire the land.

(3) After the order has been made, the prospective purchaser must—

[(za) make a copy of the order available, at a place in the vicinity of the land, for inspection by the public at all reasonable hours,][1]

(a) serve a compulsory acquisition notice [...][2] on each person to whom subsection (4) applies, and

(b) affix a compulsory acquisition notice to a conspicuous object or objects on or near the order land.

(4) This subsection applies to any person who, if the order granting development consent were a compulsory purchase order, would be a qualifying person for the purposes of section 12(1) of the Acquisition of Land Act 1981 (c. 67) (notice to owners, lessees and occupiers).

(5) A compulsory acquisition notice which is affixed under subsection (3)(b) must—

(a) be addressed to persons occupying or having an interest in the order land, and

(b) so far as practicable, be kept in place by the prospective purchaser until the end of the period of 6 weeks beginning with the date on which the order is published.

(6) The prospective purchaser must also publish a compulsory acquisition notice in one or more local newspapers circulating in the locality in which the order land is situated.

[(6A) The prospective purchaser must send a compulsory acquisition notice to the Chief Land Registrar and it shall be a local land charge in respect of the land in England or Wales to which it relates.][3]

(7) A compulsory acquisition notice is a notice in the prescribed form—

(a) describing the order land,

(b) in a case where the order granting development consent authorises the compulsory acquisition of a right over land by the creation of a new right, describing the right,

(c) stating that the order granting development consent includes provision authorising the compulsory acquisition of a right over the land by the creation of a right over it or (as the case may be) the compulsory acquisition of the land, [...][4]

[(cza) in a case where the order applies Parts 2 and 3 of the Compulsory Purchase (Vesting Declarations) Act 1981—

(i) containing a prescribed statement about the effect of those Parts, and

(ii) inviting any person who would be entitled to claim compensation if a declaration were executed under section 4 of that Act to give the prospective purchaser information about the person's name, address and interest in land, using a prescribed form,][3]

[(ca) stating where and when a copy of the order is available for inspection in accordance with subsection (3)(za), and][4]

(d) stating that a person aggrieved by the order may challenge the order only in accordance with section 118.

[...][5]

1 Inserted by Localism Act 2011, s 142(1), (2)(a) (1 April 2012).
2 Words repealed by Localism Act 2011, ss 142(1), (2)(b), 237, Sch 25, Pt 21 (1 April 2012).
3 Inserted by Housing and Planning Act 2016 (Compulsory Purchase) (Corresponding Amendments) Regulations 2017, SI 2017/16, reg 2, Schedule, para 6 (2 February 2017).
4 Inserted by Localism Act 2011, s 142(1), (3) (15 January 2012 for the purpose of conferring power on the Secretary of State to make regulations; 1 April 2012 otherwise).
5 Repealed by Localism Act 2011, ss 142(1), (4), 237, Sch 25, Pt 21 (1 April 2012).

Miscellaneous

135 Orders: Crown land

(1) An order granting development consent may include provision authorising the compulsory acquisition of an interest in Crown land only if—

(a) it is an interest which is for the time being held otherwise than by or on behalf of the Crown, and

(b) the appropriate Crown authority consents to the acquisition.

(2) An order granting development consent may include any other provision applying in relation to Crown land, or rights benefiting the Crown, only if the appropriate Crown authority consents to the inclusion of the provision.

(3) The reference in subsection (2) to rights benefiting the Crown does not include rights which benefit the general public.

(4) For the purposes of this section 'the Crown' includes—

(a) the Duchy of Lancaster;

(b) the Duchy of Cornwall;

(c) the Speaker of the House of Lords;

(d) the Speaker of the House of Commons;

(e) the Corporate Officer of the House of Lords;

(f) the Corporate Officer of the House of Commons.

136 Public rights of way

(1) An order granting development consent may extinguish a public right of way over land only if the [Secretary of State][1] is satisfied that—

(a) an alternative right of way has been or will be provided, or

(b) the provision of an alternative right of way is not required.

(2) The following provisions of this section apply if—

(a) an order granting development consent makes provision for the acquisition of land, compulsorily or by agreement,

(b) the order extinguishes a public right of way over the land, and

(c) the right of way is not a right enjoyable by vehicular traffic.

(3) The order granting development consent may not provide for the right of way to be extinguished from a date which is earlier than the date on which the order is published.

(4) Subsection (5) applies if—

(a) the order granting development consent extinguishes the right of way from a date ('the extinguishment date') which is earlier than the date on which the acquisition of the land is completed, and

(b) at any time after the extinguishment date it appears to the [Secretary of State][2] that the proposal to acquire the land has been abandoned.

(5) The [Secretary of State][2] must by order direct that the right is to revive.

[…][3]

(7) Nothing in subsection (5) prevents the making of a further order extinguishing the right of way.

1 Words substituted by Localism Act 2011, s 128(2), Sch 13, paras 1, 66(1), (2) (1 April 2012).
2 Words substituted by Localism Act 2011, s 128(2), Sch 13, paras 1, 66(1), (3) (1 April 2012).
3 Repealed by Localism Act 2011, ss 128(2), 237, Sch 13, paras 1, 66(1), (4), Sch 25, Pt 20 (1 April 2012).

137 ...

Repealed by Growth and Infrastructure Act 2013, s 23(3) (25 June 2013).

138 Extinguishment of rights, and removal of apparatus, of statutory undertakers etc.

(1) This section applies if an order granting development consent authorises the acquisition of land (compulsorily or by agreement) and—

(a) there subsists over the land a relevant right, or

(b) there is on, under or over the land relevant apparatus.

(2) 'Relevant right' means a right of way, or a right of laying down, erecting, continuing or maintaining apparatus on, under or over the land, which—

(a) is vested in or belongs to statutory undertakers for the purpose of the carrying on of their undertaking, or

(b) is conferred by or in accordance with the electronic communications code on the operator of an electronic communications code network.

(3) 'Relevant apparatus' means—

(a) apparatus vested in or belonging to statutory undertakers for the purpose of the carrying on of their undertaking, or

(b) electronic communications apparatus kept installed for the purposes of an electronic communications code network.

(4) The order may include provision for the extinguishment of the relevant right, or the removal of the relevant apparatus, [only if the Secretary of State is satisfied that the extinguishment or removal is necessary for the purpose of carrying out the development to which the order relates.][1]

[(4A) In this section 'statutory undertakers' means persons who are, or are deemed to be, statutory undertakers for the purpose of any provision of Part 11 of TCPA 1990.

[(4B) In this section—

'electronic communications apparatus' has the meaning given in paragraph 5 of the electronic communications code;

'electronic communications code' means the code set out in Schedule 3A to the Communications Act 2003;

'operator of an electronic communications code network' has the meaning given in paragraph 1(1) of Schedule 17 to the Communications Act 2003;][2]][3]

[...][4]

1 Words substituted by Growth and Infrastructure Act 2013, s 23(4)(a) (25 June 2013).
2 Substituted by Communications Act 2003 and the Digital Economy Act 2017 (Consequential Amendments to Primary Legislation) Regulations 2017, SI 2017/1285, reg 2, Schedule, para 12 (28 December 2017).
3 Inserted by Growth and Infrastructure Act 2013, s 23(4)(b) (25 June 2013).
4 Repealed by Growth and Infrastructure Act 2013, s 23(4)(c) (25 June 2013).

139 Common land and rights of common

(1) An order granting development consent may not include provision the effect of which is to exclude or modify the application of a provision of or made under the Commons Act 2006, except in accordance with section 131 or 132.

(2) For the purposes of section 38(6)(a) of the Commons Act 2006, works carried out under a power conferred by an order granting development consent are not to be taken to be carried out under a power conferred by or under an enactment, except in a case to which section 131 or 132 applies.

(3) An order granting development consent may not authorise the suspension of, or extinguishment or interference with, registered rights of common, except in accordance with section 131 or 132.

(4) 'Registered rights of common' means rights of common registered under—

(a) the Commons Act 2006, or

(b) the Commons Registration Act 1965.

140 Operation of generating stations

An order granting development consent may include provision authorising the operation of a generating station only if the development to which the order relates is or includes the construction or extension of the generating station.

141 Keeping electric lines installed above ground

An order granting development consent may include provision authorising an electric line to be kept installed above ground only if the development to which the order relates is or includes the installation of the line above ground.

142 Use of underground gas storage facilities

An order granting development consent may include provision authorising the use of underground gas storage facilities only if the development to which the order relates is or includes development within section 17(2), (3) or (5).

143 Diversion of watercourses

(1) An order granting development consent may include provision authorising the diversion of any part of a navigable watercourse only if the condition in subsection (2) is met.

(2) The new length of watercourse must be navigable in a reasonably convenient manner by vessels of a kind that are accustomed to using the part of the watercourse which is to be diverted.

(3) In deciding whether the condition in subsection (2) is met, the effect of any bridge or tunnel must be ignored if the construction of the bridge or tunnel is part of the development for which consent is granted by the order granting development consent.

(4) If an order granting development consent includes provision authorising the diversion of any part of a navigable watercourse, the order is also to be taken to authorise the diversion of any tow path or other way adjacent to that part.

144 Highways

(1) An order granting development consent may include provision authorising the charging of tolls in relation to a highway only if a request to that effect has been included in the application for the order.

(2) If an order granting development consent includes provision authorising the charging of tolls in relation to a highway, the order is treated as a toll order for the purposes of sections 7 to 18 of the New Roads and Street Works Act 1991 (c. 22).

[(2A) Subsection (2) does not apply to an order that includes provision authorising other charges in respect of the use or keeping of motor vehicles on roads.

(2B) In subsection (2A)—

'motor vehicle' has the meaning given in section 185(1) of the Road Traffic Act 1988, except that section 189 of that Act (exceptions: certain pedestrian controlled vehicles and electrically assisted pedal cycles) applies as it applies for the purposes of the Road Traffic Acts;

'road' has the meaning given in section 142(1) of the Road Traffic Regulation Act 1984.][1]

[...][2]

1 Inserted by Growth and Infrastructure Act 2013, s 27(1), (2) (25 June 2013).
2 Repealed by Growth and Infrastructure Act 2013, s 27(1), (3) (25 June 2013).

145 Harbours

(1) An order granting development consent may include provision for the creation of a harbour authority only if—

(a) the development to which the order relates is or includes the construction or alteration of harbour facilities, and

(b) the creation of a harbour authority is necessary or expedient for the purposes of the development.

(2) An order granting development consent may include provision changing the powers or duties of a harbour authority only if—

(a) the development to which the order relates is or includes the construction or alteration of harbour facilities, and

(b) the authority has requested the inclusion of the provision or has consented in writing to its inclusion.

(3) An order granting development consent may include provision authorising the transfer of property, rights or liabilities from one harbour authority to another only if—

(a) the development to which the order relates is or includes the construction or alteration of harbour facilities, and

(b) the order makes provision for the payment of compensation of an amount—

(i) determined in accordance with the order, or

(ii) agreed between the parties to the transfer.

(4) An order granting development consent which includes provision for the creation of a harbour authority, or changing the powers or duties of a harbour authority, may also make other provision in relation to the authority.

This is subject to subsection (6).

(5) Subject to subsection (6), the provision which may be included in relation to a harbour authority includes in particular—

(a) any provision in relation to a harbour authority which could be included in a harbour revision order under section 14 of the Harbours Act 1964 (c. 40) by virtue of any provision of Schedule 2 to that Act;

(b) provision conferring power on the authority to change provision made in relation to it (by the order or by virtue of this paragraph), where the provision is about—

(i) the procedures (including financial procedures) of the authority;

(ii) the power of the authority to impose charges;

(iii) the power of the authority to delegate any of its functions;

(iv) the welfare of officers and employees of the authority and financial and other provision made for them.

(6) The order may not include provision—

(a) which, by virtue of any other provision of this Act, is not permitted to be included in an order granting development consent;

(b) conferring power on a harbour authority to delegate, or makes changes to its powers so as to permit the delegation of, any of the functions mentioned in paragraphs (a) to (f) of paragraph 9B of Schedule 2 to the Harbours Act 1964.

146 Discharge of water

(1) This section applies if—

(a) an order granting development consent includes provision authorising the discharge of water into inland waters or underground strata, and

(b) but for the order, the person to whom development consent is granted would have had no power to take water, or to require discharges to be made, from the inland waters or other source from which the discharges authorised by the order are intended to be made.

(2) The order does not have the effect of conferring any such power on that person.

147 Development of Green Belt land

(1) This section applies if an order granting development consent includes provision—

(a) authorising the acquisition of Green Belt land, compulsorily or by agreement,

(b) authorising the sale, exchange or appropriation of Green Belt land, or

(c) freeing land from any restriction imposed upon it by or under the Green Belt (London and Home Counties) Act 1938 (c. xciii), or by a covenant or other agreement entered into for the purposes of that Act.

(2) The [Secretary of State][1] must notify the relevant local authorities of the provision made by the order.

[...][2]

(4) The relevant local authorities are—

(a) each local authority in whose area all or part of the land is situated,

(b) any local authority in whom all or part of the land is vested, and

(c) each contributing local authority.

(5) In this section 'local authority' and 'contributing local authority' have the same meanings as in the Green Belt (London and Home Counties) Act 1938 (c. xciii) (see section 2(1) of that Act).

1 Words substituted by Localism Act 2011, s 128(2), Sch 13, paras 1, 68(1), (2) (1 April 2012).
2 Repealed by Localism Act 2011, ss 128(2), 237, Sch 13, paras 1, 68(1), (3), Sch 25, Pt 20 (1 April 2012).

148, 149 ...

Repealed by Marine and Coastal Access Act 2009, ss 112(1), 321, Sch 7, para 4(7)(a), (b), Sch 22, Pt 2 (6 April 2011).

[149A Deemed consent under a marine licence

(1) An order granting development consent may include provision deeming a marine licence to have been issued under Part 4 of the Marine and Coastal Access Act 2009 (marine licensing) for any activity only if the activity is to be carried out wholly in one or more of the areas specified in subsection (2).

(2) The areas are—

(a) England,

(b) waters adjacent to England up to the seaward limits of the territorial sea,

(c) an exclusive economic zone, except any part of an exclusive economic zone in relation to which the Scottish Ministers have functions,

(d) a Renewable Energy Zone, except any part of a Renewable Energy Zone in relation to which the Scottish Ministers have functions,

(e) an area designated under section 1(7) of the Continental Shelf Act 1964, except any part of that area which is within a part of an exclusive economic zone or Renewable Energy Zone in relation to which the Scottish Ministers have functions.

(3) Subsections (4) and (5) apply if an order granting development consent includes provision—

(a) deeming a marine licence to have been granted under Part 4 of the Marine and Coastal Access Act 2009 subject to specified conditions, and

(b) deeming those conditions to have been attached to the marine licence by the Secretary of State [or the Welsh Ministers][1] under that Part.

(4) A person who fails to comply with such a condition does not commit an offence under section 161 of this Act.

(5) Sections 68 (notice of applications) and 69(3) and (5) (representations) of the Marine and Coastal Access Act 2009 do not apply in relation to the deemed marine licence.][2]

1 Words inserted by Wales Act 2017, s 69(1), Sch 6, para 74 (1 April 2018).
2 Inserted by Marine and Coastal Access Act 2009, s 112(1), Sch 8, para 4(1), (2) (6 April 2011).

150 Removal of consent requirements

(1) An order granting development consent may include provision the effect of which is to remove a requirement for a prescribed consent or authorisation to be granted, only if the relevant body has consented to the inclusion of the provision.

(2) 'The relevant body' is the person or body which would otherwise be required to grant the prescribed consent or authorisation.

151 Liability under existing regimes

An order granting development consent may not include provision the effect of which is to exclude or modify the application of—

(a) any provision of the Nuclear Installations Act 1965 (c. 57);

(b) section 28 of, and Schedule 2 to, the Reservoirs Act 1975 (c. 23) (liability for damage and injury due to escape of water from a reservoir constructed after 1930);

(c) section 209 of the Water Industry Act 1991 (c. 56) (civil liability of water undertakers for escapes of water from pipes);

(d) section 48A of the Water Resources Act 1991 (c. 57) (civil remedies for loss or damage due to water abstraction).

152 Compensation in case where no right to claim in nuisance

(1) This section applies if, by virtue of section 158 or an order granting development consent, there is a defence of statutory authority in civil or criminal proceedings for nuisance in respect of any authorised works.

(2) 'Authorised works' are—

(a) development for which consent is granted by an order granting development consent;

(b) anything else authorised by an order granting development consent.

(3) A person by whom or on whose behalf any authorised works are carried out must pay compensation to any person whose land is injuriously affected by the carrying out of the works.

(4) A dispute as to whether compensation under subsection (3) is payable, or as to the amount of the compensation, must be referred to the [Upper Tribunal][1].

(5) Subsection (2) of section 10 of the Compulsory Purchase Act 1965 (c. 56) (limitation on compensation) applies to subsection (3) of this section as it applies to that section.

(6) Any rule or principle applied to the construction of section 10 of that Act must be applied to the construction of subsection (3) of this section (with any necessary modifications).

(7) Part 1 of the Land Compensation Act 1973 (c. 26) (compensation for depreciation of land value by physical factors caused by use of public works) applies in relation to authorised works as if—

(a) references in that Part to any public works were to any authorised works;

(b) references in that Part to the responsible authority were to the person for whose benefit the order granting development consent has effect for the time being;

(c) sections 1(6) and 17 were omitted.

(8) An order granting development consent may not include provision the effect of which is to remove or modify the application of any of subsections (1) to (7).

1 Words substituted by Transfer of Tribunal Functions (Lands Tribunal and Miscellaneous Amendments) Order 2009, SI 2009/1307, art 5(1), (2), Sch 1, paras 291, 293 (1 March 2010: substitution came into force on 1 June 2009 but could not take effect until the commencement of Planning Act 2008, s 152(4) on 1 March 2010).

Chapter 2 Changes to, and revocation of, orders

153 Changes to, and revocation of, orders granting development consent

Schedule 6 (changes to, and revocation of, orders granting development consent) has effect.

Chapter 3 General

154 Duration of order granting development consent

(1) Development for which development consent is granted must be begun before the end of—

(a) the prescribed period, or

(b) such other period (whether longer or shorter than that prescribed) as is specified in the order granting the consent.

(2) If the development is not begun before the end of the period applicable under subsection (1), the order granting development consent ceases to have effect at the end of that period.

(3) Where an order granting development consent authorises the compulsory acquisition of land, steps of a prescribed description must be taken in relation to the compulsory acquisition before the end of—

(a) the prescribed period, or

(b) such other period (whether longer or shorter than that prescribed) as is specified in the order.

(4) If steps of the prescribed description are not taken before the end of the period applicable under subsection (3), the authority to compulsorily acquire the land under the order ceases to have effect.

155 When development begins

(1) For the purposes of this Act (except Part 11) development is taken to begin on the earliest date on which any material operation comprised in, or carried out for the purposes of, the development begins to be carried out.

(2) 'Material operation' means any operation except an operation of a prescribed description.

156 Benefit of order granting development consent

(1) If an order granting development consent is made in respect of any land, the order has effect for the benefit of the land and all persons for the time being interested in the land.

(2) Subsection (1) is subject to subsection (3) and any contrary provision made in the order.

(3) To the extent that the development for which development consent is granted is development within section 17(3), the order granting the consent has effect for the benefit of a person for the time being interested in the land only if the person is a gas transporter.

157 Use of buildings in respect of which development consent granted

(1) If development consent is granted for development which includes the erection, extension, alteration or re-erection of a building, the order granting consent may specify the purposes for which the building is authorised to be used.

(2) If no purpose is so specified, the consent is taken to authorise the use of the building for the purpose for which it is designed.

158 Nuisance: statutory authority

(1) This subsection confers statutory authority for—

- (a) carrying out development for which consent is granted by an order granting development consent;
- (b) doing anything else authorised by an order granting development consent.

(2) Statutory authority under subsection (1) is conferred only for the purpose of providing a defence in civil or criminal proceedings for nuisance.

(3) Subsections (1) and (2) are subject to any contrary provision made in any particular case by an order granting development consent.

159 Interpretation: land and rights over land

(1) This section applies for the purposes of this Part.

(2) 'Land' includes any interest in or right over land.

(3) Acquiring a right over land includes acquiring it by the creation of a new right as well as by the acquisition of an existing one.

Part 8 Enforcement

Offences

160 Development without development consent

(1) A person commits an offence if the person carries out, or causes to be carried out, development for which development consent is required at a time when no development consent is in force in respect of the development.

(2) A person guilty of an offence under this section is liable [on summary conviction, or on conviction on indictment, to a fine][1].

(3) [...][2]

1 Words substituted by Legal Aid, Sentencing and Punishment of Offenders Act 2012 (Fines on Summary Conviction) Regulations 2015, SI 2015/664, reg 4(1), Sch 4, para 41(1), (2)(a) (12 March 2015).
2 Repealed by Legal Aid, Sentencing and Punishment of Offenders Act 2012 (Fines on Summary Conviction) Regulations 2015, SI 2015/664, reg 4(1), Sch 4, para 41(1), (2)(b) (12 March 2015).

161 Breach of terms of order granting development consent

(1) A person commits an offence if without reasonable excuse the person—

(a) carries out, or causes to be carried out, development in breach of the terms of an order granting development consent, or

(b) otherwise fails to comply with the terms of an order granting development consent.

(2) Subsection (1) is subject to [section 149A(4)][1].

(3) It is a defence for a person charged with an offence under this section to prove that—

(a) the breach or failure to comply occurred only because of an error or omission in the order, and

(b) a correction notice specifying the correction of the error or omission has been issued under paragraph 2 of Schedule 4.

(4) A person guilty of an offence under this section is liable [on summary conviction, or on conviction on indictment, to a fine][2].

(5) [...][3]

1 Words substituted by Marine and Coastal Access Act 2009, s 112(1), Sch 8, para 4(1), (3) (6 April 2011).
2 Words substituted by Legal Aid, Sentencing and Punishment of Offenders Act 2012 (Fines on Summary Conviction) Regulations 2015, SI 2015/664, reg 4(1), Sch 4, para 41(1), (3)(a) (12 March 2015).
3 Repealed by Legal Aid, Sentencing and Punishment of Offenders Act 2012 (Fines on Summary Conviction) Regulations 2015, SI 2015/664, reg 4(1), Sch 4, para 41(1), (3)(b) (12 March 2015).

162 Time limits

(1) A person may not be charged with an offence under section 160 or 161 after the end of—

(a) the relevant 4-year period, or

(b) if subsection (3) applies, the extended period.

(2) The 'relevant 4-year period' means—

(a) in the case of an offence under section 160, the period of 4 years beginning with the date on which the development was substantially completed;

(b) in the case of an offence under section 161, the period of 4 years beginning with the later of—

(i) the date on which the development was substantially completed, and

(ii) the date on which the breach or failure to comply occurred.

(3) This subsection applies if during the relevant 4-year period—

(a) an information notice has been served under section 167, or

(b) an injunction has been applied for under section 171.

(4) The 'extended period' means the period of 4 years beginning with—

(a) the date of service of the information notice, if subsection (3)(a) applies;

(b) the date of the application for the injunction, if subsection (3)(b) applies;

(c) the later (or latest) of those dates, if both paragraphs (a) and (b) of subsection (3) apply.

Rights of entry

163 Right to enter without warrant

(1) This section applies in relation to any land if the relevant local planning authority has reasonable grounds for suspecting that an offence under section 160 or 161 is being, or has been, committed on or in respect of the land.

(2) A person authorised in writing by the relevant local planning authority may at any reasonable hour enter the land for the purpose of ascertaining whether an offence under section 160 or 161 is being, or has been, committed on the land.

(3) A person may enter a building used as a dwelling-house under subsection (2) only if 24 hours' notice of the intended entry has been given to the occupier of the building.

164 Right to enter under warrant

(1) This section applies if it is shown to the satisfaction of a justice of the peace on sworn information in writing—

(a) that there are reasonable grounds for suspecting that an offence under section 160 or 161 is being, or has been, committed on or in respect of any land, and

(b) that the condition in subsection (2) is met.

(2) The condition is that—

(a) admission to the land has been refused, or a refusal is reasonably apprehended, or

(b) the case is one of urgency.

(3) The justice of the peace may issue a warrant authorising any person who is authorised in writing for the purpose by the relevant local planning authority to enter the land.

(4) For the purposes of subsection (2)(a) admission to land is to be regarded as having been refused if no reply is received to a request for admission within a reasonable period.

(5) A warrant authorises entry on one occasion only and that entry must be—

(a) before the end of the period of one month beginning with the date of the issue of the warrant, and

(b) at a reasonable hour, unless the case is one of urgency.

165 Rights of entry: supplementary provisions

(1) A person authorised to enter land in pursuance of a right of entry conferred under or by virtue of section 163 or 164 ('a relevant right of entry')—

(a) must, if so required, produce evidence of the authority and state the purpose of entry before entering the land,

(b) may take on to the land such other persons as may be necessary, and

(c) must, if the person leaves the land at a time when the owner or occupier is not present, leave it as effectively secured against trespassers as it was found.

(2) A person commits an offence if the person wilfully obstructs a person acting in the exercise of a relevant right of entry.

(3) A person guilty of an offence under subsection (2) is liable on summary conviction to a fine not exceeding level 3 on the standard scale.

(4) If any damage is caused to land or chattels in the exercise of a relevant right of entry, compensation may be recovered by any person suffering the damage from the local planning authority that authorised the entry.

(5) Except so far as otherwise provided by regulations, any question of disputed compensation under subsection (4) is to be referred to and determined by the [Upper Tribunal][1].

(6) In relation to the determination of any such question, the provisions of [section][2] 4 of the Land Compensation Act 1961 (c. 33) apply subject to any necessary modifications and to any other prescribed modifications.

1 Words substituted by Transfer of Tribunal Functions (Lands Tribunal and Miscellaneous Amendments) Order 2009, SI 2009/1307, art 5(1), (2), Sch 1, paras 291, 294(a) (1 March 2010: substitution came into force on 1 June 2009 but could not take effect until the commencement of the Planning Act 2008, s 165(5) on 1 March 2010).

2 Words substituted by Transfer of Tribunal Functions (Lands Tribunal and Miscellaneous Amendments) Order 2009, SI 2009/1307, art 5(1), (2), Sch 1, paras 291, 294(b) (1 March 2010: substitution came into force on 1 June 2009 but could not take effect until the commencement of the Planning Act 2008, s 165(5) on 1 March 2010).

166 Rights of entry: Crown land

Sections 163 and 164 do not apply to Crown land.

Information notices

167 Power to require information

(1) This section applies in relation to any land if it appears to the relevant local planning authority that an offence under section 160 or 161 may have been committed on or in respect of the land.

(2) The relevant local planning authority may serve an information notice.

(3) The information notice may be served on any person who—

(a) is the owner or occupier of the land or has any other interest in it, or

(b) is carrying out operations on the land or is using it for any purpose.

(4) The information notice may require the person on whom it is served to give such of the following information as may be specified in the notice—

(a) information about any operations being carried out in, on, over or under the land, any use of the land and any other activities being carried out in, on, over or under the land, and

(b) information about the provisions of any order granting development consent for development of the land.

(5) An information notice must inform the person on whom it is served of the likely consequences of a failure to respond to the notice.

(6) A requirement of an information notice is complied with by giving the required information to the relevant local planning authority in writing.

168 Offences relating to information notices

(1) A person commits an offence if without reasonable excuse the person fails to comply with any requirement of an information notice served under section 167 before the end of the period mentioned in subsection (2).

(2) The period referred to in subsection (1) is the period of 21 days beginning with the day on which the information notice is served.

(3) A person guilty of an offence under subsection (1) is liable on summary conviction to a fine not exceeding level 3 on the standard scale.

(4) A person commits an offence if the person—

(a) makes any statement purporting to comply with a requirement of an information notice which he knows to be false or misleading in a material respect, or

(b) recklessly makes such a statement which is false or misleading in a material respect.

(5) A person guilty of an offence under subsection (4) is liable on summary conviction to a fine not exceeding level 5 on the standard scale.

Notices of unauthorised development

169 Notice of unauthorised development

(1) Subsection (2) applies if a person is found guilty of an offence under section 160 committed on or in respect of any land.

(2) The relevant local planning authority may serve a notice of unauthorised development on the person requiring such steps as may be specified in the notice to be taken—

(a) to remove the development, and

(b) to restore the land on which the development has been carried out to its condition before the development was carried out.

(3) Subsection (4) applies if a person is found guilty of an offence under section 161 committed on or in respect of any land.

(4) The relevant local planning authority may serve a notice of unauthorised development on the person requiring the person to remedy the breach or failure to comply.

(5) A notice of unauthorised development—

(a) must specify the period within which any steps are required to be taken, and

(b) may specify different periods for different steps.

(6) Where different periods apply to different steps, references in this Part to the period for compliance with a notice of unauthorised development, in relation to any step, are to the period within which the step is required to be taken.

(7) A notice of unauthorised development must specify such additional matters as may be prescribed.

170 Execution of works required by notice of unauthorised development

(1) If any of the steps specified in a notice of unauthorised development have not been taken before the end of the period for compliance with the notice, the relevant local planning authority may—

(a) enter the land on which the development has been carried out and take those steps, and

(b) recover from the person who is then the owner of the land any expenses reasonably incurred by it in doing so.

(2) Where a notice of unauthorised development has been served in respect of development—

(a) any expenses incurred by the owner or occupier of the land for the purposes of complying with it, and

(b) any sums paid by the owner of the land under subsection (1) in respect of expenses incurred by the relevant local planning authority in taking steps required by it,

are to be deemed to be incurred or paid for the use and at the request of the person found guilty of the offence under section 160 or 161.

(3) Regulations may provide that all or any of the following sections of the Public Health Act 1936 (c. 49) are to apply, subject to such adaptations and modifications as may be specified in the regulations, in relation to any steps required to be taken by a notice of unauthorised development—

section 276 (power of local authorities to sell materials removed in executing works under that Act subject to accounting for the proceeds of sale);

section 289 (power to require the occupier of any premises to permit works to be executed by the owner of the premises);

section 294 (limit on liability of persons holding premises as agents or trustees in respect of the expenses recoverable under that Act).

(4) Regulations under subsection (3) applying all or any of section 289 of that Act may include adaptations and modifications for the purpose of giving the owner of land to which such a notice relates the right, as against all other persons interested in the land, to comply with the requirements of the notice.

(5) Regulations under subsection (3) may also provide for the charging on the land on which the development is carried out of any expenses recoverable by the relevant local planning authority under subsection (1).

(6) A person commits an offence if the person wilfully obstructs a person acting in the exercise of powers under subsection (1).

(7) A person guilty of an offence under subsection (6) is liable on summary conviction to a fine not exceeding level 3 on the standard scale.

Injunctions

171 Injunctions

(1) A local planning authority may apply to the court for an injunction if it considers it necessary or expedient for any actual or apprehended prohibited activity to be restrained by injunction.

(2) Prohibited activity means activity that constitutes an offence under section 160 or 161 in relation to land in the area of the local planning authority.

(3) On an application under this section the court may grant such an injunction as the court thinks fit for the purpose of restraining the prohibited activity.

(4) In this section 'the court' means the High Court or [the county court][1].

1 Words substituted by Crime and Courts Act 2013, s 17(5), Sch 9, para 52(1)(b), (2) (22 April 2014: subject to transitional provision specified in Crime and Courts Act 2013 (Commencement No. 10 and Transitional Provision) Order 2014, SI 2014/954, art 3).

Isles of Scilly

172 Isles of Scilly

(1) The Secretary of State may by order provide for the exercise by the Council of the Isles of Scilly in relation to land in the Council's area of any functions exercisable by a local planning authority under any provision of this Part.

(2) Before making an order under this section the Secretary of State must consult the Council of the Isles of Scilly.

The relevant local planning authority

173 The relevant local planning authority

(1) This section applies for the purposes of this Part.

(2) The relevant local planning authority in relation to any land is the local planning authority for the area in which the land is situated. This is subject to subsections (3) to (5).

(3) Subsections (4) and (5) apply if the land is in an area for which there is both a district planning authority and a county planning authority.

(4) If any of the relevant development is the construction or alteration of a hazardous waste facility within section 14(1)(p), the relevant local planning authority is the county planning authority.

(5) In any other case, the relevant local planning authority is the district planning authority.

(6) 'The relevant development' is—

(a) if the relevant offence is an offence under section 160 or 161(1)(a), the development referred to in section 160(1) or 161(1)(a);

(b) if the relevant offence is an offence under section 161(1)(b), the development to which the order granting development consent mentioned in section 161(1)(b) relates.

(7) 'The relevant offence' is the offence by reference to which a provision of this Part confers a function on a local planning authority.

Part 9 Changes to existing planning regimes

Chapter 1 Changes related to development consent regime

174–177 ...

Amend Town and Country Planning Act 1990 and Town and Country Planning (Scotland) Act 1997.

Grants

178 Grants for advice and assistance: Scotland

(1) The Secretary of State may make grants for the purpose of assisting any person to provide advice and assistance in connection with any matter which is related to the application of this Act to Scotland.

(2) The Secretary of State may, as respects any such grant, provide that it is to be subject to such terms and conditions as the Secretary of State thinks appropriate.

179 ...

Repealed by Local Democracy, Economic Development and Construction Act 2009, s 146(1), Sch 7, Pt 4 (1 April 2010 as SI 2009/3318).

Chapter 2 Other changes to existing planning regimes

180 ...

Amends Planning and Compulsory Purchase Act 2004.

181 ...

Repealed by Local Democracy, Economic Development and Construction Act 2009, s 146(1), Sch 7, Pt 4 (1 April 2010 as SI 2009/3318).

182–186 ...

Amend Planning and Compulsory Purchase Act 2004.

Determination of applications

187 Power to decline to determine applications: amendments

Schedule 7 (power to decline to determine applications: amendments) has effect.

188–192 ...

Amend Town and Country Planning Act 1990.

Trees

193 Existing tree preservation orders: transitional provision

(1) This section applies to a tree preservation order made before the appointed day.

(2) With effect from the beginning of the appointed day, a tree preservation order to which this section applies shall have effect with the omission of all of its provisions other than any that have effect for the purpose of identifying the order or for the purpose of identifying the trees, groups of trees or woodlands in respect of which the order—

(a) is in force, or

(b) may at any later time be in force.

(3) In this section—

'the appointed day'—

(a) in relation to England means the day on which subsection (1) comes fully into force in relation to England, and

(b) in relation to Wales means the day on which subsection (1) comes fully into force in relation to Wales;

'tree preservation order' means an order made under, or an order having effect as if made under, section 198(1) of TCPA 1990.

Use of land

194 Use of land: power to override easements and other rights

(1) [...][1]

(2) The Welsh Ministers may by order amend Schedule 4 to the Welsh Development Agency Act 1975 (c. 70) for the purpose of authorising the use in accordance with planning permission of land acquired under section 21A of that Act, even if the use involves—

(a) interference with an interest or right to which paragraph 6 of that Schedule applies, or

(b) a breach of a restriction as to the user of land arising by virtue of a contract.

(3) The power to make an order under subsection (2) is exercisable by statutory instrument.

(4) The power includes—

(a) power to make different provision for different purposes (including different areas);

(b) power to make incidental, consequential, supplementary, transitional or transitory provision or savings.

(5) No order may be made under subsection (2) unless a draft of the instrument containing the order has been laid before, and approved by resolution of, the National Assembly for Wales.

1 Repealed by Housing and Planning Act 2016, s 206, Sch 19, paras 13, 14 (13 July 2016).

195–196 ...

Amend Town and Country Planning Act 1990, Planning (Listed Buildings and Conservation Areas) Act 1990 and Planning (Hazardous Substances) Act 1990.

Appeals

197 Appeals: miscellaneous amendments

Schedule 11 (appeals: miscellaneous amendments) has effect.

198–201 ...

Amend Town and Country Planning Act 1990 and Planning and Compensation Act 1991.

Part 10 Wales

202 ...

Repealed by Wales Act 2017, s 69(1), Sch 6, para 75 (1 April 2018).

203 Power to make provision in relation to Wales

(1) The Welsh Ministers may by order make provision—

(a) which has an effect in relation to Wales that corresponds to the effect an England-only provision has in relation to England;

(b) conferring power on the Welsh Ministers to do anything in relation to Wales that corresponds to anything the Secretary of State has power to do by virtue of an England-only provision.

(2) The England-only provisions are—

section 184 (correction of errors in decisions);

section 189 (compensation where development order or local development order withdrawn);

section 190 (power to make non-material changes to planning permission);

section 194(1) and Schedule 9 (use of land: power to override easements and other rights);

section 195 (applications and appeals by statutory undertakers);

section 196 and Schedule 10 (determination of procedure for certain proceedings);

paragraphs 2(3) and (4) and 3(3) of Schedule 7.

(3) Before an England-only provision is brought into force—

(a) the reference in subsection (1)(a) to the effect an England-only provision has is to be read as a reference to the effect the provision would have, if it were in force;

(b) the reference in subsection (1)(b) to anything the Secretary of State has power to do by virtue of an England-only provision is to be read as a reference to anything the Secretary of State would have power to do by virtue of the provision, if it were in force.

(4) The Welsh Ministers may by order make provision for the purpose of reversing the effect of any provision made in exercise of the power conferred by subsection (1).

(5) The Secretary of State may make an order in consequence of an order under subsection (1) for the purpose of ensuring that an England-only provision continues to have (or will when brought into force have) the effect in relation to England that it would have had if the order under subsection (1) had not been made.

(6) An order under this section may amend, repeal, revoke or otherwise modify a provision of—

(a) an Act, or

(b) an instrument made under an Act.

(7) The powers of the Welsh Ministers to make orders under this section are exercisable by statutory instrument.

(8) Those powers include—

(a) power to make different provision for different purposes (including different areas);

(b) power to make incidental, consequential, supplementary, transitional or transitory provision or savings.

(9) No order may be made by the Welsh Ministers under this section unless a draft of the instrument containing the order has been laid before, and approved by resolution of, the National Assembly for Wales.

204 Wales: transitional provision in relation to blighted land

(1) During the transitional period the repeal by PCPA 2004 of paragraphs 1 to 4 of Schedule 13 to TCPA 1990 in relation to Wales is subject to subsection (2).

(2) That repeal does not affect anything which is required or permitted to be done for the purposes of Chapter 2 of Part 6 of TCPA 1990 (interests affected by planning proposals: blight) in relation to land falling within any of paragraphs 1, 2, 3 and 4 of Schedule 13 to TCPA 1990.

(3) The transitional period is the period during which—

(a) in the case of land falling within paragraph 1 of Schedule 13 to TCPA 1990, a structure plan continues to be or to be comprised in the development plan for an area in Wales by virtue of Part 3 of Schedule 5 to the Local Government (Wales) Act 1994 (c. 19) and Part 1A of Schedule 2 to TCPA 1990;

(b) in the case of land falling within paragraph 2 of Schedule 13 to TCPA 1990, a local plan continues to be or to be comprised in the development plan for an area in Wales by virtue of Part 3 of Schedule 5 to the Local Government (Wales) Act 1994 and Part 1A of Schedule 2 to TCPA 1990;

(c) in the case of land falling within paragraphs 3 or 4 of Schedule 13 to TCPA 1990, a unitary development plan continues to form part of the development plan for an area in Wales by virtue of article 3(1) and (2) of the PCPA No.6 Order 2005.

(4) In this section 'PCPA No.6 Order 2005' means the Planning and Compulsory Purchase Act 2004 (Commencement No.6, Transitional Provisions and Savings) Order 2005 (S.I. 2005/2847).

(5) This section is deemed to have come into force on the same day as the repeal of paragraphs 1 to 4 of Schedule 13 to TCPA 1990 came into force in relation to Wales (see Article 2(e) and (g) of the PCPA No.6 Order 2005).

Part 11 Community Infrastructure Levy

205 The levy

(1) The Secretary of State may with the consent of the Treasury make regulations providing for the imposition of a charge to be known as Community Infrastructure Levy (CIL).

(2) In making the regulations the Secretary of State shall aim to ensure that the overall purpose of CIL is to ensure that costs incurred in [supporting][1] the development of an area can be

funded (wholly or partly) by owners or developers of land [in a way that does not make development of the area economically unviable][2].

(3) The Table describes the provisions of this Part.

Section	Topic
Section 206	The charge
Section 207	Joint committees
Sections 208 and 209	Liability
Section 210	Charities
Section 211	Amount
Sections 212 to 214	Charging schedule
Section 215	Appeals
[Sections 216 to 216B][3]	Application
Section 217	Collection
Section 218	Enforcement
Section 219	Compensation
Section 220	Procedure
Section 221	Secretary of State
Section 222	CIL regulations and orders: general
Section 223	Relationship with other powers
Section 224	Amendments
Section 225	Repeals

(4) In those sections regulations under this section are referred to as 'CIL regulations'.

1 Words substituted by Localism Act 2011, s 115(1), (2)(a) (15 January 2012 subject to transitional and savings provisions specified in SI 2012/57, arts 6, 7, 9, 10 and 11).

2 Words inserted by Localism Act 2011, s 115(1), (2)(b) (15 January 2012 subject to transitional and savings provisions specified in SI 2012/57, arts 6, 7, 9, 10 and 11).

3 Words substituted by Localism Act 2011, s 115(1), (3) (15 January 2012 subject to transitional and savings provisions specified in SI 2012/57, arts 6, 7, 9, 10 and 11).

206 The charge

(1) A charging authority may charge CIL in respect of development of land in its area.

(2) A local planning authority is the charging authority for its area.

(3) But—

(a) the Mayor of London is a charging authority for Greater London (in addition to the local planning authorities),

(b) the Broads Authority is the only charging authority for the Broads (within the meaning given by section 2(3) of the Norfolk and Suffolk Broads Act 1988 (c. 4)), and

(c) the Council of the Isles of Scilly is the only charging authority for the Isles of Scilly.

(4) CIL regulations may provide for any of the following to be the charging authority for an area, or in the case of Greater London one of the charging authorities, in place of the charging authority under subsection (2), (3)(b) or (c)—

(a) a county council,

(b) a county borough council,

(c) a district council,

(d) a metropolitan district council, and

(e) a London borough council (within the meaning of TCPA 1990).

(5) In this section, 'local planning authority' has the meaning given by—

(a) section 37 of PCPA 2004 in relation to England, [except that a Mayoral development corporation is a local planning authority for the purposes of this section only if it is the local planning authority for all purposes of Part 2 of PCPA 2004 in respect of the whole of its area and all kinds of development,][1] and

(b) section 78 of PCPA 2004 in relation to Wales.

[(6) CIL regulations may make transitional provision in connection with, or in anticipation of, a Mayoral development corporation—

(a) becoming a charging authority as a result of the operation of subsection (2), or

(b) ceasing to be a charging authority as a result of the operation of that subsection.][2]

1 Words inserted by Localism Act 2011, s 222, Sch 22, paras 59, 61(2) (15 January 2012).
2 Inserted by Localism Act 2011, s 222, Sch 22, paras 59, 61(3) (15 January 2012).

207 Joint committees

(1) This section applies if a joint committee that includes a charging authority is established under section 29 of PCPA 2004.

(2) CIL regulations may provide that the joint committee is to exercise specified functions, in respect of the area specified in the agreement under section 29(1) of PCPA 2004, on behalf of the charging authority.

(3) The regulations may make provision corresponding to provisions relating to joint committees in Part 6 of the Local Government Act 1972 (c. 70) in respect of the discharge of the specified functions.

208 Liability

(1) Where liability to CIL would arise in respect of proposed development (in accordance with provision made by a charging authority under and by virtue of section 206 and CIL regulations) a person may assume liability to pay the levy.

(2) An assumption of liability—

(a) may be made before development commences, and

(b) must be made in accordance with any provision of CIL regulations about the procedure for assuming liability.

(3) A person who assumes liability for CIL before the commencement of development becomes liable when development is commenced in reliance on planning permission.

(4) CIL regulations must make provision for an owner or developer of land to be liable for CIL where development is commenced in reliance on planning permission if—

(a) nobody has assumed liability in accordance with the regulations, or

(b) other specified circumstances arise (such as the insolvency or withdrawal of a person who has assumed liability).

(5) CIL regulations may make provision about—

(a) joint liability (with or without several liability);

(b) liability of partnerships;

(c) assumption of partial liability (and subsection (4)(a) applies where liability has not been wholly assumed);

(d) apportionment of liability (which may—

(i) include provision for referral to a specified person or body for determination, and

(ii) include provision for appeals);

(e) withdrawal of assumption of liability;

(f) cancellation of assumption of liability by a charging authority (in which case subsection (4)(a) applies);

(g) transfer of liability (whether before or after development commences and whether or not liability has been assumed).

(6) The amount of any liability for CIL is to be calculated by reference to the time when planning permission first permits the development as a result of which the levy becomes payable.

(7) CIL regulations may make provision for liability for CIL to arise where development which requires planning permission is commenced without it (and subsection (6) is subject to this subsection).

(8) CIL regulations may provide for liability to CIL to arise in respect of a development where—

(a) the development was exempt from CIL, or subject to a reduced rate of CIL charge, and

(b) the description or purpose of the development changes.

209 Liability: interpretation of key terms

(1) In section 208 'development' means—

(a) anything done by way of or for the purpose of the creation of a new building, or

(b) anything done to or in respect of an existing building.

(2) CIL regulations may provide for—

(a) works or changes in use of a specified kind not to be treated as development;

(b) the creation of, or anything done to or in respect of, a structure of a specified kind to be treated as development.

(3) CIL regulations must include provision for determining when development is treated as commencing.

(4) Regulations under subsection (3) may, in particular, provide for development to be treated as commencing when some specified activity or event is undertaken or occurs, where the activity or event—

(a) is not development within the meaning of subsection (1), but

(b) has a specified kind of connection with a development within the meaning of that subsection.

(5) CIL regulations must define planning permission (which may include planning permission within the meaning of TCPA 1990 and any other kind of permission or consent (however called, and whether general or specific)).

(6) CIL regulations must include provision for determining the time at which planning permission is treated as first permitting development; and the regulations may, in particular, make provision—

(a) about outline planning permission;

(b) for permission to be treated as having been given at a particular time in the case of general consents.

(7) For the purposes of section 208—

(a) 'owner' of land means a person who owns an interest in the land, and

(b) 'developer' means a person who is wholly or partly responsible for carrying out a development.

(8) CIL regulations may make provision for a person to be or not to be treated as an owner or developer of land in specified circumstances.

210 Charities

(1) CIL regulations must provide for an exemption from liability to pay CIL in respect of a development where—

(a) the person who would otherwise be liable to pay CIL in respect of the development is a relevant charity in England and Wales, and

(b) the building or structure in respect of which CIL liability would otherwise arise is to be used wholly or mainly for a charitable purpose of the charity within the meaning of [section 2 of the Charities Act 2011][1].

(2) CIL regulations may—

(a) provide for an exemption from liability to pay CIL where the person who would otherwise be liable to pay CIL in respect of the development is an institution established for a charitable purpose;

(b) require charging authorities to make arrangements for an exemption from, or reduction in, liability to pay CIL where the person who would otherwise be liable to pay CIL in respect of the development is an institution established for a charitable purpose.

(3) Regulations under subsection (1) or (2) may provide that an exemption or reduction does not apply if specified conditions are satisfied.

(4) For the purposes of subsection (1), a relevant charity in England and Wales is an institution which—

(a) is registered in the register of charities kept by the Charity Commission under [section 29 of the Charities Act 2011][2], or

(b) is a charity within the meaning of [section 1(1) of the Charities Act 2011 but is not required to be registered in the register kept under section 29 of that Act][3].

(5) In subsection (2), a charitable purpose is a purpose falling within [section 3(1) of the Charities Act 2011;][4] but CIL regulations may provide for an institution of a specified kind to be, or not to be, treated as an institution established for a charitable purpose.

1 Words substituted by Charities Act 2011, 354(1), Sch 7, para 136(1), (2) (14 March 2012: substitution has effect subject to transitional provisions and savings specified in Charities Act 2011, s 354(1), (2), Sch 7, para 2, Sch 8).
2 Words substituted by Charities Act 2011, 354(1), Sch 7, para 136(1), (3)(a) (14 March 2012: substitution has effect subject to transitional provisions and savings specified in Charities Act 2011, s 354(1), (2), Sch 7, para 2, Sch 8).
3 Words substituted by Charities Act 2011, 354(1), Sch 7, para 136(1), (3)(b) (14 March 2012: substitution has effect subject to transitional provisions and savings specified in Charities Act 2011, s 354(1), (2), Sch 7, para 2, Sch 8).
4 Words substituted by Charities Act 2011, 354(1), Sch 7, para 136(1), (4) (14 March 2012: substitution has effect subject to transitional provisions and savings specified in Charities Act 2011, s 354(1), (2), Sch 7, para 2, Sch 8).

211 Amount

(1) A charging authority which proposes to charge CIL must issue a document (a 'charging schedule') setting rates, or other criteria, by reference to which the amount of CIL chargeable in respect of development in its area is to be determined.

(2) A charging authority, in setting rates or other criteria, must have regard, to the extent and in the manner specified by CIL regulations, to—

(a) actual and expected costs of infrastructure (whether by reference to lists prepared by virtue of section 216(5)(a) or otherwise);

(b) matters specified by CIL regulations relating to the economic viability of development (which may include, in particular, actual or potential economic effects of planning permission or of the imposition of CIL);

(c) other actual and expected sources of funding for infrastructure.

(3) CIL regulations may make other provision about setting rates or other criteria.

(4) The regulations may, in particular, permit or require charging authorities in setting rates or other criteria—

(a) to have regard, to the extent and in the manner specified by the regulations, to actual or expected administrative expenses in connection with CIL;

[(aa) to have regard, to the extent and in the manner specified by the regulations, to actual and expected costs of anything other than infrastructure that is concerned with addressing demands that development places on an area (whether by reference to lists prepared by virtue of section 216(5)(a) or otherwise);

(ab) to have regard, to the extent and in the manner specified by the regulations, to other actual and expected sources of funding for anything other than infrastructure that is concerned with addressing demands that development places on an area;][1]

(b) to have regard, to the extent and in the manner specified by the regulations, to values used or documents produced for other statutory purposes;

(c) to integrate the process, to the extent and in the manner specified by the regulations, with processes undertaken for other statutory purposes;

(d) to produce charging schedules having effect in relation to specified periods (subject to revision).

(5) The regulations may permit or require charging schedules to adopt specified methods of calculation.

(6) In particular, the regulations may—

(a) permit or require charging schedules to operate by reference to descriptions or purposes of development;

(b) permit or require charging schedules to operate by reference to any measurement of the amount or nature of development (whether by reference to measurements of floor space, to numbers or intended uses of buildings, to numbers or intended uses of units within buildings, to allocation of space within buildings or units, to values or expected values or in any other way);

(c) permit or require charging schedules to operate by reference to the nature or existing use of the place where development is undertaken;

(d) permit or require charging schedules to operate by reference to an index used for determining a rate of inflation;

(e) permit or require charging schedules to operate by reference to values used or documents produced for other statutory purposes;

(f) provide, or permit or require provision, for differential rates, which may include provision for supplementary charges, a nil rate, increased rates or reductions.

(7) A charging authority may consult, or take other steps, in connection with the preparation of a charging schedule (subject to CIL regulations).

[(7A) A charging authority must use appropriate available evidence to inform the charging authority's preparation of a charging schedule.

(7B) CIL regulations may make provision about the application of subsection (7A) including, in particular—

(a) provision as to evidence that is to be taken to be appropriate,

(b) provision as to evidence that is to be taken to be not appropriate,

(c) provision as to evidence that is to be taken to be available,

(d) provision as to evidence that is to be taken to be not available,

(e) provision as to how evidence is, and as to how evidence is not, to be used,

(f) provision as to evidence that is, and as to evidence that is not, to be used,

(g) provision as to evidence that may, and as to evidence that need not, be used, and

(h) provision as to how the use of evidence is to inform the preparation of a charging schedule.][2]

(8) The regulations may require a charging authority to provide in specified circumstances an estimate of the amount of CIL chargeable in respect of development of land.

(9) A charging authority may revise a charging schedule.

(10) This section and sections 212, 213 and 214(1) and (2) apply to the revision of a charging schedule as they apply to the preparation of a charging schedule.

1 Inserted by Localism Act 2011, s 115(1), (4) (15 January 2012 subject to transitional and savings provisions specified in SI 2012/57, arts 6, 7, 9, 10 and 11).
2 Inserted by Localism Act 2011, s 114(1), (2) (16 November 2011: insertion does not apply in relation to cases where an examiner submits recommendations to a charging authority before the coming into force of Localism Act 2011, s 114, but subject to that the cases in relation to which this amendment applies include a case in which steps in relation to the charging schedule have been taken before then).

212 Charging schedule: examination

(1) Before approving a charging schedule a charging authority must appoint a person ('the examiner') to examine a draft.

(2) The charging authority must appoint someone who, in the opinion of the authority—

(a) is independent of the charging authority, and

(b) has appropriate qualifications and experience.

(3) The charging authority may, with the agreement of the examiner, appoint persons to assist the examiner.

[(4) In this section and sections 212A and 213 'the drafting requirements' means the requirements of this Part and CIL regulations (including the requirements to have regard to the matters listed in section 211(2) and (4)), so far as relevant to the drafting of the schedule.

(7) The examiner must consider whether the drafting requirements have been complied with and—

(a) make recommendations in accordance with section 212A, and

(b) give reasons for the recommendations.][1]

(8) The charging authority must publish the recommendations and reasons.

(9) CIL regulations must require a charging authority to allow anyone who makes representations about a draft charging schedule to be heard by the examiner; and the regulations may make provision about timing and procedure.

(10) CIL regulations may make provision for examiners to reconsider their decisions with a view to correcting errors (before or after the approval of a charging schedule).

(11) The charging authority may withdraw a draft.

1 Section 212(4) and (7) substituted for s 212(4)–(7) by Localism Act 2011, s 114(1), (3) (16 November 2011: substitution does not apply in relation to cases where an examiner submits recommendations to a charging authority before the coming into force of Localism Act 2011, s 114, but subject to that the cases in relation to which this amendment applies include a case in which steps in relation to the charging schedule have been taken before then).

[212A Charging schedule: examiner's recommendations

(1) This section applies in relation to the examination, under section 212, of a draft charging schedule.

(2) If the examiner considers—

(a) that there is any respect in which the drafting requirements have not been complied with, and

(b) that the non-compliance with the drafting requirements cannot be remedied by the making of modifications to the draft,

the examiner must recommend that the draft be rejected.

(3) Subsection (4) applies if the examiner considers—

(a) that there is any respect in which the drafting requirements have not been complied with, and

(b) that the non-compliance with the drafting requirements could be remedied by the making of modifications to the draft.

(4) The examiner must—

(a) specify the respects in which the drafting requirements have not been complied with,

(b) recommend modifications that the examiner considers sufficient and necessary to remedy that non-compliance, and

(c) recommend that the draft be approved with—

(i) those modifications, or

(ii) other modifications sufficient and necessary to remedy that non-compliance.

(5) Subject to subsections (2) to (4), the examiner must recommend that the draft be approved.

(6) If the examiner makes recommendations under subsection (4), the examiner may recommend other modifications with which the draft should be approved in the event that it is approved.

(7) If the examiner makes recommendations under subsection (5), the examiner may recommend modifications with which the draft should be approved in the event that it is approved.][1]

1 Inserted by Localism Act 2011, s 114(1), (4) (16 November 2011: insertion does not apply in relation to cases where an examiner submits recommendations to a charging authority before the coming into force of Localism Act 2011, s 114, but subject to that the cases in relation to which this amendment applies include a case in which steps in relation to the charging schedule have been taken before then).

213 Charging schedule: approval

[(1) A charging authority may approve a charging schedule only if—

(a) the examiner makes recommendations under section 212A(4) or (5), and

(b) the charging authority has had regard to those recommendations and the examiner's reasons for them.

(1A) Accordingly, a charging authority may not approve a charging schedule if, under section 212A(2), the examiner recommends rejection.

(1B) If the examiner makes recommendations under section 212A(4), the charging authority may approve the charging schedule only if it does so with modifications that are sufficient and necessary to remedy the non-compliance specified under section 212A(4)(a) (although those modifications need not be the ones recommended under section 212A(4)(b)).

(1C) If a charging authority approves a charging schedule, it may do so with all or none, or some one or more, of the modifications (if any) recommended under section 212A(6) or (7).

(1D) The modifications with which a charging schedule may be approved include only—

(a) modifications required by subsection (1B), and

(b) modifications allowed by subsection (1C).][1]

(2) A charging authority (other than the Mayor of London) must approve a charging schedule—

(a) at a meeting of the authority, and

(b) by a majority of votes of members present.

(3) The Mayor of London must approve a charging schedule personally.

[(3A) Subsection (3B) applies if—

(a) the examiner makes recommendations under section 212A(4), and

(b) the charging schedule is approved by the charging authority.

(3B) The charging authority must publish a report setting out how the charging schedule as approved remedies the non-compliance specified under section 212A(4)(a).

(3C) CIL regulations may make provision about the form or contents of a report under subsection (3B).][2]

(4) CIL regulations may make provision for the correction of errors in a charging schedule after approval.

[(5) In this section 'examiner' means examiner under section 212.][3]

1 Section 213(1)–(1D) substituted for s 213(1) by Localism Act 2011, s 114(1), (5) (16 November 2011: substtitution does not apply in relation to cases where an examiner submits recommendations to a charging authority before the coming into force of Localism Act 2011, s 114, but subject to that the cases in relation to which this amendment applies include a case in which steps in relation to the charging schedule have been taken before then).
2 Inserted by Localism Act 2011, s 114(1), (6) (16 November 2011: insertion does not apply in relation to cases where an examiner submits recommendations to a charging authority before the coming into force of Localism Act 2011, s 114, but subject to that the cases in relation to which this amendment applies include a case in which steps in relation to the charging schedule have been taken before then).
3 Inserted by Localism Act 2011, s 114(1), (7) (16 November 2011: insertion does not apply in relation to cases where an examiner submits recommendations to a charging authority before the coming into force of Localism Act 2011, s 114, but subject to that the cases in relation to which this amendment applies include a case in which steps in relation to the charging schedule have been taken before then).

214 Charging schedule: effect

(1) A charging schedule approved under section 213 may not take effect before it is published by the charging authority.

(2) CIL regulations may make provision about publication of a charging schedule after approval.

(3) A charging authority may determine that a charging schedule is to cease to have effect.

(4) CIL regulations may provide that a charging authority may only make a determination under subsection (3) in circumstances specified by the regulations.

(5) A charging authority (other than the Mayor of London) must make a determination under subsection (3)—

(a) at a meeting of the authority, and

(b) by a majority of votes of members present.

(6) The Mayor of London must make a determination under subsection (3) personally.

215 Appeals

(1) CIL regulations must provide for a right of appeal on a question of fact in relation to the application of methods for calculating CIL to a person appointed by the Commissioners for Her Majesty's Revenue and Customs.

(2) The regulations must require that the person appointed under subsection (1) is—

(a) a valuation officer appointed under section 61 of the Local Government Finance Act 1988 (c. 41), or

(b) a district valuer within the meaning of section 622 of the Housing Act 1985 (c. 68).

(3) Regulations under this section or section 208(5)(d)(ii) may, in particular, make provision about—

(a) the period within which the right of appeal may be exercised,

(b) the procedure on an appeal, and

(c) the payment of fees, and award of costs, in relation to an appeal.

(4) In any proceedings for judicial review of a decision on an appeal, the defendant shall be the Commissioners for Her Majesty's Revenue and Customs and not the person appointed under subsection (1).

216 Application

(1) Subject to [sections 216A(1), 216B(2) and][1] 219(5), CIL regulations must require the authority that charges CIL to apply it, or cause it to be applied, to [supporting development by funding the provision, improvement, replacement, operation or maintenance of infrastructure][2].

(2) In [this section (except subsection (3)) and sections 216A(2) and 216B(2)][3] 'infrastructure' includes—

(a) roads and other transport facilities,

(b) flood defences,

(c) schools and other educational facilities,

(d) medical facilities,

(e) sporting and recreational facilities, [and][4]

(f) open spaces [.][5]

[...][6]

(3) The regulations may amend subsection (2) so as to—

(a) add, remove or vary an entry in the list of matters included within the meaning of 'infrastructure';

(b) list matters excluded from the meaning of 'infrastructure'.

(4) The regulations may specify—

(a) works, installations and other facilities [whose provision, improvement or replacement may or is to be, or may not][7] be, funded by CIL,

[(aa) maintenance activities and operational activities (including operational activities of a promotional kind) in connection with infrastructure that may or are to be, or may not be, funded by CIL,

(ab) things within section 216A(2)(b) that may or are to be, or may not be, funded by CIL passed to a person in discharge of a duty under section 216A(1),

(ac) things within section 216B(2)(b) that may or are to be, or may not be, funded by CIL to which provision under section 216B(2) relates,][8]

(b) criteria for determining the areas [that may benefit from funding][9] by CIL in respect of land, and

(c) what is to be, or not to be, treated as funding.

(5) The regulations may—

(a) require charging authorities to prepare and publish a list of [what is][10] to be, or may be, wholly or partly funded by CIL;

(b) include provision about the procedure to be followed in preparing a list (which may include provision for consultation, for the appointment of an independent person or a combination);

(c) include provision about the circumstances in which a charging authority may and may not apply CIL to [anything][11] not included on the list.

(6) In making provision about funding the regulations may, in particular—

(a) permit CIL to be used to reimburse expenditure already incurred;

(b) permit CIL to be reserved for expenditure that may be incurred [in the future][12];

(c) permit CIL to be applied (either generally or subject to limits set by or determined in accordance with the regulations) to administrative expenses in connection with infrastructure [or anything within section 216A(2)(b) or 216B(2)(b)][13] or in connection with CIL;

(d) include provision for the giving of loans, guarantees or indemnities;

(e) make provision about the application of CIL where [anything][14] to which it was to be applied no longer [requires][15] funding.

(7) The regulations may—

(a) require a charging authority to account separately, and in accordance with the regulations, for CIL received or due;

(b) require a charging authority to monitor the use made and to be made of CIL in its area;

(c) require a charging authority to report on actual or expected charging, collection and application of CIL;

(d) permit a charging authority to cause money to be applied in respect of things done outside its area;

(e) permit a charging authority or other body to spend money;

(f) permit a charging authority to pass money to another body (and in paragraphs (a) to (e) a reference to a charging authority includes a reference to a body to which a charging authority passes money in reliance on this paragraph).

1 Word substituted by Localism Act 2011, s 115(1), (5)(a)(i) (15 January 2012 subject to transitional and savings provisions specified in SI 2012/57, arts 6, 7, 9, 10 and 11).
2 Words substituted by Localism Act 2011, s 115(1), (5)(a)(ii) (15 January 2012 subject to transitional and savings provisions specified in SI 2012/57, arts 6, 7, 9, 10 and 11).
3 Words substituted by Localism Act 2011, s 115(1), (5)(b) (15 January 2012 subject to transitional and savings provisions specified in SI 2012/57, arts 6, 7, 9, 10 and 11).
4 Word inserted by Community Infrastructure Levy Regulations 2010, SI 2010/948, reg 63(1), (2) (6 April 2010).
5 Word substituted by Community Infrastructure Levy Regulations 2010, SI 2010/948, reg 63(1), (3) (6 April 2010).
6 Repealed by Community Infrastructure Levy Regulations 2010, SI 2010/948, reg 63(1), (4) (6 April 2010).
7 Words substituted by Localism Act 2011, s 115(1), (5)(c) (15 January 2012 subject to transitional and savings provisions specified in SI 2012/57, arts 6, 7, 9, 10 and 11).
8 Inserted by Localism Act 2011, s 115(1), (5)(d) (15 January 2012 subject to transitional and savings provisions specified in SI 2012/57, arts 6, 7, 9, 10 and 11).
9 Words substituted by Localism Act 2011, s 115(1), (5)(e) (15 January 2012 subject to transitional and savings provisions specified in SI 2012/57, arts 6, 7, 9, 10 and 11).
10 Words substituted by Localism Act 2011, s 115(1), (5)(f) (15 January 2012 subject to transitional and savings provisions specified in SI 2012/57, arts 6, 7, 9, 10 and 11).
11 Word substituted by Localism Act 2011, s 115(1), (5)(g) (15 January 2012 subject to transitional and savings provisions specified in SI 2012/57, arts 6, 7, 9, 10 and 11).
12 Words substituted by Localism Act 2011, s 115(1), (5)(h) (15 January 2012 subject to transitional and savings provisions specified in SI 2012/57, arts 6, 7, 9, 10 and 11).
13 Words inserted by Localism Act 2011, s 115(1), (5)(i) (15 January 2012 subject to transitional and savings provisions specified in SI 2012/57, arts 6, 7, 9, 10 and 11).
14 Words substituted by Localism Act 2011, s 115(1), (5)(j)(i) (15 January 2012 subject to transitional and savings provisions specified in SI 2012/57, arts 6, 7, 9, 10 and 11).
15 Word substituted by Localism Act 2011, s 115(1), (5)(j)(ii) (15 January 2012 subject to transitional and savings provisions specified in SI 2012/57, arts 6, 7, 9, 10 and 11).

[216A Duty to pass receipts to other persons

(1) CIL regulations may require that CIL received in respect of development of land in an area is to be passed by the charging authority that charged the CIL to a person other than that authority.

(2) CIL regulations must contain provision to secure that money passed to a person in discharge of a duty under subsection (1) is used to support the development of the area to which the duty relates, or of any part of that area, by funding—

(a) the provision, improvement, replacement, operation or maintenance of infrastructure, or

(b) anything else that is concerned with addressing demands that development places on an area.

(3) A duty under subsection (1) may relate to—

(a) the whole of a charging authority's area or the whole of the combined area of two or more charging authorities, or

(b) part only of such an area or combined area.

(4) CIL regulations may make provision about the persons to whom CIL may or must, or may not, be passed in discharge of a duty under subsection (1).

(5) A duty under subsection (1) may relate—

(a) to all CIL (if any) received in respect of the area to which the duty relates, or

(b) such part of that CIL as is specified in, or determined under or in accordance with, CIL regulations.

(6) CIL regulations may make provision in connection with the timing of payments in discharge of a duty under subsection (1).

(7) CIL regulations may, in relation to CIL passed to a person in discharge of a duty under subsection (1), make provision about—

(a) accounting for the CIL,

(b) monitoring its use,

(c) reporting on its use,

(d) responsibilities of charging authorities for things done by the person in connection with the CIL,

(e) recovery of the CIL, and any income or profits accruing in respect of it or from its application, in cases where—

(i) anything to be funded by it has not been provided, or

(ii) it has been misapplied,

including recovery of sums or other assets representing it or any such income or profits, and

(f) use of anything recovered in cases where—

(i) anything to be funded by the CIL has not been provided, or

(ii) the CIL has been misapplied.

(8) This section does not limit section 216(7)(f).][1]

1 Inserted by Localism Act 2011, s 115(1), (6) (15 January 2012 subject to transitional and savings provisions specified in SI 2012/57, arts 6, 7, 9, 10 and 11).

[216B Use of CIL in an area to which section 216A(1) duty does not relate

(1) Subsection (2) applies where—

(a) there is an area to which a particular duty under section 216A(1) relates, and

(b) there is also an area to which that duty does not relate ('the uncovered area').

(2) CIL regulations may provide that the charging authority that charges CIL received in respect of development of land in the uncovered area may apply the CIL, or cause it to be applied, to—

(a) support development by funding the provision, improvement, replacement, operation or maintenance of infrastructure, or

(b) support development of the uncovered area, or of any part of that area, by funding anything else that is concerned with addressing demands that development places on an area.

(3) Provision under subsection (2) may relate to the whole, or part only, of the uncovered area.

(4) Provision under subsection (2) may relate—

(a) to all CIL (if any) received in respect of the area to which the provision relates, or

(b) such part of that CIL as is specified in, or determined under or in accordance with, CIL regulations.][1]

1 Inserted by Localism Act 2011, s 115(1), (6) (15 January 2012 subject to transitional and savings provisions specified in SI 2012/57, arts 6, 7, 9, 10 and 11).

217 Collection

(1) CIL regulations must include provision about the collection of CIL.

(2) The regulations may make provision for payment—

(a) on account;

(b) by instalments.

(3) The regulations may make provision about repayment (with or without interest) in cases of overpayment.

(4) The regulations may make provision about payment in forms other than money (such as making land available, carrying out works or providing services).

(5) The regulations may permit or require a charging authority or other public authority to collect CIL charged by another authority; and section 216(7)(a) and (c) apply to a collecting authority in respect of collection as to a charging authority.

(6) Regulations under this section may replicate or apply (with or without modifications) any enactment relating to the collection of a tax.

(7) Regulations under this section may make provision about the source of payments in respect of Crown interests.

218 Enforcement

(1) CIL regulations must include provision about enforcement of CIL.

(2) The regulations must make provision about the consequences of late payment and failure to pay.

(3) The regulations may make provision about the consequences of failure to assume liability, to give a notice or to comply with another procedure under CIL regulations in connection with CIL.

(4) The regulations may, in particular, include provision—

(a) for the payment of interest;

(b) for the imposition of a penalty or surcharge;

(c) for the suspension or cancellation of a decision relating to planning permission;

(d) enabling an authority to prohibit development pending assumption of liability for CIL or pending payment of CIL;

(e) conferring a power of entry onto land;

(f) requiring the provision of information;

(g) creating a criminal offence (including, in particular, offences relating to evasion or attempted evasion or to the provision of false or misleading information or failure to provide information, and offences relating to the prevention or investigation of other offences created by the regulations);

(h) conferring power to prosecute an offence;

(i) for enforcement of sums owed (whether by action on a debt, by distraint against goods or in any other way);

(j) conferring jurisdiction on a court to grant injunctive or other relief to enforce a provision of the regulations (including a provision included in reliance on this section);

(k) for enforcement in the case of death or insolvency of a person liable for CIL.

(5) CIL regulations may include provision (whether or not in the context of late payment or failure to pay) about registration or notification of actual or potential liability to CIL; and the regulations may include provision—

(a) for the creation of local land charges;

(b) for the registration of local land charges;

(c) for enforcement of local land charges (including, in particular, for enforcement—

(i) against successive owners, and

(ii) by way of sale or other disposal with consent of a court);

(d) for making entries in statutory registers;

(e) for the cancellation of charges and entries.

(6) Regulations under this section may—

(a) replicate or apply (with or without modifications) any enactment relating to the enforcement of a tax;

(b) provide for appeals.

(7) Regulations under this section may provide that any interest, penalty or surcharge payable by virtue of the regulations is to be treated for the purposes of sections 216 to 220 as if it were CIL.

(8) The regulations providing for a surcharge or penalty must ensure that no surcharge or penalty in respect of an amount of CIL exceeds the higher of—

(a) 30% of that amount, and

(b) £20,000.

(9) But the regulations may provide for more than one surcharge or penalty to be imposed in relation to a CIL charge.

(10) The regulations may not authorise entry to a private dwelling without a warrant issued by a justice of the peace.

(11) Regulations under this section creating a criminal offence may not provide for—

(a) [...][1]

(b) a maximum term of imprisonment exceeding 6 months on summary conviction, or

(c) a maximum term of imprisonment exceeding 2 years on conviction on indictment.

(12) The Secretary of State may by order amend subsection (11) to reflect commencement of section 283 of the Criminal Justice Act 2003 (c. 44).

(13) In this Part a reference to administrative expenses in connection with CIL includes a reference to enforcement expenses.

1 Repealed by Legal Aid, Sentencing and Punishment of Offenders Act 2012 (Fines on Summary Conviction) Regulations 2015, SI 2015/664, reg 4(2), Sch 4, para 92 (12 March 2015).

219 Compensation

(1) CIL regulations may require a charging authority or other public authority to pay compensation in respect of loss or damage suffered as a result of enforcement action.

(2) In this section, 'enforcement action' means action taken under regulations under section 218, including—

(a) the suspension or cancellation of a decision relating to planning permission, and

(b) the prohibition of development pending assumption of liability for CIL or pending payment of CIL.

(3) The regulations shall not require payment of compensation—

(a) to a person who has failed to satisfy a liability to pay CIL, or

(b) in other circumstances specified by the regulations.

(4) Regulations under this section may make provision about—

(a) the time and manner in which a claim for compensation is to be made, and

(b) the sums, or the method of determining the sums, payable by way of compensation.

(5) CIL regulations may permit or require a charging authority to apply CIL (either generally or subject to limits set by or determined in accordance with the regulations) for expenditure incurred under this section.

(6) A dispute about compensation may be referred to and determined by the [Upper Tribunal][1].

(7) In relation to the determination of any such question, the provisions of [section][2] 4 of the Land Compensation Act 1961 (c. 33) apply subject to any necessary modifications and to the provisions of CIL regulations.

1 Words substituted by Transfer of Tribunal Functions (Lands Tribunal and Miscellaneous Amendments) Order 2009, SI 2009/1307, art 5(1), (2), Sch 1, paras 291, 296(a) (1 June 2009).

2 Word substituted by Transfer of Tribunal Functions (Lands Tribunal and Miscellaneous Amendments) Order 2009, SI 2009/1307, art 5(1), (2), Sch 1, paras 291, 296(b) (1 June 2009).

220 Community Infrastructure Levy: procedure

(1) CIL regulations may include provision about procedures to be followed in connection with CIL.

(2) In particular, the regulations may make provision about—

(a) procedures to be followed by a charging authority proposing to begin charging CIL;

(b) procedures to be followed by a charging authority in relation to charging CIL;

(c) procedures to be followed by a charging authority proposing to stop charging CIL;

(d) consultation;

(e) the publication or other treatment of reports;

(f) timing and methods of publication;

(g) making documents available for inspection;

(h) providing copies of documents (with or without charge);

(i) the form and content of documents;

(j) giving notice;

(k) serving notices or other documents;

(l) examinations to be held in public in the course of setting or revising rates or other criteria or of preparing lists;

(m) the terms and conditions of appointment of independent persons;

(n) remuneration and expenses of independent persons (which may be required to be paid by the Secretary of State or by a charging authority);

(o) other costs in connection with examinations;

(p) reimbursement of expenditure incurred by the Secretary of State (including provision for enforcement);

(q) apportionment of costs;

(r) combining procedures in connection with CIL with procedures for another purpose of a charging authority (including a purpose of that authority in another capacity);

(s) procedures to be followed in connection with actual or potential liability for CIL.

(3) CIL regulations may make provision about the procedure to be followed in respect of an exemption from CIL or a reduction of CIL; in particular, the regulations may include provision—

(a) about the procedure for determining whether any conditions are satisfied;

(b) requiring a charging authority or other person to notify specified persons of any exemption or reduction;

(c) requiring a charging authority or other person to keep a record of any exemption or reduction.

(4) A provision of this Part conferring express power to make procedural provision in a specified context includes, in particular, power to make provision about the matters specified in subsection (2).

(5) A power in this Part to make provision about publishing something includes a power to make provision about making it available for inspection.

(6) Sections 229 to 231 do not apply to this Part (but CIL regulations may make similar provision).

221 Secretary of State

The Secretary of State may give guidance to a charging authority or other public authority (including an examiner appointed under section 212) about any matter connected with CIL; and the authority must have regard to the guidance.

222 Regulations and orders: general

(1) CIL regulations—

(a) may make provision that applies generally or only to specified cases, circumstances or areas,

(b) may make different provision for different cases, circumstances or areas,

(c) may provide, or allow a charging schedule to provide, for exceptions,

(d) may confer, or allow a charging schedule to confer, a discretionary power on the Secretary of State, a local authority or another specified person,

(e) may apply an enactment, with or without modifications, and

(f) may include provision of a kind permitted by section 232(3)(b) (and incidental, supplemental or consequential provision may include provision disapplying, modifying the effect of or amending an enactment).

(2) CIL regulations—

(a) shall be made by statutory instrument, and

(b) shall not be made unless a draft has been laid before and approved by resolution of the House of Commons.

(3) An order under section 218(12) or 225(2)—

(a) shall be made by statutory instrument, and

(b) may include provision of a kind permitted by subsection (1)(a), (b) or (f) above, but may not amend an Act of Parliament in reliance on subsection (1)(f).

(4) An order under section 218(12) shall be subject to annulment in pursuance of a resolution of either House of Parliament.

(5) An order under section 225(2) shall be subject to annulment in pursuance of a resolution of the House of Commons.

223 Relationship with other powers

(1) CIL regulations may include provision about how the following powers are to be used, or are not to be used—

(a) section 106 of TCPA 1990 (planning obligations), and

(b) section 278 of the Highways Act 1980 (c. 66) (execution of works).

(2) CIL regulations may include provision about the exercise of any other power relating to planning or development.

(3) The Secretary of State may give guidance to a charging or other authority about how a power relating to planning or development is to be exercised; and authorities must have regard to the guidance.

(4) Provision may be made under subsection (1) or (2), and guidance may be given under subsection (3), only if the Secretary of State thinks it necessary or expedient for—

(a) complementing the main purpose of CIL regulations,

(b) enhancing the effectiveness, or increasing the use, of CIL regulations,

(c) preventing agreements, undertakings or other transactions from being used to undermine or circumvent CIL regulations,

(d) preventing agreements, undertakings or other transactions from being used to achieve a purpose that the Secretary of State thinks would better be achieved through the application of CIL regulations, or

(e) preventing or restricting the imposition of burdens, the making of agreements or the giving of undertakings, in addition to CIL.

(5) CIL regulations may provide that a power to give guidance or directions may not be exercised—

(a) in relation to matters specified in the regulations,

(b) in cases or circumstances specified in the regulations,

(c) for a purpose specified in the regulations, or

(d) to an extent specified in the regulations.

224 ...

Amends Local Government Act 1972, Norfolk and Suffolk Broads Act 1988, Deregulation and Contracting Out Act 1994 and Greater London Authority Act 1999.

225 Community Infrastructure Levy: repeals

(1) The following provisions of PCPA 2004 shall cease to have effect—

(a) sections 46 to 48 (planning contribution), and

(b) paragraph 5 of Schedule 6 (repeal of sections 106 to 106B of TCPA 1990 (planning obligations)).

(2) The Treasury may by order repeal the Planning-gain Supplement (Preparations) Act 2007 (c. 2).

Part 12 Final provisions

The Crown and Parliament

226 The Crown

(1) This Act binds the Crown, subject to subsections (2) and (3).

(2) Sections 40, 54, 135, 166, 228 and 231 make special provision in relation to the application of some provisions of this Act to the Crown.

(3) The amendments made by this Act bind the Crown only to the extent that the provisions amended bind the Crown.

227 'Crown land' and 'the appropriate Crown authority'

(1) In this Act, 'Crown land' and 'the appropriate Crown authority' must be read in accordance with this section.

(2) 'Crown land' is land in which there is a Crown interest or a Duchy interest.

(3) For the purposes of this section, a Crown interest is any of the following—

(a) an interest belonging to Her Majesty in right of the Crown or in right of Her private estates;

(b) an interest belonging to a government department or held in trust for Her Majesty for the purposes of a government department;

(c) an interest belonging to an office-holder in the Scottish Administration or held in trust for Her Majesty for the purposes of the Scottish Administration by such an office-holder;

(d) the interest of the Speaker of the House of Lords in those parts of the Palace of Westminster and its precincts occupied on 23 March 1965 by or on behalf of the House of Lords;

(e) the interest of the Speaker of the House of Commons in those parts of the Palace of Westminster and its precincts occupied on 23 March 1965 by or on behalf of the House of Commons;

(f) the interest in any land of—

(i) the Corporate Officer of the House of Lords;

(ii) the Corporate Officer of the House of Commons;

(iii) those two Corporate Officers acting jointly;

(g) such other interest as the Secretary of State specifies by order.

(4) For the purposes of this section, a Duchy interest is—

(a) an interest belonging to Her Majesty in right of the Duchy of Lancaster, or

(b) an interest belonging to the Duchy of Cornwall.

(5) 'The appropriate Crown authority' in relation to any land is—

(a) in the case of land belonging to Her Majesty in right of the Crown and forming part of the Crown Estate, the Crown Estate Commissioners;

(b) in relation to any other land belonging to Her Majesty in right of the Crown, the government department or, as the case may be, office-holder in the Scottish Administration, having the management of the land [or the relevant person][1];

(c) in relation to land belonging to Her Majesty in right of Her private estates, a person appointed by Her Majesty in writing under the Royal Sign Manual or, if no such appointment is made, the Secretary of State;

(d) in relation to land belonging to Her Majesty in right of the Duchy of Lancaster, the Chancellor of the Duchy;

(e) in relation to land belonging to the Duchy of Cornwall, such person as the Duke of Cornwall, or the possessor for the time being of the Duchy, appoints;

(f) in the case of land belonging to a government department or held in trust for Her Majesty for the purposes of a government department, the department;

(g) in the case of land belonging to an office-holder in the Scottish Administration or held in trust for Her Majesty for the purposes of such an office-holder, the office-holder;

(h) in relation to Westminster Hall and the Chapel of St Mary Undercroft, the Lord Great Chamberlain and the Speakers of the House of Lords and the House of Commons acting jointly;

(i) in relation to Her Majesty's Robing Room in the Palace of Westminster, the adjoining staircase and ante-room and the Royal Gallery, the Lord Great Chamberlain.

(j) in relation to land in which there is a Crown interest by virtue of subsection (3)(d) or (f)(i), the Corporate Officer of the House of Lords;

(k) in relation to land in which there is a Crown interest by virtue of subsection (3)(e) or (f)(ii), the Corporate Officer of the House of Commons;

(l) in relation to land in which there is a Crown interest by virtue of subsection (3)(f)(iii), those two Corporate Officers acting jointly.

[(5A) In subsection (5), 'relevant person', in relation to any land to which section 90B(5) of the Scotland Act 1998 applies, means the person who manages that land.][1]

(6) If any question arises as to what authority is the appropriate Crown authority in relation to any land it must be referred to the Treasury, whose decision is final.

(7) References to Her Majesty's private estates must be construed in accordance with section 1 of the Crown Private Estates Act 1862 (c. 37).

(8) References to an office-holder in the Scottish Administration are to be construed in accordance with section 126(7) of the Scotland Act 1998 (c. 46).

1 Inserted by Crown Estate Transfer Scheme 2017, SI 2017/524, art 8, Sch 5, para 40 (1 April 2017).

228 Enforcement in relation to the Crown and Parliament

(1) No act or omission done or suffered by or on behalf of the Crown constitutes an offence under this Act.

(2) For the purposes of this section 'the Crown' includes—

(a) the Duchy of Lancaster;

(b) the Duchy of Cornwall;

(c) the Speaker of the House of Lords;

(d) the Speaker of the House of Commons;

(e) the Corporate Officer of the House of Lords;

(f) the Corporate Officer of the House of Commons.

Service of notices and other documents

229 Service of notices: general

(1) A notice or other document required or authorised to be served, given or supplied under this Act may be served, given or supplied in any of these ways—

(a) by delivering it to the person on whom it is to be served or to whom it is to be given or supplied,

(b) by leaving it at the usual or last known place of abode of that person or, in a case where an address for service has been given by that person, at that address,

(c) by sending it by post, addressed to that person at that person's usual or last known place of abode or, in a case where an address for service has been given by that person, at that address,

(d) by sending it in a prepaid registered letter, or by the recorded delivery service, addressed to that person at that person's usual or last known place of abode or, in a case where an address for service has been given by that person, at that address,

(e) in a case where an address for service using electronic communications has been given by that person, by sending it using electronic communications, in accordance with the condition set out in subsection (2), to that person at that address,

(f) in the case of an incorporated company or body—

(i) by delivering it to the secretary or clerk of the company or body at their registered or principal office,

(ii) by sending it by post, addressed to the secretary or clerk of the company or body at that office,

(iii) by sending it in a prepaid registered letter or, or by the recorded delivery service, addressed to the secretary or clerk of the company or body at that office.

(2) The condition mentioned in subsection (1)(e) is that the notice or other document must be—

(a) capable of being accessed by the person mentioned in that provision,

(b) legible in all material respects, and

(c) in a form sufficiently permanent to be used for subsequent reference.

(3) For the purposes of subsection (2), 'legible in all material respects' means that the information contained in the notice or document is available to that person to no lesser extent than it would be if served, given or supplied by means of a notice or document in printed form.

(4) Subsection (1)(c), (e) and (f)(ii) do not apply to the service, giving or supply of any of the following—

(a) notice under section 53(4)(b);

(b) a compulsory acquisition notice under section 134;

(c) notice under section 163(3);

(d) an information notice under section 167;

(e) a notice of unauthorised development under section 169.

(5) This section is without prejudice to section 233 of the Local Government Act 1972 (c. 70) (general provisions as to service of notices by local authorities).

(6) This section is subject to any contrary provision made by or under this Act.

230 Service of documents to persons interested in or occupying premises

(1) Subsection (2) applies if—

(a) a notice or document is required or authorised to be served on or given or supplied to any person as having an interest in premises, and the name of that person cannot be ascertained after reasonable inquiry, or

(b) a notice or document is required or authorised to be served on or given or supplied to any person as an occupier of premises.

(2) The notice or document is to be taken to be duly served, given or supplied if either the condition in subsection (3) or the condition in subsection (4) is met.

(3) The condition is that the notice or document—

(a) is addressed to the person either by name or by the description of 'the owner' or, as the case may be, 'the occupier' of the premises (describing them), and

(b) is delivered or sent—

(i) in the case of a notice mentioned in section 229(4), in the manner specified in section 229(1)(a), (b) or (d), and

(ii) in any other case, in the manner specified in section 229(1)(a), (b), (c) or (d).

(4) The condition is that the notice or document is so addressed and is marked in such a manner as may be prescribed for securing that it is plainly identifiable as an important communication and—

(a) it is sent to the premises in a prepaid registered letter or by the recorded delivery service and is not returned to the authority sending it, or

(b) it is delivered to a person on those premises, or is affixed conspicuously to an object on those premises.

(5) Subsection (6) applies if—

(a) a notice or other document is required to be served on or given or supplied to all persons who have interests in or are occupiers of premises comprised in any land, and

(b) it appears to the authority required or authorised to serve, give or supply the notice or other document that any part of that land is unoccupied.

(6) The notice or other document is to be taken to be duly served on or given or supplied to all persons having interests in, and on any occupiers of, premises comprised in that part of the land (other than a person who has given to that authority an address for the service of the notice or document on him) if—

(a) it is addressed to 'the owners and any occupiers' of that part of the land (describing it), and

(b) it is affixed conspicuously to an object on the land.

(7) This section is subject to any contrary provision made by or under this Act.

231 Service of notices on the Crown and Parliament

(1) Any notice or other document required under this Act to be served on or given or supplied to the Crown must be served on or given or supplied to the appropriate Crown authority.

(2) Sections 229 and 230 do not apply for the purposes of the service, giving or supply of such a notice or document.

(3) For the purposes of this section 'the Crown' includes—

(a) the Duchy of Lancaster;

(b) the Duchy of Cornwall;

(c) the Speaker of the House of Lords;

(d) the Speaker of the House of Commons;

(e) the Corporate Officer of the House of Lords;

(f) the Corporate Officer of the House of Commons.

General

232 Orders and regulations

(1) Subsections (2) and (3) apply to a power to make an order or regulations conferred on the Secretary of State by this Act, except—

(a) power to make an order granting development consent;

(b) a power conferred by paragraph 1(4) of Schedule 4;

(c) a power to make changes to, or revoke, an order granting development consent;

(d) a power conferred by Part 11 or section 237 or 241.

(2) The power is exercisable by statutory instrument.

(3) The power includes—

(a) power to make different provision for different purposes (including different areas);

(b) power to make incidental, consequential, supplementary, transitional or transitory provision or savings.

(4) A statutory instrument containing an order or regulations under this Act is subject to annulment pursuant to a resolution of either House of Parliament.

This is subject to subsection (5) (and section 222(5)).

(5) Subsection (4) does not apply to a statutory instrument containing—

(a) an order granting development consent;

(b) an order made by virtue of paragraph 1(8) of Schedule 4;

(c) an order changing or revoking an order granting development consent;

(d) an order under section 14(3), [33(5),][1] 111, 160(3), 161(5), 172(1), 203(5) or 227(3)(g);

(e) regulations under section [35(2)(a)(ii),][2] 104(2)(c) or 105(2)(b).

(6) No order may be made under section 14(3), [33(5),][3] 111, 160(3), 161(5), 203(5) or 227(3)(g) unless a draft of the instrument containing the order has been laid before, and approved by resolution of, each House of Parliament.

(7) No regulations may be made under section [35(2)(a)(ii),][4] 104(2)(c) or 105(2)(b) unless a draft of the instrument containing the regulations has been laid before, and approved by resolution of, each House of Parliament.

1 Word inserted by Localism Act 2011, s 131(1), (3)(a) (1 April 2012).
2 Words inserted by Growth and Infrastructure Act 2013, s 26(1), (4)(a) (25 April 2013).
3 Word inserted by Localism Act 2011, s 131(1), (3)(b) (1 April 2012).
4 Words inserted by Growth and Infrastructure Act 2013, s 26(1), (4)(b) (25 April 2013).

233 Directions

(1) A direction given under this Act must be in writing.

(2) A power conferred by this Act to give a direction includes power to vary or revoke the direction.

234 Abbreviated references to Acts

In this Act—

'the Hazardous Substances Act' means the Planning (Hazardous Substances) Act 1990 (c. 10);

'the Listed Buildings Act' means the Planning (Listed Buildings and Conservation Areas) Act 1990 (c. 9);

'PCPA 2004' means the Planning and Compulsory Purchase Act 2004 (c. 5);

'TCPA 1990' means the Town and Country Planning Act 1990 (c. 8).

235 Interpretation

(1) In this Act (except in Part 11)—

'airport' has the meaning given by section 82(1) of the Airports Act 1986 (c. 31);

'alteration', in relation to an airport, must be read in accordance with section 23(6);

'alteration', in relation to a highway, includes stopping up the highway or diverting, improving, raising or lowering it;

'appropriate Crown authority' has the meaning given by section 227;

'building' has the meaning given by section 336(1) of TCPA 1990;

[...][1]

'construction', in relation to so much of a generating station as comprises or is to comprise renewable energy installations, has the same meaning as in Chapter 2 of Part 2 of the Energy Act 2004 (c. 20) (see section 104 of that Act) (and related expressions must be read accordingly);

'construction', in relation to a pipe-line, includes placing (and related expressions must be read accordingly);

[...][1]

'cross-country pipe-line' has the same meaning as in the Pipe-lines Act 1962 (c. 58) (see section 66 of that Act);

'Crown land' has the meaning given by section 227;

[...][1]

['deployable output' means, in relation to a given facility, the annual average volume of water that can be produced per day from that facility under drought conditions, having regard in particular (where applicable) to—

(a) the hydrological yield of the facility;

(b) the quantity of water licensed for abstraction;

(c) the state of the local environment;

(d) the properties of any—

(i) pumping plant;

(ii) well;

(iii) aquifer;

(iv) raw water main;

(v) aqueduct;

(vi) transfer main;

(vii) output main;

(e) any water treatment processes;

(f) any requirements relating to water quality;

'desalination plant' means a facility for the extraction of mineral components from saline water;][2]

'development' has the meaning given by section 32;

'development consent' has the meaning given by section 31;

['drought conditions' means conditions resulting from a shortage of precipitation that has a 0.5% chance of occurring within a 12 month period;][2]

'electric line' has the same meaning as in Part 1 of the Electricity Act 1989 (c. 29) (see section 64(1) of that Act);

'extension', in relation to a generating station, has the meaning given by section 36(9) of the Electricity Act 1989 (and 'extend' must be read accordingly);

'gas' includes natural gas;

'gas reception facility' must be read in accordance with section 19(3);

'gas transporter' has the same meaning as in Part 1 of the Gas Act 1986 (c. 44) (see section 7(1) of that Act);

'generating station' has the same meaning as in Part 1 of the Electricity Act 1989 (see section 64(1) of that Act);

'goods' has the meaning given by section 83(1) of the Railways Act 1993 (c. 43);

'Green Belt land' has the meaning given by section 2(1) of the Green Belt (London and Home Counties) Act 1938 (c. xciii);

'harbour' and 'harbour authority' have the meanings given by section 57(1) of the Harbours Act 1964 (c. 40);

'highway' has the meaning given by section 328 of the Highways Act 1980 (c. 66);

'highway authority' has the same meaning as in the Highways Act 1980 (c. 66) (see sections 1 to 3 of that Act);

'improvement', in relation to a highway, has the meaning given by section 329(1) of the Highways Act 1980;

'inland waters' has the same meaning as in the Water Resources Act 1991 (c. 57) (see section 221(1) of that Act);

'land' includes buildings and monuments, and land covered with water, and in relation to Part 7 must be read in accordance with section 159;

'LNG facility' must be read in accordance with section 18(3);

'local planning authority' has the same meaning as in TCPA 1990 (see section 336(1) of that Act);

'monument' has the same meaning as in the Ancient Monuments and Archaeological Areas Act 1979 (c. 46) (see section 61 of that Act);

'nationally significant infrastructure project' has the meaning given by Part 3;

'national policy statement' has the meaning given by section 5(2);

'natural gas' means any gas derived from natural strata (including gas originating outside the United Kingdom);

'navigable watercourse' has the same meaning as in Part 6 of the Highways Act 1980 (see section 111(1) of that Act);

'non-navigable watercourse' means a watercourse that is not a navigable watercourse;

'pipe-line' has the meaning given by section 65 of the Pipe-lines Act 1962 (c. 58);

'planning permission' means permission under Part 3 of TCPA 1990;

'prescribed' means prescribed by regulations made by the Secretary of State (except in relation to matters authorised or required by this Act to be prescribed in another way);

'rail freight interchange' means a facility for the transfer of goods between railway and road, or between railway and another form of transport;

'railway' has the meaning given by section 67(1) of the Transport and Works Act 1992 (c. 42);

'renewable energy installation' has the same meaning as in Chapter 2 of Part 2 of the Energy Act 2004 (c. 20) (see section 104 of that Act);

'Renewable Energy Zone' has the meaning given by section 84(4) of the Energy Act 2004;

'special road' means a highway which is a special road in accordance with section 16 of the Highways Act 1980 or by virtue of an order granting development consent;

'standard', in relation to a volume of gas, means the volume of gas at a pressure of 101.325 kiloPascals and a temperature of 273 Kelvin;

'trunk road' means a highway which is a trunk road by virtue of—

(a) section 10(1) or 19 of the Highways Act 1980,

(b) an order or direction under section 10 of that Act, or

(c) an order granting development consent,

or under any other enactment;

'underground gas storage facilities' must be read in accordance with section 17(6);

'use' has the meaning given by section 336(1) of TCPA 1990.

(2) A reference in this Act to a right over land includes a reference to a right to do, or to place and maintain, anything in, on or under land or in the air-space above its surface.

(3) Subsection (4) applies to the question of which parts of waters up to the seaward limits of the territorial sea—

(a) are adjacent to Wales (and, in consequence, are not adjacent to England), or

(b) are not adjacent to Wales (and, in consequence, are adjacent to England).

(4) The question is to be determined by reference to an order or Order in Council made under or by virtue of section 158(3) or (4) of the Government of Wales Act 2006 (c. 32) (apportionment of sea areas) if, or to the extent that, the order or Order in Council is expressed to apply—

(a) by virtue of this subsection, for the purposes of this Act, or

(b) if no provision has been made by virtue of paragraph (a), for the general or residual purposes of that Act.

(5) Subsection (6) applies to the question of which parts of waters up to the seaward limits of the territorial sea—

(a) are adjacent to Scotland (and, in consequence, are not adjacent to England), or

(b) are not adjacent to Scotland (and, in consequence, are adjacent to England).

(6) The question is to be determined by reference to an Order in Council made under section 126(2) of the Scotland Act 1998 (c. 46) if, or to the extent that, the Order in Council is expressed to apply—

(a) by virtue of this subsection, for the purposes of this Act, or

(b) if no provision has been made by virtue of paragraph (a), for the general or residual purposes of that Act.

1 Definitions repealed by Localism Act 2011, ss 128(2), 237, Sch 13, paras 1, 69, Sch 25, Pt 20 (1 April 2012).

2 Definitions inserted by Infrastructure Planning (Water Resources) (England) Order 2019, SI 2019/12, art 2(1), (6) (9 January 2019).

236 Application of Act to Scotland: modifications

The modifications set out in Schedule 12 have effect in the application of this Act to Scotland for the purpose mentioned in section 240(4).

237 Supplementary and consequential provision

(1) The Secretary of State may by order made by statutory instrument make—

(a) such supplementary, incidental or consequential provision, or

(b) such transitory, transitional or saving provision,

as the Secretary of State thinks appropriate for the general purposes, or any particular purpose, of this Act or in consequence of, or for giving full effect to, any provision made by this Act.

(2) The power conferred by subsection (1) includes power to make different provision for different purposes (including different areas).

(3) An order under subsection (1) may amend, repeal, revoke or otherwise modify—

(a) an Act passed on or before the last day of the Session in which this Act is passed, or

(b) an instrument made under an Act before the passing of this Act.

(4) An order under this section which amends or repeals any provision of an Act may not be made unless a draft of the instrument containing the order has been laid before, and approved by resolution of, each House of Parliament.

(5) A statutory instrument containing an order under this section which does not amend or repeal any provision of an Act is subject to annulment pursuant to a resolution of either House of Parliament.

(6) In this section any reference to an Act (other than this Act) includes a reference to an Act of the Scottish Parliament.

[237A Variation and replacement of section 33 consents: transitional provision

(1) This section applies where a section 33 consent ('the original consent') has been granted or made as a result of an application made before Part 4 came into force.

(2) Nothing in section 33 prevents the original consent, or a section 33 consent that replaces it, from being varied or replaced.

(3) If the original consent, or a section 33 consent that replaces it, is varied or replaced, section 31 does not apply to the development to which the consent as varied, or the replacement consent, relates (and so development consent is not required for that development).

(4) A section 33 consent replaces an earlier section 33 consent for the purposes of this section if (but only if)—

(a) it is granted or made on an application for consent for development without complying with conditions subject to which the earlier section 33 consent was granted or made, and

(b) it is granted subject to, or made on, different conditions, or unconditionally.

(5) In this section 'section 33 consent' means a consent, authorisation, order, notice or scheme mentioned in section 33(1), (2) or (4).][1]

1 Inserted by Growth and Infrastructure Act 2013, s 22(1) (1 March 2010: insertion deemed to have had effect from 1 March 2010).

238 Repeals

Schedule 13 contains repeals (including repeals of spent provisions).

239 Financial provisions

There is to be paid out of money provided by Parliament—

(a) any expenditure incurred under or by virtue of this Act by the Secretary of State, and

(b) any increase attributable to this Act in the sums payable under or by virtue of any other Act out of money so provided.

240 Extent

(1) The following provisions of this Act extend to England and Wales only—

(a) in Part 2, section 13;

(b) in Part 3, sections 15 to 20 and 22 to [30A][1];

(c) in Part 6, section 118;

(d) in Part 7, sections 133 and 139 to 149;

(e) in Part 9, sections 193 and 194;

(f) in Part 10, sections 203 and 204;

(g) Part 11.

(2) Section 178 extends to Scotland only.

(3) The following provisions of this Act extend to England and Wales and (subject to subsection (4)) to Scotland—

(a) Parts 1 to 8 (except the sections listed in paragraphs (a) to (d) of subsection (1));

(b) this Part.

(4) Those provisions extend to Scotland only so far as required for the purpose of the construction (other than by a gas transporter) of an oil or gas cross-country pipe-line—

(a) one end of which is in England or Wales, and

(b) the other end of which is in Scotland.

(5) Subsections (3) and (4) are subject to subsection (6).

(6) So far as it amends or repeals an enactment, this Act has the same extent as the enactment amended or repealed.

(7) An order under section 225(2) extends to each part of the United Kingdom.

1 Word substituted by Infrastructure Planning (Radioactive Waste Geological Disposal Facilities) Order 2015, SI 2015/949, art 2(1), (4) (27 March 2015).

241 Commencement

(1) The following provisions of this Act come into force on the day on which this Act is passed—

(a) the provisions of Parts 1 to 9 (except section 194(2) to (5) and paragraph 7 of Schedule 7) which—

(i) confer power to make orders (other than orders granting, or making changes to orders granting, development consent), regulations or rules, or

(ii) make provision about what is (or is not) permitted to be done, or what is required to be done, in the exercise of any such power;

(b) Part 11, except sections 206, 211(7), 224 and 225;

(c) this Part, except section 238.

(2) Nothing in subsection (1)(a) affects the operation of section 13 of the Interpretation Act 1978 (c. 30) in relation to this Act.

(3) Except as provided by subsection (1)(a), the provisions listed in subsection (4) come into force on such day as may be appointed by order made by—

(a) the Welsh Ministers, in relation to Wales;

(b) the Secretary of State, in relation to England.

(4) The provisions are—

(a) sections 183, 185, 187, 188, 191(1) and (3), 192, 193 and 197 to 200;

(b) paragraphs 1, 2(1) and (2), 3(1), (2) and (4) and 4 to 6 of Schedule 7;

(c) Schedules 8 and 11;

(d) the repeals in—

(i) TCPA 1990 (except those in Schedules 1 and 1A to that Act);

(ii) the Environmental Protection Act 1990 (c. 43);

(iii) the Planning and Compensation Act 1991 (c. 34);

(iv) sections 42(3) and 53 of PCPA 2004.

(5) Section 186 and the repeal in Schedule 1A to TCPA 1990 come into force on such day as the Welsh Ministers may by order appoint.

(6) Sections 194(2) to (5), 201, 202, 203 and 225 (together with related entries in Schedule 13), and paragraph 7 of Schedule 7, come into force at the end of two months beginning with the day on which this Act is passed.

(7) Section 204 comes into force in accordance with subsection (5) of that section.

(8) The other provisions of this Act come into force on such day as the Secretary of State may by order appoint.

(9) The powers conferred by this section are exercisable by statutory instrument.

(10) An order under this section may—

(a) appoint different days for different purposes (including different areas);

(b) contain transitional, transitory or saving provision in connection with the coming into force of this Act.

242 Short title

This Act may be cited as the Planning Act 2008.

Schedule 1 ...

Repealed by Localism Act 2011, ss 128(2), 237, Sch 13, paras 1, 2, Sch 25, Pt 20 as from 1 April 2012.

Schedule 2 ...

Amends Green Belt (London and Home Counties) Act 1938, Pipe-lines Act 1962, Harbours Act 1964, Gas Act 1965, Energy Act 1976, Ancient Monuments and Archaeological Areas Act 1979, Highways Act 1980, Electricity Act 1989, Town and Country Planning Act 1990, Planning (Listed Buildings and Conservation Areas) Act 1990, Planning (Hazardous Substances) Act 1990, New Roads and Street Works Act 1991, Water Industry Act 1991, Transport and Works Act 1992, Town and Country Planning (Scotland) Act 1997, Planning (Hazardous Substances) (Scotland) Act 1997, Housing and Regeneration Act 2008, Crossrail Act 2008 (c. 18).

Schedule 3 ...

Repealed by Localism Act 2011, ss 128(2), 237, Sch 13, paras 1, 54, Sch 25, Pt 20 (1 April 2012).

Schedule 4 Correction of errors in development consent decisions

1 Correction of errors

(1) This paragraph applies if—

(a) the [Secretary of State][1] makes an order granting development consent, or refuses development consent, and

(b) the decision document contains a correctable error.

(2) The decision document is—

(a) in the case of an order granting development consent, the order;

(b) in the case of a refusal of development consent, the document recording the refusal.

(3) A correctable error is an error or omission which—

(a) is in a part of the decision document which records the decision, and

(b) is not part of the statement of reasons for the decision.

(4) The [Secretary of State][2] may correct the error or omission if (but only if) the conditions in sub-paragraphs (5) and (7) are met.

This is subject to sub-paragraph (11).

(5) The condition is that, before the end of the relevant period—

(a) the [Secretary of State][2] receives a written request to correct the error or omission from any person, or

(b) the [Secretary of State][2] sends a statement in writing to the applicant which explains the error or omission and states that the [Secretary of State][2] is considering making the correction.

(6) The relevant period is—

(a) if the decision document is an order granting development consent, the period specified in section 118(1)(b);

(b) if the decision document is the document recording a refusal of development consent, the period specified in section 118(2)(b).

(7) The condition is that the [Secretary of State][2] informs each relevant local planning authority that the request mentioned in sub-paragraph (5)(a) has been received or the statement mentioned in sub-paragraph (5)(b) has been sent (as the case may be).

(8) If—

(a) the decision document is an order granting development consent, and

(b) the order was required to be contained in a statutory instrument,

the power conferred by sub-paragraph (4) may be exercised only by order contained in a statutory instrument.

[...][3]

(10) As soon as practicable after the instrument [containing the order is made, the Secretary of State][4] must deposit a copy of it in the office of the Clerk of the Parliaments.

(11) The power conferred by sub-paragraph (4) may not be exercised in relation to provision included in an order granting development consent by virtue of [paragraph 30A or 30B of Schedule 5 (deemed marine licence under Marine and Coastal Access Act 2009)][5].

1 Words substituted by Localism Act 2011, s 128(2), Sch 13, paras 1, 70(1), (2) (1 April 2012).
2 Words substituted by Localism Act 2011, s 128(2), Sch 13, paras 1, 70(1), (3) (1 April 2012).
3 Repealed by Localism Act 2011, ss 128(2), 237, Sch 13, paras 1, 70(1), (4), Sch 25, Pt 20 (1 April 2012).
4 Words substituted by Localism Act 2011, s 128(2), Sch 13, paras 1, 70(1), (5) (1 April 2012).
5 Words substituted by Marine and Coastal Access Act 2009, s 112(1), Sch 8, para 4(1), (4) (6 April 2011).

2 Correction notice

(1) If paragraph 1(5)(a) or (b) applies the [Secretary of State][1] must issue a notice in writing (a 'correction notice') which—

(a) specifies the correction of the error or omission, or

(b) gives notice of the decision not to correct the error or omission.

(2) The [Secretary of State][1] must issue the correction notice as soon as practicable after making the correction or deciding not to make the correction.

(3) The [Secretary of State][1] must give the correction notice to—

(a) the applicant,

(b) each relevant local planning authority, and

(c) if the correction was requested by any other person, that person.

(4) The Secretary of State may [give the correction notice to persons other than those to whom sub-paragraph (3) requires it to be given.][2]

1 Words substituted by Localism Act 2011, s 128(2), Sch 13, paras 1, 70(1), (6) (1 April 2012).
2 Words substituted by Localism Act 2011, s 128(2), Sch 13, paras 1, 70(1), (7) (1 April 2012).

3 Effect of a correction

(1) If a correction is made in pursuance of paragraph 1—

(a) the original decision and the decision document containing it continue in force, and

(b) the decision document is treated as corrected as specified in the correction notice issued under paragraph 2 with effect from the date the correction notice is issued, or, if the correction is required to be made by order contained in a statutory instrument, the date specified in the order.

(2) If a correction is not made—

(a) the original decision continues to have full force and effect, and

(b) nothing in this Schedule affects anything done in pursuance of or in respect of the original decision.

(3) 'The original decision' means the decision to—

(a) make an order granting development consent, or

(b) refuse development consent.

4 Interpretation

In this Schedule—

'the applicant' means the person who made the application to which the decision relates;

[...][1]

'a relevant local planning authority' means a local planning authority for all or any part of the area in which the land to which the decision relates is situated.

1 Definition repealed by Localism Act 2011, ss 128(2), 237, Sch 13, paras 1, 70(1), (8), Sch 25, Pt 20 (1 April 2012).

Schedule 5 Provision relating to, or to matters ancillary to, development

Part 1 The matters

1

The acquisition of land, compulsorily or by agreement.

2

The creation, suspension or extinguishment of, or interference with, interests in or rights over land (including rights of navigation over water), compulsorily or by agreement.

3

The abrogation or modification of agreements relating to land.

4

Carrying out specified excavation, mining, quarrying or boring operations in a specified area.

5

The operation of a generating station.

6

Keeping electric lines installed above ground.

7

The use of underground gas storage facilities.

8

The sale, exchange or appropriation of Green Belt land.

9

Freeing land from any restriction imposed on it by or under the Green Belt (London and Home Counties) Act 1938 (c. xciii), or by a covenant or other agreement entered into for the purposes of that Act.

10

The protection of the property or interests of any person.

11

The imposition or exclusion of obligations or liability in respect of acts or omissions.

12

Carrying out surveys or taking soil samples.

13

Cutting down, uprooting, topping or lopping trees or shrubs or cutting back their roots.

14

The removal, disposal or re-siting of apparatus.

15

Carrying out civil engineering or other works.

16

The diversion of navigable or non-navigable watercourses.

17

The stopping up or diversion of highways.

18

Charging tolls, fares [(including penalty fares)][1] and other charges.

1 Words inserted by Localism Act 2011, s 128(2), Sch 13, paras 1, 71(1), (2) (1 April 2012).

19

The designation of a highway as a trunk road or special road.

20

The specification of the classes of traffic authorised to use a highway.

21

The appropriation of a highway for which the person proposing to construct or improve a highway is the highway authority.

22

The transfer to the person proposing to construct or improve a highway of a highway for which that person is not the highway authority.

23

The specification of the highway authority for a highway.

24

The operation and maintenance of a transport system.

25

Entering into an agreement for the provision of police services.

26

The discharge of water into inland waters or underground strata.

27–30 …

Repealed by Marine and Coastal Access Act 2009, ss 112(1), 321, Sch 7, para 4(7)(a), (b), Sch 22, Pt 2 (6 April 2011).

[30A

Deeming a marine licence under Part 4 of the Marine and Coastal Access Act 2009 to have been given by the Secretary of State [or the Welsh Ministers][1] for activities specified in the order and subject to such conditions as may be specified in the order.][2]

1 Words inserted by Wales Act 2017, s 69(1), Sch 6, para 76 (1 April 2018).
2 Inserted by Marine and Coastal Access Act 2009, s 112(1), Sch 8, para 4(1), (5) (6 April 2011).

[30B

Deeming any such conditions to have been attached to the marine licence by the Secretary of State [or the Welsh Ministers][1] under that Part.][2]

1 Words inserted by Wales Act 2017, s 69(1), Sch 6, para 74 (1 April 2018).
2 Inserted by Marine and Coastal Access Act 2009, s 112(1), Sch 8, para 4(1), (5) (6 April 2011).

31

The creation of a harbour authority.

32

Changing the powers and duties of a harbour authority.

[32A

The making of byelaws by any person and their enforcement.][1]

1 Inserted by Localism Act 2011, s 128(2), Sch 13, paras 1, 71(1), (3) (1 April 2012).

[32B

(1) The creation of offences within sub-paragraph (2) in connection with—

(a) non-payment of tolls, fares or other charges,

(b) a person's failure to give the person's name or address in accordance with provision relating to penalty fares,

(c) enforcement of byelaws, or

(d) construction, improvement, maintenance or management of a harbour.

(2) An offence is within this sub-paragraph if—

(a) it is triable only summarily,

(b) a person guilty of the offence is not liable to imprisonment, and

(c) any fine to which a person guilty of the offence may be liable cannot be higher than level 3 on the standard scale.][1]

1 Inserted by Localism Act 2011, s 128(2), Sch 13, paras 1, 71(1), (3) (1 April 2012).

33

The transfer of property, rights, liabilities, or functions.

34

The transfer, leasing, suspension, discontinuance and revival of undertakings.

35

The payment of contributions.

36

The payment of compensation.

37

The submission of disputes to arbitration.

38

The alteration of borrowing limits.

Part 2 Interpretation

39

(1) This paragraph applies for the purposes of this Schedule.

(2) 'Transport system' means any of the following—

- (a) a railway,
- (b) a tramway,
- (c) a trolley vehicle system,
- (d) a system using a mode of guided transport prescribed by order under section 2 of the Transport and Works Act 1992 (c. 42).

(3) 'Maintenance', in relation to a transport system, includes the inspection, repair, adjustment, alteration, removal, reconstruction or replacement of the system.

(4) The following terms have the meanings given by section 67(1) (interpretation) of the Transport and Works Act 1992 (c. 42)—

'guided transport',

'tramway',

'trolley vehicle system'.

Schedule 6 Changes to, and revocation of, orders granting development consent

Preliminary

1

(1) This paragraph applies for the purposes of this Schedule.

(2) 'The applicant', in relation to a development consent order, means the person who applied for the order.

(3) 'A successor in title of the applicant' means a person who—

(a) derives title to the land from the applicant (whether directly or indirectly), and

(b) has an interest in the land.

[...][1]

(5) 'Development consent order' means an order granting development consent.

(6) 'The land', in relation to a development consent order, means the land to which the order relates or any part of that land.

1 Repealed by Localism Act 2011, ss 128(2), 237, Sch 13, paras 1, 72(1), (2), Sch 25, Pt 20 (1 April 2012).

Non-material changes

2

(1) The [Secretary of State][1] may make a change to a development consent order if [the Secretary of State][2] is satisfied that the change is not material.

This is subject to sub-paragraph (13).

(2) In deciding whether a change is material, the [Secretary of State][1] must have regard to the effect of the change, together with any previous changes made under this paragraph, on the development consent order as originally made.

(3) The power conferred by sub-paragraph (1) includes power—

(a) to impose new requirements in connection with the development for which consent is granted by the development consent order;

(b) to remove or alter existing requirements.

(4) The power conferred by sub-paragraph (1) may be exercised only on an application made to the [Secretary of State][3] by or on behalf of—

(a) the applicant or a successor in title of the applicant,

(b) a person with an interest in the land, or

(c) any other person for whose benefit the development consent order has effect.

(5) An application under sub-paragraph (4) must be made in the prescribed form and manner.

(6) Sub-paragraph (7) applies in relation to an application under sub-paragraph (4) made by or on behalf of a person with an interest in some, but not all, of the land to which the development consent order relates.

(7) The application may be made only in respect of so much of the order as affects the land in which the person has an interest.

(8) The [Secretary of State][1] [and the person who has made the application under subparagraph (4)][4] must comply with such requirements as may be prescribed as to consultation and publicity in relation to the exercise of the power conferred by sub-paragraph (1).

This is subject to sub-paragraphs (9) to (11).

[(8A) The power to make regulations under sub-paragraph (8) includes power to allow the Secretary of State or the person who has made the application under sub-paragraph (4) to exercise a discretion.][5]

(9) If the development consent order was required to be contained in a statutory instrument, the power conferred by sub-paragraph (1) may be exercised only by order contained in a statutory instrument.

[...][6]

(11) As soon as practicable after the instrument [containing the order][7] is made, the [Secretary of State][1] must deposit a copy of it in the office of the Clerk of the Parliaments.

(12) If a change is made to a development consent order under the power conferred by sub-paragraph (1)—

(a) the order continues in force,

(b) the [Secretary of State][1] must give notice of the change to the order to such persons as may be prescribed, and

(c) the change to the order takes effect from the date on which the notice is issued, or, if the change to the order is required to be made by order contained in a statutory instrument, the date specified in the order making the change.

(13) The power conferred by sub-paragraph (1) may not be exercised in relation to provision included in an order granting development consent by virtue of [paragraph 30A or 30B of Schedule 5 (deemed marine licence under Marine and Coastal Access Act 2009)][8].

1 Words substituted by Localism Act 2011, s 128(2), Sch 13, paras 1, 72(1), (3) (1 April 2012).
2 Word substituted by Localism Act 2011, s 128(2), Sch 13, paras 1, 72(1), (4) (1 April 2012).
3 Word substituted by Localism Act 2011, s 128(2), Sch 13, paras 1, 72(1), (5) (1 April 2012).
4 Words inserted by Infrastructure Act 2015, s 28(1), (2)(a) (12 February 2015).
5 Inserted by Infrastructure Act 2015, s 28(1), (2)(b) (12 February 2015).
6 Repealed by Localism Act 2011, ss 128(2), 237, Sch 13, paras 1, 72(1), (6), Sch 25, Pt 20 (1 April 2012).
7 Words inserted by Localism Act 2011, s 128(2), Sch 13, paras 1, 72(1), (7) (1 April 2012).
8 Words substituted by Marine and Coastal Access Act 2009, s 112(1), Sch 8, para 4(1), (6)(a) (1 October 2011: substitution came into force on 6 April 2011 but cannot take effect until the commencement of Planning Act 2008, Sch 6, para 2 on 1 October 2011).

Changes to, and revocation of, orders granting development consent

3

(1) The [Secretary of State][1] may by order make a change to, or revoke, a development consent order.

(2) The power conferred by sub-paragraph (1) may be exercised only in accordance with—

(a) the following provisions of this paragraph, and

(b) paragraphs 4 and 5.

(3) The power may be exercised without an application being made if the [Secretary of State][1] is satisfied that—

(a) the development consent order contains a significant error, and

(b) it would not be appropriate for the error to be corrected by means of the power conferred by paragraph 1 of Schedule 4 or paragraph 2 of this Schedule.

(4) The power may be exercised on an application made by or on behalf of—

(a) the applicant or a successor in title of the applicant,

(b) a person with an interest in the land, or

(c) any other person for whose benefit the development consent order has effect.

(5) The power may be exercised on an application made by a local planning authority if the [Secretary of State][1] is satisfied that—

(a) the development consent order grants development consent for development on land all or part of which is in the local planning authority's area,

(b) the development has begun but has been abandoned, and

(c) the amenity of other land in the local planning authority's area or an adjoining area is adversely affected by the condition of the land.

[(5A) The Secretary of State may refuse to exercise the power on an application made under sub-paragraph (4) or (5) if, in particular, the Secretary of State considers that the development that would be authorised as a result of the change should properly be the subject of an application under section 37 for a development consent order.][2]

[...][3]

(7) [The][4] power may be exercised without an application being made if the Secretary of State is satisfied that—

(a) if the development were carried out in accordance with the development consent order, there would be a contravention of [relevant retained EU law][5] or any of the Convention rights, or

(b) there are other exceptional circumstances that make it appropriate to exercise the power.

(8) In this paragraph—

['relevant retained EU law' means—

(a) any right, power, obligation, liability or restriction that—

(i) was created or arose by or under the EU Treaties before exit day, and

(ii) forms part of retained EU law, and

(b) any remedy or procedure that—

(i) was provided for by or under the EU Treaties before exit day, and

(ii) forms part of retained EU law,

as modified from time to time.][6]

'the Convention rights' has the same meaning as in the Human Rights Act 1998 (c. 42).

1 Words substituted by Localism Act 2011, s 128(2), Sch 13, paras 1, 72(1), (3) (1 April 2012).
2 Inserted by Infrastructure Act 2015, s 28(1), (3) (12 February 2015).
3 Repealed by Localism Act 2011, ss 128(2), 237, Sch 13, para 1, 72(1), (8), Sch 25, Pt 20 (1 April 2012).
4 Words substituted by Localism Act 2011, s 128(2), Sch 13, paras 1, 72(1), (9) (1 April 2012).
5 Words substituted by Environmental Assessments and Miscellaneous Planning (Amendment) (EU Exit) Regulations 2018, SI 2018/1232, reg 4(1), (2)(a) (31 December 2020).
6 Definition substituted by Environmental Assessments and Miscellaneous Planning (Amendment) (EU Exit) Regulations 2018, SI 2018/1232, reg 4(1), (2)(b) (31 December 2020).

Changes to, and revocation of, orders: supplementary

4

(1) An application under paragraph 3 must be—

(a) made in the prescribed form and manner, and

(b) accompanied by information of a prescribed description.

(2) Sub-paragraph (3) applies in relation to an application under paragraph 3(4) made by or on behalf of a person with an interest in some, but not all, of the land to which the development consent order relates.

(3) The application may be made only in respect of so much of the order as affects the land in which the person has an interest.

(4) The Secretary of State may by regulations make provision about—

(a) the procedure to be followed before an application under paragraph 3 is made;

(b) the making of such an application;

(c) the decision-making process in relation to the exercise of the power conferred by paragraph 3(1);

(d) the making of the decision as to whether to exercise that power;

(e) the effect of a decision to exercise that power.

(5) Paragraphs (c) to (e) of sub-paragraph (4) apply in relation to the exercise of the power conferred by paragraph 3(1)—

(a) on an application under paragraph 3, or

(b) on the initiative of the [Secretary of State][1] under paragraph 3(3) or (7).

[(5A) The power to make regulations under sub-paragraph (4) includes power to allow a person to exercise a discretion.][2]

(6) If a development consent order is changed or revoked in the exercise of the power conferred by paragraph 3(1), the [Secretary of State][1] must give notice of the change or revocation to such persons as may be prescribed.

(7) If a development consent order was required to be contained in a statutory instrument, an order changing or revoking the development consent order made in the exercise of the power conferred by paragraph 3(1) must also be contained in a statutory instrument.

[...][3]

(9) As soon as practicable after the instrument [containing the order][4] is made, the [Secretary of State][1] must deposit a copy of it in the office of the Clerk of the Parliaments.

1 Words substituted by Localism Act 2011, s 128(2), Sch 13, paras 1, 72(1), (3) (1 April 2012).
2 Inserted by Infrastructure Act 2015, s 28(1), (4) (12 February 2015).
3 Repealed by Localism Act 2011, ss 128(2), 237, Sch 13, paras 1, 72(1), (10), Sch 25, Pt 20 (1 April 2012).
4 Words inserted by Localism Act 2011, s 128(2), Sch 13, paras 1, 72(1), (11) (1 April 2012).

5

(1) This paragraph applies in relation to the power conferred by paragraph 3(1) to make a change to, or revoke, a development consent order.

(2) The power may not be exercised after the end of the period of 4 years beginning with the date on which the relevant development was substantially completed.

(3) Sub-paragraph (2) does not prevent the exercise of the power—

(a) in relation to requirements imposed by the development consent order in connection with the relevant development, or

(b) to revoke the development consent order.

(4) The power includes power—

(a) to require the removal or alteration of buildings or works;

(b) to require the discontinuance of a use of land;

(c) to impose specified requirements in connection with the continuance of a use of land;

(d) to impose new requirements in connection with the relevant development;

(e) to remove or alter existing requirements.

(5) Subject to sub-paragraph (4)(a), the exercise of the power does not affect any building or other operations carried out in pursuance of the development consent order before the power is exercised.

(6) The power may not be exercised in relation to provision included in an order granting development consent by virtue of [paragraph 30A or 30B of Schedule 5 (deemed marine licence under Marine and Coastal Access Act 2009)][1].

(7) 'The relevant development' is the development for which consent is granted by the development consent order.

1 Words substituted by Marine and Coastal Access Act 2009, s 112(1), Sch 8, para 4(1), (6)(b) (1 October 2011: substitution came into force on 6 April 2011 but cannot take effect until the commencement of Planning Act 2008, Sch 6, para 5 on 1 October 2011).

Compensation

6

(1) This paragraph applies if—

(a) in exercise of the power conferred by paragraph 3, the [Secretary of State][1] makes a change to, or revokes, a development consent order,

(b) the case in which the power is exercised is one falling within sub-paragraph (3) […][2] or (7) of that paragraph,

(c) on a claim for compensation under this paragraph it is shown that a person with an interest in the land, or for whose benefit the development consent order has effect—

(i) has incurred expenditure in carrying out work which is rendered abortive by the change or revocation, or

(ii) has otherwise sustained loss or damage which is directly attributable to the change or revocation, and

(d) the claim is made to the [Secretary of State][1] in the prescribed manner and before the end of the prescribed period.

(2) Compensation in respect of the expenditure, loss or damage is payable to the person [by the Secretary of State.][3]

(3) The reference in sub-paragraph (1)(c)(i) to expenditure incurred in carrying out any work includes a reference to expenditure incurred—

(a) in the preparation of plans for the purposes of the work, or

(b) on other similar matters preparatory to carrying out the work.

(4) Subject to sub-paragraph (3), no compensation is to be paid under this paragraph—

(a) in respect of any work carried out before the development consent order was made, or

(b) in respect of any other loss or damage arising out of anything done or omitted to be done before the development consent order was made (other than loss or damage consisting of depreciation of the value of an interest in land).

(5) The Secretary of State may by regulations make provision about the assessment of compensation payable under this paragraph.

(6) The regulations may in particular include provision—

(a) for the reference of disputes about compensation for depreciation to, and the determination of such disputes by, […][4] the Lands Tribunal for Scotland, the First-tier Tribunal or the Upper Tribunal;

(b) applying, with or without modifications, a provision of or made under an Act.

1 Words substituted by Localism Act 2011, s 128(2), Sch 13, paras 1, 72(1), (3) (1 April 2012).
2 Word repealed by Localism Act 2011, s 237, Sch 25, Pt 20 (1 April 2012).
3 Words substituted for para 6(2)(a)–(b) and words by Localism Act 2011, s 128(2), Sch 13, paras 1, 72(1), (12) (1 April 2012).
4 Words repealed by Transfer of Tribunal Functions (Lands Tribunal and Miscellaneous Amendments) Order 2009, SI 2009/1307, art 5(1), (2), Sch 1, paras 291, 297 (1 June 2009).

7

(1) In this paragraph 'compensation for depreciation' means compensation payable under paragraph 6 in respect of loss or damage consisting of depreciation of the value of an interest in land.

(2) The Secretary of State may by regulations make provision about the apportionment of compensation for depreciation between different parts of the land to which the claim for the compensation relates.

(3) The regulations may in particular include provision about—

(a) who is to make an apportionment;

(b) the persons to whom notice of an apportionment is to be given;

(c) how an apportionment is to be made;

(d) the reference of disputes about an apportionment to, and the determination of such disputes by, [...][1] the Lands Tribunal for Scotland, the First-tier Tribunal or the Upper Tribunal.

(4) The Secretary of State may by regulations make provision for, and in connection with, the giving of notice of compensation for depreciation.

(5) The regulations may in particular include provision about—

(a) the persons to whom notice of compensation for depreciation is to be given;

(b) the status of such a notice;

(c) the registration of such a notice.

1 Words repealed by Transfer of Tribunal Functions (Lands Tribunal and Miscellaneous Amendments) Order 2009, SI 2009/1307, art 5(1), (2), Sch 1, paras 291, 297 (1 June 2009).

Schedule 7 ...

Amends Town and Country Planning Act 1990, Planning (Listed Buildings and Conservation Areas) Act 1990 and Planning and Compulsory Purchase Act 2004.

Schedule 8 ...

Amends Forestry Act 1967, Town and Country Planning Act 1990 and Planning and Compensation Act 1991.

Schedule 9 ...

Amends Local Government, Planning and Land Act 1980, New Towns Act 1981, Housing Act 1988, Town and Country Planning Act 1990 and Leasehold Reform, Housing and Urban Development Act 1993.

Schedule 10 …

Amends Town and Country Planning Act 1990, Planning (Listed Buildings and Conservation Areas) Act 1990 and Planning (Hazardous Substances) Act 1990.

Schedule 11 …

Amends Town and Country Planning Act 1990, Planning (Listed Buildings and Conservation Areas) Act 1990 and Planning (Hazardous Substances) Act 1990.

Schedule 12 …

Modifies Town and Country Planning (Scotland) Act 1997,

Schedule 13 …

Amends Forestry Act 1967, Town and Country Planning Act 1990, Environmental Protection Act 1990, Planning and Compensation Act 1991, Planning and Compulsory Purchase Act 2004 and Greater London Authority Act 2007.

Index

[all references are to page numbers]

www.ingramcontent.com/pod-product-compliance
Lightning Source LLC
LaVergne TN
LVHW082002200926
848481LV00010B/2788